David C. A Agnew

The Theology of Consolation

Or, an account of many old writings and writers on that subject

David C. A Agnew

The Theology of Consolation
Or, an account of many old writings and writers on that subject

ISBN/EAN: 9783337386009

Printed in Europe, USA, Canada, Australia, Japan

Cover: Foto ©Lupo / pixelio.de

More available books at **www.hansebooks.com**

THE
THEOLOGY OF CONSOLATION;

OR,

AN ACCOUNT OF MANY OLD WRITINGS AND WRITERS
ON THAT SUBJECT.

BY

REV. DAVID C. A. AGNEW,

AUTHOR OF "PROTESTANT EXILES FROM FRANCE"

"God is paid when man receives;
To enjoy is to obey."

EDINBURGH:
OGLE & MURRAY, 15 CHAMBERS STREET.
LONDON: REEVES & TURNER.
1881.

TABLE OF CONTENTS.

INTRODUCTORY ESSAY.

ON THE TEACHINGS OF SCRIPTURE CONCERNING CONSOLATION, ... PAGE 1

BOOK FIRST.
WRITINGS.—PART I.
CONSOLATION AS THE FIRST ASPECT OF THE GOSPEL.

PREFATORY QUOTATIONS FROM LUTHER, ... 25

CHAPTER I.
THE HEIDELBERG CATECHISM, ... 31

CHAPTER II.
"CHRIST ALONE EXALTED"—BY REV. DR CRISP, RECTOR OF BRINKWORTH, ... 42

CHAPTER III.
"THE MARROW," PART FIRST—BY EDWARD FISHER, GRADUATE OF OXFORD, ... 60

CHAPTER IV.
"THE MARROW," PART SECOND—BY THE SAME AUTHOR; ALSO, EXTRACTS FROM VARIOUS AUTHORS ON THE ORIGIN OF CHRISTIAN OBEDIENCE, ... 70

CHAPTER V.
THE GOSPEL MYSTERY OF SANCTIFICATION, BY REV. WALTER MARSHALL, VICAR OF HURSLEY IN THE SEVENTEENTH CENTURY; ALSO, WRITINGS OF THE EIGHTEENTH CENTURY IN HARMONY THEREWITH, ... 81

TABLE OF CONTENTS.

CHAPTER VI.

Various Writings and Discussions of the Seventeenth and Eighteenth Centuries in harmony with "The Marrow," 91

CHAPTER VII.

Guyse's Coward Lecture on Preaching Christ; also, Allusions in various Writings to such Preaching, or to the Neglect of it, . 114

CHAPTER VIII.

"Hints on Christian Experience," by Rev. Charles Watson, Minister of Burntisland, . . . 127

WRITINGS.—PART II.

Consolation Revived and Confirmed.

Preliminary Explanation, 133

CHAPTER I.

A Denial of an Assertion that all a Believer's Consolation is Delayed until after his Consciousness of Sanctification, . . . 134

CHAPTER II.

On Self-Examination and Consolation, . 139

CHAPTER III.

On Holiness and Comfort, 143

CHAPTER IV.

On the Promises to him that Overcometh, 163

CHAPTER V.

On Love to God, Christian Love, and Forgiveness of Injuries, 170

CHAPTER VI.

On the Enjoyment of God's Presence in Ordinances, 179

TABLE OF CONTENTS. vii

CHAPTER VII.

On Growth in Grace, ... 181

CHAPTER VIII.

On Love for Christ's Appearing, ... 189

BOOK SECOND.
WRITERS.

Preliminary Explanation, ... 197
Dictionary of Writers on Consolation, illustrative of Book First, . 199

Additional Memoirs, ... 395

INDEX.

I. Texts of Scripture, . 407
II. Writers Memorialised, 411
III. Writers Quoted, . . . 412
IV. Surnames for Students or Genealogists, 412

Two hundred and fifty copies having been disposed of and circulated privately, the Author now produces his work as a publication.

The *First Book*, which is an account of *writings*, is re-issued without any change. The *Second Book*, being a dictionary of *writers*, has been revised; and some needful corrections and improvements have been made.

INTRODUCTORY ESSAY.

INTRODUCTORY ESSAY

ON THE TEACHINGS OF SCRIPTURE CONCERNING CONSOLATION.

CONSOLATION has been defined by the venerable John Brown of Haddington to be *that refreshful pleasure of the soul, which ariseth from the consideration of what God in Christ is to us, and of what He has done for, and infallibly promised to us.* It describes both what God as the Saviour has prepared and prescribed, in order to create a "great calm" in the human soul, and also the great calm itself, the heavenly tranquillity, which arises from reconciliation with God through the forgiveness of sins. This Essay, it should be understood, does not treat of consolation provided for the alleviation of temporal sorrows. The idea, that no consolation is required unless there be worldly adversity and bodily distress, is too common; and it ought, in the true interests of mankind, to be discountenanced. It ought to be known that every man who wishes to be saved must become a mourner, and that God offers to him comfort, which is the mourner's desideratum. For the sake of distinction, it is usual to give the name of *spiritual consolation* to the comfort provided for souls in spiritual distress. " Happy are they that mourn, for they shall be comforted."

The work, prefaced by this Essay, has been undertaken, because of the essayist's belief that consolation does not form a separate topic in modern systems of theology—that, looking to the scriptural statements on the subject, he finds that some of those statements have not their proper place, and that others have no place, in those theological systems.

There is, however, an old literature on this branch of truth to which it is his object to introduce the inquiring reader. Those authors who have put the neglected portion of the subject in its right place, shall be introduced first. Then we can cull, from many other authors, instructive sentences as to that other part of the subject, to which our theologians have given a large amount of attention.

What is usually overlooked by professional theologians is, that consolation is the first aspect of the Christian system as presented in the Scriptures to inquirers. Salvation is offered to me as a sinner, and God offers Himself as a Saviour. Christianity, as distinguished from religious teaching in general, is a *motive-power*, named after the Lord Jesus Christ. Christ is lifted up to attract

THE THEOLOGY OF CONSOLATION.

man—Christ, as the Lamb of God, both the atoning sacrifice and the priest. This is the first aspect in which Christ is introduced to the sinner.

Although our blessed Lord is a teacher of practical religion in the end, He is first a Redeemer and a ransom. His teaching says, I will give you rest as soon as you come to Me. And then it adds, "Take My yoke upon you and learn of Me."

"We who have believed," says the Apostle, "do enter into rest."[1] It is the first step, and not the last, that is decisive of our reconciliation with God, and of our consolation in Christ. The characteristic of the Christian hope is not that all is well that ends well, but that all is well at the beginning, and that all may begin well to-day, however long it may have been of beginning. To retain the consolation with which our Christian life began, and to retain it upon exactly the same foundation, is what is required; or (to use the above-quoted Apostle's language) what is required is to hold the beginning of our confidence steadfast unto the end[2]—to hold fast the confidence and the rejoicing of the hope firm unto the end.[3] It is evident, therefore, that consolation is possible from the first, and that it may be presented to sinners as the first aspect of that Divine Biblical Gospel which offers to save their souls.

Consolation, as it is usually treated by theologians (this is the other department at which I have already hinted), is a lively hope founded upon our progress in practical religion—a hope that because our affections, our character, and our works are becoming holy, therefore God is preparing us for His habitation of holiness and glory, and will not shut us out, but does indeed intend us to dwell there for ever. We are consoled by such evidence that He has taught us to love and to praise Him, and that He will not abandon us to spend our eternity among those who hate and blaspheme Him. The consolatory reasoning is something like this—he who believes in the Lord Jesus Christ fears God and loves God: I fear God, therefore I believe in Christ; I love God, therefore I know Him. Such consolation begins at an onward stage of life, and reaches its perfection at the end. The right verdict as to this, the only theological, consolation seems to be, that there is nothing to be objected to it, if it be regarded as one of the elements of scriptural consolation. A sinful man who has found rest in Christ is more troubled about his sins than he ever was, and finds them a heavy burden, and a great discouragement in the school and service of Christ. His Christian experience may rightly prompt and enable him to thank God, and to take courage, especially at an advanced stage of life, and as the end draws nigh. But we ought to object to this theology as radically defective, if it debars the comer to Christ from consolation at the beginning, and tells him to wait for consolation till an advanced stage, or till the end. How can the beginning of a scriptural confidence be held through life, and to the end, if, scripturally, there is no such confidence until the

[1] Heb. iv. 3.   [2] Heb. iii. 14.   [3] Heb. iii. 6.

INTRODUCTORY ESSAY.

end? How can we, at the beginning, or at the early stages of our true Christianity, hold fast the confidence and the rejoicing of the hope, if there be no such confidence or rejoicing permitted at the beginning?

The scriptural statements as to consolation are of two classes: *first*, those which point to consolation as the first aspect of the Gospel of salvation; *second*, those which respect consolation as revived and strengthened by the experience of holy and heavenly life upon earth. Modern theology has confined itself to the second series of scriptural teachings, and whenever it successfully reproduces scriptural teaching, it is true and useful. But it errs in neglecting the first series. Theology errs as to the right position of consolation, if it reserves it for the end, or for a place near the end. Its scriptural place is at the beginning of those topics which are seasonable for sinners inquiring for a Divine Saviour, and for salvation according to His word.

But, at this point, an interruption (by no means impertinent) may be occasioned by some reader protesting that there is now from many pulpits a preaching of consolation for the sinner who believes in Christ—an immediate consolation, grounded upon Christ and His Gospel, before the lapse of sufficient time for the acquisition of Christian experience.

Yes, but it is *preaching* in defiance of *theology*. The theologian may tolerate it; the theologian, as a man, may say nothing against it; but he leaves his theology on the shelf, or keeps it buttoned up in his pocket. His theology is good as a part of the truth, but it has not the fulness of the Scriptures. Therefore, though a theologian, he is also a Bible Christian; and whatever theology may utter as to the delay of consolation, he will not refuse to tell his child of the present consolation that is in Christ, nor, in recommending Christ to a fellow-sinner, whose death is, or may be, as near as was the death of the thief on the cross, will he insist that there can be no felt consolation before many years.

The question is, Is it advisable that such preaching, as cannot be spoken against in Christian converse, should receive from theology antagonistic sentences, or at best a silent toleration? Could not the consolation, which is at the beginning of a believer's course, be introduced into our theological teaching, to bless our future teachers and successive generations of hearers of the word?

I.

Reverting to the two grand heads of scriptural consolation, we may, under the first head, search the Scriptures for proof that consolation is the first aspect of the Gospel of salvation as offered to sinners.

The first principle of Christianity is that there is consolation in Christ.[1] The sinner, in the full light of Gospel day, receives this direction: "Acquaint

[1] Luke i. 77-79; ii. 25; Phil. ii. 1.

now thyself with HIM, and be at peace: thereby good shall come unto thee. Receive, I pray thee, the law from His mouth, and lay up His words in thy heart."[1] Here peace, at the very beginning of acquaintance, is evidently declared. Theology would have kept it back till the end of the sentence.

No sinners could be worse than the Corinthians. Yet to the Christian converts, natives of Corinth, the Apostle Paul mentions what their own memory could recal—"I delivered unto you first of all that which I also received, how that Christ died for our sins according to the Scriptures; and that He was buried, and that He rose again the third day according to the Scriptures."[2] We are here informed about that special and peculiar department of the Apostle's teaching called "the Gospel," or *the glad tidings*. It finds in the inquirer some degree of self-accusation and self-condemnation; the Apostle says, "for our sins," *i.e.*, for my sins and for your sins. Here is the conviction of our own sinfulness which makes the fact of an expiation both desirable and welcome. And yet the Messiah and His apostles did not come on a mission of condemnation. No such mission was required while mankind had consciences. Mankind, without Christ's teaching, is pictured as a race of beings employed either in accusing or in excusing one another. The Messiah Himself said, "God sent not His Son into the world to condemn the world; but that the world through HIM might be saved."[3] The first aspect of this mission from heaven is salvation; or (in other words) consolation for sinners who have fled for refuge to lay hold of the hope set before them. The first aspect is hope; and we are saved by hope.

To all this it is a fair objection that the Apostle Paul was requested by Felix, the Roman governor, to expound "the faith in Christ," and that it appears that he had got no further than an introductory exposition of "justice, temperance, and judgment to come," when he was stopped. The reply is that he certainly was stopped when reasoning concerning morality and immorality, and responsibility and retribution, but that we need not admit that it was the very first part of the exposition. The narrative is quite consistent with the conjecture that what he declared first of all to Felix, was similiar to his historical introduction to his Corinthian sermons. Thus, the moral appeals and denunciations would follow, as throwing convincing light upon the Roman ruler's need of Christ for his own salvation. It is one thing to have a conscience suggesting or corroborating the accusation of sinfulness; it is another thing to believe that we need a Saviour, and cannot be saved without Him. It is the work of God the Holy Spirit to create this conclusive conviction, and to shut up the sinner to accept the only Saviour. And yet while, in one point of view, it is the first work of the Holy Ghost to convince us of sin, we should carefully observe that He acts in this work consistently with His office as "the Comforter"—the Comforter sent from the Father of mercies by the Lord Jesus Christ. Christ has said, The Comforter

[1] Job xxii. 21, 22.   [2] 1 Cor. xv. 3, 4.   [3] John iii. 17.

"will reprove [or convince] the world of sin, of righteousness, and of judgment: of sin, because they believe not on Me."[1] As inquirers, we see, not only that there is a refuge for us in Christ, but also that we ought to have taken refuge in Him long ago—that this was not only a permission, but a commandment. "This is His commandment," says the Apostle John, "that we should believe in the name of His Son Jesus Christ."[2] And when the Jews asked of Christ, "What shall we do, that we might work the works of God?" His own answer was, "This is the work of God, that ye believe on Him whom He hath sent."[3]

The difficulty may, perhaps, be got over thus. As a general rule, a sinner is dealt with by the Comforter, who is God the Holy Ghost, in the following manner:—First, his interest is excited as to his salvation, both as to its necessity and its possibility. And next, the serious business is begun of securing Christ as his Saviour, and the sinner's motto is, "I will not let Thee go except Thou bless me." As to the serious business, it is the Holy Spirit's first work to convince of sin; for how can I feel that I need the Saviour of sinners if I do *not* feel that I myself am a sinner? But, as to the beginning of interest, or even of curiosity, regarding the Gospel, the first aspect, according to the Scriptures, is an aspect of consolation. *There is hope*, therefore I will inquire. If there were no hope, I should only disquiet myself in vain. Jesus came to save His people from their sins; and if the result of His coming were not to be the promotion of the fear of God, salvation and the Saviour would never have been offered—would never have been heard of. The object is, not that the sinner may continue in sin with impunity, but that the sinner may be won over from sin. The first object of the Gospel is attractive, if there appear no more than possibilities rising as a vision across the sinner's future—a contrast to the sin and misery of the past. This is the Psalmist's ideal. "If Thou, Lord, shouldest mark iniquities, O Lord, who shall stand? But there is forgiveness with Thee, that Thou mayest be feared."[4] The first aspect is the possibility of forgiveness. And this, among inquirers from Christian families or congregations, includes the scriptural information as to the actual provision and purchase of forgiveness. This is the first thing that is seen; the life of Godly fear is second. This is the door of Hope—the entrance into the way of holiness.

If consolation is the last thing that the inquirer ought to dream of, and not the first, what interpretation are we to give to this array of Biblical information? And how are we to interpret the following exhortation? "Having therefore, brethren, boldness to enter into the holiest by the blood of Jesus, by a new and living way, which He hath consecrated for us, through the veil, that is to say, His flesh; and having an high priest over the House of God; let us draw near with a true heart in full assurance of faith."[5] Without examining

---

[1] John xvi. 8, 9.   [2] 1 John iii. 23.   [3] John vi. 28, 29.
[4] Ps. cxxx. 3, 4.   [5] Heb. x. 19-22.

any of the vast and deep literature regarding what our theologians mean by "assurance," it is enough to regard it as a scriptural term, and as practically synonymous with the phrases, "a strong consolation,"[1] and "everlasting consolation."[2] And it is plain that, as wedded with the invitation, "Let us draw near," it implies consolation at the very beginning of the life of faith. The consolation so freely offered, is grounded, not on self-examination—not on any autobiography, or long experience of the Christian life—but entirely on the facts concerning Christ Himself, and His finished work as our substitute and mediator. It has been sometimes said that the apostle Paul could describe his experience of assured consolation for, probably, the first time when he wrote the Second Epistle to Timothy, and that then he was an aged man. But in that account of his spiritual sensations there is nothing which even hints that his experience was different from "the beginning of his confidence," especially as the grounds of his consolation are, not his own attainments in religion, but the old and only grounds of the person of Christ, and the power of Christ to save—"I am not ashamed, for I know whom I have believed, and am persuaded that He is able to keep that which I have committed unto Him against that day."[3]

Owing to the loose and inaccurate style of our table-talk, there is often a blundering separation between belief or trust, and assurance or certainty, in men's thoughts regarding scriptural statements. I allude to passing remarks, such as—" I do not know, but I believe so ;" "I am not sure, but I trust so." And this conversational style creeps into popular theology, so that it is supposed, as a matter of course, that a believer has hold of probabilities only, and not of certainties ; and that " we believe " is essentially different from " we are sure." I find no such difference in the language of Scripture—no such limitation of the word " to believe." For instance, the Apostle Peter, as the spokesman of his colleagues, said, "We believe and are sure ;"[4] and when the disciples, on another occasion, exclaimed, "Now we are sure," Jesus replied, "Do ye now believe ?"[5] At present I am not expounding the scope of texts ; I am speaking only as a dictionary-maker might speak. Unless there is an adverb, or a similar graft upon the verb (as when the Apostle says, " I partly believe it "), " to believe" includes the idea of " being sure."[6] Illustrative texts are John viii. 46, xix. 35 ; Acts xxvii. 25 ; Rom. iv. 20, 21.

The conversational curtailment of the meaning of the word " hope " is also misleading. We often say, and hear our neighbours say, " I hope so," and apply

[1] Heb. vi. 18.   [2] 2 Thes. ii. 16.   [3] 2 Tim. i. 12.   [4] John vi. 69.   [5] John xvi. 31.

[6] The mixture of hesitation in the meaning popularly attached to the verb "to believe" may be explained thus :—In table-talk or letter-writing, I say "I believe" when I mention a probable fact, but have neither the time nor the means of immediately ascertaining its certainty. But, in the question of salvation according to the Scriptures, I have the means, and am commanded to take the time, for ascertaining the certainty of the promise. As to any alleged fact, if I apply to the person who is the first authority in connection with it, he himself being an

the phrase to what is probable or barely possible, but neither sure nor certain. Preachers will sometimes quote a text beginning with the words "we know," and they proceed to direct us to cogitate that the inspired writer says *more* than "we hope"—does not say *only* "we hope." But the scriptural meaning of the word "hope" in connection with "the things that are most surely believed among us," is a confident expectation as to future good—a strong confidence, bringing before the mind an almost pictorial representation and realization. "We KNOW," writes the Apostle John, "that when He shall appear, we shall be like Him, for we shall see Him as He is." And what does he call this assured knowledge?— "this hope."[1] The Apostle Paul amplifies his account of "everlasting consolation" by calling it "good hope through grace." Are we to suppose that he is abridging, rather than enlarging?—that "good hope" means only a fair probability, or a plausible likelihood? Certainly not. In this inspired declaration, "hope" means "certainty"—the adjective "good" points to the quality of the bliss hoped for, and not to the phenomena of the believer's sentiment or sensation. Illustrative texts are Acts xxiv. 15; Titus i. 2; Heb. vi. 19.

Another difficulty as to apprehending the possibility of consolation at the outset of the Christian cause is the twofold meaning of the word "forgiveness." It is sometimes said that although we have the promise of the forgiveness of sins, yet no sin can actually be forgiven until it has been committed; therefore our future sins are not yet forgiven, for, until our last sin has been committed, *i.e.*, until our last moments of earthly existence, we cannot be completely and finally forgiven. Assured consolation (it is therefore said) must be delayed until our last moments.

There is something in this difficulty which may be expressed thus:— "Actual forgiveness extends only to sins that are past;" and it is strengthened by the biblical sound of the phrases, "sins that are past,"[2] and "former iniquities."[3] The difficulty can be at once removed as far as these phrases are concerned, because they do not apply to any individual case. They concern Old Testament believers as a body, or nations in the mass. The prayer, "Remember not against us former iniquities," means "Remember not against us the iniquities of those who lived before us." And the Apostle Paul's statement as to "the forgiveness of sins that are past, refers to the forgiveness provided for believers in the promised Messiah who were not alive at that present time, having died before the actual coming of Christ.

If we apprehend the twofold meaning of the word "pardon," or "pardoned,"

undoubtedly truthful man, I hear what he tells me, and I say "I believe you, and I believe the information which you have given me." Here the verb "to believe" includes assurance. This fairly illustrates the scriptural phrases, "the hearing of faith" (Gal. iii. 2), and "Lord, I believe" (John ix. 38).

[1] 1 John iii. 3. [2] Rom. iii. 25. [3] Ps. lxxix. 8.

we shall see that a complete forgiveness, according to the Gospel propositions, is not delayed. The sovereign of a nation gives a free pardon to a condemned criminal: the man was in law a dead man; but now he lives, for he is a pardoned man. In his new lease of life, as an imperfect being, he will often give offence, and will as often be in need of pardon for his offences; but the grant of life, which his sovereign gave him, will be as valid as ever; the only question now is as to his living in the light of the king's countenance. This twofold pardon, and need of pardon, is essentially the same in the matter of the soul's salvation.

When God forgives us for Christ's sake, upon our faith and our willingness to be pardoned on His terms, He gives us eternal life, and we shall never perish. We were condemned already; but we have received the King's free pardon—so much so, that God justifies us. We are justified, we are declared to be righteous in His sight. The decision of the judgment-day is already given and published. "Who shall lay anything to our charge? It is God that justifieth." "There is therefore now no condemnation."[1] ["Now," that is, at the beginning of the life of faith]. Believers are like a family of adopted children, to whom has been given an eternal home—who were not cast out when they came, and who shall never be cast out. These children are ignorant, and have to add knowledge to their faith; the home of the Father is the school of Christ. These children were rebels, and have to be trained to obedience. Like children, they give continual provocation, and receive continual forgiveness. But their need of such forgiveness does not raise a question as to their reception into the home, and as to their remaining there. On their first admission they may feel an immortal consolation. "Christ is a Son over His own house; whose house are we, if we hold fast the confidence and the rejoicing of the hope firm unto the end."[2]

So much as to the words, "believing," "hoping," "forgive," as now used in conversation. But besides a confusion in the present-day use of words, there is a confusion arising from the usages of conversation in the days of "the high and mighty prince, James." The translators who worked under his royal patronage produced a Bible in conversational English, on the grand and heaven-born principle implied in such statements as, "to the poor the Gospel is preached," and, "the common people heard HIM gladly." And in most cases the pure and simple English tongue has helped to make our Bible all the more easily understood. Only in a few cases has an ancient and practically forgotten style of speech produced confusion in men's thoughts.

One, however, of the latter class of cases is the use of the word "accepted." In the original Greek there are three definite ideas, distinctly expressed by different words, for which our translators furnish us with one word only, namely, "accepted."

[1] Rom. viii. 1, 34.   [2] Heb. iii. 6.

INTRODUCTORY ESSAY.

The first of the three ideas is expressed by the word DEKTOS. "No prophet is accepted [*dektos*] in his own country;"[1] that is, the neighbours who knew him as a boy do not feel drawn to him as a prophet, and are not inclined to listen favourably to him. In this first and preliminary meaning of the word, some individuals are accepted with God—such as, the infant children of believers, and moral and devout persons who have not yet had an opportunity for hearing the way of salvation through Christ. Not by virtue of their baptism, but in consequence of their birth or pedigree, the children of any believing parent are regarded as standing apart from other children, and favourably regarded.[2] And yet the children are not actually saved until they have been effectually called by God.[3] In the beginning of the Apostle Peter's sermon to Cornelius, there is a statement to the point—" Of a truth I perceive that God is no respecter of persons: but in every nation he that feareth Him, and worketh righteousness, is accepted [*dektos*] with Him."[4] Cornelius had already been *dektos*; but he could not become a saved man until Christ was preached to him and believed by him. As the Apostle said, "Cornelius shewed us how he had seen an angel in his house, who stood and said unto him, Send men to Joppa, and call for Simon, whose surname is Peter; who shall tell thee words, whereby thou and all thy house shall be saved."[5]

The second idea is founded on the phrase, "accepted in THE BELOVED."[6] This corresponds with the inspired prayer, "Take away [*cancel*] all iniquity [*all accusations against us as guilty men*], and receive us graciously.[7] It is *the beloved*, the Lord Jesus Christ, who has earned this justification and reconciliation for us. *In Him*—on the legal footing of His merits—we who believe are accepted, justified, and reconciled, now and for ever.

But there is a third idea expressed by the word EU-ARESTOS (well-pleasing, or acceptable). This distinct topic is suggested in 2 Corinthians, chapter v., verses 8 and 9—" We are willing rather to be absent from the body and present with the Lord; wherefore we labour, that, whether present or absent, we may be accepted [*eu-arestoi*] of HIM." The second and third ideas of acceptance illustrate what has already been said as to the twofold idea of forgiveness. At first and at once, as a pardoned criminal, I have a free pardon and am perfectly safe; but as a servant or adopted son of Him who forgave me, I offend and often require paternal forgiveness for the healthful welfare and serviceable activity of my new and endless life. Thus, as a believer, I am accepted for eternity, and there can be no change in this covenant arrangement; but as a living, immortal, spiritual being, I require daily supplies of "grace, whereby I may serve God acceptably with reverence and godly fear."[8] Without any doubt as to my "acceptance in

---

[1] Luke iv. 24.   [2] Acts ii. 39; 1 Cor. vii. 14.   [3] Acts ii. 39.
[4] Acts x. 34, 35.   [5] Acts xi. 13, 14.   [6] Eph. i. 6, 7.
[7] Hosea xiv. 2.   [8] Heb. xii. 28.

the Beloved," I am anxious that my services may be acceptable—*well-pleasing* to my Father and Redeemer. And this anxiety will, by God's grace, be more or less gratified here until my last moments; and in heaven itself it will be His grace that shall enable me to continue to serve Him acceptably.

According to the third idea, therefore, the believer's expectation is, that he will be accepted at the end of his course. And only through a confusion of the second and third ideas can it ever be argued, that the assurance of an *acceptance in the Beloved* is impossible at the beginning of the life of faith, and must necessarily be delayed until the end. We hope to be found serving God in a course of well-pleasing at the end; but that is quite consistent with our being certainly and for ever "accepted" at the beginning.

In the writings of theologians we find such statements as the following:— "Let us consider all good works as acceptable through the merits of Christ, and remind our hearers that, could we do all, we were but unprofitable servants; and that we must seek to be found at last, not having our own righteousness, but that which is of God by faith." [Jennings on Preaching Christ (1723), quoted in "Williams' Christian Preacher" (1800)].

This statement is partly wrong, if it means that there is no assurance of a sinner's final acceptance until the last. It cannot be a right and safe statement unless it means that, as far as a confirmatory and reviving hope is concerned, our good works are helpful and encouraging to us through life, but that at the end we fall back, absolutely and entirely, upon the beginning of our confidence, and upon the rejoicing of the hope which began at that beginning. If, however, the statement really intends us to believe that we are not accepted finally and for eternity until the end of our time, it is misleading; even although some one may say that it is a repetition of the Apostolic saying, "We believe that through the grace of the Lord Jesus Christ we shall be saved."[1] We are bound to regard that saying as quite consistent with another which is also Apostolic, "God hath saved us, and called us with an holy calling, not according to our works, but according to His own purpose and grace, which was given us in Christ Jesus before the world began."[2] In the discourses of Christ there is no such postponement of assurance. "Verily, verily, I say unto you, He that believeth on Me hath everlasting life." "Verily, verily, I say unto you, He that heareth My word, and believeth on Him that sent Me, hath everlasting life, and shall not come into condemnation; but is passed from death unto life."[3] Let the inquiring reader therefore remember that, for practical purposes, the Bible word "accepted" is not one word but three; and that whatever kind of acceptance is necessarily delayed to a future period, it is not the believer's *acceptance in the Beloved*, which is secured to Him at once and once for all.[4]

[1] Acts xv. 11.   [2] 2 Tim. i. 9.   [3] John vi. 47; v. 24.
[4] The quotation from Jennings calls the reader's attention to the Apostle Paul's celebrated declaration to the Philippians concerning "counting all things but loss for Christ" (Phil. iii.)

II.

To the above views regarding consolation as the first aspect of the Gospel invitation and system, a few observations should be added as to the subsequent confirmation and revival of consolation in the new life of the believer.

And we should begin with the thought of the frequent necessity for the revival and confirmation of a scriptural confidence, reposing upon the Saviour, upon His finished work, and upon His written word. What the prophet said about a nation and national deliverances has a large application to the believer in Christ, and to a conscious joy of salvation. "Behold, the Lord's hand is not shortened, that it cannot save; neither His ear heavy, that it cannot hear: but your iniquities have separated between you and your God, and your sins have hid His face from you, that He will not hear."[1]

The terminus of the course that began with "the confidence and the rejoicing of the hope," is deliverance from sin—the cure of our sinfulness. "Thou shalt call His name Jesus: for He shall save His people from their sins."[2] When we awake to a remorseful consciousness of having fallen into sin, we see that our desire to be delivered from sin has been temporarily suspended and non-existent. And remembering that a believer not only believes the Promiser and His words of promise, but also desires the things promised, we feel more or less misgiving as to the reality of our belief in the truth and our reliance upon the Saviour. When the Apostle Peter enumerates "fortitude, knowledge, temperance, patience, godliness, brotherly kindness, charity," as things requiring faith as their necessary foundation, and arising from faith as commanded additions, he goes on to say, "He that lacketh these things is blind, and cannot see afar off, and hath forgotten that he was purged from his old sins."[3]

In such circumstances we feel, not only that we have been neglecting or stifling holy affection, but also that we have been offending God as God and as the Saviour. For such disgraceful behaviour, we feel that we cannot forgive our-

---

Certainly the clause "that I may win Christ and be found in Him" does point to the future, and yet not exclusively to the future. The Apostle describes himself as one of those "who rejoice in Christ Jesus" at present, and whose rejoicing dates from the past—"What things were gain to me, those I counted loss for Christ." Therefore the assurance that he had actually won Christ, and was found in Him, was not reserved for the future. As to the expression, "to be found in Him," he by it simply acknowledges the duty of abiding in Christ, along with the privilege of being accepted in Christ. As to the verb "to win," applied to a superior, it means to gain his friendship; the Apostle, as one who had acquainted himself with the Lord, and had become at peace with Him, did also desire to live continually in the sunshine of His friendship. Is not, then, the whole declaration just another way of describing the holding fast the beginning of our confidence and rejoicing?

[1] Isa. lix 1, 2.   [2] Matt. i. 21.   [3] 2 Pet. i. 9.

selves; and this leads us to fear that God cannot forgive and has never forgiven us. Such thoughts, however, are a part of the Holy Spirit's merciful discipline. Perhaps our faith as to our being forgiven by God has had some support from our being too ready to forgive ourselves, in forgetfulness of the truth that the happy man is not the man who can forgive himself, or can get his polite neighbours to forgive him, but that the only happy man is "the man to whom the Lord imputeth not iniquity,"[1]—whom the Lord forgives, because He is well pleased with the righteousness of Jesus, the Divine substitute. Our prayer for forgiveness at first was, or ought to have been, "Pardon mine iniquity, for it is great;" the greatness of our iniquity can be no argument against the fulfilment of the promised forgiveness, "for Thy name's sake, O Lord."[2]

That in us, considered as "of ourselves," or having only ourselves to depend on, "there dwelleth no good thing,"[3] is also a lesson learnt in addition to our faith, and learnt in the school of Christ as our Redeemer, who teacheth us to profit. "The beginning of our confidence" was truly our own, and yet not entirely our own: "No man can say that Jesus is the Lord, but by the Holy Ghost."[4] Yet as our confidence was truly our own, we may not have sufficiently considered that it was the result of the creating power of God and of the leadings of the Holy Spirit. That we should continue as we began is a good thing; but our confidence must be, not only that *we began*, but primarily that *God began*, as the Apostle said, intending the Philippian Christians to shape their own confidence accordingly—"Being confident of this very thing, that HE who hath begun a good work in you will perform it until the day of Jesus Christ."[5] Our sins of heart and life, detected after the beginning of our life of faith, may be overruled for good, in enabling us to observe and remember that "every good gift and every perfect gift is from above, and cometh down from the Father of lights."[6]

Our confidence often requires revival and consolidation. And it stands in need of confirmation for another reason, namely, that we have an adversary the Devil, and that his temptations, although only by sufferance, are sometimes permitted to assail our confidence. Far more than the law the Gospel of the sinner's salvation is dreaded and abhorred by Satan; and he directs his efforts, not so much against our earnest strivings and elaborate projects for holiness, as against our holding on by the simplicity that is in Christ, and standing fast in the liberty wherewith Christ hath made us free. He tempts believers to sin, not only that they may sin, but that after sinning they may doubt and despair.

Sometimes the tempter may be permitted to try our faith and principles when we are not in a backsliding state, but only to the praise of the glory of God's grace and of the glorious Gospel of the grace of God—as, for instance, he was permitted to tempt Job. And in the time of affliction, if a weak body

[1] Ps. xxxii. 2. [2] Ps. xxv. 11. [3] 2 Cor. iii. 5.; Rom. vii. 18.
[4] 1 Cor. xii. 3. [5] Phil. i. 6. [6] James i. 17.

somewhat enfeebles the mind, and if both are out of tune and out of sweet working order, the tempter takes a vile and violent advantage of our infirmities. We become overwhelmed by realizing the Almighty power of God and the vast expanse of eternity as we never realized them before, and we imagine that we never had any true feeling of spiritual realities. Through the power of temptation we feel special difficulty in grasping consolatory realities—the realities of divine mercy and salvation. Now we have to fall back upon the beginning of our confidence and (above all) upon God as the beginner of the good work which He cannot abandon. But now, also, we have materials for thankfulness, not only in consolation as the first and essential aspect of the Gospel, but also in the means for confirming and reviving our own consolation through the continued and progressive working of Him who intends to answer the prayer which he prompts us to address to Him, "Restore unto me the joy of Thy salvation, and uphold me with Thy free spirit."[1]

Such confirmation and revival being seen to be necessary, we search for and collect the scriptural evidence that has been provided.

The Apostle Paul is our first witness, speaking as he was moved by the Holy Ghost. He says, "Being justified by faith, we have peace with God through our Lord Jesus Christ: by whom also we have access by faith into this grace wherein we stand, and rejoice in hope of the glory of God. And not only so, but we glory in tribulations also: knowing that tribulation worketh patience; and patience, experience; and experience, hope: and hope maketh not ashamed; because the love of God is shed abroad in our hearts by the Holy Ghost which is given unto us."[2] Here we have presented to view both the immediate consolation and the subsequent confirmatory or reviving consolation. There is the joy of hope arising simply from what faith hears; but there is also a confirmatory hope arising from Christian experience. That experience is Christian experience which produces a scriptural joy and love towards God through Jesus Christ in a Christian's heart. Hell is the abode of hatred and blasphemy; heaven is the abode of love and praise. Love and praise are the atmosphere and breezes of heaven.

"Of such a man let this just praise be given,
Heaven was in him, before he was in heaven."

Such confirmatory hope is also acquired by diligence. At this stage we begin by referring to the Epistle to the Hebrews (vi. 11, 12). "We desire that every one of you do shew the same diligence to the full assurance of hope unto the end: that ye be not slothful, but followers of them who through faith and patience inherit the promises." This statement is usually expounded as signifying that in the end of your life alone can the full assurance of hope be obtained, and that, as the result of diligence as opposed to slothfulness. A distinction may be

[1] Ps. li. 12. [2] Rom. v. 1-5.

THE THEOLOGY OF CONSOLATION.

made between "the full assurance of faith" and "the full assurance of hope,"—the former, resting upon the sure truthfulness of our Divine Teacher and Redeemer, and therefore attainable at the very first; the latter, describing the actual expectation and realizing anticipations of the believer personally, and not attainable until the end, or nearly the end, of his course. Without dogmatically contradicting this interpretation, we can see that the words are capable of a larger signification—an interpretation quite consistent with the expressions in the former part of the epistle as to the stedfast holding of the beginning of our confidence, which is the same as the fast and firm holding of the confidence and the rejoicing of the hope. The phrase "unto the end" is quite different from "at the end," or "not till the end;" it means "until the end." The precept is, "Until the end give diligence in the direction of the full assurance of hope—the same diligence as formerly: diligence in works of faith and labours of love which you began in the childhood of Christian life." He who has Christian hope desires that it may be increased and enlarged—as Christian life grows older, labours and consolations together may abound more and more. No apostle has declared that labours are for the young Christian, and assured consolations for the old or dying Christian only. Long before the end of the life of faith—in the childhood and prime of Christian life, as described by the Apostle Paul—the characteristic of "rejoicing in hope" may go side by side with such characteristics as "not slothful in business," "fervent in spirit," "serving the Lord," "patient in tribulation," "continuing instant in prayer."[1] Far from denouncing assurance as dangerous at the beginning, the Apostle John is forward to declare: "I write unto you, little children, because your sins are forgiven you for His name's sake;"[2] while at the same time he urges that by love and obedience, in deed and in truth, they should assure their hearts in God's felt presence. Diligence in the Christian life is fitted to revive and confirm the hope of the pardoned sinner.

This truth is fully stated by the Apostle Peter. His words are, "Give diligence to make your calling and election sure: for if ye do these things, ye shall never fall: for so an entrance shall be ministered unto you abundantly into the everlasting kingdom of our Lord and Saviour Jesus Christ."[3] Here we have the phrase "give diligence," which is a fair translation of the verb in the original. But more to the point is the clause, "if ye do these things," or rather, "doing these things, ye shall never fall." Walking in the narrow way, you keep out of the broad way. Living in a state of salvation, you cannot be in a state of damnation. The object "to make your calling and election sure" means, to make sure in your own consciousness that you have been called and elected by God the Saviour.

From the Scriptures we obtain genuine metal to coin such words as "conversion" and "effectual calling." These terms are synonymous; and the latter is

[1] Rom. xii. 11, 12.   [2] 1 John ii. 12; iii. 18, 19.   [3] 2 Pet. i. 10, 11.

derived from the miraculous power of the Redeemer to call the dead out of their graves and into life. Mourning friends call, but call ineffectually; and why?—because a corpse will not arise at their call. The Saviour, as in the case of Lazarus, calls, and calls effectually; and why?—because the dead man came at His call. The evidence of a believer having been effectually called is, that he has come to Christ—that whereas he was blind, now he sees—that whereas he was dead, he is spiritually alive—that whereas he was unforgiven, now he accepts forgiveness on the gospel terms—that whereas he was impenitent and rebellious, now he is repentant and obedient. Thus our actions are proofs of our state of salvation—proofs of our having been effectually called, or of "our calling." And if we have been "called" in time, then we were "elected" to this new and everlasting life from all eternity. It is at this stage of our experience that the consolations arising from God's electing love come into the mind calmly, reverentially, joyfully, and profitably. Thus, by our dutiful scriptural activity, we make our calling and election sure—we have a feeling of the certainty of what our belief held to be certain before.[1] This is a confirmatory hope and consolation. As to the remaining phraseology in the quotation from the Apostle, we ought to observe that as "ye shall never fall" applies to the life of faith in its course, and not only at its end, so the promise "so an entrance shall be ministered unto you abundantly into the everlasting kingdom" applies to *the kingdom of grace* that is within us upon earth, and not only to the kingdom of glory.

"Thee in Thy glorious realms they praise, and bow before Thy throne;
We—in the kingdom of Thy grace—the kingdoms are but one.
The holy to the holiest leads—from thence our spirits rise:
And he who in Thy statutes treads shall meet Thee in the skies."

As the Apostle Paul fastens attention on the love of God shed abroad in the heart, so the Apostles Peter and John are memorably urgent as to love to the brotherhood, for so their Master had said in most affecting circumstances: "A new commandment I give unto you, that ye love one another, as I have loved you, that ye also love one another. By this shall all men know that ye are my disciples, if ye have love one to another."[2] The Apostle John gives a harmonizing statement, "This commandment have we from Him, that he who loveth God love his brother also."[3] And as to a confirmatory hope, he thus expresses himself, "We know that we have passed from death unto life, because we love the brethren."[4] And he also furnishes the practical exhortation, "My little children, let us not love in word, neither in tongue; but in deed and in truth. And hereby we know that we are of the truth, and shall assure our hearts before

---

[1] Or, according to Dr Gill's interpretation, thus may the men of the world be certified and assured, by the best evidence that they are capable of receiving or we of giving, that we are what we profess to be.
[2] John xiii. 34, 35.   [3] 1 John iv. 21.   [4] 1 John iii. 14.

Him; for if our heart condemn us, God is greater than our hearts, and knoweth all things. Beloved, if our heart condemn us not, then have we confidence toward God."[1]

An additional means for the confirmation and revival of consolation is the act and habit of prayer to God. "We assure our hearts before Him," said the Apostle, "and whatever we ask we receive of Him;"[2] and, again, "These things have I written unto you that believe on the name of the Son of God; that ye may know that ye have eternal life, and that ye may believe on the name of the Son of God. And this is the confidence that we have in Him, that if we ask anything according to His will, He heareth us: And if we know that He hear us, whatsoever we ask, we know that we have the petitions that we desired of Him."[3] Prayer and its answers are eminent workers in the working out of "experience" that "worketh hope." There is the word of promise for immediate consolation, "As thy days so shall thy strength be."[4] And there is an operative experience for confirmatory and reviving consolation, expressed thus—"In the day when I cried Thou answeredst me, and strengthenedst me with strength in my soul." "I love the Lord, because He hath heard my voice and my supplications."[5]

The spiritual condition of a Christian, when he sadly feels the need of confirmatory and reviving consolation, is not a penance worthily submitted to or meritoriously self-inflicted. The true specimen case is not that of a soul refusing all comfort, conscious of all the desolation of an unconverted condition, and recanting all his professions as to having begun a scriptural confidence in Christ. And, more than this—the true specimen case is not that of an utterly disconsolate man abstaining from all "looking unto Jesus," and from all study of doctrines, and confining himself to self-inspection, watching for some good workings of the heart and life on which to build his individual consolation. There is the grand old counsel of the Holy Spirit to a Christian "that walketh in darkness and hath no light;" the remedy is not to produce some good works of his own to revive him—but "let him trust in the name of the Lord, and stay upon his God."[6] So even in the alarming words of the Apostle John as to our hearts, either condemning us or condemning us not, we are pointed back to a beginning of confidence: "Whatever we ask, we receive of Him, because we keep His commandments, and do those things that are pleasing in His sight: And this is His commandment, That we should believe on the name of His Son Jesus Christ, and love one another, as He gave us commandment."[7]

Finally, the Apostle Paul, in stating the theory of Christian good works, points us, both to consolation at the beginning of the life of faith, and to equally

[1] 1 John iii. 18-21.   [2] 1 John iii. 22.   [3] 1 John v. 13-15.
[4] Deut. xxxiii. 25.   [5] Ps. cxxxviii. 3; cxvi 1.   [6] Isa. l. 10.
[7] 1 John iii. 22, 23.

unbought consolation at any stage of the life of faith, as the source and origin and only manufactory of good words and works. "Now our Lord Jesus Christ Himself, and God, even our Father, who hath loved us, and hath given us everlasting consolation and good hope through grace, comfort your hearts, and stablish you in every good word and work."[1]

NOTES ON THE RELATION OF THE ABOVE STATEMENTS TO THE WESTMINSTER STANDARDS.

Note A.—*On Assurance.*

Many students of the Holy Scriptures feel a hesitation as to declaring that "everlasting consolation" is appropriate to the very beginning of the life of faith, because of the apprehension that they would come into collision with the Westminster Confession of Faith. A number of orthodox ministers in friendly conference are told by the first speaker on the subject that we must always remember that, as believers in the Westminster Standards, we hold that assurance is not of the essence of saving faith. A second says that he is constrained to admit the force of this *caveat* and inference; and in this concur a third and fourth; and so as to all the company. But in order to quiet an inquirer's apprehension, it is sufficient to allow the Confession of Faith to speak for itself. This is the sentence which is often imperfectly reproduced by the memory:—"This infallible assurance doth not so belong to the essence of faith, but that a true believer may wait long and conflict with many difficulties before he be partaker of it" (chap. xviii. sec. 3.)[2]

Although assurance is not exactly the subject of my essay, yet I may here add my reminiscences of some hints from the preaching of the late Principal Candlish in the earlier years of his ministry. His view was, that the three expressions, "full assurance of faith," "full assurance of hope," "full assurance of understanding," are more than expressions, and are the definite and distinct designations of different stages of experience. The full assurance of "faith" relies upon the truth of the Gospel as the testimony of God, and upon the value of Christ's finished work, and upon the facts as to that complete work of redemption, as to all which a full assurance is appropriate at the very beginning of Christian life. The full assurance of "hope" is a realizing expectation and anticipation of heaven—a picturing of ourselves as in possession of the things

[1] 2 Thess. ii. 16, 17.
[2] The Larger Catechism may seem (in Q. 81) to be more decided; but the Confession of Faith is the best interpreter of the personal opinions of the Westminster Divines.

promised (hope having peculiarly to do with *things* promised, as faith with *words* of promise); this stage of full assurance presupposes some experience in the Christian life, and is not to be expected at the beginning. Then the full assurance of "understanding" arises from the study of God's word in the light of inward experience, resulting in our growth in knowledge; it has to do with the revealed methods of salvation, both of salvation from wrath and of salvation from sin, and it also has to do with any glimpses which the Scriptures give of electing love.

Whether Dr Candlish's printed works include discourses to the above effect I am not informed; but I have before me a tract[1] by an English evangelical divine, Dr John Stevenson, which distinguishes "the three full assurances" thus:—"The *glad tidings* of a Saviour and His finished work are called in one word the *gospel*."

"By faith we look *unto* it trustfully," Hebrews x. 22; Isaiah xlv. 22.
"By understanding we look *into* it intelligently," Col. ii. 2; Eph. i. 17-23.
"By hope we look *through* it expectantly," Hebrews vi. 2; 1 Peter i. 13.
"Each prepares for its successor, and all aid each other. We first believe, then we feel or realize."

"By 'faith' we come to 'understanding,' and by these two we attain to a clear and lively 'hope.' The term 'full assurance' refers to their *degree*, which, from the lowest to the highest, is the alone work of the Divine Spirit."

This note may be usefully concluded by the following extracts from "Aphorisms concerning the Assurance of Faith," by the Rev. William Cudworth of Norwich:—

"8. Justifying Faith is such an appropriation of, and trusting on, Christ, as that therein we assure ourselves of present and eternal salvation by Him; and that, not from any previous external or internal evidence that we shall be saved by Him, *but as warranted by the Word of God*, Isa. li. 1-5; John iii. 16; Rev. xxii. 17—*bound by the command of God*, 1 John iii. 23; 2 Cor. v. 14, 19, 20; *and led by the Spirit of God*, John vi. 44, 45, 63 (comp. 65), John xvii. 9,— *thus to assure ourselves;* and encouraged by His promise that we shall not be deceived or confounded in so doing, John vi. 37, iii. 15; Rom. ix. 33, x. 11; but that according to our faith, so shall it be to us. It is therefore an assuring of our souls of salvation by Christ, that we may be saved according to His promise; and is the soul's echo or obedience to the voice of God in such Scriptures as these: 'Believe on the Lord Jesus Christ and thou shalt be saved' (Acts xvi. 31); 'Look unto Me and be ye saved, all the ends of the earth' (Isa. xlv. 22.)"

"20. Self-examination, with a secondary assurance thereby, is not discarded" . . . .

[1] "The Three Full Assurances of Holy Scripture," by the Rev. John Stevenson, D.D., author of "Expositions of Psalms xxii., xxiii., and ciii." Edinburgh: J. Taylor.

Note B.—*On Divine Decrees.*

In describing the redemption of sinners the Westminster Standards begin with the Decrees of God, because these are first in order if the subject is to be treated historically. It is, perhaps, to be regretted that any such history was undertaken by man. "The secret things belong unto the Lord our God; but those things which are revealed belong unto us" (Deut. xxix. 29). What God has revealed concerning His decrees does not afford materials for a history.[1] He has been pleased to lift the veil, and to allow us no more than two glimpses into what has been decreed concerning individuals of mankind.

1st.—In order to give strong consolation to those who have fled for refuge to lay hold on the hope set before us, He has given us a glimpse which may assure each believer of God's love to himself, or herself, individually, from all eternity.

2dly.—In order to warn the rebellious that no decision or opposition on their part defeats any decree or purpose of the Almighty, He has, as in the case of Pharaoh, given them a glimpse through which He practically protests to them that in every case what is done has been decreed by the Most High.

Such glimpses were not intended to be filled up so as, along with our inferences, to swell into a book of history. And as to the additional consolation to the believer in Christ, the assurance of being an object of electing love belongs not to the beginning of faith, but to a later stage.

Such is the order observed in the Epistle to the Romans. And Dr Chalmers, following out this apostolic order, arranged his course of revealed theology, thus :—

1. The Disease for which the Gospel Remedy is provided.
2. The Nature of the Gospel Remedy.
3. The Extent of the Gospel Remedy.

Both the inspired Apostle and the Bible-loving professor of theology introduce the Divine Decrees in what may be called an appendix. And as to the first section of such a system, it is not inconsistent with the idea that consolation is the first aspect of the Gospel. It proceeds upon the belief that because there is a Divine remedy, therefore we are to inquire concerning the disease not despondently, but hopefully.

Such a method of study, or rather of practical inquiry, has been happily sketched in the following sentences of Sir Henry Moncreiff:[2]—

[1] Wollebius states the history as the *Salutis catena:* "Deus ordinavit; Verbum promittit; Christus meruit; Sacramenta obsignant; fides recipit; os fatetur; opera testantur."

[2] "The Old Temptation in its Modern Forms." A Sermon preached at the opening of the General Assembly of the Free Church of Scotland on 19th May 1870. By Sir Henry Wellwood Moncreiff, Bart., D.D.

THE THEOLOGY OF CONSOLATION.

"Let me bow before the majesty of the unseen ruler over all. I cannot account for the Devil and his works. Let me not dare to think or act as if I could. I am instructed what to make of moral evil, though not to know its origin. I am encouraged by the revelation of what God makes of it, so far as concerns my own position and that of my fellows. I have His love manifested to me in the Gospel of His Son, as a message of peace and deliverance addressed to all sinners. I see myself invited to come and fight against the Devil and all his works, through the strength of a conquering Captain of salvation. I see the heart of God reflected in the heart of the man Christ Jesus, and urging with loving entreaty the most abandoned transgressors to come and enjoy pardon and peace through faith in the blood of the Lamb. *Turn ye, turn ye,* says the voice of God, *for why should ye die?* Christ has died : ' His blood cleanseth from all sin ;' ' Look unto Him and be ye saved.' I see here no hard counsels, no ungenerous arrangements, no embarrassing limitations in my way. I see an open door of entrance into everlasting life, through the free and gracious invitation of the Lamb of God, which taketh away the sin of the world. The door is open. I welcome my opportunity. No dark thought concerning God—no profane meddling with what I cannot understand in His ways—no distrust of His promises—keeps me back. But I humbly and cordially accept of what His love has tendered to my soul. That love has brought home to me a fountain of joy, and I delight in its waters as the waters of eternal life.

"But when I have thus believed in Jesus, when I have entered thoroughly into His fellowship, and when by faith I have realized the value both of His invitations and of His promises—then I behold with reverence and adoration the heights and depths of the Divine sovereignty and the Divine love. Then I see Jesus, the substitute of a chosen people. Then I see the sure efficacy of His death."

PLAN OF THE WORK.

BOOK FIRST.—WRITINGS.

PART 1. CONSOLATION AS THE FIRST ASPECT OF THE GOSPEL.
PART 2. CONSOLATION REVIVED AND CONFIRMED.

BOOK SECOND.—WRITERS.

THEOLOGY OF CONSOLATION.

BOOK FIRST.

THE THEOLOGY OF CONSOLATION.

BOOK FIRST.—WRITINGS.

Part I. Consolation as the First Aspect of the Gospel.

PREFATORY QUOTATIONS FROM LUTHER.

It is unnecessary, and it would be impossible within the limits of my plan, to give a memoir of the writings of an author so copious and so famous as Martin Luther. It is, however, important to note that Luther's discourses and expositions of Scripture struck the key-note of the theology of consolation.

Luther's Table-Talk—a volume which, however mysterious in its origin as a formal compilation, bears internal evidence of a virtual genuineness—suggests an explanation of the usual omission of consolation from the topics of theological systems. The Reformer is quoted as having said, that *hope*, if viewed separately from *faith*, belongs to the department of admonition or exhortation, rather than to that of doctrine. The following is the paragraph:—

"297. Faith and hope are variously distinguishable. And, *first*, in regard of the subject wherein everything subsists: faith consists in a person's understanding, hope in the will; these two cannot be separated—they are like the two cherubims over the mercy seat.

"*Secondly*, In regard of the office: faith indites, distinguishes, and teaches, and is the knowledge and acknowledgment; hope admonishes, awakens, hears, expects, and suffers.

"*Thirdly*, In regard to the object: faith looks to the word or promise, which is truth; but hope to that which the Word promises, which is the good or benefit.

"*Fourthly*, In regard of order and degree: faith is first, and before all adversities and troubles, and is the beginning of life, Heb. xi. But hope follows after, and springs up in trouble, Rom. v.

"*Fifthly*, By reason of the contrariety: faith fights against errors and heresies; it proves and judges spirits and doctrines. But hope strives against troubles and vexations, and among the evil it expects good.

"In divinity, faith is the wisdom and providence, and belongs to doctrine; but hope is the courage and joyfulness, and pertains to admonition. Faith is the *dialectica*, for it is altogether prudence and wisdom; hope is the *rhetorica*, an elevation of the heart and mind. As wisdom without courage is futile, even so faith without hope is nothing worth; for hope endures and overcomes misfortune and evil. And as a joyous valour without understanding is but rashness, so hope without faith is spiritual presumption. Faith is the key to the sacred Scriptures, the right *cabala* or exposition. . . . Faith is not a quality as the schoolmen say, but a gift of God."[1]

Another paragraph of the same singular repository calls attention to consolation as the first aspect of the Gospel, or glad tidings:—

"701. Luther, at Wittenberg, seeing a very melancholy man, said to him: Ah! human creature, what dost thou? Hast thou nothing else in hand but to think of thy sins, on death and damnation? Turn thine eyes quickly away, and look hither to this man Christ, of whom it is written, *He was conceived of the Holy Ghost, born of the Virgin Mary, suffered, died, buried, descended into hell, and ascended up into heaven*, &c. Dost think all this was done to no end? Comfort thyself against death and sin; be not afraid nor faint, for thou hast no cause; Christ suffered death for thee, and prevailed for thy comfort and defence, and for that cause He sits at the right hand of God, His heavenly Father, to deliver thee."

Luther's "Commentary on the Epistle to the Galatians" is a manual of consolatory doctrines. As the English translation expresses it, it is addressed "to all afflicted consciences which groan for salvation." Bishop Sandys, in licensing it to be printed, takes the opportunity "to commend it to the reader, as a treatise most comfortable to all afflicted consciences in the school of Christ." The Bishop adds, "The author felt what he spake, and had experience of what he wrote, and was therefore able more lively to express both the assaults and the salving, the order of the battle and the means of the victory. Satan is the enemy; the victory is only by faith in Christ, as John recordeth. If Christ justify, who can condemn? saith St Paul. This most necessary doctrine the author hath most substantially cleared in this his Commentary."

A specimen of Luther's exposition of "this most necessary doctrine," we take from the comments on chap. i. ver. 4, clause 1—"Who gave Himself for our sins."

"Paul in every word handleth the argument of this epistle. He hath

[1] "Luther's Table-Talk;" Hazlitt's translation. [The above paragraph is the substance of an essay appended to Luther's comment on verse 5 of chapter v. of Galatians.]

nothing in his mouth but Christ, and therefore in every word there is a fervency of spirit and life. Weigh diligently every word of Paul, and specially mark well this pronoun, OUR; for the effect altogether consisteth in the well applying of the pronoun which we find very often in the Scriptures, wherein also there is ever some vehemency and power. Thou wilt easily say and believe that Christ the Son of God was given for the sins of Peter, of Paul, and of other saints, whom we account to have been worthy of this grace; but it is a very hard thing that thou, which judgest thyself unworthy of this grace, shouldst from thy heart say and believe that Christ was given for thine invincible, infinite, and horrible sins. Therefore, generally, and without the pronoun, it is an easy matter to magnify and amplify the benefit of Christ, namely, that Christ was given for sins, but for other men's sins, who are worthy. But when it cometh to the putting to of this pronoun, *our*, there our weak nature and reason starteth back, and dare not come nigh unto God, nor promise to herself that so great a treasure shall be freely given unto her, and therefore she will not have to do with God, except first, she be pure and without sin; wherefore, although she read or hear this sentence, *which gave Himself for our sins*, or such like, yet doth she not apply this pronoun, *our*, unto herself, but unto others which are worthy and holy; and as for herself, she will tarry till she be made worthy by her own works. This, then, is nothing else but that man's reason fain would that sin were of no greater force and power than she herself dreameth it to be. Hereof it cometh that the hypocrites, being ignorant of Christ, though they feel the remorse of sin, do think, notwithstanding, that they shall be able easily to put it away by their good works and merits; and secretly in their hearts they wish that these words, *which gave Himself for our sins*, were but as words spoken in humility, and would have their sins not to be true and very sins indeed, but light and small matters. Herein consisteth the effect of eternal salvation, namely, in taking these words to be effectual, true, and of great importance. I say not this for nought, for I have oftentimes proved by experience, and I daily find, what a hard matter it is to believe (especially in the conflict of conscience) that Christ was given not for the holy, righteous, worthy, and such as were his friends; but for wicked sinners, for the unworthy, and for his enemies, which have deserved God's wrath and everlasting death.

"Let us therefore arm ourselves with these and such like sentences of the holy Scripture, that we may be able to answer the devil (accusing us and saying, *Thou art a sinner, and therefore thou art damned*) in this sort, Because thou sayest I am a sinner, therefore I will be righteous and saved. *Nay*, saith the devil, *thou shalt be damned*. No (say I), for I fly unto Christ, *who hath given Himself for my sins*. Therefore, Satan, thou shalt not prevail against me, in that thou goest about to terrify me in setting forth the greatness of my sins, and so to bring me into heaviness, distrust, despair, hatred, contempt, and blaspheming of God. Yea, rather, in that thou sayest I am a sinner, thou givest me armour and weapons against thyself, that with thine own sword I may cut thy throat and tread thee under my feet; for Christ died for sinners. Moreover, thou thyself preachest unto me the glory of God; for thou puttest me in mind of God's fatherly love towards me, wretched and damned sinner. God so loved the world, that He gave His only begotten Son, that whosoever believeth in Him shall not perish, but have everlasting life (John iii. 16). And as often as thou objectest that I am a sinner, so often thou callest me to remembrance of the benefit of Christ my Redeemer, upon whose shoulders, and not upon mine, lie all my sins; for the Lord hath laid all our iniquity upon Him (Isaiah liii. 6); for the transgressions of His people was He smitten (Isaiah liii. 8). Wherefore, when thou sayest I am a sinner thou dost not terrify me, but comfortest me above measure.

"And this is the cause why I do so earnestly call upon you to learn the true and proper definition of Christ out of these words of Paul, *which gave Himself for our sins*. If He gave Himself to death for our sins, then undoubtedly He is no tyrant or judge which will condemn us for our sins. He is no caster-down of the afflicted, but a raiser-up of those that are fallen, a merciful reliever and comforter of the heavy and broken-hearted. Else should Paul lie in saying, *Which gave Himself for our sins*. If I define Christ thus, I define Him rightly, and take hold of the true Christ, and possess Him indeed. And here I let pass all curious speculations concerning the Divine Majesty, and stay myself in the humanity of Christ, and so I learn truly to know the will of God. Here there is no fear, but altogether sweetness, joy, peace of conscience, and such like."

In the year 1523, Luther issued a summary of Gospel doctrine in the German language for popular use; its title was a "Preface to the Epistle to the Romans." His definition of doctrinal terms have been of use to all subsequent writers and preachers. Take one or two specimens—

"LAW.—The word *law* must not be understood in the sense which man usually attaches to it, namely, a rule teaching us what actions must be done, or left undone. The law of man is satisfied with the outward actions, though the heart does not harmonize with them. Where there is not a cheerful delight in well-doing, the heart obeys not the law of God. The works of the law are all that man does, or can do, of his own will, and in his own strength; but because, under and along with such works, there remains in the heart enmity and hatred to the law, such works are altogether lost and of no use."

"GRACE.—Grace differs from gift. Grace properly signifies the mercy or favour which God of His own accord bears to us. The grace of God does not divide or distribute itself by degrees, but accepts us at once and completely, through the mercy that is in Christ, our Mediator and Redeemer; and on this account the gifts are begun to be wrought in us."

"FAITH.—Faith is not the human conceit and dream, which some take it

CONSOLATION AS THE FIRST ASPECT OF THE GOSPEL.

to be—namely, such hearers of the Gospel as imagine that in their own strength they can say, I believe. This they take to be true faith, but it is only a fiction and imagination of man; it acts not, and no improvement of life or good works follow. Faith is the gift of God. Faith is a living, all-venturing confidence in the grace of God; so firm that it would brave a thousand deaths. Such confidence in, and perception of, the mercy of God imparts joy and peace, and love towards God and all His creatures. These are the fruits of faith through the operation of the Holy Ghost. The result of this is, that man without constraint becomes willing and desirous to do good to all—to be of service to all—to suffer all—for the love and the glory of that God who has shown such mercy to him. Oh! faith is a living, active, efficacious, powerful thing; it is impossible that it should not bring forth good works without ceasing. It asks not if good works should be done, but, before that question, it has done them, and it is ever doing them."

In the year 1527, Luther, who was a poet and musical composer of undoubted genius, published the first edition of his Hymn Book. His hymns are here alluded to, because they were instructive hymns. He says in the Preface, "The blessed patriarchs and prophets of the old times composed and sang hymns, in which, like ourselves, they praise God's mercies rather than men's works." And "St Paul, in his Epistles to the Corinthians and to the Colossians, delivers it as a commandment, that from the heart we should sing to the Lord psalms and hymns, and spiritual songs, that the Word of God and the doctrines of Christianity may in every possible manner be published and practised. Therefore have I, along with some others, and in order to serve as a beginning, and an encouragement to those who are able to do better things than myself, brought together some hymns to extend the holy Gospel, which, through the mercy of God, has again appeared in the world."

After the publication in several centuries of many editions of Luther's Spiritual Songs, down to the year 1817, the work fell into temporary neglect until the year 1844, when a new edition appeared in Germany. This was the occasion of their first introduction to the British public by the Rev. John Anderson, minister of the Free Church of Scotland in Helensburgh, who published a translation in 1846. One of the hymns on mercy is a practical illustration of the use of the personal pronoun, as to the importance of which we have already heard the great Reformer discoursing. The following rendering of it in the English language is taken almost entirely from Mr Anderson's version :—

" Christians all with me rejoice,
Come and sing with cheerful voice ;
What the Lord has done for me
I will tell you joyfully.
Captive once by Satan led,

I was lost in sin, and dead ;
Lawful captive, night and day,
More and more I went astray ;
Mercies slighted—grace withstood—
There was in me nothing good.

"If I strove to break my chain
All my striving was in vain;
Poor and wretched, blind and proud,
Free-will hates the will of God.
Thus I liv'd, in trespass dead,
Yet my heart with anguish bled,
Standing on hell's fiery brink,
Dreading hourly there to sink;
Then did God, in mercy great,
Look upon my lost estate.

"'Go!' (said God to His dear Son),
'Go, My heart-beloved One,
Save that child of guilt and wrath,
Turn him from his sinful path.
Save him by Thy mighty hand,
From the burning pluck the brand,
From his bondage set him free,
Let him My salvation see.'
Cheerfully the Son obey'd,
Earthward, as my Brother, sped.

"Virgin-born, He dwelt with man,
Told His gracious, glorious plan.
'Look (He said), look thou to Me,
Captive, I will set thee free;
Surety I for thee will stand,

None shall pluck thee from My hand;
I am thine, and thou shalt be
Conqueror of hell through Me.
Falling in the fearful strife,
I for thee will give My life.

"'Blood of Mine, on Calvary spilt,
Cancel shall thy bond of guilt.
Dying, I'm the death of Death,
Gladdening the eye of faith.
When for thine My life I've giv'n,
I will then ascend to heav'n,
There thy Lord and Leader be,
And My Spirit pour on thee:
He will comfort thee and guide,
And till death with thee abide.

"What I've taught and done for thee,
Go and let thy brethren see.
Go, My love and truth commend,
And My kingdom wide extend.
Guard against each worldly lure,
Keep thy heart and actions pure.
Jewel, bought with blood of Mine,
Stain not thou the heav'nly shine.
Keep this counsel carefully,
'Tis thy Saviour's legacy.'"

As the first of the writings, about to be described, proceeded from what has since been called an Evangelical or Reformed Church, as distinguished from, and as somewhat opposed to, the Lutheran, a brief explanation may be required after the above testimony of an agreement with Luther himself.

In the first place, then, the division of Protestant Churches into Lutheran and Reformed was not the doing of the latter Church, neither did the latter Church arrogate anything to itself by the name whereby it was popularly known.

In the second place, neither Luther nor Melancthon founded a separate Church with the title of Lutheran. It was not until both those noble reformers were dead that a separation was contemplated.

In the third place, at the date of the separation, which may be regarded either as 1569 or 1577, there were English, French, Swiss, Belgic, &c., as well as German, Reformed Churches. And the new Church, which assumed the name of Lutheran, was a separation from the Foreign Reformed Churches on the part

CONSOLATION AS THE FIRST ASPECT OF THE GOSPEL. 31

of some Germans. All German Protestants who remained in union with their brethren of other nations retained their own name of the Reformed Church. And this was the occasion of the separatists calling themselves Lutherans.

On the whole, those who differed most from the Lutherans agreed best with Luther, as to the justification of the sinner by the grace of God through faith alone, both as to the truth of that doctrine, and as to its supreme importance. The first characteristic Catechism of the Reformed was issued before either of the above-stated dates in the history of (what was more correctly styled) *Neo-Lutheranism*.

CHAPTER I.

THE HEIDELBERG CATECHISM.

THE first book in order of time, and the most deeply interesting in itself, in which consolation is put forward as the first aspect of the Gospel, is the Heidelberg Catechism. Heidelberg, as the seat of a far-famed Reformed College, was the residence of great Protestant theologians and literati; and, as the city surrounding the palace of the Elector-Palatine, it was the capital of Evangelical Christendom. The Catechism, named after this city, was issued in 1563, under the sanction of the Elector Frederick III., being the work of Ursinus and Olevianus, two of the theological professors in the University.

This Catechism beautifully exhibits the manner in which the Gospel, coming with the message of consolation, leads the believer onward into practical Christianity. I shall transcribe enough to illustrate this.

In collections of church formularies it is usual to print this Catechism in Latin. While, however, the Latin edition is authoritative as a generally faithful version, a greater authority belongs to the German original. The English and German[1] are therefore given here in parallel columns.

1. *What is thy only consolation in life and in death?*

That both in soul and body, whether I live or die, I am not mine own, but belong unto my faithful Saviour, Jesus

1. *Was ist dein einiger Trost[2] im Leben und im Sterben?*

Dass ich mit Leib und Seele, beides im Leben und im Sterben, nicht mein, sondern meines getreuen Heilandes, Jesu

---

[1] In the English I have obtained much assistance from the translation so carefully and successfully edited by the Rev. A. Thelwall in 1850. The German is the modern text, compared with the first edition as reprinted in facsimile in 1864, under the editorship of Albrecht Wolters, pastor at Bonn.

[2] In case the English reader should think that the primary meaning of TROST is *trust*, it may be as well to note that *Vertrauen* is the German for "trust," and that *Trost* means "consolation."

Christ, who, by His precious blood, hath fully satisfied for all my sins, and hath redeemed me from all the power of the devil, and hath also certified that, without the will of my Father in Heaven, not a hair can fall from my head, yea, even that all things must be serviceable to me for my salvation. Wherefore He also, through His Holy Spirit, assureth me of everlasting life, and maketh me willing and prepared henceforth from the heart to live unto Him.

2. *How many things are necessary for thee to know, that thou, enjoying this consolation, mayest live and die happily?*

Three things. The first, What is the greatness of my sin and misery. The second, How I am redeemed from all my sin and misery. And the third, What thanks I owe unto God for this redemption.

3. *Whence knowest thou thy misery?*

Out of the law of God.

4. *What then doth the Divine Law require of us?*

This, in a summary, Christ teacheth us in the 22d chapter of Matthew.

Thou shalt love God thy Lord with all thy heart, with all thy soul, with all thy mind, and with all thy strength. This is the first and greatest commandment. And the second is like to this: Thou shalt love thy neighbour as thyself. On these two commandments hang the whole law and the prophets.

5. *Art thou able to keep all these things perfectly?*

No; for by nature I am prone to the hatred of God and of my neighbour.

Christi eigen bin, der mit seinem theuern Blut für alle meine Sünden vollkömmlich bezahlet, und mich aus aller Gewalt des Teufels erlöset hat, und also bewahret dass ohne den Willen meines Vaters im Himmel kein Haar von meinem Haupt kann fallen, ja auch mir alles zu meiner Seligkeit dienen muss. Darum er mich auch durch seinen heiligen Geist des ewigen Lebens versichert, und ihm forthin zu leben von Herzen willig und bereit macht.

2. *Wie viel Stücke sind dir nöthig zu wissen, dass du, in diesem Trost, seliglich leben und sterben mögest?*

Drei Stücke. Erstlich, Wie gross meine Sünde und Elend sei. Zum andern, Wie ich von allen meinen Sünden und Elend erlöset werde. Und zum dritten, Wie ich Gott für solche Erlösung soll dankbar sein.

3. *Woher erkennest du dein Elend?*

Aus dem Gesetz Gottes.

4. *Was erfordert denn das göttliche Gesetz von uns?*

Dies lehret uns Christus in einer Summa, Matth. am 22 Capitel.

Du sollst lieben Gott, deinen Herrn, von ganzem Herzen, von ganzer Seele, von ganzem Gemüth, und allen Kräften. Dies ist das vornehmste und grösste Gebot. Das andere aber ist dem gleich: Du sollst deinen Nächsten lieben als dich selbst. In diesen zweien Geboten hanget das ganze Gesetz und die Propheten.

5. *Kannst du dies alles vollkömlich halten?*

Nein; denn ich bin von Natur geneigt Gott und meinen Nächsten zu hassen.

CONSOLATION AS THE FIRST ASPECT OF THE GOSPEL.

6. *Did God then create man so wicked and perverse?*

No; but God created man good and after His own image, that is, in true righteousness and holiness, in order that he might rightly know God his Creator, and from the heart love Him, and in everlasting happiness live with Him, to praise Him, and to glorify Him.

7. *Whence then ariseth this corrupt nature of man?*

From the Fall and disobedience of our first parents, Adam and Eve, in Paradise; hence is our nature become so corrupt, that we are all conceived and born in sins.

8. *But are we so corrupt, that we are altogether unfit to any good and prone to all evil?*

Yes, except we be regenerated by the Holy Ghost.

9. *Doth not God then do injustice to man, in that He in His law requireth of him what he is not able to perform?*

No. For God hath created man such a one that he was able to perform it; but man, at the instigation of the devil, and by his own wanton disobedience, hath bereaved himself and all his posterity of those Divine graces.

10. *Will God leave such disobedience and apostacy unpunished?*

By no means; on the contrary, He is angry in the most dreadful manner, both on account of inborn and of actual sins, and in most just judgment punisheth them with temporal and everlasting

6. *Hat denn Gott den Menschen also bös und verkehrt erschaffen?*

Nein; sondern Gott hat den Menschen gut und nach seinem Ebenbild erschaffen, das ist, in wahrhaftiger Gerechtigkeit und Heiligkeit, auf dass er Gott seinen Schöpfer recht erkennte, und von Herzen liebte, und in ewiger Seligkeit mit ihm lebte, ihn zu loben und zu preisen.

7. *Woher kommt denn solche verderbte Art des Menschen?*

Aus dem Fall und Ungehorsam unserer ersten Eltern, Adam und Eva, im Paradies; da unsere Natur also vergiftet worden, dass wir alle in Sünden empfangen und geboren worden.

8. *Sind wir aber dermassen verderbt, dass wir ganz und gar untüchtig sind zu einigem Guten und geneigt zu allem Bösen?*

Ja; es sei denn, dass wir durch den Geist Gottes wiedergeboren werden.

9. *Thut denn Gott dem Menschen nicht unrecht, dass er in seinem Gesetz von ihm fordert was er nicht thun kann?*

Nein. Denn Gott hat den Menschen also erschaffen dass er's konnte thun; der Mensch, aber hat sich und alle seine Nachkommen, aus Anstiftung des Teufels, durch muthwilligen Ungehorsam derselbigen Gaben beraubet.

10. *Will Gott solchen Ungehorsam und Abfall ungestraft lassen hingehen?*

Mit nichten: sondern er zürnet schrecklich, beides über angeborne und wirkliche Sünden, und will sie aus gerechtem Urtheil zeitlich und ewig strafen, wie er gesprochen hat: *Verfluche*

punishments, even as He hath spoken: "Cursed be every one that continueth not in all things written in the book of the law to do them."

11. *Is not God then also merciful?*

Truly God is merciful, but He is also just. Wherefore His justice requireth that the sin which is committed against the Most High Majesty of God should also be punished with the highest, that is, everlasting punishments both of body and soul.

12. *Seeing then that, according to the just judgment of God, we have merited both temporal and eternal punishments; how might it be possible for us to escape these punishments, and again to come into favour?*

It is the will of God that His justice should be satisfied; therefore it is necessary that we satisfy, either by ourselves, or by another.

13. *But are we able to satisfy for ourselves?*

By no means; but we even make our guilt daily greater.

14. *But is there any one, who is a mere creature, able to satisfy for us?*

None; for, *first*, God will punish no other creature for the sin which man hath committed. *Secondly*, No mere creature is able to sustain the weight of the eternal wrath of God against sin, and to redeem others from it.

15. *What manner of Mediator and Redeemer must we seek for, then?*

Such a one, who is a real and a just man, and yet in power above all creatures, that is, who at the same time also is the true God.

sei Jedermann der nicht bleibet in allem dem, das geschrieben stehet in dem Buch des Gesetzes, dass er's thue.

11. *Ist denn Gott nicht auch barmhertzig?*

Gott ist wohl barmhertzig, er ist aber auch gerecht. Derhalben seine Gerechtigkeit erfordert dass die Sünde, welche wider die allerhöchste Majestät Gottes begangen ist, auch mit der höchsten, das ist, der ewigen Strafe an Leib und Seele gestraft werde.

12. *Dieweil wir denn nach dem gerechten Urtheil Gottes zeitliche und ewige Strafe verdient haben; wie möchten wir dieser Strafe entgehen, und wiederum zu Gnaden kommen?*

Gott will, dass seiner Gerechtigkeit genug geschehe: desswegen müssen wir derselben entweder durch uns selbst, oder durch einen Andern vollkommene Bezahlung thun.

13. *Können wir aber durch uns selbst Bezahlung thun?*

Mit nichten: sondern wir machen auch die Schuld noch täglich grösser.

14. *Kann aber irgend eine blosse Kreatur für uns bezahlen?*

Keine: denn erstlich, will Gott an keiner andern kreatur strafen was der Mensch verschuldet hat. Zum andern, so kann auch keine blosse kreatur die Last des ewigen Zornes Gottes wider die Sünde ertragen und andere davon erlösen.

15. *Was müssen wir denn für einen Mittler und Erlöser suchen?*

Einen solchen, der ein wahrer und gerechter Mensch, und doch stärker denn alle Kreaturen, das ist, zugleich wahrer Gott sei.

16. *Wherefore is it necessary that he should be a real and a just man?*
Because the justice of God requireth that the same human nature which hath sinned should satisfy for sin. But one that was a sinner himself could not satisfy for others.

17. *Wherefore is it necessary that he at the same time also should be the true God?*
That he might by the power of his Godhead sustain in his human nature the burden of God's wrath, and might earn and restore to us (the) righteousness and (the) life.

18. *But who is this Mediator who is at the same time the true God and a real and a just man?*
Our Lord Jesus Christ, who is given unto us for complete redemption and righteousness.

19. *Whence knowest thou that?*
Out of the Holy Gospel which God Himself first made known in Paradise, and afterwards did spread abroad by the holy patriarchs and prophets, foreshadowed it by the offerings and other ceremonies of the law, but lastly accomplished by His beloved and only Son.

20. *Shall then all men be again happy through Christ, just as through Adam they became lost?*
No; but only those who by true faith are engrafted [incorporated] into Him, and who accept all His benefits.

21. *What is true faith?*
It is not only a sure knowledge whereby I firmly hold as true all things

16. *Warum muss er ein wahrer und gerechter Mensch sein?*
Darum, dass die Gerechtigkeit Gottes erfordert, dass die Menschliche Natur, die gesündigt hat, für die Sünde bezahle. Aber einer, der selbst ein Sünder wäre, nicht könnte für andere bezahlen.

17. *Warum muss er zugleich wahrer Gott sein?*
Dass er aus Kraft seiner Gottheit die Last des Zornes Gottes an seiner Menschheit ertragen, und uns die Gerechtigkeit und das Leben erwerben und wieder geben möchte.

18. *Wer ist aber derselbige Mittler, der zugleich wahrer Gott und ein wahrer gerechter Mensch sei?*
Unser Herr Jesus Christus der uns zur vollkommenen Erlösung und Gerechtigkeit geschenket ist.

19. *Woher weisst du das?*
Aus dem heiligen Evangelio, welches Gott selbst anfänglich im Paradies hat geoffenbaret; folgends durch die heiligen Erzväter und Propheten lassen verkündigen, und durch die Opfer und andere Ceremonien des Gesetzes vorgebildet; endlich aber durch seinen eingeliebten Sohn erfüllet.

20. *Werden denn alle Menschen wiederum durch Christum selig, wie sie durch Adam sind verloren worden?*
Nein: sondern allein diejenigen, die durch wahren Glauben ihm werden einverleibt, und alle seine Wohlthaten annehmen.

21. *Was ist wahrer Glaube?*
Es ist nicht allein eine gewisse Erkenntniss dadurch ich alles für wahr

which God hath revealed unto us in His Word, but also a hearty trust which the Holy Ghost worketh in me through the Gospel—that the forgiveness of sins, everlasting life and salvation, are bestowed by God out of mere grace, and on account of the merit of Christ, not upon others only, but even upon me.

[Questions 22 to 85 are occupied with an exposition of the Apostles' Creed, Baptism, the Lord's Supper, Preaching and Ecclesiastical Discipline.]

86. *Since then we are redeemed out of our misery, entirely without merit of our own, because of the grace of God through Christ, for what cause are we to do good works?*

Because Christ, after He hath bought us with His blood, reneweth us by His Holy Spirit to His own image, that we all our life-time may manifest ourselves thankful to God for His benefits, and that through us He may be glorified. Thereafter also, that we severally may be assured of our faith by its fruits, and that by our godly course of life we may also win our neighbours unto Christ.

87. *Can those then not be in a state of salvation who do not turn unto God from their unthankful and impenitent course of life?*

They cannot; for as the Scripture saith, No unchaste person, no idolator, no adulterer, no thief, no covetous person, no drunkard, no reviler, no robber, nor the like, shall inherit the kingdom of God.

88. *In how many parts consisteth*

halte was uns Gott in seinem Wort hat geoffenbaret, sondern auch ein herzliches Vertrauen welches der heilige Geist durchs Evangelium in mir wirket, dass nicht allein andern, sondern auch mir Vergebung der Sünden, ewige Gerechtigkeit und Seligkeit von Gott geschenket sei, aus lauter Gnaden, allein um des Verdienstes Christi willen.

86. *Dieweil wir denn aus unser Elend, ohne all unser Verdienst, aus Gnaden durch Christum erlöset sind, warum sollen wir gute Werke thun?*

Darum, dass Christus, nachdem er uns mit seinem Blut erkauft hat, uns auch durch seinen heiligen Geist erneuert zu seinem Ebenbild, dass wir mit unserm ganzen Leben uns dankbar gegen Gott für seine Wohlthaten erzeigen, und er durch uns gepriesen werde. Darnach auch, dass wir bei uns selbst unsers Glaubens aus seinen Früchten gewiss seien, und mit unsern gottseligen Wandel unsern Nächsten auch Christo gewinnen.

87. *Können denn die nicht selig werden, die sich von ihrem undankbaren, unbussfertigen Wandel zu Gott nicht bekehren?*

Keineswegs; denn wie die Schrift sagt, Kein Unkeuscher, Abgöttischer, Ehebrecher, Dieb, Geiziger, Trunkenbold, Lästerer, Räuber, und dergleichen, wird das Reich Gottes ererben.

88. *In wie viel Stücken besteht die*

CONSOLATION AS THE FIRST ASPECT OF THE GOSPEL. 37

the true Penitence or Conversion of man?

In two parts: In the mortification of the old man, and the quickening [resurrection] of the new man.

89. *What is the Mortification of the old man?*

From the heart to cherish grief on account of sin, and to hate and shun it ever more and more.

90. *What is the Quickening [resurrection] of the new man?*

To have heartfelt joy in God through Christ, and affectionate desire to live in all good works according to the will of God.

91. *But what are good works?*

Only those that proceed from a true faith, according to the law of God to His glory, and not such as are grounded upon our own notions of what is good, or upon human institutions.

[Questions 92 to 115 contain an explanation of the Ten Commandments. Questions 116 to 129 are concerning prayer, including a paraphrase of the several petitions of the Lord's Prayer.]

wahrhaftige Busse oder Bekehrung des Menschen?

In zwei Stücken: In Absterbung des alten, und Auferstehung des neuen Menschen.

89. *Was ist die Absterbung des alten Menschen?*

Sich die Sünde von Herzen lassen leid sein, und dieselbe je länger je mehr hassen und fliehen.

90. *Was ist die Auferstehung des neuen Menschen?*

Herzliche Freude in Gott durch Christum und Lust und Liebe haben, nach dem Willen Gottes in allen guten Werken zu leben.

91. *Welches sind aber gute Werke?*

Allein die aus wahrem Glauben, nach dem Gesetz Gottes, ihm zu Ehren geschehen, und nicht die auf unser Gutdünken oder Menschensatzung gegründet sind.

The general arrangement of this Catechism might suggest to readers, who are acquainted with the Westminster Catechisms of the following century, that there is a remarkable family likeness between them. But the fact is that, in the Christian Church, catechetical instruction originally required the committing to memory of the Apostles' Creed, the Ten Commandments, and the Lord's Prayer. Christian teachers gave conversational explanations for the enlightenment of their scholars. Long experience would enable a teacher to transfer these *vivâ voce* explanations into lucid questions and answers. Thus catechisms, as we now have them, would at length be put into circulation. An introduction would to a practical man seem to be desirable; the ingenuity of the author of a catechism would be taxed to compose prefatory questions and answers. The Catechism of Calvin started with the *summum bonum*. The Heidelberg Catechism found a characteristic gospel starting-point in Divine consolation. The authors of the Westminster Catechisms thought that a preface more suitable to the grand themes of eternal salvation and new obedience was the glory of God, but almost in the same breath they put forward the happiness of man.[1] De Witte, in his catechetical commentary on the Heidelberg Catechism, combines the prefaces. His first head is, " Of man's chief comfort ; " and his first question and answer are :—

" What is that which a Christian ought most of all to wish and to desire?— In respect of God, the promoting of His glory as the uttermost end of all things. In respect of himself, the enjoyment of the chiefest good, His salvation, His comfort, both in life and in death."

An esteemed critic (Thomas M'Crie, *secundus*, D.D., LL.D.) would at once dismiss the Heidelberg Catechism from use, because it suggests to a pupil that as soon as he can repeat the first answer he is in actual possession of consolation for eternity. But such an off-hand decision is not worthy of the judge. Personal acquaintance with pupils would soon dispose of the alleged danger as imaginary. The compendious Commentary of Pastor Mohn of Dierdorf gives the evident meaning of the answer to the first question, namely, " Christianity offers consolation to man who is in misery." And any parent or teacher using the catechism might (if necessary) modify the question thus :—" What doth the Gospel offer to thee as thy only consolation in life and in death ? "—Or, " What is the consolation which God in the Gospel doth put within thy reach as thy only consolation in life and in death ? "

The Heidelberg Catechism acquired and retained great reputation, being adopted by the Evangelical German and Dutch Churches, and being extensively read and studied by Protestants of other nations. It was celebrated under various names. Through the Latin translation it was known as the " Catechism of the Palatinate and the Belgic Catechism."[2] In the English translation of the first commentary upon it, in 1587, it was called " The Catechisme authorised by the noble Prince Fredericke throughout his dominions." The English phrase *Elector-Palatine* is a translation of the German title *Churfürstlicher Pfalz*. Usually this prince was simply called the Pfalz, which our ancestors translated into Pfaltzgrave, or Palsgrave ; and hence the first English translation, which was bequeathed to us in 1568 by the learned Dr Turner, has been briefly styled *The Palsgrave's*

---

[1] " Man's chief and highest end is to glorify God, and fully to enjoy Him for ever."—*Westminster Larger Catechism*.

" Man's chief end is to glorify God, and to enjoy Him for ever."—*Westminster Lesser (or Shorter) Catechism*.

[2] The Catechism was translated into Greek by Fridericus Sylburgius, and, along with the Belgic Confession, printed by Elzevir, 1635.

CONSOLATION AS THE FIRST ASPECT OF THE GOSPEL. 39

Catechism. Thomas Boston calls it *Ursin's Catechism,* after Ursinus, its principal author and the first commentator.

Throughout Germany, and notably in Holland, a regular system of catechising resulted in the publication of many commentaries on the Heidelberg Catechism. It is not only divided into questions, but also into sections, one for each Lord's day of the year. There was an accredited staff of catechists whom it was the duty of the pastors to train for their functions; and hence it was incumbent upon professors of theology to give a similar training to candidates for the Gospel ministry. In Book Second of this publication I propose to give some account of the commentators. There does not appear to be much quotable matter concerning consolation in their works; but there is an evident agreement on one point, namely, that the fact that consolation is the first aspect of a scriptural gospel is specially proved by one favourite apostolical statement, "Whatsoever things were written aforetime were written for our learning, that we, through patience and comfort of the Scriptures, might have hope" (Romans xv. 4).

In this place I must single out Dr Henry Alting, author of Three Volumes of Heidelbergensian Theological Writings (*Scripta Theologica Heidelbergensia*) in and after 1613. On *question* 90, concerning the vivification of the new man, he declares this quickening, or spiritual resurrection, to manifest itself in three ways, namely, "(1) a man's joy in God through Christ arising from a sense of the gratuitous forgiveness of his sins; (2) the love of piety; (3) the serious and most unfeigned pursuit of piety." Among the questions which he undertakes to answer are these :—"*Question.* Is true joy in God through Christ a part of vivification, or is it not rather a result following the work of the Holy Ghost ?— *Answer.* It is both, though from different points of view. It is a part—inasmuch as rejoicing in God, reconciled to me through Jesus Christ, is an agent in vivification. It is also a result, as an effect wrought by the life-giving Spirit, because it is kindled within me by the Spirit of adoption."

"*Question.* Does not true joy in God, which the catechism places first in order, rather follow the desire and pursuit of obedience to the will of God ? Ought not such desire and pursuit to be placed first in order ?—*Answer.* These as to time are simultaneous, but in the order of nature or causation, joy is first, and the pursuit of good works follows. Joy animates men to the pursuit of good works (Luke xix. 6, 8; 2 Cor. v. 14), and joy arises from *justification;* for being justified by faith we have peace together with joy and exhilaration of heart (Romans, v. 1, &c). But the pursuit of good works arises from *sanctification* (Colossians iii. 1, 2, &c.; Titus ii. 14). Thus the order of the causes being known, the effects are correctly described in the same order (Rom. viii. 30; 1 Cor. i. 30). At the same time by the pursuit of good works, as a most sure evidence of true faith, and as a living testimony of the hope of the heavenly inheritance, joy is nourished, increased, and confirmed."

My attention has just been called to Professor Schaff's[1] panegyric on this Catechism, which he had already called "an acknowledged masterpiece." "The genius of the catechism (he remarks) is brought out at once in the first question, which contains the central idea and strikes the key-note. It is unsurpassed for depth, comfort, and beauty; and, once committed to memory, can never be forgotten. It represents Christianity in its evangelical, practical, cheering aspect, not as a commanding law, not as an intellectual scheme, not as a system of outward observances; but as the best gift of God to man, as a source of peace and comfort in life and in death. What can be more comforting—what at the same time more honouring and stimulating to a holy life—than the assurance of being owned wholly by Christ our blessed Lord and Saviour, who sacrificed His only spotless life for us on the cross? The first question and answer of the Heidelberg Catechism is the whole Gospel in a nutshell.

. . . .

"The Catechism is a work of religious enthusiasm, based on solid theological learning, and directed by excellent judgment. It is baptized with the pentecostal fire of the great Reformation, yet remarkably free from the polemic zeal and intolerance which characterised that wonderfully excited period—by far the richest and deepest in church history next to the age of Christ and His inspired apostles. It is the product of the heart as well as of the head, full of faith and unction from above. It is fresh, lively, glowing, yet clear, sober, self-sustained. The ideas are Biblical and orthodox, and well fortified by apt scriptural proofs. The language is dignified, terse, nervous, popular, and often truly eloquent. It is the language of devotion as well as instruction. Altogether the Heidelberg Catechism is more than a book; it is an institution, and will live as long as the Reformed Church."

The affectionate and grateful veneration felt for this Catechism was usefully and widely extended in the year 1863, which was observed as the Tercentary of the Heidelberg Catechism. The preparation for spoken orations and written papers, worthy of the occasion, in Germany, Holland, and America, resulted in new light thrown upon the history of the Catechism, and in greater accuracy in copies put into circulation for the use of schools and churches. Another result was the discovery of one copy of the original edition; this unique relic has been printed in facsimile. At Elberfeld a collection of sermons, in honour of the Tercentary, was published with the title, *Der einzige Trost im Leben und Sterben* [the only consolation in life and in death.][2]

---

[1] "A History of the Creeds of Christendom," with translations. By Philip Schaff, D.D., LL.D., Professor of Biblical Literature in the Union Theological Seminary, New York, U.S.A. London: Hodder & Stoughton, 1877.

[2] Schaff. I expect to be largely indebted to this distinguished author in *Book Second* of this work.

NOTE.

In this chapter, when I arrived at the Creed, I had to be content with simply referring to the questions and answers in which it is expounded. But there are two remarkable questions and answers for which I must find room here. There appears to an English reader a singularity arising from the circumstance that in German "*Christus*" is the word for "Christ," and "*ein Christ*" means "a Christian."

31. Warum ist er Christus, das ist, ein Gesalbter, genannt?

Dass Er von Gott dem Vater verordnet und mit dem heiligen Geist gesalbet ist, zu unserm obersten Propheten und Lehrer, der uns den heimlichen Rath und Willen Gottes von unserer Erlösung vollkommen offenbaret—und zu unserm einigen Hohenpriester der uns mit demeinigen Opfer seines Leibes erlöset hat und immerdar mit seiner Fürbitte vor dem Vater vertritt—und zu unserm ewigen König der uns mit seinem Wort und Geist regiert und bei der erworbenen Erlösung schützet und erhält.

32. Warum wirst du aber ein Christ genannt?

Dass ich durch den Glauben ein Glied Christi und also seiner Salbung theilhaftig bin, auf dass auch ich seinen Namen bekenne, mich ihm zu einem lebendigen Dankopfer darstelle, und mit freiem Gewissen in diesem Leben wider die Sünde und Teufel streite, und hernach in Ewigkeit mit ihm über alle Kreaturen herrsche.

31. Why is He called Christ, that is, Anointed One?

Because He was ordained by God the Father, and anointed with the Holy Ghost, to be our chief Prophet and Teacher, who hath fully revealed unto us the secret counsel and will of God concerning our redemption—and to be our only High Priest, who with the one only offering of His body hath redeemed us, and doth continually appear before the Father with His intercession—and to be our eternal King, who ruleth us with His Word and Spirit, and who defendeth and maintaineth the redemption which He hath earned.

32. But why art thou called a Christian?

Because through faith I am a member of Christ and am also a partaker of His anointing [unction], in order that I may own His name, may dedicate myself to Him as a living thank-offering, and may, in this life, with a free[1] conscience, fight against sin and the devil, and may hereafter in eternity reign with Him over all creatures.

---

[1] The Latin version says *libera et bona* [free and good.]

CHAPTER II.

"CHRIST ALONE EXALTED."

By the Rev. Dr Crisp, Rector of Brinkworth.

"*Christ alone exalted*" was the peculiarly appropriate motto for the sermons of the admirable English rector, Dr Tobias Crisp. These sermons were printed and published after his death, at the age of forty-two, so that the title-page was not dictated by himself; but it informs us that the sermons were "taken from his own mouth in *shortwriting*, whereof severall copies were diligently compared together and with his owne notes." One volume was published in 1643, containing Sermons on Christ the Only Way, and similar subjects. Another volume appeared in 1644,[1] and its chief contents were fourteen sermons on Isaiah liii. 6. A third volume, containing, among others, seven sermons on 1 John ii. 1, 2, was published in 1646; it was entitled, "Christ Alone Exalted in the perfection and encouragements of the saints notwithstanding sins and trialls." In 1690 all the above were republished by the author's son, Samuel, who added ten sermons from his father's manuscripts, including four upon Free Grace exhibited as the Teacher of Good Works (Titus ii. 11, 12). The modern editions, the first of which was issued in 1755, were under the editorship of the Rev. Dr Gill, who declared that his "sole view in republishing" them was the same as Dr Crisp's in preaching them, "namely, the relief of distressed minds and consciences burdened with a sense of sin and seeking deliverance from it."

The fundamental doctrines of Dr Crisp are simple and safe—for instance, "Christ is our way, so that there is no coming to the Father but by Him." "Christ gives a free welcome to all comers." "Only Christ's righteousness dischargeth the sinner." "The righteousness which obtains the discharge of the believer's sin, and wins his cause, is Christ's righteousness, and not the believer's act of believing." "Wheresoever the grace of God brings salvation, it is not bestowed in vain, but inclines a man's heart to new obedience, and makes him fruitful in his life in all well-pleasingness."

There have been frequent censures of these sermons as unsafe. But any censures that were at all warrantable, were directed against strong expressions and discursive remarks, which the author might have softened or pruned down if he had lived to superintend the printing of his sermons. The learned and orthodox Witsius undertook to review the sermons along with the books of other writers, with whom Dr Crisp had no connection; and he wrote an *Irenicum*,

---

[1] In the copies before me, vol. i. is dated 1644; and vol. ii., 1643—so that perhaps they were issued together.

which (as far as the Doctor is concerned, for Witsius mentions no author by name) may be fairly said to absolve him from all accusations, except as to what were called some paradoxical assertions concerning the utility of holiness and good works, which (says the *Irenicum*) "appear with quite another face when the hideous vizard of the most rugged phrases is torn off."

"Rugged phrases" roused the attention of hearers who had been put to sleep by academical homilies on Christian morals; but there is another observation that must be made, namely, that no faithful preacher of the Word of God will undertake to construct a scheme of salvation that will not, from some point of view, appear dangerous to morality. Pretentiously safe schemes have been attempted, but they differ from the Scriptures in this, that they are schemes to save saints and not to save sinners. They are schemes which date our first sensation of consolation from the perception of reformation in ourselves, not from the reception of a free pardon from God. They are schemes which leave out of consideration such facts as this one, that the promise of justification is to the sinner "who worketh not, but believeth in Him that justifieth the ungodly (*justificat impium*)." If any preacher's scheme be like the scheme of the Apostle Paul, it will raise the objection that by preaching faith he makes void the law of God and encourages men to continue in sin that mercy may abound.

To call men's attention to the old evangelical truth, that there is forgiveness with God that a sinner may fear Him, the Apostle Paul used startling expressions, and he, being inspired, said all things well. Dr Crisp, as an uninspired teacher, could not say all things perfectly; but he is not censurable where he follows out the Apostle's principles, motives, and temper. In the present day our esteemed authors use, without giving offence, a greater latitude in their expressions than Dr Crisp's critics could tolerate. And in all generations some allowances ought to be made for one or two imperfections in a valuable posthumous publication. The following extracts from "Christ Alone Exalted" have much of the style and tone of our soundest modern authorship.

Crispiana.[1]

The whole strain of the Gospel runs continually thus: "Christ came to save the lost; He died for the ungodly; while we were sinners, Christ died for us; He received gifts for the rebellious that the Lord might dwell among them," and such like, are the terms of the Gospel upon which Christ is tendered to our souls. Now, then, I say to every afflicted soul, Art thou rebellious, an enemy, ungodly, a harlot, lost? . . . Christ came for thee while thus, though no better

[1] The extracts were made by me from Dr Gill's edition, but I have now collated them with the first edition, 1643-1646.

than thus; He comes to tender Himself unto thee to take Him whilst thou art thus, before thou art any better.—*Sermon IV.*

What doth Christ mean by coming unto Him? In [John vi.] verse 35, Christ will give you His mind Himself—"He that comes unto Me shall not hunger, and he that believes in Me shall not thirst." Mark it well, beloved, he makes "coming" and "believing," in sense, all one; for if you observe it, such as Christ deals with are unsatisfied and empty ones: now He satisfies the empty, and whose emptiness will He fill?—even of those that believe in Him, that come to Him. Believing and coming are therefore all one, so that to come to Christ is to believe in Christ. But you will say, We are as far to seek as we were; what is that believing on Christ? In John i. 12, you shall see what it is to believe on Him—"As many as received Him, to them He gave power to become the sons of God, even to them that believe on His name." Here He makes receiving and believing all one, as before He made coming and believing. The sum in brief is this— the coming to Christ is no more but the receiving of Him for shelter and succour. A man is said to come to a stronghold when he enters into it for his security and safety; he doth not stand hacking and hammering—shall I? or shall I not?—but danger forces him, and in he gets (the door being open), and comes to his stronghold. So a person comes to Christ; Christ opening, he slips in, and ventures himself with Him, and casts himself into His arms, and He will sink or swim with him. Beloved, whoever you are, that can but come to Him, to venture yourselves upon the rock Christ; to sink or to swim, as Christ will support or sink under you; counting Him a refuge, to have Him for your succour—*in no wise will He cast you out.*—*Sermon XIV.*

Peradventure, though the text seem to be clear, yet you will say, "Surely the grace of God is not so large as you seem to express it; there must be something expected and considered in the person coming, or there will be no receiving and entertaining by Christ."

Beloved, it were an easy thing (if time would give leave) to show that, through the whole Scriptures, the Lord Christ hath such a purpose, to set forth the glory of the grace of His Father, as that He will have men know, that all the fitness of persons to communicate or participate of Christ is their desperate sinfulness. I say, nothing but sinfulness is that which is the fitness that Christ looks for in persons.—*Sermon XIV.*

Mark well this passage, "I will in no wise cast him out." Our Saviour doth plainly import that there neither is nor can be devised—no, not by God Himself—any one consideration whatsoever which might occasion Him to put off or say *nay* to any person that doth come. No consideration in the world, I say, can so aggravate a man's condition, could he make it as bad as the devils themselves, yet, if there be a coming to Christ, there can be no consideration in the highest pitch of sinfulness for Christ to reject, or put by, a person coming to Him. For you must know, beloved, Christ is well acquainted with all the objections the heart of man (nay, the devil) can object against the freeness of His grace and life by Him. To save labour, therefore, in this one passage (*I will in no wise cast out*), Christ at once answers all the objections that could be made. And I dare be bold to maintain, in the name and stead of Christ, let a person but say and lay down this for granted, that come he would—that he would have Christ rather than his life,—let this be granted for a truth, I will be bold with Christ out of this passage to answer ten thousand objections, even fully to the silencing of every objection that can be made; "I will in no wise cast him out;" *I will in no wise*, that is, I will upon no consideration that can be imagined and conceived.—*Sermon XIV.*

If this be truth that you say, that such and such filthiness stands between Christ and you; that though you come there could be no entertainment with Christ for you;—supposing this to be true, this that Christ speaks is most certainly false. For, saith Christ, *I will in no wise cast you off*, that is, upon no consideration will I cast you off; you say, upon this consideration I am so abominably vile there will be casting off. If this you say be true, that which Christ saith must be false. There is a point blank contradiction between these two, and therefore either Christ must call in these words again thus generally delivered, and must put in this exception that you put in, or else Christ's word and yours cannot agree.

You say, upon such considerations there is no admittance, and upon such-and-such considerations there is admittance. Christ saith, "I will in no wise cast you out;" notwithstanding this consideration I will receive you. Be what you will, do but come; and, for all that, you shall be welcome.—*Sermon XIV.*

It is a common doctrine among the rigid troublers of the Israel of God, that men must have many legal preparations, and that they must sensibly find these wrought in themselves, before they may dare to apply Christ by faith for justification, otherwise their faith is mere presumption. As, for instance—suppose a sinner hath lived in all manner of licentiousness (as Mary Magdalen), then, before he may believe that Christ hath justified him, he must forsake, and by reflecting on himself that he hath forsaken, all his former evil ways, and must be stricken with inward terror, and feel the pangs of the new birth, and be, I know not how much or how long (for their expressions intimate a strange depth), under the bondage of a kind of hellish conscience tormenting and racking him; nay, more, he must be changed too, and find a delight in the law of the Lord, and a ready cheerfulness in obedience thereunto, and that not by a fit, but constantly. Till he finds all this, and much more of a like nature, his time of believing in Christ is not come. Before this his faith is but a dream, and skinning over the sore. All this occasions so much fear, as keeps many poor souls in bondage all their lives long, suspecting still that the humiliation is not deep enough.

Is not this to put the cart before the horse?—or rather, to set the cart agoing, and the horse must come after?—to have men sanctified before they can be justified? If men must be thus qualified before they can believe to justification, how can Christ be said to justify the ungodly? By this rule He rather justifies the godly.—*Sermon LII.*

"Jesus saith unto him, I am the way, the truth, and the life; no man cometh unto the Father but by ME." . . . Christ is our way, so that there is no coming to the Father but by Him. . . . Every way, highway, or pathway, necessarily imports two terms, *From whence,* and *Whereunto.* When a man enters into a way, he leaves the place where he was, and goes to the place where he was not. . . .

The state, *from which* Christ is our way to the Father, is twofold—first, a state of sin; and, secondly, a state of wrath. The state, *whereunto* Christ is the way, is indeed expressed here to be to the Father; the meaning is, To the grace of the Father and to the glory of the Father. The sum is this, Christ is so our way from a state of sin and wrath to a state of grace and glory, that there is no coming from the one to the other but by Christ.—*Sermon I.*

Grace (in Scripture) admits of a double acceptation, proper and improper. We usually take grace for that which is improperly grace; for we commonly call "grace" those divine qualities and virtues, and holy conditions and actions, wherewith we are possessed, by which we do improve and employ ourselves in the world; this we usually call grace, and in some sense it is grace. But that which is most properly grace is nothing else but merely favour and bounty, and loving-kindness itself; and so, consequently, all sanctification is not so properly grace itself as the fruit of grace. God first casts His favour and loving-kindness upon a person, then out of His favour flow the several fruits of loving-kindness; and the fruits are those "Fruits of the Spirit" frequently mentioned by the Apostle. Now Christ is a way to grace in both these respects. Christ is a way to favour and loving-kindness in God; Christ is a way to all fruits, or graces (as you call them).—*Sermon II.*

"He hath mercy upon whom He will have mercy." Christ becomes unto them a way, not out of their will, not out of their disposition, not out of their holy walkings—but out of that mercy that proceeds out of the mere will of God; His own good pleasure is the only fountain and spring of it. Beloved, I beseech you, seriously ponder and consider, that the gospel is therefore called the gospel because it is glad tidings unto men; and so the angel interpreted it, "Behold, I bring glad tidings." Why glad tidings? In this regard, *glad*; the poor sinner, he is a broken creature; nay, more, he is a dead creature—"ye who were dead in trespasses and sins." Life is reached out unto such a person, that is, a dead person; herein it is plain, that there comes forth grace from the Lord, so that a creature, being dead, who can act nothing towards life, yet he shall receive life. "The hour is coming, and now is, when the dead shall hear the voice of the Son of God: and they that hear it shall live" (John v. 25). How come they by life? Is there any action of theirs towards life? They are dead; it is the voice of the Son of God puts life into their dead souls. And it is glad tidings, that though the creature can do nothing, yet Christ brings enough with Him from the fountain of the Father to bestow upon them, to bring them to Him.— *Sermon III.*

Christ is delivered over unto men to be their way unto the Father, of mere gift—of free gift. What is freer than a gift? That Christ is delivered over to be a way to the Father by a mere and absolute gift is most plainly expressed in Isaiah xlii. 6, "I will give Thee to be a covenant to the people." In matter of gift, what is there in the richest man in the world more than in the veriest beggar to partake of it, supposing the thing that comes to him is a gift? A beggar can take a gift as well as the richest man.—*Sermon III.*

Christ is a free way for all comers to enter into, without any cause of fear that they shall trespass by entering. He is a free way, I say,—a way that costs nothing, a way barred up to no person whatsoever, a way whose gates are cast off from the hinges,—nay, rather, a way that hath no gates at all unto it—a cheap way to us—a costly way, indeed, unto the Father, and to Christ too. . . .

If we look upon God and Christ as making a way for men, it is not a free way, it is not a cheap way. But looking upon ourselves, that have received the benefit of this way and this Christ, it is a free way indeed; free for man, without any cost or charge—free, as He is a way to all sorts of men, none excepted, none prohibited. "Whosoever will" may set footing in Christ. There is nothing can bar one person more than another from entering into Christ as a way. I know, beloved, this seems harsh to the ears of some people, that there is no difference to be made among men, not only poor as well as rich, but that the wicked as well as the godly are admitted; that is strange. But let me tell you, beloved, Christ is a free way for a drunkard, for a harlot, an enemy to Christ; I say, Christ is as free a way for such a person to enter into Him as for the most godly person in the world. But do not mistake me. I dare not say, Christ is a free way to walk in Him, and yet to continue in such a condition. Christ will never leave a person in such a filthiness, to whom He hath given to enter into Himself. But for entrance into Him Christ is as free a way for the vilest sort of sinners as for any person under heaven. If Christ has given a heart to a sinner to set footing into Himsef, that is, to receive, to take Him for his Christ—if Christ hath given him a heart to take Him for his Christ in reality, to take Him truly and unfeignedly—Christ is a way for such a person to the Father, though he be the vilest person under heaven.—*Sermon III.*

Christ is the way, and the absolute and complete way, to rid every soul that comes to God by Him from all filthiness; so that the person to whom Christ is the way stands in the sight of God as having no fault at all in Him. Beloved, these two are contradictions, for a person to be reckoned a faulty person, yet that person to be reckoned a just or an innocent person: if he be faulty he is not innocent; if he be innocent he is not faulty. Now, it is the main stream of the whole Gospel that Christ justifies the ungodly; if Christ justifies him, there is no fault to be cast upon him. Mark it well, consider it, as that wherein consists your honey, the life of your soul, and the joy of your spirits; I say, it holds forth the Lord Christ as freely tendering Himself to people, considering people only as ungodly persons receiving Him. You have no sooner received Him but you are instantly justified by Him; and in this justification you are discharged from all the faults that may be laid to your charge. There is not one sin you commit after you receive Christ that God can charge upon your person.—*Sermon I.*

Here is the sum of this part of this free grace of God, "the blotting out of transgression." You know, beloved, the use of writing debts in a book, namely, that a creditor may turn over at pleasure or leisure to them; and so, when he looks there, he may find what every person oweth, and, at discretion, may take the groundwork of his action that he lays against a person; and, upon this action, may arrest him, and lay him up in prison till he pays the debt. And, likewise, you know what the end of this "blotting out," too, is; namely, that when men come to look over their books, they may overlook and skip over what was written; and when the book is looked over, no notice shall be taken of such a person's name, who, though he was entered in the book, yet all is blotted out again; which imports to us this much as to the thing in hand, namely, that though the Lord, according to the usual manner of taking notice of actions against men, hath His time when He will take notice of these debts, when He enters the debtor, when He will arrest and clap him up for them; yet, when He shall look over His book, He shall take no notice of such persons of His whose parcels are crossed out. Therefore, in Jeremiah l. 20, see how the prophet alludes to this expression, and how he explains the words, *blotting out of transgression*. "In those days, and at that time, saith the Lord, shall the iniquities of Israel be sought for, and there shall be none; and the sins of Judah, and they shall not be found: *for I will pardon them* whom I reserve." Here the prophet seems to represent the Lord as one that begins to look over His books, to see what debts are owing unto Him, as if He were making a search. Well, saith the Holy Ghost, though at such a time the sins of this people be sought for, yet there shall be none. It is true they were all entered into the knowledge of God from all eternity, yet there shall be none; that is, though they were entered, they are blotted out again. Therefore, as it is in a debt-book, though there be never so many parcels entered—though entered ever so truly there—yet when once that which was entered is blotted out again, there is no more debt than if there never had been any; for all that was ever in is blotted out. So, though the Lord be privy to what they do, and hath recorded them in His own thoughts, yet He Himself draws a blot upon them, and makes them to be nothing. . . . .

And this He doth, not simply in respect of forgiveness. In regard of us, it is true, it is a forgiveness. Yet, in respect of Him, it is not merely forgiveness. For the reason and ground of blotting out of iniquity is, there is a second Head to which these debts are translated, that shall pay them better than those whose debts first they were; so that, the debt being paid, God loseth nothing, forasmuch as another hath paid all.—*Sermon XI.*

When the text saith, "The Lord hath laid on Him the iniquity of us all," the meaning is, that Christ Himself becomes the transgressor in the room and stead of the person that had transgressed; so that, in respect of the reality of being a transgressor, Christ is as really the transgressor as the person that did commit it was a transgressor before Christ took this transgression upon Him. Beloved, mistake me not; I say not that ever Christ was, or that He ever could be, the actor or committer of any transgression, for He never committed any sin Himself. But the Lord laid iniquity upon Christ; and this act of God's laying it upon Him makes Christ as really a transgressor as if He Himself had actually committed transgression.—*Sermon XVII.* [*Vol. II., Sermon 3.*]

God gives the person of Christ to men. God gives Christ to stand in the room of men, and men stand in His room. So that, in the giving of Christ, God is pleased (as it were) to make a change [*an exchange*]; Christ represents our persons to the Father, we represent the person of Christ to Him. All the loveliness the person of Christ hath is put upon us, and we are lovely with the Father even as the Son Himself. On the other part, all that hatefulness and loathsomeness in our nature is put upon Christ; He stands, as it were, the abhorred of the Father for the time, even the forsaken of the Father, as He represented our persons, bare our blame, sustained our wrath, and drank the dregs of our cup. Here is the gift of the person—that which is Christ's is ours; that which is ours is His. There is an admirable expression in 2 Cor. v. 21, "He was made *sin for us* who knew no sin, that we might be made the righteousness of God in Him." It is plainly manifested that that which we were Christ became ("sin for us"); then that which Christ was we became ("the righteousness of God"): for we are made the righteousness of God in Him, saith the Apostle.—*Sermon XII.*

The Apostle [Paul], in his time, found that the preaching of this free grace unto men as they are sinners, raised the very objection that is on foot to this day, and (I believe) will be to the end of the world. He had ended a great discourse, and laid down his foundation and ground, "That a man is justified by faith without the works of the law;" and the objection comes in, "Do we make void the law through faith?" . . . . Why, say some, this gives liberty to all uncleanness, for a man to know that notwithstanding his wicked estate he shall be justified freely, and he shall be saved; it is impossible he should miscarry. Who will not take liberty to sin when he knows that, though he doth sin, though his sins be ever so great, all shall be done away—he shall not receive any hurt at all by them? Is not this to make void the law? you will say.

Mark the Apostle's answer, "God forbid; nay, rather, we establish the law;" that is, the preaching of this doctrine to you that are believers, little children, that have fellowship with the Father and the Son, will not make void the law; you cannot take liberty from this free grace revealed. The preaching and publishing of this free grace of God more effectually wins believers to obedience, and to forbearance from sin, than any other course in the world that can be taken. This, saith the Apostle, is a doctrine that doth establish the law, and not make it void; that is, it doth establish men in obedience to the will of God, and brings them nearer in conformity to the law, and doth not set them loose to the breaking and violating and frustrating of the law, and to profaneness.—*Sermon XXXIV.* [*Vol. III., Sermon 3.*]

The advocateship of Christ consists in pleading the discharge of His people on the principle of right and justice.

Whereas it is objected, and, indeed, seems a thing irreconcilable, that this discharge from sin goes all along under the notion of grace, and free grace, and pardon; how can this be, if it be merely an act of justice for God to forgive sins?

This may easily be reconciled, with a distinction. Discharge from sin, in respect of us, or of what we can bring by way of recompense [*compensation*] for the sin committed, is merely free grace—we can bring nothing at all; also in respect of Christ, as He is allowed to stand in our room, it is grace too. But, Christ being allowed and admitted, and the Lord having taken the full payment

He could ask at the hands of Christ, and acknowledging satisfaction upon such payment, this act of Christ makes it an act of justice and right that God should forgive sins. And, therefore, the Apostle, in 1 John i. 7, tells us, that "The blood of Jesus Christ the Son of God cleanseth us from all sin;" and, therefore, he concludes that "He is faithful and just to forgive us our sins."—*Sermon XXXVI.* [*Vol. III., Sermon 5.*]

This advocateship of Christ is a plea founded or grounded upon justice. Christ doth not appeal in His plea to mere mercy; but His client shall stand or fall as justice itself shall pronounce the sentence. Christ doth exercise this office in heaven rather virtually than vocally; He speaks as His blood doth speak. *We are come to the blood of sprinkling* (saith the Apostle in Heb. xii. 24) *that speaks better things than the blood of Abel.*

Whose cause is it that Christ doth maintain and plead? The cause of all believers—the cause of little children, even when they have sinned without limitation of the sin they commit: for He expresses Himself in general terms, it is the cause of those that sin, "If any man sin" (1 John ii. 1); yea, the cause not only of present believers, but also of all the elect—believers or unbelievers—if they be elected. It is true, they shall believe in time; but yet I say, Christ is an advocate of them, while unbelievers, if they be elected. There is not a sin in the world, but as it is damnable in its own nature in the rigour of justice, so it doth not allow of any forbearance. It is only Christ that makes the forbearance, even until they are called.—*Sermon XXXVII.*

What is that righteousness which has efficacy and prevalency with the Father for the discharge of a member of Christ when he sins?

There is not any righteousness of a believer which he acts, which can possibly have any force in plea with the Father for the discharge of a person that hath committed a sin. I mention that righteousness "which he acts," because the very righteousness of Christ Himself is indeed the righteousness of a believer, for HE is "The Lord our Righteousness." As He was made sin for us, and became our sin by imputation, so we are made the righteousness of God in Him; that is, Christ's righteousness is as much become our own righteousness, as our sins became Christ's sins. And as Christ bore the whole fruit of our sins by being made sin for us, so we enjoy the whole fruit of Christ's righteousness by being made righteous in Him. Therefore I say, not simply no righteousness of a believer, but none which he himself doth act, hath the least force in plea to prevail for the discharge of sin.

I must tell you, there is no divine rhetoric—there is no omnipotent excellency—in any righteousness whatsoever which a believer can put up unto God. It is not your turning from your evil ways; it is not your repentance, though never so cordial and large; it is not your departing from iniquity; it is not your doing good—hath the least force or power of plea with the Father to prevail with Him, for your righteousness, for your discharge, or to move Him to give the sentence upon you that you are discharged. No righteousness, I say, whatsoever you can do; for the best righteousness that ever man did perform, Christ only excepted, hath more in it to make against the person that did it, than it hath to make for him to obtain a sentence of discharge. And my reason is this. In the best righteousness of man, in turning from sin, or in repenting or mourning, or whatever else there is to be thought of, there is abundance of sin even in the very best actions that are performed; and where there is sinfulness, there is a plea against the person.—*Sermon XXXVII.*

The righteousness which obtains the discharge of a believer's sin is no righteousness of our own; no, not so much as the righteousness of faith as it is our act of believing. . . . .

There are some things to be considered even about our believing, as it hath a stroke in the discharge from sin, or in the pardon of sin. The truth is, beloved, some hand faith hath in this business; but it is not any righteousness in the act of believing that carries any stroke in it. If you will consider it well, you shall easily see there is no more righteousness in our believing, as we do act believing, than there is in any other gracious act whatsoever that we do—than is in our love to God. Nay, more, there is as much sinfulness in our act of believing as in our acting of other gifts. There is no man under heaven hath attained unto that height of believing, or that strength of faith, but there is still something wanting, some imperfection and sinfulness in it; and as there is weakness and imperfection in believing, so it is not possible that this should give forth such a righteousness as to constitute a person, who is unrighteous in himself, to be righteous before God. That which cannot set itself complete and righteous before God, can never set another righteous before God. Faith must be first just itself, or else it is not possible it should be imagined it can ever, by the righteousness of its own act, justify another.

Beloved, whatever the Scriptures speak concerning faith justifying, it must, of necessity, be understood either objectively or declaratively. Either, faith is said to be our righteousness, in respect of Christ only, who is believed on; and so it is not the righteousness of our own act of believing, but the righteousness of HIM that is apprehended by the act of believing. Or else, you must understand it declaratively; that is, whereas all our righteousness, and all our discharge from sin, flowing from the righteousness of Christ alone, is a hidden thing—that which in itself is hid to men becomes evident by believing: and as faith doth make the righteousness of Christ evident to the believer, so it is said to justify by its own act declaratively, and no otherwise.—*Sermon XXXVIII.*

The new covenant is without any conditions whatsoever on man's part....

But, you will say, there are many conditions mentioned in this covenant; it is said, that there must be "a law put in the mind, and written in their heart," with many other such things.

I answer, It is true God saith, "I will put My law in their inward parts, and write it in their hearts," &c. But do you find in this, or in any other mention of the covenant, that this is the condition to be performed as man's part. There is no such thing in the text.

But you will say, conditions—or, no conditions: a man must have his heart in this manner.

I answer, It is true, by way of consequence, that after we are in covenant with God, He will bestow these things upon us as fruits and effects of that covenant. But it is not true, by way of antecedence, that God doth require these things at our hands, before we shall be partakers of the covenant.....

The covenant, in the actual substance of it, is made good to a person before he can do anything. The main thing in the covenant is God being the God of a people; and the model and draft of that is God's love. The covenant is nothing but God's love to man—God's love to give HIMSELF to man; God's love to take man to HIMSELF.—*Sermon VI.*

Sanctification of life is an inseparable companion with the justification of a person by the free grace of Christ. But withal I must tell you, that all this sanctification of life is not a jot the way of that justified person unto heaven. It is the business of a person that he hath to do in his way—Christ; but it is not the way itself to heaven. If there be no more to clear it but this very text, it is enough; Christ here saith, "I am the way; no man cometh to the Father but by Me." Now I ask this question, Are our works of sanctification Christ Himself, or are they not? If they be Christ Himself, then there are thousands of Christs in the world. If they be not Christ, then there is no coming to the Father by them; because the coming to the Father is by Christ alone, and by Him as He is the sole way.—*Sermon IV.*

Christ comes and brings justification, loving-kindness, and salvation; He lays them down, presents them, delivers them to the heart. When we are ungodly He enters into covenant, that we should become His. What needs, then, all this travel for life and salvation, seeing it is here already?

Objection.—But seeing we get nothing by it, this is a discouragement for men to work, may some say.

Answer.—It is true, it is a discouragement to all selfish men to work; and whether a man work, or work not at all, it is all one, if he be but for himself. If a man work never so much—if he be wholly selfish for himself, God rejects it.

But when a man will work for Christ, for a man that hath a touch of the loving-kindness of Christ, and therefore stands ready to speak for the praise of the glory of HIS grace that hath so freely saved him—for such a man to work is as welcome to Him for Christ's sake as if he were to work for his own salvation. You have many ingenuous spirits in the world, who will be more free to serve a friend that hath already raised them, than others will be to serve a master that they may be raised. There is a service of thankfulness which is usually more cordial, more sedulous, than all mercenary services that are forced. This is the true service of a believer in serving Christ. His eye is to the glory of Christ, in regard of what Christ hath already done for him; and not in expectation of anything Christ hath to do, which He hath not yet done. He looks upon all as perfectly done for him in the hand of Christ, and ready to be delivered out into his hand as several occasions require. Being thus completed by Christ, not to be mended by the creature, having nothing now to do for himself—all he doth, he doth for Christ.—*Sermon III.*

Let Christ be the Alpha and Omega. In all things begin in Christ, end in Christ. Do all in Christ; get all by Christ. . . . . Assure yourselves, while you look to get by what you do, you will get but a knock, because of so much sinfulness in the duty. But if you will have any good, you must get it by Christ.—*Sermon V.*

I. Our righteousness serves as a real way to manifest our thankfulness to God for what we have already received of God. Mark well, I pray, in the 103rd Psalm, all that is within us must be praise, and nothing but praise. And the ground is this, God doth pardon our sins, heal our infirmities, and supply all our wants. In consideration of this, all that is within us should continually express His praise.

II. Again, there is this usefulness in our righteousness, namely, that we may serve our generation. The Apostle gives this charge, that *men study to maintain good works*, because, saith he, *these things are profitable to men.* As we therefore may do good to men, so, according to our ability and talent received, we must employ ourselves to the utmost for that end and purpose. The heathen men could say, *They were not made for themselves, but for others.* There is, therefore this usefulness in our righteousness, that others may receive benefit by it. *Let your light so shine before men, that they, seeing your good works, may glorify your Father which is in heaven.* That men may be drawn on to glorify God, we must shine before men in a godly conversation.

III. Our righteousness is useful, as it is the ordinance of God, wherein the Lord hath appointed us to meet with Him, and wherein He will make good those things which before He hath promised.—*Sermon IX.*

The end and ground of our fasting, and prayer, and mourning, in our exigents and extremities, is not that these duties do at all prevail with God, or at all move Him. It is God that doth move these services; and all the spiritualness in us, in these services, He moves in us. When we are moved by His Spirit and come forth to meet Him, according to His will, where He doth appoint, there He will pour out Himself in grace and love, according to His promise, not according to our performances. Thus, the great objection may be answered easily, *Why do we fast and pray and mourn in adversity, if they do us no good?*

"I say, though they do us no good yet we fast and pray, because the Lord saith, Come to Me, meet Me in this ordinance and in that ordinance, and I will come with My hands full. Then and there I will pour out that which My own freeness hath engaged Me to do for you. Is it not injustice not to meet Him then? We do confess our sins to Him; but what is the ground of forgiveness?—Not our confession of sins—not our fastings, and prayers, and mournings, and tears—but, *I, even I, am He that blotteth out thine iniquities for My own name's sake, and will remember thy sins no more.—Sermon. IX.*

All afflictions to believers are to keep them *from* sin, rather than punishment unto them *for* sin. . . . . For my own part, I cannot see how a man can say Christ bore all the punishment of sin, if we bear any of it ourselves. And if Christ did not bear it all, I cannot see how Christ can be a sufficient Saviour, without some other to help Him out, in that which He Himself did not bear. I speak all this, beloved, the rather because when poor believers are crossed and afflicted in any kind, they are presently ready to suspect God hath cast them off for their sins, and is angry with them for sinning against Him. I say, in respect of sin he hath committed, though he thus suspects, there is not the least drop of the displeasure of God; the fruit of such displeasure comes not near him. But "every son *whom I love* I rebuke and chasten," saith the Lord. God seeth that afflictions will purge, therefore He gives them.

The father gives not his child a purge to make him sick, but to take away some bad humours that made him sick, and for the prevention of diseases, or for the removal of some disease; that is the father's end in purging the child. And this is the end why God afflicts His people—not for their sins, but to take them away; that is, to prevent the hastiness and inconsiderateness of a believer, that he may not be so rash, running headstrong in his own ways, but may be more considerate for the time to come. It is most certainly true, beloved, that as soon as ever a person is a believer, he is so ingratiated into God, and with Him, that there is nothing in the world from that instant unto a believer but mercy— God managing His mercy in His own way for the best to His, sometimes by the rod as well as by sweatmeats; but still He runs in a way of mercy.

"All things shall work together for good;" this is God's way to believers.

And if this could but be received by them—and that even then, when they are as gold cast into the fire, God all the time they are in the fire (as the prophet Malachi speaks) "sits as a refiner"—then they would be more quiet in the expectation of that purity, in which they shall come forth, when the time of their coming forth is. When you see the refiner cast his gold into the furnace do you think he is angry with the gold, and means to cast it away? No, he sits as a refiner, that is, he stands warily over the fire, and over the gold, and looks into it that not one grain be lost; and when the dross is severed, he will out with it presently; it shall no longer be there. Even so doth Christ sit as a refiner. . . . . But still I say, as a fruit of wrath God never doth punish or afflict or chastise His child.—*Sermon II.*

I have not said, God is not offended with the sins that believers commit; but God stands not offended with the persons of believers, for the sins committed by them. He hath that everlasting indignation against sin as ever. And as there is the same contrariety in sin against His nature, so there is the same contrariety in God's nature unto sin. All contrarieties have a mutual contrariety against each other: as water is contrary to fire, so fire is contrary to water; as sin is contrary to the nature of God, so the nature of God is contrary to sin. There is an abhorrence of God to that sinfulness, but not an offence in God to the person that commits that sin; because the offence of God for that sin hath spent itself on the person of Christ. . . . .

Yet there is none of God's indignation against sin lost in all this, because He is not offended at all with the believer. For He hath satisfied His own offence in His Son more fully than He would have satisfied it in our own persons; we must have been everlastingly suffering before God would have been fully satisfied. Now, therefore, as the payment of a great sum all at one payment, and at a day, is a better payment than by a penny a-year, till a thousand years be out—so Christ's satisfying the Father at once, by one sacrifice of Himself, is a better satisfying of Him than if we should have been infinite days in paying that which His justice requires, and His indignation to sin doth expect.— *Sermon II.*

Christ is the way from wrath, not only in respect of the present, but also in respect of the future; I mean, a way from everlasting damnation. Give me a believer that hath set his footing truly in Christ, and you blaspheme Christ if you dare serve a writ of damnation upon that person. Suppose a believer to be overtaken in a gross sin, it is a desperate thing in any man so much as to serve a writ of damnation upon this believer; it is absolutely to frustrate the mediatorship and saviourship of Christ, to say that any believer (though he be fallen by infirmity) is in the estate of damnation. And I say unto thee, thyself, whoever thou art, thou that art ready to charge damnation upon thyself when thou art overtaken--thou doest the greatest injury to the Lord Jesus Christ that can be; for in it thou directly overthrowest the fulness of the grace of Christ, and the fulness of the satisfaction of Christ to the Father.—*Sermon II.*

It is but a sordid and gross conceit in the heart of men to think that there can be no humiliation for sin except they be in despair. I say, beloved, that when Christ doth reveal Himself to your spirits, you shall find your hearts more wrought upon with sweet meltings and relentings of heart, and breakings of spirit, when you see your sins pardoned, than in the most despairing condition you can be in. It hath been often taken notice of, of many malefactors, that though when they have come to the place of execution, their hearts have been so hard that they could not shed a tear; yet, when they have heard their pardon read, and see themselves out of danger, their hearts, that were so hard before, have melted into floods of tears. And so, I say, that heart that could not relent to see the filthy loathsomeness of sin while he did not see his pardon; yet, after the knowledge of the pardon thereof, doth melt into tears, and hath such relenting that none in the world can have but he that knoweth it. The grace of God, which brings salvation, having appeared unto men, doth more teach them to live soberly, righteously, and godly in this present world, than all arguments besides can persuade men—for the glory of their God, the manifestation of their thankfulness to Him, and the being fruitful unto others. We are to walk in every way that God hath chalked out unto us; but if we think our righteousness and our deep humiliation, and large relents of spirit, and sorrow for sin, and our confession thereof, must make our way to the bowels of Christ, take heed lest ye set up a false Christ. When you bring anything to Christ, you deprive Him of that which is His greatest prerogative, and give it to your fastings and humiliation. It is the prerogative of Christ alone to bring you to Himself.—*Sermon XIV.*

Why must not hell and damnation be a bridle to keep men in, will you say?

I answer, mark what the Psalmist speaks, Psalm cx. 3, "Thy people shall be a willing people." Here you see how tame the people of Christ are. Thy people are a willing people. How so? by fear of damnation? No such thing; but "in the day of Thy power," "in the beauty of holiness," they shall be a willing people. First, the power of Christ comes over a person; this frames his spirit to a willingness and aptness. Then comes the beauty of holiness, that wins, persuades, allures, and draws them to willingness. And where there is a willing spirit to walk with Christ, there is no danger of taking liberty.

The philosophers observe a rule, that the will is not compelled; a man cannot constrain his will. Let the will of a person but be to the pleasure of

Christ, nothing can constrain him to go beyond Christ; he may happily be overreached and be overtaken, but he will never break loose—he will never run away, though the gate stand open on every side. The grass and pasture is so sweet that Christ hath put a believer into, that though there be no bounds to keep in such a soul, yet it will never go out of this fat pasture to feed in a barren common. Therefore, in answer to the objectors who naturally think there is a way opened to licentiousness by taking away all wrath from a believer, and that, therefore, he will break forth into all manner of excess, I tell you, the power of Christ restrains him.—*Sermon II.*

Beloved, there is no better way to know your portion in Christ, than, upon the general tender of the Gospel, to conclude absolutely He is yours; and so, without any more ado, to take Him, as tendered to you, on His word. This taking of HIM, upon a general tender, is the greatest security in the world that Christ is your Christ. Say unto your soul (and let not this be contradicted, seeing Christ hath reached Himself out to sinners as sinners), My part is as good as any man's. Set down thy rest here; question it not, but believe it; it is as good security as God can make thee; He hath promised, venture thy soul upon it without seeking for further security. But some will say, He doth not belong to me. Why not to thee? He belongs to sinners as sinners; and if there be no worse than sinfulness, rebellion, and enmity in thee, He belongs to thee as well as to any in the world. There is nothing at all can give thee a certainty He is thine, but receiving [*welcoming*] Him on these terms. "He came to His own, and His own received Him not; but to as many as received Him (mark that) He gave power to become the sons of God."—*Sermon VII.*

I do not determine peremptorily that a man cannot, by way of evidence, receive any comfort from his sanctification. I will give you somewhat for the clearing of my judgment, which I know is according to truth.

The Spirit of the Lord must first reveal the gracious mind of the Lord to our spirits, and give us faith to receive that testimony of the Spirit, and to sit down as satisfied with His testimony, before ever any work of sanctification can possibly give any evidence. But when the testimony of the Spirit of the Lord is received by faith, and the soul sits down satisfied with that testimony of the Lord, then also all the gifts of God's Spirit do bear witness, together with the Spirit of the Lord and with the faith of a believer.—*Sermon XXXI.*

The consideration of Christ, as a free way to all comers, is the only way to build men up in a more enlarged course of holiness and righteousness than all the devices in the world can raise them to.—*Sermon IV.*

CONSOLATION AS THE FIRST ASPECT OF THE GOSPEL.

For my own part, whatever others may think, I abhor nothing in the world so much as this, namely, a licentious undertaking to continue in any sin, because that such fulness of grace hath abounded. And I hope assuredly that the God of grace and mercy will keep by His power to salvation all those persons He doth deliver; and that He will so sow the seed of grace in their hearts that they may not sin, that is, may not presumingly break out of purpose in hope of pardon beforehand. And I hope also God will meet such as are disturbers of the truth of Christ and peace of the Gospel by their base and vile conversation [*conduct*]. And I shall recommend to them (if there be any such here) the reading of the Epistle of Jude, where they may see the fearful wrath of God upon such persons as abuse the grace of God to sin; because God freely pardons it, therefore they will sin and presume to do that which is never so filthy. O beloved, let not the love of the Lord God in Jesus Christ, thus manifested, be so basely requited at your hands; seeing He hath so freely loved you and given Christ to you, that you might be to the praise of the glory of His grace, in a godly and Christian conversation whereunto you are ordained; "for you are God's workmanship, created in Christ Jesus unto good works, that you should walk in them" (Eph. ii. 10). And I beseech you always to remember, that you cannot answer the free love of God towards you any other way, but by showing it in a fruitful conversation in the world, and considering that one end, for which the Lord did redeem you, was, that you might be a peculiar people to Himself, zealous of good works. —*Sermon XXXI.*

According to the plan of this work, I reserve all notices of the opponents of Dr Crisp's sermons for the second or biographical part. But I may allude here to one critic, the Rev. Mr Warner, a Wiltshire clergyman and a neighbour, who suspected that Dr Crisp did not teach the regenerating work of the Holy Spirit, and to whom the Doctor wrote in explanation. My collection of *Crispiana* proves that Dr Crisp did acknowledge the work of the Holy Spirit in conversion. The real difference between the correspondents was not as to the precedency of Christ or the Holy Spirit; but it was as to the question, whether Christ Himself or some good qualities in the sinner be the first and grand source of consolation. "I never said," writes Dr Crisp to Mr Warner, "that men should not be troubled on account of sin, or labour to get a broken heart. I said that men begin at the wrong end of the bottom, who think to wind any graces from God first, and then to seek Christ. This I called pumping at a dry pit.[1] Whoever will go smoothly on must begin with getting Christ first, if ever they mean

---

[1] "Whither do men run?—they run to their inherent righteousness, to their qualifications, to their prayers, to their tears, to their humiliations and sorrows, universal obedience, and the like. But is this to run to free grace and free mercy in Christ? Nay, Christ, alas, He is never thought of. Christ is clean forgotten and wholly neglected, and not considered all this while.

to be one jot better than corrupt nature can make them." Dr Crisp was contending against the notion of *the unfitness for Christ of a person who is impure and unholy,* and accordingly he urged, "I pray you, consider the end of Christ's coming; was it for the whole and righteous, or for the sick and sinners? Suppose men pure and holy, what need is there of Christ? If anything could rid the sink of man's filthy heart and life but Christ Himself, His coming were but vain—you make the death of Christ of none effect. You know that Christ died for the ungodly (Romans v. 6); by Himself He purged our sins (Heb. i. 3). But, you say, there can be no communion between purity and impurity. I answer, No more will there be, though Christ come to a filthy sinner. I say, no *communion,* because Christ makes clean as He goes; after He is come, He presently perfumes all the rooms of the heart, as soon as He comes with the odours of His own sweetness. He that shall stay for Christ till he be pure, holy, and fit for Him before God will give HIM, he shall stay long enough."

"Christ Alone Exalted" was discovered by Dr Crisp's hearers to be his grand aim. He himself had as a watchword a rhyming translation of a well-known Latin refrain:—

> If Christ thou know, it will suffice,
> Though else thou knowest nought;
> If Christ be hid, thou art not wise,
> Though all else thou be taught.

CHAPTER III.

THE MARROW, PART FIRST. 1645.

By Edward Fisher, Graduate of Oxford University.

READERS of religious biography have been puzzled by meeting with the phrases, "The Marrow," "Marrowmen," and "Anti-Marrowmen." These phrases arose from an unpretending but celebrated book, called "The Marrow of Modern Divinity."

Again, as these party names were first coined about the year 1720, it has

---

Beloved, here is ploughing with a wooden plough. Here is a working upon a dead horse, or rather with a dead horse. . . . . Run to Christ; so shall you prosper in everything you take in hand. . . . . Let this be your everlasting cry and song, *None but Christ, None but Christ;* or rather (in the language of the Apostle) *I desire to know nothing but Jesus Christ and Him crucified."*—Dr CRISP, *Sermon VII.*

been supposed that the doctrines of that book were new, and that the opposition to the book was a defensive war against the introduction of novelties. But the commotion was occasioned by the republication of an old book. As one of its editors remarked, "This book has outlived the fitness of its title. The divinity therein taught is now no longer the modern but the ancient divinity." Its theology is the theology of the Protestant Reformers—the grand Reformation theology.

Neither was the book of Scottish origin. It was a compilation by a graduate of Oxford, a layman who had been a gentleman-commoner in that University. The author was Edward Fisher, described by Anthony a-Wood as the eldest son of a knight, a royalist, and "a noted person among the learned for his great reading in Ecclesiastical History and in the Fathers, and for his admirable skill in the Greek and Hebrew languages."

The design of the "Marrow," however, was not to epitomize all the topics of theology, like many a Latin work of the 17th century, also styled "Medulla." What this little book was occupied with was what our own title-page describes as the theology of consolation. I copy its full and descriptive title from the second edition (the *imprimatur* of the first edition is dated 1 May 1645):—

"The Marrow of Modern Divinity, touching both the covenant of works and the covenant of grace, with their use and end both in the time of the Old Testament and in the time of the New. Wherein every one may clearly see how far forth he bringeth the law into the case of justification, and so deserveth the name of Legalist; and how far forth he rejecteth the law in the case of sanctification, and so deserveth the name of Antinomist.

With the middle path between them both, which by Jesus Christ leadeth to eternall life.

In a dialogue betwixt *Evangelista*, a minister of the Gospel; *Nomista*, a Legalist; *Antinomista*, an Antinomian; and *Neophytus*, a young Christian.

The second edition, corrected, amended, and much enlarged by the author, E. F. London: 1646."

Before going into details as to "The Marrow," I should say a word as to the opposition to it. The opposition in the following century arose from the circumstance that this First Part (which was the only part printed in Scotland at first) dealt chiefly with the foundation of Christian hope, the Pauline doctrine of the justification of the ungodly man by the grace of God and through faith alone. It was (as I have said) a compilation. It contained many of the bold utterances of Luther; and it was against these utterances that the criticisms of a more or less lukewarm churchism were chiefly directed. At the time of its original publication, it was ushered into the world under the sanction of Joseph Caryl, W. Strong, and other sound preachers. Coming in the wake of Crisp's "Christ Alone Exalted," it was valued as a temperate work, agreeing with the ardent Doctor in essentials, and yet avoiding any statements which had or seemed to have an air of extravagance.

I shall endeavour to give the substance of the doctrine of the *First Part* of "The Marrow" in a very few paragraphs.

The "Marrow" was intended to throw light upon questions concerning consolation to the individual sinner through his personal faith in the Lord Jesus Christ. Faith (it should be remembered) not only believes a doctrine but welcomes a person, a personal deliverer or saviour. It takes Christ, who is actually offering Himself in the Gospel to every sinner who has ears to hear. A believer cleaves to Christ as his living Saviour, brother, and friend ; and all this, through his private personal dealing with the Saviour, not through a notion of the safety of the company of believers and of himself as one of them. "The life that I live in the flesh," said Paul, "I live by the faith of the Son of God, who loved *me* and gave Himself for *me*." Therefore, the most scriptural theologians tell us, that in the nature of true faith there is an actual appropriation. And (says a modern writer) "The Marrowmen wanted to bring back the appropriating persuasion, still more strongly put by many Reformation Theologians."[1]

The "Marrow" proceeds generally upon the circumstance that the anxious inquirer finds his way to consolation obstructed by difficulties in the language of Scripture, and specially upon the fact that these obstructions practically disappear when the language of Scripture is understood. One of the difficult words is "law."

The word "law" is scripturally explained to involve two separate ideas in connection with one code of commandments ; the one idea being to bargain (or to enter into covenant) for eternal life, and the other idea simply being to obey dutifully. Thus, "the law of works" is censured, although it is occupied with God's good and perfect commandments, while "the law of faith," otherwise called "the law of Christ," is approved, although occupied with the very same commandments. But this seeming inconsistency is explained by a difference in the plans and motives of men. And the men who are condemned under "the law of works" may be defined to be every man who sees a meritorious value in his works of righteousness, and who imagines that he can bargain (or enter into covenant) with God to receive eternal life in exchange for them. On the other hand, the men who are saved may be described as every man who through faith looks to Christ alone for eternal life, of which life he has a foretaste in dutiful obedience to God his Saviour. And thus the same commandments are to the one class of men the law of works, and to the other class the law of faith and the law of Christ. The former class are described theologically as being under the covenant of works, and the other under the covenant of grace.

[1] "The Cunningham Lecture for 1870-71," by James Walker, D.D., page 54.

CONSOLATION AS THE FIRST ASPECT OF THE GOSPEL.

But it would be a mistake to say that the covenant of works reigned in Old Testament times, and that the covenant of grace did not begin to reign till New Testament times. On the contrary, the covenant of grace was put within Adam's reach when the triumphs of the promised Saviour were prophetically made known. Faith in Old Testament prophecy then was equivalent to faith in New Testament history now—both including confidence in God, and reliance upon what God says.

To save space, I have been compelled to express in my own words the above summary of Marrow doctrine. On looking over it, I find that I have not stated that there is an entire chapter[1] on "the law of faith," and another on "the law of Christ." And yet I have correctly represented the author's opinions by saying "the law of faith, otherwise the law of Christ," because in the believer's life the two are really one, that is, one seen from two points of view;—the first, refusing good works, whether past, present, or future, as the purchase-money of the sinner's salvation; the second, appointing good works as the business of the new life of the saved sinner.

I shall now quote some specimens of the author's style. After showing the additional prophetic views of Christ given to Abraham and to believers after him up to the era of the coming of Christ, he thus describes the mental condition of the Jews at that era:—

"The Scripture seems to hold forth that there were three several sorts of people [among the Jews] who endeavoured to keep the law of God, and they did all of them differ in their ends.

"The first sort of them were true believers who, according to the measure of their faith, did believe the resurrection of their bodies after death, and eternal life in glory, and that it was to be obtained not by their own works, but by faith in the Messiah or promised seed. And answerably as they believed this, answerably they yielded obedience to the law freely, without fear of punishment or hope of reward; but, alas, the spirit of faith was very weak in the most of them, and the spirit of bondage very strong; and therefore they stood in need to be induced and constrained to obedience for fear of punishment and hope of reward.

"The second sort of them were the Sadducees and their sect; and these did not believe that there was any resurrection, nor any life but the life of this world. And yet they endeavoured to keep the law, that God might bless them here, and that it might go well with them in this present life.

"The third sort, and indeed the greatest number of them in the future ages after Moses, were the Scribes and Pharisees and their sects; and they held and maintained that there was a resurrection to be looked for, and an eternal life after death; and therefore they endeavoured to keep the law, not only to obtain

---
[1] The headings of the chapters, and the scheme of division into chapters, are by Boston, I suppose; they are not in the author's editions.

temporal happiness but eternal also. For though it had pleased the Lord to make known unto His people, by the ministry of Moses, that the law was given not to retain men in the confidence of their own works, but to drive them out of themselves, and lead them to Christ the promised seed ; yet after that time the Priests and the Levites, who were the expounders of the law, and whom the Scribes and Pharisees did succeed, did so conceive and teach of God's intention, in giving the law, as though it had been that they, by their obedience to it, should obtain righteousness and eternal life. And this opinion was so confidently maintained and so generally embraced amongst them, that in their book *Mechilta* they say and affirm that there is no other covenant but the law; and so in very deed they conceived that there was no other way to eternal life than the covenant of works" (page 70).

In the dialogue the above statement is by Evangelista, who is the oracular speaker. In other quotations I shall give his statements in ordinary type, and the remarks of his auditory in italics, without specifying, as to the latter, whether the speaker was Nomista, Antinomista, or Neophytus.[1]

"*Well, sir, now I do perceive there was little difference betwixt the Jews' covenant of grace and ours.*"

"Truly the opposition betwixt the Jews' covenant of grace and ours was chiefly of their own making. They should have been driven to Christ by the law ; but they expected life in obedience to it, and this was their great error and mistake."

"*And truly, sir, it is no great marvel though they in this point did so much err and mistake, who had the covenant of grace made known to them so darkly; when many amongst us, who have it more clearly manifest, do the like.*"

"And truly it is no marvel though all men naturally do so. For man naturally doth apprehend God to be the great Master of heaven, and himself to be His servant; and that therefore he must do his work before he can have his wages, and the more work he doth, the greater wages he shall have. And hence it was that, when Aristotle came to speak of blessedness, and to pitch upon the next means to that end, he said it was operation and working ; with whom also agreeth Pythagoras, when he saith, It is man's felicity to be like unto God (as how ?) by becoming righteous and holy.

"And let us not marvel that these men did so err who never heard of Christ nor of the covenant of grace, when those to whom it was made known by the apostles of Christ did the like—witness those to whom the Apostle Paul wrote

---

[1] Boston, in his Notes, mentions an edition of "The Marrow" *with some interwoven additions*, namely, the Ninth Edition, London, 1699 ; but the additions at that date cannot be by Edward Fisher. Whether Boston used that edition to any extent in preparing the text of his annotated edition, I am not informed. If any quotations, now presented to my readers, are not to be found, *word for word*, in Boston's edition, the reason is, that it is more satisfactory to make use of the author's (second) edition.

his epistles, and especially the Galatians, for although he had, by his preaching, when he was present with them, made known unto them the doctrine of the covenant of grace, yet after his departure, through the seducement of false teachers, they were soon turned to the covenant of works, and sought to be justified either in whole or in part by it. Nay, what saith Luther?—' It is (saith he) the general opinion of man's reason throughout the whole world, that righteousness is gotten by the works of the law. And the reason is, because the covenant of works was engendered in the minds of men in the very creation, so that man naturally can judge no otherwise of the law than as a covenant of works which was given to make righteous, and to give life and salvation.' 'This pernicious opinion of the law, that it justifieth and maketh righteous before God (saith Luther again), is so deeply rooted in man's reason, and all mankind are so wrapped in it, that they can hardly get out.' 'Yea, I myself (saith he) have now preached the Gospel almost twenty years, and have been exercised in the same daily by reading and writing, so that I may well seem to be rid of this wicked opinion ; yet, notwithstanding, I now and then feel this old filth cleave to my heart, whereby it cometh to pass that I would willingly so have to do with God that I would bring something with myself, because of which He should give me His grace' " (page 89).

What is considered peculiar to " The Marrow " is the phrase, " *The deed of gift;* " therefore I quote the passage which contains and explains this phrase. [I have before me Boston's edition of 1726, as reprinted in 1828 ; and I find that the paragraphs *in this passage* are arranged quite differently from the author's second edition, with variations in the connecting clauses and sentences. Being without the means of information whether these alterations were (or were not) editorial, I follow the author's own second edition, beginning at the foot of page 118.]

"The covenant for life and salvation, since the Fall, is not that *covenant of works* that was betwixt God and Christ. For none of Christ's have anything to do with that, but Christ only.

"But the covenant of life and salvation is that covenant of grace which is betwixt Christ and *His* [John xvii. 6]. And in that covenant there is not any condition or law to be performed, on man's part, by himself. No ; there is no more for him to do, but only to know and believe that Christ hath done all for him. Wherefore, my dear neighbour Neophytus, I beseech you, be persuaded that here you are to work nothing, here you are to do nothing, here you are to render nothing unto God, but only to receive the treasure, which is Jesus Christ, and apprehend Him in your heart by faith, although you be never so great a sinner ; and so shall you obtain forgiveness of sins, righteousness, and eternal happiness, not as an agent but as a patient, not by doing but by receiving. Nothing here cometh betwixt, but faith only, apprehending Christ in the promise. This then is perfect righteousness, to hear nothing, to know nothing, to do

THE THEOLOGY OF CONSOLATION.

nothing of the law or works—but only to know and believe that Jesus Christ is now gone to the Father, and sitteth at His right hand, not as a judge, but 'is made unto you of God wisdom, righteousness, sanctification, and redemption'; wherefore saith the Apostle, 'Believe on the Lord Jesus Christ and thou shalt be saved.'

"*But, sir, hath such a one as I any warrant to believe in Christ?*

"I beseech you, consider that God the Father, as He is in His Son Jesus Christ, moved with nothing but His free love to mankind lost, hath made A DEED OF GIFT AND GRANT unto them all, that whosoever, of them all, shall believe in this His Son, shall not perish but have eternal life. And hence it was that Jesus Christ Himself said unto His disciples, 'Go and preach the Gospel to every creature under heaven,' that is, go and tell every man without exception that here is good news for him, Christ is dead for him; and if he will take HIM, and accept of HIS righteousness, he shall have HIM. Therefore (saith a godly writer) forasmuch as the Holy Scripture speaketh to all in general, none of us ought to distrust himself, but believe that it doth belong particularly to himself.

. . . . . .

"Do not you say (*i.e.*, do not say), It may be I am not elected, and therefore I will not believe in Christ. But rather say, I do believe in Christ, and therefore I am sure I am elected. And check your own heart for meddling with God's secrets, and prying into His hidden counsel; and go no more beyond your bounds, as you have done in this point. For election and reprobation is a secret, and the Scripture tells us that "secret things belong unto God, but those things that are revealed belong unto us.' Now this is God's revealed will, for indeed it is His express command, that you should believe on the name of His Son; and it is His promise, that if you believe you shall not perish, but have everlasting life. Wherefore you, having so good a warrant as God's command, and so good an encouragement as His promise, do your duty; and by the doing thereof you may put it out of question, and be sure that you are one of God's elect.

"Say then, I beseech you, with a firm faith, The righteousness of Jesus Christ belongs to all that believe, but I believe, therefore it belongs to me. Yea, and say with Paul, I live by faith in the Son of God, who loved me and gave Himself for me. He saw in me (saith Luther on the text, Galatians ii. 20) nothing but wickedness, going astray, and flying from Him; yet this good Lord had mercy on me, and of His mere mercy He loved me: yea, He so loved me that He gave Himself for me. Who is this *me*? Even I, wretched and damnable sinner, was so dearly beloved of the Son of God, that he gave Himself for me. O print this word in your heart, and apply it to your own self; not doubting but you are one of those to whom this *me* belongeth.

"*But may such a vile and sinful wretch as I am be persuaded that God commands me to believe, and that He hath made a promise to me?*

"Why do you make a question where there is none to be made? Go (saith Christ) and preach the Gospel to every creature under heaven, that is, go tell every man, without exception, whatsoever his sins be—go and tell him these glad tidings, that if he will come in, I will accept of him, his sins shall be forgiven him, and he shall be saved."

Having undertaken to give my readers a description of "The Marrow," I must here mention that although Evangelista speaks in this assuring manner when he gives God's good news to his well-beloved Neophytus, yet for the sake of having a good hit at Antinomista, he elsewhere brings forth the following statement:—

"True faith is produced by the secret power of God by little and little, so that sometimes a true believer himself neither knows the time when, nor the manner how, it was wrought; so that we may perceive that true faith is not ordinarily begun, increased, and finished all in a moment, as it seems yours was, but groweth by degrees according to that of the Apostle, Rom. i. 17, 'The righteousness of God is revealed from faith to faith,' that is, from one degree of faith to another, from a weak faith to a strong faith, or from faith of adherence to faith of assurance; but so was not yours. And, again, true faith according to the measure of it produceth holiness of life, but it seems yours doth not so" (page 110).

The last clause of this quotation is excellent—the clause concerning faith as the producer of holiness. But it belongs to the department of self-examination, to which we come afterwards.

But as to the laudation of hearers, who, in spite of the counsel scripturally given to them as well as to Neophytus, refuse to draw near to the Saviour with full assurance of faith—such laudation should not have been indulged in, even for the sake of having a good hit at Antinomista. It is no part of the duty of a Gospel minister to fabricate good hits against any sinner whatsoever. If any hits are truly good, they are to be found in God's Word: these as a messenger he may repeat with a wise and loving discretion. But the above-quoted hit is not in the Scriptures, and therefore is neither good nor right.

The author does quote Scripture, but not to the point; and therefore his foundation is not scriptural. The interpretation of Romans i. 17 is unsatisfactory. The text of his paragraph is our Lord's parable (Mark iv. 26); but that refers to the gradual growth of the kingdom of Christ in the world, and to the gradual sanctification of individuals; and what may be truly said in biography or history, is not always appropriate to Gospel preaching. In uninspired biographies we sometimes read of believers who are said to have had no consolation at the early stages of the life of faith. But perhaps we ought also to have been informed that theologians warned those persons that sensations of joy and consolation are irregular and unbecoming in a new convert. Such a warning being unscriptural, any experience, occasioned by subjection to it, is unworthy of commendation or imitation.

When, in a later portion of the dialogue, Evangelista proceeds to recommend self-examination, he is on scriptural ground, and his remarks are worthy of universal attention. In answer to Antinomista's suggestion—" If an unbeliever may have a resemblance of every grace that is wrought in a believer, then it must needs be a hard matter to find out the difference; and therefore I conceive it is best for a man not to trouble himself at all with marks and signs"—Evangelista replies, " Give me leave to deal plainly with you in telling you that although *we cannot say*, every one that hath a form of godliness hath also the power of godliness; yet *we may truly say*, that he who hath not the form of godliness hath not the power of godliness. For though all be not gold that glistereth, yet all gold doth glister. And therefore I tell you truly, if you have no regard to make the law of Christ your rule, by endeavouring to do what is required in the ten commandments, and to avoid what is there forbidden, it is a very evil sign, and therefore, I pray you, consider of it " (page 168).

A conversation with a young believer, concerning 2 Cor. xiii. 5, 6, is recorded, a part of which I quote :—

"*Truly, sir, I was thinking of that place of Scripture, where the Apostle exhorts us to examine ourselves whether we be in the faith or no. . . . I would gladly hear how I may be sure that I am in the faith.*

"I would not have you to make any question of it, since you have grounded your faith upon such a firm foundation as will never fail you. . . .

". . . *I would fain know how I may be assured that I have done so.*

" Well, now I understand you what you mean. It seems you do not want a ground for your believing [in Christ], but for your believing that you have believed. . . . Look back and reflect upon your own heart, and consider what actions have passed through there; for, indeed, this is the benefit that a reasonable soul hath, that it is able to return upon itself to see what it has done, which the soul of a beast cannot do. Consider then, I pray you, whether the free and full promise of God in Christ hath not been so cleared unto you that you had nothing to object why it did not belong particularly to you—and whether you have not seen a readiness and willingness in Christ to receive and embrace you as His beloved spouse—and whether you have not thereupon consented, and resolved to take Christ and to give up yourself to Him—and whether you have not, since that, found in your heart a love to Christ and His law, and a readiness and willingness to do your duty to God as a child to his father, freely, without fear of hell or hope of heaven.

. . . .

"*I desire to hear how a man may know that Jesus Christ is in him.*

" Why, if Christ be in a man, HE lives in him, as saith the Apostle, ' I live not, but Christ liveth in me.'

" *But how then shall a man know that Christ lives in him?*

CONSOLATION AS THE FIRST ASPECT OF THE GOSPEL.

"Why, in what man soever Christ liveth, according to the measure of his faith, HE executes His threefold office in him, namely, His Prophetical, Priestly, and Kingly office" (page 213).

In Boston's edition of "The Marrow," there is interwoven with the dialogue a lengthened essay, endeavouring to explain, with greater accuracy and caution than Dr Crisp, some doctrinal statements intended for the consolation of believers. Because, however, I cannot find this essay in the author's own (second) edition, I content myself with quoting nothing except the statements themselves, and the judicious verdict of the Essayist.

THE STATEMENTS.

"1. That a believer is not under the law, but it is altogether delivered from it.

"2. That a believer does not commit sin.

"3. That the Lord can see no sin in a believer.

"4. That the Lord is not angry with a believer for his sins.

"5. That the Lord doth not chastise a believer for his sins.

"6. That a believer hath no cause, neither to confess his sins nor to crave pardon at the hand of God for them, neither yet to fast, nor mourn, nor humble himself before the Lord for them."

THE VERDICT.

"These points which you have now mentioned have occasioned many needless and fruitless disputes, and that because men have either not understood what they have said, or else not declared whereof they have affirmed. For, in one sense, they may all of them be truly affirmed; and, in another sense, they may all of them be truly denied."[1]

The Gospel theory that the moral law is the rule of life to believers, is more fully treated in the Second Part of "The Marrow." But, in the First Part, that fundamental truth finds its place. In former quotations this has sufficiently appeared. To the same effect are the following sentiments quoted from Luther:—

"Do you say, If the law do not justify, then it is vain, and of none effect; if faith be only and alone sufficient unto righteousness, we may go play then, and work no working at all?

"Will you say, Money doth not justify or make a man righteous, therefore it is unprofitable—the eyes do not justify, therefore they must be plucked out—the hands make not a man righteous, therefore they must be cut off?

[1] See chapter VI. of this part of my work.

"This also is naught, that the law doth not justify, therefore it is unprofitable,

"We do not, therefore, destroy and condemn the law because we say it doth not justify. But we say with Paul, the law is good if a man do rightly use it; and that this is a faithful saying, that they which have believed in God might be careful to maintain good works: these things are good and profitable unto men."

CHAPTER IV.

The Marrow, Part Second. 1648.

By Edward Fisher, Graduate of Oxford University.

ALSO,

Extracts from various Authors on the Origin of Christian Obedience.

"The Marrow," as originally compiled, was not intended to be regarded otherwise than as a complete book. However, in the course of three years, the author issued a *Second Part*, and thus gave his final answer to all the adversaries of his scriptural faith who had misrepresented it as if it made void the law of God. This work is fully described in its title-page:—

"The Second Part of the Marrow of Modern Divinity. Touching the most plain, pithy, and spiritual Exposition of the Ten Commandments; the examination of the heart and life by them; the reason why the Lord gave them; and the use that both unbelievers and believers are to make of them.

"Profitable for any man who either desires to be driven out of himself to Christ, or so to walk as that he may please Christ.

"In a dialogue betwixt *Evangelista*, a minister of the Gospel; *Nomologista*, a prattler about the law; and *Neophytus*, a young Christian.

"By E. F., Author of the First Part.

"1 Tim. i. 8. *We know the law is good, if a man use it lawfully.*"

Comparing the speakers in this second dialogue with those in the first, we find that the scene is changed. Antinomista has been satisfactorily silenced in the first dialogue, where also Nomista has renounced the hope of establishing a righteousness of his own. Now, in the Second Part, Neophytus both asks for more instruction for himself, and also introduces another friend named Nomologista, who has not Nomista's high standard, but "is persuaded that he goes very near the perfect fulfilling of the law of God;" and this "prattler of the law" acknowledges the truth of his neighbour's allegation concerning him.

With the twofold view of instructing Neophytus in everyday duty, and of convincing Nomologista of his need of the Saviour of sinners, Evangelista occupies the most of this volume in expounding the Ten Commandments, according to a system that brings out their grand spirit and their extensive application.

For the awakening of religionists of the Nomista type, he makes the following allusion to the manner in which our Saviour was pleased to "deal with that young expounder of the law (Matt. xix. 16), who, it seems, was sick of the same disease." "Good Master," saith he, "what shall I do that I may inherit eternal life. *He doth not* (saith Calvin) *simply ask, which way or by what means he should come to eternal life, but what good he should do to get it.* Whereby it appears that he was a proud justiciary—one that swelled in fleshly opinion that he could keep the law and be saved by it. Therefore he is worthily sent to the law to work himself weary, and to see his need to come to Christ for remedy."

To Nomologista the reverend Evangelista appropriately speaks in a somewhat different strain. The following is a part of the dialogue :—

"Truly, neighbour Nomologista, if I may speak it without offence, I fear me you are still of the works of the law, and therefore still under the curse.

"*Why, sir, I pray you what is it to be of the works of the law?*

"To be of the works of the law is for a man to look for, or hope, to be justified or accepted in the sight of God for his own obedience to the law.

"*But surely, sir, I never did so. For though, by reason of my being ignorant of what is required and forbidden in every commandment,*[1] *I had a conceit that I came very near the perfect fulfilling of the law, yet I never thought I did do all things that are contained therein; and therefore I never looked for, nor hoped, that God would accept me for my own obedience without Christ's being joined with it.*

"Then it seemeth that you did conceive that your obedience and Christ's obedience must be joined together, and so God would accept you for that.

"*Yea indeed, sir, there hath been my hopes, and indeed there is still my hopes.*

"Aye, but neighbour Nomologista, as I told my neighbour Neophytus and others not long since, so I tell you now, that as the justice of God requires a perfect obedience, so doth it require that this perfect obedience be a personal obedience, namely, it must be the obedience of one person only. The obedience

[1] Nomologista had listened attentively to the whole of Evangelista's exposition of the Ten Commandments.

of two must not be put together to make up a perfect obedience. And indeed, to say as the thing is, God will have none to have a hand in the justification and salvation of any man, but Christ only; for, saith the Apostle Peter, Acts iv. 12, *Neither is there salvation in any other, for there is none other name under heaven given among men whereby we must be saved.* Believe it, then, I beseech you, that Christ Jesus will either be a whole Saviour or no Saviour; He will either save you alone, or not save you at all."

Although Nomologista is ultimately convinced, yet, in the process of skirmishing, the following objection and its answer occur :—

Objection.—" Why then, sir, it should seem that not only natural men, but regenerate men also are under the curse of the law. For if every one that keepeth not the law perfectly be concluded under the curse, and if regenerate men do not keep the law perfectly, then they also must needs be under the curse."

Answer.—" The conclusion of your argument is not true. For, if by regenerate men you mean true believers, then they have fulfilled the law perfectly in Christ, or rather Christ hath perfectly fulfilled the law in them, and was made a curse for them, and so hath redeemed them from the curse of the law, as you may see (Gal. iii. 13.)"

The true doctrine of the necessity of everyday obedience in a believer's life appears, when you accurately observe the difference between being delivered from the curse of the law, and being set free from obedience to it. Perhaps some non-theological readers have misapprehended the meaning of the words, " the curse of the law," and may have thought that they implied the irreligious sentiment that the law is " a curse," or, in everyday language, that it is " a nuisance" —" a great bother "—" an unbearable tax or exaction." Such, of course, is not the meaning. In the Scriptures, the meaning of " a curse " is a sentence of condemnation ; " the curse of the law " is the law's curse, or the lawgiver's curse, the sentence pronounced by God the lawgiver against the lawless and disobedient. A man suffering the execution of a legal sentence is also said to be " cursed," or to be " made a curse." The Divine Redeemer came forward and suffered the execution of the sentence of God's law in the stead of all those sinners who became believers in HIM ; and thus He hath redeemed us from the curse of the law, having been made a curse instead of us. We who believe in Christ are delivered from eternal punishment, but not from the eternal obligation to keep God's commandments. In fact, we receive a new and special charge to keep them ; this is well put in the Second Part of " The Marrow," and may be here quoted as defining the origin of Christian obedience.

" So soon as any man doth truly believe, and so is justified in the sight of God, then (as the Holy Ghost from the testimony of holy writ doth warrant us to conceive), Jesus Christ, or, which is all one, God in Christ, doth deliver unto him whatsoever is required and forbidden in the Ten Commandments, saying, This handwriting, even this law of commandments, which was against thee, and contrary unto thee, . . . My Father hath delivered it into Mine hands, and I have blotted out the curse or penalty, so that one letter or tittle remains not for thee to see. Yea, I have taken it out of thy way, and fastened it to My cross, yea, and torn it in pieces with the nails of My cross; so that it is altogether frustrate, and hath no force at all against thee.

"Yet, notwithstanding, the matter contained in this law, even those precepts and prohibitions which I have now delivered unto thee, being the mind and will of My Father, and the eternal and unchangeable rule of righteousness, and that which is in My heart (Psalm xl. 8)—yea, and that which I have promised to write in the hearts of all those that are Mine (Jeremiah xxxi. 33)—yea, and that which I have promised to make them yield willing obedience unto (Psalm cx. 3)—I and My Father do commend it unto thee as that rule of obedience whereby thou art to express thy love and thankfulness unto us for what we have done for thee. And, therefore, I say no more unto thee but this, If thou love Me, keep My commandments (John xiv. 15), and thou art My friend if thou do whatsoever I command thee (John xv. 14)."

Here, also, is an eloquent passage which gives a summary of the motives and principles of Christian obedience:—

"Though faith in the blood of Christ hath made your peace with God as a Judge, yet obedience must keep your peace with Him as a Father. Yea, the more your conscience witnesseth that you do that which pleaseth God, the more encouragement you will have, and the more confidently you will approach towards God in prayer. *Beloved*, saith the loving Apostle, *if our hearts condemn us not, then have we boldness towards God.* Furthermore you are to know, that the more obedience you yield unto the Ten Commandments, the more temporal blessings, outward prosperity, and comfort of this life (in the ordinary course of God's dealing) you shall have. O, saith the Lord, that My people had hearkened unto Me, and Israel had walked in My ways, He should soon have fed them with the finest of the wheat, and with honey out of the rock should I have satisfied thee. Besides, the more obedience you yield unto the Ten Commandments, the more glory you will bring to God, according to that of our Saviour, John xv. 8, 'Herein is My Father glorified, that ye bear much fruit.' To conclude, the more obedience you yield unto the Ten Commandments, the more good you will do unto others, according to that of the Apostle, Titus iii. 8, This is a faithful saying, and these things I will that thou affirm constantly, that they which have believed in Christ might be careful to maintain good works; these things are good and profitable unto men."

With regard to the exposition of the Ten Commandments, a curious literary story might be told. Edward Fisher's preface was dated 21st September 1648. During the interval between 1645 and 1648, the Westminster Assembly of

Divines had been engaged in the preparation and publication of their famous catechisms. Both their larger and lesser catechisms were presented to the House of Commons in the latter part of 1647 (they were adopted by the General Assembly of the Church of Scotland in 1648). Fisher seems to have been greatly impressed by their catechetical commentary on the Ten Commandments; yet, apart from treatises, the only catechism to which he refers as an authority is the Heidelberg Catechism, and the expositions of it by Ursinus and Bastingius. Being a royalist, and intimately associated with cavalier comrades, he evidently felt that any recognition of catechisms issued by the Assembly of Divines would hinder them from reading his own book, and shut them out from any religious edification which otherwise they might consent to receive from him. His plan being to place at the beginning of the book a summary of rules for interpreting the commandments, he produces six admirable rules, but takes no notice of the Westminster Larger Catechism, to which he is substantially indebted. Much of the language, however, is his own, and, therefore, it may be interesting to read his version of the rules.

" He that would truly understand and expound the Commandments must do it according to these six rules :—

" *First*, He must consider that every commandment hath both a negative and an affirmative part contained in it; that is to say, where any evil is forbidden, the contrary good is commanded; and where any good is commanded, the contrary evil is forbidden : for, saith Ursinus's Catechism, the Lawgiver doth in an affirmative commandment comprehend the negative, and, contrarywise, in a negative he comprehendeth the affirmative.

" *Secondly*, He must consider that, under one good action commanded, or one evil action forbidden, all of the same kind or nature are comprehended ; yea, all occasions and means leading thereunto, according to the saying of judicious Virel, The Lord minding to forbid divers evils of the same kind, He comprehendeth them under the name of the greatest.

" *Thirdly*, He must consider that the law of God is spiritual, reaching to the very heart or soul, and all the powers thereof. For it chargeth the understanding to know the will of God ; it chargeth the memory to retain ; and the will to choose the better and to leave the worse. It chargeth the affections to love the things that are to be loved, and hate the things that are to be hated; and so bindeth all the powers of the soul to obedience, as well as the words, thoughts, and gestures.

" *Fourthly*, He must consider that the law of God must not only be the rule of our obedience, but it must also be the reason of it. We must not only do that which is there commanded, and avoid that which is there forbidden ; but we must also do the good because the Lord requireth it, and avoid the evil because the Lord forbiddeth it; yea, and we must do all that is delivered and prescribed in the law for the love we bear to God. The love of God must be the fountain, the impulsive and efficient cause, of all our obedience to the law.

"*Fifthly*, He must consider that as our obedience to the law must arise from a right fountain, so it must be directed to a right end, and that is, that God alone may be glorified by us; for otherwise it is not the worship of God but hypocrisy, saith Ursinus's Catechism. So that, according to the saying of another godly writer (Mr Whatley), the final cause, or end, of all our obedience must be God's glory, or (which is all one) that we may please Him ; for in seeking to please God we glorify Him, and these two things are always coincident.

"*Sixthly*, He must consider that the Lord doth not only take notice what we do in obedience to His law, but also after what manner we do it. And, therefore, we must be careful to do all our actions after a right manner, namely, humbly, reverently, willingly, and zealously."

Some peculiarly consolatory matter as to the origin of Christian obedience is to be found in the Westminster Exposition of the *Preface to the Ten Commandments*. While quoting this, I shall include those questions and answers in the Larger Catechism which explain the distinct uses of the law to the unregenerate, and to the regenerate—which explanations coincide with " Marrow " doctrine.

THE LARGER CATECHISM.

" 94. *Is there any use of the moral law to man since the fall ?*

" Although no man, since the fall, can attain to righteousness of life by the moral law; yet there is great use thereof, as well common to all men, as peculiar either to the unregenerate or the regenerate.

" 95. *Of what use is the moral law to all men?*

" The moral law is of use to all men, to inform them of the holy nature and will of God, and of their duty binding them to walk accordingly; to convince them of their disability to keep it, and of the sinful pollution of their nature, hearts, and lives ; to humble them in the sense of their sin and misery, and thereby help them to a clearer sight of the need they have of Christ, and of the perfection of His obedience.

" 96. *What particular use is there of the moral law to unregenerate men ?*

" The moral law is of use to unregenerate men to awaken their consciences to flee from wrath to come, and to drive them to Christ ; or upon their continuance in the estate and way of sin to leave them inexcusable and under the curse thereof.

" 97. *What special use is there of the moral law to the regenerate?*

" Although they that are regenerate and believe in Christ be delivered from the moral law as a covenant of works, so as thereby they are neither justified nor condemned; yet, besides the general uses thereof common to them with all men, it is of special use to show them how much they are bound to Christ for fulfilling it, and enduring the curse thereof in their stead and for their good, and thereby to provoke them to more thankfulness, and to express the same in their greater care to conform themselves thereunto as the rule of their obedience.

"101. *What is the preface to the ten commandments?*

"The preface to the ten commandments is contained in these words, '*I am the Lord thy God, which have brought thee out of the land of Egypt, out of the house of bondage.*' Wherein God manifesteth His sovereignty as being Jehovah, the eternal, immutable, and Almighty God, having His being in and of Himself, and giving being to all His words and works; and that He is a God in covenant, as with Israel of old, so with all His people, who, as He brought them out of their bondage in Egypt, so He delivereth us from our spiritual thraldom; and that, therefore, we are bound to take Him for our God alone, and to keep all His commandments."

THE LESSER CATECHISM.

(*Now called The Shorter Catechism*).

"44. *What doth the preface to the ten commandments teach us?*

"The preface to the ten commandments teacheth us, that because God is the Lord, and our God, and Redeemer, therefore we are bound to keep all His commandments."

When we consult the commentators, we find Dr Ridgley observing that "some think that this is a part of the first commandment, ... or else they suppose it to be a reason annexed to this commandment in particular. But (says Dr R.) it seems most probable that it is a preface to all the commandments, and, accordingly, to be applied as a motive to enforce obedience to every one of them." "As to what respects God's having brought Israel out of the land of Egypt, out of the house of bondage,—this is to be extended farther than that particular providence which was fresh in their memories. And, therefore, it denotes all the deliverances which God is pleased to vouchsafe to His people, whether temporal or spiritual; and, in particular, that which was procured for us by Christ from the bondage and thraldom of sin and satan, the condemnation and sentence of the law, together with that salvation which is inseparably connected with it; which is to be improved by us as an inducement to yield universal obedience to all God's commandments." The moral law, addressing itself to the regenerate, "is said [in the Catechism] to show them how much they are bound to Christ for fulfilling it, and enduring the curse thereof in their stead, and for their good. In Romans x. 4, *Christ* is said to be *the end of the law for right-*

CONSOLATION AS THE FIRST ASPECT OF THE GOSPEL. 77

cousness; that is, He has answered the end and demand of the law by performing that obedience which it requires, and thereby procuring a justifying righteousness, which is applied to every one that believes. This lays them under a superadded obligation to obedience, peculiar to them as believers; so that they are not only engaged to the practice of universal holiness from the consideration of the sovereignty of God commanding, in common with all others, but from *the love of Christ* which does (as it were) *constrain* them hereunto. And hereby they are provoked to more thankfulness, as they have greater inducements hereunto than any others; and this gratitude cannot be better expressed than by the utmost care to approve themselves to Him in all things. Therefore the grace of God is so far from leading to licentiousness, that all who have experienced it are hereby put upon the exercise of that obedience which they owe to God as their rightful Lord and Sovereign, and to Christ as their gracious Redeemer, whom they love entirely, and therefore keep His commandments."

In his Exposition of the Shorter Catechism, Flavel has the following questions and answers:—

What is the third argument unto obedience? The benefits of redemption that they receive from God. Benefits persuade to duty; and "the goodness of God leads to repentance" (Rom. ii. 4).

How can deliverance out of Egypt be an argument to them that never were in Egypt? As that deliverance was a type of our deliverance, so 'tis an argument to us, and [as] an argument from the less to the greater so it obligeth us more than them, Luke i. 74, 75, "That He would grant unto us, that we being delivered out of the hand of our enemies might serve Him without fear, in holiness and righteousness before Him, all the days of our life."

What is the deliverance we have? and how doth it oblige us to obedience? Our deliverance is not from Egypt but from hell, "Who hath delivered us from the power of darkness, and hath translated us into the kingdom of His dear Son" (Col. i. 13). And our persons are bought by the Redeemer to glorify God, 1 Cor. vi. 19, 20, "What? know ye not that your body is the temple of the Holy Ghost which is in you? for ye are bought with a price: wherefore glorify God in your body, and in your spirits, which are God's."

Is it not mercenary to serve God upon the account of benefits received or to be received? He that makes religious duties mediums to attain carnal advantages only, is of a worse than mercenary spirit. But to be quickened by mercy to duty is not mercenary but evangelical. Hosea iii. 5, "They shall fear the Lord and His goodness."

Similar sentiments are more amply expressed in Boston's "Body of Divinity":—

"All true obedience to the ten commandments now must run in the channel of the covenant of grace, being directed to God as our God in that covenant."

"This obedience is performed not for righteousness, but to testify our love to the Lord our Righteousness; not in our own strength, but in that of our Lord God and Redeemer; not be accepted for its own worth, but for the sake of a Redeemer's merits; not out of fear of hell, or hope to purchase heaven, but out of love and gratitude to Him who has delivered us from hell, and purchased heaven and everlasting happiness for us."

"The true way to attain to the obedience of these commandments is first to believe that God is our God in Christ, and then to set about the performance of them; first to believe, and then to do. The attempting it the contrary way, placing obedience first before faith, is entirely contrary to the Lord's method. Thus to believe strengthens the soul for obedience."

"Benefits received are most powerful engagements to duty, and the greatest benefits are the strongest engagements."

"Can we reflect on the great salvation wrought for us by Jesus Christ, by which we were saved from all the sorrows of sin and hell, rescued from the power of satan, and delivered from the present evil world, and the pollutions thereof—can we reflect on these great and glorious benefits which afford astonishment to men and angels—and our hearts not glow with the warmest fire of love and gratitude to Him who hath done such excellent things for us? Can we hesitate a moment to say, Good is Thy will, O God; just and holy are Thy laws; and we will cheerfully obey what Thou commandest us?"

It should be remembered that the above comments do not necessarily open a door for historical criticism. They answer the question, What doth the preface to the Ten Commandments teach us? The teachings which have been just quoted are good, whether the text be appropriate or not. Dr Ridgley says that it is probably a suitable text. To readers who dissent even from this probability, we suggest another text, Psalm cxxx. 4, "There is forgiveness with Thee, that Thou mayest be feared."

On that text the eminent Dr Bates writes, " 'Tis both the duty and disposition of those who have received the pardon of their sins, *to fear the Lord and His goodness*. There is no principle more clearly natural and sensible than this —dependence includes observance; the receiving of benefits obliges a person to the benefactor. Accordingly, the Psalmist expresses the affections of the human and the holy nature, What shall I render to the Lord for all His benefits? and breaks out in an ecstasy of thankfulness, O Lord, truly I am Thy servant; I am Thy servant, Thou hast broken my bands. The repenting believer receives pardon from God with joyful admiration, that fastens his mind in the contemplation of His glorious mercy. The serious thought of it kindles a sacred fire in the breast, as 'tis said of Mary Magdalene, *Much was forgiven her* (for she loved much). Love to God that results from His pardoning love to us is singular and supreme, and necessarily produces an ardent desire to please and glorify Him, and an

CONSOLATION AS THE FIRST ASPECT OF THE GOSPEL. 79

ingenuous grateful fear of offending Him. The soul that has felt the terrors of the Lord as the holy and righteous Judge of the world, and afterward has been revived by the light of His countenance, and has tasted how good the Lord is—how is it possible to resist such dear and immense obligations? How prodigious to turn the strongest and sweetest engagement to reverence and obedience into an encouragement to do that which is odious and offensive in His sight! To sin against light heightens sin into rebellion, but to sin against revealed love makes it above measure sinful. This is so contrary to natural conscience and supernatural grace, that 'tis the leprosy of the wicked, not the spot of God's children. *Do ye thus requite the Lord, O foolish people and unwise?*—the upbraiding reduces them to a defenceless silence, and covers them in black confusion. When divine grace pardons our past sins, it cures our depraved inclination to future sins.

"The clearest discovery of the heart is by reflections on God's mercy. The fear of God's justice is natural, the reverent regard of His goodness is a spiritual affection. There is a great difference between filial fear of the divine goodness (that is so becoming the breast of a Christian and so congruous to our present state) and servile fear (that is the proper character of one in the bondage of sin).

"The filial fear of God is an ingenuous voluntary affection flowing from love, and freely exercised, and esteemed the treasure of the soul. It makes us more circumspect but not less comfortable. It opposes security, but establishes the assurance of faith. The fear of the Lord and hope in His mercy are united graces. Filial fear keeps the soul close to God, makes it solicitous lest any sin should intercept the light of His countenance, and obstruct communion with Him which is the paradise of a saint."

President Witherspoon has an equally able and instructive discourse on the same text. He says—

"If we take *the fear of God* in the text to signify the whole of that duty and obedience we owe to Him, their connection between forgiveness with God and His being feared appears from the following considerations.

"A discovery of the mercy of God is absolutely necessary to His being loved and served by those who have once been sinners. Despair of mercy drives the sinner from God, presents Him only as the object of terror and aversion, and (instead of having the least influence in bringing us to obedience) confirms the guilty in his rebellious opposition to his Maker. This must be manifest to every hearer. There can be no religion at all, either in inclination or performance, if there be no forgiveness with God. How should any so much as attempt what they believe to be an unprofitable labour?

"As a discovery of the mercy of God is absolutely necessary to our serving Him at all, so it is perhaps of all others the most powerful motive to induce us to serve Him in sincerity. Nothing whatever more illustrates the divine glory.

It presents Him as the proper object of worship, of confidence, and of love. When a sinner is once burdened with a sense of guilt, sees the demerit of His transgressions, and feels the justice of his own sentence, what an inconceivable relief must it give him to see the divine mercy! and how infinitely amiable must the God of mercy appear in his eyes! Others may reason at ease upon the subject; *he* is transported with unspeakable joy on the prospect. His heart is immediately taken captive; he feels His constraining power, and yields himself willing to every demand of duty and gratitude.

"From what hath been said, you may see of how much moment it is to the Christian to keep clear views of the mercy of God, as well as of his own interest in it. The moment he loses the comfortable sense of peace with God, his chariot-wheels are troubled, and he drives heavily. It makes his duty burdensome, and his trials unsupportable. . . . Hear what your Saviour says, John xvi. 33, 'These things I have spoken unto you, that in Me ye might have peace. In the world ye shall have tribulation; but be of good cheer, I have overcome the world.'"

Dr Gill's comments will fittingly conclude this chapter:—

"*There is forgiveness with Thee;* or, there is *a propitiation* with Thee, as the septuagint and vulgate Latin versions render it. God had found out Christ to be the propitiatory sacrifice for sin and the ransom of His people, and set Him forth in His purposes and decrees for that end, which was made known by the sacrifices of the law typical of it. And in the fulness of time He sent Him to be the propitiation for sin; and He is become so, and has made reconciliation for sin, and reconciled His people to God by the sufferings of death, and reconciled all the divine perfections of justice and holiness, grace and mercy, together, in the salvation of men; and is now an advocate with the Father for them, pleading the propitiatory sacrifice of Himself before Him.

"*That Thou mayest be feared.* Were it not for pardon and the hope of it, men would be desperate, and, having no hope, would resolve upon taking their swing of sin, and be entirely negligent of the worship and service of God. Was there no forgiveness of sin, there would be no more fear of God among men than there is among devils for whom there is no forgiveness; there might be dread and trembling as among them, but no godly fear. Yea, if God was strictly to mark iniquity and not pardon it, there would be none to fear Him; all must be condemned and cut off by Him. But, in order to secure and preserve His fear among men, He has taken the step He has, to pardon sin through the propitiatory sacrifice of His Son. And a discovery, and an application, of His grace teaches men to fear to offend Him, influences them to serve Him acceptably with reverence and godly fear, and engages them to fear Him and His goodness, and Him for His goodness' sake."

CHAPTER V.

THE GOSPEL MYSTERY OF SANCTIFICATION.

By Rev. Walter Marshall, M.A., Vicar of Hursley in the Seventeenth Century;

ALSO,

WRITINGS OF THE EIGHTEENTH CENTURY IN HARMONY THEREWITH.

ALTHOUGH the republication of "The Marrow" in Scotland in the eighteenth century might seem to be the topic next in order, and therefore most suitable for this chapter, yet the good influences of the seventeenth century upon the eighteenth cannot be understood without some acquaintance with *Marshall on Sanctification*, a book which elucidated "The Marrow" in its scriptural theory of the origin of Christian obedience.

The author, the Rev. Walter Marshall, Fellow of New College, Oxford (afterwards Fellow of the College at Winchester), was Vicar of Hursley until the passing of the Black Bartholomew Act. He died in 1680, and it was in the twelfth year after his death that his celebrated book was published. Its title was: "THE GOSPEL MYSTERY OF SANCTIFICATION opened in sundry practical directions, suited especially to the case of those who labour under the guilt and power of indwelling sin. To which is added a Sermon of [on] Justification—1 Cor. i. 27, 28, 29, 30, 31: *God hath chosen the foolish things of the world to confound the wise; and God hath chosen the weak things of the world to confound the things which are mighty; And base things of the world, and things which are despised, hath God chosen, yea, and things which are not, to bring to nought things that are: That no flesh should glory in His presence. But of Him are ye in Christ Jesus, who of God is made unto us wisdom, righteousness, sanctification, and redemption: That, according as it is written, He that glorieth, let him glory in the Lord.* By Mr WALTER MARSHALL, late Preacher of the Gospel.

"London: Printed for T. Parkhurst, at the Bible and Three Crowns in Cheapside, near Mercers Chappel. 1692."

The word "sanctification" in the title-page means the purification of a believer's heart and life. The phrase, "the gospel mystery of sanctification," reminds us that sanctification is the work of God the Father, Son, and Holy Ghost, and therefore mysterious; also that it is a *Gospel energy*, and therefore mysterious to the self-righteous and to the profane, but not to them alone. The earnest inquirer and striver after a new life finds, in his infant experience, how mysterious his own failures are—

> How long beneath the law I lay in bondage and distress ;
> I toiled the precept to obey, but toiled without success ;

and there is a great mystery in the truth as it dawns upon him, that the pathway to good works is entered upon by ceasing to work, and by believing in HIM that justifieth the ungodly.

The sentiments of Marshall are fully summed up in a series of directions, and these directions are expounded in a corresponding number of chapters. Before copying these directions, I extract a few statements which occur here and there throughout the book, and which serve the purpose of an introduction.

His main doctrine is, that "the true practice of holiness cannot be secure except the persuasion of our justification and reconciliation with God be first obtained without works of the law." He says, "This is a great mystery (contrary to the apprehensions, not only of the vulgar, but of some learned divines) that we must be reconciled to God, and justified by the remission of our sins and imputation of righteousness, before any sincere obedience to the law, that we may be enabled for the practice of it. They account that this doctrine tendeth to the subversion of a holy practice, . . . and that the only way to establish sincere obedience is to make it rather a condition, to be performed before our actual justification and reconciliation with God. Therefore some late divines have thought fit to bring the doctrine of former Protestants concerning justification to their anvil, and to hammer it into another form." (Chapter II.)

In reply to such misleading divines, our author concisely says, "The difference between the law and the Gospel doth not at all consist in this, that the one requireth perfect doing—the other, only sincere doing—but in this, that the one requireth doing—the other, no doing, but believing—for life and salvation." (Chapter VI.)

The following paragraph I cannot omit, it being perhaps the best known as well as the best abused portion of the book. (Chapter X., *Fourthly*) :—

"Let it be well observed, that the reason why we are to assure ourselves in our faith, that God freely giveth Christ and His salvation to us particularly, is not because it is a truth before we believe it, but because it becometh a certain truth when we believe it, and because it will never be true except we do in some measure persuade and assure ourselves that it is so. We have no absolute promise or declaration in Scripture that God certainly will or doth give Christ and His salvation to any one of us in particular, neither do we know it to be true already by Scripture, or sense, or reason, before we assure ourselves absolutely of it; yea, we are without Christ's salvation at present, in a state of sin and misery, under the curse and wrath of God. Only I shall prove that we are bound, by the command of God, thus to assure ourselves; and the Scripture doth sufficiently warrant us, that we shall not deceive ourselves in believing a lie, but according to our faith so shall it be to us (Matt. ix. 29). This is a strange kind of assurance, far different from other ordinary kinds; and therefore no wonder if it be found weak and imperfect, and difficult to be obtained, and assaulted with many doubtings. We are constrained to believe other things on the clear evidence we have that they are true, and would remain true whether we believe them or no; so that we cannot deny our assent without rebelling against the light of our senses, reason, or conscience. But here our assurance is not impressed on our thoughts by any evidence of the thing; but we must work it out in ourselves by the assistance of the Spirit of God: and thereby we bring our own thoughts in captivity to the obedience of Christ. None but God can justly require of us this kind of assurance, because He only calleth those things that are not as though they were (Rom. iv. 17). He only can give existence to the things that yet are not, and make a thing true upon our believing it that was not true before. He only can make good that promise, *What things soever ye desire, when ye pray, believe that ye receive them, and ye shall have them* (Mark xi. 24)."

All that I need say at present as to this celebrated passage is, that it was quite easy for a logician like the Rev. Dr Joseph Bellamy of Connecticut (born 1719, died 1790) to appeal to a miscellaneous audience to condemn the absence of human reason and logic. But an intelligent inquirer will not be so easily convinced that this pious graduate of Oxford had forgotten the logic which he had learned in that celebrated university, and by which he had earned a Fellowship. In fact, the following simple morsel of reasoning refuted by anticipation all Dr Bellamy's dialectical display:—" If an honest rich man say to a poor woman, I promise to be thy husband, if thou wilt have me—say but the word and I am thine; may not she presently answer confidently, Then thou art my husband, and I claim thee for my husband? And should she not rather say so, than say, I believe not what thou sayest?" (*ibid*). This is a good illustration of what was ironically called *believing a thing which was not true until you believed it*.

Taking into consideration that many disconsolate hours in many believers' lives seem to throw suspicion on the truth that a feeling of consolation is right at the very first in a believer's experience, we may here note that there are two extremes of opinion in reference to this matter. One extreme is, that a man is not a true believer unless he is full of joy and consolation; the other and the common extreme is, that such joy and consolation at the beginning of the life of faith is presumptuous and dangerous, and that to be without joy is Christian self-denial. According to the one extreme, any doubts as to our eternal safety convict us of being unconverted and unbelieving; according to the other extreme, a young convert should not aspire to joy in the Lord Jesus Christ, because in the meantime such aspira-

THE THEOLOGY OF CONSOLATION.

tions are neither suitable nor desirable for him. A thoughtful paragraph by Marshall is a valuable contribution to the solution of this question. He says :—
"A great reason why many Protestants have receded from the doctrine of their ancestors on this point is, because they think there can be no true assurance of salvation in any that are troubled with doubtings, as they find many be, whom they cannot but own as true believers and precious saints of God. True, indeed, this assurance must be contrary to doubtings in the nature of it; and so, if it were perfect in the highest degree, it would exclude all doubting out of the soul, and it doth now exclude it in some degree. But is there not flesh as well as spirit in the best saints on earth ?—Is there not a law in their members warring against the law of their minds ? May not one that truly believeth say, *Lord, help my unbelief?* Can any one on earth say they have received any grace in the highest degree, and that they are wholly free from the contrary corruption ? Why then should we think that assurance cannot be true except it be perfect, and free the soul from all doubtings ? The Apostle accounts it a great blessing to the Thessalonians that they had *much assurance*—intimating that some true assurance might be in a less degree. . . . . It is strange if the flesh and the devil should never oppose a true assurance and assault it with doubtings. A believer may be sometimes so overwhelmed with doubtings, that he may not be able to perceive an assurance in himself. . . . . Yet if at that time he can blame his soul for doubting, *Why art thou cast down, O my soul? and why art thou disquieted within me? hope thou in God, for I shall yet praise Him*—if he can condemn his doubting as sinful, and say with himself, *This is mine infirmity*; these doubtings are of the flesh and of the devil . . . . such an one hath some true assurance, though he must strive to grow to a higher degree . . . . Do but grant that it is the nature of saving faith, thus to resist and struggle with slavish fears of wrath, and doubting of our own salvation ; and you grant, in effect, that there is and must be something of assurance of our salvation in saving faith whereby it resisteth doubtings." (Chapter X).

Our author holds to the truth that consolation is the first aspect of the Gospel. Viewing the Gospel as a doctrine according to godliness, he shows how consolation is the door of hope into the way of holiness.

"The usual method of Gospel doctrine, as it is delivered to us in the Holy Scriptures, is, first to comfort our hearts, and thereby to establish us in every good word and work." (Chapter IX).

"The nature of the duties of the law requireth a comfortable state of the soul for the performance of them." (*Ibid.*)

"Both Scripture and experience show that this is the method whereby God bringeth His people from sin to holiness. Though some of them are brought under terrors for a while, that sin may be the more embittered, and the salvation of Christ rendered more precious and acceptable to them; yet such are again delivered from their terrors by the comfort of God's salvation that they may be fitted for holiness. And generally a holy life beginneth with comfort and is maintained by it. God gave to Adam at His first creation the comfort of His love and favour, and the happiness of paradise, to encourage him to obedience; and when he had lost these comforts by the Fall, he was no longer able to obey, until he was restored by new comfort of the promised seed. . . . . David telleth us for our instruction how he was brought to an holy conversation : 'Thy loving kindness [is] before my eyes, and I have walked in Thy truth. Lord, I have hoped for Thy salvation, and done Thy commandments.' . . . . What comfortless religion do those make that allow people no comfort beforehand to strengthen them for holy performances that are very cross, displeasing, and grievous to their natural inclinations (as the plucking out of a right eye—cutting off a right hand); but would have them first do such things with love and delight, under all their present fears, despondencies, and corrupt inclinations." (*Ibid.*)

Before copying out Mr Marshall's directions, I introduce the name of the Rev. James Hervey, the distinguished English rector of the eighteenth century, who agreed both with the Marrow divines and with Marshall as to the justification of the ungodly and the sanctification of believers. Hervey intended to take up Marshall's theme in a fourth volume of *Theron and Aspasio*, but he felt that the state of his health would in all probability prevent him from writing more. He therefore encouraged a bookseller to reprint *The Gospel Mystery of Sanctification*, saying humorously, "I do, by these presents, nominate and depute Mr Marshall to supply my lack of service." In his letter, dated 5th November 1756, Hervey said that if his health would enable him to write his fourth volume—his subject being, " A dissertation on practical holiness or evangelical obedience,"—"justification, free justification through the righteousness of Jesus Christ, is the sacred fleece from which he [the writer] would spin his thread and weave his garment, agreeably to that important text, *Ye are bought with a price, therefore glorify God.*"

Hervey was willing to give due consideration to all objections that might be made to Marshall's phraseology. A paper was accordingly drawn up by him, probably with the assistance of Cudworth, containing Fourteen Assertions concerning sanctification, which were Marshall's Directions revised. All worthy attempts at the improvement of standard books of human authorship must be interesting to students and inquirers; the Directions and Assertions shall therefore be presented in parallel columns.

Marshall's Directions.	*Hervey's Assertions.*
1. That we may acceptably perform the duties of holiness and righteousness required in the law, our first work is, to learn the powerful and effectual means	1. That practice and manner of life which the Scripture calls holiness, righteousness, or godliness, obedience, true religion, is not attained by our

whereby we may attend to so great an end.

2. Several endowments and qualifications are necessary to enable us for the immediate practice of the law. Particularly we must have an inclination and propensity of our hearts thereunto; and therefore we must be well persuaded of our reconciliation with God, and of our future enjoyment of the everlasting heavenly happiness, and of sufficient strength both to will and perform all duties acceptably, until we come to the enjoyment of that happiness.

3. The way to get holy endowments and qualifications necessary to frame and enable us for the immediate practice of the law is, to receive them out of the fulness of Christ and fellowship with Him; and that we may have this fellowship we must be in Christ, and have Christ Himself in us, by a mystical union with Him.

4. The means or instruments whereby the Spirit of God accomplisheth our union with Christ, and our fellowship with Him in all holiness, are the Gospel —whereby Christ entereth into our hearts to work faith in us—and faith, whereby we actually receive Christ Himself with all His fulness into our hearts. And this faith is a grace of the Spirit, whereby we heartily believe the Gospel, and also believe on Christ, as He is revealed and freely promised to us therein, for all His salvation.

5. We cannot attain to the practice of true holiness by any of our endeavours, while we continue in our natural

most resolved endeavours, but is given through the knowledge of HIM that has called us to glory and virtue.

2. No man can love God till he knows HIM, nor till he knows HIM to be his everlasting friend. Therefore the spring of true holiness is a well-grounded persuasion of our reconciliation with God, and of our future enjoyment of the everlasting heavenly happiness, and of sufficient strength given in HIM for all HE calls us unto.

3. These endowments, so necessary to the obedience of love, are contained in the fulness of Christ, and are enjoyed only by union and fellowship with Him.

4. The mean or instrument whereby the Spirit of God accomplisheth our union with Christ, and our fellowship with Him in all holiness, is the Gospel, whereby Christ entereth into our hearts, begetting us to the faith, whereby we actually receive Christ Himself, with all His fulness, unto the hope of eternal life by Him. And then by the influence of the Spirit of truth we unfeignedly believe the Gospel, and also believe on Christ as He is revealed and promised to us therein, for all His salvation.

5. The practice of true holiness is not attained by any endeavours of our natural state, but is a blessing of that

state, and are not partakers of a new state by union and fellowship with Christ through faith.

6. Those that endeavour to perform sincere obedience to all the commands of Christ, as the condition whereby they are to procure for themselves a right and title to salvation, and a good ground to trust on Him for the same, do seek their salvation by the works of the law, and not by the faith of Christ as He is revealed in the Gospel; and they shall never be able to perform sincerely any true holy obedience by all such endeavours.

7. We are not to imagine that our hearts and lives must be changed from sin to holiness, in any measure, before we may safely venture to trust on Christ for the sure enjoyment of Himself and His salvation.

8. Be sure to seek for holiness of heart and life, only in its due order where God hath placed it, after union with Christ, justification, and the gift of the Holy Ghost; and in that order seek it earnestly by faith, as a very necessary part of your salvation.

9. We must first receive the comforts of the Gospel, that we may be able to perform sincerely the duties of the law.

10. That we may be prepared by the comforts of the Gospel to perform sincerely the duties of the law, we must get some assurance of our salvation, in that very faith by which Christ Himself is received into our hearts; therefore, we must endeavour to believe on Christ confidently, persuading and assuring ourselves, in the act of believing,

new state given in Jesus Christ, and partaken of by union and fellowship with Christ through faith.

6. Those that endeavour to perform sincere obedience to all the commands of Christ, as the condition whereby they are to procure for themselves a right and title to salvation, and a good ground to trust on Him for the same, do seek their salvation by the works of the law, and not by the faith of Christ as He is revealed in the Gospel; and they shall never be able to perform sincerely any true holy obedience by all such endeavours.

7. We are not to imagine that our hearts and lives must be changed from sin to holiness, in any measure, before we may safely venture to trust in Christ for the sure enjoyment of Himself and His salvation.

8. True holiness of heart and life hath its due order where God hath placed it, that is, after union with Christ, justification, and the gift of the Holy Ghost. It is not, therefore, to be expected but in that order, as what accompanies salvation.

9. It is only by the comforts of the Gospel revealing a just God and a Saviour that God works in us to will and to do of His good pleasure.

10. The comforts of the Gospel necessary to Christian obedience contain sufficient grounds of assurance of our salvation, not because we believe, but in a way of immediate trust and confidence. Therefore, instead of seeking other methods of peace and holiness, we must endeavour to believe or trust in Christ confidently, persuading and as-

that God freely giveth to us an interest in Christ and His salvation, according to His gracious promise.

11. Endeavour diligently to perform the great work of believing on Christ in a right manner without any delay, and then also to continue and increase in your most holy faith, that so your enjoyment of Christ, union and fellowship with Him, and all holiness by Him, may be begun, continued, and increased in you.

12. Make diligent use of your most holy faith for the immediate performance of the duties of the law, by walking no longer according to your old natural state, or any principles or means of practice that belong unto it, but only according to that new state which you receive by faith, and the principles and means of practice that properly belong thereunto, and strive to continue and increase in such manner of practice. This is the only way to attain to an acceptable performance of those holy and righteous duties, as far as it is possible in this present life.

13. Endeavour diligently to make the right use of all means appointed in the Word of God for the obtaining and practising holiness, only in this way of believing in Christ, and walking in Him according to your new state by faith.

14. That you may seek holiness and righteousness only by believing in Christ, and walking in Him by faith, according to the former directions, take encouragement from the great advantages of this way and the excellent properties of it.

suring ourselves, according to the Divine declarations, that God freely gives to us an interest in Christ and His salvation, according to His gracious promise.

11. It is therefore belonging to the practical part of the Christian life to maintain the same immediate trust and confidence, in dependence on the Divine faithfulness not to suffer us to be confounded, that so our enjoyment of Christ, union and fellowship with Him, and all holiness by Him, may be continued and increased in us.

12. The Scripture calls upon Christians to walk no longer according to the principles or means of practice that belong unto the natural or original state of man, but only according to that new state given in Christ which we receive by faith, and the principles and means of practice that properly belong thereunto; and to strive to continue and increase in such a manner of practice.

13. All ordinances of Divine appointment, for the establishment and increase of our faith and love, are to be considered only in this way of believing in Christ, and walking in Him according to this new state given in Him.

14. That we may be confirmed in holiness only by believing in Christ, and walking in Him by faith, according to the former assertions, we may take encouragement from the great advantages of this way and the excellent properties of it.

CONSOLATION AS THE FIRST ASPECT OF THE GOSPEL.

The Rev. John Brown of Haddington, the eminent Scotch Theologian and Commentator, Professor of Divinity to the Associate Synod, followed in the same track as Marshall and Hervey. His "Compendious View of Natural and Revealed Religion" (published in 1782), under the head of "Sanctification," formulates the Gospel Rules thus :—

1. The true nature of sanctification and its manifold ingredients must be learned with the utmost care and attention.

2. The proper methods of attaining true holiness of nature and practice must be learned with the utmost accuracy and diligence.

3. There can be no proper study of true holiness without being, first in order, furnished with an inward inclination to it—a real persuasion of our reconciliation with God through the imputed righteousness of Christ—a well-grounded hope of eternal life through his obedience and death—and a cordial belief that God will, by His grace, enable us to perform our duty in an acceptable manner.

4. All our furniture for the study of Gospel holiness must be received from the fulness of Christ, by spiritual union to, and fellowship with Him.

5. As God's justification of our persons, and renovation of our nature, must necessarily precede all our study of holiness, we must receive Christ in all His offices as offered in the Gospel, in order to our beginning and carrying it on.

6. To promote the study of true holiness, we (depending on no change of our nature or practice, as our warrant or ground of right), as sinful and wretched men, must unite with Jesus Christ, as made of God to us, in the Gospel offer, wisdom, and righteousness, and sanctification, and redemption.

7. Gospel holiness must be earnestly sought after, by faith, as a necessary and principal part of our salvation, enjoyed in consequence of our union with Christ, justification by His blood, and reception of His Spirit.

8. Not only at first, but as long as we live on earth, we must always receive the comforts of the Gospel, in order to qualify us for obeying the law as a rule of life.

9. In order to promote our study of true holiness, we must receive these comforts of the Gospel, in Christ, by an assured faith in the declarations and promises of it as offering and giving Him and all His blessings of salvation in Him to us in particular.

10. In order that our fellowship with Christ in His comforts and grace, and our study of Gospel holiness by means of it, may be begun, continued, and more and more increased, we ought, with great diligence, to exercise this assured faith in a right manner, and to abound in it more and more.

11. We must act this assured faith only in a manner suited to our state of union with Christ, in order to promote holiness according to it, and not at all according to our legal or natural state.

12. We must diligently attend upon and improve every Gospel ordinance

answerable to our condition, agreeably to our new covenant state, that we may therein have fellowship with Christ in His blood and Spirit for the sanctification of our nature and life.

13. For our excitement to such earnest and evangelical study of holiness, we ought carefully to consider and thoroughly to understand the peculiar excellency and advantage of this method.

Brown was the editor of a reprint of one century of Meditations ["Devout Breathings of a Pious Soul"], and the author of a second century. The latter he prefaced with the following sentence:—

"Never do I read Kempis's 'Imitation of Christ,' Sale's 'Devotions,' Scougal's 'Life of God in the Soul of Man,' without lamenting that so many precious thoughts should be thrown away to erect a castle in the air—a practical religion not founded on, or cemented by, Jesus' imputed righteousness, or by His indwelling Spirit and grace."

His own meditations are good examples of Gospel teaching as to the duty and privilege of holiness ; for instance—

"19. In order to our leading a religious life, we must be united to Christ, who is so full of grace and truth, as made of God unto us wisdom, righteousness, sanctification, and redemption. We must, by His indwelling Spirit, have our heart renewed, and all its powers filled with His grace. We must be daily constrained by His love, and receive out of His fulness grace for grace. While His Word is our only rule, He and His Spirit must perform all our work in and for us. Under His influence we must sincerely purpose and earnestly endeavour to stand fast in the faith, and walk worthy of the Lord unto all well-pleasing. We must deny ungodliness and worldly lusts, and live soberly, righteously, and godly in the present world, looking for the blessed hope and glorious appearing of the Lord Jesus Christ. In the faith of our future judgment, we must frequently call ourselves to an account, always live under God's eye, and as if every day were our last."

"74. If I wish to gain much ground in religion, I must live, always forsaking and fleeing from myself to God in Christ—in fleeing from my guilt to His pardoning grace—from my pollution to His cleansing grace—from my wisdom to His instruction—from my will to His law and good pleasures—from my wants to His fulness. My resignation of myself to Him must be hearty, steadfast, complete, and often renewed. The more it be so, the greater shall be the inward peace, purity, and order of my heart. The more I die to myself and other creatures, the more delightfully shall I for ever live to God."

"87. Let me never commit myself to God but as my Father in Christ. To Him as my gracious Father let me give up all my guilt to be pardoned, all my wants to be supplied, all my plagues to be healed. To Him as my righteous Father let me apply for all the blessings that my Saviour purchased for me, and which Himself hath promised to me, and that He would avenge me of all the injuries which my spiritual enemies have done me. To Him as my holy Father let me look for all sanctifying grace and glory, for all freedom from sin, and growth in grace. To Him as my wise Father let me look for all necessary instruction and direction. And to Him as my tender and compassionate Father let me kindly submit in all the corrections and troubles I meet with."

CHAPTER VI.

Various Writings and Discussions of the Seventeenth and Eighteenth Centuries in Affinity with "The Marrow."

As we have seen, the principal writings of the seventeenth century in harmony with "The Marrow," were Crisp's *Christ Alone Exalted*, and Marshall's *Gospel Mystery of Sanctification*.

At the time when the latter work was published, discourses and disputations contradicting and crushing out the consolations of the Gospel, and yet assuming the name of Gospel truth, were much in vogue. The consequence was, that a son of the long ago deceased Dr Crisp reprinted his father's sermons. However welcome this republication was in friendly circles, the effect on the so-called Christian public was not pacifying. The stern and dogmatic disputers turned all their artillery against Dr Crisp. They were reinforced by an able, useful, and honoured divine of the Church of England, Dr John Edwards, of Cambridge, who thought it his duty to write a severe book, entitled, "Crispianism Unmasked." Dr Daniel Williams, the great Presbyterian divine, in his celebrated treatise, entitled, "Gospel-Truth stated and vindicated," composed in his own language a series of errors, which he said were necessary inferences from Dr Crisp's phraseology, and were, therefore, Dr Crisp's errors. The accusations against the preachers of consolation, viewed as the first aspect of the Gospel, were summed up in the one portentous word, *Antinomianism*.

As I have often had occasion to say, if all that those divines alleged was correct, then the Apostle Paul was an Antinomian. But as to the offensive word in its association with the end of the seventeenth century, two remarks may make the state of the question plain.

1. It is not denied that there is such a deplorable error in opinion and in action as Antinomianism.

Antinomianism means opposition to the law of God.

Antinomianism, as an opinion, is the assertion that a believer in Jesus Christ—a sinner who accepts salvation from Jesus Christ on the footing of the only Saviour's merits and atoning sacrifice—that such a believer is set free from all necessity to keep God's moral law as summed up in the ten commandments, that he is under no obligation except love towards God and free choice as to himself.

Antinomianism, as a manner of life, is a career of transgression against the moral law, carried on under a profession of relying upon Christ alone for salvation, and not upon the works of the law.

While it is admitted that there is such a thing as Antinomianism, it is denied that because the everlasting consolation, which comes from Christ alone, may, when very briefly stated, seem to overthrow the authority of the moral law, therefore I must refuse and disown such consolation, or else accept the name of Antinomian. The good John Flavel goes rather too far in his tract, "A blow at the root," and seems occasionally to strike a blow at the grace of God, on the ground that some men turn that grace into licentiousness.

2. Admitting that that man is an Antinomian, who, on the plea of his reliance on Christ alone, systematically transgresses the old and eternal principles concerning right and wrong as set down in God's moral law, I cannot plead guilty to the accusation, when the law which I do not acknowledge is a new law compiled by Dr Williams and his committee.

The Apostle Paul was no Antinomian when he said, "By the works of the law shall no flesh be justified in God's sight." And his saying has been proved to be even more weighty than our English Bible represents, because it really says, that "by works of law" shall no flesh be justified. This Pauline principle is, however, ignored by Dr Williams, who says, that the law, which is not to be resorted to for the purchase-money of the heavenly inheritance, is the law of the ten commandments; but that there is a new law which requires repentance, faith, and godly dispositions and virtues, from which law our justification must proceed.

Let us suppose that we see Samuel Crisp and Dr Williams pleading before us. It is admitted that Crisp is a Christian of moral principles and of moral life, who has no wish that God's moral law should be removed from the entire direction of his conduct. Does Williams say that such a man is an Antinomian? A denial is given by Crisp's well-known practice and principles, in which he was the worthy son of a worthy father. He says, I am for the old law as the rule of my life, while like Paul, I glory in nothing but in the cross of our Lord Jesus Christ. But he adds, turning to Williams, You preach a new law; you are therefore a Neonomian. I am no Antinomian in being against a new law.

Those who are anxious to understand the doctrinal differences of those times, should remember that the men who were most loudly and publicly called

CONSOLATION AS THE FIRST ASPECT OF THE GOSPEL. 93

Antinomians were not lawless, licentious men. They were called Antinomians because they were not Neonomians. And Neonomians were theoretically wrong, because by works of law shall no flesh be justified, and that man is accepted who worketh not, but believeth on Him who justifieth the ungodly.

But as the plan of this work is to give an account of writings, my readers' attention is now directed to a brochure by the Rev. Robert Trail, of London, entitled, "A Vindication of the Protestant Doctrine concerning Justification, and of its Preachers and Professors, from the Unjust Charge of Antinomianism. In a Letter from the Author to a minister in the country." This letter is dated London, Sept. 1, 1692. In introducing this author, we enter upon the substance of this chapter, namely, the correspondence between England and Scotland as to (what may be called) Marrow Doctrines.

Trail was a Scotch minister settled in London, a son of a father of the same name, who was minister of the Greyfriars' Church of Edinburgh, and a sufferer for Christ's crown and covenant. The son had also suffered in the covenanting times, and had been a prisoner on the Bass Rock. The friend to whom he wrote was probably his brother, a parish minister; and if so, then "the country" of his friend was Scotland.

In his letter, Trail declares his sentiments regarding the scriptural doctrine of Gospel consolation. He says, "Dr Owen's excellent book of Justification, and Mr Marshall's book of the Mystery of Sanctification by Faith in Jesus Christ, are vindications and confirmations of the Protestant doctrine against which I fear no effectual opposition." As to Marshall's book, he adds, "Its excellency is, that it leads the serious reader directly to Jesus Christ, and cuts the sinews, and overturns the foundation of the new divinity, by the same argument of Gospel holiness by which many attempt to overturn the old." As to Dr Crisp, he protests, "Let not Dr Crisp's book be looked upon as the standard of our doctrine. There are many good things in it, and also many expressions in it that we generally dislike." Again he says, "Let us take and cleave to the test of the Assembly's Confession of Faith and Catechisms. More we own not ourselves, more we crave not of our brethren; and because we deal fairly and openly, I shall set it down *verbatim*. 'Conf., Chap. XI., Of Justification.—"Art. 1. Those whom God effectually calleth, He also freely justifieth —not by infusing righteousness into them, but by pardoning their sins, and by accounting and accepting their persons as righteous in his sight—not for any thing wrought in them or done by them, but for Christ's sake alone—not by imputing faith itself, the act of believing, or any other evangelical obedience, to them as their righteousness, but by imputing the obedience and satisfaction of Christ unto them, they receiving and resting on Him and His righteousness by faith: which faith they have not of themselves— it is the gift of God.'"

" 'Larger Catechism. "Q. 73. *How doth faith justify a sinner in the sight of God?* Ans. Faith justifies a sinner in the sight of God, not because of those other graces which do always accompany it, or of good works that are the fruits of it—nor as if the grace of faith, or any act thereof, were imputed to Him for His justification—but only as it is an instrument by which He receiveth and applieth Christ and His righteousness."'

"Let these weighty words be but heartily assented to in their plain and native sense, and we are one in this great point of justification. But can any considering man think that the new scheme of a real change, repentance, and sincere obedience, as necessary to be found in a man that may lawfully come to Christ for justification—of faith's justifying, as it is the spring of sincere obedience—of a man's being justified by, and upon, his coming up to the terms of *the new law of grace* (a new word, but of an old and ill-meaning)—can any man think that this scheme and the sound words of the Reverend Assembly do agree?"

With regard to the storm of controversy which I lately described, he says, "Some think that the reprinting of Dr Crisp's book gave the first rise to it. But we must look farther back for its true spring. It is well known, but little considered, what a great progress Arminianism had made in this nation before the beginning of the civil war. And surely it hath lost little since it ended. . . . But that which concerneth our case is, that the middle way betwixt the Arminians and the Orthodox had been espoused and strenuously defended and promoted by some Nonconformists of great note for piety and parts; and usually such men that are for middle ways in points of doctrine, have a greater kindness for that extreme they go half-way to, than for that which they go half-way from."

In order to describe this interesting tract a little further, I shall quote some passages which are of use for all times:—

"As to the party suspected of Antinomianism and Libertinism in this city, it is plain that the churches, wherein they are concerned, are more strict and exact, in trying them that offer themselves unto their communion, as to their faith and holiness, before their admitting them; in the engagements laid on them to a Gospel-walking at their admission; and in their inspection over them afterwards. As to their conversations, they are generally of the more regular and exact frame; and the fruits of holiness in their lives, to the praise of God and honour of the Gospel, cannot with modesty be denied. Is it not unaccountable to charge [such] a people with licentiousness?

"What shall we do for peace with our brethren? . . . Is it desired that we should forbear to make a free offer of God's grace in Christ to the worst of sinners? This cannot be granted by us, for this is the Gospel *faithful saying and worthy of all acceptation* (and therefore worthy of all our preaching of it) *that Jesus Christ came into the world to save sinners and the chief of them* (1 Tim. i. 15). This was the Apostolic practice according to their Lord's command. They began at Jerusalem, where the Lord of life was wickedly slain by them; and yet life in and through His blood was offered to, and accepted and obtained, by many of them. Every believer's experience witnesseth to this, that every one that believes on Jesus Christ acts that faith as the chief of sinners. Every man, that seeth himself rightly, thinks so of himself, and therein thinks not amiss. God only knoweth who is truly the greatest sinner, and every humbled sinner will think that he is the man.

"Shall we tell men, that unless they be holy, they must not believe on Jesus Christ? and that they must not venture on Christ for salvation till they be qualified and fit to be received and welcomed by Him? This were to forbear preaching the Gospel at all, or to forbid all men to believe on Christ. For never was any sinner qualified for Christ. He is well qualified for us; but a sinner out of Christ hath no qualification for Christ but sin and misery. Whence should we have any better, but in and from Christ? Nay, suppose an impossibility, that a man was qualified for Christ, I boldly assert that such a man would not, nor could ever believe on Christ—for faith is a lost, helpless, condemned sinner's casting himself on Christ for salvation, and the qualified man is no such person.

"Shall we warn people that they should not believe on Christ too soon? It is impossible that they should do it too soon. Can a man obey the great Gospel command too soon? (1 John iii. 23); or do the great work of God too soon? (John vi. 28, 29)."

Trail's numerous printed sermons were most acceptable to the "Marrow-men" of Scotland, and have been often reprinted in Edinburgh and Glasgow. But the tract before us contains a sufficient number of sentences, which may be quoted as good specimens of his style.

"As to the new rational method of divinity, *rational* is a fitter commendation of a philosopher than of a divine. Yet it is somewhat better applied to a divine than to divinity; for true divinity hath a higher and nobler original than man's reason, even divine revelation; and it can never be rightly learned by them that have no higher principle in them than reason, even the teaching of the Holy Ghost.

"If men's hearts were seen by themselves; if sin were felt; if men's consciences were enlivened; if God's holy law were known in its exactness and severity, and the glory and majesty of the lawgiver shining before men's eyes; if men were living as leaving time and launching forth into eternity;—the Gospel-salvation by Jesus Christ would be more regarded.

"The poor wearied sinner can never believe on Jesus Christ till he finds he can do nothing for himself; and in his first believing doth always apply himself to Christ for salvation, as a man hopeless and helpless in himself.

"The doctrine of free justification by faith alone hath this advantage, that it suits all men's spirits and frames in their serious approaches to God in worship.

Men may think and talk boldly of inherent righteousness and of its worth and value—of good works, and frames, and dispositions; but when men present themselves before the Lord, and have any discoveries of His glory, all things in themselves will disappear and be looked upon as nothing.

"Sincere obedience is as impossible to a dead unrenewed sinner, as perfect obedience is.

"God *justifieth the ungodly*, neither by making him godly before He justify him, nor leaving him ungodly after He hath justified him; but the same grace that justifies him doth immediately sanctify him.

"*Do not some abuse the grace of the Gospel, and turn it into wantonness?* Yes, some do, ever did, and still will do so. But it is only the ill-understood and not believed doctrine of grace that they abuse. The grace itself no man can abuse, for its power prevents its abuse. Let us see how Paul, that blessed herald of this grace (as he was an eminent instance of it), dealeth with this objection (Rom. vi.) What doth he to prevent this abuse? Is it by extenuating what he had said, that *grace abounds much more where sin had abounded?* Is it by mincing grace smaller, that men may not choke upon it, or surfeit by it? Is it by mixing something of the law with it, to make it more wholesome? No; but only by plain asserting the power and influence of this grace wherever it really is.

"The plain old Protestant doctrine is, that the place of faith in justification is only that of a hand or instrument, receiving the righteousness of Christ for which only we are justified.

"A *direct act* of saving faith is that by which a lost sinner goes out of himself to Christ for help, relying upon Him only for salvation. A *reflex act* ariseth from the sense that faith gives of its own inward act upon a serious review—the truth and sincerity of which is further cleared up to the conscience by the genuine fruits of an unfeigned faith, appearing to all men in our good lives and holy conversation. But for as plain as these things be, yet we find we are frequently mistaken by others, and we wonder at the mistake; for we dare not ascribe to some learned and good men the principles of ignorance or wilfulness, from whence mistakes in plain cases usually proceed. When we do press sinners to come to Christ by a direct act of faith consisting in a humble reliance on Him for mercy and pardon, they will understand us (whether we will or not) of a reflex act of faith by which a man knows and believes that his sins are pardoned, and that Christ is his (when they might easily know that we mean no such thing). Mr Walter Marshall, in his excellent book lately published, hath largely opened this, and the true controversy of the day, though it be eight or nine years since he died."

From Robert Trail's discourse we pass to the introduction of the "Marrow of Modern Divinity" into Scotland. That minute but eventful circumstance arose from the conflicts of the old civil war. A soldier had brought from England the copy which fell into the hands of Thomas Boston of Ettrick. Boston read every word of it with the most thrilling interest and delight, and took every opportunity of speaking about it. The consequence was, that stray copies, as they came into the book market, were picked up by his friends. Thus a copy came into the hands of the Rev. James Hog of Carnock, who put it into the hands of a printer. This eventful reprint was issued at a time when a good fight against the opponents of free grace was being fought in Scotland. The truth which was most offensive to the majority of those opponents was, that sinners ought to fly for refuge to Christ just as they are. The self-styled orthodox met this by saying that a man must forsake his sins before he can come to Christ, thus using the sound, but abusing or confounding the sense, of a text in the Bible. Mr Hog was struck with the doctrine of "The Marrow" on this point :—

"*Nomista.* Truly, sir, I do now plainly see that I have been deceived, and have gone a wrong way to work ; for I verily thought that holiness of life must go before faith, and so be the ground of it, and produce and bring it forth ; whereas I do now plainly see that faith must go before, and so produce and bring forth holiness of life.

"*Evangelista.* I remember, a man, who was much enlightened in the knowledge of the Gospel, saith, There be many that think that as a man chooseth to serve a Prince, so men choose to serve God ; so likewise they think that as those who do best service obtain most favour of their Lord—and as those who have lost it, the more they humble themselves the sooner they recover it—even so they think the case stands betwixt God and them. Whereas (saith he) it is not so, but clean contrary ; for He Himself saith, *Ye have not chosen Me, but I have chosen you,* and not for that we repent and humble ourselves and do good works. He giveth us His grace, therefore we humble ourselves, do good works, and become holy. The good thief on the cross was not illuminated because he did confess Christ, but he did confess Christ because he was illuminated. For, saith Luther, the tree must first be and then the fruit, for the apples make not the tree, but the tree maketh the apples; so faith first maketh the person which afterwards bringeth forth works. Therefore to do the law, without faith, is to make the apples of wood and earth without the tree—which is not to make apples, but mere *fantacies.* Wherefore, neighbour Nomista, let me entreat you, that whereas before you have reformed your life that you might believe, why not believe that you may reform your life ; and do not any longer work to get an interest in Christ, but believe your interest in Christ that so you may work. . . .

"*Antinomista.* Sir, what think you of a preacher that in my hearing said, he durst not exhort nor persuade sinners to believe their sins were pardoned before he saw their lives reformed, for fear they should take more liberty to sin ?

"*Evangelista.* Why, what should I say, but that I think that preacher was ignorant of the mystery of faith" ("The Marrow," Part I., 2d edition, p. 186).

Against all this, the text already hinted at may be quoted :—"Let the wicked forsake his way, and the unrighteous man his thoughts: and let him return unto the Lord, and He will have mercy upon him; and to our God, for He will abundantly pardon" (Isa. lv. 7). But this text speaks of the affections of the heart, as with a repentant faith it looks to Jesus for mercy and pardon. God does not here demand a certificate of a long course of reformation—evidence of years of apprenticeship in the new life, and of a long campaign in the war against our own sins. The phrase "forsaking" implies a divorce between our affections and our sins, a declaration of war against sin—sin being viewed not only as our transgression of the law, but also as our unbelief and neglect of the Gospel and of the Saviour.[1] This declaration of war and our dedication of our souls to the Saviour are so truly simultaneous, that here we have not two things but one. The faith of the sinner that hastens to Christ for salvation, according to the Gospel, is a repentant faith.

Several divines of the Church of Scotland were striving to impress and enforce upon candidates for the ministry that a preacher of the Gospel ought to invite sinners to come to Christ just as they are; and to beware of what had been set up as a contrary dogma, namely, that a sinner must forsake his sins in order to be qualified to come to Christ, *i.e.*, must come as godly not as ungodly, as a saint not as a sinner—"the forsaking of sin" being unscripturally interpreted

---

[1] The following is Dr Gill's exposition of the duty of *forsaking:*—

Let the wicked forsake his way.] His evil way, as the Targum paraphrases it, his wicked course of life—which is his own way, of his own choosing, and in which he delights; and a very dangerous one it is, and yet he is bent upon it, and nothing can turn him from it but efficacious grace; nor will he ever forsake it, till he sees the evil, danger, and loathsomeness of it; and when he does forsake it, it is so as not to make sin the course of his life, though he does not and cannot live without sin. The word for *wicked* signifies restless, troublesome, and ungodly, and is expressive of the pollution and guilt of sin all men are under. Some are notoriously wicked, and all men are wicked in the account of God, though they may think otherwise themselves; and they become so in their own apprehensions, when they are thoroughly awakened and convinced of sin, and of the evil of their ways, and are enabled to forsake them.

Though this may also be understood of *his* own *way* of saving himself, which is by works of righteousness he has done, in opposition to God's way of saving men by Jesus Christ; which way of his own must be relinquished, and Christ alone must be applied unto, and laid hold on, for salvation.

And the unrighteous man his thoughts.] Not his natural thoughts, but his sinful ones—his wrong thoughts of religion, righteousness, and salvation—particularly his thoughts of being justified by his own righteousness—which thoughts are to be forsaken, as being contrary to God's way of justifying sinners. And as all men are unrighteous—are destitute of righteousness and full of unrighteousness—so is the self-righteous person; and he must be divested of all thoughts of his own righteousness, and acknowledge himself an unrighteous man, ere he receives mercy, forgiveness, righteousness, and salvation at the hands of the Lord.

to imply an apprenticeship or period of probation or course of preparation. This contrary dogma was, however, the one which the leaders of the church espoused. In these circumstances Mr Hog reprinted the First Part of the "Marrow of Modern Divinity," of which he wrote a preface, dated 3d December 1717.

In May of that year the General Assembly had taken into consideration a proposition enforced in the examination of divinity students by the Presbytery of Auchterarder, "That it is not sound and orthodox to teach that we must forsake sin in order to our coming to Christ, and instating us in covenant with God." The decision of the Assembly was, that that proposition is "unsound and detestable." Christians were grieved that the Church of Scotland should thus deny "the immediate access to Christ which the Gospel gives to a sinner."[1] Mr Hog, in his preface to "The Marrow," declared, "The wounds of Antichrist are cured, and he receives new strength and spirits through a darkening of the glorious Gospel and perversion thereof.... This renders the essays for a further diffusion of evangelical light the more necessary and seasonable."

Mr Hog's Preface may be regarded as the first of the writings in Scotland that were occasioned by "The Marrow." To give a bibliographical account of these writings is not the plan of this chapter. When that stage in my labours has been reached, I shall have to give my readers some biographies of authors regarding consolation, and then a considerable number of these writings will be noticed.

The documents which issued from, or were presented to, the General Assembly of the Church of Scotland are quite a large bundle of theological literature—not condensed like ordinary ecclesiastical enactments. These, with a varied and useful mass of biographical and doctrinal lore, are to be found in a modern volume, entitled, "Gospel Truth accurately stated and enforced," by Rev. John Brown, minister at Whitburn, son of Rev. John Brown of Haddington.

The General Assembly of 1720 issued a Paper filled with quotations of sentences in "The Marrow," marked as having an unorthodox sound. This "Act" is described by the biographer of Ebenezer Erskine to have been "severely condemnatory of that little book as heretical and dangerous," and also as "enjoining all ministers of the church, not in any way to recommend that book, but to warn their people against perusing it or receiving its doctrine."

The next document was a Petition to the General Assembly of 1721, drawn up by Rev. Thomas Boston, and finally revised by Rev. Ebenezer Erskine, praying for the repeal of the Act against "The Marrow." The petitioners also complained of an Act of the same Assembly containing directions for preaching catechetical doctrine, which gave countenance to "the erroneous doctrine of justification for something wrought in, or done by, the sinner as his righteousness, or keeping of the new or Gospel law." This petition was signed by twelve ministers—Hog,

[1] Fraser's "Life of Ebenezer Erskine," p. 234.

Boston, Ebenezer and Ralph Erskine, &c. One of them was Rev. John Williamson, who had reprinted the Second Part of "The Marrow," so that both parts seem to have been before the General Assembly.

Although there were only twelve signatures, yet there was a considerable party of sympathizers in the church courts, and in the country.

In the discussions that followed, it must be understood that if the controversy had been only between parties who earnestly differed as to the most scriptural terms in which the Gospel should be preached, there would have been no majority in favour of a severe condemnation. The majority was occasioned by the crowd of careless ministers who had found their way into the pulpits of Scotland. This voting crowd allowed a few learned theologians to make speeches, and to frame documents. And these leading theologians had departed from the simplicity of the Gospel, and disliked the endeavour to revive the fresh and fervid tones of the old Reformers' sermons. There were also some good evangelical ministers, whose fears were excited by the bold phraseology of Martin Luther, and of the early English Puritans with which, as we have already seen, "The Marrow" was mainly filled. Such men gave an appearance of seriousness to the doings of the majority.

But the real question at stake was, the warrant of sinners to take comfort from the Gospel of Christ, and the warrant of preachers to offer the Gospel to every sinner—the "Marrow-men" taking the same side as Robert Trail, who held that the Lord Jesus is to be offered to, and believed by men in the plight the first Adam brought them to and left them in—in the plight the law finds them and leaves them in—guilty, filthy, condemned.[1]

The above remarks are designed as my apology for not discussing the detailed statements on theology which the Anti-Marrow leaders amused themselves (and still more amused their worldly followers) by uttering—all which statements were intended only to distract attention from the main questions of Gospel consolation, and Gospel sanctification.

The petition for the repeal of the Act of 1720 was referred by the General Assembly to its Commission. A committee of management set to work to prepare written questions to be put to the petitioners, or (as they were called) representers. After a few testing questions had been agreed to, it was resolved that the twelve representers must have one question a-piece. After much ingenious toil, the committee succeeded in producing twelve questions, which were adopted and formally issued by the November Commission.

The answers to these questions were very full, and contained a long appendix

[1] Trail's language being a little obscure, the above is somewhat of a paraphrase for the benefit of modern readers. His exact words were :—"We call men to believe on the Lord Jesus Christ—in that case the first Adam brought them to and left them in—in that case that the law finds and leaves them in—guilty, filthy, condemned; out of which case they can be only delivered by Christ and by believing on Him."

of quotations from the most esteemed divines of the preceding two centuries. This valuable paper was drawn up by Ebenezer Erskine, and revised and completed by Rev. Gabriel Wilson, who was the possessor of an extensive library. It was discussed in the General Assembly of 1722; and the result was, an explanatory Act, modifying some of the terms of the one petitioned against, but virtually confirming it. The contest went on in provincial Synods, but was at last allowed to slumber, the winding up of the controversy being the publication in the year 1726 of the standard Scottish edition of "The Marrow," with Preface and Notes by Boston.

The most useful document for the information of modern readers is an Act issued to their congregations by those ministerial admirers of "The Marrow," who seceded from the Church. Between the years 1717 and 1733, we speak of the Erskines as ministers of the Establishment, with an evident national prestige. But such was the perverse course of one General Assembly after another, on every subject, and in every case, where the best traditions of the Church came into view and claimed practical recognition, only to be slighted by a tyrant majority, that four ministers, headed by Ebenezer Erskine, seceded in 1733, and were joined in 1737 by other four, including Ralph Erskine, thus swelling the number of ministers into eight, of what was called "The Associate Presbytery;" or, "Some ministers associate together for the exercise of Church government and discipline in a presbyterial capacity." Notwithstanding their secession, these ministers never lost their national prestige. We accept the testimony and acknowledge the excellence of the Erskines in their state of secession, just as if they had continued united to all their friends, not only in spiritual fellowship, but also in ecclesiastical organization. The serviceable document, to which I call attention, is the Act of the Associate Presbytery concerning the Doctrine of Grace (Edinburgh, 21st October 1742).

The chief subject of this Act is the General Assembly's censure of "The Marrow" in 1720 and 1722. The Associate Presbytery's opinion of the book is thus expressed :—" The difference between the law and the Gospel, and between the covenant of works and the covenant of grace, as also the true way of attaining Gospel holiness, are set forth in a very clear light in that book entitled 'The Marrow of Modern Divinity.'" The "Act" goes on to discuss the principal heads of doctrine, giving full statements of the arguments *pro* and *con*, and concluding each head with a verdict or decision. These decisions I quote, placing in parallel columns the truths defined, and the errors condemned.

I.—THE DEED OF GIFT TO MANKIND.

"The Presbytery hereby do acknowledge, declare, and assert, that God the Father, moved by nothing but His free

"The Presbytery hereby reject and condemn the following tenets and opinions :—

love to mankind lost, hath made a deed of gift and grant of His Son Jesus Christ unto mankind in the Word, that whosoever of them all shall receive this gift, by a true and lively faith, shall not perish, but have everlasting life. Or (which is the same thing) that there is a revelation of the Divine will in the Word, affording a warrant to offer Christ unto all mankind without exception, and a warrant to all freely to receive Him, however great sinners they are or have been; and that this gift is made to mankind only, and not to fallen angels."

"(1.) That the free, unlimited, and universal offer of Christ in the Gospel, to sinners of mankind as such, is inconsistent with particular redemption; or, that God the Father—His making a deed of gift unto all mankind, that whosoever of them shall believe on His Son shall not perish, but have everlasting life—infers a universal atonement, or redemption as to purchase.

"(2.) That this grant or offer is made only to the elect, or to such who have previous qualifications commending them above others."

II.—SAVING FAITH.

"The Presbytery do hereby acknowledge, declare, and assert, that in justifying faith there is a real persuasion in the heart of a sinner, that Christ is his —that he shall have life and salvation by HIM—and that whatever Christ did for the redemption of mankind, He did it for him; upon the foundation and ground of the gift, or promise of Christ in the Gospel that is made to sinners of Adam's family as such; and so there is in it a resting upon HIM alone for the whole of his salvation."

"The Presbytery do hereby reject and condemn the following doctrines:—

"(1.) That saving and justifying faith is NOT a persuasion in the heart, that Christ is ours—that we shall have life and salvation by Him—and that whatever Christ did for the redemption of mankind He did it for us.

"(2.) That all the persuasion in justifying faith is only *a belief and persuasion of the mercy of God in Christ, and of Christ's ability and willingness to save all that come to Him*—this being such a faith as Papists and Arminians can subscribe unto, in a consistency with their other errors and heresies.

"(3.) That one must first come to Christ and be a true believer, before he appropriates Christ and the whole of His salvation to himself, upon Scripture ground and warrant."

III.—THE JUSTIFYING RIGHTEOUSNESS.

"The Presbytery do hereby declare and assert—

"(1.) That the Gospel, properly and strictly taken, as contradistinct from the law, is a promise containing glad tidings of a Saviour—with grace, mercy, and salvation, in HIM—to lost sinners of Adam's family; and consequently all precepts (those of faith and repentance not excepted) do in a strict and proper sense belong to the law.

"(2.) That as the suffering of Jesus Christ, our Surety, is the believer's only plea in answer to the law's demand of satisfaction to justice; so the complete and perfect conformity of the Surety to law, both in nature and life, is the believer's only plea, in answer to the law's demand of perfect obedience."

"The Presbytery hereby do condemn the following tenets and opinions:—

"(1.) That the Gospel, strictly taken, is a new, proper, and preceptive law with sanction—binding to faith, repentance, and the other duties which are consequential to the revelation of the grace of God.

"(2.) That though the righteousness of Christ, only, founds our title to eternal glory, yet it is our personal holiness, or our own obedience to the new law, upon which we obtain the possession thereof.

"(3.) That our personal holiness or good works have a causal influence upon our eternal salvation, and are a federal condition and mean thereof; (*in which sense* the Assembly's directing ministers to preach the necessity of a holy life, in order to the obtaining of everlasting happiness, is of very dangerous consequence to the doctrine of free grace)."

IV.—FEAR OF PUNISHMENT AND HOPE OF REWARD.

"The Presbytery hereby do assert, maintain, and declare—

"(1.) That it is a precious Gospel truth that believers, being heirs of the heavenly inheritance, and having it, not by the law, but by free promise, through Jesus Christ, ought not to be influenced

"The Presbytery do condemn the following positions as dangerous, unsound, and erroneous:—

"(1.) That there is a legal connection instituted between the obedience of believers and their enjoying rewards, with escaping punishments, temporal and eternal; or that the law deals with in their obedience by the hopes of obtaining the possession and enjoyment of the inheritance by any works of righteousness or obedience done by them.

"(2.) That, as they should be moved to obedience from the consideration of the excellency of the heavenly inheritance—even God in Christ as their inheritance and exceeding great reward—and by many other motives ; so, particularly, they are to be influenced by this motive, that they have got the begun possession of this inheritance, and have the full possession thereof secured, by rich grace and free promise through Jesus Christ, being made heirs of God and joint-heirs with Christ.

"(3.) That though the believer ought to entertain a holy awe and dread of the majesty of God, and of the awfulness of His threatenings and judgments, both temporal and eternal, against sin and sinners, and to consider from them what even his sins in themselves deserve ; yet he is not called to be moved or excited to obedience to the precepts of the law (either as it is a covenant of works, or as it is a rule of life) by the fear of his falling into hell for omitting duty or committing sin ; but he is called fully to believe his infallible security from going down into that pit through the ransom which God has found out ; so as, through the firm and lively faith of this his safety in a state of favour with God, to have his heart more and more filled with that love which casteth out tormenting fear, and will be natively exercised in a cheerful Gospel obedience to all the Lord's commandments.

them in this manner upon law terms ; and that their hopes of enjoying the one, and escaping the other, are to rise and fall according to the measure of their obedience.

"(2.) That a person's being moved to obedience by the hope of heaven cannot be said to be mercenary in any other sense than that of a hope of obtaining a right to heaven by his own works; and that the believer ought to be moved to obedience, or to eschew evil and do good, by the hopes of his enjoying heaven, or any good temporal or eternal, by his own obedience as the federal, conditional means and cause thereof."

" (4.) That, though believers should remember and seriously consider that there is discipline in their Father's family, and believe that they may expect it when they transgress His law and keep not His commandments; yet as this discipline is instituted on account of remaining corruption in them, so the consideration thereof ought to excite them more and more to improve [*make use of*] the blood of Jesus Christ, by faith, for draining and mortifying this corruption, and, particularly, subduing and mortifying the legal bias and disposition, which is the strength of sin in them, that thus they may be more and more made to serve in newness of spirit, and not in the oldness of the letter."

V.—THE RULE OF LIFE.

" The Presbytery do acknowledge, assert, and declare—

" (1.) That—whatever the law, as a covenant of works, promiseth or threatens in itself, and as to them that are under it—yet the law, as to the believer, is really divested of the promise of life and threatening of death; and that the believer holds his legal right and claim to eternal life, only by the perfect obedience of Christ to the law in his room, and his legal security from eternal death, only by the complete satisfaction of Christ to the justice of God in the threatening of the law—and not by any law having promise of life to his own obedience, or threatening of death to his disobedience; for, *where sin abounded, grace did much more abound; that as*

" The Presbytery do condemn these following positions:—

" (1.) That the doctrine, of the believer being freed from the law as a covenant of works, whether in its commanding or condemning power, is a doctrine of licentiousness, tending any way to free the believer from obligation to the law as it is a rule of life. (Do we make void the law through faith? God forbid; yea, we establish the law.)

sin hath reigned unto death, even so might grace reign through righteousness unto eternal life by Jesus Christ our Lord. (Rom. v. 20, 21.)

"(2.) That, as the moral law doth for ever bind all, as well justified persons as others, to the obedience thereof; so to assert that the moral law, strictly and properly considered as a covenant of works, is what the believer is wholly and altogether set free from, will never prove against the asserter thereof, that he maintains the believer is not under the law as a rule of life. And to the same purpose the Presbytery maintain that, as the law is a covenant of works, believers are wholly and altogether set free from it—set free both from the commanding and condemning power thereof; or, as our Larger Catechism expresses it, *delivered from the moral law as a covenant of works, so as thereby they are neither justified nor condemned*; and that, from the maintaining of this truth it will no ways follow that the believer is not under the law as a rule of life.

"(3.) That though it be the duty of all who hear the Gospel to seek after life and justification by the obedience of Christ, and not by their own—yet, while through unbelief they do not so, they remain under the law as a covenant of works both in its commanding and condemning power; and that it is the peculiar privilege of believers in Christ to be free therefrom.

"(4.) That though all unbelievers do remain under the law as a covenant of works, both in its commanding and condemning power, yet none of them

"(2.) That the believer, *his not being under the law*, and, *his not being obliged to seek life by his own obedience*, are propositions of the same import; as if unbelievers, under a Gospel dispensation, were equally free from the commanding power of the law, as a covenant of works, with believers (since they are not obliged to seek justification by their own works any more than believers). The Presbytery, therefore, condemn this doctrine as highly prejudicial to the truth, relating both to the Law and the Gospel, and [highly prejudicial] to the distinguishing privilege of the believer in Christ, his being not under the law but under grace.

"(3.) That the law as to believers is vested with a promise of life and threatening of death; so as their obedience is properly a federal or conditional means, in order to their obtaining eternal glory.

"(4.) That unbelievers, in their being under the law as a covenant of works, are obliged to seek justification by their own obedience."

are obliged to seek justification by their own obedience; but, on the contrary, it is the great duty of all hearers of the Gospel, and also their inestimable privilege, to seek justification only through the obedience and satisfaction of Christ."

VI. THE SIX ANTINOMIAN PARADOXES,

As the General Assembly falsely called them.

[These are the doctrinal statements for the consolation of believers to which I have referred in the chapter describing the First Part of "The Marrow." They are not by Edward Fisher. At least, I have already hinted at a conjecture that they were first inserted in an edition printed after his death, perhaps in the ninth edition, published in 1699. As it is certain that they were in the reprint which was examined by the General Assembly, we are glad to hear what the good ministers of Scotland had to say about them.]

"In order to clear and maintain the foundations of Gospel obedience, and the springs of the believer's consolation, the Presbytery do acknowledge, assert, and declare—

(1.) That the distinction, as explained in "The Marrow," is good and scriptural, viz., That there is a wide difference between the law as a covenant of works and the law as a rule of holy obedience.

(2.) That a believer in Christ is neither under the commanding nor condemning power of the law as a covenant of works; although he is still under the law as a rule of obedience in the hand of a Mediator.

(3.) That God seeth not iniquity in Jacob or in true believers, as it is a transgression of the covenant of works; but only as it is the transgression of the law in the hand of Christ who bore our sins in His own body on the tree.

"The Presbytery do condemn and reject the following erroneous and dangerous positions taught by the General Assembly:—

(1.) That believers are under the law, and not altogether freed from it, as a covenant of works.

(2.) That when a believer sins he sins against the law of works, and therefore must be liable to the penalty thereof.

(3.) That God seeth iniquity in believers—that it is a violation of the old covenant of works made with Adam in innocency—and consequently that he sees it with an eye of vindictive justice, notwithstanding of the satisfac-

(4.) That, though the elect be by nature the children of wrath even as others; yet, through the death and satisfaction of Christ, the Lord's vindictive anger is turned away from them. Fury is not in Him against any soul that is come to the blood of sprinkling. And yet He may and will be angry with His dear children so as to visit their iniquity with the rod and their transgressions with stripes; but because He will not take His love from Christ, nor break His covenant with HIM, therefore not with them who are HIs seed.

(5.) That when a believer fasts, mourns for, and confesseth his sins, he ought not to do it in a legal way, as one standing under a covenant of works, either as to its precept or penalty; but he ought to do it with the hand of faith upon the head of the great sacrifice and atonement, as one whose person and duties are accepted in the Beloved. And thus he ought to fast, mourn for, and confess his sins before his reconciled God and Father, believing that God, according to His promise, is merciful to his unrighteousness, and will remember his sins no more."

tion of Christ, and their being under the covert of His law-magnifying righteousness.

(4.) That when God is angry with believers for their sins, He pursues them upon the footing of the law of works—or, which is the same thing, with the same anger wherewith He pursued the Surety when He was made a curse for them.

(5.) That when God corrects His children, He does it in His vindictive or revenging wrath, and not in a way of fatherly chastisement.

(6.) That when a believer fasts, mourns for, confesseth, and seeks pardon of sin, he is to view himself as guilty of the violation of the law of works, notwithstanding of his being dead to the law through faith in Jesus Christ."

The whole narrative of the Marrow controversy, contained in the Associate Presbytery's Act, is an intelligent and leisurely theological review, well worthy of study. A letter written by Ebenezer Erskine, while he was still a minister of the Established Church, summarizes the essential truths involved in the controversy.[1] I quote a few sentences:—

"1. Believers are freed from the law as the covenant of works, freed both from the commanding and condemning power of that covenant.

"2. There is and ought to be a difference put betwixt the law as *the law of works*, and the law as *the law of Christ*, or the law as a rule of obedience in the hands of a Mediator.

"This distinction goes upon a scriptural foundation, though declared groundless by the Act of Assembly—which [Act] has a manifest tendency to confound the two covenants, and to stop some of the principal sources of the believer's comfort.

"3. When the law, as a covenant of works, comes upon the believer with the demand of perfect obedience as a condition of life and salvation, his only relief in this case is to plead the perfect obedience and complete righteousness of his ever-blessed Surety.

"This plea is so far from weakening his study of holiness, that it is one of the principal springs thereof.

"4. There is a fiducial act or appropriating persuasion in the very nature of justifying and saving faith.

"To exclude this from the nature of faith is to abandon and condemn our Reformers, and all our polemic writers who have been ever since the Reformation contending, as *pro aris et focis*, against Papists, for this fiducial act under the name of *the assurance of* faith (which *toto cœlo* differs from the assurance of faith of which our Westminster Confession speaks, when it excludes assurance from the nature of faith). We are afraid lest our quitting of this act of faith be a receding from our National Covenant, where *the general and doubtsome faith* of Papists is abjured.

"5. There is a deed of gift or grant made by the Father to all the hearers of the Gospel, affording warrant to ministers to offer Christ unto all, and a warrant unto all to receive Him."

The most popular writing in this consolatory strain is the elaborate work known as *Hervey's Theron and Aspasio*, a series of Dialogues and Letters by Rev. James Hervey, Rector of Weston-Favell, whose preface was dated 6th January 1755. It was in a later month of that very year that Hervey first read *The Marrow*, with Boston's Notes. But he was mainly indebted for his bright and clear views of faith to Ebenezer Erskine.

It is quite unnecessary to make quotations from Hervey's well-known work. His American opponent, Dr Bellamy, gives, within inverted commas, a Herveian definition of faith:—

[1] Fraser's "Life of Erskine," Appendix, No. X.

"Justifying faith hath for the special object of it the forgiveness of sins. A man doth not believe that hiss ins are forgiven him already before the act of believing, but that he shall have forgiveness of sins. In the very act of justification he believes his sins are forgiven him, and so receives forgiveness. Faith is a real persuasion that the blessed Jesus hath shed His blood for me—fulfilled all righteousness in my stead—that through His great atonement and glorious obedience He has purchased, even for my sinful soul, reconciliation with God, sanctifying grace, and all spiritual blessings. The language of faith is this, *Pardon is mine, grace is mine, Christ and all spiritual blessings are mine.* God has freely loved me; Christ has graciously died for me; and the Holy Ghost will assuredly sanctify me in the belief—the appropriating belief—of these precious truths."

It should be known that these sentences were not flung out in this abrupt and dogmatical manner. They are brought together by an adverse critic from various parts of Hervey's book, where they may be found separately, and always interwoven with an abundant mass of modest, candid, and patient thought and argument.

Erskine and Hervey being really one, a sufficient discussion of objections may be founded upon some strictures by Dr Dick, the greatest Divinity Professor of the Associate Synod (a large and influential church which sprang from the evangelical root of the Associate Presbytery). It is singular that from the lips of an ecclesiastical son of such ancestry it should be our lot to quote an "Anti-Marrow" argumentation, as follows:—

"In opposition to Papists, who made faith consist in an assent to the truth of the Scriptures in general, and denied that any man could be certain of his final salvation, the Reformers represented it as a firm persuasion that Christ died for us in particular, and that our sins are forgiven. The founders of our religious society adopted this notion; and in one of their public deeds have defined faith to be a persuasion on the part of the sinner that Christ is his, that what He did and suffered He did and suffered for him, and that he shall have life and salvation by Him. (*Act of Associate Presbytery,* 21st Oct. 1742.)

"It may be questioned whether, in avoiding one extreme, they have not run into another, or (at least) have not employed language which must be explained and qualified, in order to make it accord with the truth.

"A sinner cannot say, in the first instance, *Christ is mine in possession;* because this becomes true only when he has believed, and cannot belong to the nature of faith, as it is a consequence of it. If the words mean only, that Christ is his in the offers of the Gospel, or is offered to him in particular, we allow it, but have a right to complain that a fact, about which there is no dispute, should be expressed in terms which are apt to suggest a quite different sense.

CONSOLATION AS THE FIRST ASPECT OF THE GOSPEL. 111

"The sinner cannot say till he have believed that Christ died for him, unless He died for all men without exception; but, consistently with the doctrine of particular redemption, no man can be assured that he was one of the objects of the sacrifice of the cross, unless he have first obtained an interest in it by faith. Neither can every sinner say, in the first moment of faith, that he shall certainly have eternal salvation. He desires salvation, no doubt, and his faith implies an expectation of it; but how many believers have been harassed with doubts at first, and during the whole course of their lives, and have rarely been able to use the language of confidence! This the advocates of this definition are compelled to admit; and it is curious to observe how, in attempting to reconcile it with their system, they shift and shuffle and almost retract, and involve themselves in perplexity and contradiction, as those must do who are labouring to prove that, although it is a fact that many believers are not assured of their salvation, yet assurance is of the essence of faith. It is manifest that, if assurance is of the essence of faith, it can never be separated from it.

"The exercise of faith is regulated by the Word of God, and its object is there defined. But it is nowhere revealed in the Scriptures that Christ died for any particular person, and that his sins are forgiven. How, then, can assurance of these things belong to the nature of faith? How can it be our duty to believe what is not in the testimony?

"It is an objection against this definition, that it makes faith consist rather in the belief of something regarding ourselves, than in the belief of the testimony of God; in the belief of the goodness of our state, rather than of the all-sufficiency and willingness of Christ.

"It may be farther objected that it confounds the inferences from faith with faith itself—nothing being plainer than that these propositions, *Christ died for me, my sins are forgiven*, are conclusions to which the mind comes from the previous belief of the doctrines and promises of the Gospel.

"Farther, it is chargeable with this error, that it defines faith in its highest and most perfect state, and excludes the lower degrees of it; and thus lays a stumbling-block before thousands of the people of God, who, not finding in themselves this assurance, are distressed with the melancholy thought that they are unbelievers."

In humbly replying to Professor Dick, I would remark—

1. That his climax is directed against an extreme strength of phraseology, and does not apply to the language used by the Associate Presbytery in its Act. There is nothing in that Act which is inconsistent with Dr Dick's own definition of faith. "Faith is not a doubting hesitating assent, but the substance of things hoped for—the evidence of things not seen. The Christian is firmly persuaded of every doctrine and fact which God has attested, and of every promise which He has made. He believes that Jesus Christ is the Son of God and Saviour of sinners

—that His death was an atonement for guilt—that there is redemption through His blood, even the forgiveness of sins—that He is freely offered to him and others in the Gospel—and that every man who trusts in Him shall be saved."[1] In consistency with that definition, we say what the "Marrow-men" say concerning the Gospel offer, that although a man's name is not there, his portrait is there. And there is in the written Gospel what serves the purpose of a blank space in which he may, and ought to, insert his own name; a phrase such as "whosoever," "any man," "him that cometh," &c., being a blank in which any name may be inserted.

2. As Dr Dick's own definition omits the doctrine of particular redemption, we are agreed that the comer to Christ is not at his stage of experience to be burdened with such questions. The question whether the atonement is limited or universal belongs to the department of Divine Decrees, and therefore it is not a question to be forced upon the attention of inquirers after salvation. It belongs neither to the preface nor to the first chapter of the life of faith, but to the appendix, as in my Introductory Essay I have already stated, and as was stated long ago in the quaint aphorism, "No man should go to the university of predestination, till he be well trained up in the Grammar School of faith and repentance." The sinner as a sinner should fly to Christ for pardon, determined to know nothing but Jesus Christ and Him crucified, and that He is able to save them to the uttermost that come unto God by Him. The "Anti-Marrow-men" insisted that inquirers should be reined in and curbed by the doctrine of a limited atonement. The Marrow-men believed the doctrine, but denied that it was "the present truth" for the anxious sinner, or that as scriptural food it was milk for babes.

3. The assertion that the things promised cannot be ours until after we have believed the words of promise, takes the question out of the field of action into the cloisters of mere speculation. It is to immediate action that the sinner is called, both by his own fears and necessities, and also by God's promises and invitations. When the Gospel says to me, *Whosoever will, let him take the water of life*, I may say, *The water of life is mine*, as soon as I run in order to take it. If a candid friend were to say, by way of objection, "The water is not yours until you have actually swallowed it," he would talk nonsense. Some such objection would be reasonable if I were to say, "The water is mine because it is offered to me, and because I am at liberty to take it if I will, and when I will, although I mean to wait a little." But it is not reasonable, if, as a famishing sufferer, I actually run to take it. In this view, the words, "*Christ is mine, pardon is mine*," &c., declared by Hervey to be essentially characteristic of faith, are thoroughly scriptural and defensible. We have a warrantable assurance, on the

[1] Dick's "Lectures on Theology," Lecture 68; the longer quotation is from that Lecture also.

CONSOLATION AS THE FIRST ASPECT OF THE GOSPEL. 113

ground of faith in the promise, and at the foot of the throne of grace, without having to serve any previous apprenticeship in the experience of possession.

4. To undertake to infer what is the accurate preaching of the Gospel-salvation from the common or frequent experience of believers, is to lead inquirers off from the genuine source of all valuable and real information. Dr Dick informs us that "Marrow-men" "are compelled to admit," that "many believers have been harassed with doubts at first, and during the whole course of their lives." But going further back, we must say, that "Anti-Marrow-men" compel and force conversation into the channel of human experience. The question to be answered, and from the pursuit of which we ought not to be diverted, is, What is the doctrine of Scripture on the subject? If, from human experience, a doctrine is framed and submitted to our inspection, asserting that it is inconsistent with genuine faith to have strong consolation in the infancy of the Christian life, and that it is a sign of genuine faith to be harassed with doubts, we reply that there is no such doctrine in the Scriptures; but that according to Scripture there ought to be at the "beginning" what an apostle called "the confidence and the rejoicing of the hope." It is strange that Professor Dick should characterize our believing *in Him who justifieth the ungodly* as a "belief in the goodness of our state." It is quite the opposite; and the charge would be more plausible against the opposite teaching, which suspends our personal consolation until we have evidence of our personal godliness. The essential danger is, that we should mistake our doubts for virtues. Let us know them to be defects; while we also know that for all our defects, both as to believing and as to doing, there is forgiveness with God that He may be feared.

The consolatory system of the "Marrow-men," and of Hervey, and of John Brown of Haddington, includes the risen Saviour's precept that the Gospel is to be preached to every creature. Give them *the Gospel*—not mere scriptural reproof, advice, and instruction in righteousness—but the offer of mercy through the Saviour. As to this, it will be sufficient to quote John Brown, whom we find engaged in answering objections:—

"OBJECTION. *Only the thirsty, the willing, the heavy-laden labourers are invited to receive Christ and His salvation* (Isa. lv. 1 ; John vii. 37 ; Rev. xxii. 17 ; Matt. xi. 28).

"ANSWER. The *thirsty* (in Isa. lv. 1) cannot mean only those who earnestly desire Christ and His righteousness and blessings; for, in verse 2, they are said to be spending money for that which is not bread, and labouring for that which satisfieth not; but must mean such as desire happiness in any form.

"*Whosoever will* (in Rev. xxii. 17) denotes the universality of the invitation, not the qualification of the persons invited (John vi. 37, and vii. 37).

"The *heavy-laden labourers* (in Matt. xi. 28) include such as have fatigued themselves in sinful courses, and are laden with the guilt and enslaving power of sin.

P

"OBJECTION. *It would be infinitely unbecoming for men, who had just been wallowing in their wickedness, to approach to or receive the Holy Jesus before some change be made upon them.*

"ANSWER—1. God must indeed make them new creatures, before they be able to receive Him; but it is not as *new men* but as *sinful men* that they are warranted and required to receive Him for their salvation (Matt. ix. 13, and xviii. 11; 1 Tim. i. 15).

"2. How is it unbecoming for the dangerously diseased to approach to or admit the all-skilful physician, before they be almost cured? for the unclean to apply the purifying water, before they be partially cleansed? for the starving to take any wholesome provision till they be almost satisfied? (Exod. xv. 6; Hos. xiv. 4; Ezek. xxxvi. 25; Zech. xiii. 1; Isa. i. 18; Acts iii. 26; Rom. xi. 26, 27; Prov. ix. 5; Isa. lv. 1-3, 7; Rev. xxii. 17). How is it unbecoming for ignorant men to come directly to the only effectual Teacher? unbecoming for guilty men to receive the Lord their righteousness, who is made of God unto them righteousness? unbecoming for lost men to come to the only—the divinely appointed—Saviour of men? (Isa. xlviii. 17, and xlv. 17, 22, 24; Luke xix. 10; Hos. xiii. 9).

"3. It is impossible for men to attain to any true sincerity, humility, or reformation of heart, before they receive Christ (Job xiv. 4; Prov. xx. 9; Ps. li. 5; Eph. ii. 1-3, 10; Rom. viii. 7, 8, 2; John xv. 5; Jer. xvii. 9, and xiii. 23; Titus i. 15, and iii. 3-7).

"4. In receiving Jesus Christ, as made of God to us wisdom, righteousness, sanctification, and redemption, we cannot continue cleaving to our sin, as we receive Him in order to purge away and destroy it."

CHAPTER VII.

GUYSE'S COWARD LECTURE ON PREACHING CHRIST; ALSO, ALLUSIONS IN VARIOUS WRITINGS TO SUCH PREACHING OR TO THE NEGLECT OF IT.

MR. COWARD was an aged gentleman, a layman in communion with the English Dissenters in the eighteenth century, whose name is associated with a lectureship instituted by him for the special purpose of reminding and stimulating Christian ministers to preach Christ. The Coward Lecture was founded in 1725. It provided preachers, but it did not contemplate the printing of an annual volume. It appears that only one volume was printed, which contained the discourses for

CONSOLATION AS THE FIRST ASPECT OF THE GOSPEL. 115

1728 and 1729, and was edited by the Rev. John Hubbard of Stepney. The title was "Christ's Loveliness and Glory in His personal and relative characters and gracious offers to sinners—consider'd in twelve sermons, preach'd at Mr Coward's Lecture. By several ministers. London, 1729."

The public attention accorded to this excellent volume arose chiefly from the two sermons by the Rev. John Guyse, preached at St Hellen's, in April 1729, with the heading, "Christ, the Son of God, the great subject of a Gospel ministry."

A young minister, who was afterwards a celebrated D.D., the Rev. Samuel Chandler, bitterly attacked these sermons. To this attack we owe a valuable pamphlet, dated 1 Dec. 1729, "The Scripture-notion of preaching Christ further clear'd and vindicated, in a Letter to the Reverend Mr Samuel Chandler, in answer to one from him to the author—in which Mr Chandler's charitable temper, his treatment of sacred things, his misrepresentations, his notion of preaching Christ, and his charge of uncharitableness, &c., are considered. By John Guyse. London, 1730."

The grievance which drew forth the Coward Lecture, was not exactly the same as that which suggested Dr Crisp's *Christ Alone Exalted* and *The Marrow*. The older grievance was, as we have seen, a diseased anxiety lest the preaching of free unconditional mercy should encourage an inquiring sinner to be licentious or careless. The later grievance was a style of preaching which seemed to deny that there are any sinners in a Christian congregation; and which asserted that because Christianity is the parent and nurse of the actual morality of each individual Christian, therefore to preach morality is to preach Christianity, and further, that to preach such Christianity is what is meant by preaching Christ.

Mr Coward's preachers held, that though a congregation is a Christian auditory, yet the true Christians in the congregation are sinners who depend upon Christ, while the larger proportion, being merely nominal Christians, are sinners who have not yet accepted the offer of their own personal salvation through Christ. Thus, however numerous the true Christians may be among such an audience, it is solemnly necessary and dutiful that the preacher should announce and insist upon it as a mutual understanding that the audience consists of two classes, unbelievers and believers. As to this Dr Isaac Watts had said, "Have we not been too often tempted to follow the modish way, and speak to our hearers in general terms, as though they were all converted already, and sufficiently made Christians by a national profession?"[1]

While this was the special grievance against which the Coward Lecture contended, the preachers did not lose sight of the older grievance. The Rev. James Wood preached, on 29th November and 13th December 1728, from the text,

[1] Watts' preface to Rev. John Jennings' discourses of "Preaching Christ."

"In the last day, that great day of the feast, Jesus stood and cried, If any man thirst, let him come to Me and drink" (John vii. 37); and he thus stated the universal offer of Christ in the Gospel.

"The invitation extends to all sinners of whatever tribe, nation, kindred, or language, that should hear the joyful sound, and will justify me in saying to the oldest offender in this assembly, Be of good cheer, He calleth *thee*. Paul was a famous instance of the riches of Christ's pardoning mercy, the freeness and fulness of it to the chief of sinners. . . . . . What we read in his remarkable case was written for our instruction, that we, through patience and comfort of the Scriptures, might have hope. He tells us so when he said, For this cause I obtained mercy, that in me first Jesus Christ might show forth all long-suffering for a pattern to them who should hereafter believe on Him to life everlasting. See in me, as if he had said, that Christ is no respecter of persons, that He scatters His pardons alike to Jew and Gentile, among the circumcision and the uncircumcision; that no circumstances, by which sin is aggravated and rendered more heinous, should discourage their applications to Him, who can as easily forgive ten thousand talents as a few pence."

Mr Wood also defended this universal offer against a misapplied mention of Divine decrees; the language of his defence has a good "Marrow" ring.

"Our Lord did well know that but few were chosen, though many were called; and that such only would believe as were ordained to eternal life. Yet His invitations were general, and none were excluded by Him who did not shut out themselves. The apostles set out upon the same principles, yet had they no cramp upon their spirits when preaching the Gospel to every creature. They left secret things to God—had no discriminating marks of elect or reprobate to guide them in the exercise of their ministry."

With regard also to perils to morality, enlarged upon by Anti-Pauline objectors, Mr Guyse quotes, with approbation, a rejoinder of his esteemed predecessor in the same field, Mr Jennings:—

"Why should not we introduce the peculiarities of the Gospel on all occasions —as frequently as the apostles did? If our schemes of theology will not allow us, we have reason to suspect that we are in a different scheme from the apostles. Are we afraid men will make perverse use of such doctrines as the apostles used for motives? The apostles chose to venture it, and why should not we? If we will not dare to preach such a Gospel as may be perverted by men of corrupt minds to their own injury, we must not expect to be instruments of any good. If we'll be *the savour of life* to some, we must expect to be *the savour of death* to others, or not preach at all."

The chief business of this chapter is with the later grievance, which demanded and drew forth Christian words of scriptural philanthropy in Mr Coward's days. To be informed of Mr Guyse's own principles as to preaching

Christ is what my readers are entitled to ask. No more, therefore, need be said regarding Mr Chandler than this, that the task which he, as the champion of too many similar preachers, imposed upon Mr Guyse, was to refute some such theorem as the following :—" To preach upon any doctrine or precept contained in the Christian religion—to preach against any vices condemned by it, or upon anything virtuous and praiseworthy inculcated in it, because they are become part of Christ's religion enjoined by His authority, and the text is taken out of the Bible, and now and then Scripture is brought to confirm what is preached—is as directly and immediately preaching Christ, as preaching the doctrines of His sufferings, death, atonement, righteousness, exaltation, and advocacy, or anything else that is most peculiar to Him." [1] Mr Chandler also ridiculed the endeavour to preach about the person of Christ as a theme distinct from the principles and requirements of Christianity.

Mr Guyse preached the *person of Christ*, the *finished work of Christ*, and *Christian morals*.

As to the person of Christ, revealed in the Scriptures as a distinct theme for preachers, his sentiments are summed up in his allusions to the assertion that there could be no such separate topic. "What! (he says) Is there no glory in His character as the Son of God, and His being the only proper person pitched upon by the eternal Father for the redemption of the Church? or in His own free and gracious willingness, in His acceptance of that trust, and engagement in eternal transactions with the Father about it, and coming in the fulness of time to discharge it? Is there no glory to be seen or spoken of, in the wonderful constitution of His person God-man, in His condescension as God therein to man, and in the honour He therein put upon man? Is no personal glory to be seen in all the infinite perfections of His Divine nature, and in all the matchless purity and lovely qualities of His human nature, as they are united in Him? Are there no glories of God to be seen in His person, who is the representative image of God to us, *the brightness of the Father's glory, and the express image of His person?* Is there no glory in His visible appearances as the Jehovah of Israel under the Old Testament? no glory in His fitnesses and capacities for His office-work, as a Person divinely qualified for it in Himself, and enriched with the unction of the Holy Spirit? no glory in the infinite dignity that His person gives to His sacrifice, and the sure efficacy that it gives to all His offices and administrations? no glory in His person as the object, on account of His own Divine perfections, of all the adoration, worship, faith, love, and obedience of men and angels, and as designed to be made to appear glorious in Himself by the whole of the Gospel dispensation? And is there no glory in the illustrious exalted state of His person at the Father's right hand, where crowds of angels surround Him with prostrate reverence? and no glory redounding to His person in the whole of our

[1] Guyse's Pamphlet, p. 75.

redemption and salvation by Him, or in the execution of His offices now and when He shall come to judge the world at the last day? Are all these things (and more than I am able to sum up) so worthless, so contemptible and mean, as to be left out, or to be but now and then, at most, slightly touched upon, in our preaching Christ? Are not these sufficiently revealed, and made so far plain in the Gospel, as to bear a part in our holy ministrations concerning Him, and to open a theme for our solemn admiration, and even for our thoughts to expatiate upon Him?

"Did not God design a personal glory to His eternal Son in the whole of the mediatorial scheme? And is not the advancement of Christ's personal glory, and of the glory of the Father in Him, the ultimate end of a Gospel ministry? The Lord keep me from overlooking or neglecting these glories. I cannot think that Christ is preached as He ought to be, if all or most of these things concerning His person are suppressed."

With regard to Mr Guyse's preaching of the work of Christ, a few sentences may be culled from his Coward Lecture:—

"According to the Apostle Paul's method of preaching Christ, He is to be proposed and recommended to sinners and to believers.

"1. *To sinners* Christ is set forth to be a propitiation through faith in His blood (Rom. iii. 25). He is to be preached to all sorts and degrees of sinners as such. He is to be recommended to them as chosen, appointed, and accepted of God to be a Saviour; as having, in His great love to sinners, freely taken upon Him a saving office; and as having gone through a humble state of obedience, sufferings, and death, in their nature, and in their room and stead, that He might effectually save them. He is to be recommended to them as living in heaven to employ Himself in His saving office. He is to be preached as the free gift of God to sinners, and as a Saviour that hath grace enough in His heart not only to invite them to Himself, but likewise to enable them to come at His invitation and call, and to receive all that come to Him. This preaching of Christ is to be directed in the ministerial way to all people where the Gospel comes. They are the objects of it; they are nearly concerned in it; and it hath to do with them promiscuously and indefinitely, none knowing who are God's elect among them till the event declares it. They are to be treated, not like brutes or machines, but like men of rational faculties, capable of attending to, and considering what is proposed to them, and capable of being wrought upon by the Spirit of God in a way suitable to their reasonable natures, and of being *drawn* under His gracious influence *with cords of a man, with bands of love*. The stupid, careless minds of sinners are to be roused by proper considerations for convincing them of their need of Christ. They are to be expostulated with, entreated and persuaded, in the bowels of compassion, to embrace Him as He is freely offered to them in the Gospel. They are to be dealt with by all the arguments of authority and grace, of duty and interest, of danger and safety, of gain and loss, of honour and disgrace, of pleasure and pain, of eternal happiness in receiving Him, and of eternal misery for rejecting Him. All arguments are to be used with them suited and appointed by God to work upon their judgments and consciences, their understandings, wills, and affections—suited to their desires and aversions, joys and sorrows, hopes and fears. They are to be warned hereby to flee from the wrath to come, and encouraged, under a sense of their guilt and danger, to flee for refuge, to lay hold on the hope that in Christ is set before them.

"2. [As] *to believers*—they are to be helped who have believed through grace (Acts xviii. 27). Christ is to be preached to them for their farther acceptance of Him and devotedness to Him. They are to be exhorted to cleave with purpose of heart to the Lord; and as they have received Christ Jesus the Lord, so to walk in Him, rooted and built up in Him, and established in the faith as they have been taught, abounding therein with thanksgiving (Col. ii. 6, 7). And He is to be recommended to them that they may have fellowship with Him, and with the Father through Him, and that their joy may be full (1 John i. 3, 4). We have no dominion over their faith, but are to be helpers of their joy (2 Cor. i. 24). All His glories, as far as we can discover them, are to be opened up before them—what He is in His wondrous person, office, and love—what He has undertaken and engaged on their behalf from eternity, and performed in time—what He has done and suffered for them on earth, and is doing for them in heaven, and will do for them at the last day and for ever afterwards—what He has purchased, provided, and secured in Himself for them—what He has already bestowed on them and promised to them—and what He expects and demands from them; in a word, all that He is in Himself and is to them, and all that they are made to be in and by Him, and are obliged to be to Him. All this should be proposed to them, to encourage their continual and increasing faith, love, hope, and joy, admiration, worship, obedience, gratitude, and praise. All this should be attempted and enforced upon them in the name of Christ, and with an expectation of His presence and blessing, that they may know their privileges in Him and their duty toward Him; and that their hearts may be comforted, strengthened, and animated in His ways, till the whole design of His grace toward them shall be perfected in their endless glory."

It may be mentioned that the text of Mr Guyse's Lecture is Acts ix. 20. His heads are—I. The Subject—"Christ, that He is the Son of God." II. The Apostle Paul's acts—" He preached." The acts he states as having been *three*—

(1.) To publish or declare these things concerning Christ.

(2.) To confirm and defend what is published concerning Him.

(3.) To propose and recommend Him to the acceptance of those to whom He is preached.

As to the *third*, he says, "The verb in our text carries such a sense of preaching as consists in proclaiming public edicts and commands, and in inviting slaves and captives to come in to a deliverer for their liberty, and in ordering things to be disposed of to the people. We may consider it as transferred to the use of preaching the Gospel, in which the ministers of Christ go forth in His name, proclaiming Him to the people, proposing liberty to the captives, and inviting sinners to come in to Him for all salvation. Their business is, among other things, to declare that this is the command of God, that they should believe on the name of His Son Jesus Christ, and to propose Him to their acceptance, that they, by Divine grace, may be brought to believe that Jesus is the Christ, the Son of God, and that, believing, they may have life through His name. Thus our Apostle preached Christ, saying, in an address to the Jews, To you is the word of this salvation sent. Be it known unto you, therefore, men and brethren, that through this man is preached unto you the forgiveness of sins ; and by Him all that believe are justified from all things, from which ye could not be justified by the law of Moses."

In answer to a doubt whether the Apostle Paul ever preached Christ as the Saviour of sinners, except when the main subject of discourse was the enforcing of Christian morals, Mr Guyse produced the following instances, among many others:—

"He tells the Corinthians that *he determined not to know* (or to preach as if he did not know) *anything among them, save Jesus Christ and Him crucified.* This, he declared, had been and should be the grand subject of his ministry amongst them. Or, as good Mr Flavel descants upon it, 'It is as if he should say, It is my stated settled judgment—the produce and issue of my most serious and exquisite inquiries—that all other knowledge (how profitable, how pleasan: soever) is not worthy to be named the same day as the knowledge of Jesus Christ. This, therefore, I resolve to make the scope and end of my ministry, and the end regulates the means. Christ shall be the centre to which all the lines of my ministry shall be drawn—*Christ* above all other subjects—*Christ crucified* above all things in Christ.'"

"Acts xvii. 2, 3. Paul, *as his manner was*, went in unto the Jews, and three Sabbath days reasoned with them out of the Scriptures, &c.

" This is an account of his usual manner, of his stated and customary way, κατὰ τὸ εἰωθός—which may relate not only to his preaching first to the Jews, but to *the way or manner of his preaching* to them. And so it is a good clue to guide our thoughts about the manner of his preaching Christ to the Jews, wherever it is spoken of. And what did he preach ? Was it not concerning Christ, *opening and alleging*, explaining and proving to them, the necessity and reality of His sufferings and resurrection, with the nature, design, and truth of His Messiahship, that He is indeed the Christ, whom God anointed to the office of a Saviour, and whom their ancient prophets had foretold and described ?

Was not Christ the principal subject of this preaching? The consequence of it was, that some believed, and others cried out against him and Silas, saying, 'These that have turned the world upside down, are come hither also.' What could he preach, to be the means of faith in some, and of all this rage in others of the Jews, but the doctrines peculiar to Christ, or concerning Him? Mr Henry's[1] note on this place is, 'Gospel ministers should preach Jesus; that must be their principal subject; their business is to bring people acquainted with Him.' And on another occasion, in his address to Mr Samuel Clark (page 77) about the method of preaching, he says, 'Manage it as an ordinance of Christ, instituted for the advancing of His honour and interest; and therefore preach not yourself, but Christ Jesus the Lord, as one that hath determined to know nothing but Christ, and Him crucified, and desires to acquaint others with Him. *Preach Christ, brother* (said an aged minister to one that asked his advice); *whatever you do, preach Christ.*'"

Mr Guyse did not condemn, but both approved and practised, the preaching of Christian morals, while he denied that such preaching is all that is meant by the phrase and commission, "to preach Christ." His statements on this department were the following:—

"*Preaching Christ* (in a latitude of the expression) takes in the whole compass of Christian religion considered in its reference to Christ. It extends to all its noble improvements of natural light and principles, and to all its glorious peculiarities of the supernatural and incomprehensible kind, as each of these may, one way or other, be referred to Him. In this sense there is no doctrine, institution, precept, or promise—no grace, privilege, or duty toward God and man—no instance of faith, love, repentance, worship, or obedience, suited to the Gospel state and to the design and obligations of the Christian religion—that don't belong to preaching Christ.

"But to bring all these with any propriety under this denomination, they must be considered, according to their respective natures or kinds, in their reference to Christ, that He may be interwoven with them and appear to be concerned in them. They must be preached, not with the air of a heathen moralist or Platonic philosopher, but with the spirit of a minister of Christ, referring them up to Him, as revealed or enjoined or purchased by Him—as shining in their brightest lustres and triumphing in all their glories through Him—as built upon Him and animated by Him—as lodged in His hands who is head over all things to the church—as standing in the connections, uses, and designs in which He hath placed them—as known, enjoyed, or practised by light and grace derived from Him—as to be accounted for to Him—as acceptable to God, and advantageous to our salvation, alone through Him, by faith in Him—as enforced upon

---

[1] "Rev. Matthew Henry's Commentary."

us by motives and obligations taken from Him—and as tending to His glory and the glory of God in Him.

"Whatever is the immediate subject of the discourse, it may be called *preaching Christ*, if it is managed in such a manner as shows His concern in it, and leads our thoughts either to the glory of His person and offices, or to His kingdom of providence and grace—as all things were created by Him and for Him —as He is before all things, and by Him all things consist—as He is the head of the body the Church, the beginning, the first-born from the dead, that in all things He might have the pre-eminence—and as it pleased the Father that in Him all fulness should dwell. In this sense the apostles preached the riches of the glory of the mystery among the Gentiles, which was Christ in them the hope of glory; warning every man, and teaching every man in all wisdom, that they might present every man perfect in Christ Jesus. Whereunto, says our Apostle, I also labour, striving according to His working, which worketh in me mightily (Colossians i. 16-19, 27-29). They gave an evangelical turn to moral duties, and enforced them with a reference to Christ and by considerations taken from Him.

"'Twould be to transcribe a great part of the apostolic writings to give you a full view of this strain of preaching Christ; how they intermingled the doctrines that peculiarly relate to Him, as enforcing and evangelizing the duties that have a foundation in natural light. In this latitude of the expression, all their sermons and epistles were full of Christ. And after their example, Christ should triumph in all our discourses. His name should throw life and lustre upon all our holy ministrations."

In his pamphlet the lecturer enforces these views by quotations from influential English authors. The following is one from Dr Bates:—

"He [Dr Jacomb] preached Christ crucified, our only wisdom, righteousness, sanctification, and redemption. His design was to convince sinners of their absolute want of Christ; that with flaming affections they might come to Him, and from His fulness receive divine grace. This is to water the tree at the root, whereby it becomes flourishing and fruitful; whereas the laying down of moral rules for the exercise of virtue and the subduing of vicious affections, without directing men to derive spiritual strength, by prayer, and in the use of divine ordinances, from the Mediator, the fountain of all grace—and without representing His love as the most powerful motive and obligation to obedience—is but pure philosophy, and the highest effect of it but unregenerate morality."

Mr Guyse could not but complain, with much feeling and force of language, of many professedly Christian ministers' neglect to preach Christ. Such lamentations by him, and by other truly philanthropic Christians, have been made, not for the sake of attacking any preacher, but in order to call attention to Christ, and to the preaching of the person and work of Christ as the grand desideratum for the salvation of men, and for the success of ministers. It is as suggesting views of the consolation that is in Christ that I present the reader with the following collection of testimonies as to this prevalent neglect. Among them Mr Guyse's own testimony appears in its place in the chronological arrangement:—

JOHN OWEN, D.D.—" It is evident to me, who have some advantage to consider things, as much as ordinary men, that the apostacy, the cursed apostacy that spreads itself over the nation, and whose fruits are in all ungodliness and uncleanness, consists in an apostacy from and forsaking the person of Christ. Some write of how little use the person of Christ is in religion—none, but to declare the doctrine of the Gospel to us. Consider the preaching and talk of men. You have much preaching and discourse about virtue and vice (so it was among the philosophers of old), but Jesus Christ is laid aside quite as a thing forgotten, as if He was of no use—no consideration in religion; as if men knew not at all how to make use of Him, as to living to God. This being the general plague, as is evident, of the apostacy of the day wherein we live, if we are wise we shall consider very carefully, whether we ourselves are not influenced, more or less, with it."

REV. INCREASE MATHER, 1689.—" It was a wise reproof which a grave divine administered to a young preacher who entertained his auditory with an elaborate discourse. After he had commended his parts and pains, *There was* (said he) *one thing wanting in the sermon—I could not perceive that the Spirit of God was in it.* Though morality is good and necessary to be taught and practised, yet it is much to be lamented that many preachers in these days have hardly any other discourses in their pulpits than what we may find in Seneca, Epictetus, Plutarch, or some such heathen moralists. Christ, the Holy Spirit, and (in a word) the Gospel is not in their sermons."

BISHOP GIBSON (*Bp. of London*), 1724.[1]—" It must be always remembered, in the first place, that we are Christian preachers, not barely preachers of morality. The several branches of what we may call *the Mediatorial Scheme*, with the several duties annexed to it resulting from each branch, are, without doubt, the main ingredients of the Gospel state—these by which Christianity stands distinguished from all other religions, and Christians are raised to far higher hopes, and far greater degrees of purity and perfection—in which views it would seem strange if a Christian preacher were to dwell only upon such duties as are common to Jews, heathens, and Christians, and were not more especially obliged to

---

[1] " Directions given to the clergy of the Diocese of London in the year 1724, to which are now added Directions given to the Masters and Mistresses of the Charity Schools." By Edmund, Lord Bishop of London. Second edition. (London, 1727), p. 13.

dwell on, and inculcate those principles and doctrines which are the distinguishing excellence of the Christian religion. But yet so it is, that these subjects are too much forgotten amongst young preachers, who, being better acquainted with morality than divinity, fall naturally into the choice of moral rather than divine subjects, and will, of course, do so till the two subjects are better considered and understood."

REV. JOHN GUYSE, 1729.[1]—"There are but few in our days that preach Christ, and but few that regard Him. The greatest number of preachers and hearers seem contented to lay Him aside; and too many there are among us who set themselves against Him. His name is seldom heard of in conversation, unless in a way of strife and debate, or (which is infinitely worse) in a way of contempt, reproach, and blasphemy.

"The present modish turn of religion looks as if we began to think that we have no need of a Mediator, but that all our concerns were to be managed with God as an absolute God. The religion of nature makes up the darling topics of our age; and the religion of Jesus is valued only for the sake of that, and only so far as it carries on the light of nature, and is a bare improvement of that kind of light. All that is *restrictively* Christian, or that is peculiar to Christ—everything concerning Him that has not its apparent foundation in natural light, or that goes beyond its principles—is waived, and banished, and despised. And even moral duties themselves, which are essential to the very being of Christianity, are usually harangued upon without any evangelical turn or reference to Christ as fruits of righteousness to the praise and glory of God by Him. They are placed in the room of Christ, are set up independent of Him, and are urged upon principles, and with views ineffectual to secure their practice, and more suited to the sentiments and temper of a heathen than of those that take the whole of their religion from Christ.

"How many sermons may one hear that leave out Christ, both name and thing, and that pay no more regard to Him than if we had nothing to do with Him! What a melancholy symptom—what a threatening omen is this! Do we not already feel its dismal effects in the growth of infidelity, in the rare instances of conversion-work, and in the cold, low, and withering state of religion among the professors of it beyond what has been known in some former days? May not these things be chargeable in great measure on a prevailing disuse of preaching Christ? and where will they end if the disuse goes on, and little or nothing concerning Him is to be heard among us? How should all the ministers of Christ that heartily love Him, that are concerned for His honour, and for the honour of religion as *Christians*, be affected at these thoughts! And how should

[1] He became D.D. in 1732.

they be excited, by the too general neglect of others, to be so much the more frequent, earnest, and explicit in preaching Christ themselves!"

REV. JOHN CURRIE, 1732.—"It is regretted, and I wish it be not on too just grounds, especially concerning our younger ministers and preachers, who are said often and ordinarily to entertain their hearers with bare harangues of morality; their discourses having little, and sometimes no more in them but what might have been said by such as never saw a Bible, having nothing but what the light of nature doth suggest, so that a stranger, at hearing, might doubt whether the preacher was a Christian or a Deist."
Sermon before the Synod of Fife, 26th Sept. 1732.—[The above sentence suggested the title of a small tract printed at Glasgow in 1746:—"A Short Essay to prevent the dangerous consequences of the Moral Harangues now so common in Scotland, especially to prevent the dangerous consequences of Mr Leechman's Sermon on Prayer, being a collection of some of the sentiments of several judicious divines in opposition to these moral harangues," &c.]

REV. JOHN WITHERSPOON, D.D., 1753.—[The prevalence of mere philosophizing and moralizing in the pulpit, as well as the opposition of such clergymen to preachers of Christ, occasioned the publication of an energetic protest by Dr Witherspoon. In order that it might be read in quarters to which access was almost impossible, the author adopted the style of burlesque, and entitled his pamphlet, "Ecclesiastical Characteristics; or, The Arcana of Church Policy—being an humble attempt to open up the Mystery of Moderation, wherein is shown a plain and easy way of attaining to the character of a Moderate Man, as at present in repute in the Church of Scotland." A Moderate Man is supposed to enunciate a number of Maxims—one of which is the following:—]

"Maxim IV.—A good preacher must not only have all the above and subsequent principles of Moderation in him as the source of everything that is good, but must, over and above, have the following special marks and signs of a talent for preaching:—1. His subjects must be confined to social duties. 2. He must recommend them only from rational considerations, viz., the beauty and comely proportions of virtue, and its advantages in the present life, without any regard to a future state of more extended self-interest. 3. His authorities must be drawn from heathen writers—none (or as few as possible) from Scripture. 4. He must be very unacceptable to the common people."

WILLIAM COWPER, 1783.

"All truth is from the sempiternal source
Of light divine. But Egypt, Greece, and Rome
Drew from the stream below.

Their rules of life,
Defective and unsanctioned, proved too weak
To bind the roving appetite, and lead
Blind Nature to a God not yet revealed.
'Tis Revelation satisfies all doubts,
Explains all mysteries except her own,
And so illuminates the path of life
That fools discover it, and stray no more.
" Now tell me, dignified and sapient sir,
My man of morals, nurtured in the shades
Of Academus, is this false or true ?—
Is Christ the abler teacher, or the schools ?
If Christ, then why resort at every turn
To Athens or to Rome, for wisdom short
Of man's occasions, when in HIM reside
Grace, knowledge, comfort, an unfathomed store ?
How oft, when Paul has served us with a text,
Has Epictetus, Plato, Tully preached !"—*The Time-Piece.*

EDWARD MEYRICK GOULBURN, D.D., 1861.—" Some of us can remember the time when sermons were nothing more than moral essays, setting forth some duty or some grace of the Christian character, with little or no reference to those evangelical motives from which alone an acceptable obedience can spring, and no suggestions of any value as to the method in which the particular grace recommended might be obtained. You were told that humility and self-denial and contentment were excellent things, and worthy of being pursued by all men ; but as to the considerations which alone can move to the pursuit, and as to any practical method of maintaining them under difficulties, you were left in ignorance. But when it pleased God to quicken the dry bones of the Church with new life, men began to see that to divorce the moral code of Christ from His constraining love, which alone can enable us to keep it, was an unhallowed act, upon which God's blessing can never rest, and the exhortations of the Christian preacher should be something warmer and more genial and more persuasive than the moralizings of Seneca."—*Thoughts on Personal Religion,* Chap. I.

CHAPTER VIII.

"HINTS ON CHRISTIAN EXPERIENCE."

By Rev. Charles Watson, Minister of Burntisland.

Second Edition, 1833.

HAVING had occasion to remind my readers, that narratives of human experience are not the materials out of which the Gospel offer is constructed, I think that they will be both pleased and profited by hearing Dr Watson's able and accurate observations bearing upon this matter. If his book is not one of the "old writings," it contains the "old wine" which the grapes of the written Gospel supply.

In the preface to his little work, entitled, "Hints on Christian Experience and the Christian's duty with respect to it," he says:—

"The distinction between *Christian Experience* and *The Experience of the Christian* appears to afford the only general principle by which, in ordinary circumstances, Christians can determine the extent to which it is their duty to proceed [in conversing] on the subject of Christian experience. It is not intended to limit the communications of one Christian friend with another. In the intercourse warranted by long-tried intimacy, many things may form the subject of communication which will not bear to be repeated in more general society."

In the body of the work, after some cautions against "an indiscriminate disclosure of facts," the author proceeds thus:—

"These remarks apply with particular force to that species of experience commonly denominated Christian, but of which we may be permitted to doubt, whether (strictly speaking) it deserves to be considered *Christian* experience. The reference here is to those conflicting and painful exercises—occasioned by the resistance of a depraved nature and evil habits to the energy of divine grace —and to that state of dejection and melancholy into which the mind is often, in consequence, thrown. Unfortunately it happens that more of this experience than of any other has been brought before the public; and to this circumstance must doubtless be traced most of the objections that have at any time been urged against the communication of religious experience in general.

"Now, Christian experience is really a very different thing from what too many seem disposed to consider it. Its source and its test are the divine word; and its nature and characteristics are defined by the nature and characteristics of the truths which that word contains. It is neither more nor less than divine truth embodied in a living example. This is Christian experience. It is not everything that may be associated with a man's feelings while believing, but everything that enters essentially and properly into the act of believing, or that follows naturally as a consequence of believing. And if this be a correct view of the nature of Christian experience, then, in order to distinguish it from its counterfeits and accidental concomitants, we have only to consider what both Scripture and reason tell us must be the effects of cordially and fully believing the various testimonies of God in their due order and connection. On this principle, one cannot help seeing, that however gloomy and depressed, however unstable and unhappy some Christians may be, the experience that legitimately claims the appellation of Christian, must partake largely of *righteousness and peace, and joy in the Holy Ghost.*

"It may be true that, in consequence of the peculiar circumstances of a fallen creature, every act of believing the truths of the Gospel may be attended, more or less, with internal commotions and struggles; but who does not perceive that these are owing not to the Gospel, which has a directly opposite tendency, but to the deranged and debilitated constitution of the mind resisting the native influence of the Gospel? So far from being the natural and proper effects of a reception of the Gospel, or of a suitable experience of its power, these struggles and internal conflicts are to be regarded and deplored as so many efforts of the mind to thwart and resist it. When, therefore, we hear a man complaining of his weakness and corruptions, of his doubts and fears, we may allow, from our knowledge of his general character, that this may be the experience of a Christian; but if we call such experience by the name of Christian, we do unintentional injustice to the Gospel, which has no tendency in itself to produce these effects. In fact, to dignify an experience, which a firmer faith in the doctrines and promises of the glorious Gospel of the blessed God is intended and exactly fitted to remove, with the title *Christian*, is not only to confound two things which, happily for us, are essentially distinct, but to foster in the Christian the erroneous and mischievous conception, that that—which he ought to regard as a proof of languid faith, and defective grace—is a healthful symptom of his spiritual state.

"While on the subject of this distinction, it may not be out of place to remark, that nothing can be of greater importance to a Christian than a firm conviction that the tendency of the Gospel, and its assured effect if he will not hinder the effect by unbelief, are to make him triumphant and happy. In its first effect on a sinner's conscience and heart it may, indeed, operate with the power of *the whirlwind, the earthquake, and the fire,* but it is sure to act upon him at last with the gentle influence of *a still small voice* that speaketh peace. All its discoveries point to this result; and the glorious object—a crucified Saviour, whom it enjoins us as our first duty to keep continually in view—tends immediately to produce it.

"A man cannot be a believer, to the full extent to which it is his duty to be a believer, without experiencing a satisfaction, a serenity, and a joy, above any feeling of the sort that takes its rise in worldly causes. If any Christian who is of a different opinion will but make the experiment, and ask himself when dejected and sorrowful, 'Why am I thus?—Am I believing God, appropriating His promises, and exercising a suitable trust in that gracious Saviour who died for me, and who is now alive to protect and enrich me?'—he will be sensible of the truth of what is now affirmed; he will be sensible that his want of comfort is owing to his want of faith—to the defective exercise of that grace which is peculiarly Christian. We may conceive that his circumstances are calculated, in a remarkable degree, to produce dejection;—we may conceive him beset by all the trials, whether of an external or spiritual nature, that can enter into the lot of any human being;—but while faith in the word and promises of God is in his power, we cannot conceive him destitute of resources.

"The saddest feature in outward trials or spiritual conflicts is their tendency to weaken faith; and of this the Christian, in order to the preservation of his comfort, or the recovery of it if lost, ought to be aware. The thing to be deprecated is not their immediate tendency to make him unhappy—for this they cannot immediately do. On some Christians they have the very opposite effect; and the reason is obvious—these Christians meet them in the exercise of faith. They oppose the blood of the cross to the accusations of conscience. They resist temptation in the strength of Him who has said, My grace is sufficient for thee. They look at afflictions through the medium of promises; and, while the world fails them, they cling only closer to their portion and their treasure, God.

"Why trials and conflicts should not have the same effect, in every case, is owing not to any peculiarity in them, but solely to the state of mind of him who is the subject of them. In almost every case their first effect is to absorb and occupy the mind,—to leave room for nothing but an absorbing sense of helplessness and misfortune; and so long as this effect is yielded to, it is obvious that the mind must droop and suffer. In such a case the Christian's duty is to prevent this tendency of spiritual or temporal evils to occupy his mind—to turn his thoughts to the hopes and promises of the Gospel—to apply himself to those parts of Divine truth that bear a more immediate reference to his situation—and to keep in mind that what he reads in his Bible is the word of an immutable, an omnipotent, and gracious Being, who never says more than He means His creatures to believe, and who never requires them to believe what He is not both competent and willing to perform. The sooner this is done the better for the Christian; and he who displays most aptitude and facility in doing it, is the farthest advanced in Christian duty and Christian attainment.

"A man can never be said to be destitute of the means of comfort—whatever his circumstances may be—so long as the views, the objects, and the exercises of faith are left him for a resource. Let him only set his heart on bringing faith into lively exercise on every occasion; let him commune with conscience in the language of faith—oppose to his spiritual enemies the shield of faith—contemplate vexations and crosses with the eye of faith; and he will learn by experience, what it is a pity he should ever have doubted or forgotten, that *according to his faith so it is unto him*, and that a *believing* must always be a *rejoicing* Christian.

"The distinction that has given rise to these remarks, viz., that between the experience of a Christian and Christian experience, goes a great way (if the writer is not mistaken) to obviate some of the difficulties connected with the inquiry, how far it is the duty of Christians to communicate their experience to others. If the distinction be correct, it may convince us that there are many details, connected with the experience of almost every Christian, on which it were better for him to be silent."

Note A. of the Appendix contains the author's views on the Gospel foundation of Christian experience. The following is an extract from it:—

"It is unnecessary to multiply words on a point so plain, as the connection between the exercise of faith and the enjoyment of spiritual comfort. . . . . From the nature or quality of the objects of faith, it is manifest that faith involves the enjoyment of peace, on the same principle that opening the eye on sunshine involves the perception of light, or accepting a treasure the possession of wealth.

"Yet how important at the same time is the lesson which such passages as the following teach us with respect to the dependence of the Christian, even while engaged in exercises which have the closest natural connection with privilege, on the great efficient source of all spiritual blessings. 'THOU wilt keep him in perfect peace, whose mind is staid on Thee: because he trusteth in Thee' (Isaiah xxvi. 3). 'Now *the God of hope* fill you with joy and peace in believing, that ye may abound in hope, *through the power of the Holy Ghost* ' (Rom. xv. 13).

"While the God of hope is to be regarded as the primary fountain whence all genuine enjoyment issues, He is also to be considered as directing the stream in the channel of His word, and as calling upon men, by the lively and habitual exercise of faith, to drink of the water of life freely. By presenting the blessings of the Gospel as gratuities, which any of the children of Adam may lawfully appropriate, He has removed the only obstruction that could have prevented a sinful creature, who is willing to believe, from participating in the Saviour's legacy of peace.

"When the Holy Spirit is described in His office as the Comforter, what is He represented as doing? *He shall teach you all things* (said our Lord), *and bring all things to your remembrance, whatever I have said unto you. He shall glorify Me: for He shall receive of Mine, and shall shew it unto you* (John xiv. 26; xvi. 14). In other words, He sheds light upon the objects of faith, and excites to exercise the principle of faith. This is the appointed ordinary course of His procedure, in promoting both the sanctification and comfort of the individuals committed to His care."

THEOLOGY OF CONSOLATION.

BOOK FIRST.—PART SECOND.

BOOK FIRST.—WRITINGS.

PART II. CONSOLATION REVIVED AND CONFIRMED.

PRELIMINARY EXPLANATION.

I HAVE not met with any special book devoted to the second branch of the subject of Gospel consolation. Instead, therefore, of a review of separate books, a number of classified extracts from books must now pass in review before my readers.[1] In these extracts the authors speak in their own language entirely; though sometimes their long passages and chapters are reduced to paragraphs.

This is the plan intimated in the Introductory Essay; namely, first (as has been done), to describe books in which consolation is put in the front as the first aspect of the Gospel; and, secondly (as I shall now do), to cull from many authors instructive sentences as to the revival and confirmation of the consolation of individual believers.

There are many authors who are, more or less, committed to the opinion that consolation has no place within a sinner, either in theory or in experience, except after a feeling of conscious sanctification. Yet, many of their scriptural expositions are quite consistent with the view that the consolation, which follows sanctification, is a revival and confirmation of consolation rather than the beginning of it.

In the First Chapter of this Part, I shall give the substance of Boston's Commentaries on those questions of the Westminster Shorter Catechism, which throw light on this matter. The exact theoretical difference between the last-mentioned authors, and other authors whose views seem to be the most evangelical, will thus appear.

Except, perhaps, in the first chapter, all authors who, as servants of Christ, are really one in sentiment, although they may sometimes differ in statement or in phraseology, may walk together, as those who are agreed, in this Second Part of the First Book of the Theology of Consolation.

[1] Colquhoun on "Spiritual Comfort" might have been reviewed; but more profit may, perhaps, be obtained from detached extracts from that truly evangelical and genial book.

CHAPTER I.

A Denial of an Assertion that all a Believer's Consolation is delayed until after his Consciousness of Sanctification.

This chapter proceeds upon the circumstance that many theologians affirm what we deny, namely, that a believer's consolation is all delayed until he is conscious of his sanctification. We now discuss that affirmation in the form of an inquiry as to what is taught on this subject in several questions of the Westminster Shorter Catechism.

31. *What is "effectual calling"* [conversion]?
Effectual calling is the work of God's Spirit, whereby convincing us of our sin and misery, enlightening our minds in the knowledge of Christ, and renewing our wills, He doth persuade and enable us to embrace Jesus Christ, freely offered to us in the Gospel.

32. *What benefits do they that are "effectually called"* [converted] *partake of in this life?*
They that are effectually called, do in this life partake of justification, adoption, and sanctification, and the several benefits which in this life do either accompany or flow from them.

33. *What is justification?*
Justification is an act of God's free grace, wherein He pardoneth all our sins, and accepteth us as righteous in His sight, only for the righteousness of Christ imputed to us, and received by faith alone.

34. *What is adoption?*
Adoption is an act of God's free grace, whereby we are received into the number, and have a right to all the privileges of the sons of God.

35. *What is sanctification?*
Sanctification is the work of God's free grace, whereby we are renewed in the whole man after the image of God, and are enabled more and more to die unto sin, and live unto righteousness.

36. *What are the benefits which in this life do accompany or flow from justification, adoption, and sanctification?*
The benefits which in this life do accompany or flow from justification, adoption, and sanctification, are assurance of God's love, peace of conscience, joy in the Holy Ghost, increase of grace, and perseverance therein to the end.

The reader may now observe what interpretation is given to No. 36 by those who believe in no consolation at first—all delayed to the last. A sinner knows Christ enough to embrace or accept Him as the offered Saviour; (no consolation.) God accepts him as righteous in His sight; (no consolation, only a consciousness of sin and misery.) God adopts him as a son with divine and eternal privileges; (no consolation yet.) God begins to sanctify him, he is conscious of purification of heart and of life; (now consolation begins). That is one interpretation of the teaching of the catechism founded upon the circumstance that the answer has no such sound as "assurance of God's love," until all the three words, "justification, adoption, and sanctification," have been uttered—until the sound of sanctification is heard, there is no place for the assurance of God's love.

This is an interpretation which seems to have a very slender support of its own; and it overlooks the fact that the catechism claims no more than to be an interpreter of Scripture. The Scripture says (Rom. v. 1, 2), "Being justified by faith, we have peace with God through our Lord Jesus Christ: by whom also we have access by faith into this grace wherein we stand, and rejoice in hope of the glory of God." Interpreting the catechism in the light of this text, Thomas Boston of Ettrick gives the better interpretation. There are two commentaries upon this portion of the catechism by Boston, one included in a series of sermons on the whole catechism known as his *Body of Divinity*, and the other in *An Explication of the First Part of the Assembly's Shorter Catechism*. From these commentaries I make a few extracts.

Boston's doctrine is, "Assurance, spiritual peace and joy, are benefits flowing from a state of justification." And "the justification of a sinner before God is of free grace, through the satisfaction of Christ."

"Pardon cuts the knot, whereby guilt ties sin and wrath together, cancels the bond obliging the sinner to pay his debt, reverses the sentence of condemnation, and puts him out of the law's reach.

"God justifying a sinner does not only pardon his sin, but accepts and accounts his person righteous in His sight.

"(1.) The bar in the way of abounding mercy is taken away, so that the rivers of compassion may flow to the believer (Rom. v. 1, &c). The believer being accepted as righteous, the law's mouth is stopped—justice and truth have nothing to object against mercy flowing to him.

"(2.) The person is by this means adjudged to eternal life, even agreeably to the constitution of the law. Life was promised in the first covenant, upon the fulfilling of the law. Now the law, having all it can demand of the believer, is very agreeable thereto, that he be adjudged to eternal life. Thus, what sets salvation far from unbelievers contributes to the believer's security.

"(3.) The accusations of Satan and the clamours of an evil conscience are hereby to be stilled. See how the Apostle triumphs over and bids a defiance to all the believer's accusers (Rom. viii. 33, 34), 'Who shall lay anything to the charge of God's elect? It is God that justifieth. Who is he that condemneth?

It is Christ that died, yea rather, that is risen again, who is even at the right hand of God, who also maketh intercession for us.'

"Sanctification follows. [By justification] that has been removed which was the stop of sanctifying influences. A communication is opened betwixt heaven and the soul again, upon its reconciliation with God.

"Faith is the great means of communication between Christ and us. It empties the soul of all confidence in self for sanctification, and relies upon Him for it according to His word.

"When God in the depths of infinite wisdom laid His measures for the salvation of sinners, He had their sanctification in His eye, to bring it about by the death of His own Son.

"Ye may do what ye can to reform—ye may bind yourselves with vows to be holy, watch against sin, and press your hearts with the most affecting considerations of heaven, hell, &c. ; but ye shall as soon bring water out of the flinty rock, as holiness out of all these, nutil ye believe and unite with Christ.

"Wherefore, be persuaded of your utter inability to sanctify yourselves, and receive Christ for sanctification as He is offered to you ; and thus alone shall you attain to holiness both in heart and life.

"True spiritual joy is sanctifying. It makes one forward in the duties of universal obedience ; 'I will run the way of Thy commandments when Thou shalt enlarge my heart' (Ps. cxix. 32).

"It is not God's allowance for His children to harden themselves in sorrow and refuse to be comforted. 'Rejoice in the Lord always, and again I say, Rejoice' (Phil. iv. 4). As it is uncomfortable to themselves, it is dishonouring to God, and is the fruit of unbelief.

"Doubts and fears are no friends to holiness of heart and life. It is little faith that breeds them in the hearts of the people of God. And little faith will always make little holiness."

The doctrine of Boston therefore is, that there is consolation from justification; and that such consolation fosters sanctification—that sanctification flows from justification, but does not bid consolation wait behind, and only appear after it. He therefore may be quoted as denying that all a believer's consolation is delayed until after his consciousness of sanctification.

But there is an additional doctrine of consolation arising from sanctification (Rom. v. 3, 4, 5) which Boston largely expounds. I quote two or three sentences :—

"The Spirit shines on His own work of grace in the heart, and the believer discerns it. The Spirit of God clears up to the man the truth of grace in him —lets him see, for instance, that he loves God. And (says the Spirit) this is My work. The Spirit of the Lord sometimes gives a joint testimony with the spirit of the saints, to the truth to the conclusion that they are the children of God.

"It is the office of the Spirit of God to assure believers of this. He has given us the word for this end. He is given to lead His people into all truth, particularly to discover the grace of God to them and in them (1 Cor. ii. 1, 2)—to witness with their Spirits to their adoption (Rom. viii. 16)—to be a *seal*, which is properly to ensure an evidence (Eph. iv. 30)—to be *an earnest*, i.e., a part of the price and pledge of the whole (2 Cor. v. 5).

"Christians may thank themselves for the uncomfortable lives they lead. What sovereignty may do, we know not; but surely it is sloth and unbelief that the want of assurance is ordinarily owing to. Stir up yourselves then to seek it. Be frequent in self-examination; cry to the Lord for the witness of the Spirit. Believe the word and be habitually tender in your walk, if ever ye would have assurance."

The above extracts are from Boston's "Body of Divinity." I quote a sketch of the two departments of consolation from the brief "Explication" of the same author.

I.

"There is some assurance in justifying faith itself.

"1 Thess. i. 5, 'Our Gospel came not unto you in word only, but also in power, and in the Holy Ghost, and in much assurance.' Heb. x. 22, 'Let us draw near with a true heart in full assurance of faith, having our hearts sprinkled from an evil conscience, and our bodies washed with pure water.' Jer. iii. 19, 'But I said, How shall I put thee among the children, and give thee a pleasant land, a goodly heritage of the hosts of nations? and I said, Thou shalt call Me, My Father; and shalt not turn away from Me.' Hosea ii. 23, 'And I will say to them which were not My people, Thou art My people; and they shall say, Thou art my God.'

"The assurance which is in justifying faith itself is that whereby, in believing on Christ for salvation, the party is persuaded, in greater or lesser measure, of God's good-will to him, and that Christ will save him from sin and wrath. 1 John iv. 14, 16, 'And we have seen and do testify that the Father sent the Son to be the Saviour of the world. And we have known and believed the love that God hath toward us.' Chap. v. 10, 11, 'He that believeth on the Son of God hath the witness in himself: he that believeth not God hath made Him a liar; because he believeth not the record that God gave of His Son. And this is the record, that God hath given to us eternal life, and this life is in His Son.' Acts xv. 11, 'We believe that through the grace of the Lord Jesus Christ we shall be saved, even as they.' James i. 6, 7, 'But let him ask in faith, nothing wavering; for he that wavereth is like a wave of the sea driven with the wind and tossed. For let not that man think that he shall receive anything of the Lord.'

"The ground from whence this assurance is raised is the Word of God *allenarly* [only], demonstrated by the Spirit in the work of saving illumination.

"1 Cor. ii. 4, 5, 'And my speech and my preaching was not with enticing words of man's wisdom, but in demonstration of the Spirit and of power: that your faith should not stand in the wisdom of men, but in the power of God.'

"There may be doubting of God's will and of salvation, where this assurance of them hath place. These are contraries capable of various degrees, the one weakened as the other gathers strength.

"Matt. xiv. 31, 'And immediately Jesus said unto Peter, O thou of little faith, wherefore didst thou doubt?' Mark ix. 24, 'And straightway the father of the child cried out, and said with tears, Lord, I believe; help Thou mine unbelief.'

"But where doubts are reigning, to the barring of any assurance of these things at all, true faith is barred too. (Jas. i. 6, 7; Isa. l. 10; 1 John v. 10, 11)."

II.

"The assurance of God's love, which proceeds from the evidence of grace, is, That whereby a true believer is certainly assured of God's love and complacency in him, and that he is in the state of grace, and shall persevere therein.

"Rom. v. 4, 5, 'Experience worketh hope, and hope maketh not ashamed; because the love of God is shed abroad in our hearts by the Holy Ghost which is given unto us.' John xiv. 21, 'He that hath My commandments, and keepeth them, he it is that loveth Me: and he that loveth Me shall be loved of My Father, and I will love him, and will manifest Myself to him.'

"A believer may attain unto this assurance, in the use of ordinary means, without extraordinary revelation. And the special means for that end are close walking with God, self-examination, and the right use of the holy sacraments.

"The grounds from whence a believer may raise this assurance are the infallible truth of the word of grace to him in the Scriptures, and the evidence of grace in his own heart. And a believer is enabled to discern these grounds of assurance, so as to be assured upon them by the Spirit's shining in his heart, on the word of grace, and on the work of grace there: he sees the one to be the Spirit's infallible word to him, and the other His gracious work in him.

"1 Cor. ii. 12, 'Now we have received, not the spirit of the world, but the Spirit which is of God; that we might know the things which are freely given to us of God.'

"True assurance distinguishes itself from presumption, by its humbling the soul, making the conscience tender, and the heart heavenly. It is a necessary duty to seek true assurance. The excellency of it in the Christian life is, that it fits men to live most usefully for God, and most comfortably for themselves.

"But there may be true faith, justification, adoption, and sanctification, without this assurance.

"1 John v. 13, 'These things have I written unto you that believe on the name of the Son of God; that ye may know that ye have eternal life, and that ye may believe on the name of the Son of God.' Isa. l. 10, 'Who is among you that feareth the Lord; that obeyeth the voice of His servant; that walketh in darkness, and hath no light? Let him trust in the name of the Lord, and stay upon his God.'"

CHAPTER II.

Self-Examination and Consolation.

It was said by many theologians that there is no personal assurance of salvation arising from "the hearing" of faith; but that all such assurance must come by reflection. By reflection they meant the testimony of the judgment and conscience, resulting from an inquiry into the state of the feelings with regard to the offered salvation and the offered Saviour. Therefore the saying amounts to this, that all assurance of salvation arises from a favourable report furnished by self-examination. It is (as I have already said) an extreme opinion, and a misleading opinion, that there is no strong and everlasting consolation, except what can be obtained from self-examination.

But there is an opposite extreme. Men are apt to suppose that personal consolation is what they are most prone to, and that it is the province of self-examination to undeceive and disturb them. That self-examination is a duty, every believer in the Scriptures must believe; and the imagination, that self-examination necessarily refuses to bring consolation to the soul, is therefore to be regretted. For this reason I quote a few extracts from venerable authorities, to show how self-examination is associated with consolation, and may even pave the way for it in discouraging circumstances.

"If we would wish to discover whether there were any particles of steel in a large quantity of rubbish, it would not be the wisest way to search for them, and especially in the dark, but to hold a large and efficacious magnet over it. This, if it be there, is the way to discover true religion in our souls. The truths and promises of God are, to a principle of religion in the mind, that which the magnet is to the steel. If there be any in us, the proper exhibition of the Gospel will ordinarily draw it forth. If it be a matter of doubt with you whether you be truly converted, far be it from me to endeavour to persuade you that you are so. Your doubts may be well founded for aught I can tell; and supposing they should be so, the door of mercy is still open.

"The consolations I have to recommend are addressed to you not as converted nor as unconverted—not as elect nor as non-elect—but as *sinners;* and this character, as I suppose, you have no doubt of sustaining. All the blessings of the Gospel are freely presented for acceptance to sinners. Sinners, whatever may have been their character, have a complete warrant to receive them; yea, it is their duty to do so, and their great sin if they do not. Nothing but ignorance, unbelief, self-righteous pride, or some such evil state of mind, prevents it. The Gospel supper is provided; all things are ready; and the King's servants are commissioned to persuade, and, as it were, compel them to come in.

"If you accept this invitation, all [the consolations] are yours. I ask not whether you be willing to be saved in God's way in order to determine your right to accept spiritual blessings (the message sent you in the Gospel determines this), but in order to ascertain your interest in them. If you cordially believe the Gospel, you have the promises of eternal life. If its blessings suit your desires, they are all your own; if, for example, it does not offend you, but accords with your very heart, to sue for mercy as the chief of sinners—if you be willing to occupy that place which the Gospel assigns you, which is *the dust,* and to ascribe to Jesus that which God has assigned to Him, power, and riches, and wisdom, and strength, and honour, and glory, and blessing—if you can unreluctantly give up all claim to life on the footing of your own worthiness, and desire nothing so much as to be found in Christ, not having your own righteousness—if the salvation you seek be a deliverance from the dominion of sin, as well as from its damning power—finally, if the heaven you desire be that which the Scriptures reveal, a state of pure and holy enjoyment—there can be no just cause to doubt of your interest in these things.

"To imagine that you believe all that God has revealed concerning His Son (and that, with all your heart, receiving the love of the truth that you may be saved), and yet that something else is wanting to denominate you believers, is to imagine that believing is not believing.

"Read the Holy Scriptures, pray to the Fountain of light for understanding, attend the preaching of the Word—and all this, not with the immediate view of determining what you are, but what Christ is; and, if you find in HIM that in which your whole soul acquiesces, this, without your searching after it, will determine the question as to your personal interest in Him."—ANDREW FULLER, *Sermon XII.*

"If the believer would attain increasing tranquillity of mind, he must frequently examine his heart and conduct, in order that he may the more clearly discern his evidences of personal interest in spiritual consolation. The more clearly he perceives his personal interest in Christ, and in the covenant of grace, the higher will the degree of his holy comfort usually be. The more diligently he scrutinizes his heart and life, comparing them with the word of God; and the more frequently and clearly he perceives, in consequence of the witnessing of the Holy Spirit, his evidence of union and communion with Christ—the more will his heart be comforted and encouraged; the more will he know that he is of the truth, and with the greater confidence will he assure his heart before God.

"When he has it in view, at any time, to examine himself, let him begin it by renewing his act of trusting in Christ for all his salvation, as well as for the joy of his salvation. For if he begin this inquiry by fearing that the Lord Jesus will not save him, or by yielding to distrust and despondency, he will be afraid to search deeply into his heart, or to know the worst of himself. But if he begin it by an act of humble and direct confidence in Christ Jesus for salvation to himself in particular, he will be disposed, as well as encouraged, to deal impartially with himself; he will be willing to find out the worst as well as the best of himself. He will not be afraid to find that his heart, so far as it is unrenewed, is deceitful above all things, and desperately wicked. Besides, by means of that acting of faith, his other graces will be invigorated and excited to lively exercise; and the more he exercises them, the more easily and the more clearly will he perceive them. Further, let him begin it [the inquiry], also, by praying that the Holy Spirit may shine upon the graces which, he trusts, are implanted in his heart, and so *bear witness with his own spirit that he is a child of God.*

"He may then proceed to try his graces; and he should try them by their nature, rather than by the degree of their strength or liveliness. Let him more especially examine himself *whether he be in the faith,* and so prove himself. If he do not discern true faith in his heart; yet, if he is conscious of an earnest desire to believe cordially in Jesus Christ, accompanied by frequent endeavours to do so, he ought to conclude that he hath some measure of that precious faith.

"An earnest and habitual desire of grace is grace, in the account of God. A man's desire of faith, of love, of hope, and of all the other graces of the Spirit is sincere and earnest when he desires them for their own intrinsic excellence and amiableness, and chiefly for the glory of God in Christ; and when, though he do not perceive them, he yet feels his need of them, and is conscious that he desires them, and desires even the perfection of them. Let the believer, then,—trusting that the Lord Jesus giveth him grace, and that the Holy Comforter will, in every time of need, shine upon that grace in his soul, and render it apparent to him,—enter frequently upon the trial of his state and conduct; and if he find but one scriptural evidence of his being in a state of grace, he ought for his comfort to conclude that he has all the other evidences of being in it, though he cannot at present clearly perceive them. Nevertheless, he should frequently pursue the important inquiry, till he have the comfort of discerning clearly all his evidences; for, the more knowledge he has of his personal interest in the blessings of salvation, the more consolation he will enjoy.

" Moreover, let the believer search daily into his heart and life, in order to find out more of his *sins* and of his *wants;* that, by a deep and affecting sense of them, he may be urged to apply and plead, frequently, the promises of pardon and sanctification. This is a necessary means of *walking in the comfort of the Holy Spirit.*"—COLQUHOUN *on Spiritual Comfort, Chapter VIII.*

" No sooner does a good man arrive at some degree of settled comfort, than Satan (if permitted) will tempt him to look with great intenseness upon his evidences for heaven. That enemy of his holy comfort will often suggest to him, *You cannot be sure enough that you are not deceiving yourself.* [He will suggest this] that, by occupying him continually with laying the foundation, and trying it, he may keep him from diligence in the exercise of grace, and performance of duty.

" Were the believer to be as diligent in exercising himself to have always a conscience void of offence toward God, and toward men, as in trying his evidences, he would advance more speedily than he does in the assurance of sense. It is indeed the duty of Christians, *often* to examine their state and their frame, and to see that they are not deceiving themselves, but not to be doing *it only* and *incessantly*—not to be occupying themselves with that, when they are called to faith and love, to patience and holy activity for God.

" Were those of the saints, who are favoured with comfortable discoveries of their evidences of inherent holiness, to take frequent occasion from those evidences to think of Christ, and to set their hearts the more on His consummate righteousness as the only ground of their title to holiness and comfort, they would thereby attain more assurance of their personal interest in Him, and more establishment in pure consolation. When the Apostle Paul was assured that Christ already lived in him, he took occasion from that to live the more by faith on the righteousness and fulness of Christ. 'I live (says he), yet not I, but Christ liveth in me; and the life which I now live in the flesh, I live by the faith of the Son of God, who loved me and gave Himself for me.' At the very time on which the same Apostle had his eye fixed upon his having the excellent knowledge of Christ, he had his heart taken up with the Righteousness of Christ. If the believer, then, would maintain solid and stable comfort, let him think more of the Lord Jesus, and delight more in Him and in His righteousness and fulness, than in his own evidences of grace. To pore upon his inherent holiness, more than upon his imputed righteousness, would soon interrupt and lessen his tranquillity of mind. Evidences are, indeed, delightful to an exercised Christian; but Christ ought to be far more delightful to him."—COLQUHOUN *on Spiritual Comfort, Chapter IX.*

CHAPTER III.

HOLINESS AND COMFORT.

THE compound theological term, "holiness and comfort," implies a consolation that follows sanctification. It occurs in the Westminster Shorter Catechism in the answer to Q. 89, "The Spirit of God maketh the reading, but especially the preaching, of the word an effectual means of convincing and converting sinners, and of building them up in holiness and comfort through faith unto salvation." This paragraph is enlarged in the answer to Q. 155 of the Larger Catechism :— "The Spirit of God maketh the reading, but especially the preaching, of the word an effectual means of enlightening, convincing, and humbling sinners, of driving them out of themselves, and drawing them unto Christ, of conforming them to His image, and subduing them to His will, of strengthening them against temptations and corruptions, of building them up in grace, and establishing their heart in holiness and comfort through faith unto salvation."

It is for the sake of a characteristic heading for this chapter that I begin by collecting some observations on a phrase quoted from catechisms, instead of at once quoting illustrative texts of the word of God, and instructive comments upon them.

The Associate Presbytery, in the middle of last century, appointed the Rev. Ebenezer and Ralph Erskine, and James Fisher, to draw up a commentary on the Westminster Shorter Catechism, the explanations being in the form of questions and answers. A few of these may be quoted as describing the relations between holiness and comfort :—

"Whence ariseth the necessity of holiness or sanctification ? From the holy nature and will of God, for it is written, Be ye holy, for I am holy (1 Pet. i. 16), and, This is the will of God, even your sanctification (1 Thess. iv. 13) ; and from the death of Christ, who gave Himself for us, that He might redeem us from all iniquity, and purify to Himself a peculiar people, zealous of good works (Titus ii. 14).

"For what good end and use is sanctification necessary ? Not for justification before God, but for evidencing our justification and faith (James ii. 18). It is necessary for glorifying God (Matt. v. 16), and showing forth His praise (1 Pet. ii. 19), for adorning the doctrine of God our Saviour (Titus ii. 10), for proving our union to Christ (John xv. 5, 6), for promoting inward peace and rejoicing (Psalm cxix. 165 ; 2 Cor. i. 12), for maintaining fellowship and communion with God (John xiv. 21, 23), for making us meet for heaven, because without holiness no man shall see the Lord (Heb. xii. 14), for making us useful to men on earth

(Titus iii. 18), for stopping the mouth of calumny when we are reproached as evil-doers (1 Pet. iii. 16).

"Why are the saints said to be built up in holiness? Because the work of sanctification, like a building, is gradually carried on towards perfection at death.

"How doth the Spirit make the reading and preaching of the word an effectual means of building up the saints in holiness? By giving them in the glass of the word such clear and repeated discoveries of the glory of Christ, as thereby they are more and more transformed into the same image with Him (2 Cor. iii. 18).

"How doth He by means of these ordinances build them up in comfort? By conveying with power unto their souls the great and precious promises which contain all the grounds of real and lasting comfort (Gal. iii. 29; iv. 28).

"Through what instrument is it that the Spirit makes these means effectual for building up the saints in holiness and comfort? It is through faith (1 Thess. iii. 13).

"What instrumentality has faith, in the hands of the Spirit, for building up the saints in holiness and comfort? It rests upon God's faithful word for the promoting of both—Psalm cxxxviii. 8, *The Lord will perfect that which concerneth me.*"—JAMES FISHER and RALPH ERSKINE.

"What is *sanctification*? It is a principle of grace savingly wrought, whereby the heart becomes holy, and is made after God's heart. A sanctified person bears not only God's *name* but *image*.

"How may *sanctification* be *attained* to? Be conversant with the word of God—John xvii. 17, *Sanctify them through Thy truth*. The word is both a glass to show us the spots of our soul, and a laver to wash them away. Get faith in Christ's blood—Acts xv. 9, *Purifying their hearts by faith*. Nothing can have a greater force upon the heart to sanctify it than faith; if I believe Christ and His merits are mine, how can I sin against Him? Justifying faith doth that in a spiritual sense which miraculous faith does; it removes mountains —the mountains of pride, lust, envy. Faith and the love of sin are inconsistent. Pray for sanctification. Breathe after the Spirit; it is called (2 Thess. ii. 13) the sanctification of the Spirit. Associate with sanctified persons. As the communion of saints is in our creed, so it should be in our company. He that walketh with the wise shall be wise (Prov. xiii. 20). Association begets assimilation.

"Are you sanctified? Heaven is begun in you; happiness is nothing but the quintessence of holiness."—THOMAS WATSON.

"All true solid comfort is fetched out of the word. The leaves of Scripture, like the leaves of the tree of life are for the healing of the nations. Is it not a comfort to find our evidences for heaven? and where shall we find them but in the word?—1 Thess. i. 4, 5, The word written is a sovereign elixir or comfort in an hour of distress; Psalm cxix. 50, This is my comfort in my affliction, for Thy word hath quickened me."—THOMAS WATSON.

"Heaven is a state in which grace is brought to perfection, which at present is only begun in the soul; nevertheless, the beginning thereof affords ground of hope that it shall be completed. As a curious artist, when he draws the first lines of a picture, does not design to leave it unfinished—or he that lays the foundation of a building determines to carry it on gradually, till he has laid the top stone of it—so the work of grace, when begun by the Spirit, is a ground of hope that it shall not be left unfinished. As God would never have brought His people out of Egypt with a high hand and an outstretched arm, and divided the Red Sea before them, if he had not designed to bring them into the promised land; so we may conclude that when God has magnified His grace in delivering His people from the dominion of darkness, and translating them into the kingdom of His dear Son—when He has helped them hitherto, and given them a fair and beautiful prospect of the good land to which they are going—He will not leave His work imperfect, nor suffer them to fall and perish in the way to it. Christ in believers is said to be *the hope of glory;* and the joy which they have in believing is said, not only to be *unspeakable,* but *full of glory*—that is, it bears a small resemblance to that joy which they shall be filled with when brought to glory, and therefore may well be styled the earnest or first-fruits of it. (An earnest is a small sum given in part of payment, whereby they who receive it are encouraged hereafter to expect the whole)."—RIDGLEY. Q. 83.

Having expounded the theological formula of "holiness and comfort," we come to the direct scriptural teaching concerning it. The fullest instruction is in the second chapter of the Epistle of James; and it accords with our plan to take Dr Manton as our guide in its interpretation.

With regard to the imaginary difference of the Apostle James from the Apostle Paul, Dr Manton quotes the orthodox accounts which "do very well suit with the scope of the Apostle," being all "to the same effect, either subordinate to one another, or differing only in expression":—

"Paul disputeth of the cause of justification, and so excludeth works; James of the effects of justification, and so enforceth a presence of them.

"Paul disputeth how we are justified, and James, how we shall evidence ourselves to be justified; the one taketh justification for acquittance from sin, the other for acquittance from hypocrisy; the one for the imputation of righteousness, the other for the declaration of righteousness.

"Paul speaketh of the office of faith, James of the quality of faith; Paul pleadeth for saving faith, James pleadeth against naked assent; the one speaketh of the justifying of the person, the other of the justifying of the faith."

With regard to the difference between consolation viewed as the first aspect of the Gospel, and revived or confirmatory consolation, Dr Manton notes:— "Works are not a ground of confidence, but an evidence; not the foundations of faith, but the encouragements of assurance. Comfort may be increased by the sight of good works, but is not built upon them. They are seeds of hope, not props of confidence; sweet evidences of election, not causes; happy presages and beginnings of glory. In short, they can manifest an interest [in Christ], but not merit it. We have peace with God by the righteousness of Christ, and peace of conscience by the fruits of righteousness in ourselves."

While therefore we are to know, that "works are the evidence of true faith," and while it is our duty and happiness to "judge ourselves," "to try our graces by their fruits and operations," our motto, as suggested by Dr Manton, must be, "Believers, though they justify their profession, still are monuments of free grace," and our foremost obligation is to "be loyal to Christ." Let us "go to work this way," as Manton counsels us, "Let there be a thorough going out of yourselves. If any might have confidence in the flesh, Paul might; but he renounceth all, nay, counts it *loss*, that is, dangerous allurements to hypocrisy and self-confidence. It is good to have such actual and fresh thoughts in ourselves when we proceed to trial, that our souls may be rather carried to, than diverted and taken off from, CHRIST. Usually assurance is given after a solemn and direct exercise of faith—Eph. i. 13, *After ye believed, ye were sealed by the Holy Spirit of promise.* The order of the Spirit's sealing is after believing or going to Christ; and the quality, under which the Spirit sealeth, is as a *Spirit of promise,* implying that when our thoughts have been newly and freshly exercised in the consideration of our own unworthiness and God's free grace and promises, then are we fittest to receive the witness and certioration of the [Holy] Spirit. In the very view and comfort of your graces, still keep the heart upon Christ. The most regenerate man durst not adventure his soul upon the heavenliest thought that he ever conceived. In the presence of the greatest evidences, you should see free grace is the surest refuge. In the fairest train of graces, you should still keep Christ in the eye of faith, and let the soul stay upon Him. Or, as in a pair of compasses, one part is fixed in the centre, while the other wandereth about in the circumference; so must the soul stay on Christ—be fixed on Him—while we search after evidences and additional comforts."

Those who go about the dutiful and profitable search of these "additional comforts," may be interested in reading another representation by Dr Manton about the reconciliation between James and Paul:—"Paul speaketh of the justifying of a sinner from the curse of his natural condition, &c., and accepting him into the favour of God, which is of grace and not of debt. James speaketh of the justifying and approbation of that faith, whereby we are thus accepted with God; God giveth us the comfort of our former justification by the experiences and fruits of faith, for in them we are found faithful."

So much as to the setting about the work; now as to the work itself. "Works are an evidence of true faith. This is the evidence by which we must judge ourselves. It is the drift of many Scriptures to lay down evidences taken from sanctification and the holy life; they were written for the very purpose, as more especially, the 119th Psalm, and the First Epistle of John. Yea, conclusions are drawn to our hands; it is said, *Hereby we may know*, &c. (see 1 John iii. 14 and 19). In many places promises are given out with descriptions annexed, taken from the meekness, piety, good works of the saints. Good works are the most sensible discovery [information, or disclosure]. All causes are known by their effects. The apples, leaves, and blossoms are evident, when the life and sap is not seen."

"You had need look to your faith and confidence, that it may be justified —justified by your works; this is a sensible evidence and most in sight. Some think that, because there are so many shifts, and circuits, and wiles in the heart of man, it is an uncertain, if not an impossible way of trial. I confess, if in trial we were only to go by the light of our conscience and reason, the objection would have some weight in it. The main certainty lieth in the Spirit's witness, without which the witness of water is silent. Graces shine not without this light. God's own interpreter must show a man his righteousness (Job xxxiii.); otherwise there will be many shifts in the heart, and we shall still be in the dark. Under the law everything was to be established by the mouth of two or three witnesses; so here are two witnesses, the Spirit with our spirits (Rom. viii. 16), the Spirit with our renewed consciences. It is the Holy Ghost that giveth light, whereby we may discern the truth of grace, imprinteth the feeling and comfort, and, by satisfying the soul, begetteth a serenity and calmness within us."

"To look after works is the best way to prevent delusion. Fanatic spirits are often deceived by sudden flashes of comfort. Works, being a more sensible and constant pledge of the Spirit, beget a more solid joy. Learn to approve yourselves to God, with all good conscience, in times of trial. When God trieth your faith or obedience with some difficulty, then is the special time to gain assurance by being found faithful."

The Heidelberg Catechism illustrates the great principle of the Epistle of James. Q. 86. Since then we are redeemed out of our misery, entirely without merit of our own, because of the grace of God through Christ, for what cause are we to do good works? Because Christ, after He hath bought us with His blood, reneweth us by His Holy Spirit to His own image, that we all our life-time may manifest ourselves thankful to God for His benefits, and that through us He may be glorified. Thereafter also, that we severally may be assured of our faith by its fruits, and that by our godly course of life we may also win our neighbours unto Christ.

The clause "that we severally may be assured of our faith by its fruits," may be explained in the language of Ursinus, edited by Parèus.[1]

"1. By our good works we may make testimony of our faith and may be assured thereof. Every good tree bringeth forth good fruit (Matt. vii. 18); Filled with the fruits of righteousness which are by Jesus Christ unto the glory and praise of God (Philipp. i. 11). That faith, which is without works, is dead (James ii. 20). Now, by our works, we must needs know that we have faith, because the effect is not without his cause, and we must know the cause by his proper effect. When as therefore, we find not in ourselves good works or new obedience, we are hypocrites, neither have we faith but an evil conscience. For true faith only (which never wanteth all her fruits) bringeth forth, as a fruitful tree, good works, obedience, and amendment of life; and these fruits likewise discern and distinguish true faith from historical and temporary faith, and so also from hypocrisy.

"2. By our good works we may be assured that we have obtained remission of sins through Christ, and are for Christ's sake justified before God. For justification and sanctification are benefits linked together, which so cleave together (and that necessarily) as they can never be severed or pulled asunder. For Christ obtained both for us at once, namely, both remission of sins and the Holy Ghost, who stirreth up in us by faith the study and desire of good works and new obedience.

"3. By our good works we may be assured of our election and salvation. Give diligence to make your calling and election sure (2 Peter i. 10). These proceed from the cause next going before. For God hath chosen from everlasting of His free mercy those only which are justified for the merit of His Son. Whom He predestinated, them also He called, and them also He justified (Rom. viii. 30). Therefore we are assured of our election through justification; and that we have received from Christ justification, which is never given unto the elect without sanctification, we know by faith; and that we have faith, we perceive by the works of faith, true obedience, and true conversion."

Henry Alting says as to Q. 86, "Although the end on account of which we perform good works be not to merit eternal life, there may be as to this, and as to many other performances, more ends than one. The catechism sets forth three ends in the matter before us, which have respect (1) to God, (2) to ourselves, and (3) to our neighbours. Good works are the fruits of faith, from which each believer can be assured concerning his own faith."

[1] The English translation of "Ursinus and Parèus," Quarto Edition. London, 1617.

Dr Manton, quoting 1 John iii. 19, "Hereby we know we are of the truth and shall assure our hearts before Him," explains "hereby" as meaning "by real acts of love and charity." We pass to the consideration of this text and its context.

"The soul's studying conformity to the Divine will does not found peace, yet much peace flows therefrom, for *great peace have they that love Thy law* (Psalm cxix. 165). Though this be not the cause of their acceptance, yet from this they have the more holy boldness; *if our heart condemn us not, we have confidence toward God* (1 John iii. 21). This will be the evidence of a new covenant state, and of the begun accomplishment of the promises thereof, when thou canst show thy faith by thy works. And though thy faith be founded upon a more sure bottom, yet thy hands are strengthened hereby in believing. We have this comfortable evidence of being the sons of God when [we are] in the way of holiness, led by the Spirit of God. This is an ornament to Christianity. This is useful to others; when they see thy good works they will glorify thy Father which is in heaven. And upon this doth the sentence of the reward of grace proceed (Matt. xxv. 35, 36)—all which may induce us to the study of holiness."—BRISBANE, 1718.

1 JOHN iii.	EXTRACTS FROM GILL'S NOTES.
18. *My little children, let us not love in word, neither in tongue;*	This, though it holds good of love to God and to Jesus Christ, is here to be understood of love to the brethren, as the context shows. We should not love in this manner only. It is very lawful and right to express our love to one another and to all men in words—to give good words and use courteous language—to speak in a kind, tender, and affectionate manner, and especially to persons in distress; but this should not be all.
but in deed and in truth.	True love is a laborious and operative grace—actual love, love in fact, apparent and evident—love in reality, and not in show only—the work and labour of love, cordially and heartily done, with cheerfulness and without grudging.
19. *And hereby we know that we are of the truth,*	True, sincere, and upright persons, true believers in Christ, whose faith works by love, and who are real lovers of Him and His.
and shall assure our hearts before Him.	We shall arrive to a full assurance of faith, hope and understanding, that we are of the truth, do belong to God, are loved by Him with an everlast-

ing love, are chosen by Him unto salvation, and are His adopted and regenerated ones, having passed from death to life.

Some render the words, *shall pacify—shall make our hearts tranquil, or quiet.* This only the blood of Christ can do. It is true, indeed, that one that loves his brother, heartily and sincerely, has peace of mind in it, though not for it.

Or this passage may refer to that holy confidence before God, which true believers in Christ, and cordial lovers of the brethren have—both now *at the throne of grace,* where they can come with boldness, intrepidity, and freedom to ask for what they want, and confidently believe they shall receive what is proper and needful for them; and also hereafter *at the throne of judgment,* and in the day of judgment, when they shall have boldness and not be ashamed before the Judge at His coming, who will particularly take notice of their love in feeding, clothing, and visiting the least of His brethren, which He takes as done to Himself.

20. *For if our heart condemn us,*

The conscience, which is here meant by the heart, is accuser, witness, and judge, as to want of love to the brethren, and hypocrisy in it, as well as any other sin.

God is greater than our hearts, and knoweth all things.

God is a swifter witness than conscience, and a superior Judge to it. He knoweth all things that are in the heart, the principles of actions, all the actions of men, all the sinfulness in them and the aggravations of them; as He knows them more perfectly, He judges of them more exactly. It is a fearful thing to fall into the hands of the living God.

21. *Beloved, if our heart condemn us not,*

This does not designate such a purity of heart and life in believers, as that their hearts do not smite, reproach, or condemn them for sin at any time (for such a state of perfection is not to be attained to and expected in this life). It is best to confine it to the case of brotherly love—if our heart condemn us not of the want of brotherly love and sincerity.

then have we confidence toward God; " toward God," rather " with God," at the throne of His grace. Cain's heart condemned him, his conscience smote him, and he went from the presence of the Lord—and this applies to such as hate the brethren. But those that love the brethren have confidence of their relation to God—can draw nigh to God as their Father, and call Him so.

22. *And whatsoever we ask, we receive of Him,* Whatever is asked according to the will of God —in the name of Christ and for His sake—and in faith, nothing wavering, but believing in God, in His covenant and promises.

because we keep His commandments, Keeping the commands of God is a necessary adjunct, or what necessarily belongs unto and enters into the character of those who are heard and answered by God.

and do those things that are pleasing in His sight; So the keeping of His commandments is—not that these things ingratiate into the love and favour of God, or are the causes and condition of it, for the love of God is prior to anything of this kind; nor are they the causes of men's acceptance with God, for the acceptance both of persons and services is only in Christ the Beloved. But these things are what God approves of, when done in faith, from a principle of love, and with a view to His glory. Here, therefore, is a reason strengthening their confidence in Him, who hears such persons as are worshippers of Him and do His will.

21. *And this is His commandment, That we should believe on the name of His Son Jesus Christ, and love one another, as He gave us commandment.* Having mentioned the keeping of the commandments of God, the Apostle proceeds to show what they are—that they are faith in Christ, and love to one another—which two are reduced to one because they are inseparable; where the one is, the other is; faith works by love. To believe is called *a commandment,* and comes under the notion of one, not that it is properly a law, or belongs to the law of works. It is to go forth in special and spiritual acts upon Jesus Christ, such as—looking at Him, coming to Him, venturing on Him, trusting in Him for life and salvation, committing all into His hands, and expecting all from Him.

Another method of describing confirmatory consolation is to be found in the first Epistle of John also, namely, in chapter iii. 24, "Hereby we know that He abideth in us, by the Spirit which He hath given us;" and in chapter iv. 13, "Hereby know we that we dwell in Him and He in us, because He hath given us of His Spirit." The interpretation of such statements may be found in comments upon parallel passages in Romans viii., (1.) "They that are in Christ Jesus walk not after the flesh but after the Spirit; (2.) they that are after the Spirit mind the things of the Spirit; (3.) if any man have not the Spirit of Christ he is none of His; (4.) as many as are led by the Spirit of God, they are the sons of God."

I quote the comments of a very old divine of the Church of England:—
"(1.) V. 1. What profit comes there of these things? First, it reproves such as boast that they are in Christ, and yet show the contrary by their walking after the flesh. Secondly, it assureth them that walk after the Spirit that they are the very members of Christ. Finally, it teacheth all men that sanctification of the Spirit is an inseparable companion and fruit of our justification by faith.; moisture and water, heat and fire, light and sun, are not more firmly united than faith and holiness.

"(2.) V. 5. First, it teacheth that all believing justified persons must exercise themselves in such works as are commanded of God; for, justification by faith—wheresoever it is, it hath always annexed with it sanctification, or study of an holy life, which can no more be separated from it than a living man can be separated from the soul. Secondly, here is a special comfort for such as endeavour to do good things pleasing to God, with love and delight in them; because such have the Spirit of Christ, and therefore are certainly justified, free from sin and death, and shall never be condemned, but eternally saved in heaven.

"(3.) V. 9. This reproves such as use to excuse their sins by saying they are flesh and blood, and not spiritual; which is as much as to say that they are no Christians; for if they be of the body of Christ, they must of necessity have His Spirit and be spiritual. Also, this reproves such as say, we must always doubt whether we have the Spirit of Christ or no—which we ought no more to doubt of, than whether we be Christians or no.

"Aye, but many pretend themselves to be one with Christ and to have His Spirit, and so to be good Christians, which yet are not. How, then, shall we be sure of these things?

"We shall surely know it, by the effects of our spiritual union, to wit, justification and the fruits thereof as they are laid down, Rom. v. 1, 2, 3, 4, 5, 11; also by the effects of our sanctification, as they are laid forth, Rom. vii. 16-20; 2 Pet. i. 6, 7; Ps. xv.

"(4.) V. 14. *To be led by the Spirit* is a word borrowed from the blind that cannot see their way, but must have one to lead them—or from the lame that cannot go, but must have one to help them—or from infants and young children, which can very hardly go without another to lead them.

"This leading is, First, information or instruction outwardly given by the word, concerning things agreeable to God's will. Secondly, an illumination from the Spirit to see and know such instructions to be from God Himself. Thirdly, inclination and bowing of the will, voluntarily to will and readily to obey such divine instructions.

"As the Spirit doth not enlighten us but by the word expounded and opened, so it is in vain to know what we should do by the light of the Spirit and word, unless will and strength be given us to do it ; and it were not enough to have will and strength given us to do it, if we want [lack] knowledge of that which we are to do. Therefore unto 'leading,' these three things be necessary, first, to be instructed by the word—secondly, to be enlightened by the Spirit in our minds—and thirdly, to be mightily strengthened in our wills and affections, that we will well effect what we do soundly affect."—Rev. THOMAS WILSON, 1614.

"Hebrews v. 9. Christ *became the author of eternal salvation unto all them that obey Him.* Christ is the sole author of eternal salvation, and all the glory of it should be given to Him. Those to whom He is the author of salvation are such as hearken to the voice of His Gospel and obey Him in His ordinances. Christ is not the author of salvation to all men ; all men do not obey Him. All those whom Christ saves He brings to an obedience to Himself ; for His obedience for them does not exempt them from obedience to Him, though their obedience is no cause of their salvation—Christ Himself is the alone author of that."—GILL's *Commentary.*

"Titus ii. 14. Christ *gave Himself for us, that He might . . . purify unto Himself a peculiar people, zealous of good works.* These people for whom Christ has given Himself, and whom He has redeemed and purified, are a peculiar people, for whom Christ has a peculiar love, in whom He takes a peculiar delight, and to whom He grants peculiar nearness to Himself, and bestows peculiar blessings on them, and makes peculiar provisions for them, both for time and eternity. These are Christ's own—His possession—His substance—what He has a peculiar right to by His Father's gift, His own purchase, and the conquest of His grace. They are a distinct and separate people from all others in election, redemption, effectual vocation, and in Christ's intercession, and will be so in the resurrection morn, at the day of judgment, and to all eternity. They are, as the word also signifies, an excellent and valuable people ; they are Christ's portion and inheritance ; they are His peculiar treasure, His jewels, whom as such He values and takes cares of ; the Syriac version renders it, *a new people.*

They who are redeemed and purified by Christ, through the power of His grace upon them, become zealous of good works, not in order to their justification and salvation, but in obedience to the will of God, and to testify their subjection and gratitude to Him, for His honour and glory, for the credit of religion and the good of men. They not only perform them, but perform them from principles of truth and love—with a zeal for the glory of God and honour of His Gospel—and with an holy emulation of one another, striving to go before and excel each other in the performance of them."—GILL's *Commentary.*

HEBREWS xiii.   EXTRACTS FROM GILL'S NOTES.

15. *By Him* — By His assistance—for Him, and blessings in Him—on Him, as the altar which sanctifies the gift—through Him, as the High Priest and Mediator.

therefore — On account of temporal and spiritual mercies, particularly for sanctification, and the expiation of sin by the blood of Christ, and for heaven, the continuing city that is to come.

let us offer — It is the reasonable service of us who believe in Christ. For being made by Him priests to God, and having faith in Him, such are capable of offering aright.

the sacrifice of praise to God continually, — The Apostle, having shown that all legal sacrifices were superseded and abolished by the sacrifice of Christ, points out what sacrifices believers should offer up to God under the Gospel dispensation. The Jews themselves say, that *in future time* (*i.e.*, in the days of the Messiah) *all sacrifices shall cease, but* THE SACRIFICE OF PRAISE *shall not cease.*

that is, the fruit of our lips — The sacrifice of praise is so called in allusion to the offering of the first fruits under the law,—see Hosea xiv. 3, *the calves* of our lips ; Isaiah lvii. 19, *the fruit* of the lips.

giving thanks — We are to praise God with our lips—to do which we are under the greatest obligations ; since He is always bestowing mercies upon us, of one kind or another, and therefore should be continually praised, even in times of adversity, affliction, and temptation, in the midst of reproach and persecution, even when unsettled in mind, body, and estate; since there is a continuing city to come; nor can a believer be in any state of life but he has something to be thankful for. The word *giving thanks* signifies *a speaking together*, and may design not only the conjunction of the heart and tongue in praise, but a social giving thanks to God by the saints as a body together.

to His name. To the glory of His name—to the honour of His Divine perfections—as the Creator and Preserver of us in our beings—as the Father of mercies—as the Father of Christ, and as our Covenant God and Father in Him.

16. *But to do good and to communicate* —which is to be understood, not of doing good works in general, but of acts of beneficence, or *communicating to the poor*, as the Syriac version renders it. Besides the fruit of the lips, another sort of sacrifice continues under the Gospel dispensation, and that is alms. Alms should be given, or beneficence be exercised, to all men in need, even to our enemies as well as to our friends and relations, and especially to poor saints and ministers of the Gospel.

forget not: This believers should not forget—which shows that it is a duty of importance, and that men are too apt to neglect it, and should be stirred upon unto it.

for with such sacrifices God is well pleased. —not that they are meritorious of the favour of God, and of eternal life—for what a man gives in a way of charity, is but what God has given him, and cannot be profitable to God though it is to a fellow-creature—nor is there any proportion between what is given, and grace and glory which the saints receive. Yet doing good in this way—when it is done in faith, springs from love, and is directed to the glory of God—is well-pleasing to Him. Yea, these sacrifices are preferred by Him to legal ones (Hosea vi. 6); and the Jews also say that greater is he that does alms than if he offered all sacrifices.

"If the believer would attain established consolation, he should endeavour diligently, according to the opportunities afforded him, to promote the extension

THE THEOLOGY OF CONSOLATION.

and establishment of the Redeemer's spiritual kingdom. This is a sure means of his arriving at solid and durable comfort. 'Pray for the peace of Jerusalem : they shall prosper that love thee' (Ps. cxxii. 6). 'Let them shout for joy, and be glad, that favour my righteous cause : yea, let them say continually, Let the Lord be magnified, who taketh pleasure in the prosperity of His servant' (Ps. xxxv. 27). 'Rejoice ye with Jerusalem, and be glad with her, all ye that love her : rejoice for joy with her, all ye that mourn for her : that ye may suck, and be satisfied with the breasts of her consolations ; that ye may milk out, and be delighted with the abundance of her glory' (Isa. lxvi. 10, 11). When the Apostle Paul had reviewed the success of his ministrations among them, he addressed them thus : 'Great is my glorying over you : I am filled with comfort, I am exceeding joyful in all our tribulation' (2 Cor. vii. 4).

"The constant and earnest endeavours of the saints to promote and extend, according to the law of Christ's kingdom, the interests of His church-militant, do not indeed entitle them to stable comfort ; but they are usually connected with it. The glorious King of Zion hath decreed that they who by His grace are habitually disposed to contribute, by their prayers, their labours, and their substance, to promote so great and so glorious a design, shall, even in this valley of tears, participate with Him of that ineffable joy wherewith He always rejoiceth over His Church (Zephaniah iii. 16, 17, 18).

"If a Christian, instead of being of a liberal and a public spirit, is contracted in his views, and concerned mainly for his own welfare, and that of a particular party, he is not qualified for strong and durable consolation. Established comfort, like fame, will elude the grasp of him who pursues it, merely or chiefly, for himself and for its own sake.

"One reason, perhaps, why some believers at this day have little spiritual and lasting comfort is, that in comparison of it they care little for anything else. If they were more employed in seeking the glory of Christ, the success of His blessed Gospel, and the extension of His spiritual kingdom, both 'at home and abroad, than in seeking ease and comfort for themselves, they should find that holy and lasting consolation would come, as it were, of its own accord, and flow freely into their souls. Were they to seek first the kingdom of God and His righteousness, they should experience more frequently, and in a higher degree, that righteousness, and peace, and joy in the Holy Ghost, of which His kingdom consisteth (Rom. xiv. 17)."—COLQUHOUN, *Chapter IX.*

2 Peter i. 10. *Give diligence to make your calling and election sure : for if ye do these things, ye shall never fall.* This is the last text which I quote here to illustrate the theory of confirmatory consolation. The following comments are from "The Saint Indeed," by Rev. John Flavel, 1667 (though his actual text is Prov. iv. 23, Keep thy heart with all diligence), and from the marvellous

commentary on the Second Epistle of Peter, by Rev. Thomas Adams, 1633; in extracts from the latter, Latin quotations are removed to the margin.

"The comfort of our souls doth much depend on the keeping of our hearts; for he that is negligent in attending his own heart is (ordinarily) a great stranger to assurance and the sweet comforts flowing from it. It is the work and office of the [Holy] Spirit to assure you; yet, if ever you attain assurance in the ordinary way wherein God dispenses it, you must take pains with your own hearts. You may expect your comforts upon easier terms, but I am mistaken if you ever enjoy them upon any other; *Give all diligence—Prove your own selves*—this is the Scripture way. . . .

"The Spirit of God dwelling in us is a mark of our adoption. The Spirit cannot be discerned in His essence, but in His operations; to discern these is to discern the Spirit. And how these should be discerned without serious searching and diligent watching of the heart, I cannot imagine. . . .

"A neglected heart is so confused and dark that the little grace, which is in it, is not ordinarily discernible. The most accurate and laborious Christians, that take most pains and spend most time about their hearts, do yet find it very difficult to discover the pure and genuine workings of the Spirit there, how then shall the Christian, who is comparatively negligent and remiss about heart-work, be able to discover it? Sincerity, which is the *quæsitum*—the thing sought for—lies in the heart like a small piece of gold in the bottom of a river; he that will find it must stay till the water is clear and settled, and then he shall see it sparkling at the bottom. And that the heart may be clear and settled,—how much pains and watching—care and diligence—will it cost!

"God doth not usually indulge lazy and negligent souls with the comforts of assurance. . . . His command hath united care and comfort together. . . . Suppose it possible for a careless Christian to attain assurance, yet it is impossible he should long retain it. For—as for these hearts that are filled with the joys of assurance—if extraordinary care be not used, it is a thousand to one if ever they long enjoy it. A little pride, vanity, carelessness, will dash to pieces all that for which they have been labouring a long time, in many a weary duty. Since then the joy of our life, the comfort of our souls, rises and falls with our diligence in this work, keep your heart with all diligence."—FLAVEL.

2 PETER i. 10.

The mercy of God in our salvation requires our actual obedience; we must *do these things*. All the bells of Aaron ring this peal (Deut. iv. 1), "Hearken unto the statutes and judgments which I teach you *for to do them*." (Gal. iii. 10), "Cursed is every one that continueth not in all things written in the law *to do them*"—not sufficient to know them, but to do them; (Rom. ii. 13) "not the hearers of the law are just before God, but the doers of the law shall be justified." There was a woman (Luke xi. 27) that blessed the womb which bare Christ. But He replied, "Yea, rather, blessed are they that hear the word of God and keep it"— yea, that thou sayest is true, she is blessed indeed, and all generations shall call her blessed; but there are others also blessed, even as many as hear the truth and do it. Blessedness is desired of all, but few will go to the price of it. (Ps. cvi. 3), "Blessed are they that keep judgment and do righteousness" —that keep within the bounds of the one and live in the practice of the other—the one being as it were their ore [oar?] and the other their compass. (Eph. v. 1), "Be ye followers of God as dear children"—the abstract of religion is to imitate Him whom thou dost worship.[1] Such a one hath done me insufferable wrong, how can I forgive him? God would. Another is gotten into my debt and abuseth my patience, how can I forbear him? God would. Be then a follower of God in grace, that thou mayest ascend to His glory. A man is travelling to this city—at least in his own opinion, he thinks so, and tells all he meets that he is going to London—yet still he keeps his back upon it and bends his course the contrary way. So ridiculous a thing is it for men to profess that they are going to heaven, when their whole life is directly forwarding themselves to hell. All men would come to God, but few will be persuaded to follow after God.[2] "Not every one that saith unto Me, Lord, Lord, shall enter the kingdom of heaven" (Matt. vii. 21), for many call Christ their Lord, yet serve the devil. "He that hath My commandments, and keepeth them, he it is that loveth Me" (John xiv. 21); we must have the Gospel in our hearts and keep it in our lives—have it in hearing, keep it in obeying— our understanding must contain it, our actions express it.[3] Let us endeavour to turn the scriptural

---

[1] Summa religionis est imitari quem colis.

[2] Omnes ad Deum ire volunt, post Deum pauci.—*Augustin.*

[3] Qui habet in memoriâ et servat in vitâ—qui habet in sermonibus et servat in moribus—qui habet audiendo et servat obediendo. Or, qui habet faciendo et servat perseverando — qui habet lectione et servat dilectione.—*Augustin.*

CONSOLATION REVIVED AND CONFIRMED.

[1] Scripturarum cupimus verba in opera vertere, et non modo dicere sancta sed facere.—*Hieron.*

[2] Frustrà Scriptura lecta nisi intellecta, frustra intellecta nisi præstita.

[3] Noluit intelligere ut bene ageret.

[4] De virtute loqui minimum, virtutibus uti, Hic labor, hoc opus est.—*Persius.*

[5] Magna dicere Goliæ sonus est—magna facere Sampsonis opus est.—*Tertullian.*

[6] When the one doth *proponere quid agendum*, the other *exponere quid propositum*.

words into works, and not only to speak holy things but to do them.[1] For in vain we read the Scripture if we understand it not; in vain we understand it if we obey it not.[2] (James i. 22), "Be ye doers of the word, and not hearers only, deceiving your own selves." We must first be hearers, for David hath branded the wicked man with this mark, *he would not hear nor understand that he might do well.*[3] A man may know the will of God and not do it, but he cannot do it unless he know it. Then, not hearers only, but doers—and that without any plea or excuse, or fear of danger by holy obedience. The dove will not leave her flight, because there are some ravens in the air, so the good Christian will always keep obedience upon the wing. (Psalm xxxiv. 14), "Depart from evil" (what, and speak good only? no, but) "do good." To speak of virtue is nothing—the labour is to show the power of it in virtuous actions.[4] To speak bravely, this is but the sound of a swelling giant—but to do heroically this is the work of a valiant champion.[5] . . . No man can work unless he believes; no man can believe unless he works. Christian religion is more practicall than theoricall—rather an occupation than a mere profession—dwelling, like the artisan's wit, at the fingers' ends."

"Idleness never had the testimony of God's acceptance; it is a vice that damns itself. The idle person seems to be God's outlawry—out of the compass of His protection. Art and nature bring forth nothing suddenly; there must be growing degrees in the one, and intervenient labours in the other. (Matt. xx. 8), the penny had never been theirs, if they had stood in the market idle till sunset. . . . Nothing better pleaseth God than the sweet composition of a man's hand with his heart; when the heart doth direct what the hand should do, and the hand doth do what the heart directs.[6] For the hand is the best commentary of the heart; what a man does I am sure he thinks, not always what he speaks. We must serve God (as one said he would marry), *pro amore,* for love.

THE THEOLOGY OF CONSOLATION.

Now there are four things comprehended in that word, and they are found by cutting off the first letter—AMORE, with love (as life in the body, so devotion in the soul, begins at the heart)—MORE, with the conversation (practical obedience, doing that which is good)—ORE, with the mouth (setting forth God's praise)—RE, with the estate (when we do not offer sacrifice to the Lord, of that which costs us nothing). There must be hearty love, lively practice, kindly thanks, costly service."

"*Ye shall never fall.* Falling is twofold—of infirmity and of apostacy; the one is a falling into sin, the other a falling into the state of damnation; there is weakness in the one, there is presumption or obstinateness in the other. The former of these falls may befal the faithful, but not the latter; for there is no damnation to them that are in Jesus Christ (Rom. viii. 1). Indeed, he may fall into divers sins, but not into that sinning sin; they be slips not foils; or if foils, not falls; or if falls, yet falling forward to repentance, not backward from mercy. The faithful shall not fall into apostacy from the Lord; the reason is, because God establisheth his goings (Psalm xl. 2), the Lord will preserve him and keep him up. If that were understood of sin that Solomon speaks, The just man falleth seven times a day, yet it implies his repentance; for he could not properly be said to fall seven times unless he had rose six times. He doth not more often fall by sinning, than he riseth again by repenting.[1] Thus he may fall into infirmity, but shall never fall into apostacy. And this is a sweet comfort, that those which are upheld by God's power shall never fall away from Jesus Christ. . . . . Whosoever is in Christ shall never fall. Indeed, he may fall into affliction, but not into destruction. . . . . Death may trip down his body, Satan cannot get down his soul; *in abyssum non cadet.* His name is written in heaven; and until that name fall, which will not be though heaven fall, himself shall never fall. Though he wrestles with giants—against principalities and powers, and wicked spirits, in high places—yet he shall stand. Though death lay his body in the dust, yet it hath no power to touch his soul; he shall stand."

"They that trust in the Lord shall be as mount Zion, which cannot be removed, but abideth for ever. The dove makes moan, to her fellow birds, of the tyranny of the hawk. One counsels her to fly aloft, but the hawk can mount as high as she. Another adviseth her to keep below, but the hawk can stoop for his prey. Another, to shroud herself in the woods, there she shall be sure; but, alas, that was the hawk's manor, the place where he kept his court. Another bids her keep the town, there she was sure from the hawk; but so she became a prey to man, and had her eyes put out to make the hawk sport. At last one bids her nest herself in the hole of a rock, there she should be safe; violence itself could not surprise her. The dove is man's soul. . . . . There is no

[1] Toties resurgit pœnitendo, quoties cecidit peccando.

sureness in thy lands, none in thy money, none in thy honours, none in thy pleasures. Neither court, nor city, nor country, neither castles nor forts, can save thee; yet there is a rock for this dove, O my dove that art in the clefts of the rock (Cant. ii. 14). The clefts of this rock are the wounds of Jesus Christ; fly thither, O my soul, and be safe. Psalm lv. 6, O, that I had wings like a dove! then would I fly away, and be at rest. The wings are faith and prayer; hie thee to this rock, there only thou art sure. All the devils in hell shall not pluck thee from the merciful arms of Christ (John x. 28). How are we sure that we are in His hand?—if His Spirit be in our heart. It was a good argument of Manoah's wife (Judg. xiii. 23), If the Lord were pleased to kill us, He would never have accepted of our sacrifice. So conclude thy own conscience, If the Lord were pleased to reject me, He would never have given me His Spirit. If I were a vessel of wrath, such a Comforter would never have come into my soul. Psalm xli. 11. By this I know that Thou favourest me, because my enemy doth not triumph against me. If Satan prevailed not, sure then I am in favour, and the Lord Jesus hath reserved me to His eternal kingdom."

"'But, alas, (saith the humbled soul), my godliness is so small, that I despair of assurance.' Be comforted; strive against thy corruptions, and by the Spirit of Jesus Christ thou shalt overcome. Paul was a sanctified man; yet he complains (Rom. vii. 15), What I would, that I do not; but what I hate, I do. O wretched man that I am! who shall deliver me from the body of this death? Albeit he groaned under the weight of his infirmities, and felt the buffets of Satan, yet he knew that nothing could separate him from the love of God in Christ. Thou canst will that which is good (*velle bonum*); then hear God speak comfort—2 Cor. viii. 12, If there be first a willing mind, it is accepted according to that a man hath, and not according to that it hath not. Indeed, where this want of grace is, content in that want, love of that content, indulgence to all these—there is neither ornament of sanctification nor argument of salvation. But dost thou feel thy wants?—hath that feeling bred sorrow?—that sorrow, desire?—that desire, prayer?—that prayer, increased faith? Faith shall bring down mercy. In thee there is the sense of infirmity; in the other is the infirmity of sense. The feeling of sin doth not annihilate the assurance of salvation. We feel the ache of a finger more sensibly than the health of the whole body; yet is the health of the whole body far more than the ache of a finger. Sanctification is itself, though joined with some imperfection."

"To conclude—let me now characterize to you the man in whose heart there is this assurance. He stands like an impregnable fort, upon whom misery and malice would spend all their shot; much they do to their own shame, to his glory. Sin, like a flattering neighbour, hath often knocked at his door, and would have come in, but found cold welcome; and, if it was importunate, was sent away, not without repulse and blows. Perhaps it lurks about his outhouses, and (spite of him) will be his tenant, but shall never be his landlord. He hath some faults, but God will not see them. He meets at every turn with his railing and accusing adversary, Satan; but he stops his throat with a pardon sealed in the blood of Jesus Christ. He is never out of war, never without victory. Those roaring fiends set upon him proudly, and he bears them down triumphantly. The shield he always bears with him was never pierced—faith. He hath been often tripped, once or twice foiled, was never vanquished. His hand hath been scratched, his heart is whole. Tyranny bends on him a stern brow, but could never dash him out of countenance. Is he threatened with the surgery of the sword?—he sees Esay under the saw, John in Patmos cutting [being cut] in pieces. Is he threatened drowning?—he sees Jonas diving into that inextricable gulf; burning?—he sees those three servants in their fiery walk, and the Son of God amongst them. Is he threatened devouring?—he sees Daniel in that sealed den of terrible lions; stoning?—he sees that protomartyr of the Gospel sleeping in peace under so many gravestones; heading?—he sees the Baptist's neck bleeding in Herodias's platter. He is sure that the God, which gave them such strength, is not weak in him; what could they suffer without God?—what cannot he suffer with God? If he must endure their pain, he looks for their faith, their patience, their strength, their glory. The terrors of death amaze him not; for, first, he knows whom he hath trusted, and, then, whither death shall lead him. He is not more sure to die than to live again, and outfaceth death with his assured resurrection. Like Enoch he walks every day with God, and confers familiarly with his Maker. When he goes in, humbly to converse with Him in meditation and prayer, he puts off his own clothes, and takes a rich suit out of the wardrobe of his Redeemer; then confidently he entereth the presence-chamber, and faithfully challengeth a blessing. He hath clean hands and a white soul, fit to give lodging to the Holy Ghost; not a room is reserved for the enemy; He that gave all finds all returned to Himself. He is so certain of his eternal election and present justification, that he can call God Father, His Saviour Brother, the Holy Ghost his Comforter—the devil his slave, earth his footstool, heaven his patrimony, and everlasting life his inheritance. Those celestial spirits do not scorn his company, nor refuse to do him service. His heart is so devoted to Christ, that if misery, if death, if torments stood in his way on the right hand, he would disdain all obstacles, and break through all difficulties, to come unto Him whom his soul loveth. He fixeth his spiritual eye upon the eternal things that are not seen; others see that [which] is present, He that [which] is to come. He walks upon earth as a stranger, his heart is at home. He hath laid up a sure treasure in heaven—a portion that shall never be taken away. He vexeth not himself with cares; he knows that he lives not at his own cost. Without omitting good means, he rests on a *Providebit Deus*, the Lord's providence. Without the warrant of God he dares do nothing—with it, anything. Nor is his faith more valiant than his bowels are compassionate. He hath his tears plenty, both for his own sins and others' sufferings. He is no niggard of these showers on earth; he is sure never to weep hereafter. When he departs this life, his body sleeps in a peaceful grave; and those glorious angels bear his soul with triumphant songs to the glorified saints, where it is married to the Bridegroom, Jesus Christ, for ever."—ADAMS.

CHAPTER IV.

ON THE PROMISES TO HIM THAT OVERCOMETH.

READERS of the Apocalypse must have been struck with the abundant promises "to him that overcometh," recommended to the earnest attention of all the members of the seven Christian churches in Asia Minor. All these are summed up in a general promise (chapter xxi. 7), "He that overcometh shall inherit all things; and I will be his God and he shall be My son."

I cannot quote any concise and instructive comments upon these promises, as my search has been in vain. The plan of my work has been to speak for myself only in the Introductory Essay to this volume, and thereafter to collect an apparatus of doctrine on the theology of consolation from old and valued authors. Not being able to find in Dr Gill's Commentary on the Book of Revelation the explanations which inquirers after consolation desire, I begin this chapter by collecting from his comments on other Scriptures the principles on which his desired article would have been framed, if he had not been quite absorbed by the glorious future to the neglect of the anxious present. All of my own, that I present to the readers of this chapter, shall be one or two preliminary sentences to the effect that man's achievement, called "overcoming," does not begin his "consolation in Christ," but confirms or revives it, after it has begun. It does not unite him to God in Christ; but after his union it may be the occasion of his "thanking God and taking courage." It comes in the course of obedience to the precepts, "Fight the good fight of faith; lay hold on eternal life." This fight is fought not in order to earn a right to eternal life (this none but the Lord our righteousness can earn), but in order to take possession of eternal life, which begins on this side of heaven. So the psalmist built all his hope of occupying the Land of Promise on the Lord's own "holy promise;" "God has spoken in His holiness (he said) and therefore I will rejoice." Then, triumphing in the Lord's word only, he proceeded to take possession of the land (Psalms lx. and cviii.). Thus he might be described both as "he that believeth" and as "he that overcometh,"—the former, characteristically; and the latter, incidentally.

THE THEOLOGY OF CONSOLATION.

Before quoting Dr Gill's comments on other Scriptures, I extract two remarks bearing upon our subject in his comments on Revelation, chapters xiv. and xvii.

xvii. 14. "The Lamb shall overcome; for He is Lord of lords and King of kings, and they that are with Him are called, and chosen, and faithful." "The Lamb shall overcome, partly through the constancy of His people, who will not love their lives to the death, but freely lay them down for Him; nor can anything separate them from the love of Christ, or prevail upon them to desert Him, His truths and ordinances, cause and interest. They are more than conquerors through Him, and so He overcomes in them."

xiv. "Blessed are the dead which die in the Lord .... their works do follow them,"—"they don't go before them to prepare heaven and happiness for them; nor do these persons take them along with them and use them as pleas for their admission into the heavenly glory; but they will follow them, and will be found to praise and honour and glory, and will be taken notice of by Christ, and graciously rewarded by Him at His appearing and kingdom."

The other illustrative comments from Dr Gill are founded on James i. 25; 1 John ii. 17; and Psalm xix. 11.

I.

"This man shall be blessed in his deed." He shall be blessed, *doing*, and whilst he is doing; not that he is blessed *for* what he does, but *in* what he does. He has, in hearing the word and looking into it, &c., the presence of God, the discoveries of His love, communion with Christ, and communication of grace from Him by the Spirit. So that wisdom's ways become ways of pleasantness, and all her paths are peace."—GILL on James i. 25.

II.

"He that doeth the will of God abideth for ever." He abideth in the love of God (which will never depart from him nor shall he be separated from that), and in the hands and arms of Christ (out of which none can pluck him), and in the family and household of God (where he as a son abides for ever and shall never be cast out), and in a state of justification (he shall never enter into condemnation), and in a state of grace and holiness (from which he shall never fall totally and finally). The reason of this his abiding is not his doing the will of God, which is only descriptive of him manifestatively, and not the cause of his perpetuity and immovableness. . . . ." GILL on 1 John ii. 17.

III.

"In keeping of them there is great reward." This is to be understood not of keeping the law of Moses . . . . but of observing the word of God—by diligent searching into it, reading and learning it, and meditating on it, to get and obtain knowledge of divine things—which carries its own reward with it, and is better than thousands of gold and silver. Laying up the word of God and the truths of the Gospel, and keeping them in mind and memory, is very profitable and serviceable to promote spiritual peace and comfort, and to preserve from sin. . . . ." GILL on Psalm xix. 11.

On such principles, then, the promises to him that overcometh suggest to believers that they are henceforth enlisted into the service of God, as God and as the Saviour, that it is their duty and privilege and honour to be on the Lord's side, and to contend joyfully and constantly—to fight the good fight of faith, content with nothing less than victory.

1 John ii. 14. *The word of God abideth in you, and ye have overcome the wicked one.* The Scripture is a magazine out of which we may fetch our spiritual artillery to fight against Satan. When the devil tempted our Saviour he fetched armour and weapons from Scripture, *it is written.* . . . Contend for Scripture. Though we should not be contentious, yet we ought to contend for the word of God. The Scripture is beset with enemies, heretics fight against it; we must therefore contend for the faith once delivered to the saints (Jude 3). The Scriptures is our book of evidences for heaven; and shall we part with our evidences ?—THOMAS WATSON, QQ. 2 and 89.

"Moses, when he prayed for Israel when engaged in battle with Amalek, represented a praying saint in his conflict with spiritual enemies. A stone was put under him, on which he sat while lifting up his hands—an emblem of Christ, the Eben-Ezer, the stone of help in time of need. Aaron and Hur, the one on one side and the other on the other, held up his hands and stayed them. Aaron, who could speak well, was a type of Christ, the advocate and spokesman of His people, by whose mediation they are encouraged and supported in prayer. Hur is a name which has the signification of liberty, and may point to the Spirit of God who is a *free Spirit*, and, as such, supports the saints in the exercise of grace and discharge of duty.

"*Prayer is the speech of the soul to God—though we whisper, not opening our lips, but pray in silence, cry inwardly, God incessantly hears that inward discourse* (said Clement of Alexandria). Prayer is one part of the saints' spiritual armour, and a principal one, though mentioned last in the sixth chapter of the Epistle to the Ephesians. Satan has often felt the force of this weapon. Resist the devil, by faith in prayer, and he will flee from you. When the Apostle Paul was buffeted and distressed by him, he besought the Lord thrice that the temptation might pass from him, and had for answer, *My grace is sufficient for thee.*

Jacob had the name of Israel given him, because as a Prince he had power with God and prevailed—prevailed by prayer and supplication.

"Mental prayer may be performed without the motion of the lips, and is what we call an ejaculatory prayer, from the suddenness and swiftness of its being put up to God, like a dart shot from the bow. But there is vocal prayer in language to be heard and understood by men as well as by God, and to this kind of prayer the church is directed by the Lord Himself (Hosea xiv. 2)."—GILL, *Body of Divinity*, Vol. III., Book iii., Chap. 5.

"The Christian has a good cause in which he is engaged; he wars a good warfare, and fights the good fight of faith; he has a good Captain, under whose banner he fights—the great Captain of salvation. Saints have good weapons wherewith they are acccoutred—the shield of faith, the helmet of salvation, and the sword of the Spirit; which weapons are not carnal but spiritual, and mighty through God, and are such as are proved, and may with confidence be made use of. They are sure of victory beforehand, for all their enemies are conquered, sin is made an end of—Satan, who had the power of death, is destroyed—the world is overcome by Christ. The warfare is accomplished, and believers are made more than conquerors through HIM that loved them, and therefore may be sure of the crown of life, righteousness and glory, laid up for all that love the appearing of Christ.

"Though saints are to be humble, self-denying, submissive to the will of God, and patient towards all men, and in all things; yet they are not to give way to pusillanimity and to a meanness of spirit, but to show firmness of mind, resolution, an undaunted courage and fortitude. 2 Tim. i. 7, 'For God hath not given us the spirit of fear; but of power, of love, and of a sound mind.' 1 Cor. xvi. 13, 'Quit you like men, be strong'—which respects not strength of body, but fortitude of mind.

"One of Christian fortitude will strive against sin, be an antagonist to it, and act the manly part against it. Those young men, who are strong, and in whom the word of God dwells, overcome the Wicked One. The world also, with its flattering lusts and frowning fury, is overcome by the saints in the exercise of faith (1 John v. 4, 5). Not only ministers of the Word, but all professors of religion, and members of the churches of Christ, should stand fast in one spirit, striving together for the faith of the Gospel, and should contend earnestly for the faith once delivered to the saints—strong in the Lord and in the grace that is in Christ Jesus—strengthened with might by His Spirit in the inner man."—GILL, *Body of Divinity*, Vol. III., Book i., Chap. 18.

"*Ye are strong, and the word of God abideth in you, and ye have overcome the wicked one.*—1 John ii. 14.

"They overcome him by the strength of their faith; they hold fast their confidence in the Lord's promised strength, and He fights for them. That mighty arm which bruised the serpent's head brings them victory.

"*They overcame the accuser of the brethren by the blood of the Lamb, and by the word of their testimony, and they loved not their lives unto the death* (Rev. xii. 11).

"Through faith in His blood they were pardoned and justified freely, and they knew that in Him they had righteousness and strength; therefore they were at peace with God, and the accuser of the brethren could not lay anything to their charge. Thus they were delivered from his power, and translated into the kingdom of God's dear Son; and they testified this by adhering to the Word of Truth. They believed that whatever Christ had therein promised, He would fulfil to them, and they bore their testimony to their being safe in depending on His Word in the most trying circumstances. They would not give it up whatever they lost by trusting to it; nay, they stuck stedfastly to its truth, although it cost them their lives for maintaining their testimony. They loved the truth more than life; they were not afraid publicly to own that their trust and confidence was in the blood of the Lamb; and they believed they should be infinite and everlasting gainers by holding fast the word of their testimony unto death."
—ROMAINE *on the Life of Faith.* Edition of 1793.

"Such were the heroes of Christianity. They fought the Lord's battles, and in the power of His might they subdued sin; they obtained dominion over it through faith in Jesus.

"And the same faith in the same Jesus is still mighty through Him to obtain as great victories. The truth of His promise, the faithfulness of the promiser, the strength of His arm to fulfil His promise—these did not fail Moses nor Paul, never did—never can—fail any believer. Thus speaketh the Lord unto them, *Sin shall not have dominion over you.* Having pardoned it by My blood, I will subdue it by My Spirit. Trust Me, you shall find strong faith an overmatch for strong sin; because it fights in the strength of Jesus to whom all things are possible, and who must reign till He hath put all His enemies under His feet; and sin and death shall be no more. Say, is it a besetting sin? This only gives more employment for faith, and for the power of Jesus. It may be a sin of constitution, breaking out into wrath and passion, that the man has no government of himself; but the Spirit of Christ can make him a new creature, and can enable him to put off the old man with his deeds, and put on the new man, which, after God is created in righteousness and true holiness. It may be a long habit of sin; but is anything too hard for the Lord? Has He not promised, A new heart will I give you, and I will put My Spirit within you, and I will cause you to walk in My statutes, and ye shall keep My commandments and practise them.

"Wherever grace reigns, this scripture is fulfilled. The armies of the Lord of Hosts fight under His banner, and no weapon formed against them can prosper. Kept by His mighty power, they are daily more than conquerors, marching on triumphant over all opposition; for He enables them to hold fast the confidence and the rejoicing of hope firm unto the end. Thus they were commanded to pray, Order my steps, O Lord, according to Thy Word, and let not any iniquity have dominion over me. And the power of Christ resting upon them, they were kept in this spirit of prayer. They looked to His Word and to His arm for the right ordering of their steps, believing that He would keep the feet of His saints, and sin should not have dominion over them, now they were no longer under the law, but under the kingdom of His grace. The victory, which He had promised, they expected; and He did put forth His power, according to that good word wherein He had caused them to place their trust. They found His grace sufficient to subdue the tyranny of iniquity; yea, where sin had abounded, grace did much more abound in daily victory over its wiles and assaults.

"O thou God and Father of our Lord Jesus Christ, strengthen me mightily by Thy Spirit in the inner man, that Christ may dwell in my heart by faith, and I may have His strength to set against the power of my sins and mine enemies."
—ROMAINE *on the Triumph of Faith*, Chapter VI.

"Drawn by that power, without which *none can come unto Him*, their hearts are broken, their wills are renewed, and all the powers and faculties of their souls are inclined to subscribe to the government of Christ, as King of saints. They solemnly withdraw themselves from—renounce and testify their abhorrence of—those to whom they have formerly been in subjection, whose interest is contrary to, and subversive of, Christ's government. These they count to be their greatest, yea, their only enemies, and proclaim open war against them, and that with a fixed resolution, by the grace of God, to pursue it to the utmost.

"The courageous soldier, having drawn his sword, throws away the scabbard, as one that will not leave off fighting till he has gained a complete victory; and this resolution is increased by that hatred which he entertains against sin, and is exercised in proportion to it. The enemies against whom he engages are the world, the flesh, and the devil. The motives that induce him thereunto, are that they are enemies to Christ, and stand in the way of his salvation. That he may manage this warfare with success, he takes to himself *the whole armour of God* (Eph. vi. 11-17), which is both offensive and defensive. He also considers himself obliged to shun all treaties or proposals made by them to turn him aside from Christ, and all correspondence with them, and to avoid everything that may prove a snare or temptation to him, or tend to Christ's dishonour. Also, he hath a due sense of his obligation to endeavour to deliver others from their servitude to sin and Satan, and to encourage those who are almost persuaded to submit to Christ."—RIDGLEY, Q. 45.

If we had time to go into full details in the description of a true believer in Christ as *one that overcometh*, we might enlarge on the habit of self-denial. Self-denial may be called a victory over self, and such a definition is suggested by the book of Proverbs (xvi. 32), where the sentence occurs, "He that ruleth his spirit is better than he that taketh a city." This sentiment has been thus expounded:—

"One that has the command of his temper—that can govern himself and not suffer his passions to exceed due bounds—is superior in strength to him that can storm a castle or take a fortified city. It is easier to do the one than the other; courage of mind, joined with wisdom and assisted by a proper number of persons, may do the one; but it requires the grace of God, the assistance of His Spirit, thoroughly to do the other. Cicero says (Epistles xv. 4), In all ages fewer men are found who conquer their own lusts, than that overcome the armies of enemies."—GILL's *Commentary.*

The above note refers to the inner man of the heart; the Apostle James expatiates on "the bridling of the tongue" (James i. 26; iii. 2)—on the uncomfortable inconsistency of a professedly religious man, who with one and the same tongue both blesses God, even the Father, and curses men who are made after the similitude of God (James iii. 9, 10). Self-denial in this department consists (as Dr Manton expresses it) in "abstaining from the evils of the tongue, such as, railing, reviling, censuring, and detracting." "Speak only a known truth, and that seasonably, charitably, without vanity or folly, or obscenity or rash oaths, as Gregory Nyssen fully expoundeth it." "To be able to bridle the tongue (says Manton) is an argument of some growth and happy progress in grace. . . . As we must avoid the evil of the tongue, so we must commune one with another more fruitfully, quickening one another to a sweet apprehension of the benefits of God."

For the purpose in hand, I may here repeat a note already quoted from Manton, "Learn to approve yourselves to God, with all good conscience, in times of trial. When God trieth your faith or obedience with some difficulty, then is the special time to gain assurance by being found faithful." The meaning of this is elucidated in the following additional notes:—

James ii. 21, *He* [Abraham] *had offered up Isaac his son upon the altar.* The great trial of faith is in acts of self-denial. Such was Abraham's. A man is not discovered, when God's way and his own lie together. Your great inquiry should be, Wherein have I denied myself for God? thwarted any lust? hazarded any concernment? No trial like that, when we can part with some conveniency in sense, upon the proper and sole encouragements of faith.

Rahab's faith, how weak soever, yielded some self-denying act or fruit. She

Y

incurred present danger, and the tortures which the rage of her citizens would inflict upon her for harbouring spies.

Those who would have Abraham's privileges, must look to it that they have Abraham's faith. You claim kin of him as believers. How was it with Abraham? Who would not stick at those commands wherewith Abraham was exercised and tried? God calleth every believer, more or less, to deny something that is near and dear to him. Can you give up all that is near and dear to you? Public duties, if well done, are usually against carnal interests—private duties, against carnal affections. Can you offer up your Isaac—your ease and pleasure for private duties—your interests for public? Every action is not a trial of faith, but such as engageth to self-denial.

He was called the friend of God. "Ye are my friends [saith Christ] if ye do whatsoever I command you." Here is comfort to the righteous—to those that have found any friend-like affection in themselves towards God—any care to please Him. O this is *your* comfort, that delight in His presence—that walk in His ways as much as you can, though not as much as you should.—MANTON *on James*.

CHAPTER V.

ON LOVE TO GOD, CHRISTIAN LOVE, AND FORGIVENESS OF INJURIES.

THIS partnership of Christian graces, residing in the heart of the believer, ministers to his personal consolation. I quote instructive illustrations from various old writers.

"After faith and hope, follows love; for in this order they stand (1 Cor. xiii. 13). Faith is of more use to the believer himself, and such things are ascribed to it as cannot be ascribed to love; but love is more diffusive of its benefits to others, and is of longer duration. Love, in order of nature, follows faith and hope, as the effect [follows] its own cause, as Dr Ames observed; for because by faith and hope we taste how good the Lord is, therefore we love Him. Faith spies eternal life in the promise, and hope rejoices in it; and both attract the affections to God the giver of it.

"Love to God manifests itself in a desire to be like Him. One that loves another endeavours to imitate him; and such as love God are followers of Him as dear children—beloved ones—and walk in love, and are obedient ones, and desirous of being holy, as He is holy in all manner of conversation; nor can they be thoroughly satisfied and contented until they awake in His likeness.

"Such as love the Lord are loved by Him, not that their love is the cause of the love of God to them. His love is prior to theirs, and is the cause of that. But greater manifestations of His love are made to them, and more instances of it shown.

"*If any man love God, the same is known of* Him (1 Cor. viii. 3); he is taken notice of by Him—owned and acknowledged as His. To him God makes Himself known, uses him familiarly, and favours him with communion with Himself, knows his soul in adversity, supports him in it, and delivers him out of it; the knowledge He has of him is special, peculiar, and distinct, and is joined with love and affection to him. The Lord knoweth them that are His (2 Tim. ii. 19).

"Benefits bestowed are not *in quality* the chief motives to love God; yet they are *in order* first, and chiefly strike the affections and stir them up towards the Lord. We cannot come at a view of the Divine perfections but by these means; yet hereby we are led into a view of His nature and perfections, and to love Him for the sake of Himself. Such love, though it is not first in order, is chief and ultimate, and comes nearest to the love which the Divine Persons bear to each other, and nearest to the love with which God loves His people, which arises not from any goodness shown to Him or received by Him.

"1 John iv. 7, The Apostle John expressly says, *Love is of God*—that is, from God the Father, Son, and Holy Spirit. It stands, in the first place, among the fruits of the Spirit (Gal. v. 22.) It is wrought in the soul in regeneration, and is an evidence of it, for *every one that loveth is born of God*. There can be no love to God where there is no knowledge of Him (according to that phrase, *ignoti nulla cupido*). Where there is knowledge of Him—especially of Him in Christ, as gracious and merciful—there will be love to Him. The seat of love is the heart of a regenerate man; and true love to God is a love of Him with all the heart, soul, and strength.—GILL, *Body of Divinity*, Vol. III., Book i., Chap. 9.

James ii. 8. If ye fulfil the royal law according to the Scripture, Thou shalt love thy neighbour as thyself, *ye do well*; ye do that which is right and which is a man's duty to do. This, when done from right principles and to a right end, is a good work, and is doing a good work well. The law of love to men, without distinction of rich and poor, high and low, bond and free, is called *the royal law*, because it is the law of the King of kings; hence the Syriac version renders it, *the law of God*. It is the law of Christ, who is King of saints. As love to God is the sum of the first and great commandment in the law, and may be called the king of laws, so love to the neighbour is the second and next unto it, and may very well bear the name of queen of laws, and so has royalty in it; and indeed this last is said to be the fulfilling of the law (Rom. xiii. 8, 9, 10; Gal. iii. 14).

It is also submitted to and obeyed by those who are made kings and priests to God—and that, in a royal manner, with a princely spirit, willingly and with all readiness. In the Hebrew language the same word signifies "princes," and "to be willing."—GILL'S *Commentary.*

There seems to be a difference between the nature of Christian charity and that love which is required in the second great command. The latter is love to our neighbour, the former is love to a Christian; the latter is love for his own sake, the former is love for Christ's sake; the latter is pure benevolence, the former includes complacency. The Scriptures denominate Christian charity to be a *brotherly love,* or a love to Christians as brethren. "Be ye kindly affectioned one to another with brotherly love, in honour preferring one another (Rom. xii. 10); "Let brotherly love continue" (Heb. xiii. 1). According to this the object of Christian love must be one who is esteemed a Christian brother; but the object of the second great command extends to all mankind, irrespective of their moral qualities.

Christian love is by our Lord called "a new commandment." Speaking to His disciples, He says, "A new commandment I give unto you, That ye love one another" (John xiii. 34). Some indeed have supposed that it is so called on account of its being revived by our Lord, after having been neglected by the Jews, and discountenanced by their teachers; others have thought that it so called by way of excellence. But the peculiar phraseology of the passage is not satisfactorily accounted for by either of these suppositions. It rather seems that Christian charity or love is called "a *new* commandment," because of its being a love to Christians as such, which, though virtually contained in the second great command, was not specifically required by it. The church of God was now no longer to be national, but should be formed of Christians individually, amongst whom there should be no other bond of union but that of pure Christianity. Hence it is that this "new commandment" is suited to a new dispensation.—ANDREW FULLER.

Christ says, A new commandment I give unto you, That ye love one another —which yet (as the Apostle John says) is both old and new (1 John ii. 7, 8)— *an old commandment,* being founded upon the original law of God—*a new commandment,* being *a new edition* under the Gospel dispensation. Being given out anew by Christ, the law-giver in His house, it is called *the law of Christ*; the law of love, with a new pattern and exemplar, a new motive and argument, mentioned by Christ Himself, *As I have loved you, that ye also love one another.*

The comfort and joy of ministers should be an argument with saints to mutual love; with the greater pleasure they pursue their studies and labour in their ministrations for the good of souls. Yea, when it is otherwise, the comfort of the saints themselves and their edification are greatly hurt. Wherefore, the Apostle exhorts to love and unity, and that brotherly love continue; for the love of God and Christ continues; nothing can separate from it; they love to the end.—GILL, *Body of Divinity*, Vol. III., Book i., Chap. 9.

They are poor men and you may do your pleasure with them, but if God be in them, take heed, "touch not Mine anointed" (Ps. cv. 15). If it be "the Divine nature" (2 Pet. i. 4) that is in them, be never so unnatural and ungracious as to hate, despise, or oppose it. But, on the contrary, let us own, love, and honour it wherever we find it. Let us own God and His image in His poorest servants. Let it be evident to us that we ourselves are *partakers of the Divine nature*, when even naturally, and from a Divine natural instinct and sympathy, we close and clasp with it; love, honour, and cherish it in others—both it, and them for it—how mean and abject and despised soever they may be otherwise. That the dunghill cock should prefer the barley corn before the gem—that a stranger should ask the spouse what is her Beloved above another beloved—is no wonder; no more is it for an ignorant carnal worldling, who knoweth not the spiritual worth of the things of God, to undervalue the children of God, and to count them the filth of the world and the offscouring of all things. But for professed Christians to think goodly of him that hath a gold ring on and gay apparel, and meanwhile to tread under their footstool a saint rich in faith, as a child of God, partaker of the Divine nature and heir of the kingdom, because of his poor raiment and mean outside, is most unworthy.

Let me ever value a diamond, though in the dirt, above a pebble or clot of earth though set in gold—a poor Christian "all glorious within," though clad with sheep skins and goat skins, above all the satins and velvets and ruffling gaieties of other bug men who have little or nothing of God in them. Any appearance of God is glorious; but this of saving grace in His saints (which rendereth them most precious and honourable), next after that which appeared in Christ, is most glorious. As Christ [said] of John the Baptist, What went you out to see—a man clothed in soft raiment—or a prophet? Yea, I say unto you, more than a prophet—more than a bare man—one that hath much of God in him, a *Theophoros*, as Ignatius explained it to Trajan.

Though the godly be partakers of the Divine nature, yet they may not be of divine worship. But yet, upon this account, there is due to them—

1. Great honour and reverence—for if we ought so to reverence the image of God, looking out in magistrates and superiors (who are therefore called "gods," Psalm lxxxii. 6), in regard of their greatness, is there none due to the saints who resemble Him in His holiness and goodness? The hollow of a Paphnutius eye, put out for Christ's sake, is worthy of the kiss of an emperor.

2. Singular and transcendent love—and this in the fruits and effects of it, in bounty if they need; for if they be partakers of the Divine nature, what we give to them we lend to the Lord; however, in most ardent affection, let this Divine nature kindle this Divine flame, and more to them than to other men, and to them most in whom most of God appears.

Good is to be done unto all, but "especially unto them which are of the household of faith" (Gal. vi. 10). "Be reconciled (as your phrase is) to the whole creation," and let your love be as universal as it can to all mankind; "to brotherly kindness" we must "add love" (2 Pet. i. 7). Be we not so prodigal of our love to the saints that we prove so niggardly that we have none for others; but yet, on the contrary, though our love should be universal, yet it should not be equal—extended to all, but yet so as more intensely set on such whom He bestows His peculiar love upon; and ours should imitate His, be discriminant as His. "Honour all men," but especially "Love the brotherhood" (1 Pet. ii. 17). Let, at least, humanity prevail with us to esteem and love all that partake with us of human nature, for so far we love ourselves—but so as to put more abundant honour on them who are made partakers of the Divine nature, for so we shall love God in them.—TUCKNEY, 1657.

"Love is not an empty thing, the voice and sound of love is not an uncertain sound or an empty voice, for saith the Apostle (1 Cor. xiii. 1), 'Though I speak with the tongue of men and have not love, I am become as a sounding brass or a tinkling cymbal.' A man's heart may be purged from grosser sins, and he may be garnished with parts and gifts, and yet his soul left empty for Satan to return in again (as you read in Matt. xii.). But grace and love is a filling thing, yea, saith the Apostle (ver. 8), *Love never fails*, but it continues; it is that garment that never waxeth old; but gifts do, and are soon threadbare. Though these gifts are fine sweet flowers, yet, therewithal, the mower filleth not the hand. A gracious heart cannot be satisfied with gifts alone; gifts alone are not able to satisfy; love and grace doth. But wherein doth love work beyond gifts?

"Saith the Apostle here, I will tell you. *Love suffereth long;* better read thus, Love is slow to anger, parts and gifts are not so. But a man may be slow to anger, and yet not kind and bountiful. True, *but love is kind*, or bountiful; gifts are not so. The Apostle speaks of the effects of love, in opposition to parts and gifts, all along. Love, saith he, is slow to anger, and is kind, or bountiful.

"Aye, but though a man be kind or bountiful, yet, notwithstanding, he may envy at the good of others. True, if he have parts and gifts only; but love, true love—*that envies not*. Aye, but though a man do not envy at the good of others, yet he may not consider the wants of others. True, but love will; for in the next words, *Charity* or love *vaunteth not*—rather, according to the Greek, *love is not light* or inconsiderate, but considers, and weigheth all things. Aye, but though you do all this, yet, notwithstanding, a man may be proud when he hath done. True, if he have gifts alone; but *love is not puffed* up—is not swelled or blown, and filled with wind as bellows are.

"At the 5th verse, saith he, *Love doth not behave itself unseemly*. This may be understood two ways, saith Peter Martyr. Love will do no unseemly thing—or, love counts nothing unseemly for the person loved. Our Saviour washed His disciples' feet; one would think it an unseemly thing for the Lord and Master to do this for the servants, but He loved them, and counts nothing unseemly for the person loved. Judas comes and betrays his Master with a kiss; this was an unseemly thing. Judas had parts and gifts, but he had not love, and therefore he did an unseemly thing. Love doth not behave itself unseemly, that is, it doth no unseemly thing, and yet counts nothing unseemly for the person loved. It *seeks not her own*—but the good of the person loved; *is not easily provoked*—rather, is not easily embittered, or is not sharp, doth not speak bitter language; gifts and parts will.

"*Love thinks no evil*—verse 6, it *rejoiceth not in iniquity, but rejoiceth in the truth*. It rejoiceth not in injustice, but rejoiceth with the truth—so the words are to be read, and it is thus. If a man be oppressed, love cannot rejoice in his oppression; but if a man be freed and delivered from his oppression, and the truth heard and known, love rejoiceth with such a man when the truth is discovered; it rejoiceth not in injustice, but rejoiceth with the truth when that comes to light. Well, but suppose all this, yet, notwithstanding, a man may labour under some sinful infirmities, what will love do then?

"Verse 7. Love *covereth all things;* though men have many infirmities, yet true love will cover them all; and it *believeth all things:* though a man may have done that which is evil in itself, yet love believes he had a good intention in the doing it;[1] and though a man may go very far in sin, yet if another have love, he hopeth that God will bring him back again, for love *hopeth all things;* and if another do me wrong, if I have love I shall bear that too, for love *endureth all things*. But now will gifts and parts do these things? Surely no; gifts and parts will not cover all things, believe all things, hope all things, endure all things. Aye, but love doth and love will.

"Now, if you look into 1 Cor. viii., you will find that it is said concerning love, that it edifies. *Knowledge puffeth up, but charity* or love *edifieth*. Knowledge, that is, the gift of knowledge, doth puff us up. The end of gifts is edification; it is the proper work of gifts to edify; yet, saith the Apostle, love edifies. Comparing love and gifts together, he shows that love edifies rather than gifts.

[1 A Christian has within him a court of justice, called to settle the claims of his neighbours upon his good opinion. There are several commissioners on the bench, such as, conscience, good information, &c., and *one* commissioner is *love*, which is always *inclined to believe all things*, especially in favour of a Christian brother or sister.—D. C. A. AGNEW.]

Now, I say, if love do thus outshoot gifts in their own bow, then certainly there is a great deal more excellency in love than in all gifts, though they be never so great."—W. BRIDGE, *Sermon before the Lord Mayor*, 1649.

The Shorter Catechism, in expounding the Lord's Prayer, says, "In the fifth petition (which is, *And forgive us our debts as we forgive our debtors*) we pray, That God, for Christ's sake, would freely pardon all our sins—which we are the rather encouraged to ask, because by His grace we are enable from the heart to forgive others."

The Larger Catechism's exposition is, "In the fifth petition (which is, *Forgive us our debts as we forgive our debtors*), acknowledging that we and all others are guilty both of original and actual sin, and thereby become debtors to the justice of God, and that neither we nor any other creature can make the least satisfaction for that debt—we pray for ourselves and others, that God of His free grace would, through the obedience and satisfaction of Christ apprehended and applied by faith, acquit us both from the guilt and punishment of sin, accept us in His Beloved, continue His favour and grace to us, pardon our daily failings, and fill us with peace and joy, in giving us daily more and more assurance of forgiveness—which we are the rather emboldened to ask, and encouraged to expect, when we have this testimony in ourselves that we from the heart forgive others their offences."

With regard to the requisite state of the petitioner's heart, the Heidelberg Catechism uses very happy and instructive phraseology. According to a frequent popular understanding of the Lord's Prayer, some persons have represented an acceptable petitioner's language as amounting to this, We have always forgiven, or we have in past times forgiven. And, according to this interpretation, all petitioners who have been hitherto unforgiving, are finally and for ever forbidden to say, Forgive us our debts as we forgive men their trespasses against us.

The truth nevertheless is, that whenever a forgiving spirit dawns within us, —even if it be felt for the first time after we have knelt down to pray,—we may say that we forgive—that we do now forgive, however unforgiving we have hitherto been. We forgive, when the feeling and the resolution begins, before there has been time for a public manifestation or personal declaration to him who is, or whom we think to be, an offender against us. What we declare to the Hearer of Prayer is a firm purpose, or resolve—*firmum propositum*, as Conrad Mylius expresses it; or, as the Latin version of the Catechism has it, "firmiter nobis propositum habemus."

126. *Was ist die fünfte Bitte?*
Vergieb uns unsere Schulden, wie auch wir vergeben unsern Schuldigern ;

126. *What is the fifth petition?*
Forgive us our debts as we forgive our debtors, that is, may it please thee

das ist, du wollest uns armen Sündern unsere Missethat, auch das Böse so uns noch immerdar anhanget, um des Blutes Christi willen nicht zurechnen, wie auch wir dies Zeugniss deine Gnade in uns befinden, dass unser ganzer Vorsatz ist unserm Nächsten von ganzem Herzen zu verzeihen.

for the blood of Christ, not to impute to us poor sinners our misdeeds—also the evil which still adheres to us— even as also we find this evidence of Thy grace in us, that it is our full resolution to pardon our neighbours from the whole heart.

The following is a portion of Boston's Discourse, illustrating the answers in the Westminster Catechisms:—

When we find that we, who are such evil and malignant creatures—so hateful and ready to hate one another—are by the power of God's grace enabled to forgive those who have injured us, we have ground to hope that the most gracious God will forgive the injury against Himself. From our disposition to forgive we may confirm our confidence in God as our God, and firmly believe that our feet shall be washed, where the whole body has been washed before. The petition, *Forgive us our sins, for we also forgive every one that is indebted to us,* denotes our forgiving to go before the forgiveness here asked of God for ourselves. And this is a demonstrative proof that the forgiveness the saints here ask for themselves is only the pardon of the guilt of fatherly anger,[1] and the manifestation of pardon—and not the pardon of the guilt of eternal wrath,[2] which concerns their state. For till this last be obtained one cannot sincerely forgive others. No man can sincerely forgive his brother who does not love him; and none can love his brother but he who loves God; and none loves God but he who is forgiven of God—Luke vii. 47, "I say unto thee, Her sins, which are many, are forgiven; for she loved much: but to whom little is forgiven, the same loveth little."— BOSTON.

"We may observe a variation of expression in Matthew and Luke. In the former it is said, Forgive us our debts as we forgive our debtors; and in the latter, Forgive us our sins, for we also forgive every one that is indebted to us. There is a little difficulty in the sense of the particles AS and FOR.

"In Matthew the particle AS is not a note of equality but of similitude; and accordingly it signifies that we are to forgive others even as God, for Christ's sake, has forgiven us; or, as we hope to obtain forgiveness from Him. Though, if we compare those two together, there is an infinite disproportion between them, as to the injuries forgiven and other circumstances that attend the action.

[1] "*Of* fatherly anger," means "implying the fatherly anger of God."
[2] "*Of* eternal wrath," means "implying the eternal wrath of God."

"In Luke the particle FOR is not causal but demonstrative, and therefore we are not to understand it as though our forgiving others were the ground or reason of God forgiving us (since that would be to put it in the room of Christ's righteousness); but the meaning is, that we are encouraged to hope that He will forgive us, from the demonstrative evidence that He has given us that grace which inclines and disposes us to forgive others.

"Our forgiving injuries is an evidence of our having obtained forgiveness when—

"1. We do it out of a humble sense of the many crimes that we have committed against God. It is joined with and flows from the grace of repentance.

"2. It also contains in it several acts of faith; as hereby we do, in effect, acknowledge that all we have is in God's hand, who has a right to take it away when He pleases; if He suffers us to be deprived of our reputation and usefulness in the world, or of our wealth and outward estate therein, by the injurious treatment we meet with from those who without cause are our enemies—we are sensible that this could not be done without His permissive providence, which we entirely acquiesce in, hoping and trusting that He will overrule this and all other afflictive providences for our good.

"3. We forgive those that have injured us, with an earnest desire that God would give them repentance; that thereby His name may be glorified and His interest promoted, whatever becomes of our name and usefulness in the world."—RIDGLEY, Q. 195.

"Aye, but suppose that a man doth me wrong, stirs and provokes me, and that he hath first made the breach, should I love him then?

"Yes, else there were no labour of love. God is not unmindful to forget your labour of love. That faith is a faith worthy of God that steps over difficulties; and that love is a love worthy of God that steps over provocations. You see how it is with a glass that hath sweet liquor in it: the more you stir that glass the more savoury sweet smell it sends forth. Art thou provoked, and art thou stirred?"—WILLIAM BRIDGE, 1649.

"This great duty of forgiving others is a crossing the stream; 'tis contrary to flesh and blood. Men forget kindnesses but remember injuries. But it is an indispensable duty to forgive; we are not bound to trust an enemy, but we are bound to forgive him. We are naturally prone to revenge. Revenge (says Homer) is sweet as dropping honey. The heathen philosophers held revenge lawful; ulcisci te lacessitus potes (Cicero). But we learn better things out of the oracles of Scripture; Mark xi. 25, When ye stand praying, forgive; Col. iii. 13, If a man have a quarrel against any, even as Christ forgave you, so do ye.

"Lay up a stock of faith; Luke xvii. 4, 'If thy brother trespass against thee seven times in a day, and seven times a day turn again unto thee and say, I repent, thou shalt forgive him. And the apostles said to the Lord, Increase our faith,'—as if they had said, We can never do this without a great deal of faith: Lord, increase our faith. Believe that God hath pardoned you and you will pardon others. Only faith can throw dust upon injuries, and bury them in the grave of forgetfulness.

"To forgive is one of the highest evidences of grace. As the sun draws up many thick noxious vapours from the earth, and returns them in sweet showers; so a gracious heart returns the unkindnesses of others, with the sweet influences of love and mercifulness; Ps. xxxv. 12, They rewarded me evil for good; but as for me, when they were sick, my clothing was sackcloth: I humbled my soul with fasting.

"Forgiving others is a sign of God's forgiving us; it is not a cause of God's forgiving, but a sign. We need not climb up into heaven to see whether our sins are forgiven; let us look into our hearts and see if we can forgive others. Then we need not doubt but God hath forgiven us. Our loving others is nothing but the reflection of God's love to us."—THOMAS WATSON.

CHAPTER VI.

OF THE ENJOYMENT OF GOD'S PRESENCE IN ORDINANCES.

"THE sweet enjoyment of ordinances together[1] is a great help to our love. Swelling gifts despise ordinances, and neglect love. Gifts thrive best when they live under grace, and grace thrives best when it lives under ordinances. Now, the girdle of all the ordinances is the Lord's Day, which doth surround and combine all the rest. May it please the magistrate to be a friend to this good day; Christ will surely be a friend to him in an evil day. You cannot make people sanctify this day, for the hearts of men are not in your hands; but you may restrain them much from public profaning this day. Job is said to sanctify his sons, because he commanded them to sanctify themselves, used all means for their sanctification, and prayed for them. So, though the magistrate cannot sanctify the people as to the infusion of grace, yet by his prayers and gracious endeavours of love, mixed with some power as just occasion requires, he also may be said to sanctify them."—WILLIAM BRIDGE, 1649.

[1] [*Together*, that is, in a congregation "assembled and met together."]—*See* my Book Second, *art.* HUNTER.

THE THEOLOGY OF CONSOLATION.

"Praying *with* and *for* others" is a piece of the communion of saints. It is one of the privileges of God's family on earth, that they have the prayers of all the family here. God is a rich Father, who has blessings for all. He is a forgiving God. Why does He teach us to pray for pardon to ourselves and others, but that there is a fulness of mercy for pardon with Him?

Use not "Amen" superficially at the end of your prayers, but with earnestness and faith. As for those who think it superstition to say "Amen," they are ignorant of the Word of God; and I would recommend them to consult their Bible and Catechism, in order to cure them of that senseless conceit. "Amen" imports two things—(1.) Our desire to be heard = "so be it"—Rev. xxii. 20, "Amen. Even so, come, Lord Jesus." And the believer uses this word properly as a testimony of his desire when by faith he is emboldened and emboldened to plead with God, that He would fulfil his requests (2 Chron. xx. 6, 11). (2.) Our confidence and assurance that we shall be heard = "so certainly it shall be"—Rev. i. 7, "Even so, Amen." And the sincere Christian uses the word with great propriety in the conclusion of his prayers, in testimony of his assurance to be heard, when he is by faith emboldened quietly to rest upon the Lord, that He will fulfil the desires of his heart (2 Chron. xiv. 11).—BOSTON, *Body of Divinity.*

"*I went into the sanctuary of God* (Psalm lxxiii. 17). The Psalmist went into the tabernacle or house of God, where the word of God was read and explained, and prayer was made, and where fellowship was had with the saints, and communion with God Himself—which, for one hour or moment, is preferable to all the prosperity of the wicked during their whole life. This shows that though he was beset with temptation, it did not so far prevail with him as to cause him to neglect public worship, and relinquish the house of God, and the ordinances of it. It is right, under temptations, doubts, and difficulties, to attend the public ministrations, which is the way and means to have relief under temptation, to have doubts resolved, and difficulties removed."

"It is the duty of the saints to assemble together for public worship, on the account of God who has appointed it, who approves of it, and whose glory is concerned in it; and on the account of the saints themselves, that they may be delighted, refreshed, comforted, instructed, edified, and perfected; and on account of others, that they may be convinced, converted, and brought to the knowledge and faith of Christ. They ought not to forsake such an assembling of themselves together (Heb. x. 25); for it is a forsaking God and their own mercies."—GILL's *Commentary.*

"In order to his being established in pure consolation, the believer must endeavour, with all diligence, to make a right and profitable use of the holy sacraments. These are the seals of the covenant of grace, for they were instituted in order to confirm that holy covenant with true believers. In the hand of the Holy Comforter they are special means of confirming that everlasting covenant with them; and they confirm it with them not by making it firmer in itself than it is already, but by confirming their faith of it, and by clearing up or confirming to them their personal interest in it, and in all the blessings promised in it."—COLQUHOUN.

"The believer may be called either to present a child for baptism, or to witness the dispensation of baptism to the child of another. Seeing baptism, in the room of circumcision, is a seal, especially of the righteousness of the faith (Rom. iv. 11), he should, in witnessing the dispensation of it, renew his cordial application of the righteousness of Jesus Christ which, in the Gospel, is revealed from faith to faith. Since the water in baptism represents the cleansing virtue of the blood and Spirit of Christ, he should, when he sees the baptismal water applied to the body, seize the precious opportunity afforded to his soul of applying the justifying blood of Christ to his conscience for cleansing it from the guilt and pollution, and the sanctifying Spirit of Christ to his heart for cleansing it from the power of sin. Relying on the righteousness or blood of Jesus for a complete title to deliverance from the guilt, the power, and the pollution of sin—and trusting in the Lord Jesus Himself for all his salvation—he should then within himself say, As certainly as I have now seen the baptismal water sprinkled upon the body of that infant,—the blood and the Spirit of Christ are mine not only in offer but in possession; they are mine to justify, sanctify, and comfort me; Christ Himself is mine, as my Covenant Head; God is mine as my Covenant God from henceforth and for ever.

"Seeing that the child is, in its baptism, solemnly dedicated to the Lord, the believer [witnessing the baptism] ought further to say, O Lord, I devote myself, and all that I am, to Thee, to be Thine wholly, only, and for ever, to be saved by Thy grace, and to be employed for Thy glory."—COLQUHOUN, *Chapter IX.*

Address at the Lord's Supper.

There is nothing in this world which true Christians more earnestly desire than to be well assured and satisfied of the love of Jesus Christ to their souls. You are now come to a sealing ordinance, instituted on purpose for this noble end and use. O that we could pray and plead for it, as the spouse doth, "Set me as a seal upon thine heart, a seal upon thine arm; for love is strong as death."—*Sol. Song,* viii. 6.

Surely you have now before you the greatest motive in the world to inflame your love to Jesus Christ. Behold Him, as He is here represented to you, wounded for your iniquities—yea, sacrificed to the wrath of God, for your peace, pardon, and salvation. O what manner of love is this! Behold how He loved thee! If Christ's love draw forth thine, it will so far clear thy interest in His love, as it shall engage thy heart in love to Him.

The activity of your love will be according to the activity of your faith. Therefore I advise you to make it the main work and business of this hour to exercise your faith upon Jesus Christ.

1. Realise the sufferings of Christ for you, and behold them here represented in a true glass to the eye of faith. See you that bread broken and that wine poured out? As sure as this is so, Jesus Christ endured the cross, suffered the wrath of the great and terrible God, in His soul and in His body, upon the cursed tree, for, and in the room of, poor condemned sinners. Your faith for the one hath as much—yea, more—certainty that your sense hath for the other. "This is a faithful saying, and worthy of all acceptation, that Jesus Christ came into the world to save sinners" (1 Tim. i. 15). "And, without controversy, Great is the mystery of godliness, God was manifest in the flesh" (1 Tim. iii. 16).

2. Apply the sufferings of Christ this day to thine own soul; believe all this to be done and suffered in thy room and for thy sake. He offered not this sacrifice for His own sins, but ours (Isa. liii. 9; Heb. vii. 27). He was incarnate for you; Isa. ix. 6, "For unto us a child is born; to us a son is given." His death was for you and in your stead—Gal. iii. 13, "He was made a curse for us;" and when He rose from the dead, "He rose for our justification" (Rom iv. 25). And now He is in glory at the right hand of God, He is there for us; Heb. vii. 25, "He ever lives to make intercession for us." It was the pride, passion, earthliness, and unbelief of thy heart which Jesus groaned, bled, and died to procure a pardon for.

3. Infer from the sufferings of Christ those conclusions of faith that tend to assurance, as thus—

Did Christ die for me when I was an enemy? Then surely, being reconciled, I shall be saved by His life (Rom. v. 10). Again, is Christ dead for me? Then I shall never die eternally. Nothing shall separate me from the love of God; it is Christ that died (Rom. viii. 34) . . . . Engage thy soul to Him this day, to be more active, cheerful, and fruitful in His service.—FLAVEL, *Sacramental Meditations, XI.*

Praise is a comely mixture in all the parts of Divine worship. It is most directly tending to God's honour; and it is the piece of worship that will last longest; when prayers, &c., are laid by in heaven, praise will be there for ever.

God's mercies are new every morning; let therefore the sacrifice of praise be a part of the daily sacrifice ye offer unto God. Never bow a knee unto God for supplicating a mercy from Him, without praising Him for what mercies ye enjoy. This is a very promising way of obtaining the requests ye make at the throne of grace in the confidence of faith.

The Lord's Prayer begins with praise, and ends with it too. For it is necessary in the entrance (that we may have our hearts awed with the Divine glory, that so we may be the fitter to pray on) and in the end, that we may carry away high thoughts of God, for the better regulating of our life in the intervals of duty.—BOSTON, *Body of Divinity.*

"We are to inquire, What have we received from God under His ordinances?—whether we have had any sensible communion with Him, any experiences of His love, or impressions of His power on our hearts—whether we have had fellowship with the Father and with his Son Jesus Christ—whether as we have gone from one ordinance to another, we have gone from strength to strength, our faith being more lively, our love to God increased, and our spiritual joy enlarged? Let us inquire whether we have learned some doctrine from the word which we understood not (or, at least, have been more confirmed therein, after some degree of wavering) or have been affected with some truth which we never saw such a beauty and glory in before—whether we have been melted under the word, if it has been (as the prophet speaks) *like fire,* or *as the hammer that breaketh the rock in pieces,* or, as the disciples say one to another, *Did not our heart burn within us, while He talked with us by the way, and while He opened to us the Scriptures?* We may comfortably conclude that we have received good under the ordinances if we have been brought into a holy and lively frame of spirit—and if, the more we attend on them, the more our hearts are drawn forth to desire and delight in them—and especially, when public duties fit us for private—when, from the advantage that we receive from such opportunities, we are more disposed to walk with God in all the affairs and businesses of life, so that our whole conversation in the world receives a tincture, from the benefit which we gain by that communion which we enjoy with God in His ordinances on His own day."—RIDGLEY, Q. 117.

O it would be pleasant if our experience in ordinances were such here as that they would fit us for the exercises of heaven—our prayers here, a stretching forth of our desires for the enjoyment of God and of the Lamb—and our praises here, a tuning of our hearts for the songs above! . . . O what must Christ be in Himself, when it is HE that sweetens heaven, sweetens Scriptures, sweetens ordinances, sweetens earth, and even sweetens trials! O what must Christ be in Himself!—JOHN BROWN of Haddington.

CHAPTER VII.

ON GROWTH IN GRACE.

"IF a believer would reach establishment in spiritual comfort, he must study daily to grow in grace. It must be his earnest and continual endeavour, in the faith of God's free favour to him, to grow stronger and stronger in the habit—and to abound more and more in the exercise—of every grace implanted by the Holy Spirit in his soul. By so doing, spiritual declension and the loss of comfort will, under sanctifying and consoling influences, be happily prevented. The Apostle Peter, in order to prevent the believers, to whom he wrote, from being so led away by the error of the wicked as to fall from their own steadfastness, directed them to grow in grace (2 Pet. iii. 18). Believers, holding the Head and having nourishment administered, ought, in point of duty, as well as of privilege, to increase with the increase of God (Col. ii. 19). It is their duty to grow up into Christ who is the Head (Eph. iv. 15), not only in all things, but at all times. Their path should always be as the morning light that shineth more and more unto the perfect day. They ought at all times to grow inwardly, by faith and love, cleaving more firmly to Christ, the head of gracious influences—to grow outwardly, by being more and more fruitful in good works—to grow upward, in heavenly mindedness and joy in God—and to grow downward, in humility and self-denial."—COLQUHOUN, *Chapter XI.*

"In Hosea xiv., compared with Psalm xcii., the Holy Ghost singleth out the choicest trees and flowers in the world, on purpose to express the saints' fruitfulness, and their growth therein.

"As, first, to show the sudden springing up of the new creature, as it falls out upon some men's conversion or upon the saints' recovery again after falls, he compares them to the lily, whose stalk, though long hid in the earth, when once it begins to feel the dew, grows up oftentimes in a night. But yet a lily is a flower and soon decays.

"Therefore, secondly, to show their perpetuity and stability together with their growth, the prophet compares them to the cedar, whose wood rots not (put to express immortality, *digna cedro*), and which is not only most durable, but of all trees the tallest, and shoots up the highest.

"But yet, thirdly, suppose the new creature to be kept under and oppressed with temptations and oppositions, yet to show that still it will grow and flourish again, therefore he compareth them to a palm tree which useth to grow the more weight is hung upon it, and sprouts again even when it is cut down to the roots.

"Fourthly, to show that they grow with all kinds of growth, therefore the prophet expresseth their growth both by the spreading of their root, and also of the branches, and so in a growth both upward and downward. He shall cast forth his roots as Lebanon—that is, grow inwardly in habitual grace in the heart—and then, outwardly, spread forth their branches, and so grow in the outward profession of God's ways and truth, and external holiness in their lives.

"Neither, fifthly, is it a growth merely in bulk, but also in fruitfulness; and therefore he compares them to the olive and the vine, which are of all trees the fruitfullest, and most useful to God and man (Judges ix. 9, 13).

"But yet, sixthly, trees have a flourishing time of it but for some while, during which, although they may be thus green and fruitful, yet, in their age, they wither and rot, and their leaves fall off, and their fruit decays. The Holy Ghost, therefore, as preventing [anticipating] this exception to fall out in the saints' growth, he adds, They bring forth fruit still in their old age. When nature begins to decay, yet grace renews its strength—which, if it be wondered at and how grace should grow and multiply, the soil of our hearts being a stepmother to it, *From Me,* says Christ, *is thy fruit found.* It is God that gives the increase, and *I will be as the dew to Israel.*"—GOODWIN, *The tryall of a Christian's growth,* Chapter I.

"When our faith waxeth stronger, our charity hotter, our patience meeker, our obedience more conscionable, our conscience more sincere—this is to grow in grace. And the more we grow in goodness, which is the latter grace, our sanctification, the more assured we grow of the former, even the favour of God in Christ, which is our justification. Still the more holy, the more happy. It is true that our justification admits no latitude, we can be no more than just and righteous; but that grace is without us—no growing in that. But our sanctification admits of degrees and measure, and is within us; so that we may grow in that. We cannot be more just to-day than we were yesterday in respect of God; we may be more holy in regard of ourselves. And if we be not more beloved than we were, yet we shall feel ourselves more beloved and blessed than we were.

"Knowledge is wrought in us by the Holy Spirit. No man can say that Jesus is the Lord but by the Holy Ghost (1 Cor. xii. 3). It is the gracious work of the Holy Spirit to teach us to know Christ. Thus, in knowing Christ to be our Saviour, we know the First Person to be our Father, and the Third Person to be our Comforter. Christ is all in all; we cannot know the sun, but withal we must know his light that illuminates us, and his heat that cherisheth us. It was Paul's determination not to know anything but what concerned Jesus Christ. This is enough; we need no more knowledge to the completion of our happiness. Therefore it might well be decreed by the learned of the Christian world, that none should take their degrees in the school of learning unless they could first read and understand the title of *Christ crucified.*

"*Grace* and *knowledge* are joined together (2 Peter iii. 18), because the one helps to maintain the other. Knowledge is like a star, the darkest part of the orb till it be enlightened by the sun—a mere dark lantern till grace put a light into it. It may see much into nature before, and be cunning in this world; but it is grace that gives it eyes to see into heaven. Thus grace maintains knowledge. Again, the more we know Christ, the better we love Him; the farther we look into the joys above, the more we are ravished with them; the comfort we find in the fruits of grace, the more growth we wish to the tree of grace in our own hearts. Thus knowledge maintains grace. . . . . . . Grace is not kindled by knowledge, but by knowledge grace is cherished. Grace directs knowledge how to contemplate, and knowledge stirs up grace to practice. Grace will not suffer knowledge to want illumination, nor will knowledge suffer grace to want operation.

"In our actions there is a golden mean; and we may either neglect or overdo them. To besiege our patience the devil hath a stupidity as well as impatience. Against our devotion he raiseth diffidence on the one side, and over-boldness on the other. In justice's way there lies rigour and partiality; for charity, a prodigal and pinching hand. Thus for the satisfaction of nature—for the felicity of estate—for order and rule to the actions of our body and passions of our mind—without question, mediocrity is the best.

"But for the grace of God—for the knowledge of Christ—no mean must content us here. In these we must still be growing like fruitful trees, and never think ourselves high enough till we are in heaven. The state of that soul is doubtful that can satisfy itself with a small measure of holiness. In other things, a mediocrity will serve well enough (best of all), but not in righteousness, not in grace; no competency to be talked of here—as much measure of this as possibly we can, and all little enough. Not a child in God's family leaves off growing in grace till he be grown up into glory. . . . . . . Let every judgment we see make us wiser in the fear of God, and every mercy we feel wiser in the love of God, and let us depart from every sermon wiser in the grace of God than we came. This is to grow in the knowledge of Christ; and as HE by His knowledge doth justify many, so we by our knowledge shall get assurance that we are justified by Him.

"The growth of any plant is improved principally by three helps—the fecundity of the ground wherein it grows—the kindly heat of the sun cheering it up with his influence—the contribution of the clouds towards it with their dews and showers descending upon it.

"The ground wherein we are planted is the church. And she, like a kind and indulgent mother, accommodates us with all her helps—her doctrine to direct us that we may do well—her discipline to correct us when we do amiss—her sacraments which are cordials to our heart, like springs and veins and channels of grace to the root—her prayers to heaven for a blessing upon that she gives.

"The rain that continually falls upon us, to make us shoot up in goodness, is a frequent distillation of the word preached. If those holy dews do not soak into our hearts, we shall be dwarfs in grace. For this purpose Christ sends apostles, pastors, and teachers; those be the clouds, and from those clouds come rain and showers; the effect should be that we may grow up to the stature of Christ (Eph. iv. 11); there is our growth by it.

"The sun that ripens us, and is the principal cause of this accretion, is Christ Himself—that Sun of Righteousness. All our growth is merely beholden to His beams and saving influence. He blesseth the ground that bears us. He filleth and emptieth the clouds upon us.

"We are not only living but reasonable and holy plants, and must both labour for our own sustenance, and mature and further our own accrescence. The grace that is in us is perfect; for the least grace is grace, as a spark of fire is fire. If men see but little—so little, that they think themselves blind—yet they do see. But they may be brought to see better. We know there is a double perfection—of parts, and of degrees. The grace, that is infused into us at first, is perfect in regard of the parts; as a child is so far a perfect man, because it hath all the parts of a man. But it is not perfect in regard of degrees; for we may grow up in grace, as a child does in stature. In our conversion, when we first receive this saving grace, we are but infants in Christ; yet infants may be tall men in time.

"Faith calls to love, and love to obedience, and obedience to constancy, and one grace foreruns another. Whom God predestinates them He calleth, and whom He calls He justifieth, and whom He justifies He glorifieth. Let us grow up into Him in all things, which is the Head, even Christ (Eph. iv. 15). There is no defect on His part; let there be none on ours. As the rich grow easily richer, so the good grow quickly better."—ADAMS.

"David had his one thing (one thing have I desired), and Paul hath his one thing too—one thing for the saints—and that is this, We forget what is past and press on to that which is before (Philipp. iii. 13), labouring to increase and to grow in grace, and perfecting holiness in the fear of God (2 Cor. vii. 1).

"And this you shall find to be the end of all those afflictions which we meet withal from God the Father. God the Father is unwilling to afflict His children; He would not do it unless it were necessary; why, the end of His affliction we find to be this—John xv. 2, 'Every branch in Me that beareth fruit He purgeth it, that it may bring forth more fruit.'

"And this you shall find to be the end of Christ's coming, as you read in John x. 10, 'I am come that they might have life, and that they might have it more abundantly.' There lies a poor soul (saith Christ) dead in trespasses and sins; I am not only come to give life unto that soul, spiritual life, but that he may have it in more abundance. So that it is not only our duty to have grace, but we must *abound* therein *more and more* (1 Thess. iv. 1); we must grow therein.

"And, my beloved, it is not only the duty of the saints to do so, but they will and they do do this. And if you look into Revelations ii., you will find that this was the commendation of the church of Thyatira, that her works were more at the last than at the first. . . . . Read, I pray, what is said in Prov. iv. 18, But the path of the just is as the shining light, that shineth more and more unto the perfect day—*that shineth more and more*. Look how it is with the light of the day, so with the grace of God in the hearts of His people; the light is small and little at the beginning of the day, but it shineth more and more, it grows brighter and brighter. . . . .

"Aye, but there is a great deal of danger, through the great opposition that the saints meet withal, that their light should be quite put out; they are in great danger to lose all, for they meet with much opposition, yea and the rather, because that they do grow. But as the torch by being beaten burns the better, so the saints do by their oppositions grow stronger and stronger—as in Job xvii., 'Upright men shall be astonished at this . . . . the righteous also shall hold on his way, and he that hath clean hands shall be stronger and stronger.' His opposition should make him grow more and more. When he is chidden for following Christ and the ordinances and ways of Christ, he will cry *so much the more*, Jesus, thou Son of David, have mercy upon me. And if you look into Acts ix. you will find that Paul did increase by the opposition he met withal. When he was much opposed by the Jews, it is said (ver. 22), *But Saul increased the more in strength* and confounded the Jews. God hath a hand upon all the hands of opposition against His children; and it is so far from putting out their light, that it makes their light to grow brighter and brighter.

"The saints cannot but grow in grace, for so the promise is, To him that hath shall be given, and he shall have it in more abundance. And so in that place of Isaiah, He that waiteth upon the Lord shall renew his strength, he shall mount up as with eagle's wings; there shall be an addition of strength unto him, he shall increase and abound yet more and more."—WILLIAM BRIDGE.

"Sanctification is a progressive thing. It is growing. It is compared to seed which grows; first the blade springs up, then the ear, then the full corn in the ear. Such as are already sanctified may be more sanctified; justification doth not admit of degrees, a believer cannot be more elected or justified than he is; but he may be more sanctified than he is. Sanctification is still increasing, like the morning sun, which grows brighter to the full meridian.

Knowledge is said to increase (Col. i. 10), and faith to increase (2 Cor. x. 15). A Christian is continually adding a cubit to his spiritual stature.

"It is not with us, as with Christ who received the Spirit without measure. Christ could not be more holy than He was. But we have the Spirit only in measure, and may be still augmenting our grace; as Apelles when he had drawn a picture, he would be still mending it with his pencil. The image of God is drawn but imperfectly in us, therefore we must be still mending it, and drawing it in more lively colours. Sanctification is progressive; if it doth not grow, it is because it doth not live.

"Grace instils peace; as grace grows, so peace grows. The more we grow in grace, the more will God love us. If you would be growing Christians, be humble Christians. Let Christians be thankful for the least growth; if you do not grow so much in assurance, bless God if you grow in sincerity; if you do not grow so much in knowledge, bless God if you grow in humility. If a tree grows in the root, it is a true growth; if you grow in the root-grace of humility, it is as needful for you as any other growth."—THOMAS WATSON, QQ. 35, 36.

CHAPTER VIII.

ON LOVE FOR CHRIST'S APPEARING.

"WHAT a weight—what an eternal weight—what an exceedingly exceeding and eternal weight of glory is, by redeeming grace, secured for thee! Doth not thy heart long ardently for this? doth it not rejoice and even exult in the cheering prospect of endless felicity, of inconceivable joy? Doth it not look, beyond all transitory shadows, for that blessed hope and the glorious appearing of the great God, even our Saviour, Jesus Christ. . . . . By frequent meditation on that glorious rest which remaineth for the people of God, thou now enterest into rest; thou enjoyest more and more of holy tranquillity, of heavenly consolation. To rejoice in hope of the glory of God is to experience the sweetest and purest joy—joy which shall enable thee to rise superior to the inordinate love of life and to the disquieting fear of death. . . . .

"Having already tasted the sweetness of pure consolation, thou shouldst long with ardent and increasing desire for the marriage-supper of the Lamb. He hath, by ten thousand thousand instances of kindness, so endeared Himself to thy heart, that thou shouldst not be fully satisfied until thou have the full enjoyment of His immense and everlasting love—until thou see Him as He is, enjoy the unclouded light of His countenance, and be crowned with the unfading brightness of eternal glory."—COLQUHOUN, *Chapter IX*.

"The soul that knows herself redeemed by Christ is never thoroughly contented till either she returns to Christ or Christ returns to her. The spirit returns to Him that gave it. Hope, then, should make us *look up*; and desire enflames us to *look for* the coming of Jesus Christ."

"This eye of expectation hath three beams—vigilancy, hope, and patience. Without watchfulness we cannot look—without hope we will not look—without patience we should not look for the coming of the Lord."

"Evil is the object of fear, and that we suspect; the object of hope is good, and this we expect. *Justi expectant et expetunt.* None but the gracious can be said to look for this day; they love His appearing (2 Tim. iv. 8)."

"To us, if we be true believers, belongs the *Promise of His coming* (2 Peter iii. 4). Christ's first coming was the expectation of nations—this next is the expectation of Christians. Look up and lift up your heads, for your redemption draweth nigh (Luke xxi. 28). Our eyes are still dropping in this valley of tears; but we look for the gracious beams of that Sun of mercy that shall dry them up. No woman with child did ever more exactly count her time—no Jew did ever more earnestly wish for the jubilee—no servant so desireth the end of his years—no stranger so longs to be at home—no overladen soul so groaneth for case—no soldier so heartily contendeth to have his wars determined with conquest—as the saints expect the promise of the coming of Jesus Christ. It is the strength of their hopes, the sweet object of their faiths, in the midst of all sorrows—the comfort of their hearts, the heart of their comforts—the encouragement of their wearied spirits, the life of their encouraged souls—the common clausule, the continual period and shutting up of their prayers, *Come, Lord Jesus, come quickly. Amen.*"

"We look for new heavens and a new earth wherein dwelleth righteousness (2 Peter iii. 13). There dwelleth *righteousness;* that is, holiness, pureness, innocency, and the perfection of goodness. There dwelleth Christ, and He is righteousness, The Lord our Righteousness. Here is the full antithesis of this new world to the old. Righteousness dwells there, unrighteousness here; here sin and guiltiness, there grace and holiness; below transgression, sanctification above. This world is the orb of sin which corrupted all; that new one, the orb of righteousness which restoreth all. This is the winter wherein all things wither; that is the spring which revives them. The world was made good, only sin depraved it. . . . . . Good was before evil, before malice charity. Decay entered by sin, dishonour by sin, death by sin. . . . . . Sin is a constant incumbent of the earth, never non-resident, never out of business. No place can be rid of him, no time exclude him, no action escape him. He crept into heaven with an angel, into paradise with a devil, into man's nature with the root of that nature. Where can we devise to keep him out? . . . . . . In God's temple sin will not leave us; at our prayers it will be interrupting us. It insinuates itself into every action we do; even our best is not without some touch of sin, or, at least, some assault of sin. It may get into our beneficence and be vainglory, into our devotions and be hypocrisy, into our friendship and be flattery, into our hope and make it smell of presumption, into our humility and turn it into base dejection, into our repentance and work it down to desperation, into our best works and there be an opinion of merit which is a blow with the left heel that kicks down all our milk."

"*There dwelleth righteousness*—no sin there; altogether righteousness. Here, indeed, we have some righteousness, but it is blended with sin. In the most regenerate saint on earth there is flesh as well as spirit; and it is a question sometimes, which of them shall get the predominance. We have a righteousness that is perfect *now*, but that dwells in heaven—in the Person of Christ, and is only imputed to us; this is a justifying righteousness, and is absolute, but *extra nos*, without us. That sanctifying righteousness which is *intra nos*—inherent to our own persons—is so imperfect that sin is joined tenant with it in our mortal body, and there is a perpetual contention between them which shall have the superiority. They are like the land and sea within us; the one would keep, the other would gain; Michael and the Dragon in one heaven—Cæsar and Pompey in one empire—Nehemiah and Sanballat in one city—Isaac and Ishmael in one family—Jacob and Esau in one womb—the Ark and Dagon in one temple—grace and corruption in one Christian. Michael against the Dragon, Cæsar against Pompey, Nehemiah against Sanballat, Isaac against Ishmael, Jacob against Esau, the Ark against Dagon, Grace against Corruption, shall prevail; but *nondum*, not yet."

"We look for a new earth and new heavens; and those new heavens and earth look for new creatures. . . . . . . We *look* for a glorious place, *wherefore* let us be gracious men. Joy and honour is our expectation, wherefore let holiness and innocence take up our conversation. We hope to have an inheritance in that world wherein dwelleth righteousness, wherefore righteousness looks to have her habitation in us while we dwell here."—ADAMS.

John xiv. 3. "If I go and prepare a place for you, I will come again, and receive you unto Myself; that where I am, there ye may be also."

The presence of a beloved object is the grand preparative of any place, and that which gives it its principal charm. Such is the preparation of a place in the future world for us. Jesus is there, and that is quite enough. If anything will operate as a magnet to attract us from earth to heaven, it is the consideration of being "where Jesus sitteth at the right hand of God." Think what an accession of joy His triumphant entrance must have occasioned through all the heavenly regions, and what a source of uninterrupted bliss His presence affords. What would some societies be without certain interesting characters, which are in effect the life of them? And what would heaven be without Christ? The zest of all its bliss consists in HIS being there, and this is urged as the grand motive to "setting our affections on things above" (Col. iii. 1, 2).

There, also, He will gather together the whole family of heaven and earth. His redemption brings multitudes to glory out of every kindred and tongue, and people and nation; and every one that enters adds to the enjoyment. In order to connect us together in the closest bonds of affection, God has so ordained that both in this world and that which is to come our blessedness should be bound up with that of each other, in seeing the good of His chosen, rejoicing in the gladness of His nation, and glorifying with His inheritance. Hence it follows that every accession to the heavenly world affords an influx to the enjoyment of its inhabitants. Every one that goes before may be said to contribute to the preparing of the place for them which follow after. The pure river of the water of life has its origin in the throne of God and the Lamb, but in its progress it passes through various mediums, which swell its streams, and render it more and more delectable. From the entrance of righteous Abel into the New Jerusalem to this day it has been rising higher and higher, and will continue to do so till all the nations of the saved are gathered together.

Christ prepares a place for us in superintending the concerns of the universe, and causing all events to work together, and produce the highest ultimate good. Glory awaits the righteous immediately upon their departure from the body, but a much greater glory is in reserve. Innumerable events in the system of Providence must remain inexplicable till the mystery of God be finished. It is impossible for spectators to comprehend the use of all the parts of a complicated machine, till it is constructed and put into motion. And as our Forerunner is now preparing the scenery of this grand exhibition, and hastening it to its desired issue, it is thus that He is preparing a place for us.

Hence we are encouraged to be looking for, and hastening unto, the coming of the day of God, and directed to consider it as the period when we shall be fully "satisfied." How solemn, and yet how sweet, is the description of it! "The Lord Himself shall descend from heaven with a shout, with a voice of the archangel, and the trump of God; and the dead in Christ shall rise first." A "shout," perhaps, denotes the universal joy of heaven, for the arrival of the day when the war is terminated in victory, and the last enemy is destroyed. The blowing of a "trumpet" may probably allude to that of the jubilee, on which the prison doors were thrown open, and the captives set at liberty.—ANDREW FULLER, *Sermon XLIII.*

"Christ's appearing at His second coming is to be loved and so looked for by the saints, not only because it will be glorious in itself, in its attendants and consequences, but because it will be of great advantage to the saints. Christ will appear unto salvation to them, and so to their joy; they will appear with Him in glory, and be like Him, and enjoy the everlasting vision of Him. Such will wear the crown *who* (as the Ethiopic version renders it) *love Him at His coming;* all that love Him now will love Him then."—GILL on 2 Tim. iv. 8.

END OF BOOK FIRST.

THEOLOGY OF CONSOLATION.

BOOK SECOND.—DICTIONARY OF WRITERS.

PRELIMINARY EXPLANATION.

This Second Book was planned in order to escape from the attempt to interweave biographical incidents among reviews of books and papers.

It has also been considered undesirable to attempt to weld into distinct and complete narratives the biographies which each chapter in the First Book suggests. Such an attempt would demand wearisome endeavours after variety of language; and it would also forbid the admission of many small details which are useful to investigators.

The names of the men, whose memoirs are here collected, are therefore produced and memorialized in alphabetical order. The Book is a Biographical Dictionary. Any disadvantages in this arrangement may be obviated by stating here, in reference to the chapters of Book First, what the names in the Dictionary are.

With regard to the first part of that book, the preliminary matter makes mention of Luther, and of Bishop Sandys, who introduced the reformer's Commentary on the Galatians to English readers.

Chapter I. on the Heidelberg Catechism. The Elector Frederick III. and his dynasty; Ursinus and Olevianus, the authors of the catechism, and the following commentators, Parens, Alting, Strackius, Maresius, Bastingius, Mylius, Leydekker, Roëll, De Witte and Van Der Kemp;[1] Dean Turner, the author of the first English translation; Bishop Parry, the introducer of Ursinus' and Pareus' commentary to English Readers; Felltham, one of those readers; Dr Nevin, the great American author; and the German pastors, Gillet and Wolters. (See also the memoir of Boston.)

Chapter II. Drs Crisp, Gill, and Witsius.

Chapters III. and IV. Edward Fisher, Ridgley, Flavel, Bates, and Witherspoon.

[1] "A graduate of the University of Oxford," in the preface to his translation of the Heidelberg Catechism, printed in 1828, mentions other commentators,—Reuter, Guilnomma, Hulsius, and Cocceius—also, L'Enfant's "L'innocence du Catechism d'Heidelberg démontrée contre deux libelles d'un Jesuite du Palatinat."

Dr Schaff (1877) mentions the following commentators:—Cocceius, 1671; D'Outrein, 1719; Lampe, 1721; Stähelin, 1724; Van Alpen, 1800.

Chapter V. Marshall, Hervey, W. Cudworth, and John Brown of Haddington.

Chapter VI. Robert Trail (and his father), Thomas Cole, Walter Cross, and Thomas Goodwin, junior. The Marrow-men of Scotland, viz., Hog, Boston, Bonar, Williamson, Kid, G. Wilson, E. and R. Erskine, Wardlaw, Davidson, Bathgate, and Hunter; and their friends, Brisbane, two Hamiltons, Riccaltoun, W. Wilson, and J. Fisher.

Chapter VII. Dr Guyse, J. Hubbard, and W. Coward, Esq.

Chapter VIII. Charles Watson, D.D.

With regard to the second Part of Book First, it contains practical quotations from authors who were of various shades of opinion regarding the beginnings of consolation in the soul. These authors I memorialize in this Dictionary; and I also introduce several other authors for the sake of additional quotations. So that the reader will find some information regarding Calvin, Hooker, Adams, Thomas Wilson, and Ames; Dr Owen, Dr Goodwin, Reynolds, Tuckney, S. Simpson, Bridge, Manton, and Thomas Watson; Romaine, Dr Dwight, Andrew Fuller, and Colquhoun.

After the completion of the alphabet, some *additional memoirs* are appended, for the use of investigators—viz., Melchior Adam, James and John Anderson, Bannatine, John Brown of Whitburn, Professor Dunlop, Principal Hadow, Maxwell, Morren, and Hew Scott, D.D.

THEOLOGY OF CONSOLATION.

WRITERS.

REV. THOMAS ADAMS.

THOMAS ADAMS was a clergyman in the Diocese of London whose first publication was a Sermon preached at Paul's Cross on 29th March 1612, and his last, Two Sermons preached and published in 1653. In October 1612 he styled himself Minister at Willington (in Bedfordshire), and in 1618 Preacher of St Gregory's in London. His folio volume in 1629 was inscribed to the Parishioners of St Bennet's, near to St Paul's Wharf, " my dearly beloved charge." Except his quaint and eloquent writings, and their title pages and dedicatory epistles, which contain more or less suggestive allusions to his benefices and to his personal friends, we possess no materials for a Memoir. Homage has been done to him by three great nonconformists of modern times, the Rev. James Sherman (in 1842), President Stowell (in 1847), and Principal Angus (in 1862). President Stowell says of " this rare old preacher and expounder of the Scriptures," :—
" Though not a Nonconformist, he was a Puritan ; though a Churchman in the days of Laud, he was a Calvinist ; though unhonoured by the degrees of a university, he abounded in deep and varied learning. When he was born, or when or how he died, we know not. He has left no diary, and found no biographer. His only monument is his works."

ADAMS' WORKES are a collection of his separately printed sermons, with the addition of Meditations on the Creed, issued in a thick folio volume in the year 1629. The favourite piece used to be " The Souls Sicknesse," in which man's spiritual and moral diseases are discussed in medical language ("timber borrowed out of Galen's wood "), with reference to their symptoms, their causes, and their cure.

Mr Sherman reprinted and edited Adams' greatest work, " A Commentary or Exposition upon the divine Second Epistle Generall written by the blessed Apostle St Peter." It was this editor who introduced into the title page after the author's name, "Rector of St Gregory,"—an interpolation which has led to unnecessary discussions; for the original title page had nothing more than "By Thomas Adams,"—"London, Printed by Richard Badger, for Jacob Bloome, 1633." (A second title page was inserted before p. 800, to inaugurate "The second Tome," which is said to be "Imprinted by Felix Kyngston for Jacob Bloome, 1633." The motto on both title pages is 1 Peter v. 10.)

Adams' writings are characterised by luxuriant humour, which in his "Workes" is often delightful, although sometimes overdone and silly. But a great improvement appears in his elaborate "Commentary," in which his great object evidently was to give a conscientious exposition of the text of the second Epistle of Peter,—its words, its scope, and its application; and the humour was quite subsidiary, and also more pointed and happy. It is of this commentary only, and the author's own edition of it, that I have made use in my First Book. A few references may now be made to his other writings, which are reprinted among Nichol's Standard Divines.

Although a mild man compared with many of his Laudean brethren, his high-churchism occasions the only real fault in his writings. Volleys of poisoned arrows against nonconformists startle the reader in unexpected places. It is enough to say that his own real principles contradict high-churchism. Principal Angus quotes the following sentences (see Memoir in Nichol's Divines, p. xxv.):
—"They [Romanists] plead antiquity, as a homicide may derive his murder from Cain. They plead unity, as Pharisees, Sadducees, Herodians combined against Christ. They plead universality; yet of the ten lepers but one was thankful. When many join in the truth, there is the church, not for the many's sake, but for the truth's. The vulgar stream will bring no vessel to the land of peace."

Adams might have preached to himself the following running commentary which concludes his "Three Divine Sisters";—

"Philippians ii. 1. If there be any consolation in Christ (and there is consolation in Him when the whole world cannot afford it), if any comfort of love (and he that knows not the comforts of love knows no difference betwixt man and beast), if any fellowship of the Spirit (by whom we are all knit into one communion and enriched with the same treasures of grace), if any bowels and mercy (if uncharitableness and avarice have not turned our entrails into stone and iron), fulfil ye my joy, that ye be like-minded, and have the same love. Fulfil the Apostle's joy only? No, the joy of the Bride and Bridegroom—of the church on earth, of the saints in heaven; the joy of the blessed angels; the joy of the Father, Son, and Holy Spirit; and last of all, the joy of your own hearts, that ye love one another. Forget not that trite but true saying,

'They shall not want prosperity
That keep faith, hope, and charity.'"

With regard to Adams' sentiments on consolation as the first aspect of the

Gospel, it is in his case, as in the case of many preachers, difficult to compile a consistent system from his writings, much depending on variable sentiments as to what is good and safe for individual hearers, and on varying sensations in the preacher's own soul, inclining him at one time to be more soothing, and at another time more stern.

The following are the concluding sentences of his Folio of 1629:—

"The prophet's servant seeing the Syrian troops, cried, Alas, master, how shall we do? (2 Kings vi. 15). He looked round about. His eyes were directed upwards; there he saw relief. While we look upward to Him that hath bidden us believe, there is no point of faith so hard but it shall go easily down with us. When we shall subject all the powers of our reason and will to the word of our Maker, this is the noble proof of faith. Lord, Thou hast charged us to believe our own salvation by Christ. Be it unto us according to Thy word. All the doubt is in our believing, not in the performing; give us to believe what Thou hast promised. We need not ask Thee to perform Thy promises; for in Jesus Christ all Thy promises are Yea and Amen."

And here is the conclusion of his last printed sermon written in that period of his life which he calls "my necessitous and decrepit old age."

"Psalm xciv. 13. In the multitude of my thoughts within me, Thy comforts delight my soul. As there be no comforts like those of God, so there is nothing to which comforts are so welcome as to the soul. The pleasure which the body takes is but the body (yea, scarce the very shadow) of pleasure. The soul of pleasure is the pleasure of the soul. There be many things pleasing to the body wherein the sanctified soul takes no delight, especially in the day of trouble. In calamity, good nourishments are comfortable, good words are comfortable, the physician is comfortable, a good spouse specially comfortable; but in respect of these comforts, which do nevertheless pass all understanding, we may say of them, as Job did to his visitant friends, Miserable comforters are ye all. But blessed are the souls upon whom this Sun of comfort shineth; and happy are those showers of tears and sorrows that shall be dried up with such beams of comfort; and blessed [is] God, the Father of our Lord Jesus Christ, the Father of mercies, and God of all comfort (2 Cor. i. 3), to whom, with the Son and Holy Ghost, be all praise and glory for ever and ever! Amen."

PROFESSOR HENRICUS ALTING, D.D.

HENRY ALTING was a member of a family which was of great influence in Holland for many generations. His father, Menso Alting, was a patriotic Protestant pastor. Henry was born at Embden, 17th February 1583, and was a successful student at Groningen and Herborn. Frederick V., the Electoral Prince Palatine (afterwards King of Bohemia), was a student at Sedan in 1605, and to that university Alting went at the close of his own education, in order to be the tutor of three young noblemen, who were companions of the prince. In 1606 civil commotions in France drove the young men to Heidelberg, where they continued their studies under Alting, who became the tutor of the Elector himself in 1608, and returned with him to Sedan. This charge terminated in 1610; but in 1612 Alting was one of the train who accompanied his Highness into England and remained till the royal marriage in 1613.

The founder of the college of Heidelberg had given to it the peculiar name of the College of Wisdom. In this college Alting received the degree of D.D., and the chair of theology. He and his renowned colleague, Abraham Scultet, were the representatives of the college at the Synod of Dort in 1619 ; and both acquitted themselves with marked distinction. When the Elector was made King of Bohemia, and the tutor of his youth had risen to European celebrity, prosperity seemed to be their lot. But the Romish and Imperial party soon brought about the well-known reverse. On a day in the month of September 1622 Alting was in his study at Heidelberg, and a messenger hurriedly told him that the enemy had taken the town, and that the soldiery had already been let loose upon the inhabitants. The professor bolted his door and betook himself to prayer. But a friend, accompanied by two soldiers, urged him to retire by his back-door to the chancellor's house, which, for the sake of the official papers, was under the protection of the conquerors. The lieutenant-colonel of the regiment of Hohenzollern was standing at the door of the protected mansion when Alting approached ; and the rough soldier began to say, "With the battle-axe which I hold in my hand I have to-day killed ten men, and Dr Alting would be the eleventh in no time if I knew where to find him." Then, observing the studious man before him, he said in the same breath, " Who are you ?" Alting quietly replied, " I was a regent in the College of Wisdom." The quaint designation of the college, which was unknown to the officer, seems to have amused his fancy, and he took the collegian under his protection. The Jesuits took possession of the house on the following day, and the colonel withdrew without remembering to speak a word for the refugee. But having succeeded in hiding himself in a garret, Dr Alting was recognised by a man-cook of the Elector's household, whose services Count Tilly had secured. By the favour of the cook he paid a melancholy farewell visit to his study ; and the Count, in the course of three days, gave him a pass which enabled him to leave Heidelberg, and to join his family at Schorndorf in Wurtemberg.

In 1623 he returned to his native town, Embden, and having gone to the Hague to see his exiled master, he was persuaded to become tutor to his children. In 1627 he became professor of theology at Groningen, and there remained till his death, 25th August 1644. He continued devoted to the titular

King of Bohemia, visiting his royal children every year, and holding himself always in readiness to return to Heidelberg should fortune smile upon the old family. A gleam of hope appeared during the weary Thirty Years War in the year 1634; and on the invitation of Louis Philippe, who was then acting as administrator of the Palatinate, he in that year actually travelled as far as Frankfort in order to reopen the College of Heidelberg. But the victory of the Imperialists at Nördlingen put an end to the project, and he retraced his dangerous road to Groningen. Amidst wars and disputations Henry Alting was a peaceable divine, who fought with heavenly weapons; he ended his holy and honourable earthly warfare at the age of sixty-one. He had published in 1618 a small controversial work. His three volumes of *Scripta Theologica Heidelbergensia* were published in 1646. One of his sons became law professor at Deventer. The other was James (*born* 1618, *died* 1679), who as Jacobus Altingius, the author of five folio volumes, theological, philosophical, and epistolary, is well known in the old booksellers' catalogues. (The above article is compiled from "Bayle's Dictionary").

Henry Alting's exposition of the Heidelberg Catechism is quite in the spirit of that glowing evangelical manual; and, being characteristic of its framers, it is more valuable than the Commentary compiled by Pareus from the dry notes which he had jotted down when he attended the lectures of Ursinus. Alting calls special attention to the necessity of studying the original German as being the only authoritative and genuine form of the catechism. In addition to didactic exposition, he has appended to each section controversial questions and answers, one set being against Socinianism, and the other against Arminians, whom he calls the Innovators (Novatores).

PROFESSOR WILLIAM AMES, D.D.

THE incomparable Amesius, author of "Bellarminus enervatus," "Medulla ss. theologiæ," "An analytical exposition of both the Epistles of the Apostle Peter," &c., &c., was professor of theology at Franeker in Friesland, and a star of the first magnitude among Dutch theologians. But he was an Englishman, a native of Norfolk, born in 1576, educated at Cambridge under Dr William Perkins, and Fellow of Christ College in that University. Being opposed to priestly vestments in the church, he was persecuted by Bishop Bancroft and other leaders, and retired to the Hague in 1610. He never returned to England; and being a martyr to asthma he was on the point of emigrating to New England, when death overtook him at Rotterdam, 14th November 1633. (His widow and family sailed to the new world, from whence his son, the second William Ames, came to England, and was one of the good ministers ejected in 1662.)

The first William Ames is mentioned here on account of his book on catechetical doctrine, highly praised by Maresius. He seems to have occupied himself in his exile, in the first place, by translating "Bradshaw's English Puritanism" into Latin, for the information of Dutch Protestants. His attention, probably, in the next place, was attracted by the system of public catechizing in Holland, and by the two catechisms in use—the Heidelberg Catechism, and Calvin's Catechism, *alias*, the Catechism of Geneva. He drew up a book suggesting a scheme of catechetical doctrine, entitled—"The chiefe heads of divinitie, briefly and orderly set down, in forme of catechizing by question and answere," Dordrecht, 1612. As a professor he seems to have taught and lectured on this system; and after his death his notes were collected and published in Latin (dated Amsterdam, 1st January 1635), with the title, "Christianæ Catechescos Sciagraphia."

It is interesting to observe the opening of the Sciagraphia, which combines the Heidelberg *only consolation* with the Calvinian *summum bonum*. The orderly procession of scriptural texts is also remarkable (I quote from the Latin).

Texts.
First Lord's Day.
Psalm iv. 6. There be many that say, Who will shew us any good? Lord, lift Thou up the light of Thy countenance upon us.

Some of the Notes.
1. The chief good is what we ought to regard and to seek above all other things during our whole life.
2. The chief good of man cannot be found in the good things of this life.
3. Our true and chief good consists in the union and communion which we have with God.
4. That joy, which believers take possession of from the communion which believers have with God, excels all human delights and joys in its sweetness.
5. That joy and that consolation bring a certain holy security to the consciences of believers.

Second Lord's Day.
Rom. vii. 7. What shall we then say?—Is the law sin?—Far from it! Nay, I had not known sin, but by the law; for I had not known lust, except the law had said, Thou shalt not covet.

By nature men are so blind that, though evidently plunged in sin and death, they of themselves do not know this.

Third Lord's Day.
Rom. v. 12. By one man sin entered

into the world, and death by sin; and so death has passed upon all men, for that all have sinned.

Fourth Lord's Day.

Eph. v. 6. Let no man deceive you with vain words: for because of these things the wrath of God cometh upon the children of disobedience.

Fifth Lord's Day.

Rom. viii. 3. For what the law could not do, in that it was weak through the flesh, God, sending His own Son in the likeness of sinful flesh, and for sin, condemned sin in the flesh.

1. It is the will of God that miserable men be freed from their misery and restored to life eternal.
2. The law is not able to free miserable men from their misery.
3. No sinner is able to free himself from this misery.
4. No mere creature, existent in heaven or earth, is able to free miserable men from sin and death.

Sixth Lord's Day.

1 Tim. iii. 16. Without controversy great is the mystery of godliness: God was manifest in the flesh, justified in the Spirit, seen by angels, preached to the nations, believed on in the world, received up into glory.

All true godliness depends on faith in this mystery, so that without this faith there is no true and solid godliness, nor can this faith be true and solid unless it have godliness coupled to it.

Seventh Lord's Day.

Acts xvi. 31. And they said, Believe on the Lord Jesus Christ, and thou shalt be saved, and thy house.

1. All are not saved by Christ, but only those who are united or ingrafted into Christ.
2. That bond, by which we are first united and ingrafted into Christ, is faith.
3. The adequate object of faith, as justifying, is Jesus Christ, or the mercy of God in Jesus Christ.
4. Justifying and saving faith properly consists, not in a kind of knowledge, but in a solid and sure trust.
5. Those who truly believe in Christ can, and ought to, be sure of their salvation.

PROFESSOR JEREMIAS BASTING.

THE Bastings were a French Protestant family who had fled to the Netherlands. At the date of the birth of Jeremie Basting (better known as BASTINGIUS), 1554, his parents were in France as refugees from the Netherlands. He was born in Calais; but through his immediate ancestry, although a steadfast Protestant, he had ceased to be French. He studied at Bremen, Geneva, and Heidelberg, and became an eminent classical and Hebrew scholar. He was installed as a Protestant pastor at Antwerp, but his residence there was not of long duration. The military successes of the Duke of Parma drove off and scattered himself and all the Protestant ministers and people. Thus in the year 1585 he became an exile, and retired to Dort. It does not appear whether he settled there or set out upon travels. He employed much of his time in preparing for the press his expository discourses on the Heidelberg Catechism. The exact date of publication I have not ascertained. The book is dedicated, "To my most beloved brethren, fellow-priests, and presbyters, and remaining believers from the dispersion of the Reformed Church of Antwerp, and also to all ministers of the Word in Holland and the Palatinate, who preach in its purity the Gospel of the Eternal Son of God." The *second edition* was published at Heidelberg in 1590, "revised and enlarged;" [In Catechesin Religionis Christianæ, quæ in Ecclesiis et Scholis tum Palatinatus tum Belgii traditur, Exegemata sive Commentarii.] At that date he is simply styled "a minister of the Word of God." But soon after he was made professor of theology at Leyden—which chair he filled till his too early death, in his forty-fifth year, on 26th October 1598. His only publication was the above-named successful and valued manual—each question is illustrated by one paragraph of *exegesis*, and by another of *falsa doctrina*. And to each section of the Catechism are prefixed *Argumenta*, *i.e.*, Contents. To some of the sections there is added USUS, or practical inferences.

REV. WILLIAM BATES, D.D.

WILLIAM BATES was born in November 1625. He was a graduate of Cambridge University, from which he received the degree of D.D. in 1660. Before that date he was a London minister, and he was vicar of St Dunstan's in the West when he was ejected from the Church of England for non-conformity; his farewell sermon was preached 17th August 1662. Dr Bates was always anxious for a healing measure of union. At the Revolution of 1688 he was the acknowledged leader of the Nonconformists, and headed the deputation of congratulation to their majesties, William and Mary. To the king he said, "We humbly desire and hope that your majesty will be pleased by your wisdom and authority to establish a firm union of your Protestant subjects in the matters of religion, by making the rule of Christianity to be the rule of conformity;" and to the queen, "We hope those reverend persons who conspire with us in the main end—the glory of God and the public good—will consent to terms of union wherein all the reformed churches agree." On the death of Mary, he again headed a deputation to the king; he also preached a funeral sermon on the lamented queen. He also preached funeral sermons on Drs Manton and Jacomb, and on the Rev. Richard Baxter, David Clarkson, and Benjamin Ashurst. He spent his last years at Hackney, where he died 14th July 1699, greatly esteemed, admired, and beloved. The immortal John Howe preached his funeral sermon with the motto, "Let us also go and die with him" (John xi. 16). He said of Dr Bates, "I never knew any one more frequent and affectionate in the admiration of Divine grace upon all occasions than he was, as none had a deeper sense of the impotence and depravity of human nature. Into what transports of admiration of the love of God have I seen him break forth, when some things not immediately relating to practical godliness had taken up great part of our time! How easy a step did he make it from earth to heaven!"

The works of Dr Bates were collected in one folio volume, and dedicated by his widow to the king. (The Second Edition is the best.) He also compiled "Vitæ selectorum aliquot virorum."

REV. JAMES BATHGATE.

Mr Bathgate (who was born in 1684) was schoolmaster of Inverkeithing, but was licensed as a preacher 19th October 1715, and was ordained as minister of Orwell 6th March 1717. He was a co-presbyter of Messrs Hog, R. Erskine, and Wardlaw, and sat in the Synod of Fife with them and with Ebenezer Erskine, who said that the special animosity of the Anti-Marrowmen against Mr Bathgate diverted attention from him, during this young minister's career. He was one of the twelve representers. After the Assembly's condemnation of "The Marrow," he continued publicly to recommend this book, and, in consequence, he received a special censure from his synod. He united with Mr Hog in protesting against the appointment of fast-days and thanksgiving-days by the English government, not for the deplorable modern reason that such appointments are an interference with religious liberty, but for the reason, thus expressed by Mr Hog, "That it is the right of the Church of Scotland to appoint days for fasting and thanksgiving within her own bounds, according as her case and circumstances (being a distinct church from that of England) do demand." The reasons were printed, with the following note :—" The foresaid reasons being given in, first to the Presbytery of Dunfermline, and by them referred to the Synod of Fife which met at Kirkaldy, April 1724, the Synod, after reading, did, notwithstanding, declare Mr Hog censurable (*Mr Bathgate having died before the Synod met*) for not observing the thanksgiving." Of "the twelve" the first who died was Mr Bathgate; and on his death-bed he gloried in his testimony to the doctrines of grace, exclaiming, "O glorious cause ! O glorious cause ! I will glorify the Lord in heaven for ever for these precious truths." The day of his death was 30th March 1724 ; he was the father of Rev. James Bathgate, minister of Dalgety.

REV. JOHN BONAR, M.A.

JOHN, son of John Bonar, Esq., of Kilgraston, in Perthshire, was born at Kilgraston, 16th January 1671. His father was a bigoted Episcopalian. When John was a student at St Andrews, his father instigated the Principal to threaten him with expulsion from the university unless he took the communion in the alien Episcopal form. The threat was administered, but without success. A brighter day dawned, and old Scottish presbytery was re-established. John Bonar was licensed as a preacher (15th June 1692), and was ordained as minister of Torphichen, in the presbytery of Linlithgow, on 2d March 1693. In 1715 he preached on the covenant of grace, as absolutely and unconditionally free to sinners, for which he was attacked by Rev. John Lookup, minister of Mid-Calder. Mr Bonar was one of " the twelve " who signed the representation regarding "the Marrow" in 1721, and was altogether in sympathy with those brethren and their friends. In 1742, notwithstanding his age and infirmity, he made a journey to Cambuslang to witness the great revival of religion, and to assist at the dispensation of the communion to the assembled thousands. In his last years, on Lord's days, be was carried to his church on a chair. He died 7th August 1747. He printed a sermon preached at Whitburn 1719, upon the erection of that part of Livingstone into a new parish; also Letters on the duty and advantage of religious societies (Edin., 1743), containing counsels to prayer meetings. His widow survived him for only five days.

DICTIONARY OF WRITERS.

His descendants in the ministry make up a roll of honoured names. The following is the ecclesiastical pedigree:—

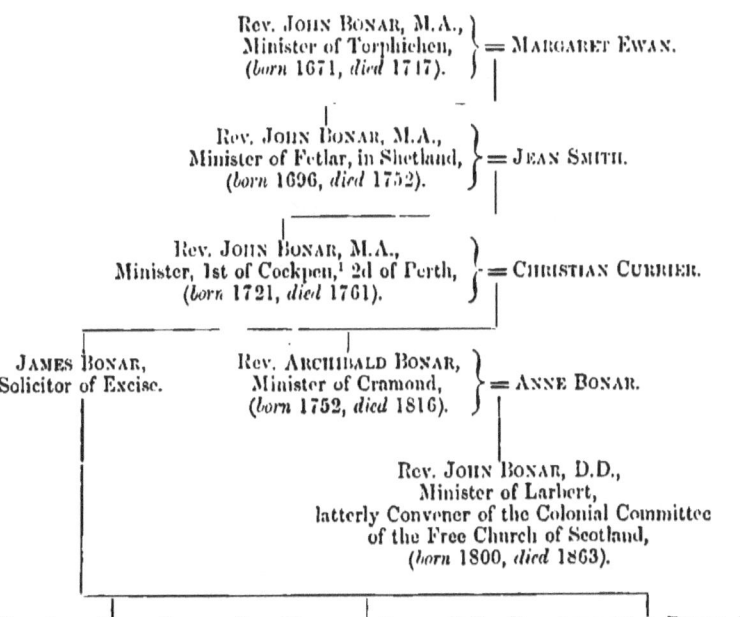

Rev. JOHN BONAR, M.A.,
Minister of Torphichen, } = MARGARET EWAN.
(born 1671, died 1717).

Rev. JOHN BONAR, M.A.,
Minister of Fetlar, in Shetland, } = JEAN SMITH.
(born 1696, died 1752).

Rev. JOHN BONAR, M.A.,
Minister, 1st of Cockpen,[1] 2d of Perth, } = CHRISTIAN CURRIER.
(born 1721, died 1761).

JAMES BONAR,
Solicitor of Excise.

Rev. ARCHIBALD BONAR,
Minister of Cramond, } = ANNE BONAR.
(born 1752, died 1816).

Rev. JOHN BONAR, D.D.,
Minister of Larbert,
latterly Convener of the Colonial Committee
of the Free Church of Scotland,
(born 1800, died 1863).

Rev. JOHN JAMES BONAR,   Rev. HORATIUS BONAR, D.D.,   Rev. ANDREW A. BONAR, D.D.,
Minister at Greenock.   Minister, 1st at Kelso,   Minister, 1st at Collace,
                         2d at Edinburgh.   2d at Glasgow.

In 1813, the Rev. Archibald Bonar, minister of Cramond, "whose spiritual worth and saintly character will not soon be forgotten," wrote to the Rev. Dr Colquhoun, author of a "Treatise on Spiritual Comfort," in the following terms:—

"I am more and more convinced that according to the degree of our spiritual consolation, and the measure of our rejoicing in glorious Immanuel as our all, so will be our steadfastness and progress in all the other graces of the divine life.

"I have often lamented in secret that even the Lord's own children seem so little impressed with the vast importance of rejoicing in the Lord, in the faith of the Gospel, and in the lively hope of purchased, promised, prepared, approaching glory. I rejoice to think that you, dear brother, have been stirred up to set

---

[1] ["John Bonar at Cockpen, though of the High party, was a man of sense—an excellent preacher; he was temperate in his opposition."—ALEX. CARLYLE.]

this important subject in a truly evangelical light. Though I trust you will be long spared to labour, with growing comfort and success, in our Lord's vineyard, yet I rejoice to think that when you and I lie mouldering in the dust, generations yet unborn will read your work with tears of gratitude, and will magnify the God of Zion for your book on Spiritual Comfort.—ARCHIBALD BONAR."
(Quoted in Memoir of Dr Colquhoun, p. 13).

REV. THOMAS BOSTON, M.A.

THOMAS, youngest son of John Boston and Alison Trotter, was born at Dunse, in Berwickshire, on 17th March 1676. Through hearing a sermon at Newton of Whitsome, by Rev. Henry Erskine, late of Cornhill, he was brought under religious impressions, when he was eleven years old. This was in the year 1687. He was educated at the grammar school of Dunse, and went to the College of Edinburgh in 1690. His four years' course in Arts cost him altogether £128, 15s. 8d. Scots, and at the close of it in 1694 he took the degree of M.A.

The Heidelberg Catechism seems at an early period of its existence to have found its way into Scotland, and often to have given a characteristically evangelical tone to the faith and piety of its readers. The English translation was first reprinted at Edinburgh in 1591. This and other editions were superseded in 1615 by a new edition, containing "arguments" and "uses" extracted from the Commentary of Bastingius. The English version, now in use in the Dutch and Reformed churches of America, was brought from Scotland in the eighteenth century. This Catechism must have exercised a most important influence on young Boston's religious thought. He says, "A minister put into my hand Pareus on Ursin's Catechism; the which I read three or four times ere I went to the school of divinity."

He entered the Divinity Hall of the University of Edinburgh about 25th January 1695, where Professor George Campbell taught privately the Theological Compendium by Ryssenius, and publicly that of Essenius. The Presbytery of Dunse and Chirnside licensed him to preach the Gospel on 15th June 1697. He says, "I began my preaching of the word in a rousing strain, and would fain have set fire to the devil's nest. . . . But speaking with Mr John Dysert, minister at Coldinghame, of the strain of preaching I had continued in, he said to me to this purpose, *But if you were entered on preaching of Christ, you would find it very pleasant.*"

In the beginning of 1699, he wrote (but did not print) a "Soliloquy on the Art of Man-Fishing," and on 21st September of that year he was ordained minister of Simprin. On Wednesday, 17th July 1700, he notes, " I, going on 25 years of my age, married Katharine Brown, going on 27, as born February 3, 1674, and baptized, the 22d, Providence having seen it meet for me to order the odds to be on her side." The father of this lady was (the then deceased) Robert Brown of Barhill, in the parish of Culross, who "had been a practitioner in physic." "What engaged me to her (says Boston) was her piety, parts, beauty, cheerful disposition fitted to temper mine, and that I reckoned her very fit to see to my health." The last item was suggested by the constant delicacy of his health.

The frightful abuse of public oaths during the reigns of the Stuarts seems to have impressed a lasting horror on the minds of good men, as appears in Mr Boston's case, who, on being appointed Clerk of the Synod of Merse and Teviotdale in 1701, declined the oath *de fideli administratione*, and the Synod accepted his promise to serve them faithfully and keep their secrets. On the accession to Queen Anne he took the oath of allegiance to her Majesty, but he adds, " Unto this day [1730] I never took another, whether of a public or private nature."

In Simprin, about the year 1700, he borrowed an old neglected book, and afterwards bought it; it was the first part of the "Marrow of Modern Divinity;" it probably "had been brought from England by the master of the house, a soldier in the time of the civil wars." Boston was at that time endeavouring to get scriptural views of the consolation that is in Christ. He had become convinced of the truth of the doctrine, in which *The Marrow* distinctly concurred, that "the sins of believers in Christ, even when not yet actually repented of, do not make them (being in a state of grace) liable to eternal punishment." In friendly conversation he brought many of his co-presbyters to the same mind, arguing thus : " If believers are liable to eternal wrath in the case mentioned, they must be so, either by the law and covenant of works, or by the Gospel and covenant of grace. But they are not so by the first, for believers are dead to it ; nor by the second, for it condemns no man." He says that people observed in his sermons "a certain tincture," " though 'The Marrow,' from whence it sprang, continued in utter obscurity ; but they were acceptable to the saints, neither did brethren [ministers] show disgust of them."

Mr Boston on 1st May 1707 obtained the parish and congregation by which he is known to posterity, being inducted as minister of Ettrick. Here he began the study of the Hebrew language, in which he became so eminently proficient. In 1711 he resigned the synod clerkship, as to his discharge of which office he received the distinguished appreciation of Lord Minto.

In Ettrick Mr Boston was one of a fraternal triumvirate, consisting of himself, and his reverend brethren Messrs Davidson of Galashiels, and Wilson of Maxton. These are the names which the reader of Boston's Memoirs must bear in mind when he reads of "my two friends and I." And they with Mr Hog of Carnock became more and more associated, when the storm occasioned by the reprinting of "The Marrow" rose and raged. The three friends rode together to Edinburgh frequently during this contest, availing themselves of the quiet and coolness of summer nights, and joining in praises to their Redeemer-God.

The doctrines of grace had been insidiously and injuriously assailed by Professor Simson of Glasgow University. And in the General Assembly of 1717 Mr Boston, being a member of the court, protested against the leniency with which the heresiarch was treated. A second sorrow was the Assembly's condemnation of the Auchterarder creed. This circumstance brought Mr Boston into conversation with Rev. John Drummond of Crieff, a minister of the Auchterarder Presbytery. To Mr Drummond he mentioned "The Marrow" and its account of the Gospel offer. Mr Drummond succeeded in buying a copy, which he showed to Mr Webster, who showed it to Mr Hog of Carnock, who prefaced and reprinted it in 1718.

Mr Boston, having as yet printed nothing, was not called to account. But "The Marrow" having been condemned by the Assembly of 1720, he in 1721 drew up a draft of a counter-representation, which was modelled into the famous representation with its twelve signatures.

Mr Boston at this time specially felt the usefulness of "The Marrow" to himself, when he was dangerously ill. He says: "July 1721.—While in my extremity death stared me in the face, the doctrine of 'The Marrow' concerning *the gift and grant,* and 1 John v. 11, accordingly understood, that God hath given unto mankind sinners (and to me in particular) eternal life, whereby it is lawful for me to take possession of it as my own, was the sweet and comfortable prop of my soul, believing it and claiming it accordingly."

It was on the suggestion of "my two friends" that Boston began his "Notes" on "The Marrow." "In the beginning of July 1722 I finished the Notes. . . . which afterwards, in the year 1726, were printed with 'The Marrow,' in the which, out of regard to the authority of the church, I took to myself the name of Philalethes Irenæus, as being my real and sincere design, namely, truth and peace therein. In compiling of these notes I had in view what was extant against 'The Marrow' in the several prints extant at that time. . . . The unacquaintedness with these prints may occasion posterity's judging several of the notes quite needless; but at that time many had been at much pains to find knots in a rush."

He wrote the Preface in the beginning of the year of publication (1726), and issued this standard edition as an instructive monument of "The Marrow" Controversy. As to this good fight for the doctrines of divine grace, he says in his Memoirs:—"Thus ended that weighty affair, by means whereof I received another sensible increase of light into the doctrine of grace, especially as to the gift and grant made of Christ unto sinners of mankind, and as to the nature of faith. In which last my friend Mr Wilson was the most clear and distinct, and my clearness and distinctness therein I owe to him. . . . Moreover, that struggle hath been, through the mercy of God, turned to the great advantage of truth in our church, both among some ministers and people, having obliged both to think of these things and inquire into them more clearly and nicely than before, inasmuch that it has been owned that few public differences have had such good effects. Meanwhile it is not to be doubted but others have, on that occasion, been carried farther to the side of legalism than they were before, and that, through the prevalence of their passions and prejudices, the Gospel of Christ is by this time with many, especially of the younger sort of divines, exchanged for rationalism. So that I believe the light and the darkness are both come to a pitch that they were both far from in this church—of which posterity may see a miserable and a glorious issue."

It would appear that Mr Boston preached for the last time in Ettrick Church on 25th March 1732 on the text, "That there should be time no longer, but the mystery of God should be finished." Unable to go out of doors, he opened a window of the Manse on the 2nd and 9th April, and preached from it to the assembled congregation. These were two short sermons, carefully composed and afterwards printed, on 2 Cor. xiii. 5, "Examine yourselves whether ye be in the faith." He died on Saturday the 20th April, aged fifty-six. His funeral sermon was preached by Rev. Gabriel Wilson, on the 28th, his text being, "He was a burning and a shining light, and ye were willing for a season to rejoice in His light" (John v. 35). His son Thomas (*born* 3rd April 1713) was at that time a student of divinity; but the benefice was kept open for him until he was a preacher, and he was ordained at Ettrick 4th April 1733. [*See* WITSIUS].

The Author of "The Fourfold State" is too well known to require my commendation. His works, having been collected, need not be enumerated. Many seem to have been printed by his reverend son, but of these I name but one, from which I have quoted in my Book First, Part Second, Chapter I., as to which I have this note : "With a view to the preservation of the doctrine of grace in the understanding and heart of the inhabitants of Scotland, an explication of the Catechism was projected by Rev. Thomas Boston of Ettrick, Gabriel Wilson of Maxton, and Henry Davidson of Galashiels. Mr Boston wrote his allotted portion and left it in manuscript; it was printed in 1755."

The printing and publishing of his "Body of Divinity" in three octavo volumes, in the year 1773, brings us down to another generation, as is manifest by the notice on the back of the title-page :—"*N.B.* As the property of this work is vested in John Reid, printer, and William Darling, bookseller, Edinburgh, and their heirs and assigns, by the Rev. Mr Michael Boston, the author's grandson, so they have entered it in Stationers' Hall, in terms of the Act of Parliament of the 8th of Queen Anne, and expect that after this public notice none will presume to invade this their property by reprinting this work or any part thereof, as the doing so will subject them to all the pains of the aforementioned Act of Parliament."

Appended to the imprint of 1755 were sermons on Isa. xxxviii. 19, "The living, the living, he shall praise Thee," &c. (preached in 1727). The following sentences illustrate Boston's own life:—"The mercy of life lies in the business of life, to wit, being serviceable for God in the world. Hezekiah counts that [to be] the great mercy of life. Which speaks (1). A high esteem of God and His service, as men count it a favour to be allowed to serve their prince. (2). An ardent love to Him, as men delight to serve the interests of those they dearly love. This will be to a spiritual man in a spiritual frame the most desirable thing in life—'according to my earnest expectation and my hope, that in nothing I shall be ashamed, but that with all boldness, as always, so now also Christ shall be magnified in my body, whether it be by life, or by death; for to me to live is Christ, and to die is gain' (Philipp. i. 20, 21)."

NOTE.

I have in my possession an autograph letter from Boston thus addressed:—

To
MISTRISS SHIELL at her lodging
in the Castlehill
Edr.

[This widow lady (see HOG) was the sister of Mr Robert Wightman, Lord Dean of Guild of the city of Edinburgh.]

"ETTERICK MANSE, *March* 23, 1732.

"DEAR MRS SHIELL,—Understanding by my son safely come home that you are under indisposition, and judging that you are under some one damp or other, it was very natural to me to express by this my concern in your trouble and cordial sympathy with you. 'Tis not strange that upon the back of your unordinary toil you had this winter, some such indisposition has seised you.

"If you are in the depths, as I apprehend you are, you have been there before, and know by experience all is not lost that is in hazard. Your Pilot is to the fore, and still keeps the direction of the tost ship in His own hand; for what concerns His people He will perfect; and, their deliverances being chain'd together by the bond of the covenant, the deliverance from six troubles is a pledge of deliverance from seven also, and the seventh a pledge of the eight and so on, till the last link come up in the resurrection of the body at the last day. And what tho' you have neither sun, moon, nor star-light in your tempest (though I hope it is not quite so), yet darkness is as the light to your Pilot. Only trust Him the conducting of you. All the generations of the saints have trusted Him with their whole weight for time and eternity. His Father trusted Him with the work of the reparation of His glory injured by sinners. And will not you trust Him? If I should trust you no farther than I see, I believe you would think that I thereby payed you out a very sorry regard. I pray you, do not you treat Christ so, when you have His word, (Joh. iii. 16; Heb. xiii. 5; Psal. ix. 18) (which see), with many others; and tho' you see nothing else without you, or within you, you have in that word all that faith in its own nature requires. And remember, you have Christ in it (Rom. x. 6, 7, 8), *q.d.*, you need neither go up nor go down for Christ, He is in the word of the Gospel. I would not have you raze foundations you laid in accepting God's covenant of free grace, when you was in better condition; do not make light of belying the Spirit of God. Go as deep as you please, and make as narrow a scrutiny as you will, in the causes of the Lord's controversy. Take up as nicely as you can what the Lord is pointing at by the rod; but I say, let alone the foundations, for none but your grand adversary bids you meddle with them in this hour of darkness. I suppose, I did with my utmost application, in my vigor, and full exercise of my faculty, establish myself in a point; then, I suppose my vigor gone, I'm not able to apply myself as formerly to trace it, so it loses its light with me that I had in it at that time. But should not I act like a fool, if therefore I should give up with it? The application is easy.

"Perhaps this is all out of the way. But I hope it can do no harm. What's not seasonable at one time may be seasonable another time. I hear your brother is gone to Newcastle and, by an acceptable letter I lately had from him, expect him here shortly.

"I'm in much distress, chastened with pain, confined to the upper rooms, with difficulty going on two stilts, but, Thanks to my kind Father and Master, hitherto getting out to my work on the Sabbath. My wife is come up to the western room bed. What the issue will be I know not; but matters go on apace in this crazy tabernacle, towards its being laid by for good and all, either in a bed or a grave. I am the Lord's; other choises I desire not to make, but to refer to Him. My love to your children, particularly Lizie. I'l expect no answer but with great respect, continue   D. Mrs. Shiell

"Yor. affectionat humble servt.
"& Brother in Christ Jesus
"T. Boston."

REV. WILLIAM BRIDGE, M.A.

WILLIAM BRIDGE was M.A. of Cambridge and Fellow of Emmanuel College. It is believed that he was a native of that county, and born in the year 1600. He resided at the university from 1618 to 1631, and then removed to Colchester, whence he was soon translated to Norwich, where he was Friday Lecturer of St George's, Tombland, and Rector of St Peter's, Hungate. In 1636 the persecuting system of the Bishop of Norwich (Wren) drove him into exile. Archbishop Laud reported to Charles I., "Mr Bridge of Norwich, rather than conform, hath left his lecture and two cures, and retired to Holland"—to this information the king added the note, "Let him go; we are well rid of him." The desire seems to have been to get rid of all persons of whom the world was not worthy; fifty ministers were censured, suspended, or silenced, for resisting the inroads of semi-Romish superstition. Mr Bridge became the pastor of the English Congregationalists at Rotterdam, where many refugees from Norwich joined his church. In 1642 he returned to the county of Norfolk, and laboured for twenty years as minister of a congregation at Great Yarmouth. He was a member of the Westminster Assembly, and associated with the Independents. In addition to his scholarship and pulpit eloquence, he possessed excellent business habits, and assisted the parliament in a scheme for the general augmentation of ministers' salaries. The black Bartholomew Act drove him from Yarmouth, and the closing years of his life were spent at Clapham, where he preached along with Rev. Dr Henry Wilkinson and Rev. Thomas Lye. He died 12th March 1670, aged seventy.

His works were collected by the Messrs Tegg, and published in London in five volumes in the year 1845, and are well worthy of study. The following is a specimen of his method of preaching :—

"Ask thine own soul these questions—

"I. Whether there be any gain by doubting—whether there is any spiritual gain to be made by doubting? Faith purifies the heart; but doth doubting purify the heart?

"II. Whether there is anything in all the world more pleasing to God than to trust the Lord in and by Jesus Christ, when all comforts are out of view, and when you see nothing but what is contrary to the thing promised?

"III. Whether you must not venture upon Christ at the last—and if you must venture upon Christ at the last, why not now, as well as at the last?

"When a man comes to go over a river, though he ride once and again into the water, and comes out saying, I fear it is too deep for me; yet, considering there is no other way for him, he resolves to venture; for (saith he) the longer I stay the higher the waters will rise, and there is no other way for me, and I must through at last, as good at the first as at the last; and so he doth venture through and is safe. Thus it is here. You must venture upon Christ at the last, there is no other way but by venturing upon Jesus Christ, thou must do it at the last; and were it not as good for you to do it at the first as at the last? Surely the longer you stay the harder you will find it to venture, and the more difficulties will arise upon the work of believing.

"You say now, O but my heart is not humbled, O but I am a great sinner; and should I venture upon Jesus Christ? But will thy heart be more humbled by keeping from Christ, and shalt thou be less a sinner by keeping from Him? No, certainly; but the longer you stay from Christ, the harder work it will be to venture upon Christ at the last. Wherefore if there be ever a poor, drooping, doubting, fearing, trembling heart in all this congregation, know, that I do here in the name of the Lord call out to you and say, O soul, man or woman, venture, venture, venture upon Christ now; for you must come to this venturing work at the last; and, if ever, it is true here, Better at the first than at the last."—*A lifting up for the downcast.* Sermon XIII.

The following is a specimen of his thoughtfulness and acuteness:—

"The more grace one hath, the more he doth see sin; and the more a man sees his sin, the more his own grace will be hidden from his own eyes. Godly men do often measure themselves by metaphors; as sometimes we that are preachers of the word—we fall upon a Scripture metaphor, as where Christ is called a *sun* or *shield* or *bread*, and we run the metaphor off its legs, further than the Holy Ghost did intend; so sometimes we do. So it is with Christians too; they fall upon a Scripture and they run it and themselves off their legs, beyond what the Holy Ghost doth intend. For example, *increase of grace*, in Scripture phrase, is called a growth; now, because a Christian cannot find his own spiritual increase answerable to all outward growth, therefore he thinks that he doth not increase in grace."—*Seasonable truths in evil times.* Sermon I.

REV. JAMES BRISBANE.[1]

JAMES BRISBANE was licensed to preach the Gospel by the Presbytery of Glasgow, February 23, 1693, and was in the same year ordained minister of Kilmalcolm, in the Presbytery of Greenock, having been called on August 8th, and settled on 21st November. He was a member of the General Assembly in 1703, and was sitting beside Mr Boston, minister of Simprin (afterwards famous as Boston of Ettrick), when the Royal Commissioner prematurely dissolved the Assembly as a

[1] Dr. Scott always calls him "Birsbane."

token of displeasure. Protestations were loudly made by many members, but, says Boston, " Mr James Brisbane pulled me down when offering to join the protesters." In December 1703 he removed to Stirling, having been translated to the second charge of that town and parish ; and in the end of 1705 he became minister of the first charge. He had not been a preacher of the free scriptural Gospel before his settlement at Stirling; but his intercourse with the eminent Mr Hamilton, minister of the adjacent parish of Airth, was the means of his conversion and the beginning of an earnest Gospel ministry. He was not only highly esteemed, but greatly admired. Boston calls him "the learned and pious Mr James Brisbane," and "a very worthy man." Ralph Erskine, in eulogizing Mr Hamilton, said, "Great Brisbane owned himself his happy proselyte." The "solemnities" connected with a communion season in old Scotland gave the ministers many opportunities of sharing each other's pulpits, and also of making the people of each parish acquainted with all the best preachers in the district. Mr Brisbane became by such brotherly services a very popular minister in Stirlingshire. In the autumn of 1718 he assisted at the communion of "an old worthy man," Mr John Watson, minister of Denny—an incident which is important, as it gave occasion to the publication (against his will) of "A Sermon preached at Denny on Monday the 11th of August 1718, being the Thanksgiving Day after the administration of the Sacrament of the Lord's Supper there," by Mr James Brisbane, minister of the Gospel at Stirling.

"The Marrow of Modern Divinity" was not altogether to Mr Brisbane's taste ; and when Mr Hog and other mutual friends reprinted it, he did not join either in recommending or defending the celebrated book. But the simple preaching of the free Gospel exposed a minister to suspicion in high quarters; and his reputation as a Gospel preacher, confirmed by his one printed sermon, led to his being summoned in the year 1720 before the General Assembly's committee for purity of doctrine. No proceedings, however, were taken against him ; and the sermon will repay our examination. It was a practical sermon on the text, " Sin shall not have dominion over you, for ye are not under the law, but under grace" (Rom. vi. 14). His teaching was that every "convinced sinner, being sensible of his being a slave to sin and Satan, is to go into a full, free, and freely offered grace, without money and without price; to take, possess, and enjoy the grace of the covenant in order to become holy, with a full faith upon the promises relative thereto, for that end : *holiness is the fruit of faith ; faith is not the product of their holiness.*"

The clauses which I have italicized are very happily expressed, and so is the following description of one danger in a believer's course. Often (he says) "a legal spirit prevails over the real believer, which makes him look more to his own resolutions than to the grace of the covenant, and to lay more weight upon his promises to God to be holy than upon God's promises of making him holy." He refutes antinomianism itself, and the accusation of antinomianism falsely directed against all Pauline preachers, by an interesting exposition of the context (viz., Romans vi. 2-11):—"The Apostle unanswerably refutes this cavil—

"I. By rejecting it with abhorrence. *Shall we sin, because grace abounds? God forbid.*

"II. By demonstrating the inconsistency betwixt justification by faith and this abominable practice, which he does by two arguments—

"(1.) That Christ died not only for the justifying the sinner and removing of his guilt, but for the sanctifying the sinner. And so to whom the value of that death is applied for pardon, the virtue of it will be applied for cleansing—these two never being separated.

"(2.) That the real believer in Christ embraces Him, not only for justification, but also for sanctification and complete redemption from sin—a sure evidence of the solid believer in Christ; and consequently, that such will not abuse the doctrine of grace, as the world does. And in a suitableness to this (*verse* 11) he discovers what these honest souls should (and would gladly) reckon, upon their embracing this doctrine, that they are dead indeed to sin but alive to God through Jesus Christ. Consequently thereupon (vers. 11, 12) he exalts the study of holiness—that they would not give sin any peaceable habitation in their souls, that they would not any more yield thereunto—but that they would yield themselves unto the Lord as those that are alive from the dead. The words that I have read seem to be an encouraging motive pressing this exhortation to holiness, answering an objection of a poor, sensible, believing sinner who may say, *It is useless to desire me to forbear sin, to yield myself to God and my members as instruments of righteousness. Sin is so engrained in my nature, and hath such an ascendant over me, that to me it seems next to an impossibility to obey.* No (says the Apostle); set about the work, for sin shall not have dominion over you, for ye are not under the law, but under grace." "Go out against every known sin and to the performance of every commanded duty, sensible of your own weakness, denied to your own strength and capacity, with faith's entire dependence upon the grace that is in the promises." "Take hold of God's method of grace for holiness, and particularly on Christ as the living Head and quickening Spirit, and in Him the Holy Ghost, as the covenanted Spirit for the application of the virtue of His death and resurrection, for killing the old man and quickening the soul in the way of God."

The reason why the General Assembly's committee looked askance at Mr Brisbane's sermon may perhaps be found in the following paragraph:—

"There is a topic that much prevails, viz., That God accepts of sincerity under the Gospel, instead of perfect obedience. This is ordinarily supported by 2 Cor. viii. 12, 'If there be first a willing mind, it is accepted according to what a man hath, and not according to what he hath not.'

"I shall not say but in some sense it may be admitted, yet I fear it is very much abused—some making their sincere obedience their righteousness in the sight of God (which is contrary to the Gospel plan)—others thinking the Lord requires no more than what they call sincerity (making the capacity of the creature the rule of his obedience).   . . . .

"As to 2 Cor. viii. 12, the Apostle is discoursing of giving alms to the poor, in which case God requires no more than what He has given them faculty in the world to bestow.   Hence the Lord reckoned the widow's two mites, thrown into the treasury, equivalent if not preferable unto the greater gifts of the rich."

Another question which agitated the members of committee was the alleged necessity for an apprenticeship in the forsaking of sin as a qualification for being a comer to Christ and for being welcomed as such.

Mr Brisbane goes briefly and yet fully into this subject; he says :—

"If any say that we are not, and need not, to part with sin in order to our closing with Christ, and consequently may close with Christ and retain idols too, I humbly conceive the case is misstated.

"For the question is not, If a person may close with Christ and keep his idols, but, If they can part with them, before they embrace Christ and by faith derive virtue from Him for that end.

"And this the Scripture seems to determine (Acts xv. 9), *He purifies the heart by faith.* The soul, by the enlightening cast of grace, sees itself not only condemned but depraved and desperately wicked, and that all its essays [efforts] for peace and for growing better are ineffectual. It now sees Christ made righteousness and sanctification, for the attaining of which it closes with Him.

"This does not say that they [believers] keep their idols when they close with Christ, but finding the power of sin an overmatch for them, they embrace Him as God's remedy, that they may be freed from such an enemy. And so it is a coming to Him, labouring and heavy-laden with the sense of guilt and wickedness that they may have relief—which I take to be the import of Isaiah lv. 7, Let the wicked man forsake his way and the unrighteous man his thoughts—*his ways and thoughts of relief*—and in returning to the Lord he will find mercy and pardon"

The incidental interpretation, which I have italicized, is favourably commented on as "The Denny gloss" by Mr Riccaltoun in his "Review of an Essay on Gospel and Legal Preaching," pp. 68 to 79.

A Stirling minister would be a member of the General Assembly only once in five or six years. Probably, therefore, Mr Brisbane was not a member either in 1718, 1719, 1720 or 1721. He was never an opponent of the Marrow-men, though he took no part in their private conferences. Mr Ralph Erskine says, " I remember a worthy and great divine, Mr James Brisbane, minister of Stirling, when the Act of 1722 was passing, openly asserted that there were not so many errors in that book [*The Marrow*] as in their [the General Assembly's] Acts condemning it." This alludes to the General Assembly of 1722, of which Mr Brisbane was a member, when he probably spoke and certainly voted against an Act explaining and confirming the Act of 1720 condemning "The Marrow." The Act, however, passed by a majority of 134 to 5. Mr Boston says of Mr Brisbane, that he never could go along with the General Assembly in this matter, and ultimately "was obliged to declare himself in favour of truth" (alluding to his vote in 1722). Mr Brisbane lived till June 1725.

REV. JOHN BROWN.

JOHN BROWN, son of an intelligent and pious weaver, was born in 1722 at Carpow village, in the parish of Abernethy (Perthshire). During a brief school life he was taught reading, writing, and arithmetic—"one month at school (he informs us) without my parents' allowance, I bestowed upon the Latin." In 1733, or soon after, he became an orphan and a shepherd-boy, and devoted much of his time to reading good books, and to teaching himself Latin and Greek. The parish minister was Rev. William Moncrieff, who was one of the founders of the Associate Presbytery, and to his ministry over the seceding congregation John Brown adhered, having found in him a faithful pastor and a kind helper in his studies. When he was nineteen years of age the country people, being informed that this country lad was a good scholar in Latin, in Greek, and in Hebrew, accused him of witchcraft; and though the law courts had ceased to receive such accusations, he suffered the penalty of adverse and malignant public opinion for a period of five years. The discomforts of his position led him to become a pedlar, and the year 1745 found him in this occupation. He narrowly escaped plunder from the Highland soldiery. Accordingly he deposited his stock-in-trade in the heart of a peat-stack. Crossing the Queen's Ferry, he enlisted in the Fife volunteers, and did duty with his regiment at Blackness and Edinburgh Castle until the suppression of the Rebellion. He spent all the balance of his pay upon books, except threepence, which enabled him to recross the ferry, and recover his pack.

In 1747 he opened a school at the village of Gairney Bridge, celebrated as the cradle of the first Associate Presbytery, near Kinross. During the vacations he studied philosophy and divinity under Rev. Ebenezer Erskine and Rev. James Fisher; and in 1751 the presbytery licensed him as a preacher. In June of the same year he became minister at Haddington. This town, according to the custom of his church, became the seat of a Divinity Hall in the year 1768, when he was made Professor of Divinity to the Associate Synod. He was an evangelical, pious, and learned professor, who, in addition to the usual learning of a Scottish minister, had a creditable knowledge of Arabic, Syriac, Persic, and Ethiopic, and also of French, Spanish, Italian, Dutch, and German. He was also familiar with literature in various departments. John Brown of Haddington was a name extensively known, as appears, for instance, from his correspondence with Rev. Charles Simeon of Cambridge, Selina, Countess of Huntingdon, and Mr Mason of New York.

He became an author in 1758, when he published "An Help for the Ignorant, being an Essay towards an easy explication of the Westminster Confession of Faith and Catechisms." He is now known as a commentator on the whole Bible, composed on his favourite principle that the Bible is self-interpreting; and as the author of a "Dictionary of the Holy Bible." His work on systematic theology, from which I have quoted in my First Book, is called "A Compendious View of Natural and Revealed Religion" (1782). His last publication, dated 1785, was a pamphlet against the travelling of the mail on the Lord's Day.

The year 1787 found him almost exhausted by the incessant and excessive labours of his life. He solemnly took leave both of his own congregation and of a miscellaneous evening congregation from his pulpit on February 25th, and died on June 9th. One of his last sayings was, "It is the finished righteousness of Christ which is the only foundation of my hopes; I have no more dependence on my labours than on my sins."

His "Essay towards an easy, plain, practical, and extensive explication of the Assembly's Shorter Catechism" was reissued by one of his sons, Rev. Ebenezer Brown of Inverkeithing, "revised and enlarged," in 1830. The following extracts contain his sentiments as to Christian Obedience, and as to a believer's expectation of reward and liability to punishment:—

"Is our serving of God a requital of His redeeming us?

"No. God neither requires, nor can any good works be, any proper requital of such amazing favours; for when we have done all, *we are but unprofitable servants*" (Ps. cxvi. 12; Luke xvii. 10).

"Why, then, doth God require obedience because He has redeemed us?

"That we may thereby acknowledge our obligation to Him for His redeeming grace, and sink deeper in its debt (Ps. cxvi. 12, 13).—Page 198.

"What is believers' obedience, to the law as a rule, rewarded with?

"With much freedom from spiritual plagues, and sweet communion with God here, and additional degrees of glory in heaven (Isa. lxiv. 4, 5).

"Why call you these *fatherly* or *gracious* rewards?

"Because, though they are given to obedient believers, yet they are not given for their obedience sake, but flow from God's fatherly grace and love (Rom. v. 21).

"If it is not for the sake of their good works that believers are rewarded, how is it that the more holy they are the more happiness they receive?

"Because the receiving of much purchased holiness prepares for receiving the more abundant purchased happiness (Dan. xii. 3).

"Is not holiness itself happiness?

"It is the very height of happiness (Ps. xvii. 15).

"Are more diligent and holy believers less indebted to Christ for their happiness than more slothful believers?

"No; they are the deeper in the debt to God's free grace, being first indebted for more grace, and then for more glory (Luke xxii. 28, 29, 30; 1 Cor. xv. 10).

"What mean you by fatherly chastisements?

"All those troubles which believers meet with in this world, after their conversion, on account of their sin (Heb. xii.).

"What are the heaviest of believers' chastisements?

"The terrors of God and hiding of His face, with the occasional prevalency of sin and Satan, which are terrible as hell to the saints (Ps. lxxxviii.; Rom. vii.).

"Why are these called *chastisements* and not punishments?

"Because they tend not to the hurt but to the advantage of the saints (Heb. xii. 6, 10, 11).

"Would it not more effectually stir up believers to obedience if it entitled them to eternal life, and their disobedience exposed them to eternal death?

"No; that would disparage the righteousness of Christ, hinder our improvement of it as the great motive to obedience, and fill us with so much of the spirit of bondage as to disqualify us for gospel obedience (2 Cor. v. 14)."—Page 40.

In the year 1831 his *Second Century* of Meditations was published as a sequel to *Devout Breathings of a Pious Soul.*

John Brown of Haddington has been honourably represented in literature by his *son*, John Brown of Whitburn; by his *grandson*, John Brown, D.D., of Edinburgh, Professor of Exegetical Theology to the United Presbyterian Synod; and by his *great-grandson*, John Brown, M.D., Author of "Rab."

The following is one of the articles in the "Dictionary of the Holy Bible," by John Brown of Haddington:—

"COMFORT—CONSOLATION—inward pleasure, joy, and cheerfulness, natural or spiritual (Job vi. 10; Ps. cxix. 50, 76). Spiritual comfort is that refreshful pleasure of the soul which ariseth from the consideration of what God in Christ is to us in respect of relation, and of what He has done for and infallibly promised to us (2 Cor. i. 5). The Holy Spirit is the author of it; the Scriptures are the established ground and means of it; and ministers and godly companions are the instruments and helpers of it (Job xvi. 7; Ps. cxix. 49, 50; 2 Cor. i. 5,

6, 7 ; vii. 6, 7). Christ is *the consolation of Israel ;* with the prediction of His coming and kingdom did the ancient prophets comfort the Jews; and in every age His person, righteousness, fulness, and love are the source and substance of His people's comfort against every trouble (Luke ii. 25). *Are the consolations of God small with thee?* (Job xv. 11); do you contemn our divine advices which we have given you for your direction and comfort? *To comfort* is to free one from grief and render him glad and joyful (Gen. v. 29). God *comforts the cast down* by supporting them under their trouble, and delivering them from it (2 Cor. vii. 6). The Holy Ghost is called *the Comforter* because, by the application of Jesus' word, blood, and fulness to our soul, He fills us with joy unspeakable and full of glory (John xiv. 26); but the word is by some rendered *Advocate."*

The best edition of the Bible Dictionary (Glasgow, 1833) contains a Memoir and some Notes by the author's grandson, Rev. John Brown Patterson, M.A., Minister of Falkirk (*born* 1804, *died* 1835).

JOHN CALVIN.

JEAN CAUVIN, latinized Joannes Calvinus, was a scholarly Frenchman, a native of Noyon in Picardy, born in 1509. His embracing of the Reformation obliged him to leave France. In 1535 he published at Basle his famous " Institutes of the Christian Religion," dedicated to the King of France, Francis I. ; this work he afterwards translated into French. Merle D'Aubigné claims him as the founder of the Reformed Church of France. In 1536 the Swiss Reformers induced him to become Professor of Divinity and Preacher at Geneva, and he established the Reformation in that community with combined persuasion and determination. But his discipline occasioning some disturbances, he was virtually banished to Strasburg, where he wrote his Commentary on the Romans. In September 1541 he re-entered Geneva in triumph, and continued there till his death in May 1564. He lived to see the end of the Council of Trent, whose proceedings he instructively and vigorously criticised. His doctrine was the doctrine of the free and sovereign grace of God, and was substantially innocent of all peculiarities, although his opponents have devised caricatures which they please to call *Calvinism.* His writings are singularly free from dogmatism and theory. Conscientious students admit the fairness of his numerous commentaries on the Books of Holy Scripture; they are carefully and copiously explanatory, rather than studiously and sternly argumentative.

When the successors of Luther organized a Lutheran party, it became a common artifice to call other adherents of the Reformation *Calvinists*. Thus in Germany and in the Dutch Republic it might be said, Calvin was French by birth, and Swiss by residence; and if you propagate his opinions here, you are supplanting what is native by what is alien, and preferring a foreigner to your own countrymen. The historian Motley, abandoning his usual research, and in the very abandonment relying upon his reputation for impartial investigation, has stooped to this artifice, wearisomely insisting on describing the evangelical faith of the Dutch States as Calvinistic. Not merely does he leave the reader to infer that such a faith was a foreign invasion, but he actually lauds each Dutch Arminian as a patriot standing up against the foreigner.

It requires no research to show that whatever may have been known of the name of Calvin, the man, Calvin, had nothing to do with the internal affairs of the Dutch Church in its contest with Arminius. The Belgic Confession was of home growth. The Belgic Catechism, adopted in preference to the one by Calvin, was the Heidelberg Catechism. Arminius, who was by his own confession, as well as in ecclesiastical estimation, an innovator (his sect being called *Novatores* or *Novantes*), was only four years of age when Calvin died; and the great opponent of the House of Orange, who strangely (perhaps through anti-Calvinistic promptings) is Mr Motley's latest hero, John Barneveldt, was in that year (1564) a youth aged seventeen, Prince Maurice being of a generation then unborn.

I have not made any study of Calvin's voluminous works for the purposes of my present work; but he was a great authority with the writers whom I have been memorializing.

Ebenezer Erskine says: "The assurance I speak of—namely, a persuasion of the promise with appropriation (as the judicious Calvin speaks)—can no more be separated from faith than light can be separated from the sun."

One of the Prefacers of "Wilson's Christian Dictionary" (1611) writes: "It is a special duty of a good teacher to know and deliver the sound and fit sense of the places and texts of Scripture . . . . In this behalf, how much the Church of God is beholding to that learned, judicious writer, Mr Calvin, all that are learned do well know and willingly confess. For when he meets with a place wherein he seeth men have made scruples, he doth in the end (after sifting the matter) strike the nail full on the head with his resolute SENSUS EST—*this is the sense and meaning of the place.*"

REV. THOMAS COLE, M.A.

THOMAS, son of William Cole of London, gent., was educated at Westminster Public School, and was thence elected student of Christchurch, Oxford, where he graduated B.A., 6th November 1649; M.A., 8th July 1651. In 1656 he became Principal of St Mary's Hall, Oxford; and losing this dignity in 1660, he founded a private academy at Nettlebed, Oxfordshire. His final residence was in London, where he became minister of a large congregation of nonconformists, and a frequent lecturer on Gospel themes. He published—

1. A Discourse in the Morning Exercise, on Luke iii. 5, 6, How we may steer an even course between presumption and despair.
2. A Discourse of Regeneration, Faith, and Repentance, preached at the Merchants' Lecture in Broad Street. 1689.
3. Sermon on Ephesians i. 19, 20—(in the Morning Exercise).
4. Funeral Sermon for Mr Edward West.
5. A discourse of Christian Religion in Sundry Points, preached at the Merchants' Lecture in Broad Street. 1692.
   (1.) Christ in us the Hope of glory.
   (2.) What it is to know God in Christ.
   (3.) Christ the only Saviour of His people from sin.
   (4.) Christ the great Redeemer of body and soul.
   (5.) Christ the only Mediator of the New Covenant.
   (6.) Christ the Foundation of our Adoption.
   (7). The necessity of preaching Christ.
6. The Incomprehensibleness, by human reason, of Imputed Righteousness for justification.

Mr Cole was a champion of the Gospel of free grace and a powerful comrade of Mr Robert Trail of London. He preached and wrote against "those who make previous conditions performed by themselves the ground of their faith in Christ for pardon." He protested to them and to all, that "the bare offer and tender of grace, made to sinners in the Gospel, is sufficient to give *them* a title to it *who thankfully accept the offer*, though they come without money, have no righteousness of their own to make way for them—coming, as they are, in their nakedness and poverty—casting themselves upon Christ for all—looking for acceptance only in the Beloved."

He was seized with fatal illness in 1697, and died in September of that year. On his death-bed he was visited by Mr Trail. The two friends conversed pleasantly about the imputed righteousness of Christ. Mr Trail said, "Have you then no kind of repenting that you gave occasion for the contention there has been about this doctrine?" Mr Cole exclaimed, "Repenting? No; I repent I have been no more vigorous in defending those truths in the confidence of which I die. If I desire to live, it is that I may be more serviceable to Christ in defending His name in the pulpit." Mr Trail continued, "We desire, Sir, to know the peace and comfort ye have from those truths as to your eternal state." "They are my only ground of comfort," Mr Cole replied; "death would be terrible indeed if it were not for the comfortable assurance faith gives me of eternal life in Christ, and were it not for the abundant flowing in of that life—not what I bring to Christ—but what I derive from Him." A long account of his dying conversations both with Mr Trail and with other persons may be studied in Palmer's "Calamy's Nonconformists' Memorial," vol. i., p. 250.

Referring to the list I have given of his publications, it is refreshing to see such a *Christian* exposition of *Christian Religion* in the volume of 1692. From it and from the volume of 1689 I give a very few extracts:—

"Did we live more by faith in Christ Jesus, we should quickly see how all good works rise out of that faith by which all true believers are already justified. All *that antinomianism* that the orthodox preachers of free grace are falsely charged with, lies here—because they maintain (and, I hope, ever will maintain) that the first thing a convinced sinner is to eye, in his turning to God, is the free grace and mercy of God in Christ for the pardon of sin.

"Evangelical conviction leads him to a reliance upon Christ, in some degree of saving faith, for the pardon of all his sins; and this faith begets in him a secret hope of pardon, and is the sprig of all *after sanctification*—viz., of mortification of sin, of repentance, and of all new obedience. Let this be remembered as the main thing we contend about—that we begin our religion at the grace of God, and [do] not think to ground our faith in Christ upon any legal preparations or works of our own."—Page 247 (1692.)

"Brethren, in common acceptation, when we say, *Come to me and I will do this and that for you*—pray, who is the doer?—he that comes to have the thing done? or he that doth it?

"Certainly if *coming* be a service, in this case, it is a service done to a man's self, and can never be urged as a service done to God.

"But they further say that this is *a conditional service.*

"Why?

"Because God has commanded us to believe that we may be justified.

"*Commanded us to believe!* And, pray, what is that? I told you before the meaning of an act of faith—even to renounce our own righteousness, to come in our nakedness and poverty to Christ—without money, or without money's worth—that we may be enriched by Him in all things. Is not this the old, honest, plain, down-right notion of believing?

"And is this the conditional service required? Why don't you do it then? Who is against it? ... Hath God required us to *believe in Jesus?* Let us know what He means, and do it; nobody is against it.

"If that be the conditional service, let them lie low before God, and seem more vile in their own eyes, and cast themselves upon Christ for all. Let them learn to come without money. This is the proper *obedience of faith*—that obedience which the doctrine of the Gospel doth require. And since you will call this *a condition*, I say, Why don't you perform it?

"Is this the performance of such a condition, according to the sense and meaning of *believing*—to tell the world that Christ is *not* our only justifying righteousness—that we must seek for something in ourselves to join with Him —if ever we will be saved? Is this the condition? Doth God mean this when He bids me believe in Jesus?

"Sirs! let us not read our Bibles backwards—wresting Scripture to our own destruction. It is strange to me that faith, which is all along in Scripture opposed to works in our justification, and is appointed by God to shut all good works out of justification, should be thus made an inlet to bring all good works into justification."—*Treatise of Faith,* page 65 (1689.)

"The doctrine of faith and the doctrine of good works are both very sound Christian doctrines, agreeing very well in their proper place and order. As no man can enter into a state of grace by good works, so no man can conclude himself to be in a state of grace without good works. 'Tis one thing to prove that I am already in a state of grace—another thing, to show how a sinner may now enter into a state of grace, and what is first to be done in order thereunto. 'Tis not said, he that worketh, but he that believeth, shall be saved; and 'tis the work of God that we believe; and none but God can bring over the heart of a sinner to trust in Christ; and under such a faith 'tis impossible not to lead a holy life.

"We had need be clear and distinct in our conceptions of these things, since our salvation depends upon our right understanding this point. I say, we had need consider what we mean and how we express ourselves, lest instead of trusting in Christ we trust in ourselves, and drop the Gospel whilst we seem to maintain it."—Page 395 (1692).

"There is much preaching and much hearing in this city, but what comes on't? Truly if faith does not come, nothing comes that will turn of any good account to you. The apostles in the primitive times so spake that many believed (Acts xiv. 1); with that evidence and power their words had a special accent in the ears and hearts of those that heard them. God gave a signal testimony to the word of His grace; then fear came upon every soul (Acts ii. 43). Those who were not savingly wrought upon were greatly astonished at the doctrine of the

Gospel. 'Tis otherwise now. How little of this astonishment does appear in our assemblies! Where is this fear that came upon every soul? 'Twas short of faith; yet I am persuaded, when faith comes in some open eminent conversion, that the whole assembly is usually struck with some present fear. The Word comes like a mighty rushing wind into the congregation—shakes all, when 'tis about to convert one. Something like this may be observed in the Acts of the Apostles and other passages in the New Testament. It is fit that grace should be solemnly attended, when it goes forth to the public conversion though but of one soul. If God intends the coming of faith into any of your hearts this day, HE'll come along with HIS work. He will prepare the way, He'll bless your hearing, and speak something inwardly to you from Himself, that shall incline your hearts to believe the Gospel. Though God speaks by the ministry of man, yet His voice is distinct from ours, and begins where that ends, carrying the word from the ear to the heart, there leaving it under those mixtures of faith that make it work effectually. Hear, I beseech you, with diligence, lest you obstruct the coming of faith by not attending to what shall be spoken to you in the name of the Lord. 'So then faith cometh by hearing, and hearing by the word of God' (Rom. x. 17)."—*Discourse of Faith*, page 4 (1689).

REV. JOHN COLQUHOUN, D.D.

JOHN COLQUHOUN, the son of a small farmer in the parish of Luss, was born 1st January 1748. His school education was received in the school at Muirland, belonging to the Society for propagating Christian Knowledge in Scotland. The master, as a faithful servant of the Society, laboured for the elementary English education and true Christianization of his pupils. It was through his catechetical examinations and personal applications of the answer to the question, "What is effectual calling?" that John Colquhoun was converted. He also recommended him to read Boston's "Fourfold State," and John walked to Glasgow and back (altogether a journey of fifty miles) and bought the book. A neighbouring farmer strongly advised him to study for the ministry. After mastering the rudiments of Latin, John became a student of Glasgow University in the year 1768, at the age of twenty. His zeal for a thorough preparation for the sacred office led him to spend ten years in Glasgow, and another year at Edinburgh University. He was licensed as a preacher by the Presbytery of Glasgow 2nd August 1780. He was ordained on 22nd March 1781 minister of the New

Kirk (afterwards called St John's Church) in Leith. He was by this time a ripe scholar and an experienced man and Christian. His was the life of a diligent and successful minister, a valued friend and correspondent, and a public-spirited citizen. His reputation obtained for him the degree of D.D. from the Marischal College and University of Aberdeen in November 1811.

It was at the age of sixty-five that Dr Colquhoun became an author, by publishing "A Treatise on Spiritual Comfort," Edin., 1813. The success of this essay led to frequent successive publications, viz. : "A Treatise on the Law and the Gospel," 1st edition, 1816 ; 2nd edition, 1819. "A Treatise on the Covenant of Grace," 1818. "A Catechism for the instruction and direction of young communicants," 1821. "A Treatise on the Covenant of Works," 1821. "A view of saving faith from the sacred records," 1824. "A view of evangelical repentance from the sacred records," 1825. "A Collection of the Promises of the Gospel, arranged under their proper heads, with reflections and exhortations deduced from them," 1825.

In his sermons and writings Dr Colquhoun was a disciple (as he had been in boyhood) of Boston of Ettrick. His most original work was the "Treatise on Spiritual Comfort," 1st edition, 1813 ; 2nd edition, 1814 ; 3rd edition, 1822.

He preached his last sermon on 18th November 1826, but he survived in feebleness of body, though strong in faith, until 27th November 1827. He nearly completed his eightieth year.

In 1836, a very brief memoir, introducing a volume of his sermons, was published. The following is a paragraph from his Sermon on Justification :—

"Faith does not justify as an act or work ; for in the article of justification it is distinguished from works. But it justifies—

"(1.) RELATIVELY. A sinner is not said to be justified for faith, but only by faith. Faith justifies in relation to Christ and His righteousness—justifies as it is a bond of that union with Jesus Christ, upon which the believing sinner has communion with Him and His righteousness.

"(2.) INSTRUMENTALLY. It, and no other grace, is the instrument appointed in the eternal covenant for applying the righteousness of Christ to the conscience. It is the very office of faith to appropriate and present this glorious righteousness as the only ground of title to justification. As the hand is said to nourish, because it is the instrument of applying food to the body, so faith justifies as the hand or instrument of applying the Redeemer's righteousness to the soul.

"(3.) OBJECTIVELY. It is not the act but the object—it is not faith itself, but the righteousness which it appropriates and on which it relies—that justifies. A sinner is justified before God, not by the act of receiving, but by the righteousness received. When we read in Scripture that the faith of the believer is counted to him for [1] righteousness, the meaning is not that the act but that the *object* of faith, is so accounted to him—the righteousness on which it relies as accounted, in law, his righteousness. It is usual in the Scriptures often to put the act of the mind for the object on which it terminates. In 1 Tim. i. 4, Christ is called our hope, that is, the object of our hope. In Heb. vi. 18, believers are said to lay hold upon *the hope* set before them, that is, the object of hope. When believers, then, are said to be justified by faith, the meaning is, by the object of faith; and faith is said to be counted for righteousness, it is the object of it which is so counted. Add to this—if the believer were counted righteous for the sake of his faith, he might depend on his faith for justification; and then there would be as many righteousnesses as there would be of persons justified. But the righteousness by which many are justified is the obedience of ONE (Rom. v. 19).

"Faith, then, justifies relatively, instrumentally, and objectively. But why is faith, rather than any other spiritual grace, thus said in Scripture to justify? Faith alone has been selected to be the instrument of justification, that the glory of redeeming grace might the more illustriously shine. 'Therefore it is of faith, that it might be by grace' (Rom. iv. 16). It is of the nature of faith, only to receive, but of the other graces, only to give. It is the property of faith never to present itself as a condition, but to receive the spotless righteousness offered in the Gospel as the only condition of a man's justification."

WILLIAM COWARD, ESQ.

THE surname *Coward* was connected with Wiltshire before 1576, the date of the Will of Robert Coward, whose son John removed to the city of Wells, and was the grandfather of William Coward, Esq., Serjeant-at-law, M.P. for Wells (*born* 1635, *died* 1705). The latter had a son, Colonel William Coward, M.P. for Wells, who had an only child, Bridget, wife of Hon. George Hamilton, M.P. for Wells, son of James, 6th Earl of Abercorn. There is a burial place, known as Coward's Chapel, in the parish church of St Cuthbert's, Wells. These details I obtained from correspondents in searching for a pedigree for the founder of the

[[1] I think that scholars might give a fuller solution of the difficulty regarding the sentence "his faith was counted for righteousness," by observing that the preposition "*for*" is not *anti* instead of), but *eis* (with a view to).—D. C. A. A.]

Coward Lecture. But the eminently hospitable and munificent William Coward, Esq., of Walthamstow, as far as genealogists know, began and ended with himself.[1] He made a fortune as a London merchant, and resided in "the quiet village of Walthamstow." He was a truly good man, of active mind, and of no small eccentricity. His wife, who is praised by Doddridge, died before him. In extreme old age he made his extensive grounds remarkable for gardens, canals, and an equestrian statue of William III. He died in May or June, 1738.

His church connection was with the Congregationalists, but he encouraged all evangelical preachers. Three lectureships, founded by him, are remembered through their published lectures. The course on Doctrinal Calvinism, known as the Lime Street Lectures, was preached between November and April, 1730-1. There was another course on *faith and practice*, including worship, preached in 1733 in the chapel of Bury Street, St Mary Axe, which through a bookseller's spelling are known as the Berry Street Sermons. What is known as "The Coward Lecture" was a regular institution, "founded and maintained by the sole generosity" of Mr Coward. It was continued every Friday morning, from the first sermon preached in Little St Helen's, by Rev. Matthew Clarke of Miles Lane in 1725, down to the first sermon preached in Camomile Street, where it took its seat in 1795, and was *left speaking* in 1808. I described its printed volume in my Book First.

Mr Coward, having no child, had intended to found by Will a college at Walthamstow for instruction in the Westminster Theology, under the presidency of Dr Doddridge. But, considering the risk of violating the provisions of the Mortmain Act recently enacted, he refrained from bequeathing his lands for that object. He willed that his whole estate should be turned into money, and founded a trust for educating candidates for the congregationalist ministry, "according to the principles of the Assembly's Catechism." His property, when realised, amounted to about £20,000. His trustees sent their students to Dr Doddridge, and so Northampton became their first academic seat. Their successors sent students to various ministers, holding the requisite doctrines, until 1832, when they opened a theological academy in Torrington Square, London, and named it Coward College. In 1849 Coward College was amalgamated with the other congregational colleges of London, and now survives in work, although not in name, within the walls of New College, St John's Wood.

---

[1] See Wilson's "Dissenting Churches," Vol. I.; "Philip Doddridge," by John Stoughton D.D.; and "Doddridge's Correspondence," Vol. III.

DICTIONARY OF WRITERS.

REV. TOBIAS CRISP, D.D.

Dr Crisp and his writings, apart from much later controversies, belong to the Established Church of England. His popularity with nonconformists, and his unpopularity with ungodly cavaliers and their soldiers, both arose from his being one of the noble army of Doctrinal Puritans. His father was Ellis Crisp, Esq., of London. Tobias was the third son, born in London in 1600, and educated at Eton and Cambridge, leaving his college as B.A. In February 1626 he removed to Oxford and was incorporated as B.A. of that University, and as a member of Baliol College; he proceeded to the degree of M.A. in 1627. In that year he was settled over the parish of Brinkworth in Wiltshire, and for fifteen years discharged the duties of rector of that parish, where (says Anthony a Wood) "he was much followed for his edifying way of preaching and for his great hospitality to all persons that resorted to his house." Having a good share of this world's wealth, and being happy in preaching Christ to his congregation, he refused all promotion, except the degree of D.D. (probably from Oxford). That he had sufficient interest to procure ecclesiastical advancement appears from the case of his brother Nicolas, who was knighted by King Charles I., and was created a baronet by Charles II. in 1665. The occasion of Dr Crisp's removal to London in August 1642, was his fears of "the insolencies of the soldiers, especially of the cavaliers." He had preached "the freeness of the grace of God in Christ to poor sinners" at Brinkworth; and the enthusiastic fervour and vigour of his preaching soon aroused attention in the great metropolis, and the opposition of a great band of theologians. There seems to have been a public disputation where he (according to A. W.) "was baited by fifty-two opponents." His sojourn in the city, though ever memorable, was brief, and reckoned by months only; for he died on the following February 27th, 1642 (old style), but 1643 (new style). A. W. says that the excitement of the theological controversy[1] occasioned his death. Probably bodily and mental exhaustion made him all the more susceptible of the infection of small-pox, to which disease he succumbed. He died in perfect peace with the Saviour of sinners; his last words were, "Where are all those that dispute against the free grace of God, and what I have taught thereof? I am now ready to answer them all."

Although (as has been related) Dr Crisp's preaching, and his sermons posthumously printed, occasioned controversy in his times, yet the great controversy with which his name was connected was in the reign of William III.

---

[1] I am not sure that there was a public disputation. Bishop Bull's biographer says, "Most of the pulpits of London were hotly contesting and fighting about the grace of God and the method of man's justification by it," page 161.

The accusation that he was an Antinomian Divine, or a preacher of the harmony of grace and licentiousness, cannot be maintained by any who have studied either his life or his sermons. The only charge that will hold water is what an excellent writer [1] calls "the fault" of "approaching too near to Antinomianism;" for, as has been said with evident truth, "that he went into real Antinomianism must be denied; his sermons upon *Free grace the teacher of good works*, and *The use of the Law*, with others, abundantly prove the contrary." [2]

Dr Ridgley complains that Dr Crisp was not more cautious in explaining his sentiments, and in carrying out his alleged design of bearing testimony against Arminianism, which in the days of Laud was propagated in England by persons of great influence. He admits that Dr Crisp's practice was far remote from Antinomianism. As to Antinomian doctrines, summed up by Dr Ridgley, the only one with which Dr Crisp is chargeable, may seem to occur in such a sentence as the following:—"All his [a believer's] sins shall be done away; *he shall not receive any hurt at all by them.*" Yet even as to this phrase it can be easily explained that it refers to hurt to the believer's inheritance or patrimony, and not to hurt to his character and moral sense. A prodigal through his father's bountiful provision may have done himself no hurt, in the sense that his inheritance is safe. "The blood of Jesus Christ the Son of God cleanseth us from all sin. And if any man sin, we have an advocate with the Father, Jesus Christ the Righteous." [Not to prolong this biographical article, I refer the reader for this and similar discussions to other memoirs in this work.—*See* RIDGLEY.]

The most favourable impression of Dr Crisp is obtained by examining the opinions advocated in opposition to his, and proposed to be substituted for his. The contrast is all in his favour. Some learned arbiters of the Established Church were unable to perceive any difference between the combatants regarding the righteousness and atonement of Christ, and expressed a suspicion as to the controversy that *there must be something behind it*—some irritating sore not brought to view. There was *something behind*—namely, the encouragement (by one party) and the discouragement (by the other party) of poor sinners going to Christ just as they are. The opponents of Crisp's sermons could state accurately the doctrines and precepts of the Gospel concerning Christ and Christianity; but they offered comfort to the godly only and not to the ungodly. Theirs was a course of instructions for Christian congregations regarded as good people; they had no offers for sinners—no robe for the prodigal—no fountain for the leper. The same question, as old Anthony a Wood had stated it, continued to be agitated in the following generation—namely, the freeness of the grace of God in Christ for poor sinners. And (as a memoir, formerly quoted, truly says) " in

---

[1] Rev. James Anderson, in "The Martyrs of the Bass," p. 229.
[2] "Life of Crisp" (prefixed to an edition of his sermons), by John Gill, D.D.

opposing the opinions of Dr Crisp, they (the opponents) condemned some important truths of the Gospel as Antinomian."

An error of mysterious and alarming sound was charged upon Dr Crisp— namely, the permutation of persons, or commutation of persons. If the perplexed reader inquires with wonder what this heresy can be, a historian tells him, it is "actually to make a Saviour of the sinner, and a sinner of the Saviour."[1] I have read Dr Crisp's sermons (which this historian and his copyists apparently have not), and there is no declaration in them which is as strong as the following by Luther: "Faith without adulteration must be taught, because by it thou mayest be so cemented with Christ that out of thee and Him there may be made one person that cannot be separated, but eternally coheres; that with confidence thou mayest be able to say, *I am Christ*—that is, Christ's righteousness is mine, His victory is mine, His existence is mine, &c. And, conversely, Christ may say, *I am that sinner*—that is, his sins are Mine, his death is Mine, &c., because he adheres to ME, and I to him. We have been joined by faith into one flesh and bone (Eph. v. 30)—we are members of Christ's body, of His flesh and of His bones. This faith unites me to Christ more closely than a husband is joined to his wife. So this faith is not a trifling quality, but its magnitude is such that it obscures and entirely sweeps away those most senseless dreams of sophistical doctrine concerning the satisfaction (atonement) made by inwrought faith and charity, concerning merits, concerning worth or qualities of our own, &c." (Quoted by Seckendorf, Index III., year 1535, in a chronological list of Luther's writings.) Crisp's alleged heresy is thus the Apostle's doctrine that "Christ was made sin," and that believers are "the righteousness of God"—the old scriptural doctrine taught by the Reformers, by "judicious Hooker," &c.—[*See* HOOKER.]

Another alleged heresy was that God the Judge feels no wrath with believers even on account of their sins, and deals out no vengeance upon them. Dr Crisp admitted God's anger against sin, and His fatherly chastisement of believers, so that he said no more than what gospel preachers say now; something both of his thought and energy of speech may be seen in their printed pages, opened almost at random. Who, for instance, would charge Mr Spurgeon with heresy on account of the following passage? "For the Christian there is no stroke from God's angry hand —nay, not as much as a single frown of punitive justice. The believer may be chastised by his Father, but God the Judge hath nothing to say to the Christian except *I have absolved thee, thou art acquitted.* For the Christian there is no penal death in this world, much less any second death."[2] Orthodox doctrine admitted all this before the publication of Dr Crisp's sermons. The doctor startled mere theorizers by his administration of personal consolation, founded upon the old doctrine,[3] but administered to each individual

---
[1] "History of Dissenters," by Bogue and Bennett, Vol. I., page 408.
[2] Spurgeon's "Evening by Evening," July 27.
[3] Afflictiones temporales fidelium non sunt poenae peccati propriè dictae.—MARCKIUS.

inquiring sinner with a freeness and a tenderness altogether new.—[As to the old doctrine, see REYNOLDS.]

It was charged against Dr Crisp as an error, that he denied that faith is the condition upon which the Lord Jesus Christ accepts a sinner, and that he considered this denial to be essential to the truth that salvation is unconditional. In sermon VI., "The New Covenant of Free Grace," he enlarges upon the axiom, *Faith is not the condition of the covenant.* To meet the charge of heresy, it is sufficient to say as to gospel preachers, that although some may approve of the word *condition*, all agree in condemning the thing that Dr Crisp had before his mind. It is only a question of phraseology; [see CROSS]. But if any readers suspect that there is an error, Dr Gill has undertaken Dr Crisp's defence; [see GILL].

The conclusion is that Dr Crisp was bent upon proclaiming the truth, that consolation is the first aspect of Christ's gospel; and that this gospel is for a sinner, for all comers, "any man," "whosoever will." He had eternal truth on his side; and, both as a preacher and an author, he had success in his labour. The great Dr Twisse,[1] President of the Westminster Assembly, said to the Rev. Christopher Fowler : " Having read Dr Crisp's sermons, I can see no reason why they have been opposed, except that so many souls were converted by his preaching, and so few by ours."

Dr Crisp once preached by appointment "before the honourable House of Commons assembled in Parliament." There he boldly declared the same gospel that he preached at home. It was a fast-day, and his theme was that " men's own righteousness is their grand idol." His text was a portion of the Apostle Paul's animadversions upon his own nation : " They being ignorant of God's righteousness, and going about to establish their own righteousness, have not submitted themselves to the righteousness of God." He said to the honourable members, " The Jews were not so easily misled, as we are apt to follow them having gone before us ; we are like sheep, leaping without looking, if any leap before us." *The righteousness of God,* spoken of in his text, Dr Crisp defined to be the righteousness of Christ; because (he said) " the righteousness that God aims at is a perfect righteousness, a righteousness that reaches to the very end of the law ; *your* righteousness can never reach to the end of the law, it is Christ's alone that doth." In explaining the special theme of his sermon, the preacher said : " When we put upon our own righteousness that which should have been put upon God's only—when we make our own righteousness the sanctuary and refuge that only God's righteousness should be—then our righteousness is set up as a grand idol. . . . If we expect that our own righteousness should bring down a gracious answer from God to our spirit—that, when we have done our work, our righteousness must, in effect, be our mediator and messenger from God, and as our righteousness will speak, so shall we either have peace or remain in bitterness of spirit—what can the righteousness of God Himself do more than this?"

[1] For information regarding Dr Twisse, see Colonel Chester's " Westminster Abbey Registers," page 140.

REV. WALTER CROSS, M.A.[1]

WALTER CROSS took the degree of M.A. at a Scotch University, and he also studied in Holland. In 1675 he became pastor of the Independent Church of Ropemakers' Alley, Moorfields, London. He took refuge from the troubles in England in 1685 in Utrecht, and preached there, along with John Howe and Matthew Mead. He returned to his London church in 1689, and died in 1701. He was an intimate friend of Mrs Elizabeth Gaunt, whom King James burnt at the stake, and of her sister, Mrs Constancy Ward, of East Smithfield, London, though he was not a Baptist like them. He preached the funeral sermon of the latter on 7th April 1697, and a friend contributed an acrostic.[2] In this sermon, which was printed with the title, *Caleb's spirit paralleled*, he gave indications of his extensive and accurate Hebrew scholarship, of which there is a perpetual remembrance in his substantial book published in 1698, called "The Taghmical Art;" [the art of expounding Scripture by the Hebrew Accents].

Before 1694 he published a tract (price sixpence) entitled, "A Compend of the Covenant of Grace;" also a Discourse on Romans iv. 1. In 1694 he brought out a quarto volume of 166 pages on Romans iv. 2; iii. 17. But he is memorialised here on account of his pamphlet (of 66 pages) published in 1695, and occasioned by Dr Crisp's Sermons, which was entitled, "The *instrumentality* of faith asserted, proved, explained—compared with and preferred to a *conditional relation* thereof (in order to pardon and happiness) when strictly taken in a legal or fœderal sense."

The conclusion of his volume of 1694 is: "We may say with the old Rabbins, *When the Messias comes, He will solve all doubts*. His coming in here [in the interpretation of the phrase 'the law of faith'] removes all these diffi-

[1] See Wilson's "London Dissenting Churches," Vol. II.

[2] C an those who have surviv'd the bloody rage
   O f *Charles* and *James*, acted on Britain's stage,
   N eglect to drop their tears upon this stone,
   S ince underneath doth lie the dust of one
   T hat, while alive, took pleasure to supply
   A nd hide such as escap'd their cruelty?—
   N o difference in judgment from her own
   C ould ever lessen her compassion;
   I t flow'd to all alike; Scots Exiles were,
   E qual with English, objects of her care.
   W isdom and knowledge, zeal and charity,
   A dorn'd her life; now let her memory
   R emain to future ages; let her praise
   D etermine thee to imitate her ways.

["When the ship of exiled Scots came into this river she, with others, carried them provision, and showed to them other kindnesses, even to their redemption." *Sermon*, page 45.]

culties [as to boasting being excluded thereby]. For [the fact] that we are not justified by our own righteousness, but [by] HIS—by a law wrought out, not by us, but by Him, and proposed to our faith—removes all boasting, establishes the law, glorifies God, saves the sinner. And it is considerable, that the first dawning of the gospel entirely placed the equity in the change of *persons*—'the seed of the woman shall bruise the head of the serpent'—that HE should have His heel or humanity bruised, suffer the curse of the law, and HE should bruise and trample on Satan's headship, free us from his sinful drudgery by His royal power. Lord hasten His kingdom of light and love."

As to his Pamphlet, his text was Hebrews xi. 1. He says: "Faith is an instrument (so Dr Owen and others before him) of substantiating *hoped-for* things and evidencing things unseen. Others think that the word *foundation* (or, principle) may be understood. . . . Yet they mean an instrumental foundation, such as planks in sandy or moorish ground. Our hopes are liable to many infirmities, waverings, and doubtings; but faith is a pillar that underprops. Hopes of heaven without faith to support them are vain. . . . Article XI. of the Church of England says, ' That we are justified by faith only is a most wholesome doctrine, and very full of comfort, as is more largely expressed in the Homily of Justification.' The which Homily says, 'It's not the act of faith that justifies—that were by some act or virtue that is within ourselves.'"—Page 7.

The author explains his title-page to this effect:—That in the economy of salvation faith bears the part of an instrument is a very discriminating doctrine. Socinians, Arians, and Papists, however they differ about explaining its conditionality, agree in the thing, that faith is, properly and in a law-sense, a condition. Protestants, on the other hand, say, if condition be taken so largely as to signify connection, priority, or instrumentality, faith may be called a condition, *but not otherwise.*—Page 6.

The Pamphlet shows the obscurity and inconvenience of the word "condition" in preaching the Gospel, because it is a word that naturally suggests "a law-sense." He explains faith to be "a luminous instrument" resembling *the eye* in the human body, and *reason* as to sublunary matters.

"Faith is a most excellent telescope; we can see through all the heaven of heavens by it; we can see from eternity to eternity by it. Abraham's aged eye could see Christ's day afar off, and Moses could see Him who is invisible. . . . . It's the only instrument we can savingly see or know a God by. It may be left among the Problems of Divinity, whether saving faith and heavenly vision differ in kind, or in degree only. The Apostle explains 'Now abideth faith' thus, that when perfection comes, that which is in part perishes. Vision is faith in perfection, they differ as the seed and tree; faith here is a grain of mustard seed in comparison of that vast tree as it is in perfection. No grace perishes; all the good work wrought in the soul is to be perfected, not destroyed; he that hath begun a good work will perfect it unto the day of Christ. But this is certainly supposed, that there is another way of seeing than by faith, and that there are some means we can see other things by that are not faith's peculiar object ; for it's reckoned faith's excellency to evidence and demonstrate what other means cannot reveal or discover."—Page 24.

The Pamphlet concludes by showing that any *term of art*, being more or less metaphysical, must describe divine things more or less obscurely—but maintains that among terms of art, "an instrument" is the most proper term to define faith's influence in the soul's salvation, especially as the Scriptures declare, *It is of faith that it might be by grace* (Rom. iv. 16). The general nature of an instrument is a passive fitness to subserve an end—"a Magnifying Glass, or Prospective, has not greater fitness to help our weak eye, than Faith our weak understanding."—Page 62.

Although offered to controversialists for study, the Pamphlet is not controversial. But I find in the volume of 1694 an allusion to the notion that faith is obedience to a new law, and that all who do not acknowledge a new law in the New Testament are Antinomians. Mr Cross turns the tables upon the champions of this notion by showing how it has led men into actual Antinomianism :—" This doctrine opens a door to Antinomianism, and history tells us it [Antinomianism] sprung from such a mistake that faith and repentance were taught and commanded by the Gospel, and they contained all [that was] necessary to salvation, so the law was needless."—Page 165.

The Dedication of the Pamphlet is interesting to genealogists.

" To the truly honourable and nobly accomplished Sir John Thomson, Kt. Baronet, patriot of his country and chief of his family.

" To the right honourable lady My Lady Frances Thomson, daughter to the late Earl of Anglesea, a consiliis sacris et sigillo privato Caroli II. Regis.

" To the much respected and renowned William Thomson, Captain, and his beloved consort Katharine Thomson, daughter to the late famous general, Lieutenant-General Drummond.

" To all the honourable and honest families of that numerous, ancient, and honest name of Thomson, especially the branches of the four famous merchants and brothers in the city of London.

" Grace, Mercy, and Peace."

A separate paragraph is devoted to each of the first three. The fourth runs thus :—

" GENTLEMEN,—There is no name better known to me than yours ; some in Scotland very ancient families, if the antiquaries' rule be true, your name is older than the use of surname—some in the north of England very numerous, in Germany some soldiers of great valour—some Divines of great learning in Scotland and England—four noted writers at one time—some merchants of great riches as the four famous brothers, Mr Maurice, the Colonel, Sir William, and the

Major, who found the stone their father in vain sought long for. But though neither divinity nor morality consist in names, I never observed any name, that uprightness and integrity did accompany with fewer exceptions and generally a love to religion, than the name of Thomson. But as there is a name better than the name of sons and daughters so than this of yours—to be sons of God, called by his name and callers on it—that this may be more generally your privilege, and that this small treatise of the feu of heaven, the fee of felicity, the hold of happiness, and tenure of eternity, may contribute to entitle you to this inheritance, and give you comfortable evidence of it, is and shall be prayer of Your Minister in Gospel Service, WALTER CROSS."

REV. WILLIAM CUDWORTH.

MR CUDWORTH was for many years the pastor of a Congregational Church in Norwich. His little work, entitled "Aphorisms concerning the Assurance of Faith," is valuable, and has been constantly reprinted. Though not at all extreme, he was viewed, and almost disliked, as a Calvinist by Wesley; but Whitefield was his friend, and visited him at Norwich. His great friend and correspondent was the sainted James Hervey, at whose rectory he was a frequent visitor. Their correspondence began in 1755, "when (says Mr Cudworth) I perceived by his first edition of 'Theron and Aspasio' that he had so publicly espoused the truths for which I had incurred the displeasure of many of his professed friends and admirers, I wrote him signifying my fellowship with him in the despised truth." Mr Cudworth gave great assistance in revising "Theron and Aspasio" for a new edition. With regard to the "Aphorisms" Hervey wrote to him in 1757: "If I should be able to publish a fourth volume of 'Dialogues,' I propose to have one conference on the assurance of faith—to state it more clearly and to establish it more strongly. In this I shall be glad to borrow several of your thoughts, and will make my acknowledgments accordingly, declaring at the same time my opinion of the piece which lends me such valuable assistance." Ten days before Mr Hervey's death, he received a line from him : " December 15 [1758]. Dear Mr Cudworth, I am so weak I am scarce able to write my name. J. HERVEY." During the last years of his life Mr Cudworth was pastor of a chapel in Margaret Street, Oxford Road, London, in which city he died in the year 1763, " in the comforts of the doctrines of grace, leaving behind him a character for eminent holiness and integrity" (says Lady Huntingdon's biographer).

REV. HENRY DAVIDSON, M.A.

HENRY DAVIDSON, only son of a gardener in the parish of Eckford, near Kelso, was born in 1687. His father, observing his talents and early piety, sent him not only to the parish school but also to the University of Edinburgh. At the close of his literary curriculum he took the degree of M.A., 27th April 1705. Thereafter he pursued his theological studies, and was licensed as a preacher by the Presbytery of Jedburgh 5th March 1712. The congregation of Galashiels gave him a unanimous call on 10th August 1714, and he was ordained over that parish by the Presbytery of Selkirk on 21st December following. He is chiefly known as the intimate friend of Boston of Ettrick and Wilson of Maxton. By the former he is eulogized as " a man of great gravity, piety, and tenderness— learned and judicious—well acquainted with books—a great preacher, delivering in a taking manner masterly thoughts in an unaffected elevated style—endowed with a gift of prayer in heavenly oratory beyond any man that ever I knew—extremely modest and reserved in his temper, but a kind and affectionate friend." In 1721 Mr Davidson signed the representation against the General Assembly's Act of 1720 on " The Marrow," and shared in the ecclesiastical persecution. He was a great sufferer from bad health, and he also deeply felt his family bereavements, as to which he wrote in 1755 : "I have often known the heart of a mourner by means of the loss of three of my nearest relations, and the removal of several of my most intimate friends." He married, on 23rd February 1727, Katharine Scott, a lady of a very respectable family in the neighbourhood, but she died in child-bed on the 6th day of the February following. On 27th February 1732 he preached a funeral sermon on his mother from the text Daniel xii. 13, " But go thou thy way till the end be: for thou shalt rest, and stand in thy lot at the end of the days." In May of the same year Boston died ; his other special friend, Wilson, survived till 1750. It was in 1732 that the flood of subserviency to lay-patronage and to the domination of the world over the church set in with vehemence. Mr Davidson did not join with Ebenezer Erskine and his section of the Marrow-men, when they formed an Associate Presbytery outside of the Establishment. But the severe measures pursued against the Seceders certainly increased Mr Davidson's irritation against the Presbyterian Church Courts of his day. And the result was that he, with his friend Wilson, adopted the principles of the Independents, and formed a small Independent congregation at Maxton (numbering twenty-four members), to whom they preached and administered the Lord's Supper on Sabbath evenings. Mr Davidson offered to resign his parochial charge, but the Presbytery requested him to retain it;[1] the only actual irregularity was that he ceased to administer the Lord's Supper in the parish church. Mr Davidson thus resided and did the other duties of the charge, as far as health would permit, until his death on 24th October 1756, aged sixty-nine. He was (said the *Scots Magazine*) the last liver of the twelve ministers, commonly called *the twelve apostles.*

In 1811 there was published a volume of his "Letters to Christian Friends." One of his letters, which is on consolation under bereavement, has the following sentences:—

"Providence sends afflictions as so many workmen to make the crown more massy and bright; *they work for us* (2 Cor. iv. 17)."

"We know that all things work together for good to them that love God; *we know*—we don't guess and conjecture so; we have an infallible assurance of it (Rom. viii. 28)."

"Something remains to the saints when they have lost all they can lose. He has more remaining than what he loseth. All created things here are by a lease: we have a lease of relations, friends, and other earthly things for so many years; and when that time expires, then we must part with them. The movables are gone; but the inheritance, Christ with His grace and glory, remains for ever to the heirs of heaven: it cannot be taken from them. There is not only an overbalancing fulness, but a direct supply in Jesus Christ for all thy losses, to fill up the blank made by Providence."

It is generally stated that Mr Davidson left no sermons behind; but Dr Scott mentions two publications: "The fulness of the Godhead dwelling in Christ," a sermon; "Dark Providences to be admired, not curiously pried into," two sermons. These I have not seen, and therefore have made the following extracts from the note-book[2] of one of his hearers:—

"Looking to Christ's sufferings without taking a look of our own sins is no better than looking to a crucifix.—(26 Aug. 1717).

"Believing communicants, it is possibly midnight with some of you, but even in that case, cast not away your confidence. It is the time of your Friend's coming. He comes at midnight, when all is darkness within and without; when

---

[1] Personal respect and weariness of strife may account for the Presbytery's forbearance. But when the Church of Scotland became harsher towards the founders of an opposition Presbytery, it became lenient towards Congregationalists. The General Assembly of 1739 took off the sentence of deposition pronounced upon Mr John Glas, minister of Tealing, in 1730, for holding the principles of Independency, and restored him to the character and exercise of a minister of the Gospel of Christ; but declared that "he is not to be esteemed a minister of the Established Church of Scotland, or capable to be called and settled therein, until he shall renounce the principles embraced and avowed by him that are inconsistent with the constitution of this Church."—*Scots Magazine*, Vol. I.

[2] John Blackhall's MS. Volume, in Edinburgh New College Library.

candles are put out, then says Christ, 'I'll go [and] visit My child, for it is dark.'—(2nd Oct. 1730.)

"Here is blood—conscience-and-justice-satisfying blood. Here is blood for the foundation of your peace with God, peace with conscience, peace spoken in the Gospel by the Spirit of God. The natural conscience speaks peace from a false court of a covenant of works.—(2nd Oct. 1730.)

"It has been often known and felt by Christ's people that it has been better with them when in the class of waiters than in the class of enjoyers; as it was with David—he flourished more in grace and holiness before he obtained the kingdom when he was kept waiting, than after.—(14th June 1731.)

"Says our Blessed Lord (John vi. 29), 'This is the great work that ye believe on the Son of God;' this is the work of works, preparatory to all good works.—(1st Aug. 1731.)

"*Believe on Him whom He hath sent*—that is, give credit to His message, to His word; and trust in Him that He'll make it good to you, and to you in particular.—(*Ibid.*)

"For the Lord's sake, beware of resting upon the Father's external sending of Christ to you; be not satisfied without [unless] Christ be in you. There are some that rest upon the Father's sending the Son into the world, and are at no pains of getting Him in their hearts by the Spirit of Faith.—(8th Aug. 1731.)

"The Lord is calling out of heaven to you, and to every one of you, as He did to the Corinthians, '*Be ye reconciled to God.*' By faith embrace the message of reconciliation, give credit to the word of reconciliation; God is requiring you to trust and place your confidence in Him as reconciling the world to Himself. He is *beseeching* you—an astonishing word. Herein God stoops low; He can stoop no lower. Nothing like this was offered to angels, and nothing beyond this can be said to men; as if He said, 'If ye have no love to your own souls, yet for My sake accept of the message of reconciliation; I'll remember it as an act of kindness; and I'll remember it as long as immortality, whose days have no end.' —(4th Oct. 1731.)

"Believing communicants, will ye return the echo of faith to Heaven's word in the words of institution?—(3rd Oct. 1731.)

"All external order and communion laid down by men's invention avails nothing, without [unless] the hearts of believing confessors be united with love to each other. . . . 'A new commandment I write unto you that ye love one another.' Why is it called new? Because enforced with a new example that was given by Christ to His disciples. Christian love—the communion of saints —is founded upon it; all the drivings and drawings of men to make a society are but like ropes of sand, and will be of no avail without [unless] this prevail. —(21st Nov. 1731.)

"The two graces—faith and hope—are very much akin to [each] other, yet there is a distinction. Faith refers to the promise, and the faithfulness of the promiser; hope refers to good things in the promise. Many pretend to faith that have no hope—that's certainly presumption; and many pretend to hope that have no faith—that's certainly delusion. Faith looks on them [good things] as absent and unenjoyed; but hope contains in it their attainment on the ground of faith trusting. Hope contains a love and valuation of the things promised, otherwise hope could not counterbalance the straits it meets with; it's compared to the helmet—the hope of salvation. The helmet bears off the weight of the strokes of the head; so hope bears off the weight of the trials of the believer's heart and mind.—(28th Nov. 1731.)

"Heb. vi. 11. Ye have here the measure of this hope—the full assurance of hope. Every true Christian will and must press after the perfection and the attainment of the highest measures of every grace. And according to the measure of the Christian's faith, so is his hope that everything will be made out to him. Diligence is laid down as the means for the attainment of the full assurance of hope; and it is the means by virtue of the Divine appointment; and it has a natural and proper tendency to it.—(*Ibid.*)

"The main causes of sloth in the duties of religion are unbelief and carnal affections. As faith is the spring of the duties of holiness, so unbelief is the chief spring or reason of laying them by; as faith comes over mountains, so unbelief makes molehills mountains.—(*Ibid.*)

"Sin will have its residence in a believer, but there is a mighty odds betwixt sin's dominion and sin's residence (Rom. vi. 14).—(21st Nov. 1731.)

"Would ye be made strong against your corruptions that sin may not have dominion nor recover strength? Then my advice to you is, Resist sin—what's said to the Christian with respect to the devil, we say to you in respect of your corruptions, Resist them, be steadfast in the faith. The Apostle recommends you to *submit yourselves* to the Lord (James iv. 7). The word is too soft: the first language reads, Subject yourselves to the Lord; it imports, Put yourselves—by faith put yourselves—under the power of Christ and His grace, so plead the promise as it's here (Rom. vi. 14), *For sin shall not have dominion over you,* and the corruption shall fly away.—(*Ibid.*)

"It's a monster for one member of the body to be useless. Uselessness in the Christian society is as great a monster.—(9th January 1732.)

"Not by works of righteousness which we have done (says the Apostle) but according to His mercy He saved us (Titus iii. 5). That's no dishonour done to good works. A man is not slighted when undue honours are not paid. An inferior magistrate has no just cause of exception when he is not honoured as the king; so it's no dishonour done to good works when the crown is set on Christ; HE must have the pre-eminence.—(23rd October 1732.)

"The good man is said to have a good treasure in his heart—graces, com-

forts, experiences in religion, the law of God in his heart. There are these three or four things or properties our actions must have, in order to constitute them to be good :—
  (1.) They must flow from a gracious principle, or principle of grace—the principle of faith.
  (2.) They must be according to the rule, the Word of God. There must be a conformity in our actions to the Word of God.
  (3.) They must have a gracious motive, the love of Christ constraining you; and so
  (4.) A gracious end, the glory and honour of God.—(16th July 1732)."

PASTOR PETRUS DE WITTE.

"DE WITTE'S Catechizing upon the Heidelberg Catechism" is one of those standard books which convey no biographical information and no chronology personal to the author. It was compiled for "the A.B.C. clarckes, that is, the children." We conjecture from the title-page and dedicatory epistles that Petrus De Witte was pastor of the Reformed Church, first, at Hoorn in West Friesland; secondly, at Delft; and finally, at Leyden. Before publication, the book, which consists of the Heidelberg Catechism with a very full catechetical commentary, was examined and approved by the Classis [the Presbytery] of Hoorn.

The Synod of Dort in 1618 had recognised three catechisms :—
  1. The articles of faith, the ten commandments, the Lord's Prayer, &c.
  2. A short compend of the Catechism of the Palatinate.
  3. The Catechism of the Palatinate.

("The Walloon Netherland Churches, who have so long used the Catechism of Geneva, may retain the same in churches and schools.")

The different Provincial Synods of Holland urged the duty of public catechizing. De Witte gives the date of many Synods, the last being the Synod of Leyden in 1649. Parenthetically, as if referring to a new book, he mentions "Hoornbeck on Catechizing," published at Leyden 1654. The States of Holland, on a representation from the Synod of South Holland, issued an order to each *classis*, that provision should be made for public catechizing in church on the afternoon of each Lord's day. This letter from the States concluded thus :—
"Reverend, religious, most learned, honest, and discreet Sirs, we commend you unto the protection of God; dated in the Hague, 29th July 1654."

Probably the first edition was in circulation a little before 1654, and a new edition was sent forth in that year, encouraged by the States.

The "advertisements" to the English translation are signed, Mauritius Bohemus. The title-page informs us that De Witte's work had already reached a sixteenth edition :—

"CATECHIZING UPON THE HEIDELBERGH CATECHISM
OF THE REFORMED CHRISTIAN RELIGION.

Published after precedent inspection and approbation of the
Rev. Classis of Hoorn

By PETRUS DE WITTE, Minister of the Word of God at Leyden,
and now, after the *Sixtienth Impression*,

Translated for the English Reformed Congregation in Amsterdam.

A. B. C."

The English Church (De Engelsche Kerk) was a Church provided by the Dutch National Church for the accommodation of English residents and travellers at Amsterdam. And it was by order of the Classis of Amsterdam that this translation of the Catechism was made, it being their principle, as to the children of foreigners as well as of natives, that none should be permitted to grow up uncatechized; and that, therefore, the catechism, which they deemed the best, and which they had reason to conclude would be acceptable to English Protestants, should be accessible to them by means of a translation.

The answer to the first question of the catechism is broken up by De Witte into sixty-eight simplified subsidiary questions, so that I cannot quote a specimen of the execution of his performance, not being able to find any sufficiently brief apparatus under any question. I may therefore take the opportunity of introducing some questions for which I could not find room in my chapter on the Heidelberg Catechism.

[After a full and practical commentary on the creed.]

59. Was hilft es dir aber nun, wenn du diess alles glaubest?

Dass ich in Christo vor Gott gerecht und ein Erbe des ewigen Leben bin.

60. Wie bist du gerecht vor Gott?

Allein durch wahren Glauben in Jesum Christum. Also, dass ob mich schon mein Gewissen anklaght, dass ich

59. But now what profit redoundeth thence unto thee that thou believest all this?

That I am righteous in Christ before God and an heir of eternal life.

60. How art thou righteous before God?

Only by a true faith in Jesus Christ, insomuch that if my conscience accuse me, that I have grievously trespassed

wider alle Gebote Gottes schwerlich gesündiget, und derselben keines nie gehalten habe, auch noch immerdar zu allen Bösen geneigt bin, doch Gott ohne all mein Verdienst, aus lauter Gnaden, mir die vollkommene Genugthuung, Gerechtigkeit, und Heiligkeit Christi schenket und zurechnet, als hätt' ich nie eine Sünde begangen noch gehabt, und selbst allen den Gehorsam vollbracht, den Christus für mich hat geleistet, wenn ich allein solche Wohlthaten mit gläubigem Herzen annehme.

against all the commandments of God, nor have kept any one of them, and moreover am still prone to all evil, yet notwithstanding, the full and perfect satisfaction, righteousness, and atonement of Christ is imputed and given unto me, without any merit of mine, of the free mercy of God (if I embrace these benefits of Christ with a true confidence of heart), even as if I had never committed any sin, or as if no spot at all did cleave unto me—yea, as if I myself had perfectly performed that obedience which Christ performed for me.

61. Warum sagst du, dass du allein durch den Glauben gerecht seiest?

Nicht dass ich von wegen der Würdigkeit meines Glaubens Gott gefalle, sonder darum, dass allein die Genugthuung, Gerechtigkeit, und Heiligkeit Christi meine Gerechtigeit vor Gott ist, und ich dieselbe nicht anders denn allein durch den Glauben annehmen und mir zueignen kann.

61. Why affirmest thou, that thou art made righteous by faith only?

Not that I please God through the worthiness of my faith, but because only the satisfaction, righteousness, and holiness of Christ is my righteousness before God; and I cannot take hold of or apply it unto myself any other way than by faith.

I quote the conclusion of De Witte's elucidations of Question 1 :—*What comfort have the Papists here?* Continual doubting, an unquiet mind, and the wrack of conscience. The Papists say—

> "Three things there are that trouble my mind,
> The first, that I the grave must find;
> The second troubleth me more yet,
> That I know not the time of it;
> The third above all troubleth me,
> That whither I must, I cannot see."

What doth a believer set against this?

> "Three things there are that cheer my mind,
> First, that in Christ I pardon find;
> The second cheers me much more yet,
> That Christ the Lord for me is fit;
> The third above all cheereth me,
> That I my place in heaven see."

REV. TIMOTHY DWIGHT, D.D., LL.D.

TIMOTHY DWIGHT was the son of an American merchant and landowner, Timothy Dwight, and Mary, his wife, third daughter of President Edwards. He was born in Northampton (Massachusetts) 14th May 1752. He was a distinguished graduate of Yale College (in the city of Elms, at Newhaven) in Connecticut, and for six years a college tutor. He left college on his father's death in 1776, and took the management of the family estate for the benefit of his mother and the other children, discharging the duties of a guardian for five years. During this period he occasionally preached. He entered the ministry as pastor of Greenfield in Connecticut in May 1783. In 1795 he became President of Yale College, which very honourable office he held till his death on 11th January 1817.

"Dwight's Theology" is a standard work, which was extensively read and is still consulted. This is not the place to criticise the system of theology; but as an earnest lover of the Gospel, as well as an accomplished scholar, President Dwight has written much that we could quote with profit and admiration. The English language is never more forcible and beautiful than when it flows from some American pens. A few detached extracts, which illustrate my First Book, I shall arrange in the order that suits it.

"Socrates doubted whether it were possible for God to forgive sin, and, in my view, expressed the real ultimatum of reason on this subject. The sins of men are so causeless, so numerous, and so great, as to leave to a sober man, solemnly considering the subject, little else beside a fearful looking for of judgment. To relieve the distress and despondency to which we are thus exposed, the Bible comes to our aid."—*Sermon XII.*

"There can be no repentance where there is no hope of acceptance; despair here is the only predominant emotion, and with despair, repentance cannot, in the physical sense, co-exist."—*Sermon XXVIII.*

"God never extends mercy to sinners because of their desert and worth, but because they need His mercy."—*Sermon LXXVI.*

"Willingness to suffer perdition is no part of Christian resignation. . . . . The professor, in thus consenting to suffer, consents in the same act to be the eternal enemy of God and of all good."—*Sermon XCV.*

"The convinced sinner feels unwilling, like the Publican, even to lift up his eyes towards heaven. . . . . But he cannot be prevented from praying. His cries for mercy—and those, at times, involuntary and ejaculatory—are forced from him by a sense of his guilt and his fears of perdition. They often break out in his walks, in the course of his daily employments, and in his occasional journeyings; they spring from his meditations, they ascend from his pillow. The question, whether a sinner shall be directed to pray, has become nugatory to him, and has been decided not by metaphysical disquisition, but by the controlling anguish of his heart."—*Sermon LXXV.*

" The declaration of Solomon, that the prayers of the wicked are an abomination, appears to me, together with others of the like import, to be descriptive of the prayers of wicked men as they are in their general nature, and not as the mere cries of a suffering creature for mercy. . . . . As the whole number of regenerated persons is formed of those who have been convinced of sin, and who have been diligently employed in prayer while under conviction, it is plain that their prayers are not abominable in such a sense as to prevent the blessing prayed for from descending upon them, and therefore not in such a sense as rationally to discourage them from praying."—*Sermon LXXVI.*

" Christ actually suffered, while yet He was perfectly holy. He therefore suffered either for Himself or for mankind.

" If He suffered for mankind, the existence of an atonement is admitted.

" If He suffered for Himself, then the objector must admit that He suffered while He was yet perfectly holy, and of course that God can inflict suffering, not only on holy beings, but for their own sake ; in other words, can retribute punishment to obedience.

" I leave the objector to choose which part of this alternative he pleases."
—*Sermon LVII.*

"That which is true is not affected by any difficulty whatever, so far as *its truth merely* is concerned ; and that which is known is not rendered less certain by that which is unknown, whatever connection may exist between them, or whatever embarrassments may arise concerning that which is unknown."—*Sermon XXXII.*

" By the *Christian System,* I intend the system of doctrines and duties by means of which apostate creatures are restored to obedience and favour. The Christian system is not substantially different in the New Testament from what it is in the Old."—*Sermon XLV.*

" 1 Thess. v. 23. As he prays that they may be sanctified wholly, it is evident that they were sanctified in part only at their regeneration, and at the time also in which this prayer was uttered. It is further evident that they were to be sanctified in a still greater degree, because this event is prayed for by the Apostle under the inspiration of the Holy Ghost."—*Sermon LXXXIII.*

" His friends, His disciples, His apostles were selected from the poor and lowly. .... Christ descended to these lowly men and these lowly circumstances, from the throne of the heavens. Shall not we then be willing to let ourselves down from the side or even the summit of our mole-hill, to visit our fellow-emmets at the bottom ? "—*Sermon XLII.*

" The prevalence of a meek and humble disposition furnishes the mind with good reason to believe that it is renewed. .... A humble mind is meek, little disposed to feel provocations deeply, uninclined to construe them in the worst manner, and still more indisposed to requite them with wrath and revenge. .... The propensity to wrath is lessened; and humility and meekness (not insensibility to injuries, but a serene and quiet soul under them) have, like beautiful twin sisters, entered the mind and made it their permanent habitation."—*Sermon LXXXIX.*

" Under the influence of evangelical love to mankind, the renewed man does that which is good, just, and sincere because it is so, and because God has required these things in His law, and not from a regard to reputation and convenience. Now he finds the promotion of happiness to be desirable and delightful in itself, and independently of a separate reward—to be done for its own sake and not merely as it is done by publicans and sinners. The great question now becomes, How, when, and where good can be done, and not, What he shall gain by doing it."—*Sermon LXXVI.*

" Christ is not only the dispenser of the good enjoyed in heaven, but the very good which is dispensed."—*Sermon LIX.*

REV. EBENEZER ERSKINE, M.A.[1]

DURING the latter half of the sixteenth century, and the former half of the seventeenth, there flourished a gentleman descended from the Earls of Mar, named

[1] See Rev. Donald Fraser's "Life of Ebenezer Erskine," Edin , 1831 ; and an abridged Memoir, by Rev. Dr. Harper, Edin. 1849.

Mr Ralph Areskine of Shielfield, who had twelve children. The ninth child was the Rev. Henry Areskine, M.A. of Edinburgh, who was born at Dryburgh in 1624, and was known as the minister of a chapel at Cornhill, in the parish of Norham, in Northumberland, from which he was ejected for nonconformity in 1662. In 1687 he was settled at Whitsome in Berwickshire, and in 1690 was translated to Chirnside (only four miles distant), where he died, 10th August 1696.

Ebenezer Ereskine, or Erskine, was the elder son of the above by his second wife (née Margaret Halcro). He was born 22nd June 1680, and became M.A. of Edinburgh in June 1697. He was licensed as a preacher by the Presbytery of Kirkcaldy in February 1703, and in September of the same year he was, by the same Presbytery, ordained minister of Portmoak. His marriage in 1704 to Miss Alison Turpie, daughter of Mr Alexander Turpie, writer, Leven, deserves to be recorded, as to her he ascribed his being brought to a saving acquaintance with the Gospel of our salvation in the year 1708.

It is well known that Mr Erskine was one of the chiefs of "The Marrow" Divines. The representation and petition addressed by them to the General Assembly of 1721 was revised and perfected by him. At the instigation of Principal Hadow, the Synod of Fife thereafter repeatedly harassed him, and the four other Marrow-men in its membership (Messrs Hog, Bathgate, Wardlaw, and Ralph Erskine). This led him to publish in 1725 his sermon on Revelation iii. 15, with an apologetical preface, so that his first appearance as an author was in the forty-fifth year of his age. At one meeting of Synod he listened to many attacks on his Gospel views in silence; but at length he rose, and with impressive dignity and energy, made this short speech :—" Moderator, Our Lord Jesus says of Himself, My Father *giveth you* the true Bread from heaven. This He uttered to a promiscuous multitude, and let me see the man who dares to affirm that HE said wrong."

In 1731 a third charge was erected in the town of Stirling, and to it Mr Erskine was translated on the 8th July of the same year. Being a member of the General Assembly of 1732, he protested against the Act anent the method of planting vacant churches. He opened the next Synod of Perth and Stirling by preaching a sermon, which as printed is entitled, " The Stone rejected by the builders exalted as the Head-stone of the Corner." In this *concio ad clerum*, he renewed his protest and denounced the Act; and when censured by the Synod, he appealed to the General Assembly. This ultimately led to "the secession," and to the formation at Gairney Bridge, near Kinross, on 6th December 1733, of *The Associate Presbytery*, of which he is regarded as the father. In 1746, in the patriotic resistance to the Jacobite Rebellion, the Stirling Seceders served in the field in two companies, headed by their intrepid minister. A new church was built for him in Stirling, where he continued his Gospel labours till his death on 2nd June 1754, having almost completed his seventy-fourth year. He was Professor of Theology from 1747 to 1749. His works have been collected; they are well known and justly valued, as both earnest and instructive.

I am indebted for the following quotations from Ebenezer Erskine to Brown's "Gospel Truth."

"The order of doctrine, laid in the dispensation of the Gospel, is *first* to lead the sinner by faith unto Christ and unto God in Him, and *thereupon* to inculcate obedience to the law as a rule of duty. This order of doctrine is laid down in our Lesser Catechism by the Westminster Assembly, where, in answer to the third question, we are told that the Scriptures principally teach what man is to believe concerning God, and then what duty God requires of man; and according to this order we have *first* the objects of faith and privileges of believers explained, and *then* the duties of the moral law inculcated upon that ground. The same method we find the Apostle Paul observes in most of his epistles, so that this is no new scheme, but the good old way."

"The assurance I speak of, namely, a persuasion of the promise with appropriation (as the judicious Calvin speaks), can no more be separated from faith than light can be separated from the sun; it takes *home* the grace and mercy of God to the soul in particular, which lay before *in common* [on the common] in the offer of the Gospel. And without this particular application, the offer and promise of the Gospel can stand us in no stead, but is like a price put into the hand of a fool who has no heart to it. Our food set before us will never feed us unless it be applied by eating; so except we eat the flesh and drink the blood of the Son of man by an applying faith, we have no life in us. . . . Faith will not quit its *my's*, though all the world should say against it. The marrow of the Gospel, as Luther observes, is in these words, *my*, and *our;* he bids us read these with great emphasis. Says another, Take away *property*, and you take away God—take away Christ. It is the common dialect of faith in Scripture, to vent itself in words of appropriation; it has a peculiar pleasure and satisfaction in these words, *my*, and *our*, and rolls them in its mouth as a sweet morsel. . . . There is a sufficient ground laid in the Gospel revelation and promise, for a sinner, even in his first approach to God in Christ, to come with full assurance of faith, . . . to come with assurance of acceptance and welcome, grounded upon His infallible word of promise, Him that cometh unto Me I will in no wise cast out."

REV. RALPH ERSKINE, M.A.[1]

THE younger brother of "The Father of the Secession" was Rev. Ralph Erskine, M.A., of the University of Edinburgh, who was born at Monilaws, in Northumberland, 15th March 1685. In later years he used to record "the Lord's drawing out my heart towards HIM at my father's death;" the date of this bereavement was 1696, when he was eleven years of age. In February 1700 the Parliament Square in Edinburgh was almost entirely destroyed by fire; and Ralph with difficulty forced his way through the flames with a number of his books. He was licensed as a preacher at Culross by the Presbytery of Dunfermline, 8th June 1709. He was ordained second minister of Dunfermline on 7th August 1711, his colleague being Rev. Thomas Buchanan. On the death of the latter in 1715, Mr Ralph Erskine was appointed first minister, and on 20th November 1718, the Rev. James Wardlaw became his colleague. The colleagues preached every Sabbath, one in the forenoon, and the other in the afternoon, and were most congenial. There was for a time a singular addition to their interchanged services to the church and to each other. There being a feud between the kirk-session and the Marquis of Tweeddale about the right of patronage to the office of precentor—a feud which lasted for more than four years—a specimen of what occurred is thus noted in Mr Erskine's diary:—

"*Sabbath, Dec.* 24, 1732.—This day my colleague and I were precentors to ourselves, and raised the Psalm because of the Marquis's decreet which he was insisting upon. *Thursday, Dec.* 28.—This day I precented for my colleague in the church. *Sabbath, Dec.* 31.—I precented for my colleague and he for me."

With regard to "The Marrow" controversy, Mr Ralph Erskine was at one with his brother, and his cordiality is attested by Boston. The brothers were in different Synods when the preliminary or presbyterial secession took place; and the younger brother did not join the Associate Presbytery at its formation, although present as a spectator. But in August 1736, at the General Assembly's Commission, Ralph Erskine declared his adherence to the testimony of that Presbytery. Thereafter (in February 1737) he formally joined that Church-court in company with the Rev. Thomas Mair of Orwell, Thomas Nairn of Abbotshall, and James Thomson of Burntisland. The original members were Rev. Ebenezer Erskine of Stirling, William Wilson of Perth, Alexander Moncrieff of Abernethy, and James Fisher of Kinclaven. These eight ministers remained in charge of their parishes and congregations. They believed that they were entitled to remain and to draw the national salaries and other emoluments—better entitled

[1] See Rev. Donald Fraser's "Life of Ralph Erskine." Edin., 1834. [The Rev. John Erskine, D.D., the great evangelical leader at a later date, was of a different family.]

than other ministers who had been unfaithful to the Gospel, and to the other standards of doctrine lawfully recognised by the State as well as by the Church. It was not till the 12th May 1740 that they were deposed by the General Assembly, and that their churches legally became vacant.

Such was the esteem in which Mr Ralph Erskine was held, that neither the magistrates nor the people sought to have the law put in force, and the Presbytery of Dunfermline did not interfere. He continued to preach once a day along with Mr Wardlaw in the parish church; and he preached from a tent to all comers at the other diet of worship. Sometimes, in the former pulpit, assertions regarding the deposed ministers were made in a forenoon to be contradicted in the afternoon. But the first step towards Mr Erskine's removal from the benefice followed the death of Mr Wardlaw, which sad event happened on 2nd May 1742. On the 2nd June, this minute was engrossed, "The Presbytery, taking into their consideration the melancholy state of the parish of Dunfermline, did, after some reasoning, agree to supply the vacancy occasioned by the deposition of Mr Ralph Erskine, as well as the vacancy occasioned by the death of Mr James Wardlaw, and did and hereby do appoint the moderator to preach at Dunfermline next Lord's day *both forenoon and afternoon.*"

In April 1739 it had been ascertained that £400 would be subscribed to build a Secession Church at Dunfermline, so hearty were the poorer people as well as the more wealthy. A large church, capable of accommodating about 2000 people, was built in Queen Anne Street. On leaving the parish church, Mr Erskine preached in the new building, with ever increasing usefulness, till his death on 6th November 1752. He was survived by his venerable brother, who, on receiving the solemn news, expressed himself to this effect, "And is Ralph gone? he has twice got the start of me: he was first in Christ; and now he is first in glory."[1]

Although Ebenezer was, in council and in affairs, the greatest man, yet Ralph Erskine is much better known, and as an author has still a world-wide popularity. He was more often before the public view than his brother, through his elegies upon deceased ministers, which have been useful to biographers. He also wrote many other sacred verses, which were studied with profit by numerous readers, and which include, among other compositions, Gospel Sonnets, and a Paraphrase on the Song of Solomon. It cannot be denied that he had much poetical taste, yet we can scarcely say that the above-named works are successful efforts. However poetical his diction may have been, he could have expressed his sentiments

[1] The late Robert Chambers, in his "Picture of Scotland," has said that it was a tradition in Dunfermline that when Mr Ralph Erskine heard of his brother's death, he exclaimed, "Ah, Yeben, Yeben! ye've won to heaven before me; but I'll no be lang ahint you, lad!" The very beginning of this anecdote proves it to be apocryphal, because Ralph died more than a year and seven months before his brother, Ebenezer.

more poetically in prose. The following is a favourable specimen of his versification:—

SONG OF SOLOMON v. 10. "My Beloved (the Lord Jesus Christ) is white and ruddy."

> "Were He not red, but only white—the lily, not the rose—
> He might suffice the angels' sight; but I am none of those.
> Were He not white, but only red—a suff'rer for His sin—
> His blood would rest upon His head, nor could I joy therein.
> But (here's my joy and confidence) both mixt I see by faith,
> The whiteness of His innocence, the redness of His death."

It has been observed in many individuals, that a turn for poetical composition has contributed to beautify their prose writing. Certainly Ralph Erskine's prose is beautiful, and seems, as we read it, to fall on the ear like music. For one specimen I refer, almost at random, to his sermon on Zechariah xiv. 7, "It shall come to pass that at evening time it shall be light."

OWEN FELLTHAM, ESQ.

OUR English ancestors were fond of soliloquizing, and they often gave their soliloquies to the reading public, in books consisting of detached miscellaneous paragraphs arranged in hundreds or "centuries." Perhaps the earliest publication of this kind was a volume of Three Centuries of "Meditations and Vows, Divine and Moral, serving for directions in Christian and Civil Practice," by Joseph Hall, D.D., afterwards Bishop of Norwich. The example of that eloquent divine was followed by a scholarly layman of the first half of the seventeenth century, who styled himself Owen Felltham, Esq.; his work comprises Two Centuries of "Resolves, Divine, Moral, Political." One century was written when the graceful writer was only eighteen years of age, and all his "Resolves" date originally from his early manhood. It is in their fresh youthful state that they are valued and have been reprinted. His pains at a later period of life to correct the style and to import a tone of maturity were thrown away.

"Felltham's Resolves" contain internal evidence of the author's acquaintance with the Heidelberg Catechism, at least with *Question* 2, "How many things are necessary for thee to know that thou, enjoying this consolation, mayest live and die happily?" and with its *Answer*, "Three things. The first, What is the greatness of my sin and misery. The second, How I am redeemed from all my sin and misery. And the third, What thanks I owe to God for this redemption."

I quote from what in the fifth edition was called the "Second Century," but which, in order of composition, was the first.

"*Three things that a Christian should specially know.*

"There are three things especially that a Christian should know—his own misery—God's love—his own thankful obedience: his misery, how just; God's love, how free, how undeserved; his own thankfulness, how due, how necessary. Consideration of one successively begets the apprehension of all: our misery shows us His love; His love calls for our acknowledgment. Want makes a bounty weightier; if we think of our needs, we cannot but admire His mercies; how dull were we, if we should not value the relief of our necessities! He cannot but esteem the benefit that unexpectedly helps him in his deepest distress. That love is most to be prized whose only motive is goodness. The thought of this will form a disposition grateful; who can meditate so unbottomed a love, and not study for a thankful demeanour? His mind is cross to nature, that requires not affection with gratitude. All favours have this success, if they light on good ground they bring forth thanks. Let me first think my misery without my Saviour's mercy—next, His mercy without my merits—and from the meditation of those two, my sincere thanks will spring. Though I cannot conceive of the former as they are—infinite and beyond my thought—yet will I so ponder them as they may enkindle the fire of my unfeigned and zealous thanksgiving. That time is well spent wherein we study thankfulness."

This delightfully concise article is altogether rewritten in the folio editions, and not at all improved except perhaps in the title, which runs, "*Of three things we ought to know*"—which are defined to be "*our own misery, God's love, and our own thankful obedience.*"

Several additional sentences, however, are worthy of the writer:—

"Though as Cato we did tear our self-made wounds to widen death's sad entrance, yet, without our wishes and against our wills, when we lay gasping in the road to ruin, by the mercy of this Great Samaritan we were again bound up for life and for the joy of being. So bats and owls that hate the sun's gay light are yet, by the influence of its gracious beams, from their dark holes, drawn out to fly and live." . . . .

"The consideration of God's love will be, as that of God Himself was to Simonides, the more thought on, the less to be comprehended. And this being infinitely above all our apprehensions, we cannot in reason give less than all our gratitude; and yet of that how small a part is all! When all we can pay is so simple a little of what we justly owe, we should immeasurably be unjust if we returned not all in our ability. Though we have not to *requite*, we may have what will *please*, when we give Him up His own and offer up His offering for us; when we yet remember what we cannot return. The best repository of a benefit is a mind that will perpetually acknowledge it. We ought to study what will please ; we ought to fly from offence. And when we have done all we can, we are still short, alive, of what the dead earth does. That yields our seed with multiplied increase ; but this *quick* earth of ours does dwindle what is cast in't. So though we meditate our own misery and God's free grace and bounty, yet the great business of our life is gratitude. For that, in all its dimensions and concomitants, will take up all we can possibly do, and yet, at last of all, will leave us still to *wish* and *pray.*"

The second and third editions of Feltham's "Resolves" appeared in 1628 (the first edition was without date, a small duodecimo volume, containing one century, which in the fourth [1631] and following editions was issued as the second century). Identical with the fourth were the fifth, sixth, and seventh editions, which were issued between the years 1634 and 1647 ; all except the first edition were quarto volumes. It was in honour of the Restoration of Charles II. that Mr Feltham issued the first folio edition, containing an epitaph which described himself as willing to die in token of his consummated happiness because his king had come back. Unfortunately he celebrated the political era by taking liberties with the text of his "Resolves," especially those in "the second century," meaning to improve and adorn, but producing the opposite result. This too loyal folio appeared in 1661 ; and it was the last edition in the author's lifetime. It was reprinted in 1670, 1677, and 1696 in folio, and 1709 in octavo ; as to the edition of 1696 (the eleventh), the title-page adds "with references made to the poetical citations, heretofore much wanted." [Mr Feltham had purposely omitted such references, on the ground, "I do not profess myself a scholar, and for a gentleman, I hold it a little pedantical."] Mr James Cumming, F.S.A., recalled the attention of the world of letters to Feltham's "Resolves" in 1806 ; but his reprint was only a modernized abridgment. Mr Pickering produced a real and beautiful reprint in 1840, following the quarto editions. The editor was anonymous ; but he dedicated the book to the Rev. Philip Bliss, D.C.L. of Oxford, the possessor of the only known copy of the first edition. Although the folio editions were justly set aside by Mr Pickering as the source of the text, yet from their interpolated sentences and paragraphs, an appendix of the author's latest "Resolves" might be compiled. The paragraphs which I have quoted from Century II., No. 77, show that the enlarged volume contains some good writing which might usefully be rescued from oblivion.

With regard to the personal history of Owen Feltham, only a few facts are known, which may be gathered from his Will (first printed by Mr Pickering) and from allusions within the boards of his book. His father was a Suffolk gentleman by birth, but became possessor of a small property in Cambridgeshire, " an ancient inheritance of his family," namely, Thomas Feltham, Esq. (born 1570, died 1632, N. S.) Owen was the second of three sons, Robert, Owen, and Thomas. Owen's patron was the Earl of Thomond, who died before 1660, to

2 K

whose widow, Mary, Conntess-Dowager of Thomond, the Folio of 1661 was dedicated, the author alluding to the contents as "being, most of them, composed under the coverture of your roof, and so born subjects under your dominion." He was dispossessed of the Cambridgeshire estate; and in his Will, dated 4th May 1667, he styles himself of Great Billing in Northamptonshire, and bequeaths two leasehold properties in Ireland, namely, Cratelagh Keale in the County of Clare, and Catherlogh. He mentions his brother Robert as having children named Owen, Elizabeth, and Frances; he mentions his brother, Thomas; also Lucas, (Rev.) Thomas, and Nathaniel, the testator's nephews. His nephew aforesaid, Owen Felltham of Gray's Inn, who was his residuary legatee, proved this Will in the Strand, in the County of Middlesex, 22nd April 1668. In all the folio editions of "The Resolves," there is a collection of small pieces called *Lusoria*, of which No. 8 is headed, "Upon my father's tomb at Babram in Cambridgeshire."

Memoriæ posterisque sacrum.

Ex suffolciæ ortus comitatu
THOMAS FELLTHAM,
vir probus, generosus, sciens, ubique colendus,
bonis ⎫ malis ⎧ amicisque
adjutor ⎭ obstes ⎩ fidelis
bene vivens, moriens pié,
filios tres, totidemque natas, superstites relinquens,
11 Martii, salutis anno 1631, sed militiæ suæ 62.
Per natu filium minorem hic in vitam beatiorem ad resurgendum positus.

It is supposed that in more remote times the head of the family was Thomas Felltham, Esq., of Sculthorpe in Norfolk, who by his wife, Mayant Jackson, left descendants—a younger son being Thomas Felltham of Mutford in Suffolk, father of the Thomas who is memorialized in the above epitaph, written by his second son, Owen Felltham, author of "The Resolves." It is further supposed that Owen's elder brother, Robert, succeeded his kinsmen of the older branches, and became Felltham of Sculthorpe (a Robert Felltham of Sculthorpe, with a son named Owen, being in a contemporary record). The fact of the Earl of Thomond having a mansion at Great Billing, is thought to account for the date of the Will of the author of "The Resolves." Mr Cumming states that the surname of Felltham has survived among the peasantry of Suffolk, and that he himself once conversed at a fair with an Owen Felltham, dealer in gingerbread.

EDWARD FISHER, B.A. OXON.

ANTHONY A WOOD tells us, "Edward Fisher, the eldest son of a knight, became a Gentleman-Commoner of Brasen-nose College, Oxford, 25th August 1627, took one Degree in Arts, and soon after left that house. Afterwards being called home by his relations (who were then, as I have been informed, much in debt) he improved that learning which he had obtained in the University so much, that he became a noted person among the learned for his great reading in Ecclesiastical History and in the Fathers, and for his admirable skill in the Greek and Hebrew languages." "This Edward Fisher was a royalist." This is all the precise information which the Oxford Historian can give regarding Mr Fisher personally, as the eminent scholar fell into poverty and became (as Wood thinks) a schoolmaster. The conjecture that his father was Sir Edward Fisher of Mickleton, in Gloucestershire, proves on investigation to be incorrect. A good many gentlemen of the name of Fisher received the honour of knighthood during the same generation; but the father of the author of "The Marrow" has not yet been ascertained, as far as my information has gone.

Anthony a Wood had no prejudice in favour of the author, or of his evangelical sentiments; and he must have known the common report that Edward Fisher was a London barber, and one of the party of the Independents. If there had been any truth in the rumour, he would not only have mentioned it, but would have readily adopted it. That the rumour has been thus virtually contradicted, I record merely in the interest of biographical truth, without resenting Mr Riccaltoun's saucy anticipation of Robert Burns' maxim, "A man's a man for a' that." Mr Riccaltoun's words were:—"I know this circumstance [that E. F. was a barber] has been publicly contradicted from the Press. But as I look upon that other account of the author, however better vouched, yet never a whit more authentic than this, so I own I value 'The Marrow' more as written by Edward Fisher the barber, than when I consider it as the work of the learned and honourable Edward Fisher."—(Sober Enquiry, page 42).

Besides "The Marrow of Modern Divinity, part i., 1645; part ii., 1648," Mr Fisher wrote "An Appeal to thy conscience, as thou wilt answer it at the great and dreadful day of Jesus Christ." Oxford, 1644.

"A Christian Caveat to the old and new Sabbatarians,"[1] 4to, London, 1650; 2nd ed. 1652; 3rd ed. 1653; 4th ed. 1655. To the fourth edition he added, "An Answer to Sixteen Queries touching the rise and observation of Christmas."

[1] *The Sabbatarians* held that the Sabbath should be observed on Saturday. The best answer to them was from the pen of John Wallis, D.D., Savilian Professor of Geometry in the University of Oxford.

Far from "The Marrow" being a contraband article, it was licensed for the Press by the Rev. Joseph Caryl, the great author on the Book of Job, and recommended by Rev. Jeremiah Burroughs and Rev. William Strong, most esteemed authors in their own and all succeeding times. As to the first part, Mr Caryl, "having perused this ensuing dialogue," recommends it as "a Discourse stored with many necessary and seasonable truths, confirmed by Scripture and avowed by many approved writers." As to the second part he writes, "Reader, The *marrow* of the second bone is, like that of the first, sweet and good. The commandments of God are marrow to the saints as well as the promises. And they shall never taste the marrow of the promises who distaste the commandments. This little treatise breaketh the bone—the hard part of commandments —by a plain exposition, that so all, even babes in Christ—yea, such as are yet out of Christ—may suck out and feed upon the marrow by suitable meditations. 6th September 1648. *Joseph Caryl.*"

The title-page gives only the author's initials, E. F. Any doubts, as to Mr Fisher being the author, are removed by the Rev. Samuel Prittie's testimonial:—

"Grace and peace to you in Jesus Christ. My loving friend in Christ—I have, according to your desire, read over your book and find it full of evangelical light and life, and I doubt not but the oftener I read it the more true comfort I shall find in the knowledge of Christ thereby. The method is Apostolical wherein the works of love, in the right place, after the life of faith, be effectually required. God hath *endewed* His *Fisher* with the net of a trying understanding, and discerning judgment and discretion, whereby, out of the *Christaline* streams of the well of life, you have taken a mess of the sweetest and wholesomest fish that the whole world can afford, which if I could daily have enough of, I should no more care for the flesh or the works thereof."

NOTE.

His book being a compilation from, and a compendium of, Protestant Divinity from the Reformation era to 1645, Mr Fisher called it *The Marrow of Modern Divinity;* he referred to his authorities in the margin of each page. The following references belong to the paragraphs concerning *the deed of gift:*—

"Luther on Galatians," pp. 69, 104. Culverwell's "Treatise of Faith, p. 15. Dr Preston "Of Faith," p. 8. A little book called "The Benefit of Christ's Death." Thos. Hooker's "Poore doubting Christian," p. 69. Dr Sibbes' "Soul's Conflict," p. 621. Dr Preston "Of Love," p. 146.

REV. JAMES FISHER.[1]

In 1693, the Rev. Thomas Fisher, a licentiate of the Presbytery of Dumbarton, was ordained minister of Barr in Ayrshire, thence in 1698 he was translated to Auchtergaven, and again in 1699 to Rhynd, both in Perthshire (*born* 1665, *died* 1721).

His third son, Rev. James Fisher, was born at Barr, 23rd January 1697, and his school education was probably received in Perth. His literary curriculum, with a view to the ministry, was spent at the Universities of Glasgow and St Andrews. For the study of divinity he chose Edinburgh, and sat under Professor William Hamilton for six years. Immediately thereafter, *i.e.*, in 1722, he was licensed as a preacher by the Presbytery of Perth, and in December 1725 he was ordained by the Presbytery of Dunkeld as minister of Kinclaven.

During the year 1721 young Mr Fisher made the acquaintance of Rev. Ebenezer Erskine, the minister of Portmoak. Having approved of this eminent minister's stand in the "Marrow" controversy, he attended his ministry in preference to that of the minister of Arngask, in whose parish he was residing temporarily with his widowed mother. In 1727 Mr Fisher married Jean, Mr Erskine's eldest daughter. He gave a life-long support to the principles of his venerated father-in-law—principles which had been dear to himself before he knew him personally.

When the Associate Presbytery was formed by the four ministers, he was chosen to be presbytery-clerk. Although deposed by the General Assembly of 1740, Mr Fisher kept possession of the parish church of Kinclaven till 13th August 1741, when the building was seized and closed by the sheriff-officers. He then preached from a tent on Kinclaven braeside. The new parish minister, whom the patron had presented in November 1740, was not inducted till 13th May 1742.

The forbearance of Mr Fisher's opponents arose from the circumstance that, in the summer of 1740, the seceding people of Glasgow invited him to be their minister. But the parishioners of Kinclaven were so unwilling to part with him, that he hesitated for a year. The resolution of the Established authorities as to Kinclaven, and his own decision as to Glasgow, seem to have mutually hastened one another. For we are informed that, on 8th October 1741, Mr Fisher was inducted " in the open air at Crosshill, in the neighbourhood of Glasgow, about a mile to the south, in the parish of Cathcart, where they had been accustomed to worship, and continued to do so till their church was built." The congregation was afterwards known as the congregation of Shuttle Street, and finally of Greyfriars, Glasgow.

[1] See "Memorials of Rev. James Fisher," by John Brown, D.D, Edinburgh, 1849.

THE THEOLOGY OF CONSOLATION.

During a part of this interval of time, Mr Fisher and his family lived in Perth. And they did not remove to Glasgow until after the addition of twin children to the family on 31st October. [*See* WILLIAM WILSON]. Mr Fisher was Theological Professor, in succession to his father-in-law, from 1749 to 1764. His wife died 1st December 1771. He himself survived till 28th September 1775—the last survivor of the first Associate Presbytery.

In 1747 the Synod appointed Messrs Ebenezer and Ralph Erskine and Mr Fisher as a committee to prepare an exposition of the Westminster Shorter Catechism. On 6th November 1752, Mr Ralph Erskine died, and thus the preface to Part First, dated February 1753, was signed by "Eben. Erskine" and "James Fisher" only. On 2nd June 1754, Mr Ebenezer Erskine died. Mr Fisher, the sole survivor, had the wisdom to proceed leisurely. On 14th January 1765, he issued a *third edition* of Part First, slightly remodelled, in order to correspond with the first edition of Part Second, the preface to which was signed, "James Fisher," "Glasgow, May 3, 1765." This Catechism was called "The Synod's Catechism," but soon obtained the name, which it has ever since retained, of "Fisher's Catechism"—and justly, because "the explanations by way of question and answer," of Questions 1 to 7, 29 to 75, and 96 to 107, were all by him—while Ebenezer Erskine's materials comprise only QQ. 8 to 28, and Ralph's, only QQ. 76 to 95. [The quotations in my Book I., Part 2, regarding "*building up* in holiness and comfort," are therefore by Rev. Ralph Erskine].

Mr Fisher's other works of enduring interest are:—
1. The inestimable value of divine truth, considered in a Sermon from Prov. xxiii. 23, "Buy the truth and sell it not." 1739.
2. Christ Jesus the Lord considered as the inexhaustible matter of Gospel Preaching. 1741.
3. The Character of a Faithful Minister of Christ. 1752.
4. Christ the Sole and Wonderful Door in the Work of Man's Redemption. 1745.
5. The Doors of the Heart Summoned to open to the King of Glory. 1755.

He also wrote a biographical preface to Ralph Erskine's Works, in which he alludes to the Marrow Controversy as "the most useful and beneficial to this Church of any other that has been broached since the beginning of this century."

Mr Fisher preached the gospel with beautiful simplicity. His sermon, "Christ the sole and wonderful Door," is from the text Judges xiii. 19; and the "doctrine," or thesis, is, "As the Lord Jesus Christ, the Angel of the covenant, is the wonderful and only door in the great work of our redemption, so it is the privilege and duty of mankind sinners to look on. The Angel did wondrously, and Manoah and his wife looked on."

The conclusion of "The Doors of the Heart summoned" is:—" O sirs! whatever be your difficulties and objections against opening to Christ in a way of believing, yet He is making none at all against His own incoming to your hearts. ... Have you made Him to serve with your sins and wearied Him with your iniquities? Yet even in that case He says—I, even I, am He that blotteth out thy transgressions for My own sake, and will not remember thy sins (Isa. xliii. 24, 25). Have you gone on frowardly in the way of your own heart? Yet He is saying to you, as He did to Israel in the like case—I have seen his ways and will heal him (Isa. lvii. 17, 18). Have you been making lies your refuge, and under falsehood hiding yourselves? Even in this case He declares, that He is the Foundation laid in Zion for you, and that the refuge of lies shall be swept away (Isa. xxviii. 15-17). Have you gone after your lovers and forgotten Me, saith the Lord? He answers Himself, *Therefore, behold, I will allure her and bring her to the wilderness, and speak comfortably unto her.* (Hosea ii. 14)."

Mr Fisher's affinity with the Erskines suggests the following Table of Representatives of the Erskine family :—

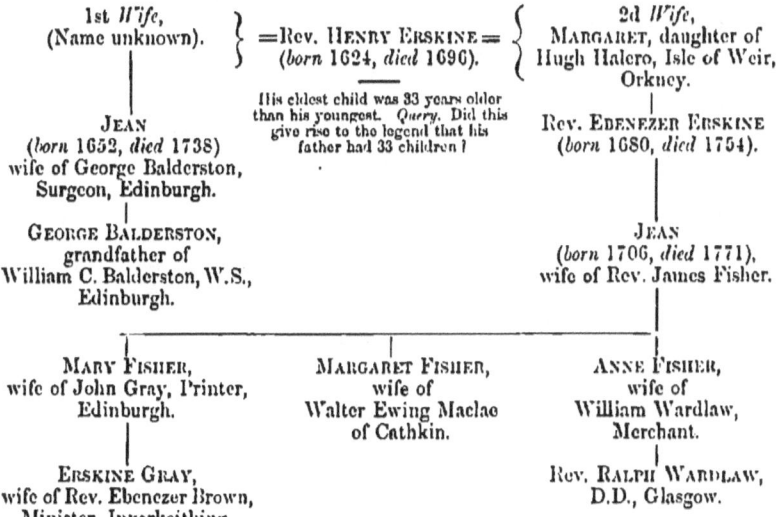

Dr John Brown, Fisher's biographer, nephew of Rev. Ebenezer Brown, dedicated the biography to the surviving grandchildren of the Rev. James Fisher —namely, Mrs Jane Crum, Thornliebank ; Humphrey Ewing Maclae, Esq. of Cathkin ; Mrs Margaret Buchan, Braeside, West Canada ; James Ewing, Esq. of Strathleven; Mrs Elizabeth Hyde, Dunoon; Rev. Ralph Wardlaw, D.D., S.S.T.P., Glasgow. Dated, 25th May 1849.

REV. JOHN FLAVEL, B.A. OXON.

JOHN, son of Rev. Richard Flavel, parish clergyman of Bromesgrove in Worcestershire, was born at Bromesgrove in 1627. He was educated at Oxford, in University College. He entered the ministry, and his first charge was at Deptford, where he was settled in 1650, but he was translated to Dartmouth in 1656, where he was eminent as an incumbent, and afterwards as a Nonconformist minister, so that immediately after his death, Dr Increase Mather, visiting Dartmouth, wrote:—" My heart bleeds to look on this desolate place, and not to see him that, whilst living, was the glory of it. I can truly say (as, sometimes, Beza of Calvin), Now Mr Flavel is dead, life will be less sweet, and death less bitter to me."

Mr Flavel in the troublous days of the Stuarts suffered many vicissitudes in his own land; and it would appear that he was once an exile in Holland, where the Earl and Countess of Sutherland prized his society; he dedicated to the Earl his sermon entitled, "Mount Pisgah, preached at the Public Thanksgiving, February 14, 1688-9, for England's Deliverance from Popery, &c." His joy at the happy Revolution was overflowing; he preached and published a volume of Sermons entitled, "England's Duty under the present Gospel Liberty;" and the same spirit appeared in his catechizing, which is described "as carried on in the Lord's Day exercises in Dartmouth, in the First Year of Liberty, 1688." He died suddenly at Exeter, 26th June 1691, aged sixty-four, and was buried in Dartmouth Church.

The works of John Flavel are well known, and have been often printed in a collected form. His practical writings are evangelical and useful. Both his learning and his experience made him familiar with controversy, and thus too ready to suspect heresy, especially Antinomianism—an apprehension which sometimes hampered the freeness of his Gospel invitations. He had, however, an eloquence and impressiveness which sprang entirely from the heart; and his desire was to preach Christ according to the Scriptures. And often he put his learning aside in order to minister, in the simplest style, to husbandmen and seamen.

In *The Seaman's Catechism* he has given his best statement of the free Gospel:—

"*Q.* 11. What is it to go to Christ?

"*Ans.* To go to Christ is to embrace Him in His person and offices, and to rest entirely and closely upon Him for pardon of sin and eternal life, being deeply sensible of the want and worth of Him (John i. 12, iii. 36; 1 Cor. i. 30; Acts iv. 12, xiii. 39; Isa. xlv. 22; Acts ii. 37).

"*Q.* 12. But will Christ receive me if I go to Him?

"*Ans.* Yes, yes; He is more ready to receive thee than thou art to come to Him. Luke xv. 20, The son doth but go, the father ran; if he had but received him into the house, it had been much, but he fell on his neck and kissed him; he bespeaks him much after that rate he expressed himself to returning Ephraim, My bowels are troubled for him, I will surely have mercy on him (Jer. xxxi. 20). There is not the least parenthesis, in all the pages of free grace, to exclude a soul that is sincerely willing to come to Christ.

"*Q.* 13. But how may it appear that He is willing to receive me?

"*Ans.* Make trial of Him thyself. If thou didst but know His heart to poor sinners, you would not question it. Believe what He saith in the Gospel; there thou shalt find that He is a willing Saviour, for therein thou hast—

'*First*, His most serious invitations (Matt. xi. 28; Isa. lv. 1). These serious invitations are—

"*Secondly*, backed and confirmed with His oath (Ezek. xxxv. 11).

"*Thirdly*, amplified with pathetic wishes, sighs, and groans (Luke xix. 42).

"*Fourthly*, yea, delivered to them in undissembled tears (Matt. xxiii. 37, 38).

"*Fifthly*, Nay, He hath shed not only tears, but blood, to convince thee of His willingness. View Him in His dying posture upon the cross, stretching out His dying arms to gather thee, hanging down His blessed head to kiss thee; every one of His wounds was a mouth opened to convince thee of the abundant willingness of Christ to receive thee.

"*Q.* 14. But my sins are dyed in grain; I am a sinner of the blackest hue; will He receive and pardon such as me?

"*Ans.* Yea, soul, if thou be willing to commit thyself to Him. Isa. i. 18, 'Come now, let us reason together, saith the Lord: though your sins be as scarlet, I will make them as snow; though they be red like crimson, I will make them as wool.'"

Flavel was considered to be peculiarly felicitous in the illustration of doctrines by anecdotes. It is curious to contrast the modern anecdotal style with his. In modern anecdotes, the speakers in a dialogue speak very precisely and even pathetically—even a boy is made to exhibit profound pathos—for instance, the boy who explained his fearlessness during a storm at sea by saying, "My father is at the helm." This anecdote is only a new edition of one told by Flavel in more homely style, as follows:—

"Remember that God, in whose hand all creatures are, is your Father. I have met with an excellent story of a religious young man who, being at sea with many other passengers in a great storm, and they being half dead with fear, he only was observed to be very cheerful, as if he had been little concerned in that danger. One of them demanding a reason, O (said he), '*tis because the pilot is my father.*" (*See* the Index to Flavel's Works).

FREDERICK III., Elector-Palatine.

The exact title of the exalted personage, briefly called the Elector-Palatine, was Count-Palatine of the Rhine and Elector of the Empire. His dominions were called the Palatinate. The beginnings of the Reformation there were in the year 1546 (the year of the death of Luther). Melancthon, who was a native of the Palatinate, was in that year requested by the Elector Frederick II. to become Professor of Theology at Heidelberg. He declined the chair, but assisted the Elector with his advice, which resulted in the establishment of a moderate Lutheranism, friendly to Calvinism. In 1556 the Elector, Otto Henry, succeeded Frederick II., and he in 1557 repeated the invitation to Melancthon, who again refused the theological professorship, but gave great assistance in reorganizing the University of Heidelberg on an evangelical basis. The national doctrinal standard was the Augsburg Confession, and the worship was of Zwinglian simplicity. In 1558, on the recommendation of Melancthon, the Elector unfortunately gave the theological professorship to Tilemann Heshusius, whose Lutheran bigotry for consubstantiation filled Heidelberg with dissensions, and evoked among the clergy mutual defiance, leading to sentences of excommunication, and even to a fight between the Professor and Deacon Klebitz in the church at the Lord's Table. The controversy had not subsided at the date of the Elector Otto Henry's death in 1559.

Frederick III. (who was born in 1514) succeeded to the Electorate amidst this fierce commotion. The date is said to be February 1559. The Elector wrote for counsel to Melancthon. The Reformer's reply was dated 1st November 1559. Melancthon recommended the avoidance of extreme dogmas on the Lord's Supper. The letter also drafted and endorsed a eucharistic doctrine, substantially Calvinistic.

The Elector deposed both Heshusius and Klebitz, and appointed a public disputation to be held in the month of June 1560. The issue was, that Melancthon's suggestion was approved of. Distinguished foreign divines were called to the University of Heidelberg, and from them Olevianus and Ursinus were selected to draw up an evangelical catechism. The Elector took the liveliest interest in its preparation, and revised and corrected it. It was submitted in manuscript to a general synod in December 1562, and was agreed to.

The first edition of the Heidelberg Catechism was printed in 1563. It had a preface written by the Elector, dated Tuesday, 19th January 1563, in which he thus described himself:—" Wir Friderich, von Gottes Genaden, Pfaltzgrafe bey Rhein, des heiligen Römischen Reichs Ertztruchses und Churfürst, Herzog in Bayern, &c." The legal title of the Empire was the Holy Roman Empire, although geographically and truly it was the German Empire.

Both a second and a third edition were published in 1563. The third edition had a note, announcing a new question and answer, " on a matter that had been hitherto omitted by an oversight, but now added by command of His Electoral Grace." The original catechism was simply didactic; instructing in the truth, and not naming the opposite errors and heresies. And such a catechism is the best for the edification of the church. But it is said that the sweeping anathema with which the Council of Trent had just closed its proceedings, aroused the Elector, so that he commanded that a question and answer exposing the Romish Mass should be inserted. It is even said that it was his own composition. It is the Eightieth Question of the Third Edition (December 1563), and of all subsequent editions :—

80. Was ist für ein Unterschied zwischen dem Abendmahl des Herrn und der päpstischen Messe?

Das Abendmahl bezeuget uns, das wir vollkommene Vergebung aller unserer Sünden haben, durch das einige Opfer Jesu Christi, so er selbst einmal am Kreuz vollbracht hat; und dass wir durch den heiligen Geist Christo werden eingeleibet, der jetzund mit seinem wahrem Leib in Himmel zur Rechten des Vaters ist, und daselbst will angebetet werden. Die Messe aber lehret, dass die Lebendigen und die Todten nicht durch das Leiden Christi Vergebung der Sünden haben, es sei denn, dass Christus noch täglich für sie von den Messpriestern geopfert werde, und dass Christus leiblich unter der Gestalt des Brods und Weins sei, und derhalben darin soll angebetet werden. Und ist also die Messe im Grund nichts anders, denn eine Verläugnung des einigen Opfers Jesu Christi, und eine vermaledeite Abgötterei.

80. What difference is there between the Supper of the Lord and the Popish Mass?

The Supper testifieth unto us, that we have the complete forgiveness of all our sins through that only sacrifice of Jesus Christ which He Himself hath once accomplished upon the cross, and that we through the Holy Ghost become incorporated with Christ, who now with His true body is in heaven at the right hand of the Father, and willeth to be worshipped there. But the Mass teacheth that the living and the dead have not the forgiveness of sins through the Passion of Christ, unless Christ shall be daily sacrificed for them by the Mass Priests, and that Christ is bodily under the species of bread and wine, and therefore ought to be worshipped therein. And so the mass upon principle is nothing else than a denial of the only sacrifice of Jesus Christ, and is accursed idolatry.

After the publication of the Catechism, great disputations occurred, chiefly regarding the Eucharist and the imagined ubiquity of the body of Jesus, which imagination was, of course, disbelieved by Frederick and his theologians. In April 1564, a colloquy was held at Maulbron. It lasted for six days, the leading divines of Wurtemberg, on behalf of the Lutherans, debating with Olevianus, Ursinus, and Boquin on the part of the Reformed Palatinate.

On account of his so-called Calvinism, Frederick III. was threatened with exclusion from the benefits of the Augsburg Treaty of Peace. At the diet of Augsburg in 1566 it was proposed that he should be excluded from *the Peace of the Empire* (Religionsfriede). He met mere threats with a defiant courage, saying that he would not renounce the truth although the whole world should forsake him. But he had convincing arguments with which he defended his ecclesiastical administration. He brought forward evidence to prove that he had acted on the advice of Melancthon, and this refuted the charge that he was actuated by hostility to the memory of Luther. As to his Catechism, he represented that it was all taken from the Bible, its definitions being fortified by marginal texts; and he called upon any member of the diet to present him with a better—that is, a more scriptural—catechism. The motion to exclude him was withdrawn, the Margrave of Baden saying, " Why do ye persecute this man?" and Augustus, the Elector of Saxony and a Lutheran, exclaiming, " Fritz ! thou art more pious than the whole of us."

Queen Elizabeth of England had in vain sought to form a European Protestant Alliance. The German Princes would go no further than to unite among themselves, being suspicious of the orthodoxy of foreign potentates, and all (except the Landgrave of Hesse and a small minority) characterizing England as Zwinglian. The Elector Frederick III. sent an ambassador to Elizabeth; and she, though without much hope of a practical result, responded by sending her ambassador, Henry Killigrew, to Heidelberg, renewing the proposal of a defensive alliance. Killigrew, along with Dr Christopher Mount, received credentials, dated at Westminster, 12th April 1569, to attend a congress at Frankfort, as a deputation to explain our queen's views. The deputies arrived too late. But the Elector did what he could by withdrawing the word "alliance." He moved "That a Christian agreement with the Queen of England be resolved upon, and that for no other purpose than the protection and safety of the true Christian faith. That the entire support of the alliance should be given to any one state, if threatened with war, or attacked on account of religion. And considering that England is rich in money especially, and that Germany is well supplied with soldiers, that the German Princes shall send an army into the field which England will maintain." This motion was referred to a conference at Erfurt, to which Wilhelm, Landgrave of Hesse, sent this message : " England may be Zwinglian, but the Pope does not care whether a man be Zwinglian or Lutheran, both being alike hated by him. Neither Zwinglians nor Lutherans should care either, as most of their articles of faith are the same." On September 10th (1569) a final answer was sent to the queen, to the following effect :—" We are fully aware of the dangers with which the Protestant princes and nations are threatened; but, on the one hand, we consider ourselves to be sufficiently protected by existing treaties, and, on the other, we have reason to hope that the Catholic German Princes will never enter into such relations with the Pope as would prejudice the welfare of their country and ours. At the same time, we rejoice to see the Queen of England giving repeated proofs of her great zeal for the cause of the Gospel; and though the present circumstances of the Empire prevent us from accepting her offer, we express our sincerest thanks for the sympathy she manifests towards the evangelical Christians of Germany." [1]

Frederick III. had to establish the Reformation in the Palatinate gradually, as parishes became vacant. The following are specimen incidents:—In 1571 the Church of Schlettenbach being vacant, the Bishop of Spire claimed the nomination on behalf of the corporation of Alfested. But the Elector replied that, by the Peace of Passau, the nominators were bound to present to him as patron, pastors whose religion he approved. Thus David Pareus was installed as pastor, and the altars and images were demolished. About three years thereafter, the Bishop of Worms dismissed the drunken priest of Hemsbach, but presented a dissolute priest as his successor. The Elector considered that a good time had come to introduce the Reformation there, and translated Pareus to Hemsbach; and the people at once concurred in removing and burning the images.

The Elector suppressed the convents in his dominions, and devoted their entire wealth to educational and charitable institutions. He lived in the most simple style, that he might contribute liberally from his private income to religion and learning. On his death-bed he praised God that he had seen such a reformation in the church and in schools, as had brought men back from human traditions to Christ and the written word. Frederick III. died on 26th October 1576. He left a confession of his faith in manuscript, which was published by his son, John Casimir.

DESCENDANTS OF THE ELECTOR.

Apart from his high personal merits, the Elector-Palatine Frederick III. deserves recognition as an ancestor of our Royal Family. He had two sons, Louis (born 4th July 1539) and John Casimir. The elder succeeded him as Louis VI., but as a Lutheran he banished the pastors and schoolmasters appointed by his father. He, however, died on 12th October 1583, leaving a son, Frederick, aged only nine. And John Casimir, who became Regent of the Palatinate during his nephew's minority, restored the ecclesiastical state as it was in his father's time. The good regent died in 1592, and the young Elector assumed

[1] Heppe's "Reformers of England and Germany in the sixteenth century—their intercourse and correspondence." English translation. London, 1859.

the government as Frederick IV. (born 5th March 1574, died 9th September 1610). He was succeeded by his son, the Elector Frederick V. (born 16th August 1596), who on 14th February 1613 married the Princess Elizabeth, elder daughter of our King James. The delight of his subjects was intense, and "Thomas Beard, Doctor of Divinitie," as their spokesman in England, penned the following glowing eulogy on His Britannic Majesty :—

" We may here see what cause we have to bless God for the religious care of our dread soveraigne in matching his only daughter, a princess peerless, with a prince of that soundness in religion as the Prince Elector is: thereby discovering his singular love to the truth and his upright heart to God : when as neither masses of treasure nor height of honour did so much preponderate in his royal heart, as did true religion, and the advancement of the Gospel and glory of God. What is to marry in the Lord, if this be not ? and what can be a truer token of a religious heart than this is ? Policy counselleth to strengthen states and kingdoms by conjoining them together by marriages ; and in this respect not only religion is often not regarded, but even nature's law contemned, as experience showeth in many places of Christendom, and especially in the house of Austria. But our religious soveraigne, esteeming it no policy but vanity, which is not grounded upon the fear of God the root of true wisdom, hath preferred true religion above all, and laboured to strengthen himself rather in the Lord than in the world." [1]

Before leaving England, the Elector matriculated at Christ Church, Oxford, and added to his signature the prayer, Rege me, Domine, secundum verbum tuum [Govern me, O Lord, according to Thy word].

The only royal grandchildren during King James' reign were the Elector's elder children. In two forms of prayer by Samuel Smith, printed in 1618,[2] the following morning petitions were suggested :—" Bee gracious unto the King's Majesty . . . Blesse that hopefull Prince, Charles his sonne, the Prince Palatine of the Rhene, and the Lady Elizabeth his wife and their Royall posterity ; " and for the evening —" Continue Thy goodnesse to our King, deliver him from all danger of soule and of body. Blesse the hopefull Prince Charles, the Princely Palsgrave of Rhene, with the Lady Elizabeth his wife and their Royall issue."

Anne, Queen Consort of England, had opposed the Electoral marriage as an unequal alliance for an English Princess. She had treated the Elector with much derision and disdain. Her Majesty died in the spring of 1619 ; but her too well remembered treatment had perhaps fired him with a visionary desire to be " a crowned head," and thus may have

---

[1] Preface (printed in 1614) to a " Declaration of the faith and ceremonies professed in the dominions of Frederick V., Prince Elector Palatine."

[2] Appendix to " David's Repentance, a Plaine and Familiar Exposition of the 51 Psalme." Sixth edition, 1623.

contributed to his decision to accept the royal title to which he was elected. He was crowned King of Bohemia, November 1619, proscribed 1621, deposed 1623 (died 19th November 1632). His Queen survived the English Civil Wars in which her sons, Prince Rupert and Prince Maurice, earned their historical reputation. Her son, Charles Louis, conformed to Romanism and became Elector-Palatine (born 22nd December 1617, died 28th August 1680), and his son Charles, who died 16th May 1685, was the last Elector of his house, the senior line, at his death, being represented by his sister, Charlotte Elizabeth, Duchess of Orleans. The youngest son of Frederick V. and Elizabeth, Edward (born 6th October 1625, died 1684), was only Count-Palatine; he and his descendants were Romanists. The Protestant heir for the British throne was therefore found in the person of the youngest daughter of Frederick V. and Elizabeth, the Princess Sophia, who in 1658 was married to Ernest Augustus of Brunswick, afterwards Elector of Hanover. The Electress Sophia might have lived to be our Queen; but her indignation on receiving a studiously offensive letter from Queen Anne, was the occasion of her sudden death. On the death of Anne a few months afterwards, the Electress Sophia's son became King George I. of Great Britain and Ireland.—(*See* Anderson's Royal Genealogies, Table cclxx).

REV. ANDREW FULLER.

THIS great man, whose praise is in all the churches, was a native of the County of Cambridge, the son of a farmer at Wicken, near Ely. He was born on the 6th February 1754. He received no regular education for the ministry; but being in his youth interested in Divine truth, and much drawn into theological controversy of a practical tendency, he developed a gift for preaching evangelically and usefully. His parents, although seatholders in a Baptist chapel, do not appear to have been Baptists in theory. But Andrew Fuller embraced this persuasion, and was immersed, in April 1770. His first charge was in the town of Soham, where he had received his school education, and had lived since 1760; the date of his settlement was 1774. But he is celebrated as the Baptist pastor of Kettering in Northamptonshire, where he laboured from October 1782 till his death on 7th May 1815. He was also one of the founders of the Baptist Missionary Society and its first secretary, in which office he served unweariedly for twenty years. His voluminous works have been collected, and frequently reprinted.

It was the lot of Andrew Fuller to live in an atmosphere of controversy. Those among whom he walked and wrestled with a truly pious (but a too pugilistic) zeal, were professed believers in the Gospel, some of whom misrepresented it, and some turned the grace of God into licentiousness. He was thus constantly provoked to correct other people's mistakes, and was in danger of modifying or narrowing the expansive Pauline doctrine by constructing pretentiously safe schemes that, unlike the scheme of the Apostle, would make theoretical Antinomianism impossible. This danger Mr Fuller did not always escape from; and in writing in a strain inconsistent with the unconditional freeness of the Gospel offer (as he sometimes did), he was inconsistent with himself. Such inconsistency need not have come prominently into notice; but it was his life-long lot that almost everything which he wrote found its way into print; so that he is continually exhibited as fighting, sometimes with a friend and sometimes with a foe, and in each case equally determined to knock his opponent down. In preaching, he could discourse evangelically on such texts as "To him that worketh not but believeth on Him that justifieth the ungodly," or, " When we were enemies we were reconciled to God by the death of His Son;" but when disputing, he would heap up arguments to prove that a sinner, before he can take refuge in Christ, must have become godly and in subjection to the Father of spirits. A dispute of this kind has the unedifying appearance of setting up one text of Scripture to overthrow another. When we approach such a question, not in order to silence a controversialist, but to speak a word in season to a weary sinner, we can calmly observe that there is no quarrel between the confronted texts, and that the quarrel between confronted Gospel teachers is practically one of mere words—the true question being, not whether a sinner has actually become godly when he takes refuge in Christ, but whether he must know himself to be godly. This is a question not as to actual godliness, but as to conscious godliness—the fact being, that the sinner in fleeing to Christ can see in himself nothing but ungodliness.

REV. JOHN GILL, D.D.

THIS prince of commentators was a native of Kettering (in Northamptonshire), where he was born in the end of 1697. His education was begun in the Grammar School of Kettering, but after 1708, owing to clerical intolerance, it had to be pursued privately. Such was the success of his studies, that another obstacle arose, and this on the part of the Dissenters, one of their metropolitan collegiate academies refusing him admittance, on the ground that if he should continue to make such marvellous progress, his education would be finished at a time of life when he would be too young to be a preacher. He had given himself to Christ when he was in his thirteenth year; and he resolved, though assisting his father, Mr Edward Gill, in the woollen trade, to pursue his studies in his home and in the bookseller's shop, with a view to the pastoral office. Thus, by his own exertions, he became an acknowledged proficient in classical and theological Latin, in Greek, and in Hebrew, as well as in all departments of modern literature. The body of Christians to which his father and himself belonged, were the Particular Baptists, the same as that in which, at a later date, the Rev. Andrew Fuller ministered, their distinctive epithet signifying that they were evangelically orthodox. To this congregation at Kettering, Mr John Gill preached his first sermon on 4th November 1716.

His first charge was at Higham-Ferrers, in his native county, where in 1718 he married Miss Elizabeth Negus. In 1719 he was translated to London, as pastor of the Baptist Church at Horsly-down, Fair Street, Southwark. He now embarked on a most laborious and distinguished life as a preacher, a controversialist, and an author. For full details the reader must have recourse to his Memoir by Dr Rippon, to which is appended an eulogium by Toplady, who humorously remarked, "It would perhaps try the constitutions of half the literati in England, only to read with care and attention the whole of what he wrote."

His first great publication was an "Exposition of the Song of Solomon"—with a translation of the Chaldee paraphrase, or Targum of that book—a folio volume, issued in 1728. In 1735 his extensive acquaintance with the Scriptures and the Fathers was serviceably shown in his book, entitled, "The Cause of God and Truth," in reply to a reprint of Dr Whitby's Arminian Discourse on the Five Points.

Soon after his settlement in London, he had bought a large collection of Hebrew and Rabbinical books, from the library of the late Rev. John Skepp, and used them during his ministry for illustrating the expository discourses which he delivered to his congregation. In 1745 he proposed to throw his expositions into the form of a complete Commentary, and to begin with the New Testament. This "Exposition on the New Testament" was published—vol. 1 in 1746, vol. 2 in 1747, vol. 3 in 1748. It was received with wide applause, and was the occasion of the resolution of the Marischal College of Aberdeen to confer on him, unsolicited, the degree of D.D. This success ultimately culminated in his splendid Commentary on the whole Bible.

Some readers, anxious only for comments suitable to the children and servants in their families, have objected to the constant quotation of Jewish sayings and writings in Dr Gill's notes. This, however, was a principal part of the plan of the author, because Rabbinical literature often suggests how the words of Sacred Scripture would strike the original hearers and readers. In fact, a collection of Dr Gill's Rabbinical and similar quotations would itself form an interesting, a useful, and even a beautiful volume.

But there is one blemish in this admirable Commentary (as in our own Spurgeon's "Morning by Morning," and "Evening by Evening"), namely, a vein of insinuation against all Christians who practice infant baptism. The insinuation is, that they are unbaptized Gentiles; and that it is because of their half-heartedness to Christ, and their deliberate conformity to the world, that they shrink from being publicly immersed in an Antipædobaptistic baptistry. In a Commentary, written by a member of the sect of the Baptists, it is quite seemly and honourable to bring forward before the eyes of hearers, not unprepared for the charge, and in connection with all relevant texts of Scripture, a full and reiterated detail of the commentator's baptismal theory and of its practical application. But it is an unseemly and unmanly style of warfare to insinuate it into the exposition of texts which deal quite generally with such topics as the means of grace and the commandments of Christ and Christian courage; and thus continually to drag that ritualistic theory before the bewildered eyes of devotional inquirers after spiritual and immortal realities.

In 1757 and 1758 Dr Gill published his "Exposition of the Prophets," in two folio volumes. The books from Genesis to Solomon's Song had now to be expounded in order to produce a complete Commentary. This object, in God's kind providence, was achieved. Vol. 1 was published in 1763, vol. 2 in 1764, vol. 3 in 1765, vol. 4 in 1766. [But in the midst of this undertaking he was bereaved of his amiable wife who died 10th October 1764.]

It was with the advantage of a head and heart saturated with the Scriptures that he wrote his "Body of Divinity," of which the doctrinal portion, in two quarto volumes, appeared in 1769, and the third volume, on Practical Divinity, in 1770. He was supported by a long array of subscribers, including the Rev. Henry Venn; Rev. Augustus Toplady; Rev. Thomas Jones, of St Edmund Hall, Oxon.; Rev. Timothy Neve, D.D.; Sir Joseph Mawbey, Bart.; Richard Hill, Esq.; and Captain Thomas Hill; also his late wife's kinsman, Mr Jeremiah Negus; and his own nephew, Rev. John Gill of St Alban's. This was his last publication, as he died 14th October 1771, having earned the reputation (as Toplady said) of being, "in every respect, a burning and a shining light."

It was in 1755 that Dr Gill published his Notes on Dr Crisp's Sermons, in a new edition of those sermons, the publication of which he superintended. The note to which I have undertaken (see CRISP) to refer in this Memoir, is on the truth, that a believer's faith is not properly termed a condition of his receiving Christ's salvation, which is essentially unconditional. Dr Gill's Notes on Sermon VI. support Dr Crisp's testimony on behalf of this truth, and contain the two following valuable quotations from the third book of *Witsius on the Covenants*.

"The Covenant of grace (or the Gospel, strictly so called, which is the formula of the Covenant) consists in mere promises, and properly prescribes nothing. It requires nothing, it commands nothing—not even, 'believe,' 'trust,' 'hope in the Lord,' and the like."—Chap. i., § 18.

"That does not seem to be accurately said, that faith is *a condition* which the law requires of us, that we may be accounted righteous and guiltless with God. The condition (properly so called) of justification is perfect obedience;

this the law requires. The Gospel does not substitute another condition, but teaches that the law is satisfied by our surety—Christ. Moreover, it is the business of faith to accept of Christ's satisfaction of the law's demand, and, by accepting, to make Christ's satisfaction its own."—Chap. viii. § 52.

Even those who think that to preach the Gospel is to tell a sinner that he is offered salvation if he himself will fulfil the required condition of believing in Christ—even they deny that faith is a condition in the most strict and proper meaning of the word, *condition*. Mr Riccaltoun represents this denial in a clever species of dialogue. Speaking of his opponent, he says—

"He owns he is not for a condition, if by condition be meant that which merits anything at the hand of God (no great wonder he rejects this, for even perfect obedience in Adam was not properly meritorious, though it was a federal condition); he rejects it also as it founds a title for heaven (I am glad of this; I hope we shall come pretty near other, on this head, if he hold on); he refuses it likewise as practicable in our own strength (very good all, I hope then 'tis freely given to us to believe). He advances and adds further, that it is not anything done by us that comes in the room of *perfect obedience under the first covenant* (excellent yet, I'm heartily pleased with all this); he concludes, ' it is not anything previous as the condition of the first grace:' this, he owns, is absolutely promised and given (Jer. xxxii. 37, &c., Ezek. xxxvi. 26, &c.)—(all this I frankly own).

"The author goes on to explain the difference between an *interesting* and an *entitling* condition, and owns that it is the righteousness of the surety that comes in place of Adam's perfect righteousness as *the entitling condition*, and that faith, as the bond of union with Christ, *interests* us in Him (well, then, I think we will not dispute about faith's being the condition of the covenant of grace in the strict and proper sense of the term ' condition ').

"The [Westminster] Assembly (Larger Cat., Q. 32) takes the word ' condition ' in a large and improper sense, as the way and mean which God makes use of for making up our union with Christ, and so not properly as the condition of union, but as the very uniting act, or mean of union."—*Review of an Essay on Gospel and Legal Preaching*, p. 104.

Ebenezer Erskine states the case thus: "*But*, say you, *is not faith the condition?* I will be loath to condemn that way of speaking, because worthy men have used it, and do use it, in a sound sense. But, sirs, I would have you to remember, that when it is called a condition, all that such learned and worthy men mean by it is only this, That you can have no saving benefit or advantage by Christ, unless He be received [*accepted by you*, or *welcomed*]; you can have no benefit by God's covenant of promise, unless you believe the promise to be true, and believe it with application to your own souls. Faith is just such a condition as shows the inseparable connection between one thing and another:

as if you should say to a beggar, There is your alms, on condition you take it; there is meat, on condition you eat it; there is a good bond for a sum of money, on condition you trust him that granted it. Now, such a condition of the covenant of grace is faith; it is just a taking what is freely given without money and price; and, let it be remembered, that itself is one of the blessings promised in this covenant."—*Sermon* on Rev. iv. 9, published in 1718.

DR J. F. A. GILLET.

DR GILLET was pastor of the congregation of the Court Church of Breslau in and before 1857, in which year he published "The Heidelberg Catechism Dissected for the Use of Schools and Confirmation Classes, and for Self-Instruction, and authenticated from Holy Scripture" [Der Heidelberger Katechismus, zum Gebrauche für Schulen, Confirmanden-Unterricht, und Selbstunterweisung zergliedert und aus der Heiligen Schrift bewährt.]

A more interesting manual was never compiled. The Scripture proofs are arranged in answer to brief simplified questions. Each section is accompanied with a lesson in Bible history; and, with a few exceptions, each question is illustrated by appropriate hymns. The hymns, if printed separately, would admirably carry out Luther's idea, of instructing the pupil systematically by means of sacred songs.

The proof that the Scripture sanctions the division of the elements of saving knowledge into the knowledge of sin, redemption, and practical thankfulness is ingenious:—

		SIN AND MISERY.	REDEMPTION.	PRACTICAL THANKFULNESS.
Rom. vii. 24, 25.		O wretched man that I am!	Who shall deliver me from the body of this death?	I thank God, through Jesus Christ our Lord.
Matt. xi. 28, 29, 30.		All ye that labour and are heavy laden!	Come unto Me, and I will give you rest.	Take My yoke upon you and learn of Me, for I am meek and lowly in heart; and ye shall find rest unto your souls; for My yoke is easy and my burden is light.

This threefold knowledge is illustrated by three hymns. [I find that although the above are not the proof-texts in the original catechism, they are those of the modern German reprints.]

REV. THOMAS GOODWIN, D.D.

THOMAS GOODWIN was a native of Norfolk, having been born in the village of Rolesby in 1600 (Oct. 5). He was educated at Christchurch in Cambridge, and became Fellow of Katharine Hall, and Bachelor of Divinity. He became also a famous preacher in that University town. It is said that Dr Sibbes remonstrated with him "because his sermons were, for the most part, if not wholly, calculated to produce conviction and terror, to alarm the conscience and wound the heart;" and gave him this advice, which he thereafter acted upon, to the incalculable benefit of his own and all following generations :—" Young man, if ever you would do good, you must preach the Gospel and the free grace of God in Christ Jesus, and the consolations that flow from these important doctrines." He was episcopally ordained, but the tyranny of the Laudean system drove him out. He resigned his preferments, and was a refugee in Holland, and pastor of an Independent congregation at Arnheim. He returned to London about the beginning of the Long Parliament, and became a member of the Westminster Assembly. In this relation his congregationalist principles were obstructive, both as to public results and as to his own personal advantage. But his principles recommended him to Cromwell. In 1650 he began his residence in Oxford as President of Magdalen College, and he received the degree of D.D. in 1653. From Oxford he was, of course, removed in 1660, and he retired to London, where he resided, chiefly in the parish of Great St Bartholomew, till his death, in his eightieth year, 23rd Feb. 1680 (new style).

The republication of Dr Goodwin's Works by Mr Nichol of Edinburgh renders a list of his writings unnecessary. They occupy twelve volumes, octavo ; as they were formerly known, they consisted of one thick quarto volume and five gigantic folios. The original editions had become very scarce, and their possessors were considered fortunate. It was thought that the reprint would be very popular ; and no doubt it has been extensively useful, like the whole of the series of Puritan Authors republished by Mr Nichol. However, the effect of the voluminous republication has, for the present, been disappointing ; the public apparently having been surfeited, and the Puritans' writings being generally neglected. There can be no doubt that modernised spelling often strips those ancient men's sayings of their fatherly and testamentary tone. For instance, to modernise

such a sentence as the following (extracted from Goodwin's "Child of Light Walking in Darkness") is to spoil it:—
"*That strange fire* of their owne righteousnesse, which is from and in nature unchanged, and the *kitching fire* of outward comforts—these are the two maine hinderances that keepe all wicked men from *Christ* and *justification* through Him."

REV. THOMAS GOODWIN, JUNIOR.

THE son and namesake of Dr Goodwin was partly educated in England, but finished his education in Holland. He was, says Calamy, "a person of great and universal literature, and of a most gentle and obliging temper, and who lived usefully upon his estate." During the reign of Charles II., he, with three other young men, carried on an evening lecture, which was supported and attended by some of the first merchants in London. In 1683 he made the tour of Europe with Mr Shower and other gentlemen. In 1685 he became assistant to Rev. Stephen Lob in Fetter Lane, London. He was during the rest of his ministerial life "Pastor of a Church of Christ at Pinnor in Middlesex." He was there in 1695, when he wrote his valuable pamphlet, "A Discourse on the true nature of the Gospel, demonstrating that it is no new law but a pure doctrine of grace. In answer to the Reverend Mr Lorimer's Apology." Mr Lorimer, though a respectable minister, was one of those combatants who condemn themselves by their condemnation of better and sounder men, and demonstrate the falsity of their own opinions in proposing them as substitutes for a scriptural and evangelical system. Mr Goodwin says, (p. 3), "As for Bradwardine and Dr Owen, on whom Mr Lorimer is pleased to bestow some disadvantageous remarks, they are . . . . great names . . . . and above his little reflections." "As for Mr Marshall, that very book, which Mr Lorimer so much vilifies, discovers a pious heart, joined with a closeness and consistency of thought." Mr Lorimer's watchword was the word "law," from which he inferred that the Gospel is a new law; but Mr Goodwin (p. 37) agreed with Calvin, that when the Gospel is called a law, only a *doctrine* of salvation is meant by that word "law." Mr Goodwin shows that Romanists, Socinians, and Arminians have advocated Mr Lorimer's views, as their respective dreams about salvation required them to do. So Luther (on Gal. ii. 5) said, "All justiciaries esteem Christ to be a new legislator. The truth is, that precepts are found in the Gospel. But they are not the Gospel; they are but expositions of the law and appendixes of the Gospel." Mr Goodwin's Pamphlet contains a full history of the true and false doctrine on this vital question. It shows him to have been a most capable Theological Professor in the Academy attached to his Church.

REV. JOHN GUYSE, D.D.

JOHN GUYSE was born in Hertford in 1680. He studied literature and theology at Saffron Walden, under Rev. John Payne, known as the friend of Dr Owen. He was a congregationalist, and began to preach in 1700 in his native town, as assistant to Mr Haworth, whom he afterwards succeeded in the full charge of the Independent Congregation. His biblical and theological learning was turned to special account when Arminianism threatened the churches. The result of the controversy and of his successful teaching of the truth as it is in Jesus, was the publication of the still celebrated books, "Guyse on the Divinity and Person of Christ" (1719), and "Guyse on the Divinity of the Holy Spirit" (1724). Mr Guyse had frequently been offered promotion, but felt bound by duty to Hertford. However, his congregational and literary labours, and the large size of his church and congregation, threatened to end his days. And the advice of Mr Bragge commended itself to him : " A minister may lawfully leave his people when, upon a full trial, his labours are too great for his health. Christ does not call upon His servants to kill themselves in His service ; He is too good a Master to require it, and too great a one to need it."[1] At the invitation of the infant congregation of New Broad Street in London, Mr Guyse became their minister in 1727. The early years of his London ministry were signalised by his preaching the Coward Lecture, and by his controversy with Mr Chandler on its publication. Mr Guyse declared his determination to preach Christ, and urged that true method of preaching upon his brethren. Young Chandler's letters were both unevangelical and rude ; so much so, that he demeaned himself by saying, that by preaching Christ Mr Guyse meant preaching well, that is, preaching better than other ministers ; and that he was advertising himself and his church in competition with others. I have already devoted a whole Chapter to this important subject, so that in this Memoir I need only quote the verdict of Bogue and Bennett (to whom I am indebted for the facts in this Memoir). " Mr Guyse had evidently the advantage both in argument and temper, and his opponent never appeared to so little advantage as in this dispute."[2] It was in London that Mr Guyse wrote his great work in three quarto volumes, "A Paraphrase on the New Testament." It differs from the similar work of Dr Doddridge in its object, which was to be a safe guide to students as to biblical interpretation, and consequently in its

---

[1] [The neglect to distinguish between burnt-offerings and thank-offerings has led some people into an opposite opinion founded on the Apostle's phrase, "a living sacrifice" (Rom. xii. 1). But that phrase justifies Mr Bragge's opinion. What it suggests is a sacrifice of praise with Hezekiah's motto, " The living, the living, he shall praise Thee." It is impossible for a man at one and the same time both to kill himself and to be a living sacrifice.—D. C. A. A.]

[2] " History of Dissenters," Vol. IV., page 443.

method, which was to collect the various senses put on the text by orthodox divines. For this task the great scholarship and studious zeal of the author made him well qualified. As a testimony to his profound and accurate knowledge of theology and biblical criticism, the University of Aberdeen conferred on him the degree of D.D. in the year 1732, to the surprise of himself and the satisfaction of his many friends. His Berry Street Sermons, and others, were collected into one volume in 1756. The age of fourscore found him faithful and diligent, though feeble in body. When his end drew nigh, he said, "Thanks be to God, I have no doubt, no difficulty in my mind, as to my eternal state; if I had, I could not bear what I now feel. I know whom I have believed, here my faith rests." —"The peculiar doctrines of the Gospel which I have long preached, are now the support of my soul. I live upon them every day, and thence I derive neverfailing comfort."—" How gracious is my God to me; how often has He made good to me that promise, As thy day so shall thy strength be."—"I am not afraid of death; I am afraid lest I should err on the other side, in being too desirous of it."

Dr Guyse died on 22nd November 1761, aged eighty-one. His funeral sermon was preached by the Rev. John Conder.

REV. ALEXANDER HAMILTON.

ALEXANDER HAMILTON, *born* in 1662, was a pious youth, reared amidst the troubles of Covenanting times. When a student in the University of Edinburgh, the head of Rev. James Guthrie of Stirling, which had been exposed, ever since his martyrdom, upon a pike affixed to the port at the Netherbow, was pointed out to him; and he took advantage of the darkness of night to climb up and remove it from the public gaze. He was ordained as minister of Ecclesmachan by the Presbytery of Linlithgow on 29th August 1694, from whence he was translated to Airth, in Stirlingshire, on 23rd April 1700. It is as "Hamilton of Airth" that his memory is embalmed in the memory and in the Church History of Scotland. Principal Hadow, having had a friendly correspondence with him from 1710 to 1712, was aware of his love for the free and full Gospel, and of his disapproval of the orthodoxy of that date, which insisted that the covenant of grace is offered to hearers of the Gospel on certain terms, and that it is "a mutual covenant containing stipulation and re-stipulation." The form of the correspondence was an examination of a catechism by Mr Hamilton, which was then in manuscript, but which Dr Scott informs us was printed at Edinburgh in 1714, with the title, "A Short Catechism concerning the Three Special Divine Covenants and the Two Gospel Sacraments, with Scripture-proofs." A manuscript copy of the correspondence is in the Edinburgh New College Library, and now lies on the table before me. Not having seen the printed catechism, I copy from one of Mr Hamilton's letters a specimen both of it and of his epistolary vindication of his doctrine.

"Part III. Concerning the covenant of grace. Q. 3. Is this covenant, then, mutual as containing stipulation and re-stipulation?

Answer. In a proper and strict sense it is not—the whole of the grace thereof being lodged in the Lord's own hand, and what actings the poor lost dead sinner has at any time toward Him being the effect of God's grace."

MS. Vindication.

"Though it must be granted that God doth not bring any under the bond of the covenant against their will, yet it must be owned that what assent or consent the elect sinner hath at any time toward Him holds entirely of God. Hence saith the Lord, 'I will betroth thee unto Me for ever in righteousness and judgment and in loving-kindness; I will even betroth thee unto Me in faithfulness: and thou shalt know the Lord. I will have mercy upon thee that hath not obtained mercy, and I will say unto them, that were not My people, Thou art My people, and they shall say, Thou art my God' (Hosea ii. 19, 20, 23). Hence, saith Gillespie, in his "Treatise upon the Covenants," Part I., p. 101, 'God's covenant with man is the sole will and pleasure of the one party.' (See also p. 143.) P. 294, he saith expressly, 'God makes the covenant with us, and not we with Him.' And in p. 208, 'It's a covenant that saith, *I will and they shall*, and saith not, If he do this I will do that, but *I will do this, and they shall do that,* I will make them do it,' &c." "ALEX. HAMILTON."
Airth, Dec. 1, 1710.

The seventh question and answer are as follow:—
"Q. 7. Wherein consists the nature and form of the covenant? *Ans.* Properly it consists in gracious promises."

Principal Hadow, whom Mr Hamilton describes as a mild man in conversation, proved to be stern in action; and accordingly the author of the above statements was summoned to answer for himself before the General Assembly's Committee on Purity of Doctrine, April 1720. He was examined ten or eleven times during eight days. He wrote an account of the affair, in which he says: "I confess, when they were putting some queries to me, which insinuated great suspicions of gross error, and others that (I thought) grated much upon special Gospel truths, my heart grew so great that I could scarce utter a word without a flood of tears." The result was, that the Committee expressed "the greatest affection and brotherly tenderness towards him," and reported favourably.

In 1725 Mr Brisbane of Stirling died; Mr Hamilton was inducted as his successor on 2nd February 1726. Mr Ebenezer Erskine became his neighbour in Stirling in 1731, and he lived in close friendship with him and his brother— a friendship which was not cooled by the secession of the Erskines from the judicatories of the Establishment. Mr Ralph Erskine said of him: "His sentiments were so much the same with *those that are now associate together by themselves* that they had a remarkable share in his daily prayers under the name of *The Reforming Society*." He died 29th January 1738, in his seventy-sixth year.

PROFESSOR WILLIAM HAMILTON, D.D.

WILLIAM, second son of Gavin Hamilton of Airdrie, a scion of the Hamiltons of Preston, was born about 1669, and, being a child of covenanting parents, "was baptized at a conventicle."[1] On 26th September 1694 he was ordained minister of Corstorphine, where he laboured for fifteen years. In 1709 he was installed as Professor of Divinity in the University of Edinburgh. In 1732 he became Principal of the University, and exchanged his chair for the collegiate charge of the New North Church in the city. But he is remembered as Professor Hamilton; for he survived the translation for only three months, dying on 12th November 1732, aged about sixty-three. He thus predeceased the Secession; and it can only be a conjecture how, as an acknowledged leader, he would have encountered the emergency. He was five times Moderator of the General Assembly. He was an excellent theological teacher. Thomas Boston of Ettrick writes in his Memoirs: "17th May 1729.—I had a conversation with Professor Hamilton, who ingenuously declared to me his satisfaction (and this of his own accord) with what we called *the deed of gift*, and his conviction that the Gospel could not be preached without it."

[His children were—Robert Hamilton, D.D., Professor of Theology, Edinburgh, from 1754 to 1787; and Ann, wife of Rev. John Horsley, M.A., and mother of Right Rev. Samuel Horsley, Bishop of St Asaph.

Professor Robert Hamilton married Jean, daughter of John Hay, Esq., of Haystoun, Peeblesshire, and had, with other children, a son, James Hamilton, M.D.; and a daughter, Grizel, wife of Benjamin Bell, surgeon, Edinburgh, author of a great work on "The Principles of Surgery."]

[1] So says Anderson's "Scottish Nation" (Vol. II., page 424). Mr Anderson makes 1675 the year of W. H.'s birth, but this would represent him as receiving ordination at the age of nineteen; I therefore follow Dr Scott.

REV. JAMES HERVEY, M.A.

This accomplished English clergyman was, for a long period, well known as the author of "Meditations among the Tombs," "Reflections on a Flower-Garden," and similar elegant pieces. The same poetical prose characterized his dialogues and letters on Gospel privileges, entitled "Theron and Aspasio." (*Theron* is an inquirer, a gentleman of fortune, and *Aspasio* is his Christian friend and instructor). In an unadorned style he wrote a defence of the latter work addressed to the Rev. John Wesley, who at that time repudiated the doctrine of the imputation of Christ's righteousness, except as a less felicitous mode of expressing forgiveness through the blood of Christ. Mr Hervey also wrote "Remarks on Lord Bolingbroke." James Hervey was born at Hardingstone in Northamptonshire, in February 1713, in the house of his father, the Rev. William Hervey, who held two family livings, Weston-Favell and Collingtree. He was educated at Northampton, and at Lincoln College, Oxford. At the University he was a friend and associate of Whitefield and Wesley. On 19th September 1736 he took Deacon's Orders and came home as curate of Collingtree. He served in curacies in Devonshire, first at Stoke Abbey, then at Bideford. In this county his delicate consumptive constitution received little or no benefit. It was in following a ploughman for the sake of generous exhalations from the newly-turned earth, that an often-repeated conversation took place. He said to the pious rustic, *What is the hardest thing in religion?* and the man having referred the question back to the reverend questioner, Mr Hervey's answer was, "To deny sinful self." The ploughman admitted that was a hard but not the hardest thing, and said that his own experience would answer the question thus, "To deny righteous self." Mr Hervey felt offended and even indignant; but his studies having been providentially directed to the writings of Witsius and Boston, and to such books as "Jenks on Submission to the Righteousness of Christ," and Marshall's "Gospel Mystery of Sanctification," he came to see that the poor man was right. And the tidings that the loving and Catholic James Hervey had *learned Christ* and now *preached Christ* rejoiced the heart of Whitefield. In 1743 he returned to Collingtree, where he had great leisure for writing. Circumstances connected with his delicate health and attacks of illness led to his long residence in London (from June 1750 to May 1752), where he associated with Whitefield, William Romaine, and Dr Gill. His father died in May 1752; and after that, James Hervey resided in his native county as rector of Weston-Favell and Collingtree, until his death, at the early age of forty-four, on 25th December 1758.[1]

As already hinted, he elaborated his compositions with great care; but he said, "I do not so much as wish to invent any new doctrine, but to dress the

---

[1] See Mr Bull's Papers on Hervey in *Sunday at Home* for 1875.

good old truths of the Reformation in such drapery of language as to allure men of all conditions."

His "Theron and Aspasio," as far as it went, was chiefly occupied with explanations and recommendations of the doctrine of justification. It was the entire failure of Mr Hervey's health and strength that hindered him from continuing those dialogues, so as completely to illustrate his religious principles, as often expressed by him in language such as the following: " Cherish faith, and you will of course cultivate obedience; water the root, and the branches of Gospel godliness will assuredly partake of the beneficial effects."

All that he wrote in contemplation of the continuation of "Theron and Aspasio" was this draft of a programme of a fourth volume :—

"Pleasure and happiness of Christ's religion (for I am of the same opinion as Mr Marshall in his treatise on sanctification, namely, that we must partake of the comforts of the Gospel before we can practise the duties of the law).

"Theron oppressed with fears, on account of his numerous sins. Discouraged with doubts, on account of his imperfect obedience. The cordials of the Gospel readministered, with some additional spirit and strength. Objections to assurance of faith, stated, discussed, answered.

"Vital holiness, its nature, necessity, excellency. Its grand efficient, the blessed Spirit. Its principal instrument, true faith; mixed with which, the Scriptures, the Lord's Supper, prayer, the Divine promises, are powerful and effectual means; disunited from which, they are a dead letter and insignificant ordinances.

"The evangelical principles of holiness, such as, *I beseech you by the mercies of God—ye are bought with a price—ye are the temples of the living God,* &c. ; all these privileges, though not hereditary, yet indefeasible; or the final perseverance of the saints.

"Our friends part—renew their correspondence. Theron desires to glorify the God of his salvation, asks advice concerning the best method of family worship, educating children, instructing servants, edifying acquaintance. On each of these particulars Aspasio satisfies his inquiry—enlarges on the subject of education, especially of daughters, as that seems to be most neglected, or the proper way of conducting it least understood.

"Letter on the covenant of grace, comprising the substance, and being a kind of recapitulation, of the three foregoing volumes.

"Aspasio seized with a sudden and fatal illness; his sentiments and behaviour in his last moments."—(Letter 142).

Although Mr Hervey never wrote the volume, of which the above was the plan, yet his design was not altogether unfulfilled. The Rev. John Brown of Whitburn, in Scotland, was a diligent student of all his writings, and published an interesting Memoir, which was welded out of the printed letters, almost every sentence being made some use of. Having thus become saturated with Hervey, Mr Brown wrote additional *Letters to Theron*. In the pages of "The Christian Repository" they were printed, and after the author's death they reappeared in a volume, as "Brown's Letters on Sanctification" (1834). The Letters are arranged thus:—1. Preliminary. 2. The Connection between Evangelical Holiness and Christ. 3. The Nature of Holiness. 4. The Exercise of Holiness. 5. The Pleasures of Evangelical Holiness. 6. The Law of Holiness. 7. The Dying Saint.

To render his letters a fitting continuation of Aspasio's Letters to Theron, Mr Brown, whose own style of writing was quite unadorned, secured the aid of his son, who had acquired a more literary style. The father wrote the letters in the style natural to himself, the son rewrote them, and the father revised the embellished draft. (This plan was carried out in every letter, except the sixth). The Letters, thus completed, were sent to the editor of the "Repository," along with the following note:—

"Sir, It is generally known that it was Mr Hervey's intention to have added another volume to his 'Theron and Aspasio' on the influence of his peculiar views of Gospel doctrine on sanctification. His ill health and premature death prevented the execution of this design. Strongly persuaded that the Gospel as understood by Mr Hervey is 'the doctrine according to godliness' (1 Tim. vi. 3), I have devoted some of my leisure hours to the composition of the enclosed letters, which, if they suit your journal, you are welcome to give to the public. How far they supply the desideratum, others must determine. I have at least this consoling reflection, I have meant well, I have done what I could.

"J. B., W."

(See the "Additional Memoirs" at the end of this volume, where a specimen of the Letters on Sanctification will be given).

REV. JAMES HOG, M.A.

THE name of Mr Hog, minister of Carnock, will always be dear to worthy Scotchmen, and his memory has long been revered in Great Britain and America. As to his parentage, which was godly and covenanting, I reserve it for a note. James Hog was born in 1658, and studied in the University of Edinburgh, where he took the degree of M.A. in 1677. His father died peacefully and triumphantly about 1680 or 1681, and young Hog went to Holland for his theological studies. We recognise his name in Professor Leydekker's class for the Heidelberg Catechism,

THE THEOLOGY OF CONSOLATION.

9th September [1682], where he is called "Jacobus Hoog, *Scoto-Brit.*" During his younger days he had enjoyed the friendship (though apparently he was no relation) of Rev. Thomas Hog, minister of Kiltearn, whom he visited as a covenanting prisoner in the Edinburgh Tolbooth, and from whom he received one or more letters from the Bass Rock. In Holland they became fast friends as fellow-exiles. [He, in the next century, wrote in the preface to his "Notes about saving illumination": "If I have attained to any improvement in this and other things pertaining to life and godliness, I owe it much, next unto free mercy, to the instruction and conduct of Mr T[homas] H[og], a burning and shining light, who was honoured to gain many souls in his day, and under whose tender and fatherly care I had the happiness to live for a little while in a foreign country, after some more transient converse before that exile."]

In his manuscript, which I shall afterwards describe, speaking of himself in the third person, James Hog writes, "It was his happiness often to enjoy a powerful dispensation of Gospel ordinances during the first periods of his sinful and much-tossed life. In those days several choice ministers adventured to preach in the face of cruel laws enacted against them." This manuscript contains his meditations during his time of anxiety as to the question whether the Gospel of our blessed Saviour was intended for such a sinner as himself. Some of us may have thought that some modern light regarding the Gospel welcome is conveyed in the lines—

"Just as I am—and waiting not
To rid my soul of one dark blot—
To Thee, whose blood can cleanse each spot,
O Lamb of God, I come!"

But James Hog came to this conclusion in his younger days. He writes, "The Gospel-calls to believe, recorded by the Spirit of God in the word, do plainly point out the sinner's state as that wherein we were left by our sin and fall in our first parents; and the wretched sinner is invited to come to Christ—[to come] as he is, in these very circumstances of death, darkness, enmity, wickedness, and extreme dangers of every sort that attend him. . . . . The wretched sinner—as ungodly (only, wholly, and exceedingly so)—is invited and welcomed to come unto Him who is the Lord our Righteousness." (*See* COLE and TRAIL.)

The last chapter in the manuscript is Chapter XI., "Wherein Philomathes [J. Hog] proposeth to account for the chief wrestlings which relate to his ministerial work, his preparation for it, entrance upon it, and conduct therein, both as to the incontested matters that belong to the common salvation, and also with respect to sundry things controverted in his time." This chapter informs us that he studied under the best professors in Holland, supporting himself as a college tutor. He returned to Scotland after the abdication of James VII., "chiefly on account of the commands of his only surviving parent." His theological education was severely tested by the Presbytery of Edinburgh, and he was licensed as a Preacher of the Gospel. In the end of 1690 he received a call to be minister of Dalserf, in the Presbytery of Hamilton, and was ordained 20th January 1690. He sat in the General Assembly as a representative of his Presbytery in May 1692. He now got into trouble about oaths to the government.

I must explain that at that epoch all godly ministers observed, with deepest feeling, how the Stuart rule had demoralized the consciences of the people by a wanton imposition of oaths. The people had been compelled to swear this thing and that thing, and even an undescribed *et cetera*, not because they believed it, but because it was commanded. Falsehood and perjury were incurred with a light heart and elastic conscience, and a sacred solemnity was rendered contemptible and ensnaring. Mr Hog, and those with whom he associated in the ministry, felt it necessary to criticize public oaths very carefully. There could be no objection to a simple oath of allegiance to William and Mary. But there were oaths in existence and in contemplation which seemed to imply the approval of the establishment of episcopacy, &c., in England, and also of the declaration as to England that the Sovereign is the Head of the church, or supreme over all persons, and in all causes, civil and ecclesiastical. The consequence was, that the most earnest ministers, as seeking the public good, refused to swear. To distinguish them from the Episcopal Non-Jurors (who disowned allegiance to William and Mary) they were usually called *non-jurants*, and the Presbyterian ministers, who were *jurors*, were regarded as lukewarm servants of their church and country.

Mr Hog shared in these scruples. But what most offended his conscience was, that an Act of Parliament had declared that men, who would not swear, should not be ministers or preachers. This was the point that brought him to a decision; "when he saw the Act of Parliament for settling the peace and quiet of the church, and understood from it that a swearing the allegiance and subscribing the assurance were required by law as a necessary qualification, without which none were allowed to be ministers and preachers within the same, this Act appearing to him to be of an Erastian strain, did heighten his reluctancy. Hence, upon these and other grounds for which he hath accounted in another way, he thought it his duty to decline the swearing required."

This declinature made him liable to severe and ruinous fines; and he and his brethren were always prepared to submit to the legal penalty. But it being notorious that they were practically the most loyal and exemplary subjects of their Majesties, no prosecution took place. Mr Hog wrote a letter to the Duchess of Hamilton, to be communicated to her noble husband, who was the Royal Commissioner to the General Assembly of the Church of Scotland, declaring in the strongest terms his dutiful and grateful loyalty to their Majesties, and protesting that his declinature was founded on conscientious objections, not to the contents of the oaths, but "to some concomitants of them." The Duke received the letter kindly, and no prosecution was instituted against him.

On one Sabbath he was absent from home, and the parishioners of Dalserf, who repaired to the nearest church, had to listen to a sermon assailing the nonjurants. On the next Sabbath Mr Hog explained his conduct from his own pulpit to his flock, which hitherto he had refrained from doing. This led to unpleasant debates in the Presbytery. Apparently to bring the matter to a climax, the Presbytery elected him, against his will, as a member of the General Assembly of 1695. As soon as Mr Hog entered the House, Lord Carmichael, the Royal Commissioner, sent for him, and, in a private interview, requested him not to take his seat. Next, the Lord Advocate, also privately, but more excitedly, conversed with him, and expressed the same desire. To both he gave the same answer, that he must keep his seat, unless the General Assembly formally resolved otherwise. No such resolution being communicated to him, he both sat and spoke as a member. But for the sake of peace he offered to retire from Dalserf. The General Assembly accepted his resignation, and granted him an *Act of transportability*, that is, a certificate that he was eligible for any vacancy in the church. Thus he was separated from his parish, and "accepted of no other for some years." And so the manuscript concludes, "At length, a way being most unexpectedly opened to him, with universal consent, to an easy and manageable congregation, he agreed to make a trial, and continueth to labour there to this day."

The delay in his settlement arose from severe illness; in fact, his health was precarious during the rest of his life. He had for this reason to resign his deed of election to a charge in the Synod of Moray. The "easy and manageable congregation," over which he was inducted on 23rd August 1699, was Carnock, in the Presbytery of Dunfermline. His first printed book, prefaced by a friend in 1701, states, "the author, being by indisposition laid aside from any other exercise of his ministry, did employ his talent in family Exercises; they come to thy hand in their native dress." Perhaps the thought, that the yearly college vacation might preserve his life, induced him to be a candidate for the Divinity Chair in Marischal College, Aberdeen, in 1711; he was, however, defeated. Though in a minority in the Synod of Fife and in the General Assembly, he was recognised as a leader in the religious community. This appears from his being employed in 1714 to write the Preface to the late Professor Halyburton's great work on the "Insufficiency of Natural Religion." Another and more celebrated preface was dated "Carnock, December 3, 1717," introducing to the Scottish public the little book called "The Marrow of Modern Divinity." I have elsewhere given the history of the Marrow and the Church-courts. Here I need only quote a short narrative by Mr Boston:—"In April 1720, a Committee of the General Assembly examined Rev. James Hog, minister of Carnock; Alexander Hamilton, minister of Airth; James Brisbane, minister of Stirling; and John

Warden, minister of Gargunnock. They were examined apart. Mr Hog being called, the first query proposed to him was, Whether he owned himself author of the preface to the last edition of "The Marrow of Modern Divinity." To which he answered affirmatively, and moreover told them that that book, whereof he knew nothing before, came most unexpectedly to his hand, and he read it over as soon as he could—that he had no thoughts of the reprinting of it, but complied with the motion thereto, after the project had been laid by others—that at the earnest desire of some who managed the business he wrote the preface—that the Lord had blessed the reading of the book to many excellent persons of divers ranks, and that he knew an eminent divine, now in glory, who left it on record that the reading an old edition thereof was the first notable means blest of the Lord for giving him some clearness of impression concerning the Gospel—and that, for his own part, he owned that he had received more light about some important concerns of the glorious Gospel by perusing that book, than by other human writings which Providence had brought into his hands."

There is no record of any public appearances by Mr Hog after the cessation of the Marrow debates. He probably was frequently disabled even from preaching, and on 21st January 1730 the Rev. Daniel Hunter was ordained his assistant and successor. Mr Hunter also became his son-in-law by his marriage to Miss Janet Hog. Mr Hog died in Edinburgh, on 14th May 1734, in his seventy-sixth year.

Mr Hog's publications were numerous, but owing to a scholastic and involved style they have fallen out of notice. As containing the counsels and opinions of one who had a masterly grasp of theology, and who wrote for the good of souls and the glory of God, they might be profitably consulted. Having facilities for giving a more complete list than has yet appeared, I present students with the following catalogue. [Where a full description is given, I have the book or tract on my table. Where Mr Hog's name is not given in my transcript of the title-page of any such book or tract, the publication is anonymous.]

(1.) *In manuscript.* Memorial written by Philomathes, and addressed to his surviving friends.

[Several copies of this manuscript were made, and have been preserved. From one copy partial reprints were taken by Rev. John Brown of Haddington, and by Rev. Archibald Bruce of Whitburn. There is a copy in the Advocates' Library, Edinburgh, from which I gleaned most of my information regarding the period of his life with which it is occupied. This copy of the MS. has been described thus:—"The life of Mr James Hog, sometime minister of the Gospel at Disserf, in Hamilton Presbytery, afterwards at Carnock, in Dunfermline Presbytery—written by himself—belonging to John Jamieson, SS.T.S., the gift of the Rev. Mr Adam Gib, minister of the Gospel, Edinburgh. Glasgow, June 20, 1776."]

(2.) Remarks concerning the Spirit's Operation, and the difference betwixt the law and the gospel. Being the heads of some Family Exercises upon

Galatians, chap. iii. ver. 2 ; Rom. x. 14, *How shall they believe in Him of whom they have not heard?* Rom. iii. 28, *Therefore we conclude that a man is justified by faith without the deeds of the law.* Edinburgh, printed by the heirs and successors of Andrew Anderson, printer to the King's most Excellent Majesty, Anno Dom. 1701. [Preface signed J. C., 3 pp.] 126 pp.

[The Preface, written by an older divine, is a link between the 17th and 18th centuries—the glowing language of the senior contrasting with the complex sentences of the junior. The old man writes both with the beauty and with the occasional (quite innocent) indelicacy of Manton :—" Mistake not the author, as if he brought thee off from the law as a rule, or as a schoolmaster to lead to Christ. As long as Hagar is Sarai's maid, she serves her. But when she goes into Abraham's bed, then cast out the bondwoman and her son."]

(3.) A Casuistical Essay upon the Lord's Prayer, wherein divers important Cases relative to the several Petitions are succinctly stated and answered. To which is subjoin'd, A Letter to a friend, in answer to Sir Hugh Campbel of Calder, and Monsieur d'Espagne, concerning the use thereof. Edinburgh, printed by John Reid, junior, 1705. xxiv. and 374 pp.

[For a specimen of this work, *see* REYNOLDS.]

(4.) A letter to a friend containing diverse remarks concerning the Sacrament of the Lord's Supper, with some hints at the Scriptural-Rules for administration of and admission to the same. Edinburgh, printed by James Watson, on the North-side of the Cross, 1706. 100 pp.

(5.) Some Select Notes towards detecting a covert mixture of the Covenant of Works and of Grace, with the danger of that evil and a few advices for remedying thereof. Contained in a letter to a friend upon the head. Edinburgh, printed by James Watson, on the North-side of the Cross, in Craig's-Closs, 1706. 32 pp.

[" The Second Edition" was published in 1718, and signed " Yours, &c., J. H."]

(6) The Covenants of Redemption and Grace Displayed. 1707.

(7.) Otia Christiana, or Christian Recreations. Being a conference betwixt Nicon and Philotheus, in which diverse important concerns of the doctrine and practice of religion are fairly and familiarly discoursed. Written by J. H., Minister of the Gospel, while in a frail estate of body and much disabled for greater labours. Divided into several Dialogues. Edinburgh, printed by James Watson, on the North-side of the Cross, 1708. viii. pp., and 220 pp.

[This Volume was very neatly reprinted, at Aberdeen, by J. Chalmers & Co., 1776.]

(8.) Notes about the Spirit's Operations, for discovering from the Word their nature and evidence. Together with diverse Remarks for detecting the enthusiastical delusions of the Covennois, Antonia Bourignon, and others. As also, Some account of the differences betwixt a legal and an evangelical administration. Being the substance of several private discourses on Gal. iii. 2. By James Hog, Minister of the Gospel. Edinburgh, printed by John Moncur, 1709. viii., 128, and 56 pp.

[This is a new edition of the "Remarks" of 1701. It is dedicated to the Right Honourable Major-General Maitland, His Lady, Theodosia Maitland. There was a "James Maitland," who became a Brigadier 1st June 1696, Major-General 1st February 1705, Lieutenant-General 1st January 1709.

There is a misprint in this second edition, the printer having failed to recognise a Scotch noun. In the first edition (p. 89) Mr Hog characterized an erroneous definition of "faith" as "works with a little gospel faird." In the second edition (part ii., p. 16) the verb "fair'd" is substituted.]

(9.) Notes about Saving Illumination. To which are subjoined Two Letters, one explaining the Lord's guiding His people by His word, and the other detecting the delusions of some of the Cevennois.

[This tract was reprinted at Aberdeen in 1778, and appended to the reprint of Mr Hog's Discourses on Job xxxvi.]

(10.) A letter to a gentleman, in which the unlawfulness of imposing Forms of Prayer, and of other Acts of Worship, is plainly demonstrated. By James Hog, Minister of the Gospel at Carnock. Edinburgh, printed by John Moncur, at his Printing-House at the foot of the Bull-Closs, foregainst the Tron, Anno 1710. 72 pp.

(11.) Some Remarks about submission to the sovereign disposure of the God of the spirits of all flesh. 24 pp.

["I add no more, but that I remain, Reverend Sir, Yours in the sweetest bonds, J. H."]

(12.) Preface to Halyburton's Natural Religion insufficient, and Revealed necessary to man's happiness in his present state. 1714.

(13.) An Abstract of Sundry Discourses on Job xxxvi. 8, 9, 10. *And if they be bound in fetters, and be holden in cords of affliction; Then He sheweth them their work, and their transgressions that they have exceeded. He openeth also their ear to discipline, and commandeth that they return from iniquity.* By James Hog, Minister of the Gospel at Carnock. Edinburgh, printed in the year 1714. Recommendatory Preface (signed Ja. Webster). and iv. pp. 72 pp.

[These discourses were reprinted at Aberdeen in 1778, but a larger type having been used, the reprint fills 102 pages.]

(14.) A Letter to a person exercised to godliness about our Natural Enmity—wherein also a singular opinion about the state of the devils and damned in hell is considered and refuted. By James Hog, Minister of the Gospel at Carnock. Edinburgh: Printed in the year 1714. 48 pp.

[This letter begins, "Madam."]

(15.) Remarks concerning the Rooting, Growth, and Ripeness of a Work of Grace in the Soul, contained in some Queries moved and answered from Mark iv. 26, 27, 28. *And He said, So is the Kingdom of God, as if a man should cast seed into the ground, And should sleep, and rise night and day, and the seed should spring and grow up, he knoweth not how. For the earth bringeth forth fruit of herself; first the Blade, then the Ear, after that the full Corn in the Ear.* By James Hog, Minister of the Gospel at Carnock. Edinburgh, printed by the heirs and successors of Andrew Anderson, Anno Dom. 1715. iv. and 38 pp.

(16.) An Essay to vindicate some Scripture Truths in five separate articles from the danger of being corrupted at this time. In answer of a letter from a gentleman to a minister. Published by a Member of the Church of Scotland. 2 Cor. xiii. 8, *We can do nothing against the truth, but for the truth.* Printed in the year 1716. [Dated, *Brittane,* Feb. 24, 1716.] 32 pp.

[" I send you a few animadversions on the R. Professor Simpson's Apologetick Answers to the R. Mr Webster's Libel against him. I think not fit to invade Mr Webster's province in medling with what the Professor denys and referrs to probation; but only will glance at a few propositions which he expressly owns and asserts."]

(17.) A Letter to a Gentleman concerning the interest of Reason in Religion. By James Hog, Minister of the Gospel at Carnock. Edinburgh, printed in the year 1716. And to be sold by John Martin, William Brown, and William Dicky, Booksellers there. 20 pp.

(18.) A Letter to a Gentleman, detecting the gangrene of some errors vented at this time. Gal. i. 6 : *I marvel that ye are so soon removed from him that called you into the Grace of Christ unto another Gospel.* 2 Tim. ii. 17 : *And their word will eat as doth a canker.* 2 Tim. iii. 13 : *Evil men and seducers shall wax worse and worse, deceiving, and being deceived.* By James Hog, Minister of the Gospel at Carnock. Edinburgh, printed in the year 1716. And to be sold by John Martin, William Brown, and William Dicky, Booksellers there. 50 pp.

[" Honoured Sir, I remember when we were last together, you were very earnest with me that I should review the Answers of Professor Simpson, &c.]

(19.) Abstract of Discourses on Psalm xli. 4. *I said, LORD, be merciful unto me: heal my soul; for I have sinned against Thee.* Published at the desire of some of the hearers. By James Hog, Minister of the Gospel at Carnock. Edinburgh, printed in the year 1716. To be sold by John Martin in the Parliament Closs at the Hand and Bible. 32 pp.

[The Author quotes the opening words of the Psalm, and as to the phrase, *that considereth the poor,* he adds, " or (as the Low Dutch render it) who demeaneth himself wisely towards one in adversity."]

(20) Three Missives written to a Minister of the Gospel in answer to one from him, Wherein the Author's grounds for remaining in communion with the Church of Scotland, as to its Judicatories and the Ordinances therein dispensed, are ingenuously and fairly stated. And the chief reasons of our separatists for setting up Ordinances and Judicatories distinct from the National Church and in Opposition to it are impartially considered and repelled, as these Reasons were printed in a late book intituled *Protesters Vindicated*, &c. Published by a gentleman into whose hands these letters came. Edinburgh, printed in the year 1717. To be sold by John Martin, William Brown, and William Dickie, booksellers there. 64 pp.

[Three letters, signed J. H., dated Carnock, Feb. 1, March 4, and April 6, 1717.]

(21.) The Right of Church Members to chuse their own Overseers, stated from the Scriptures, being the abstract of a Discourse on Acts i. 21, 22, 23. *Therefore of these men which have companied with us all the time that the Lord Jesus went in and out among us, Beginning from the Baptism of John, unto that same day that he was taken up from us, must one be ordained to be a witness with us of his resurrection. And they appointed two, Joseph called Barsabas, and Matthias.* Published at the desire of some of the hearers. By James Hog, Minister of the Gospel at Carnock. Edinburgh, printed in the year 1717. And to be sold by John Martin, William Brown, and William Dicky, Booksellers there. 20 pp.

(22.) Preface to the first Scottish edition of the Marrow of Modern Divinity. Edin. 1718.

(23.) Some Missives written to a gentleman which contain the Author's aim at detecting and refuting the Deism (as it is called) or Atheism and Libertinism of our time. Edinburgh, printed by John Mossman, William Brown, and Mr James M'Euen, and sold at Mr John Macky bookseller his shop in the Parliament-Closs, 1718. vi. pp. and 130 pp.

[The epistle "To the candid reader" is signed JA. HOG; the book consists of Twelve Letters.]

(24.) Some Proposals for Peace and Harmony, humbly offered to the consideration of the Ministers and members of the Church of Scotland. Contained in a Letter to a gentleman on the head. Edinburgh, printed by John Reid, and sold by Mr John Macky, Book-Seller in the Parliament Closs. Ann. Dom. 1718. 24 pp.

[This tract is full of Christian love to the people of God in the Church of England and in all Protestant churches. It concludes, " I shall add no more, but that I remain, Sir, Yours, &c., J. H."]

(25.) A Vindication of the Doctrine of Grace from the charge of Antinomianism, contained in a Letter to a Minister of the Gospel. Edinburgh, printed by Robert Brown, and are to be sold at Mr John Macky's shop in the Parliament-Closs, 1718. 24 pp.

["This with wonted Salutations is all at present from, my very Dear Brother, Yours as before, I. H. September 25, 1718."]

(26.) An Explication of Passages excepted against in the Marrow of Modern Divinity, taken from the book itself. Contained in a letter to a Minister of the Gospel. Edinburgh, printed by Robert Brown, and are to be sold at Mr John Macky's shop in the Parliament Closs, 1719. 24 pp.
[I remain, &c., J. H."]

(27.) A Conference betwixt Epaphroditus and Epaphras, wherein the very Reverend Principal Hadow's Sermon preached before the Synod of Fife, April 7th, 1719, is fairly enquired into, in so far as he findeth fault
with { Mr Marshal on Sanctification,
       The Marrow of Modern Divinity,
       And the Explication of Passages Excepted against in the Marrow.
Edinburgh, printed by Robert Brown, and are to be sold at Mr John Macky's shop in the Parliament Closs, 1719. Price 3d. 40 pp.
[For a quotation from this Dialogue, see MARSHALL.]

(28.) Letter to a Gentleman containing a detection of errors in a print entitled, *The Snake in the grass*, wherein that author giveth his Remarks upon the Marrow of Modern Divinity. 1720 [?]
[I have copied the title of the above tract from Brown's (of Whitburn) "Gospel Truth." The tract, to which it is an answer, was entitled "The Snake in the Grass, or Remarks upon a book entituled *The Marrow of Modern Divinity*, touching both the covenant of works and of grace, &c., originally done by E. F. about the year 1645, and lately revised, corrected, and published by the Reverend Mr James Hog, Minister of the Gospel at Carnock. 2 Tim. iii. 6 : *For of this sort are they who creep into houses and lead captive silly women, &c.* Edinburgh, printed for the Author, and sold by the Booksellers. Anno Dom. 1719. (Price 4d.) 48 pp.] [To No. 27 Mr Hog had added a P.S., "As to what concerns *The Snake*, &c., it contains nothing of difficulty and which is not cleared in *The Explication of Passages excepted against in the Marrow*. Nevertheless the Prefacer to the last edition of The Marrow intends to consider that author when he hath more leisure—and the rather, because he doubts not to demonstrate that his Print is not free of gross and dangerous errors."]

(29.) Reasons of Masters James Hog and James Bathgate, Humbly offered to the Reverend Presbytery of Dunfermline for their not observing the Day of Thanksgiving appointed by the King. Referred to the Synod of Fife, met at Kirkaldy, April 1724. The Synod having censured Mr Hog, on April 8, 1724, he tabled a Representation to the very Reverend the Synod of Fife.
[The above Reasons and Representation are printed in a tract. As to their substance, see BATHGATE].

(30.) Letters to a Private Christian on Gospel Holiness.

[Mentioned in Dr Scott's "Fasti Eccl. Scot.," as also are all the following]:—
(31.) On Covenanting. Edin. 1727.
(32.) On Professor Campbell's Divinity. Edin. 1731.
[There is a publication entitled, Answers to Campbell's " Discourse, proving that the Apostles were no enthusiasts"—described as a continuation to the above, and ascribed either to Mr Hog, or to his son-in-law and successor, Mr Hunter, or to Messrs Hog and Hunter jointly. *Query*, Ought it to be in a catalogue of Mr Hog's Works?]
(33.) Preface to Memoirs or Spiritual Exercises of Mrs Ross. Edin. 1735.

Probable Ancestry of Rev. J. Hog, Minister of Carnock.

[Dr Scott's " Fasti Eccl. Scot." furnishes me with this information. I use the adjective *probable*, only because Dr Scott speaks of Mr Hog as " son of " the minister here represented as his " father," but omits his name from the *list of the family* of the said father ; and the same observation applies to another " Hog" in this tree.]

Rev. ARCHIBALD HOG, Min. of Durris, Aberdeenshire,
from 1574 to 1594.

Rev. PATRICK HOG, Min. of Fetlar, Shetland, 1607.

Rev. THOMAS HOG, M.A., Min. of South Leith from 1616 to 1618,
and of Stobo, Peeblesshire, from 1618 to 1639.

Rev. JOHN HOG, M.A.,	Rev. THOMAS HOG, M.A.,
Min. of Linton, Peebles, from 1640 to 1646, of the Canongate, Edin., from 1646 to 1653, of South Leith from 1653 to 1662 [deprived as a godly covenanter], and of Rotterdam from 1662 to 1689. *Died* 1692.	Minister of Larbert, Stirlingshire, from 1650 to 1662 [deprived as a godly covenanter], married Marjory Murray, a descendant of the Philiphaugh family. *Died* at Edinburgh, 1680 or 1681.

Rev. THOMAS HOG, M.A. Min. successively at Delft, Campvere, and Rotterdam (*born* 1655, *died* 1723).	Rev. JAMES HOG, M.A., Min. 1st of Dalserf, 2d of Carnock, [the subject of the preceding memoir].

Letter (hitherto unpublished) *from Rev. James Hog.*

The following consolatory letter was addressed to Mrs Shiell, of Edinburgh, sister of Boston's friend, Mr Robert Wightman, Lord Dean of Guild :—

MISTRIS,—I heard not till ere yesterday of the cup of affliction it hath pleased our sovereign and gracious Lord to put into your hand, by taking your worthy husband home to himself. The account affected me deeply. And howsoever I be of little or no significancy for anything, yet I would sincerely aim, under divine influences, at somewhat of sympathy. We ought to bear one another's burdens, and so to fulfil the law of Christ (Gal. vi. 2). The trial is indeed great and sharp, and the severing that nearest relation and one so favorably stated, so endeared, and useful in the most valuable regards, cannot readily fail to be of a very uneasy digestion, without that the Lord give support, strength and consolation beyond an ordinary rate. But it ought to quiet us that He is the Lord, and assuredly it is lawful for Him to do what He will with His own (Matt. xx. 15). The posture becoming creatures, namely, as clay, to prostrate ourselves at the feet of our merciful and sovereign Lord, is the only situation for rest and quietness. (Rom. ix. 20, 21; Isa. xlv. 9, 10; Matt. xi. 28, 29; Jer. xviii. 1, 2, 3, &c.) But as this is much above our reach, so it is as much contrary to the strong bent of corrupt and haughty nature. That Infinite power, which gave us a being, is yet more gloriously exerted in subjecting us, by faith, to His sovereign and wise disposure. No persuasives by the tongues of men or angels will ever prevail to break the iron sinew, unless that Infinite power be put forth in a way of special mercy and grace. Hereunto is every, even the least, degree of this believing subjection entirely owing. The present cup is bitter indeed, but it may be remembered that you and I have tasted what in sundry regards was yet bitterer. Deliverances out of these deep pits ought never to be forgotten, and ought to allay other afflictions, though, otherways, most penetrating, I am loath to detain you by this weak yet ingenuous essay. It's sweet to consider that the bitterest cups it pleaseth the Lord to put into the hands of His children, do yet issue from everlasting love, and have nothing of vindictive wrath in them. (Jer. xxxi. 1, 2; Ps. lxxxix. 29, 30, 31, &c.) It should stay our reluctance to believe, that, how cross soever they are to the propensions of soft and selfish nature, and how strongly soever it reclaimeth, yet they are necessary, and wholesome medicaments ordered and appointed by the Lord to fit His children for glory and to render it the sweeter. (1 Pet. i. 6, 7, 8; Rom. viii. 18; 2 Cor. iv. 17, 18; Rom viii. 28, and v. 2, 3, 4, &c.) He it is, who prepareth and putteth the medicinal cups into the hands of His people, and from Him only we are to implore and expect the kindly operation by faith and the prayer of faith. (Ps. l. 15; Jas. v. 13; Job xxiii. 10, and xxxvi. 6, 7, 8.) Afflictions or chastenings for the present are not joyous but grievous, yet afterwards they yield the peaceable fruits of righteousness unto them who are exercised thereby. (Heb. xii. 11.) I add no more but that I remain,

Mistris,
Your sincerely affectionat
Friend and Servant,
Ja. Hog.

Carnock Manse, Decr. 2, 1723.

REV. RICHARD HOOKER, M.A.

It is not necessary for me to give a memoir of "Judicious Hooker" (as his epitaph named him). His name is now introduced because of his adherence to the ancient doctrine of Christ's substitution, which some degenerate Presbyterians of London, in the seventeenth century, stigmatized as the heresy of "the permutation of persons."

Richard Hooker was a native of Exeter, in which city he was born, about Easter, in the year 1554 (N. S.). His family was genteel, but poor; and his University education and Church preferments were obtained through the patronage of Bishop Jewel and Archbishop Sandys. He was M.A. of Oxford and Fellow of Corpus Christi College in 1577, and Deputy-Professor of Hebrew in 1579. He preached his first sermon at St Paul's Cross, London, in 1581; and his sojourn as a preacher and invalid in "The Shunammite's House," in the metropolis, led to his singular marriage. Thus, having to relinquish his Fellowship, he, in course of time, left Oxford; and in 1584 he became Rector of Drayton-Beauchamp, in Buckinghamshire. Bishop Sandys brought him to London, in 1585, to fill the distinguished post of Master of the Temple. The controversial atmosphere, in which he now lived for six years, made him anxious to put his thoughts on Church government into shape; and having planned a great literary work on Ecclesiastical Polity, he solicited from the Bishop a translation from the city to a country charge. In 1591 Dr Nicholas Balgay was happy to resign, in exchange for the Mastership of the Temple, his stall in Salisbury as Prebendary and Sub-Dean. These preferments Hooker accepted, along with the Rectory of Boscomb in Wiltshire. In 1595 he changed his residence to the Rectory of Bishop-Bourne (near Canterbury), where he died, 2nd November 1600, aged forty-five.

The quotation from one of Hooker's Sermons, which I have to transcribe, is the following paragraph:—

"The righteousness wherein we must be found, if we would be justified, is not our own (Philipp. iii. 8, 9); therefore we cannot be justified by any inherent quality. Christ hath merited righteousness for as many as are found in Him. In Him God findeth us, if we be faithful; for by faith we are incorporated into Christ. Then, although in ourselves we be altogether sinful and unrighteous, yet even the man which is impious in himself, full of iniquity, full of sin—him being found in Christ through faith, and having his sin remitted through repentance—him God beholdeth with a gracious eye, putteth away his sin by not imputing it, taketh quite away the punishment due thereunto by pardoning it, and accepteth him in Jesus Christ as perfectly righteous, as if he had fulfilled all that was commanded him in the law—shall I say more perfectly righteous than if himself had fulfilled the whole law? I must take heed what I say; but the Apostle saith, God made HIM to be sin for us who knew no sin, that we might be made the righteousness of God in HIM. Such we are in the sight of God the Father, as is the very Son of God Himself. Let it be counted folly, or frenzy, or fury, whatsoever, it is our comfort and our wisdom; we care for no knowledge in the world but this—that man hath sinned and God hath suffered; that God hath made himself the Son of Man, and that men are made the righteousness of God."—*Sermon on Justification,* § 6.

Beautifully worded as these sentences are, they are neither so beautiful nor so accurate as the statements on the subject by some of the early Christian fathers. Justin Martyr writes: " God gave His own Son a ransom for us, the Holy One for the transgressors, the innocent for the wicked, the righteous for the unrighteous, the incorruptible for the corruptible, the immortal for the mortal. For what else could cover our sins but His righteousness? In whom else could we the transgressors and ungodly be justified but in the Son of God only? Ὦ τῆς γλυκείας καταλλαγῆς, *O dulcis permutatio,* O the sweet exchange! O the unsearchable contrivance! O unexpected benefits! that the iniquity of many should be hid in one righteous person, and the righteousness of one should justify many transgressors!"—(*Epistle to Diognetus*).

Chrysostom has bequeathed to us the following comment on 2 Cor. v. 21:— " He hath made HIM to be sin for us, who knew no sin; that we might be made the righteousness of God in HIM." " What mind can represent these things? He made the righteous One a sinner, that He might make the sinners righteous. Rather this is not what he says, but something much greater. He says, not that He made Him *a sinner,* but that He made Him *sin,*—not only Him who had not sinned, but Him who did not know sin,—that we might be made (not righteous, but) righteousness, and the righteousness of God. For this is the righteousness of God, when we are justified, not by works (for in this case it is necessary that there should be no spot in them) but by grace, in the blotting out of all sin. This does not permit us to be lifted up, for God freely gives us all and teaches us the greatness of the gift; because the former righteousness is that of the law and of works, but this is the righteousness of God."

REV. JOHN HUBBARD.

JOHN HUBBARD was born in 1692. He was a congregationalist as to Church government, and evangelical in doctrine. His sermons were so full of Christ,

that he became prominent in the Coward Lecture, and his sermons, preached on
1 Peter i. 8. (on September 27, and October 11, 1728), were printed in the
volume already described ; he wrote the dedicatory preface, dated Stepney, 28th
May 1729. At that date he was the Independent Pastor at Stepney, having
begun his labours there as assistant to Mr Mitchel, whom he succeeded in
1721. He also took part in the Berry Street Lectures. Mr Hubbard had much
and varied learning, and was well versed in theology, his acquaintance with the
Scriptures being so extensive as to supersede the use of a concordance ; he was
therefore selected for the Theological chair in 1740 (his predecessor was Abraham
Taylor, D D., and his successor was Zephaniah Marryat, D.D.). His career was
suddenly closed by an attack of fever ; he suffered much pain, but, "tranquil and
rejoicing in spirit," he died on Wednesday, 13th July 1743, at 4.30 P.M.,
repeating the text of his last sermon, *Through Christ we are more than conquerors* (Rom. viii. 37). His funeral sermon was preached by Dr Guyse.

His sermons on love to Christ were, in their matter, useful models for
ministers, combining orthodoxy with a reality like the utterances of private friendship. Although the style is laboured, it is less laboured than Boston's, being
characterized by some of the heaviness of the ancients, and by some of the freedom
and flow of the moderns—a connecting link, as it were, between the technical
and the literary style. I quote some paragraphs :—

"Our Lord is truly, every way, so deserving of our tenderest, warmest, and
strongest love, for all manner of attractive charms that meet in Him, that *nothing*
(in a manner) should be loved but Himself—nothing (it is certain), in the whole
circle of created objects, *before* HIM—nothing *like* HIM—nothing *without* HIM—
but all of them should be loved for His sake, and used as scales and steps to
mount up our love higher and higher to Him, where only it can attain its proper
and complete rest."—Page 15.

On Christ suffering.—"This work of our Saviour for us is uncommonly
divine, as well as infinitely more than human—a work, which equally required
the power and dignity of a God to accomplish and render it effectual, and the love
and condescending grace of a God to undertake and persevere in it till it was
finished. And how can it then but commend Christ to all the love of a Christian, when it does, with such strange and unusual surprise, commend His love to
him—a love strong as death—a love which carried Him, great as He was in
Himself, to condescend so low to us as to suffer and die for us, nay, to court, to
seek, to long for, to embrace suffering and death, with as great readiness and
cheerfulness, as we can do life and happiness ? There is no need of bringing
any tragical passions and affections to the scenes of trouble and vast distress
Christ passed through in our world for us. It is love, it is love, that tender
and pleasing affection, which is first and chiefly, under the conduct of faith,
to approach them—love to answer and meet His love, which reigns all over this

field of blood, and is joined with victorious power, to make it produce nothing but the sweetest and most durable fruits for our comfort and happiness—fruits of the most costly, expensive love. For the more He lessened His person, whether in the divine or human nature, lowering and obscuring the beauties and glories belonging to each, the higher He raised His love in the meantime."—Page 76.

On Christ in glory.—" In regard to Christ's serving us by the greatest sufferings that ever were, He excuses us now, as He did the daughters of Jerusalem even when going to be crucified, from weeping at all for Himself (Luke xxiii. 28), and would have our love to Him [to be] all gratitude and joy for the good we reap from His evil without any intervening grief for His sake, whatever may properly qualify it for our own. And wherefore this? Why, because His sufferings, however great above the measure of any besides, were all of His own voluntary choice and submitting to, from pure love to His church—were all known beforehand to Him with the certain happy issue of them—were no more than what He was equal, nay, superior to, so that it was not possible for Him to be swallowed up or consumed, no, nor long exercised by them. And they are all now long since past and gone as to the smart He felt under them, though abiding in their virtue, use and excellent fruits; and so, consequently, they are all accounted, be and to Him, for trophies of honour—beauties instead of blemishes—and highest matter of glory and triumph. Whence it is that He appears in heaven with the marks of His bleeding wounds, the Lamb as it had been slain, in the midst of the throne. And thus the shame and pain of His cross is entirely alleviated, and it redounds to Him for an ensign of renown and eternal glory—a perpetual memorial of His love, merit, and victory—dear to saints and angels above, and no less precious to saints below. It is His sufferings also that formed, and lead on, all the remaining works Christ performs, for the service of His people, in heaven in His exalted state, which are of a different nature from those done on earth, being works of power and authority (whereas the other were works of humiliation), but equally necessary for His people's good, and expressive of His love still pursuing its kind design, though in a new manner, for their happiness and salvation. His love doth change with the change of His state, but it is as warm at His heart as ever. The same love that made Him endure a cross here for His people's sake, abides as firm in Him as ever, now He has a crown on His head, and makes Him use His honours and employ His high authority for their advantage. As His love was proved here by poverty and tribulations, it is now proved by a fulness of glory and power, and it answers to this proof as completely as it did to that. His love was then in labour and disgrace for us; now it is enthroned and triumphing yet still for us also. Then it emptied Himself—now it is filling us out of His immense and perfect fulness."
—Page 78.

On love to Christians.—" If we love our dearest Lord, now He is absent from us, we shall have an hearty esteem and especial love for all the members of His mystical body, nor be wanting in such offices of love to them which our mutual circumstances require and give opportunity for. For they are all of them His friends and favourites—the only ones He has in our world. They are His relations in a spiritual sense, His brethren, His children, so that if we do indeed love HIM then surely we cannot but love them that are begotten of HIM (1 John v. 1). They are also to be considered as the living images and representatives of Christ Jesus (2 Cor. iii. 3.), having His likeness stamped on them. Other pictures and representations of Christ there are (and can be) none."—Page 136.

REV. WILLIAM HUNTER, M.A.

This good minister's name is the twelfth and last of the signatures to the famous Representation in favour of "The Marrow." During the sitting of the General Assembly at Edinburgh in 1721, Mr Brown, in his narrative regarding this representation, writes: "Mr William Hunter, minister at Lilliesleaf, signed it in the church just before it was presented." Although for this reason he appears late, he was in fact one of the older ministers. His childhood, youth and early manhood were spent amidst fiery trials, and he was not enrolled as M.A. of the University of Edinburgh until 3rd July 1693, when he was thirty-six years of age. He was licensed as a preacher by the Presbytery of Kelso 29th August 1694, and he was ordained by the Presbytery of Selkirk as minister of Lilliesleaf on 2nd May 1695, having been called by the parishioners during the month of March preceding. His native place is not recorded, but he acquired the property of Lauchhill. He died 19th November 1736, in the seventy-ninth year of his age, and the forty-second of his ministry. Although he published nothing, yet he was a pleasing and rather striking preacher. In 1727, when he was in his seventieth year, he assisted Mr Boston as a sacrament at Ettrick, and that minister, who was suffering from indisposition, wrote: "Mr Hunter preached after Mr Wilson on the words, '*He is faithful that promised.*' I was so refreshed by that sermon, that I found my body in good condition when he was over." From an old manuscript[1] I extract some passages of a sermon preached three years after— i.e., when he was in his seventy-third year:—

NOTES of a SERMON Preached by Mr HUNTER at Selkirk on 15th August 1730, being a Communion Saturday.

PSALM xlii. 2.—*My soul thirsteth for God, for the living God, when shall I come and appear before God!*

[1] Jas. Blaikie's MS

Sometimes the Lord is pleased to dandle His people on the knee of His kind Providence; at other times it is not so—these are times of distance. Sometimes He smiles, at other times He is pleased to frown. David sometime enjoyed Him in ordinances; now he is driven to the wilderness of Judah. But the Lord ever knows the case of His people.

In this Psalm we have David's zeal to serve and enjoy God in His house. *As the hart panteth after the water-brooks*—the hart is a creature that is thirsty, because it feeds on dry places, and because of its violent running from other beasts that would devour it. Thirst is more vehement than hunger, so David's zeal is illustrated by thirst. But what is it for that he thirsts? It is even for God—not after idols, but after God. In the words ye have his frame, even longing after the living God. The main thing that every gracious soul seeks is the fruition and enjoyment of God Himself—as in the 27th Psalm says the Psalmist, "One thing have I desired of the Lord, and that I will seek after," &c.; it is to enjoy the Lord Himself in a life of communion with Him here below in His house, and for ever in His tabernacle above.

Many there are about the court that come not to the king's presence. Many of us see one another in the house of God, but never see God. O may it not be so with any of you!

Even believers themselves do not enjoy the like measure of His presence: some are taken up the hill of God in enjoyments; others are left at the foot of the hill. Neither after the same manner do His people enjoy Him. Sometimes He manifests Himself in such a manner as lays them in the dust; at other times He is pleased to manifest Himself for their recovery and raising them up.

(1.) He is pleased to manifest Himself in His glorious perfections and excellences, so as to make the sinner to abhor himself with Job, crying out, "I have often heard of Thee by the hearing of the ear: but now mine eye seeth Thee. Wherefore I abhor myself in dust and ashes." He comes in His Word and makes them see His stately magnificence. He comes in His Word and discovers to them His holiness; this makes them loathe themselves. Isaiah vi. O what influence this had on the prophet, as he cries out, " Woe's me, I am undone, I am a man of unclean lips."

(2.) When the discovery of the riches of His grace in Jesus Christ appears, then the sinner is ashamed. And when the Word discovers the irresistible power of God, and when he discovers that it is on his side, then he is made to speak big words (Psalm xlvi.). "God is our refuge and strength; we will not fear, though the earth be removed, and though the mountains be carried into the midst of the sea. The Lord of Hosts is with us." The Word discovers the wisdom of God for their walk in this world, and the faithfulness of God, and that there is a good foundation for their faith in this perfection of God; this is the enjoyment of God that believing souls sometimes meet with in His ordinances.

There are some who can from their experience set their seal to the truth of this.

(3.) This enjoyment of God consists in His discovering to them by His Word and Spirit the wretched and miserable state they are in, and in giving them a sight of sin so as to make them mourn for it and turn from it—this is a fruit of the presence of Christ and His sufferings.

(4.) It consists in the sweet interviews that the soul gets with Christ. Song ii. 14, "O my dove, that art in the clefts of the rock, in the secret places of the stairs, let me see Thy countenance, let me hear Thy voice; for sweet is Thy voice, and Thy countenance is comely." What does the gracious soul say? Psalm xxvii., "Hide not Thy face from me;" Psalm iv., "Lord lift on me the light of Thy countenance." This is the sweetest food that ever the soul gets; yea, it's the life of the soul. The believer can no more live without Christ than the body can do without the soul. Will not a sight of angels and ministers satisfy the soul? No; John xx.—believers are like Mary; none but Christ could satisfy her.

(5.) This enjoyment consists in the pleasure and satisfaction the Lord takes in following His word with the power of His Spirit, making it a strengthening and reviving word to them, and them to be fruitful. When thus the influences come down, then the soul starts to its feet and goes nimbly on.

(6.) When the soul is transformed into the image of Christ (2 Cor. iii. 18), as when the discoveries of Christ in the Gospel leave a stamp of Christ on the soul, then it is that the soul may be said to enjoy God. When the man comes to the ordinances polluted and guilty, and goes away clean; Psalm lxviii., "Though ye have lien among the pots, yet ye shall be as the wings of a dove"—that is, ye have lien rusty and defiled, yet there has been a discovery of the fountain. Isa. i. 18, "Come now, and let us reason together, saith the Lord: though your sins be as scarlet, they shall be white as snow; though they be red like crimson, they shall be as wool."

Why is it that gracious souls are so desirous of enjoying communion with God in ordinances?

(1.) The fundamental reason of it is, the great plot of grace—the great design and plot of grace is to bring sinners to Christ.

(2.) It flows from the experience that they have found formerly in their views of God, which makes them long to be back when they want [*lack*] it, or to sit still when they enjoy it.

(3.) Pinching need drives them to it. Whatever others say (says the soul), I know it is good for me to draw near to God.

Is it so then, that that which the gracious soul longs for and seeks after is the enjoyment and fruition of God in His ordinances; then let it be all your endeavours to have communion with Him in this ordinance that ye have before you. You can expect no good without this; for the virtue and efficacy of this ordinance depends upon the fruition and enjoyment of God. The enjoyment of God in ordinances is the very beauty of ordinances; ordinances without God are unsavoury to every gracious soul. It will be an earnest of your fruition of Him in the higher house, if ye enjoy Him in the lower house. Eating and drinking is not above; but it represents the happiness of the higher house. Labour then after the enjoyment of God while here. O, sirs, invite Him to the feast.

REV. JAMES KID.

JAMES KID was born in Scotland in troublous times, in the year 1666, and had to be taken to Holland for personal safety, so that his education for the ministry was carried on under the great Dutch professors. He was licensed as a preacher by the Presbytery of Dunfermline, 27th February 1706. On 28th September 1710, he was ordained by the Presbytery of Linlithgow as minister of Queensferry. Dr Scott reminds us that "he was one of the twelve brethren who gave in a Representation and Petition to the General Assembly, 11th May 1721, against an act of the preceding Assembly condemning The Marrow of Modern Divinity, from which they were waggishly styled *the twelve apostles.*" Mr Boston says that Mr Kid was "a man of singular boldness," and was selected to lay the representation before the committee of Assembly. His courage had already been conspicuous at the Synod of Lothian and Tweeddale, when he was the only minister who protested against a forced settlement of a presentee to the parish of Bathgate, for which protest, and for baptizing the children of Bathgate parishioners who would not acknowledge the intruded minister, he was prosecuted in the Church courts. His only separate publication is "A Letter to a Minister of the Gospel concerning the parish of Bathgate," published in 1720. Being a member of the General Assembly of 1722, which rebuked the representers, he signalized his protest by throwing down upon the clerk's table a guinea, instead of the customary shilling. He took the responsibility of publishing in 1723 the Rev. Gabriel Wilson's impugned sermon, "The Trust," and wrote a preface to it, in which he says: "The Committee of the Synod of Merse and Teviotdale, after they had got the author's papers from him, did drop their calumnious condescendence, and drew up a charge consisting of twelve remarks, twelve questions, and twelve slanders, for you must know, by the bye, that the number *twelve* is what some wanton kirkmen have taken pleasure to sport themselves with of late, though some of them have discovered how ridiculously straitened they have been to find their account" [to make up the number].

Mr Kid held communion with the seceding brethren, but did not withdraw from the Established Church. He was an excellent preacher, and popular among lovers of the Gospel. He died on 9th February 1744, in the seventy-eighth year of his age.

DR MELCHIOR LEYDEKKER.

MELCHIOR LEYDEKKER was born at Middleburg, in 1642, and was the pastor of more than one charge successively in Zeeland till 1679, when he became Professor of Theology at Utrecht. He was a Calvinist of the Heidelberg type, and entered with spirit into the exposition of the Belgic or Heidelberg Catechism to his class. The first fruits of this academical exercise he committed to the press in 1683 :—" Professor Leydekker, D.D., Marrow of Practical Divinity, or Meditations on the Heidelberg Catechism in which is made manifest the force and efficacy of the Reformed Faith for true piety. [Melchioris Leideckeri, S.S.T.D. and P. Medulla Theologiæ Practicæ seu Meditationes ad Catechesin Heidelbergensem quibus vis et efficacia Reformatæ Fidei ad veram pietatem ostenditur.] This publication proceeded as far as Q. 57, and I have not seen the continuation. But he published a complete commentary in 1694, entitled "De veritate fidei Reformatæ ejusdemque sanctitate," a quarto volume. In the meantime he had been assiduous in controversy with Coccejus, regarding his view of the three dispensations of the covenant of grace. The controversies in Holland were keen from a dread that the errors of Protestants might occasion the re-establishment of Popery—a keenness which magnified into heresy what were either harmless speculations or only inexpedient changes in phraseology. The Westminster Larger Catechism deals largely with the Divine covenants; and therefore for a popular refutation of Coccejus, I may refer the reader to Dr Ridgley's exposition (a Body of Divinity, &c.). The theologian may consult Leydekker himself, of whom Herzog's Cyclopedia says, "His method of reducing the reformed system of doctrine to definite and comprehensive principles—as also the elucidation given of the Coccejan theology—will continue to deserve regard." All the controversial works, above referred to, having been published between 1677 and 1690, were prior to his final commentary on the Heidelberg Catechism. In 1695 he published his account of Jansenism (Leidecker de Jansenismo) which contains an engraved portrait of the famous Cornelius Jansen, Bishop of Ypres—whose birth was in Holland, his bishopric in Spain, and his posthumous fame in France, as the author of "Augustinus." Dr Leydekker's greatest work was his treatise on the Hebrew Commonwealth (De Republicâ Hebræorum). He died at Utrecht, 6th January 1721.

THE THEOLOGY OF CONSOLATION.

DR MARTIN LUTHER.

MARTIN LUTHER, son of Hans Luther and Grethe his wife, was born at Eisleben on 10th November 1483 at eleven P.M. He was educated at the school of Eisenach and the University of Erfurth. He entered the monastery of the Augustines at Erfurth on 17th July 1505, and was ordained a priest two years afterwards. In 1508 he was invited by Frederick, Elector of Saxony, to be professor in the University of Wittemberg. Luther was M.A. of Erfurth, but he now studied the Scriptures in Hebrew and Greek, and obtained the degree of B.D. of Wittemberg in March 1509. In 1516 he gave out certain theses on Grace, but his famous theses against Indulgences were nailed to the door of the Castle of Wittemberg on 31st October 1517; he was by this time a doctor of theology. It is unnecessary to detail the career of the great Reformer. He died 17th February 1546, not before the assembling of the Council of Trent, but before it had done anything. His son, Paul Luther, Doctor of Physic, was a distinguished man, and is memorialized in Melchior Adam's Lives.

NOTE I.—*On some of Luther's writings quoted in* BOOK I.

With regard to his Commentary on the Galatians, he informs a correspondent on 3d September 1519 that it is now ready; and on the 22d he writes jocularly to George Spalatin, "I send you my *Foolish Galatians* famously salted" (mitto insensatos Galatas meos, multo sale conditos). Merle d'Aubigné says : "Luther, far from retreating, advanced daily. It was at this time that he aimed one of his most violent blows against error in his Commentary on the Epistle to the Galatians. The second commentary is undoubtedly superior to the first; but in the first he expounded with great power the doctrine of justification by faith . . . He also showed that this salvation transforms man, and makes him abound in good works" (*History of the Reformation of the 16th century*, vol. ii. book 5, chap. 8). "The second commentary" (according to Seckendorf, who calls it *commentarius alter* and *commentarius repetitus*) was published in 1535. It was printed from the notes of the Wittemberg students, revised and prefaced by Luther, who was amazed at the bulk to which it had grown. It was translated into German by Justus Menius. The English translation is evidently from "the second commentary;" Luther is represented as saying, "I myself have now preached the gospel *almost twenty years*." [*See* my Book I., page 65.]

As to Luther's Spiritual Songs (Geistlicher Gesänge), Seckendorf, in his third index, describes an edition dated Erfurt, 1525, containing all the thirty-eight hymns. Mr Richard Massie mentions the modern edition of Wackernagel as scrupulously adhering to the text of Luther's last edition. I have quoted the *second hymn on grace* from Rev. John Anderson's translation of 1846. Mr Massie, in 1853, produced and published an excellent translation, preserving the metres, of Luther's Hymns. I quote the the first verse of the above-mentioned hymn in its proper metre :—

> Dear Christians, one and all, rejoice,
>   With exultation springing,
> And with united heart and voice,
>   And holy rapture singing,
> Proclaim the wonders God hath done,
> How His right arm the victory won ;
>   Right dearly it hath cost Him.'

NOTE 2.—*The harmony of German Reformers with Luther himself.*

That the believers in the Heidelberg Catechism, although they differed from the Lutheran Church, were more in harmony with Luther himself than were the Lutherans, is proved in an old pamphlet entitled "A Full Declaration of the faith and ceremonies professed in the dominions of the most illustrious and noble prince, Frederick V., Prince Elector of Palatine ; published for the benefit and satisfaction of all God's people—according to the original printed in the High Dutch tongue, translated into English by John Rolte, 1614 ;" the short title was, "A full declaration of the faith and ceremonies of the Pfaltzgrave's churches ;" and there is a recommendatory preface for the English reader by "Thomas Beard, Doctor of Divinitie." I quote from this *Declaration* what concerns Luther :—

"Doctor Luther did well and right, that he would not bind himself to any writings of men, but only to the word of God."—*Chap.* iii.

"Doctor Luther was a man, and so could fail and err even as well as other men."—*Chap.* iii.

"Doctor Luther, of happy memory, both believed and taught of all and every necessary point, even as we believe and teach, that one point of the Holy Supper excepted. And yet differ we not in that same point so much from each other as many men take it. In all sacraments two things are to be considered, *first*, the tokens, and *then* the betokened riches, whereon out of all doubt more dependeth many thousand times than on the outward tokens. Doctor Luther taught that the betokened treasure in the holy Supper is not the bodily but the spiritual eating of the body and blood of Christ. Even so teach we also. Only here lies the difference, what the outward tokens be. We say the outward tokens are bread and wine. Doctor Luther understands they are not only bread and wine, but also the body of Christ in bread, and the blood of Christ in wine. And so the difference betwixt our doctrine in the Supper and Doctor Luther lieth, not in the ground of salvation, but only in the tokens, which should show us unto the ground of salvation."—*Chap.* iv.

"These are the motives, beloved reader, which move, force, and drive us to depart from Doctor Luther's opinion in this, because (1) such an opinion hath not only no ground in God's word, but (2) indeed is clear against the same, and (3) hath no testimony from the old apostolical churches, but (4) was first hatched in the blinded times of Popery, and (5) serves no other end than to underprop the popedom, and to darken the gospel of Jesus Christ."—*Chap.* v.

" The first cause were sufficient; for whatsoever hath not its foundation in the word of God, that shall no man endure to be forced upon him as an article of faith, as Doctor Luther right and truly used to sing and say—

" And take thou heed of man's device,
Thereby consumes the pearl of price,
This learn I thee, for the last."—*Ibid.*

" We are not contradictory to Doctor Luther in any sort in all the other points which at this day there is so much contention about. Even as Zwinglius also did not disagree with Dr Luther after the conference at Marpurg in any point but only this, whether Christ is bodily also in the bread and wine of the supper. (3d October 1529) . . . It is true, indeed, that there are more points controverted at present betwixt the disciples of Doctor Luther and us. But nothing at all with Dr Luther himself."—*Chap.* vi.

" Christian loving reader, it cannot be uttered what mischief the contention about the Supper hath done, and yet daily doeth, and is to be feared will do more and more in the Protestant churches."—*Preface.*

" It is manifest, and it proclaims itself daily more and more in all nations, what blood-thirsty plots the Jesuits propound to themselves against all those who are gone out from the popedom, whether they be called Lutherans or Calvinists. We confess that we fear that there will shortly befall some calamity in Deutschland except it be prevented in time. And therefore our counsel is to hold peace and unity amongst ourselves, as being the best means to stop the common misery. Will this our counsel yet be acknowledged and accepted? Well and good. If not, then have we done what appertained to us. And we will not, for all that, despair or renounce the confession of the truth though the whole world should leave us.[1] God being on our side, who can be against us? . . . And therefore do we sing merrily with Doctor Luther,—

" Though they take our life,
Goods, name, child, and wife,
See thou let all go,
They get naught but woe,
And we shall have the kingdom."— *Conclusion.*

[1] [" As Prince Frederick of blessed memory did formerly answer those that thought to daunt him."—*John Rolte.*]

NOTE 3.—*On Faith.*

We come now to the modern notion that although Luther and his comrades held assurance to be of the essence of faith, yet those divines who have differed from him have made an advance in the knowledge of divine truth.

The able and learned Riccaltoun dissents from such an eulogium. He says:—

"Until one can say with the Apostle, *Christ loved me and gave himself for me*—that is, until one sees his own interest in Christ, and (as the Apostle John expresses it) *knows and believes the love that God hath to him*—his faith is defective in a very essential point; and the spiritual life, if there be any, is at so low an ebb, that both the comfort and the fruit of it are lost.

"The question has been very warmly disputed, *Whether assurance be of the essence of faith?* And disputed it has been, until faith itself seems to be disputed away, and little left among Christians but a faint shadow of it,—that answers no manner of purpose but giving those a name to live who are really, and to all intents and purposes, dead.

"There was a time when it was the received doctrine among all Protestants, that the word of God carried in it such divine light and power as, under the conduct of the Holy Spirit, approved itself unto the hearts and consciences of men, and made faith of the things there held forth; and this was then thought agreeable unto the experience of all true Christians. And as the special mercy of God to sinners in Christ, and the love of Christ in giving himself a ransom for them, is the great import of the gospel—to believe this was thought to be the very essence and distinguishing characteristic of true faith.

"But, in time, when the belief of the Scriptures came to be founded on (what they call) rational evidence, and deductions from (what is called) natural religion—a pretended philosophical knowledge of God—and men took it into their heads to become Christians as they become philosophers or men of learning, there was no such effect felt in their faith. This they reckoned to be an argument from experience, that there was no assurance belonging to faith, but such as was gathered up by rational evidence, and by reflecting on the effects from faith felt in themselves."—*Riccaltoun's Collected Works*, vol. ii. pp. 468, 472, &c.

In his "Politick Disputant," *Instruction* 19, he had said, "Assurance in the nature of faith is what (I may say) all Protestant Divines since the Reformation have maintained—if you except some few who, upon the abuse of this way of speaking, chose *another which*, they thought, *expressed the thing as well.* What they (what the Marrow, who had it from them) understood by it is no more than such a well-grounded confidence and trust as is necessary to answer [respond to] the faithfulness of God and the all-sufficiency of Christ in the promise, and such a persuasion of one's own interest therein, as necessarily follows upon a persuasion of the honesty and sincerity of the Promiser."

THE THEOLOGY OF CONSOLATION.

REV. THOMAS MANTON, D.D.

THOMAS MANTON'S grandfather and father were ministers. His father was Rev. Thomas Manton of Whimpole, in Devonshire. He himself was born in 1620, and was educated at Oxford in Wadham College and Hart Hall. In 1640 he was ordained, receiving Deacons' Orders from the Bishop of Exeter (Hall). He was weekly lecturer at Coylton (then called Culliton) till 1643, when he was settled at Stoke Newington; and in 1650 he became Rector of St Paul's, Covent Garden. In 1654 he was made B.D., and in 1660 D.D. of Oxford. He was ejected from his rectory in 1662, and died at Stoke Newington 18th October 1677. As an author he is one of the most voluminous of the Puritans. The student has now the advantage of a complete edition in twenty-two volumes, octavo, published by Messrs James Nisbet & Co. His powers as an expositor have been displayed in my Book First; here is a specimen of his admired preaching:—

"The great duty of Christianity is *coming to Christ*, and Christians are described as those that *come to God by Him*. Now this work is not easily done. Nature is averse to it; partly, because believing or coming to Christ is a mystical duty not evident by natural light but instituted by the Gospel (and we usually bid better welcome to an acquaintance than a mere stranger); moralities, which are in part engraven on man's heart, go down sooner with us than matters of faith. Partly because nature, affecting a self-sufficiency, is loath to be beholding to another, and therefore doth not easily submit to fetch all from Christ; as a proud man will rather choose to wear a russet coat of his own than a silken garment of another's. Partly because it is a long time ere we can get men to be serious and to mind soul-affairs; and if it be so hard a matter to bring them and themselves together, what is it to bring them and Christ together? Partly because Christ and the main of his blessings lie in another—in an invisible—world, and man that is so enchanted with the pleasures of sense and biassed with fleshly lusts (which are importunate to be pleased with what is visible and present) is not easily moved with unseen hopes and induced to deny himself and lay all his affections and interests at the feet of Christ, and entirely to consecrate himself to the use and service of God. For these and many other reasons, man hangs off from Christ, and nothing but a Divine power can cure this averseness. The work of reducing man from his strayings, and bringing him to seek his happiness in *God through Christ*, is carried on among the Divine Persons, between the Father, Son, and Holy Ghost." (*Preface to* Vines, 1662).

PROFESSOR SAMUEL MARESIUS, D.D.[1]

SAMUEL DES MARETS was a French Protestant, son of David Des Marets, Seigneur du Feret and his wife, Madeline Vauquet. He was born at Oisemont, 9th August 1599. He was a delicate child, and was fed on milk for twelve years, during which time the Pasteur Esaïe Blanchard taught him Latin and Greek. At the age of thirteen he went to the University of Paris. His theological studies were carried on at Saumur and Geneva. And in 1619 he went to Paris to be taught sacred eloquence. At the Synod of Charenton, in 1620, he was set apart to the ministry, and became Pasteur of Laon, which he quitted in 1623 after a Jesuit had attempted to answer a pamphlet of his by assassination, and had escaped without punishment.

In 1625 this learned minister, now known in literature as *Maresius*, was elected Professor of Hebrew at Sedan, and during a tour before his installation he received the degree of D.D. at Leyden. Having visited London, he returned to his chair. In 1634 he was summoned into Holland as military chaplain to the Duc de Bouillon. The result was that in 1643 he became a Theological Professor in Groningen, and an ornament of a Dutch university. Here he was colleague to Dr Henry Alting, with whom he was in perfect accord. After his death, his son, Dr James Alting, became his junior colleague; but he was an innovator in theology, and began and maintained a personal quarrel. Maresius always protested that he wished brotherly love and personal friendship to continue amidst all differences in theological persuasions.

The only permanent memento of his early delicacy of health was his smallness of stature, on account of which he was known as "the little preacher." He had no illness during a long life, and was actually preparing for his translation to a chair at Leyden, when his first and fatal sickness set in. On his deathbed he had communications with James Alting, which resulted in personal reconciliation. He died at Groningen 18th May 1673.

The Messieurs Haag give a list of 104 publications by him (Art. DES MARETS). But the figure, 105, was reached; for Maresius wrote two theological systems, only one of which is described by Haag; or rather, in a professed enumeration of editions, the two are confusedly rolled into one.

The omitted one is his *Systema Theologicum;* the *privilegium*, or patent of the last edition is dated 9th April 1673. The dedication, dated 12th April, and signed by himself, is to William Henry, Prince of Orange. It is a very thick

[1] See "Bayle's Dictionary," and Haag, *La France Protestante*.

quarto volume, extending to 1057 pages, with 80 pages of appendix. I mention it, because the engraved title-page contains a portrait of the learned and venerable author, taken at the age of 73. The other system is compendious, being entitled *Collegium Theologicum*, sive *Systema Breve* universæ theologiæ 1st edition, 1645; 2nd, 1649; 3rd, 1656; 4th, 1659, &c.; it is noteworthy, because the last edition was posthumous, and contained a Life of the Author.

In 1652 Maresius published his *Fœderatum Belgium Orthodoxum*, being an exposition of the Belgic [or Dutch] Confession, compiled from the notes which he prepared for his class. The Heidelberg Catechism was known as the Belgic Catechism, and it was endeared to him by recollections of Dr Henry Alting, who had bequeathed to him the upholding of the position of the Catechism in the churches, colleges, and schools of Holland. He had among his papers, though in some disorder, materials for the Catechism similar to what had been worked up into *Fœderatum Belgium Orthodoxum*. And these in his old age he revised, arranged, and published in a separate volume, by general request. This little book was entitled :—" Catechesis Publica fœderati Belgii, et Samuelis Maresii PORISMATA THEOLOGICA ad singulas illius Dominicas, olim publicè disputata nunc verò plurimis flagitantibus recusa ex Authoris recognitione et emendatione. Groningæ, Apud Æmilium Spinniker, 1671." [The Public Belgic Catechism, and Maresius' *Theological Materials* for each of its weekly portions (or, for the lessons of each Lord's Day in the year).]

REV. WALTER MARSHALL.

THE records of New College in Oxford University contain the following interesting information :—

" John Marshall (son of Rev. Walter Marshall of *Husband* in Hampshire) of Wearemouth, in the county of Durham, at the age of nineteen was admitted a scholar of New College, September 2, 1643, and Fellow in 1645. He was ejected from his Fellowship by the Parliamentary Visitors in 1648, and restored by an order of the King's Commissioners, dated August 17, 1660. In 1661 he was elected Fellow of Winchester College. He was Rector of Morested, Hants, and died August 25, 1670, at the age of forty-seven, and was buried in the cloisters of Winchester College."

" Walter Marshall, of Wearemouth, in the bishopric of Durham, at the age of ten was admitted Scholar of Winchester, and in 1648 Scholar of New College, and Fellow two years after. He was elected Fellow of Winchester in 1657, and resigned in 1661. He was vicar of Hursley, Hants."

This information gives us the parentage of Rev. Walter Marshall and his reverend brother. Both were settled in Hampshire, and Hursley was a village near Winchester. From this vicarage he was ejected in 1662, having been "put under the Bartholomew bushel, with nigh 2000 more lights." He set up a small church in an obscure alley in Gosport, " where he shined, though he had not the public oil." He had comfort in his little flock; and a succession of Gospel preachers had multiplied the congregation fourfold at the centenary of his death. It seems that he had conversed with Richard Baxter and the older evangelical divines, especially in consequence of his troubled state of mind, and his sense of his sins. But at last he was comforted by being told to lay to heart the greatest of all his sins, namely, the sin of not believing on the Lord Jesus for pardon and sanctification. The result was not only his own Christian experience, but also his celebrated book, "The Gospel Mystery of Sanctification," "spun out of his own experiences." This book has been abridged. But I can certify, as to the complete work, that the copies in circulation are exact reprints of the first edition. The only omission is the following paragraph in the anonymous friend's Preface, whose racy phraseology I have just been quoting:—" Sometime since he was translated by death Elijah-like, dropping these sheets as his mantle for succeeding Elisha's to go forth with, for the conversion of sinners and comfort of drooping souls. These Papers are the profound experiences of a studious holy soul, learned of the Father, coming from his very heart, and smell of no party or design but for holiness and happiness; yet it is to be feared they will scarcely go down with the heady notionalists of this age, who are of the tribe of Reuben wavering with every wind of modish doctrine. But in Judah it will be praised, and we may hope that many shrubs and cedars hereby may advance in knowledge and comfort."

Mr Marshall died in 1680. His funeral sermon was preached by his neighbour, Rev. Samuel Tomlyns, M.A. of Trinity College, Cambridge, the ejected Rector of Crawley, his text being 2 Cor. v. 1. The Epistle "to my well-beloved friends, the inhabitants of Gosport in the county of Southampton," is dated August 23, 1680, and begins thus:—

" Christian Friends, It hath seemed good to the Sovereign Lord of heaven and earth to make a breach upon you by snatching away from you a faithful servant of Christ, who fed you with his doctrine and edified you by his example. He wooed for Christ in his preaching, and allured you to Christ by his walking."

Mr Marshall's book (as I formerly stated) was not printed till 1692. I have already described and reviewed it. I here insert two Notes, criticising his peculiar *dictum*.

NOTE 1.

Mr Hog of Carnock discusses it in his "Conference betwixt Epaphroditus and Epaphras," page 19 :—

Epaphras. What do you think of that expression in Mr Marshall, *That the thing we are bound by the command of God to believe* (viz., that God freely giveth Christ and salvation to us particularly) *is not a truth before we believe it.*

Epaphroditus. I cannot approve it. The words appear to me harsh and dangerous. Nevertheless I would think that the judicious reader, upon a more full, sedate, and impartial view of the whole context of that eminent author, will not find things so harsh as they appear at first view. And howsoever the expression was offensive to me at first, and I could not but be heartily sorry to find it amongst so many excellent things taught by that author, yet upon further consideration I took his meaning to be, That the gift of Christ and salvation in the Gospel offers becometh a gift beneficial to us, only upon our acceptance.

[Mr Hog then quotes, with approval, Mr Marshall's illustrations, namely, *phrases used in everyday life*, such as, "Do but take this gift and it is your own ; " " I will forgive your offence and be your friend, if I find that you can believe it and that you take me for a friend ; " " I promise to be thy husband if thou wilt have me ; say but the word and I am thine." In such instances, *the declarations to be believed become true when they are believed ;* " that becomes true upon the reception, consent, and acceptance, which yet could not have been said with verity before."]

NOTE 2.

Mr Riccaltoun in referring to the objection that to call upon some individuals to believe that God has given to them eternal life, &c., is to call upon them *to believe what is not true*, says :—

"To this an answer has been often made, *That it is indeed not true that God gives eternal life, and his Son in whom this life is, to any particular person until it is believed; but it becomes true when it is believed.* This has been thought a very bad sort of assertion ; and some have been bold enough to bestow abundance of wit to expose it.

"And yet there is nothing more obviously true. God never gave and never promised to give eternal life, or any of the blessings connected with it, *to an unbeliever.* The gift lies in common, without any determinate application to one person more than another, just as Christ Himself, in whom this life lies, is set forth as a common Saviour. And what we call Believing, or Faith, is the established method—the mean—which God has ordained for applying [appropriating] it. The proclamation is general, *Whosoever will, let him come and take.* And *coming* and *taking* are the application [appropriation] of the general gift; and these are but other words for *believing;* for in no other way can we *come and take the waters of life freely.*

"But here it must be remembered, that, however it is that by this application of [appropriation transacted by our] faith we are received, yet it is still through grace, and not according to any works of righteousness done by us. That very faith, which makes the application [appropriation] is the gift of God, wrought by the Spirit of Christ in the heart and spirit of the believer, and is no more than the first vital act of the new creature. . . . . . This makes a perfect consistency in the method of grace. God gives His Son and life in Him. He really gives or imparts life by His Spirit, and—at that very time, not sooner—the man believes He gives it; and when he does so, he must believe that Christ *has loved him and given Himself for him*—which was indeed true before, but he could not know it sooner." (*Riccaltoun's Collected Works,* Vol. II. page 477.)

PASTOR CONRAD MYLIUS.

CONRAD MYLIUS was a pastor at Neustadt, in the Palatinate, who delivered lectures on the Heidelberg Catechism during the reign of the Elector Frederick V. These Lectures were printed in Latin, the Epistle Dedicatory bearing the date, May 1618. He dates "Ex Musæo meo Lautreæ olim Cæsarum, hodie Palatinorum;" he calls Neustadt, inclyta respublica Neapolitana Nemétum, and prayerfully points to heaven as *Neapolis Cœlestis.* He indicates his native country by styling himself MIDDANUS ; but I must leave the adjective for a future translator. The exposition of the Catechism is in the form of homilies. It must have been a successful book, as the only edition I am acquainted with was published at Amsterdam more than a quarter of a century after the first appearance of the work, viz., in 1654. [Conradi Mylii, Middani, Meletemata Catechetica, sive in Catechesin Heidelbergensem homiliæ ad populum Nepolitanum Nemétum habitæ, capita religionis Christianæ, cum orthodoxe, tum methodice et populariter, secundum theoriam et praxin, proponentes atque exponentes. Editio nova, diligenter recensita, versuum seu linearum et sectionum collocatione contractior, Testimoniorum verò S. Scripturæ indicio subinde auctiora. Amstelodami, sumptibus Johannis Ravensteynii MDCLIV.]

The style of Mylius is sententious. In his exposition of QQ. 86 and 87, he says, "It has been most clearly proved that good works are not demanded from us arbitrarily, although apparently it does not affect our salvation whether we do them or omit them—nor are they needless and superfluous—much less are they pernicious, as if they hindered rather than promoted our salvation. Good works are necessary and useful to the justified. I say, to the justified; I do not say, to men who would be justified. So says Augustin, Bona opera non præcedunt justificandos, sed sequuntur justificatos." Mylius adopts the substance of Luther's rejoinder to the objection, that we need not work, if we are not justified by works. He varies the phraseology thus;—" We are not justified by agriculture, nor by any daily toil or trade ; are we therefore discouraged from cultivating our fields and vineyards, or from minding our counters and workshops ?"

REV. JOHN W. NEVIN, D.D.

DR NEVIN is the author of "The History and Genius of the Heidelberg Catechism," published at Chambersburg, in Pennsylvania, in 1848, and appreciated by Dr Schaff as the best work on the Catechism in English.

The German original of the Catechism made its first appearance on American soil in 1609, when it was conveyed from Holland to Manhattan Island by the discoverers of the Hudson. About a hundred years later, the refugees from the Palatinate brought it to Pennsylvania and other States. The English version was brought from Scotland by the Rev. Dr Laidlie, who became minister at Flushing, Long Island, in the eighteenth century; and this circumstance was the first incident in the history of its adoption by the Synod of the American Reformed Dutch Church in 1771. It has kept its place ever since. It has always been admired by the Presbyterians of America, although they adopt the Westminster Standards with slight Republican modifications. Their General Assembly, in 1870, passed the following Resolution :—" If any churches desire to employ the Heidelberg Catechism in the instruction of their children, they may do so with the approbation of this Assembly."

Dr Nevin was prominent, on the occasion of the Tercentenary of the Heidelberg Catechism in 1863, in preparing and publishing a stately quarto, containing the Catechism in German, Latin, and English. He was the author of the historical introduction to that monumental book. He has been successively Professor of Theology in the Presbyterian Seminary at Alleghany, and in the German Reformed Seminary at Mercersburg, and President of Franklin and Marshall College, Lancaster, Philadelphia.

The following are some of Dr Nevin's laudatory sentences on the Heidelberg Catechism :—" Its widespread and long-continued popularity proclaims its universal significance and worth. It is at once a creed, a catechism, and a confession ; and all this in such a manner, at the same time, as to be often a very liturgy also. Its utterances rise at times to a sort of heavenly pathos, and breathe forth almost lyrical strains of devotion. Simple, beautiful, and clear in its logical construction, the symbol moves throughout also in the element of fresh religious feeling. It is full of sensibility, and faith, and joyous childish trust."

GASPAR OLEVIANUS, LL.D.

KASPAR von der Olewig was born at Treves, 10 August 1536. He studied the ancient languages at Paris, Bourges, and Orleans. He took the degree of LL.D. at Paris, and became known as *Olevianus*. He had been converted to the gospel and joined the Reformed Church, at Paris (it is said). Some young noblemen, one of whom was a son of Frederick III., the Elector-Palatine, exposed themselves to the risk of drowning, in spite of the remonstrances of Olevianus. Plunging into the water to save them, he felt himself in danger, and vowed that if he escaped he would study theology. The results were all that could be desired. Both himself and the youths were preserved, and he went into Switzerland to study theology under Beza. Both Geneva and Zurich are said to have been the scenes of his education for the ministry. He returned to Treves and opened a class for dialectics. But taking occasion to indoctrinate his pupils with the gospel, he was interdicted from teaching and the Canons shut up his school. In some other town (name unknown) he endeavoured to preach the gospel, when a monk gave information, and the authorities cast him into prison. A friend of the Elector-Palatine procured his release and took him to Heidelberg, where Frederick III., who had not forgotten his heroic conduct towards his son, received him cordially. This was in the year 1560. Olevianus was made a Professor of Theology and the Court Preacher, and became the Elector's chief councillor in church affairs. In the composition of the Heidelberg Catechism he was associated with Ursinus, to whom he was inferior in learning, but superior in preaching and in administrative ability. He laboured for the introduction of Presbyterianism and pure discipline, but was thwarted by Thomas Lieber, Professor of Medicine in Heidelberg, and afterwards of Ethics at Basle, who advocated Cæsaro-papism. Lieber was no other then the dread Erastus.

In 1576, on the death of the Elector Frederick, Olevianus was banished from Heidelberg. He was settled at Herborn in 1584, preaching the gospel and teaching a school; there he died, 15 Mar. 1587, in most joyful hope. A friend said to him, " My brother, beyond all doubt you are certain of your salvation in Christ Jesus, as you have taught others." He replied, " Most certain."

Among authors he was known as Gaspar Olevianus Trevirus. He dedicated to Frederick III, on 19 March 1576, his *Exposition of the Apostles' Creed or*

Articles of Faith, wherein is briefly and perspicuously treated the sum of the gratuitous (or gracious) *eternal covenant between God and believers.* [Expositio Symboli Apostolici sive Articulorum Fidei in quâ summa gratuiti fœderis æterni inter Deum et fideles breviter et perspicaciter tractatur]; there is an edition printed in 1584. On 22d January 1579 Beza issued a compilation of Notes on the Romans from sermons on that epistle by Olevianus. Olevianus himself revised these "In Epistolam D. Pauli Apostoli ad Romanos Notæ" for a second edition, which was printed in 1584. In 1585 A. F. printed, at Geneva, Olevianus *On the Substance of the Gratuitous Covenant between God and the Elect, and also on the means whereby that is communicated to us;* [De substantiâ fœderis gratuiti inter Deum et Electos, itemque de mediis quibus ea ipsa substantia nobis communicatur.][1] He was perhaps the first Divine who clearly stated that in offering salvation God represents himself as a God in covenant with us. In the eighteenth century Principal Hadow misrepresented this Scriptural idea by representing a sinner's salvation as being dependent, not simply upon God's faithfulness to God's stipulation, but on the sinner's faithfulness to the sinner's re-stipulation. Principal Rainy[2] bears testimony to Olevianus: "His representations are pervaded throughout with the thought of the gratuitousness of the covenant, and of the wholly Divine efficacy which establishes it.... With him faith sums up everything in this relation [*i.e.*, as to what God claims from us]; and faith itself is not a re-stipulation, but a believing acquiescence for our own part in a covenant which establishes all things for us; and especially an acquiescence in Christ, in whom we find the covenant sealed and vitally operative."

REV. JOHN OWEN, D.D.

JOHN, son of Rev. Henry Owen, vicar of Stadham, near Oxford, and a scion of an influential Welsh family, was born at Stadham in 1616. Both his school and college education were received in Oxford; he became student of Queen's College in 1628, and M.A. in 1635. He left Oxford in 1637, on account of the superstitious ceremonials introduced by Laud as Chancellor of the University. He had been admitted to holy orders by Bishop Bancroft, and having filled two domestic chaplaincies, he in course of time came to London. For some years he had been oppressed with anxieties as to his personal salvation. One day he happened to walk to Aldermanbury Chapel to hear the oldest Edmund Calamy;

[1] His other works are (1) Notæ in Epp. ad Philipp., Col., Gal., Eph. (2) Inventio Dialecticæ. (3) Epitome Institutionis Calvini, 1586. (*See* Bodleian Catalogue.)
[2] On Federal Theology, in the *Catholic Presbyterian*, May 1881.

but an unknown country minister officiated for the great man, and preached a sermon on the text, " Why are ye fearful, O ye of little faith ? " (Matt. viii. 26), which brought " the sunshine of a settled peace " into the soul of John Owen.

We pass over his life, which, after the quiet pastorates of Fordham and Coggeshall (both in Essex), was an eventful one. On 18th March 1651 he was made Dean of Christ Church, Oxford, in the room of Dr Reynolds, and in the following September he became Vice-Chancellor of the University. On 23rd September 1653 he was made D.D. of Oxford ; " it was conferred on me " (he said) " by the University in my absence, and against my consent, as they have expressed it under their public seal ; " the diploma eulogized him as *in palestra theologica exercitatissimus, in concionando assiduus et potens, in disputando strenuus et acutus.*

During Richard Cromwell's rule, Dr Owen was superseded at Oxford, and retired to Stadham. He had for many years been an Independent or Congregationalist by conviction (as many of his writings peaceably testify), so that the National pulpits lost his services at the Restoration, and he has been ever since celebrated as the greatest of Nonconformist preachers and authors. His church and home during those dark ages of the English Church were in London, where he died on 24th August 1683, aged sixty-seven.

The peculiar value of Dr Owen's works, apart from their distinguished ability and fervent soundness in the faith, is their grasp of the meaning of the Divine Word and of the wants of the human soul, to the exclusion of all the political and personal gossip of his own generation. He deals with definite topics, knowing from the first what he is about, and not beginning with random declamations which (in the language of many authors) " lead him to consider " or to hunt some game that chances to start into view. His collected works are accessible, in their most complete and serviceable form, in the twenty-four volumes of the Rev. Dr Goold's edition.

Robert Trail and the Scottish Marrow-men always reckoned Dr Owen to be on their side, especially in his Treatise on Justification (1677). In a discourse on faith, Ebenezer Erskine said : " I shall only at present quote the definition of faith given by the great and judicious Dr Owen in his Catechism, where, having moved the

" Question—What is justifying faith ?

" His answer is—A gracious resting on the free promises of God in Christ Jesus for mercy, with a firm persuasion of heart that God is a reconciled God to us in the Son of His love."

On the theme of Gospel Consolation, it is more practical to regard him as a preacher than as an author. Anthony a Wood, as his brief required of him, has set down with animation everything, however calumnious, that was said against him. But even this furious partizan esteemed Dr Owen as a man and as a preacher. "What I myself knew of him (says Anthony a Wood), which may, I hope, be mentioned without offence, envy, or flattery, is (let rash and giddy heads say what they please) that he was a person well skilled in the tongues, Rabbinical learning, Jewish rites and customs —that he had a great command of his English pen, and was one of the most genteel and fairest writers who appeared against the Church of England, as handling his adversaries with far more civil, decent, and temperate language than many of his fiery brethren, and by confining himself wholly to the cause, without the unbecoming mixture of personal slanders and reflection. . . . His personage was proper and comely, and he had a very graceful behaviour in the pulpit, an eloquent elocution, a winning and insinuating deportment, and could by the persuasion of his oratory, in conjunction with some other outward advantages, move and wind the affections of his admiring auditory almost as he pleased." Dr Goold says: "The merits of Owen as a preacher have not been sufficiently appreciated . . . From the accounts transmitted to us, whether by his various friends and admirers (such as Clarkson, his colleague and successor), or by those who were opposed to him in principle and sentiment (such as Anthony Wood), the ability with which Owen could secure and sustain the attention of an audience must have been great. The effects of his preaching in some instances attest his usefulness in this department of his public labours. John Rogers, in his singular work, 'The Heavenly Nymph,' records the cases of two individuals, Dorothy Emett and Major Mainwaring, who ascribed their conversion to the preaching of Owen when he was in Dublin. Mr Orme remarks that the circumstance confutes a saying attributed to Owen, that he never knew an instance of a sinner converted through his instrumentality; though the saying might so far be true, that he himself might be ignorant of the extent of his own usefulness."

The second of Owen's two sermons on the text, "He staggered not at the promise of God through unbelief, but was strong in faith, giving glory to God" (Rom. iv. 20), furnishes sufficient evidence as to Dr Owen's harmony with the opinions of theologians represented, at a rather later date, by Robert Trail.

In that sermon Dr Owen stated the heresy, as to *a new law*, thus :—

"It hath been said, that faith is the receiving of Christ, as a priest *and a lord* to be saved by Him *and ruled by Him*. . . . This sounds well, makes a fair show, and there is, in some regard, truth in what is spoken. But latet anguis in herbâ [there is a snake in the grass], let men explain themselves, and it is [means] this: *The receiving of Christ as a king is the yielding obedience to Him; but that subjection is not a fruit of the faith whereby we are justified, but an essential part of it; so that there is no difference between faith and works or obedience, both being alike a condition of it.*"

Dr Owen's counter-statement was the following :—

"It is true that faith receives Christ as a lord—as a king—and it is no true faith that will not, doth not do so, and put the soul upon all that obedience which He as the Captain of our salvation requires at our hands. But faith, as it justifies (in its concurrence, whatever it be, thereunto), closeth with Christ for righteousness and acceptation with God only. And (give me leave to say) it is, in that act, no less exclusive of good works than of sin."

Is assured consolation "of the essence of faith?" Dr Owen defined it as a *necessary concomitant of faith*.

His "general description of faith, or believing (as may answer in some measure the proper and metaphorical expressions of it in the Scriptures, where it is termed looking or seeing, hearing, tasting, resting, rolling ourselves, flying for refuge, trusting, and the like)," is given under three heads:—

"1st. There must be an assent to the whole truth of the promises of God, upon this ground and bottom, that He is able and faithful to accomplish them."

"2nd. Over and above this, faith, in the Scriptures, is expressed (and we find it by experience) to be the will's consent unto, and acceptance of the Lord Jesus Christ as mediator—He that accomplished His work as the only way of going to the Father, as the sole and sufficient cause of our acceptation with Him, as our only righteousness before Him."

"3rd. Add hereunto, that which I cannot say is absolutely of the nature of faith, but in some degree or other (secret or more known to the soul) a necessary concomitant of it, that is, the soul's resting and quieting itself, and satisfying its affections, in its interest in and enjoyment of a sweet desirable Saviour."

In the course of this same sermon, Dr Owen expounds Hebrews vi. 17, 18. "*The heirs of the promise* are said to fly for refuge—they are *the fliers with speed*. The allusion, say some, is taken from those who run in a race for a prize. This they say, the word that follows, *to take fast hold on*, doth import; men that run in a race, when they attain the end, seize on and lay fast hold of the prize. Our translators, by rendering the word *flying for refuge,* manifest that they had respect to the manslayer's flying to the city of refuge under the Old Testament. And I am inclined to this acceptation of the metaphor upon a double account.

"(1.) Because I think the apostle would more willingly allude to a Hebrew custom, writing to the Hebrews touching an institution of God, and that, directly typical of the matter he had in hand, than to a custom of the Greeks and Romans in their races, which hath not so much light in it, as to the business in hand, as the other.

"(2.) Because the design of the place doth evidently hold out a flying *from* something, as well as a flying *to* something, in which regard it is said that there is *consolation* provided for them, namely, in their deliverance from the evil which they feared and fled from.

"Now in a race there is indeed a prize proposed, but there is no evil avoided.

"It was otherwise with him that fled for refuge; for as he had a city of safety before him, so he had the avenger of blood behind him; and he fled with speed and diligence to the one that he might avoid the other. Now these cities of refuge were provided for the manslayer, who, having slain a man at unawares, and being thereby surprised with an apprehension of danger (it being lawful for the avenger of blood to slay him), fled with all his strength to one of those cities, where he was to enjoy immunity and safety. Thus, a poor sinner, finding himself in a condition of guilt, surprised with a sense of it, seeing death and destruction ready to seize upon him, flies with all his strength to the bosom of the Lord Jesus—the only city of refuge from the avenging justice of God and curse of the law.

"Now this *flying* to the bosom of Christ (the hope set before us for relief and safety), is *believing*. It is here called *flying* by the Holy Ghost, to express the nature of it to the spiritual sense of believers. He hath taken all means possible to show Himself abundantly willing to receive them. He hath engaged His word and promise, that they may not, in the least, doubt or stagger, but know that He is ready to receive them and give them *strong consolation*. And what is this consolation?—whence may it appear to arise?

"Whence did consolation arise to him who, having slain a man unawares, should fly to a city of refuge? Must it not be from hence—the gates of the city would certainly be open to him, that he should find protection there and be safeguarded from the revenger? Whence then must be our strong consolation, if we thus fly for refuge by believing? Must it not be from hence, that God is freely ready to receive us—that He will in no wise shut us out, but that we shall be welcome to Him—and with the more speed we come, the more welcome we shall be?"

His well-known Exposition of Psalm cxxx. may be referred to as pulpit discourses. We may regard Dr Bates and President Witherspoon (whose expositions of *verse* 4 are quoted in my Book First, part first, chapter 4), as the pupils of Dr Owen on the great theme of the Origin of Christian Obedience; and their eloquent paragraphs may be here fortified by the quotation of one or two aphorisms of their master:—

"*First*, to take up mercy, pardon, and forgiveness, absolutely on the account of Christ—and *then*, to yield all obedience in the strength of Christ, and for the love of Christ—is the life of a believer."

"Faith of forgiveness is the principle of Gospel obedience. (Titus ii. 11, 12.)"

"True gospel obedience is the fruit of the faith of forgiveness. Whatever you do without it is but a building without a foundation, a castle in the air.

You may see the order of gospel obedience, Eph. ii. 7, 10 ; the foundation must be laid in grace—riches of grace by Christ in the free pardon and forgiveness of sin ; from here must the works of obedience proceed."

"You perform duties, abstain from sins—but with heaviness, fear, and in bondage. Could you do as well without them as with them—would conscience be quiet, and hope of eternity hold out—you would omit them for ever. This makes all your obedience burdensome. The service of God is only the drudgery of your lives, which you dare not omit, and delight not to perform. From this wretched and cursed frame there is nothing can deliver you, but this closing with forgiveness. This will give you such motives, such encouragements, as will greatly influence your hearts and souls. It will give you freedom, liberty, delight, and cheerfulness, in all duties of Gospel obedience. You will find a constraining power in the love of Christ therein—a freedom from bondage when the Son of God truly hath made you free. Faith and love will work genuinely and naturally in your spirits ; and that which was your greatest burden will become your chiefest joy. Thoughts of the love of God, of the blood of Christ, of the covenant of grace, and sense of pardon in them, will enlarge your hearts and sweeten all your duties. You will find a new life, a new pleasure, a new satisfaction, in all that you do."

"You lose all you do, and all that you hope to do hereafter, if the foundation be not laid in the receiving of pardon in the blood of Christ. . . . . All that you do is but to compound with God for your sin ; you hope, by what you do for Him and to Him, to buy off what you have done against Him, that you may not fall into the hands of His wrath and vengeance. This makes all you do to be irksome. As a man that labours all his days to pay an old debt and brings in nothing to lay up for himself, how tedious and wearisome is his work and labour to him ! It is odds but that one time or other he will give over and run away from his creditor. So it is in this case ; men, who have secret reserves of recompensing God by their obedience, every day find their debt growing upon them, and have every day less hopes of making a satisfactory payment. This makes them weary, and for the most part they faint under their discouragements, and at length they fly wholly from God. . . . . It is high time to cast down all that vain and imaginary fabric which you have been erecting, and to go about the laying of a new foundation which you may safely and cheerfully build upon—a building that will abide for ever."

"Find you not in yourselves an impotency, a disability unto the duties of obedience, as to their performance unto God in an acceptable manner ? . . . . You are not able in your obedience to answer what you aim at ; you have not strength or power for it. Now, it is this faith of forgiveness alone that will furnish you with the ability whereof ye stand in need. Pardon comes not alone, or Christ comes not to the soul with pardon only; it is that which He opens the door and enters by. But He comes with a Spirit of life and power; and as without Him we can do nothing, so through His enabling us we may do all things."

That the Marrow-men were pupils of Owen, or that he was their model, may be seen in the following sentences from his printed letter to Du Moulin:—" We are by the death of Christ freed from all sufferings [in as far] as they are purely penal and the effects of the curse, though they spring out of that root; only, Sir, you and I know full well that we are not freed from pains, afflictions, and death itself, which had never been had they not proceeded from the curse of the law. And so, sir, by the obedience of Christ we are freed from obedience to the law, as to justification by the works thereof; we are no more obliged to obey the law in order to justification than we are obliged to undergo the penalties of the law to answer its curse."

DAVID PAREUS, D.D.

DAVID WANGLER was born at Francolstein in Silesia on 30th December 1548. His father was *Echevin* or Sheriff of Francolstein, and a Lutheran. About 1564 David was at the school at Hemsberg under the rector, Christopher Schilling, who persuaded him to abandon Lutheranism and to join the Reformed Church. For this proselytism Schilling was banished. The Elector, Frederick III., invited the homeless rector to reside in the Palatinate, and made him the Principal of the new college of Amberg. Schilling had invested his young pupil with a Latin surname. The noun most resembling Wangler was Wange, a cheek, which in Greek is Paria; the Greek noun was softened into Paré, and was latinised into Paréus; as it is sometimes printed PARÆUS, in order to secure the right pronunciation.

Pareus followed the Rector to Amberg in 1566, but left him in the same year, and removed his quarters to Heidelberg, where he was enrolled as a student of the College of Wisdom under Ursinus. In May 1571, having successfully completed his education, he became pastor of Schlettenbach, but soon returned to Heidelberg as a college tutor. In 1573 he became pastor of Hemsbach, where, in 1574, he began to edify the people by the moral life of a married clergyman as contrasted with the scandalous immoralities of his Popish predecessor.

In 1577 Pareus as an exile began a life of six years in John Casimir's territory. And his patron becoming Regent of the Palatinate in 1583, Pareus in

1584 was made Professor of Theology at Heidelberg. In 1586 he published a Method of the Ubiquitarian controversy. In 1589 he edited a German Bible with notes. In 1602 he became chief of the Theological Faculty of Heidelberg, having received the degree of D.D. in 1592. In that city he built a house, with splendid accommodation for a library, in the year 1607. Upon this house, called Parcānum, several privileges and immunities were conferred by the Elector. He gave a splendid course of lectures against Cardinal Bellarmine's voluminous theological writings, which began 28th October 1611, and ended 30th November 1614. Surely some of our young divines, with a public spirit bent on construction rather than destruction, might enter this spacious garden, and might cull for public use much that is valuable from the six scores of prelections *de justificatione impii*, which are the concluding lectures of that course (Nos. 213 to 337). An "Irenicum" by Parcus was published in the last-named year, 1614. In 1617 he published a Commentary on the Romans, known on account of his exposition of the beginning of chapter 13, which our King James I. condemned as revolutionary, but which others seemed to regard as Erastian. In that year (1617) a Protestant jubilee or centenary was held, which lasted for three days; Parcus took a leading part in the celebration, and some of his papers were printed. In 1619 he was requested to proceed to Dort as a delegate to the famous synod, but declined on the plea of age and infirmity, having arrived at the stage of "threescore and ten." He, however, wrote a letter, recommending the banishment of Arminian doctrines from the churches and schools of the Dutch provinces. His fame as a professor was widespread, and many students from Hungary and Poland attended him. In 1621, foreboding the ruin of the Elector on his ill-advised acceptance of the crown of Bohemia, he set out as an emigrant from the Palatinate; but feeling his end approaching, he returned to Heidelberg to die. He expired within his beloved Parcānum in the month of June 1622, in his 74th year.

His son, Philip Parēus, showed a laudable care in collecting and editing his works, and also published a work of his own, entitled *Anti-Owenus*, being a reply to Rev. David Owen, D.D., a Cambridge divine, whose lectures against the (so-called) anti-monarchical views of David Parēus (inferred from his comments on Romans xiii.) had been printed in 1632 with the title, *Anti-Parēus*.

BISHOP PARRY.

THAT the English surname *Parry* should be associated with the Latin name *Pareus*, in the title-page of a commentary on the Heidelberg Catechism, might appear significant. But there is no etymological coincidence, *Pareus* being derived from the Greek, and *Parry* from the Welsh patronymic "ap Harry." In the beginning of the sixteenth century William ap Harry was a gentleman residing at Wormebridge in Herefordshire. He had a son, Henry, father of Henry the future bishop. As to the senior Henry, we may identify him with Henry Parry, one of the influential exiles at Frankfort during the Marian persecution, who returned to take a prominent part under Queen Elizabeth in resettling the Reformed Church of England. A royal commission for the establishment of religion was appointed on 19th July 1559, and its members were William, Earl of Pembroke, John Jewel, S.T.P., Henry Parry, licentiate in laws, and William Lovelace, lawyer. Mr Parry presided as chancellor at Salisbury, at a joint meeting of the Queen's commissioners and the chapter of the cathedral, to receive her Majesty's message relative to the election of a bishop. The younger Henry was born in Wilts about 20th December 1561, and was educated at Oxford in Corpus Christi College. The known dates of his university career are those of his entrance (13th Nov. 1576) and of his becoming a probationer (23d April 1586); at the latter date he was M.A.

In 1587 he appeared as the translator of Ursinus on the Heidelberg Catechism. His object was to spread the Gospel among the people, out of pity for the "desolation of so many distressed souls, who in so many places of this our land and country have been and are daily pined away and consumed to the bone for lack of God's sustenance, the bread of life, the word of God." And a special motive was the instruction of clergymen, who had not been educated in theology. The young author apologized for "the greenesse of my age," on the ground that "but a small and short remnant of days is allotted unto every one of us to try the hazard and adventure of this world in Christ's holy merchandise (yet forty years, and the youngest may—the oldest must depart), I being subject to this common case, and most certain uncertain tie of our life, neither knowing, if perhaps at this present my staff standeth next the door." The following is a transcript of the title-page of his octavo :—"THE SUMME OF CHRISTIAN RELIGION delivered by ZACHARIAS URSINUS in his Lectures on the Catechism autorized by the noble Prince FREDERICK throughout his dominions. Wherein are debated and resolved the questions of whatsoever points of moment which have beene or are controversed in Divinitie. Translated into English by HENRIE PARRIE, out of the last and best Latine editions, together with some supplie of wants out of his Discourses of Divinitie, and with correction of sundrie faults and imperfections which are as yet remaining in the best corrected Latine. AT OXFORD, Printed by Joseph Barnes and are to bee solde in Paules-Churchyeard at the signe of the Tygres head. 1587."

Both he and his father enjoyed the patronage of the great Protestant house of Pembroke (or *Penbroke*, as it was then called). And his book was dedicated

"To the Right Honorable Henric Earl of Pembrooke, Lorde Harbert of Cardiff, Marmion and S. Quintine, Knight of the Most Noble Order of the Garter, and Lorde President of Wales."

There appeared in 1589 another edition, or a reissue with a new title-page, in which the translator's name is spelt HENRY PARRY, the Prince is FREDERICKE, and *autorized* is changed into *authorized*. In 1591 a similar reprint or reissue was published. In 1595 Parry received the degree of D.D.; he had been the Greek Reader in his college, and was in great reputation as a scholar and theologian. He was also chaplain to Queen Elizabeth, whom he attended at her last moments, 24th March 1603. In 1605 he became Dean of Chester. His preaching was admired by King James; and a sermon, which he preached before him at Rochester in 1606, was rewarded by the gift of "a very rich ring" from the King of Denmark. In the same year, he published two sermons in latin, on *the kingdom of God* and *Christian victory.* [De regno Dei et victoriâ Christianâ, conciones duæ.] His name in latin was Henricus Parræus. He became Bishop of Gloucester on 12th July 1607, and Bishop of Worcester in September 1610. None of this eloquent and learned bishop's publications have been reprinted except his translation of Ursinus. In 1611 a quarto edition, enlarged by extracts from David Pareus, was brought out by Richard Crosse, "*with consent of the former interpreter;*" but his episcopal title was not mentioned. It was not then thought that the approbation of an English bishop was required by so eminent a man as Ursinus. Bishop Parry died of palsy at Worcester on 12th Dec. 1616, in his fifty-fifth year. Mr Thelwall begs his brethren to consider that "the doctrines of the Heidelberg Catechism come to us with the fullest sanction and commendation of this learned and pious Bishop of our Church."

NOTE.

The evidence that the youthful Henry Parry, who translated Ursinus, is the same person as Henry Parry, Bishop of Worcester, is the uncontradicted statement of Anthony à Wood. A collateral proof is the connection of father and son with the Pembroke family. William, first Earl of Pembroke, and his son Henry, Lord Herbert, were influential men at the accession of Elizabeth. The influence of the former made the senior Henry Parry an Ecclesiastical Commissioner in 1559. To the latter (who became the second Earl of Pembroke in 1569), the translator of Ursinus wrote in his dedicatory epistle in 1587:—"your annecient favor and good wil, manifoldly extended to my father who long since departed this mortality, [hath] stretched to me his son." He is called D. HENRIE PARRY, in the quarto editions of 1611, &c., and in the folio editions of 1633, &c.

BISHOP REYNOLDS.

EDWARD, son of Austin and Bridget Reynolds, was a native of the parish of Holyrood in Southampton, where he was born in November 1599. He was educated in the Grammar School in his native town and at Merton College, Oxford. After a very distinguished career at the University, being a Fellow of his College, and M.A., he entered into Holy Orders and became Rector of Braunston in Northamptonshire, and Preacher at Lincoln's Inn. He was (says Anthony a Wood) "a noted preacher, though of a hoarse voice." Amidst the troubles which Charles I. and Laud brought upon the Church, Mr Reynolds became a member of the Westminster Assembly of Divines, the Author of the Assembly's Annotations on Ecclesiastes, and a visitor of the University of Oxford. With regard to the Vice-Chancellorship of Oxford, it is interesting to note that in 1641 the Chancellor, Archbishop Laud, being a prisoner in the Tower, resigned the office and was succeeded by the Earl of Pembroke, who was turned out by the king's command in 1643 but restored in 1648. On April 12, 1648, Lord Pembroke having recommended him for the vice-chancellorship, Edward Reynolds (at that time created a D.D.), was duly installed, and was also made Dean of Christchurch. He had another tie to his University, by his marriage to Mary, daughter of John Harding, D.D., late President of Magdalen, Hebrew Professor, and one of the translators of the Bible. Being opposed to the Engagement presented to him by the Independents for signature, Dr Reynolds retired to Braunston in 1650, and soon after he became Vicar of St Lawrence-Jewry, in London, where he was famous for his eloquence and learning. By the favour of Richard Cromwell, he was in 1660 (new style) restored to his Deanery. He lost it again on the Restoration of Charles II., whose return he had promoted, but was offered the bishopric of Norwich which he accepted, and held from 1661 till his death, 28th July 1676, "a frequent preacher and constant resident."

As an author, Bishop Reynolds has always been valued by posterity, his Explication of Psalm cx. and Sermons on Hosea, chap. xiv., being still known and admired. Even more valuable is his volume entitled, "Meditations on the Holy Sacrament of the Lord's Last Supper," which was licensed for the press on 7th April 1638. It is on account of an Essay embodied in it upon the complete deliverance of believers from God's wrath that I have brought his name before my readers. The greater portion of this Essay I now transcribe; the first few paragraphs are condensed, and rearranged for the sake of lucidity.

THE PASSION OF CHRIST was His death, whereby I understand not only that last act of expiation, but the whole space between that and His nativity, wherein, being subject to the law of death and to all those infirmities which were the harbingers of death, He might in that whole space be as truly called *a man of death*, as Adam was a dead man in the virtue of the curse that very day (beyond which, notwithstanding, he lived many hundred years), that which we call death being nothing else but the consummation of it. The estate of exaltation is the resurrection of Christ (whereby the efficacy of that merit which on the cross was consummated is publicly declared) and His intercession (wherein it is proposed and presented unto God the Father as an eternal price and prayer on behalf of His Church).

"The first part of our deliverance respects [*has respect* or *reference to*] us as we are in the state of death and enmity; and it is a double deliverance, *negative* by removing us out of this estate, and *positive* by constituting us into another which is an estate of life and reconcilement.

"The next part of our redemption was from the bondage of corruption unto the liberty of glory, which likewise is by Christ performed for us, which is a deliverance from the consequents of sin.

"And if it be here demanded how it comes to pass, if all the consequents of sin be removed, that the faithful are still subject to all those temporal evils both in life and death which even in this state of nature they should have undergone, we answer in general that the faithful die in regard of *the state*, but not in regard of *the sting* of death; they are subject to a dissolution, but it is to obtain a more blessed union, even to be with Christ.

"Punishment may be considered, improperly and incompletely, as any oppressive evil, which in a reasonable creature doth so draw its origin from sin, as that [we may say] that if there were not a habitation of sin, there would be no room for such an evil—as, in the man that was born blind, though sin were not the cause of the blindness, yet it was that which made room for the blindness. If thus we consider punishments as they are dolours and pains, and as they are impressions contrary to the integrity of nature, then [we may say that] the temporal evils of the godly are punishments, because they work the very same manner of natural effects in them which they do in other men.

"Punishment may be considered properly and perfectly as an evil or pressure of nature proceeding from a Lawgiver just and powerful, and inflicted upon reasonable creatures for their disobedience and breach of His law, whereby there is intended a declaration of wrath, and satisfaction of justice. The temporal evils which do befall the godly are not formally or properly punishments, nor effects of divine malediction or vengeance towards the persons of the godly, who, having obtained in Christ a plenary reconciliation with the Father, can be by Him respected [*regarded*] with no other affection (however, in manner of appearance, it may seem otherwise) than with an affection of love and free grace.

"Those evils of nature which do occasionally follow sin, and unto which sin hath originally opened an entrance—which declare how God stands affected towards sin, with a mind purposing the rooting out and destroying of it—such afflictions of the godly may be called punishments, as God is said to have been exceeding angry with Aaron. But though inflicted on the godly because of their sins—as were the death of the child to David, the tempest to Jonah, and the like—yet they are not evils inflicted for the revenge of sin, which is the right nature of a proper punishment (so saith the Lord, *Vengeance is Mine, I will repay*); but they are evils inflicted by God's wisdom and love towards His saints, for the overthrow of sin, for weakening the violence and abating the outrageousness of our natural corruptions.

"As then, in the godly, sin may be said *to be* and *not to be*, in a diverse sense, even so punishments or consequents of sin may be said *to be* in the godly, or *not to be* in them, in a different sense. They are not in them in regard of their sting and curse as they are proper revenges of sin, although they be in them in regard of their state, substance, and painfulness, until such time as they shall put on an eternal triumph over death (the last enemy that must be overcome).

"Punishment, in the nature of it, is a thing legal, namely, the execution of the law; for divine law is ever the square and rule of that justice, of which punishment is the effect and work. All those on whom the execution of the law doth take any effect may truly be said to be so far under the law in regard of the sting and curse thereof, for the curse of the law is nothing else but the evil which the law pronounceth to be inflicted, so that every branch and sprig of that evil must needs bear in it some part of the nature of a curse, even as every part of water hath in it the nature of water. But all the godly are wholly delivered from all the sting and malediction of the law. Christ is unto us the End of the law, abolishing the shadows of the ceremonial, the curses of the moral. We are no more under the law, but we are under grace—under the precepts, but not under the covenant—under the obedience, but not under the bondage of the law. Unto the righteous *there is no law*, that is, *there is no condemnation to them that are in Christ*. We are dead unto the law by the body of Christ; it hath not the least power or dominion over us.

"The most proper nature of punishment is to satisfy an offended justice. But Christ, bearing the iniquity of us all in His own body on the tree, did therein make a most sufficient and ample satisfaction to His Father's wrath, leaving nothing wherein we should make up either the measure or the virtue of His suffering, but did Himself perfectly save us. An infinite person suffering, and the value of the suffering depending on the dignity of the person, it must needs be that the satisfaction made by that suffering must be likewise infinite, and, by consequence, most perfect.

"If we but consider (as it is, in all matters of consequence, necessary) the author of this evil, we shall find it to be no true and proper punishment. For it is a reconciled Father who chasteneth every son whom He receiveth—who, as

He often doth declare His severest wrath by forbearing to punish, doth as often, even out of tenderness and compassion, chastise His children—who hath predestinated us unto them [*unto chastisements*], doth execute His decrees of mercy in them, doth by His providence govern and by His love sanctify them to those that suffer them—in none of which things are there the points of punishment.

"But if Christ have thus taken away the malignity of all temporal punishments, why are they not quite removed? To what end should the substance of that remain, whose properties are extinguished?

"Certainly God is so good as that He would not permit evil to be, if He were not so powerful as to turn it to good. Is there not honey in the bee when the sting is removed?—sweetness in the rose when the prickles are cut off?—a medicinable virtue in the flesh of vipers when the poison is cast out? And can man turn serpents into antidotes, and shall not God be able to turn the fiery darts of that old Serpent into instruments for letting out our corruptions, and all his buffets into so many strokes for the better fastening of those graces in us, which before were loose and ready to fall out?

"Briefly—these, amongst others, are some ends of the remaining of death and other temporal evils, notwithstanding the death of Christ have taken away the malignity of them all.

"*First*—for the trial of our faith and other graces. Our faith in God's Providence is then greatest when we dare cast ourselves on His care even when to outward appearances He seemeth not at all to care for us—when we can so look on our miseries, that we can withal look through them. Admirable is that faith which can with Israel see the Land of Promise through a sea, a persecution, a wilderness, through whole armies of the sons of Anak—which can with Abraham see a posterity like the stars of heaven through a dead womb, a bleeding sword, and a sacrificed son—which can with Job see a Redeemer, a Resurrection, a Restitution, through the dunghill and the potsherd, through ulcers and blotches, through the violence of heaven and of men, through the discomforts of friends, the temptations of a wife, and the malice of Satan—which can with Stephen see Christ in heaven through a whole tempest and cloud of stones—which can with that poor Syrophenician woman see Christ's compassion through the odious name of *dog*—which can in every Egypt see an exodus, in every den of lions a Lion of Judah, in every temptation a door of escape, and in every grave an *Arise and sing*.

"*Secondly*, They are unto us for antidotes against sin, and means of humility and newness of life—by which our faith is exercised and excited, our diseases cured, our security, and slackness in the race set before us, corrected—without which good effects all our afflictions are cast away in vain upon us. He hath lost his affliction that hath not learned to endure it. The evils of the faithful are not to destroy, but to instruct them; they lose their end if they teach them nothing.

"*Thirdly*, They make us conformable unto Christ's sufferings.

"*Fourthly*, They show unto us the perfection of God's graces and the sufficiency of His love.

"*Fifthly*, They drive us unto God for succour, unto His word for information, and unto His Son for better hopes. Nothing sooner drives a man out of himself than that which oppresseth and conquereth him; insomuch that public calamities drove the heathen themselves to prayer and to consult with their Sybil's Oracles, whose author, though ignorant of, yet under false names and idolatrous representations, they laboured (as much as in them lay) to reconcile and propitiate.

"*Sixthly*, God is in them glorified, in that He spareth not His own people, and yet doth so punish that He doth withal support and amend them.

"*Lastly*, It prepareth us for glory. By these evils convincing the understanding of the slipperiness and uncertainty of this world's delights, and how happiness cannot grow in that earth which is cursed with thorns and briars; it teacheth us to groan after the revelation of that life which is hid with Christ, where all tears shall be wiped from our eyes.

"So that, in all temporal evils, that which is destructive—the sting and malediction of them—is, in the death of Christ, destroyed."—*Reynolds on the Lord's Last Supper*, Chapter XV.

In the next century the Rev. James Hog of Carnock [*see* Hog] stated the same doctrine quite as strongly in his comments on the fifth petition of the Lord's Prayer [Forgive us our debts, &c.]; the following is his preliminary doctrinal statement:—

"I. Our Lord Jesus—the Surety of that better testament—by giving Himself a sacrifice, did satisfy justice to the full, and purchased complete remission, which also is and shall be vouchsafed upon every elect person. He paid in the room of each of them that full price which justice required for its entire and thorough satisfaction.

"II. The humbled soul, having heard and learned of the Father and under His drawings, and having applied in the extremity by faith unto his only Redeemer, is hereby ingrafted into Christ and married to Him. Thus the believer is (may I use the word ?) *instated into* and *entered upon* the possession of the before-mentioned full pardon. He may, and ought to, look upon himself as one whose debt is wholly taken off, having been charged upon his glorious Head and Husband, who hath discharged it to the full; so that he is entirely freed from hell and wrath, and shall never come into condemnation.

"III. In this blessed estate of the nearest and sweetest relations to Christ which incomparably surpass anything of that kind amongst creatures (for *he who is joined to the Lord is one spirit*), the believer, as a child of the family of his heavenly Father, standeth under another kind of government than that by which the Lord ruleth reasonable creatures in a more general way. He is now under the tender care and sweet inspection of a Father, yet as strongly and indispensably obliged to obey the law in everything as ever he was in any estate. Be ye therefore perfect, as your Father which is in heaven is perfect. Do we then make void the law through grace? Nay, we establish the law.

"IV. Nevertheless, the believer, by reason of a body of death still cleaving, hath many corrupt springs running in him, which not only carry to more ordinary strayings through the sins of more daily incursion, but procure at times greater and more dangerous declinings.

"V. Every sin is displeasing to the Lord, who is of purer eyes than to behold iniquity. Every sin is therefore grievous to the child of God, both in the poisonous fruits and the hidden roots. And so its greater than ordinary prevalency bringeth him under so much of discountenance and such penetrating fatherly strokes, as are (though inflicted from everlasting love) necessary for discovering sin more clearly to the conscience, and for riveting more deeply a humbling sense thereof—that the heart may be strongly drawn *furth* towards the only Physician for taking away all iniquity.

"VI. After the Lord hath discovered [*disclosed*] His everlasting love, the believer ought strongly to hold fast His encouraging testimony who is the God of truth, whose gifts and callings are without repentance—seeing we have not received the spirit of bondage (may the Lord's children say) again to fear, but the Spirit of adoption whereby we cry, *Abba, Father*. Notwithstanding, forasmuch as they (and even the most established amongst them) offend in many things—while assaulted by enemies without, as also drawn away of their own lusts and enticed—they are liable to the Lord's hiding His face, and chastising them variously with the rods of men, although He will never take His lovingkindness from them, nor suffer His faithfulness to fail.

"VII. The intrinsic demerit of sin is still the same—viz., death in its full significancy and extent. And the privileges which believers enjoy, and which are peculiar to them, aggravate their guilt so much the more, and on that very account prove matter of deep humiliation, which maketh each of them look upon himself as *the chief of sinners*. Nevertheless, after a gracious change, and after the Lord speaking peace to their souls, their fears of wrath (attended sometimes with much of confusion and horror, as also with deep and perplexing exercise of mind about it, and with fervent deprecations of the same) are really founded upon darkness and mistake."—*Hog's Essay*, pp. 210, &c.

THE THEOLOGY OF CONSOLATION.

REV. ROBERT RICCALTOUN.

ROBERT RICCALTOUN was one of the most remarkable men that Scotland has produced. His knowledge of the Scriptures was unsurpassed and almost unrivalled, the fruit of an enthusiastic study which began when he was five years of age; "he could read the Bible distinctly before he was five years of age." He was born in 1691, and educated at the Grammar School of Jedburgh and the University of Edinburgh. His academic career was entirely a matter of choice, as he had no plan for his future life except to be a farmer. He formed for himself a system of Bible divinity, but left college without attending the divinity classes. His learning and abilities, as well as his religious character, so commended themselves to the Presbytery of Kelso, that they urged him to become a preacher of the Gospel; and they actually licensed him as a probationer on March 5, 1717, notwithstanding his never having studied at a divinity hall. His subsequent career entirely justified the Presbytery's exceptional procedure. Though "almost forced upon trials," Mr Riccaltoun was a hearty servant of the Church of Christ ever afterwards. He assisted the Rev. Archibald Deans of Bowden for seven years; and he married Anna Scott in 1724. The parish of Hobkirk (*alias* Hopekirk), in the Presbytery of Jedburgh, having been vacant for more than a year, the Presbytery exercised the *jus devolutum* in the autumn of 1725, and presented him to the charge and living. Mr Riccaltoun was ordained as minister of Hobkirk on 24th September 1725. He had thus no official concern with *The Marrow* controversy; but as a probationer he had employed his leisure in writing very much and very ably on the side of *The Prefacer* (Mr Hog) and the persecuted brethren. (His works, published by himself in his life-time, were all anonymous.)

His first publication was *Dialogue First* on the "Marrow controversy;" the copy before me has no title-page, but I have the authority of the late Principal Lee for dating it 1721. The following is the title of the second (and last) dialogue: "The Controversie concerning the Marrow of Modern Divinity considered in several familiar dialogues. Dialogue II., Acts xx. 23 : ... *Bonds and afflictions abide me, but none of these things move me,* &c. Isa. lxvi. 5 : *Hear the word of the Lord, ye that tremble at His word; your brethren that hated you, that cast you out for my name's sake, said, Let the Lord be glorified. But He shall appear to your joy, and they shall be ashamed.* Printed in the year 1722. Price sixpence stitched."

The speakers in the dialogue were "Gamaliel, a minister, defender of the Assembly Act condemning 'The Marrow,' &c.; Paul, a minister, a defender of the Representation against that Act; Philologus, a private Christian, a violent stickler for the Condemnatory Act; Apelles, a private Christian, a zealous friend of the Representation; Rufus, a well-meaning private Christian attached to neither side; Gallio, a careless libertine gentleman, who misimproves these debates to ridicule all true religion." The first dialogue has 158 pages, and the second 132; the latter concludes thus: "A particular providence interrupted this conference here. What remains may, as Providence makes it expedient, be considered in other such conferences, or in particular Essays on the subjects themselves."

His next tract was humorous and satirical, being entitled: "THE POLITICK DISPUTANT; Choice Instructions for quashing a stubborn adversary. Gathered from and exemplified in the learned Principal Hadow's conduct in his late appearances against *The Marrow of Modern Divinity* and its friends.

"Quid immerentes hospites vexas canis,
Ignavus adversus lupos?—Hon.
Edinburgh, printed in the year 1722"—80 pp.

This brochure is much in the style afterwards followed by Witherspoon in his *Ecclesiastical Characteristics*; the difference being that Riccaltoun's burlesque is confined to the *Instructions*, while the commentary is serious. The instructions are 30 in number. I copy the first two:—

"I. Study carefully whatever methods may be most proper to raise your own reputation and sink your adversary's—no matter whether by making him odious, or ridiculous and contemptible; but your best course will be to carry on both designs at once.

"II. As you must always hold in view worthy and laudable ends and designs for your own undertaking, so you must take care to provide some frightful and odious name for your adversary—made so, either by being affixed to some abominable heresy, or carrying in it somewhat harsh and shocking to the generality of readers."

The next year was eventful in Mr Riccaltoun's life, as witnessing two publications from his pen. The first was a volume extending to 446 pages, entitled: "A Sober Enquiry into the Grounds of the present Differences in the Church of Scotland, wherein the matters under debate are fairly stated, the differences adjusted, and Mr Hadow's Detectious considered and weighed. Deut. xix. 16, 18, 19: *If a false witness rise up against any man . . . . the judges shall make diligent inquisition; and, behold, if the witness be a false witness, and hath testified falsely against his brother, then shall ye do unto him, as he had thought to do unto his brother: so shalt thou put away the evil from among you.* Printed in the year 1723."

How competent this young Biblical divine was to discuss the questions may be seen from a passage at which the book happens to open—*page* 401:

"Here is the judicious, learned, and holy Dr Owen, brought in to support a cause which, while he lived, all who know anything at all about him, must know he opposed, with all the earnestness and vigour he was capable of. And what does he say? Why truly, when all is done that can be to make him serve a turn, he speaks still like himself, *That no impenitent sinner, going on in his sins, can have any part in Christ. But what is that to actual believers, or the law-curse seizing upon* THEM?

"But though the curse of the law is thus bound up and restrained by the covenant of grace, or rather exhausted by our Lord Jesus Christ, yet some threatenings there are, consistent with a covenant state; and thus the law takes hold even of the believer, *and shows what afflictions in this life they may expect for them, although freed from the curse thereof threatened in the law*,[1] and thus 'they incur God's displeasure and grieve His Holy Spirit—come to be deprived of some measure of their graces and comforts—have their hearts hardened and their consciences wounded—hurt and scandalize others, and bring temporal judgments upon themselves.' [2] But as these, nor any of them, are no part of the law-curse, they are still, notwithstanding all these, delivered from the evil of all afflictions, and the blood of Christ proves a sufficient protection against the law. All these are instituted for quite other ends, that they may be partakers of God's holiness. Until these ends are accomplished, and the means [which] God takes be made effectual to humble the believer and bring him to renew his faith and repentance, he is not to expect to have the light of God's countenance lifted up upon him.[3]

"These sins, then, may be considered either in themselves, and as to their eternal demerit as they stand in the eyes of the just, holy, and righteous law of God—and thus they are fitted to bring upon the soul the curse in its utmost extent, were it not already exhausted upon Christ.

"But if we consider them as they lie against that rule, which God hath established under the covenant of grace . . . . they bring on grievous plagues indeed many times, but still so (as all corrections are) to produce amendment. For the removal of one's liableness unto these, then, it is not only necessary that one have interest in the blood of Christ, but also that he fall in with God's end therein, and learn that lesson which God is teaching him thereby —which, whenever it is accomplished, we may assure ourselves as He afflicteth not the children of men willingly, these shall be removed and taken off. But still it must be remembered that this is not owing unto the value of our obedience, but unto God's own rich grace in Christ Jesus.

"If no more than this is meant by the expression which the Reverend Principal adduces from the second part of *The Marrow*,—*That, though faith in*

[1] "Westminster Confession," chap. xix., sect. 6.   [2] *Ibid.*, chap. xvii., sect. 3.
[3] *Ibid.*, chap. xi., sect. 5.

Christ's blood takes away that guilt which subjected to the legal curse, yet obedience must take away that guilt which subjecteth to fatherly displeasure,—there is nothing so strange in it that one needs to triumph over the author, as I find a great many doing who understand very little of the one guilt or the other. And the Principal himself might have spared the bitter jeer with which he introduces it."

Mr Riccaltoun's second publication, in 1723, was "A Review of an Essay upon Gospel and Legal Preaching. In several letters to a friend. Gal. i. 7. &c. : *There be some that trouble you and would pervert the Gospel of Christ.* 8. *But though we, or an angel from heaven, preach any other Gospel unto you, than that which we have preached unto you, let him be accursed,* &c. Edinburgh : Printed and are to be sold by Mr John M'Euen and other booksellers in Edinburgh and Glasgow. 1723. Price, stitched, 8d." 128 pp.

The Essayist, to whom this tract is an answer, used a ready pen and superior diction in a sharp onset upon "The Marrow" divines. His professed theme was "Gospel and Legal Preaching." What he practically aimed at was to show that the Marrow-men had not a monopoly of Gospel preaching, but, on the contrary, that their peculiar Gospel was Antinomianism ; while their stigmatizing other preaching as legal was a misapprehension and a misrepresentation. On this latter topic the Essayist asserted that no preaching is *legal, i.e.,* legalistic or Pharisaical, which is not boldly and unblushingly so, and does not actually teach that a man's salvation is to be obtained entirely by his own good works. Mr Riccaltoun's observations, in reply to this reckless assertion, are valuable, and also impress us favourably with his own faith and piety :—" In stating what *legal preaching* is, he (the Essayist) tells us several things which indeed are so, yet he takes no notice of *criminal omissions* . . . . which may justify the denomination of *legal* preaching (though the preacher do not directly say that perfect obedience is the condition of life—that man can obey the holy law of God without being regenerated, &c.). If some ingredients, absolutely necessary unto a prescribed potion, be left out by the apothecary to whom the care of making it up is committed, may we not say, it is not the potion prescribed? (though all the rest do also belong to the prescription, and though nothing contrary to it be put in). The application is easy. Though a man, in his preaching morality, should say nothing that is directly heterodox ; yet, if he omit these doctrines that are necessary ingredients to make his sermon a truly evangelical discourse, I will not say he is '*nick-named*' a Legal Preacher.

"Now, sir, I have heard some judicious Christians say, that they have been for a long time under the ministry of some men, and that they seldom heard them insist on any other subject but the pressing of some duty and declaiming against some vice—which they thought indeed to be *a legal strain* of preaching, not because they said anything contrary unto truth, nor because either their explications or arguments were, in themselves, wrong; but because of their habitual neglect of preaching either on the root and spring of vice, *Our fall and the corruption of our nature*, or on the source and fountain of holiness, *Union with Christ*, and many other necessary Gospel doctrines."—Pp. 7, 8.

We have no information as to the public life of Mr Riccaltoun during his forty-four years' ministry at Hobkirk, except that he preached and presided at the ordination of Mr Somervel as minister of Hawick on 29th March 1732. In his pastoral and private life he earned universal esteem and affection. He maintained his studious habits, and could cogitate deeply and write fluently, even when conversation was resounding around him. He was patient and self-possessed. While he was a probationer, he, by becoming surety for a friend, so involved himself, that his circumstances were straitened for life; but he always said that it had been so ordered by God for his best interests, " as he thought, if he had not been so borne down, his spirit might have been very haughty and overbearing." His recreations were refined and useful. He wrote a poem called " A Winter's Day," which appeared in the *Gentleman's Magazine* for May 1740, and which suggested to his young friend, James Thomson, the subject of " Winter"—the first written (and the best) of *Thomson's Seasons*. Riccaltoun's memory would deserve to be cherished, were it only for " the friendship and patronage which he showed to Thomson when young and unknown." In 1764 he lost his wife, to whom he had been married for forty years; and on 4th December 1765 his son, John, became his assistant and successor. He himself died on Sabbath the 17th September 1769 (aged seventy-eight), having been taken suddenly ill during public worship in his church on the previous Sabbath. The only work which he sent to the press during his ministry was entitled, " A Dissertation on the conduct of the Jewish Sanhedrim, and the advice offered by Gamaliel in the famous trial of the Apostles (Acts v. 17-41) considered as an argument for the truth of Christianity. Edinburgh, printed for A. Kincaid and J. Bell, and T. Cadell, London, 1769." vi. and 190 pp. 8vo. (Dedicated to the Hon. John Campbell of Calder). His son, the Rev. John Riccaltoun (who had been ordained as his successor in 1765, and lived till 9th April 1800), edited "The Works of the Rev. Robert Riccaltoun," in three volumes, *never before printed*, 1771, 1772, octavo.

The first volume, beginning with *Essays on Human Nature*, was perhaps not fitted to attract the reading public; but two-thirds of the volume was occupied with *Essays on several Doctrines of Revelation*, which are full of life and interest.

The second volume also has an unpromising opening—namely, *Treatise on the General Plan of Revelation*; but more than half the volume contains a series of dissertations (founded upon Galatians ii. 20) on *The Christian Life*, which are both edifying and readable. And the *Notes and Observations on the [whole] Epistle to the Galatians*, which compose the third volume, are so eminent for their simplicity and comprehensiveness, and exhibit such popular and scholarly endowments, that they are well worthy of being reprinted for general circulation. All his writings have this value, that their theology is drawn from the pure text of Scripture, and that they give an independent support to the system of the Marrow divines as a whole, while reserving liberty to differ in one or two details.

As an instance we may quote some beautiful sentences from his "Christian Life," which a Marrow divine would hardly approve of:—

"When the love of Christ, and of the Father in Him, is known and believed, how happy the man! . . . .

"But how shall we attain so happy a state? It is in God's hand; it is a gift of His grace; and until He shall be pleased to bestow it, and to give the Spirit of faith which leads into all truth, vain are all the attempts of man. . . . .

"He has laid down a way which He has promised to bless, and it is the way of faith; and he has warranted us to go on in an absolute dependence on, and entire confidence in Him, whatever difficulties and discouragements we may meet with in our way. And, indeed, we may be put to wait long, and even meet with many things that look like absolute refusals, as the woman of Canaan did. But we have this for our encouragement, that never any followed and waited (for faith hath always patience for its companion; they that believe never make haste) —never any, I say, waited but in the end had their errand and more. Himself has said, *Him that cometh to Me I will in no wise cast out.*

"The only direction then I would give, is that which God gave Moses for the Israelites when they were in the most desperate case men could be in, shut up between the Egyptians and the Red Sea, *Speak unto the children of Israel that they go forward."*

The Marrow divines would say, *Go forward,* by believing the Gospel which is the truth, and the Saviour who is true, while you give the glory of your believing to God the Holy Spirit alone. That a man is not to believe a faithful witness and a true testimony until he is conscious of having received the Holy Spirit, is a misstatement as dangerous as that a man is not to pray until he is conscious of having been favoured with special liberty of access to God. Such an excuse for not freely taking the water of life is often an indolent and sinful apology for delaying to give our souls to Christ.

And the Marrow divines would say further, that Mr Riccaltoun's apology for delay is contradicted by his own exposition of the text—Gal. ii. 20, "I live by the faith of the Son of God, who loved me and gave Himself for me." Both in his Dissertations on that verse, and in his Commentary on the Epistle, he gives a thoughtful and evangelical statement of the lessons which every reader of the Bible should learn from that text.

In the Dissertations on the Christian Life, speaking of the Son of God

"who loved *me* and gave Himself *for me*," he says: "In whatever view we consider the faith of Christ, it will very naturally and even necessarily land us where it did the Apostle, namely, in the particular application of His redeeming love to ourselves." (Vol. ii., p. 480). On this he enlarges in the Commentary:—
"I was saying, To live to God is to devote ourselves to Him and His work and service. And if any should put the question the Jews put to our Lord (John vi. 28), *What shall we do that we may work the works of God?* we have HIS answer to it who certainly best understood it, *This is the work of God, that ye believe on* HIM *whom* HE *hath sent.* This is the only way that man can do anything for God; and all that the best believers do, or can do, is but giving Him the glory due unto His name and acknowledging His grace. And this is the singular specialty of His service, that all the profit of their labour redounds to themselves; their Master needs none and can receive none. The Apostle understood his Master's direction; *the life he lived in the flesh* was (he says) *by the faith of the Son of God;* where this is wanting, all that can be done without it is but affronting God in the basest manner; for what the Apostle [John] says is evident in the nature of the thing : *He that believes not His testimony,* or *record concerning His Son, makes Him a liar,* and treats Him as such.

"Whosoever has so far considered this testimony as to know anything of Christ, cannot miss to find in Him the highest evidence God could give of His love to the world. God has stated it in such a manner that no one person has more or less reason than another to believe it. All who hear are called—are commanded—to believe in Him whom He hath sent; and all have equal encouragement and assurance of success in this way; insomuch that, strictly and properly, faith is no more but the application of the general declaration in the testimony to one's self. Thus, we see, the Apostle took it, and sets an example to us. He does not pretend any particular revelation, of the love of God and His ever blessed Son, to himself more than to others; nor did he need any; and therefore pleases himself with a conclusion arising so naturally and necessarily from the truth as it is in Jesus, and concludes with the strongest confidence of faith, *who loved me and gave Himself for me.* . . .

"I know not how it hath happened that many, even serious people, not only do in fact, but have even been taught to, soothe themselves in the want of this assurance of faith; as if it were their unhappiness but not their sin. But surely they must be egregiously mistaken who make such a conclusion. For nothing can be more certain, than that so much as there is of abatement of the most perfect confidence of faith, so much there is of unbelief (Rom. iv. 20), and I hope nobody will say that is no sin. It is true, there may be faith where there is much doubting; nay, one may say, there can be no doubting where there is not some faith. But weak faith cannot fail to make a weak Christian. And if the Apostle John's account of the rise and progress of the love of God in the heart of man (which, by the way, is really writing the law of God there) may be credited,— just so far as the love of God to us is known and believed, so far will this law of love be planted and rooted in the heart, for (1 John iv. 19) *we love Him because He first loved us.*" (Vol. iii. p. 135.)

REV. THOMAS RIDGLEY, D.D.

THOMAS RIDGLEY was born in London in 1667, and was educated for the ministry among the Congregationalists at their academy in Trowbridge. His first appointment was to be assistant to Rev. Thomas Gouge at the Three Cranes in Thames Street, in London; he served under this celebrated divine from 1695 till 1700, and then succeeded him in the full pastorate. To this charge there were added in 1712 the labours of Theological Professor in the chair left vacant by Dr Isaac Chauncey of London (the ejected rector of Woodborough, in Wiltshire). The classical and mathematical professor was John Eames, F.R.S. (an associate of Sir Isaac Newton), who ultimately succeeded Ridgley in the theological professorship.

Mr Ridgley faithfully resisted the Arian invasion which desolated so many churches. He defended the order for signing the Trinitarian paragraphs, extracted from the Westminster Confession and Catechisms as a test for ministerial communion among the Dissenters, and published his views as to this great theological crisis in the year 1719, in a pamphlet entitled, " The unreasonableness of the charge of imposition, exhibited against several dissenting ministers in and about London, considered. And the difference between creed-making as practised in former ages, and their late conduct in declaring their faith in the doctrine of the blessed Trinity, stated and argued."

Although strictly and heartily orthodox, Mr Ridgley was original in many of his statements. He agreed in all the conclusions usually called Calvinistic, but thought that sometimes the steps leading up to those conclusions had not been described as accurately and as simply as they might have been. It was only as to methods of reasoning and processes of proof, and not as to vital doctrines, that he ever differed from his brethren. This characterised all his writings, but especially his pamphlet entitled, " The Doctrine of Original Sin Considered, being the substance of Two Sermons preached at Pinners Hall, with a postscript explaining, correcting, or vindicating some passages therein," London, 1725. He seems to have virtually held the opinion of Augustine, who, as to the question of the origin of man's sinfulness, said, Sinfulness is *not an effect* (but *a defect*), and therefore to inquire into its *cause* is purposeless.

As he advanced in years Mr Ridgley had sometimes the affecting duty of preaching funeral sermons in memory of old friends. Sermons preached by him for Rev. Thomas Tingey (who died 1st November 1729), for Rev. John Hurrion (who died 31st December 1731), and for Rev. John Slade (who died 19th October 1733), were printed. Mr Ridgley received the degree of D.D. in or before 1731.

Dr Ridgley is still celebrated as the author of a "Body of Divinity," in two volumes folio (several times reprinted), which is the only known Exposition of the Larger Catechism of the Westminster Assembly. Volume first appeared in 1731, with a fine portrait engraved by John Vandergucht from the painting by B. Dandrige. It was patronized by six hundred subscribers, among whom were Lady Margaret Dolius, Hon. Mrs Birch of Kensington, Sir Richard Ellys, Bart., and Rev. Philip Doddridge, in England; and James Earl of Strathmore, the Lord Advocate (Duncan Forbes, Esq.), Rt. Hon. James Erskine of Grainge, one of the Senators of the College of Justice, Sir Gilbert Elliot of Stobbs, Bart., Rev. William Wishart, D.D., Rev. Robert Trail of Paubride, Rev. William Trail of Benholm, Mr John Trail of Edinburgh, Rev. John Bruce of Airth, and Rev. Henry Lindsay of Bothkennar, in Scotland.

The second volume was published in 1733; and in a postcript Dr Ridgley declared that he had relaxed none of his pastoral or professorial duties during the production of this great literary performance, and that his health had been much impaired by an attack of fever. He survived but a short time, and died in his sixty-seventh year, on the 21st March 1734.

Under Question 80, his precise topic being that assurance is attainable in the present life, Dr Ridgley expresses the following consolatory sentiments:—

"Our Saviour encourages His disciples to expect that, notwithstanding present destitute circumstances as to outward things, yet their Father, who knows that they have need of them, will supply their wants. . . . God, that He may encourage the faith of His people, gives them assurance that no temptation shall befall them but what is common to men—[that is,] that they shall not be pressed down, so as to sink and despair of help from Him under the burdens and difficulties that in the course of his Providence He lays on them. If God is pleased to give such intimations to His people with respect to their condition in this world, may we not conclude from hence that the assurance of those things that concern their everlasting salvation may be attained? If the promises that respect the one may be depended on, so as to afford relief against all doubts and fears that may arise from our present circumstances in the world, may we not with as good reason suppose that the promises which respect the other afford equal matter of encouragement—that the one is as much to be depended on as the other—so that (as the Apostle says, Heb. vi. 18) they who have fled for refuge, to lay hold on the hope set before them, may have strong consolation arising from thence?

"Sometimes the destitute state of believers as to the good things of this life is abundantly compensated by spiritual blessings, . . . while they are denied the lesser, they have the greater blessings instead thereof; so that their assurance of the accomplishment of the promises of outward blessings must be understood with a limitation. But as to spiritual blessings, which God has promised to His people, there is no foundation for any distinction of their being made good in kind or in value. If the promise of eternal life be not made good according to the letter of it, it cannot be, in any sense, said to be accomplished.

"That assurance of justification, sanctification, and salvation may be attained in this life is farther evident from the obligations that persons are under to pray for these privileges. . . . The Apostle (1 John v. 14, 15) says, that if we ask anything according to His will, He heareth us. This is said in the following words to be known by us—*we know that we have the petitions that we desired of Him;* therefore it follows that we may know, from the exercise of faith, in prayer for the forgiveness of sin, that our iniquities are forgiven. The same may be said of the subject-matter of our prayer for all other blessings that accompany salvation. Consequently, it is possible for us to know, whether God has granted us these blessings or no.

"We are not only to pray for saving blessings, but to praise God for our experience thereof; as 'tis said, *Whoso offereth praise, glorifieth Me.* Now this supposes that we know that God has bestowed upon us the blessings we prayed for. If the Psalmist calls upon his soul to *bless the Lord* for *forgiving* him *all his iniquities,* we must suppose that there was some method by which he attained the assurance of the blessing which he praises God for.

"Some have attained this privilege, and therefore it is not impossible for others to attain it. That some have been assured of their salvation is evident from the account we have thereof in several Scriptures. Thus the Apostle tells the Church he writes to (1 Thess. v. 9), 'God hath not appointed us to wrath, but to obtain salvation;' and he says concerning himself (2 Tim. i. 12), 'I know whom I have believed, and I am persuaded He is able to keep that which I have committed unto Him against that day.'"

Under Questions 93 to 97, Dr Ridgley alludes to Dr Crisp as having been unguarded in his phraseology; and he instances an Antinomian phrase, as to believers, that their sins *shall not do them any hurt.* But the word "hurt" applies to damage done to a patrimony, and not to any injury or wound inflicted upon the soul or conscience. The latter result has to do with a question distinct from the former. As to the stability of the heavenly inheritance, surely bestowed on believers (who are clothed in Christ's righteousness, though, in themselves, they are sinful and liable to sin), there is a pair of phrases, perfectly accurate in their own place, viz., that a believer's sins do him no hurt,¹ and his righteous-

---
¹ "Such expressions should be disused. I heartily join in the same wish with the excellent Witsius that nothing of this kind might drop from the mouth of a Reformed divine; for though

nesses do him no good. As to the second phrase, it is illustrated by the anecdote of a gentleman's groom who consented to give regular attendance at family prayers, but hoped that it would be considered in his wages; now, while his attendance might do him good if regarded as a religious habit and opportunity, it would do him no good in a question as to wages. The sins of a believer represent not only wrongs and transgressions committed by him, but also God's broken law demanding his punishment. The phrase, therefore, that *his sins* can do him no hurt, is the same as the phrase, that *the broken law* can do him no hurt. Thus Crisp and Trail are at one, Trail expressing Crisp's sentiments in language which no lover of a free Gospel can object to :—

"If so be (says Trail) that men will give glory to God, and renounce their own righteousness and all expectations of relief that way, and betake themselves to God's device of salvation by Jesus Christ, and believe on Him—as they can expect no good by the law, so they should fear no hurt by it; for, as sin hath made it impossible that the law of God should justify us, so the grace of God in Christ hath made it impossible that the law should condemn a believer in Him."

"Whensoever you come to have any dealings in earnest with God about salvation and your justification and eternal life, always remember these two things, *The grace of God*, and *Christ's death*. The law hath nothing to do in this case; it cannot *help* you whilst you are under it, but condemn you; and if you be believers, the law cannot *hurt* you, for you shall be absolved."—(Conclusion of Sermons on Galatians ii. 21.)

PROFESSOR HERMAN ALEXANDER RÖELL, PH.D., D.D.

IN 1728 a posthumous publication, *Explicatio Catecheseos Heidelbergensis*, by Dr Röell, was brought out at Utrecht by his son, Dionysius Andrew Röell. It is a handsome quarto volume, extending to 1048 pages, and is a sound and spirited commentary. The son modestly suggests that such a thoroughly satisfactory work proves that there was nothing to be said against the able author as to his personal faith and character, although, on some points, he was in controversy with such great and good men as Vitringa and Marckius, and although, in or about the year 1723, a Dutch Synod voted him to be in error. Between 1689 to 1723 he seems to have been busily occupied in studying and stating, and defending his statements. With Vitringa he discussed *De Geboorte des Zoons*

sin cannot do any penal hurt to a believer, yet it may damp his spiritual joy, break his peace, interrupt communion between God and him, dishonour Christ, grieve the Spirit, and cause Him to depart for a season."—*Gill's Note.*

and *De tijdelijke Dood der Geloovige*, viz., the generation of the Son of God and the temporal death of believers, in Latin, 1689 and 1690, and in the Dutch language in 1691. In 1700 we find him discussing natural theology and innate ideas. In 1723 Marckius, Fabricius, Wesselius, and Van der Honert pronounced their concurrence in a synodical condemnation of some of Dr Röell's opinions. He also published Vol. I. of a Commentary on the Ephesians; Vol. II. (which included a brief exposition of Colossians) was published posthumously in 1731.— (See the Catalogue of the Library of the New College, Edinburgh).

REV. WILLIAM ROMAINE, M.A.

WILLIAM ROMAINE, son of a corn merchant, was born at Hartlepool, in the county of Durham, 25th September 1714. He was educated at the Grammar School of Houghton-le-Spring and at the University of Oxford, of which he was a distinguished graduate. I refer my readers for the particulars of the life of this grand old London clergyman to two Memoirs—one by the Hon. and Rev. William Bromley Cadogan, and the other by Rev. Thomas Haweis, LL.B. and M.D., both of whom were respected clergymen of the Establishment. Reference may also be made to "Our Christian Classics," by James Hamilton, D.D., and to Funeral Sermons by Rev. William Goode, Rev. Thomas Wills, and Rev. Charles Edward de Coetlogon. He died on the Lord's Day, 26th July 1795. His works in a collected form have been reprinted frequently. He is chiefly known by three treatises on the Life, the Walk, and the Triumph of Faith, lately republished as one Treatise on Faith.

In 1876 the Rev. George Townshend Fox, prebendary of Durham, sympathizing with his principles and admiring his talents, which were an honour to his native county, erected a tablet to the memory of Romaine in the parish church of Hartlepool. This tablet contains four beautiful and characteristic extracts from his Treatises on Faith; and I am sure my readers will thank me for the following copy of the complete inscription:—

WILLIAM ROMAINE,

RECTOR OF ST ANN'S, BLACKFRIARS, LONDON.
BORN IN HARTLEPOOL, 1714.   DIED IN LONDON, 1795.

SPRUNG FROM THE TRULY NOBLE BLOOD OF A PROTESTANT CONFESSOR WHO TOOK REFUGE IN THIS TOWN AT THE REVOCATION OF THE EDICT OF NANTES, 1685, HE EARLY EMBRACED, BY THE GRACE OF GOD, THOSE PRINCIPLES OF SCRIPTURAL TRUTH FOR WHICH HIS FATHER SACRIFICED HIS PROPERTY AND FORSOOK HIS NATIVE LAND.

A CHRISTIAN OF EMINENT PIETY, A RIPE SCHOLAR, AND A PREACHER OF PECULIAR GIFTS, MIGHTY IN THE SCRIPTURE, HE WAS HONOURED OF GOD TO BECOME A LEADING INSTRUMENT IN ACCOMPLISHING THAT GREAT REVIVAL OF EVANGELICAL RELIGION IN THE CHURCH OF ENGLAND, WHICH TOOK PLACE LAST CENTURY.

IN ADDITION TO HIS UNWEARIED LABOURS AS A MINISTER OF THE GOSPEL OF CHRIST, AND HIS FAITHFUL PROCLAMATION OF THE DISTINCTIVE DOCTRINES OF GRACE, HE GREATLY PROMOTED THE CAUSE OF TRUTH, WAS THE INSTRUMENT OF QUICKENING AND DEEPENING VITAL PIETY IN THE HEARTS OF THOUSANDS, AND HAS BEQUEATHED A RICH LEGACY TO POSTERITY BY HIS ADMIRABLE TREATISE ON THE LIFE, WALK, AND TRIUMPH OF FAITH.

AFTER A LAPSE OF 80 YEARS, THIS TABLET IS ERECTED BY ONE WHO REVERES HIS MEMORY, LOVES THE SCRIPTURAL DOCTRINE WHICH HE EMBRACED, AND REGARDS HIS NAME AS AN HONOUR TO HIS NATIVE TOWN AND COUNTY.

I.

"I was even as others once, by nature a child of wrath, and an heir of misery. I was going on in the broad way of destruction, careless and secure, and I am quite astonished to see the danger I was in. I tremble to behold the precipice over which I was ready to fall when Jesus opened mine eyes, and, by the light of His Word and Spirit, showed me my guilt and danger, and put it into my heart to flee from the wrath to come;

O, what a merciful escape!"

II.

"The believer is reconciled to God, being no longer under the law as a covenant of works but under grace; he loves the law and walks with God in sweet obedience to it; he sets out and goes on every step in faith, trusting to the acceptance of his person and his services in the Beloved; he does not work now *in order to be saved, but because he is saved*, and he ascribes all he does to the praise of the glory of free grace; he works from gratitude—the faith of God's elect always does—

It never fails to show itself by love."

III.

"Christ as the believer's surety has taken his sins upon Himself, and the believer takes Christ's righteousness, for Christ makes over all that He has to the believer, who by faith looks upon it, and makes use of it as his own, according to that express warrant, *All things are yours, and ye are Christ's.*"

IV.

"Christ with bread and water is worth ten thousand worlds. Christ with pain is better than the highest pleasures of sin. Christ with all outward sufferings is matter of present and eternal joy.

Surely these are the only happy people!
Reader, art thou one of them?"

—*Life, Walk, and Triumph of Faith.*

The Family of Romaine.

This being a Huguenot refugee family, I refer my readers to my "Protestant Exiles from France," vol. ii., p. 279 ; vol. iii., p. 224. To those Memoirs I now add the following particulars : —

The Rev. G. T. Fox, preaching at Hartlepool in St Hilda's parish church, on 27th February 1876, said : " William Romaine was born in this town in the year 1714 ; the house is still standing within a few yards of the west end of this church in the High Street, south-west corner of St Mary's Street, and is at present used as a butcher's shop."

Mr Romaine's sister, Mrs Callander, was represented by the late William Romaine Callander, M.P.

Mr Romaine's son was the Rev. Dr Romaine, who lived for many years at Castle Hill, Reading. He left two daughters, one of whom was the wife of Rev. R. Govett (he was vicar of Staines for forty-nine years). She is represented by three daughters and eight sons. Of the sons, five are in the Christian ministry—Rev. R. Govett, minister of the Baptist Church, Norwich ; Rev. T. Romaine Govett, vicar of Newmarket ; Venerable H. Govett, an archdeacon of the Church of England in New Zealand ; and two others. The second of the eight sons has assumed the additional surname of Romaine, and resides in the neighbourhood of Windsor—namely, W. Govett Romaine, Esq., late Judge-Advocate of the troops in India.

ARCHBISHOP SANDYS.[1]

EDWIN, third son of William Sandes, or Sandys, Esq. of Easthwaite Hall, Lancashire, was born in 1519. Born in the profession of Romanism, he was converted to Gospel light and life. It is supposed that his tutor, Mr Bland (afterwards a Protestant martyr) was instrumental in his conversion. St John's College, in Cambridge, was " a house deeply tinctured with the principles of the Reformation," and to it Edwin Sandys was sent in 1533. In 1547 he was Master of Catharine Hall. In 1553 he was Vice-Chancellor of the University of Cambridge ; King Edward VI., who died that year, had made him Prebendary of Peterborough (in 1549) and of Carlisle (in 1552).

When Lady Jane Grey was proclaimed at Cambridge, Dr Sandys preached the sermon before the Royal Commissioners. He was apprehended on Queen Mary's star obtaining the ascendant, and was imprisoned in the Tower and the Marshalsea. But Her Romish Majesty treated him with leniency, and he was a

[1] See " The Sermons of Edwin Sandys, D.D."—*Parker Society*.

refugee in Strasburg during her reign. He was very staunch. His keeper in the Marshalsea taunted him thus : " You being a young man will stand in your own conceit, and prefer your own knowledge before the judgment of so many worthy prelates, ancient, learned, and grave men." Dr Sandys answered: " I know my years young and my learning small ; it is enough to know Christ crucified."

On the accession of Queen Elizabeth, Dr Sandys was consecrated as Bishop of Worcester 21st December 1559 ; he translated the books of Kings and Chronicles for the Bishops' Bible. In 1570 he became Bishop of London. The English translation of Luther on the Galatians was submitted for his approval, and he issued the following Address to the Reader :—

" This book being brought unto me to peruse and consider of, I thought it my part, not only to allow of it to the print, but also to commend it to the reader as a treatise most comfortable to all afflicted consciences exercised in the school of Christ. The author felt what he spake and had experience of what he wrote, and therefore able more lively to express both the assaults and the salving, the order of the battle and the mean of the victory. Satan is the enemy, the victory is only by faith in Christ, as John recordeth. If Christ justify, who can condemn ?—saith St Paul. This most necessary doctrine the author hath most substantially cleared in this his commentary, which, being written in the Latin tongue, certain learned godly men have most sincerely translated into our language, to the great benefit of all such as with humbled hearts will diligently read the same. Some began it according to such skill as they had. Others godly affected, not suffering so good a matter in handling to be marred, put to their helping hands for the better framing and furthering of so worthy a work. They refuse to be named, seeking neither their own gain nor glory, but thinking it their happiness if by any means they may relieve afflicted minds and do good to the church of Christ, yielding all glory unto God, to whom all glory is due.

Aprilis 28, 1575. EDWINUS LONDON."

On the following 17th May he was bereaved of his friend, Dr Matthew Parker, Archbishop of Canterbury, and was chief mourner at his funeral. Archbishop Grindall of York having succeeded Parker, Bishop Sandys became Archbishop of York, 8th March 1576. The lands and moneys belonging to the sees both of London and of York made his life in the archiepiscopal see a troubled one, the only perfectly happy incident being his founding a grammar-school at Hawkshead, in the neighbourhood of his native place. Archbishop Sandys died 10th July 1588.

His Sermons were published under his own eye in 1585. I cull from them two specimens of English Divinity :—

" All flesh hath sinned and doth need forgiveness. God is the only forgiver of our sins. Neither doth He forgive them in respect of man's merits, but of His mercy, goodwill, and free mercy. The only means that moved God to be merciful freely to sinful man, was that most acceptable sweet bloody sacrifice which the innocent Son of God offered upon the cross for our sins. All have sinned and are deprived of the glory of God, and are justified freely by His grace through the redemption that is in Christ Jesus (Rom. iii. 23, 24). He took our unrighteousness upon Himself, and clothed us with His justice; and He who knew no sin was made sin for us, that we might be made the righteousness of God in Him (2 Cor. v. 21). In Christ and for Christ we receive free remission of sins. There is no other name given us under heaven whereby we may be saved (Acts iv. 12). *I am the way, the truth, and the life; no man cometh to the Father but by Me*, saith Christ (John xiv. 6)—no sin forgiven but through Him; and through Him all sins are forgiven freely.

"The mean, whereby we are made partakers of this free remission of sins in the death and resurrection of Christ, is faith in Christ; for *All* (saith Peter) *that believe in Him shall receive remission of sins through His name* (Acts x. 43). God doth freely offer us remission of sin, and peace, in Christ; the mean and instrument to receive it withal is faith. He that believeth is made partaker of it, and not of it only, but of eternal life also; for *he that believeth on Me hath life eternal*, saith our Saviour Christ (John vi. 47). But this faith, this justifying faith, doth work through love and showeth itself by works. The good tree will be fruitful. The believing, justified child of God will fear God and work righteousness."—Page 290.

"The Gospel preacheth Christ. Christ is our peace and peace-maker. He that hath Christ hath peace with God, and he that believeth in Him hath Him. By this means we have peace of conscience, peace with God."—Page 60.

REV. SYDRACH SIMPSON, B.D.

SYDRACH SIMPSON was a graduate of Cambridge University. The date of his birth may be conjectured to be about 1600. In 1635, having been episcopally ordained, he was Curate and Lecturer of St Margaret's Church in Fish Street, London. The intolerance of Laud drove him at that date to Amsterdam. He appears in Westminster in 1643 as a member of the Assembly of Divines, and pastor of a congregation formed by himself in "Abchurch, Canon Street, London." He also appears in print on the title-pages of Sermons preached before the Parliament. In Holland he had become a congregationalist; and in the Westminster Assembly he was one of the leading Independents, prominent along with his fellow-exiles, Goodwin, Burroughs, Nye, and Bridge. He had no difficulties as to ecclesiastical toleration. The tendency to discourage *lay-preaching* (as it is now called) he lamented. His sentiments, as recorded by his friend, Philip Nye, are worthy of being quoted :—" We do not despise Ordination, nor those that in the name and authority of Jesus Christ inaugurate persons to the sacred office. It is doubtless an ordinance. But that none may preach but such—this we deny, and distinguish (with Junius) between preaching as done *ex officio* or as done *ex communi jure*. That place, Rom. x. (14, 15), evidently implieth that there must be *a church* or corporation before *officers*—believers before a church (which is *cœtus fidelium*)—the glad tidings of good things must be preached before believing, and preachers *sent* before any good tidings brought. Now this *sending* cannot be a putting into church-relation or office (because as yet there is no church), but more common and general, as when one man *ex charitate* instructs and teaches others, parents their children, governors their families, Christian kings and princes the people under their charges. . . . for the begetting of faith and gathering of believers into a church. Our [Presbyterian] brethren (*Jus Div. Min.*, part i., cap. 5) say 'The principal object of preaching is the church. Prophecy is NOT (*i.e.*, not so much) *for them that believe not, but for them that believe* (1 Cor. xiv. 22). Hence it is that God hath set His officers *in* the church (1 Cor. xii. 28) and *for* the church (Eph. iv. 12).' If there be no preaching without being ordained and in office, then there is no provision made by the Lord for the converting of souls and working faith—that is, none *principally*, or *so much as* for edification and the building up of such as are converted. Now it is very hard to imagine, that the converting of souls—a principal end for which Christ came into the world and suffered—should have no provision made for it of primary and principal intention." Mr Simpson became Master of Pembroke Hall, in Cambridge, in 1650. On the day of his death he was visited with melancholy and apprehension; but brethren and friends in his house so assisted him with their prayers that he took leave of them cheerfully, saying, "I am satisfied; the gloom which hung over my soul is wholly removed." He died the same evening—this was in the year 1658. In the same year two volumes of his Sermons were printed, each consisting of "Two Books." I have compiled this Memoir in order to call the attention of inquirers and students to these volumes, which discuss the theology of consolation more fully than any others.

The title-page of the first volume is :—

"TWO BOOKS of Mr Sydrach Simpson, late Master of Pembroke Hall in Cambridge, and Preacher of the Gospel in London, viz. :—

I. Of Unbelief; or the want of readiness to lay hold on the comfort given by Christ.

II. Not going to Christ for life and salvation is an exceeding great sin, yet it is pardonable.

In the First Book is showed (besides many other things)—
1. What Unbelief it is that is here spoken of.
2. The best way to deal with Unbelief.
3. That Unbelief is a sin against al the attributes of God.
4. That Christ will not bear with this Sin of Unbelief.
5. That we should be quick and ready to Beleeve.
6. Motives to indeavor for readiness to Beleeve.
7. Helps to attain readiness in Beleeving.

In the Second Book is showed—
1. That Unbelief is a great Sin, and exceeding provoking unto God.
2. Several arguments provoking us to beleeve the greatness of the Sin of Unbelief.
3. Many objections answered.
4. Several sorts of this Sin of Unbelief.
5. Means to convince us that Unbelief is so great a Sin.
6. Though the Sin of Unbelief be very great, yet it's pardonable.
7. God hath pardoned Unbelief, and will pardon it.

London. Printed by Peter Cole, Printer and Book-Seller, at the sign of the *Printing-press* in Corn-hill, neer the Royall Exchange. 1658."

The title-page of the other volume is:—

"Two Books, &c., viz. :—
I. Of Faith, or, That Beleeving is receiving Christ; And receiving Christ is Believing.
II. Of Covetousness.

In the First Book is showed (besides many others things)—
1. That Persons that are beleevers are Receivers.
2. That to Receive is the Principal use of Faith.
3. That nothing should hinder our Receiving—(1.) Not our Sins. (2.) Nor Gods delaies. (3.) Nor the smalness of our receipts. (4.) Nor the greatness of our wants.
4. How Faith receives.
5. That Faith Receives Christ—(1.) In the understanding. (2.) In the will.
6. The temper of a man that hath faith.
7. The necessity of Faith.
8. Though Faith be smal yet it makes us the Sons of God.
9. The Nature of True Faith.
10. There are but few that Receive Christ.
11. Three sorts that come not to Christ—(1.) Such as Receive Him not as He is. (2.) Such as delay their coming to Him. (3.) Such as give not that place to Christ in their hearts that is fitting for Him.

In the Treatise of Covetousness is showed—

1. It is the duty of all as they would obtaine eternal Life to beware of Covetousness.
2. The Reasons of the Doctrine—(1.) Its a spiritual Sin. (2.) It over spreads the whole man. (3.) Its opposite to the Nature of Godliness and Religion. (4.) Its the Womb and Seed of all Sin. (5.) Its a base Sin.
3. The Dangerousness of covetousness—(1.) Its hardly avoided. (2.) Its difficultly cured.
4. You shall have all things needful for this life if you wil look after grace.
5. Your Life lies in Grace, not in Riches.
6. There is more to be feared than to be desired in Riches.
7. We should Mortifie our desires after Riches.

London, &c."

[The Four Books have each a text—(1.) Mark xvi. 14. (2.) 1 Tim. i. 13. (3.) John i. 12. (4.) Luke xii. 15].

Here is a specimen of Sydrach Simpson's style :—"Did Christ chide His disciples for their unbelief—for want of clearness and quickness in their faith—for want of snatching at and laying greedily hold on the comforts that He brought them through His resurrection ? Chide thou then thy own self, whenever thou findest any of these in thee. When thou canst not believe, ask thy soul the reason of it—why art thou so disquieted ? why art thou so unbelieving ? If thou canst not find out the cause, yet chide and fall out with thyself, fall upon thy own heart. Christ did so now (Mark xvi. 14), being newly come to His power—to have all power in His hands, both in heaven and earth—He chides. And in this, do you exercise that kingly power which Jesus Christ hath given you. As you are *priests to God*, and so must offer to Him what He hath appointed, so you are *kings to God* (Rev. i. 6), and one piece of your dominion lies in this, that you chide and reprove yourselves, and not allow—but condemn and censure and disallow—every evil that is found in you. If you be not very much offended with yourselves because of unbelief, you are very much to blame, because your unbelief is a very great sin. Christians they are wont to foster and nourish unbelief—to lay it (as Michal did David) in the bed upon down pillows. Will you speak peace where God hath spoken war ? Will you defend that which Jesus Christ reproves ? . . . O foolish—O sluggish—O proud heart, that art always twisting and knitting of objections against thyself and the grace of Jesus Christ !"—Book i., chapter 4.

PASTOR THEODORUS STRACKIUS.

OF this author I know nothing but what can be gathered from his book which I am about to describe, the Dedicatory Epistle of which, to the Magnates of Guelderland, was written in July 1629. He seems to have been a native of Essen in Westphalia, and to have been a pupil of Brantius and Willichius at Wesel in Cleves. He was in Guelderland an exile on account of his religion, and the pastor of a congregation *apud Borcharenses et Hernenses*. He had two brothers, John, pastor at Wesel, and Henry, legal notary at Wesel.

His book arose out of a singular manual, concocted and laid at the feet of the Apostle Peter by a monk, John Andrew Coppenstein, a parish priest in Heidelberg in 1623. The title of this manual was "The Calvino-Heidelbergensian Catechism Uncalvinized. [Coppensteinii Ex-Calvinizata Catechesis Calvino-Heidelbergensis.] It was written in Latin and duly licensed.

It is remarkable that the Romanizing process began by removing *present personal consolation* from the first question and answer:—

COPPENSTEIN.

I. Quæ est unica tua consolatio in vitâ et in morte?

Quod animo pariter et corpore, sive vivam, sive moriar, non meus, sed fidissimi Domini et Servatoris mei Jesu Christi proprius sum, qui pretioso sanguine suo pro omnibus peccatis meis plenissimè satisfaciens, me ab omni potestate Diaboli liberavit, meque ita conservat ut sine voluntate Patris mei cœlestis ne pilus quidem de meo capite possit cadere, immò verò etiam omnia saluti meæ servire oporteat. Quocirca me quoque Spiritu sancto de vitâ æternâ certum facit; utque ipsi deinceps vivam promptum ac paratum reddit.

I. Quæ est unica consolatio in vitâ et in morte?

Quod animo pariter et corpore, sive vivam, sive moriar, non meus sed fidissimi Domini et Servatoris mei esse debeam ac possim proprius, qui pretioso suo sanguine pro omnibus peccatis nostris plenissimè satisfaciens nos ab omni potestate Diaboli liberavit, nosque ita conservat ut sine voluntate Patris mei cœlestis ne pilus quidem de meâ capite possit cadere, imò verò etiam omnia saluti nostræ servire oporteat. Quocirca spem quoque nostram de vitâ æternâ certam facit, utque ipsi deinceps vivamus, promptos ac paratos reddit.

After this crafty beginning, followed by a virtual adoption of the answers to QQ. 2, 3, and 4, Coppenstein became more bold, and denied that by nature we are at enmity with God and with one another. As to the two great commandments, the monk contradicted the Protestant flatly :—

V. Num hæc omnia perfectè servare potes?
Minimè. Naturâ enim propensus sum ad odium Dei et proximi.

V. Num hæc omnia perfectè servare potes?
Maximè, cum Deo. Naturâ enim, licet vitiatâ, favente gratiâ, propensus sum ad amorem Dei et proximi.

Of course also there was a similar contradiction as to Justification by faith (Q. 60), and as to the Sacrifice of the Mass (Q. 80)—in the latter *exsecranda idololatria* being changed into *sacrosancta doctrina*.

The undertaking of Strackius was, in a commentary upon Coppenstein, to reassert the evangelical doctrine of the Heidelberg Catechism. For scholars who wish to study the book I here copy the title-page:—" Vindiciæ Catecheticæ tripartitæ, pro Catechismi Palatino-Belgici perpetuâ et constanti orthodoxiâ, tam quoad Quæstionum et Responsionum contextum earundemque sententiam, quam quoad S. Scripturæ, a Catechiste passim ad Orthodoxæ vereque Catholicæ fidei confirmationem adductas, authoritates—adversus tum illius tum harum depravationem Johannis Andreæ Coppensteinii, Mandalensis, Ordinis Prædicatorum Monachi, ac Heidelbergensis p. t. Parochi.

"Institutæ operâ et studio Theodori Strackii, Essendeniensis, ecclesiæ, quæ Christo apud Borcharenses et Hernenses in Geldriâ colligitur, Pastoris. Arnhemi Geldrorum, Typis Joannis Jansonii. Anno MDCXXX."

Strackius, of course, denies that the Heidelberg Catechism was written by Calvin, it being an entirely original work by Ursinus and Olevianus, translated into Latin by Lagus and Pithopæus. As to the accusation that its admirers placed it above the Bible, he describes it as a subordinate standard, the Bible being supreme—supreme not in their judgment only, but in their affections.

Advocating what some self-sufficient moderns sneer at as *Bibliolatry*, he quotes with zest a sacred song by Ludovicus Crocius:—

"Biblia, noster amor, dulcissima Biblia, diva
Biblia, deliciæ lautitiæque meæ," &c.

REV. ROBERT TRAIL, SENIOR.

The pedigree of this excellent minister will appear from a Note in a subsequent page. He was born at Belcy, in the parish of Denino, in 1603, but, his family removing to St Andrews, both his school and college education were received in that university seat. The beginning of the commotions as to religion which surrounded him through life was the opposition of many of the students to the introduction of the Prelatic Service-Book in 1622. In 1625, before his divinity studies were quite completed, he visited France on the invitation of his brother James, who was travelling tutor to a young English gentleman. Robert Trail continued his studies at the Protestant College of Saumur, where he acquired the French language. He spent a few years as a teacher in an academy and in private families (one of his pupils being a sister of the great Duc de Rohan), and returned to Scotland in 1630. Having obtained license as a preacher he served in several subordinate posts till 1639, when he became minister of Elie, a newly erected parish, where he remained till 1649. He was a laborious pastor and zealous covenanter, his occupations being varied by frequent appointments to attend the Scotch army as a chaplain. During his incumbency there was a collection made for "the commune cause" (1640), which amounted to 600 merks; there was also raised 100 pounds Scots for the distressed poor of Argyle (1647), and 60 pounds Scots for relief of some persons of quality from Ireland.

In 1649 he quitted Fife, having been appointed minister of the Greyfriars Church in Edinburgh. In the following year he came prominently before the public as one of the ministers who visited the Marquis of Montrose in prison, and attended him on the scaffold. Like the covenanters of that period he was a royalist, and welcomed Charles II. to Scotland. He was present at his swearing the covenant and at the coronation, preaching before His Majesty on one occasion. He made no submission to Cromwell, who, however, treated him kindly. All his loyalty could not protect him at the time of the Restoration, because he incidentally reminded His Majesty that he had sworn the covenant. Having in August 1660 assembled with other ministers to draw up an Address to the King on ecclesiastical affairs, he was in September imprisoned in Edinburgh Castle. Although set at liberty by order of the parliament, he was soon apprehended again by order of the Privy Council for expounding the Scriptures in his own house, and he was on 9th November 1662 banished to Holland, and remained there as an exile, separated from wife and children, till 1674. In the last-mentioned year he returned to Scotland in bad health. His death, which was the result of palsy, took place at Edinburgh on the 10th of July 1676. His portrait, painted in Holland, was engraved in Smith's " Iconographia Scotica," published 1st January 1798, by Robert Wilkinson, 58 Cornhill, London. The senior Robert Trail published nothing ; but two beautiful letters to his children, written from Holland, have been printed.

REV. ROBERT TRAIL, OF LONDON.

ROBERT was born at Elie in May 1642, the second son of the Covenanter. He and his elder brother William were successful students both in the literary and divinity classes of the University of Edinburgh, having the invaluable superintendence of their father at home. At the Restoration he showed his piety and intrepidity by standing by the martyr, James Guthrie, on the scaffold. In the troublous times which followed, Mrs Trail (*née* Jane Annan of Auchterallan) did not shrink from running risks for the Gospel's sake, and her family shared in her zeal. Meetings for the worship of God were held in her house as frequently as possible. These did not bring down the vengeance of the Privy Council till 1666, when a search-warrant was issued in order to detect the conventicles, and especially to find a copy of Brown of Wamphray's "Apologetical Relation," a book the possession of which was illegal. The mother and children, three sons and three daughters, fled and hid themselves. All that can be said about Robert is, that at that time he was much in the society of John Welch, chiefly on the English side of the Border. Through the overthrow of Presbytery he was of no higher position than a student of theology, awaiting the exit examination required by the Church. A proclamation, dated Whitehall, 1st October 1667, declared him to be *a Pentland rebel*, and excepted him from the act of indemnity. He therefore retreated to Holland, where his exile was alleviated by the society of his father and other worthies from Scotland. Though the royal proclamation had described him as "*sometime chaplain to* [the laird of] *Scotstarvet*," he was still a divinity student, and his studies under eminent Dutch professors were carried on to his high advantage. He made himself useful in superintending the publication at Utrecht of Rutherford's "Examen Arminianismi," which had been brought to light by the widow of the author, the sainted Samuel Rutherford.

Robert Trail next comes to view in London on Thursday 22nd April 1669, in the pulpit of a Presbyterian congregation on a sacramental fast-day; he had been licensed as a preacher of the gospel a week or two before that day. He preached several times in London pulpits at this period, and in 1670 he was ordained to the charge of the Presbyterian station at Cranbrook in Kent.

He was in Edinburgh in the end of May 1677, probably on a visit to his widowed mother and the younger members of the family. Here he transgressed the law by preaching the gospel in private houses. For apprehending him, who was an outlawed Pentland rebel, as well as a holder of conventicles, Major Johnston received a reward of 1000 pounds (Scots) from the Privy Council. At his trial Mr Trail pled guilty of preaching in private houses, but refused to plead on the charge of holding field conventicles, that being a capital charge. For declining to purge himself by oath of such a charge, and for such reasons as that the old *letters of intercommuning* were still in force against him, and that he had been an associate of John Welch, the Privy Council directed the Marquis of Athol with a party of horse " to transport the person of Mr Robert Trail from the Tolbooth of Edinburgh unto the isle of the Bass, to remain prisoner there." This order was dated Edinburgh, 19th July 1677.

Thus the younger Robert Trail became one of the martyrs of the Bass, and was immured for more than two months within a cell upon that historic rock in the Firth of Forth.

On 5th October of the same year a warrant for his liberation was sent to the governor of the Bass, and Mr Trail was set at liberty, undertaking " to live orderly in obedience to law." The circumstance that the regular scene of his orderly life was England, and not Scotland, enabled him to undertake what a Scottish pastor would have declined. He returned to his charge at Cranbrook, and was afterwards translated to a Scotch church in London, where he spent a long and honoured life. He lived unmarried, and died in May 1716, aged seventy-four. This was the same age which his elder brother had attained, who died minister of Borthwick, in 1714. His other brother was Lieutenant James Trail, of the garrison in Stirling Castle. His sisters were Helen, wife of Rev. Thomas Paterson, minister of Borthwick ; Agnes, wife of Sir James Stewart of Goodtrees, Lord Advocate of Scotland ; and Margaret, wife of James Scott of Bristo, writer in Edinburgh.

In early life Mr Trail addressed the public as one of the editors of the Rev. Andrew Gray's Sermons ; but he made his first appearance as an author at the age of forty, that is, in the year 1682. It was a sermon which (he used to say) had been *extorted* from him for publication ; but it is a gem of the first water, being a succinct reply to the question—" By what means may ministers best win souls ?" Fourteen years afterwards, namely in 1696, he voluntarily published a volume of sermons, entitled, " Sermons concerning the throne of grace." These were followed in 1705 by " Sermons concerning the Lord's Prayer "—the subject of which was our Lord's Intercessory Prayer contained in John xvii. After his death twenty-one sermons were published, entitled, "The Stedfast adherence to the Profession of our Faith." His letter on the controversy among London ministers was published in his life-time ; but his sermons specially bearing on that controversy did not see the light till 1778 (*see* RIDGLEY) ; they were on the text, Gal. ii. 21. All the above are included in four volumes, frequently reprinted, a new edition of which was published by the Ogles in 1810, with a motto from Tertullian, " *Cui veritas comperta sine Deo?—cui Deus cognitus sine Christo?—cui Christus exploratus sine Spiritu Sancto?*"

As an admired minister in London, Mr Trail's services were in such constant request, that he habitually preached *ex tempore;* and his printed works, with scarcely an exception, were compiled from the notes of his hearers. Mr Anthony Trail, of Edinburgh, Writer to the Signet, lent to the Free Church of Scotland the manuscript of Robert Trail's earliest sermons ; and thus in one of the volumes of the *Free Church Publications* several sermons by him are printed, just as they came from his pen. A few sentences, from the fast-day sermon already mentioned, may therefore be quoted here :—

HEBREWS xii. 28, 29. *Wherefore we receiving a kingdom which cannot be moved, let us have grace, whereby we may serve God acceptably with reverence and godly fear : for our God is a consuming fire.*

The saints have [become familiar with] some attributes of God to move fear and dread, which others [of mankind] have not. His goodness, love, pardoning and healing mercy, the manifestations of that love and mercy (Hos. iii. 5 ; Ps. cxxx. 4)—unto a considerate soul how ready are these to stir up holy fear and dread !

Even God in covenant with His own is a dreadful God (Deut. xxviii. 58). Only such do know Him, and none can know Him but they must fear Him.

The Lord, though in covenant with His people, is still the same God, and in Him are all those things which move holy fear. It is true that His justice, having received satisfaction from their Surety ; and, upon the account of their covenant relation unto Him ; they may with comfort and delight travel through all the attributes of God, even such as are most terrifying. Yet notwithstanding all this, all those things are still in our covenanted God which are the grounds of fear and reverence.

And as He is still the same, so we are but very little changed ; and there is little of that removed that lays us open to destruction from this consuming fire. It is true that there is a change in the state of believers in their justification and adoption—which is a begun change in their natures in sanctification—yet still they are creatures ; still there is much unholiness in their hearts and lives, and all sin in itself is equally hateful to God, and contrary to His holy law ; still they are under His holy law and bound to obedience, though not as a covenant of life, yet as the rule of their life ; still they are in hazard of His anger (though not as an unappeased enemy, yet as an offended father) and of the fruits of it upon their breaking of His laws.

From the doctrine of His majesty rightly understood there is no such fear of God called for, as is in any way legal [legalistic, or Pharisaical] or opposite unto faith and love. It is deep heart-reverence and holy awe that is called for, which, as we find in some measure in the kindly affections of children to their parents, is very well consistent with love, and trusting them with the care of all their movements ; so also is it very well consistent in the Lord's people with faith in and love unto Him. And therefore when we read of the fear and fearers of

God in Scripture, we are not to take it as holding forth that passion of fear which is an apprehension of some ill coming, but rather this reverence and holy awe which may be where there is no fear of wrath as coming. And so here the *serving Him acceptably with reverence and godly* fear, on account of His being *a consuming fire*—though the exhortation, as it concerns the visible church, ought not to be taken as exclusive of the fear of consuming by Him (since many in the church are enemies to God, and so are commanded to fear that, as a mean to make them submit unto Him)—yet as it is an argument pressing the regenerate to reverent service of God (which is the scope of the Holy Ghost here), it imports no ground of such an unbelieving fear in them who have fled for refuge to lay hold of the hope set before them.

The want of a due impression of the majesty of God is so evident, and bringeth forth such sad fruits, that it is exceedingly of your concernment to endeavour to have this,—as you tender the welfare of your souls—as you would grow up in His way and bring forth fruit to His praise.

You must be endued with power from on high. There must be an impress of His own hand upon your heart, to bring out this grace to exercise. Pant therefore for it, and wait on Him; and He will manifest His glory unto you and stir up this holy fear in you.

THE FAMILY OF TRAIL.

This family has been favourably known in Scotland since 1385, when Walter Trail, Bishop of St Andrews, flourished as an ecclesiastic and a statesman. Its original territorial designation was Trail of Blebo, in Fife.

Two branches of the family acquired property in the Orkneys at an early date, and are still represented.[1]

Another branch, to which the Rev. Robert Trail, senior and junior, belonged, has been so largely represented in the Church, both in Scotland and in Ireland, as to merit a note.

This branch of the Trails was founded by Colonel Andrew Trail of Beley, in the parish of Denino (Fife), who died 13th February 1608; his wife was Helen, daughter of Thomas Myrton of Cambo, by the Hon. Catherine Lindsay, daughter of John, sixth Lord Lindsay.

Colonel Andrew Trail had a son, James Trail of Beley (*died* 1635), who by his first marriage had two sons :—

---

[1] They spell the surname TRAILL, for what reason I know not. The booksellers think proper to spell in the same manner the name of the reverend author who has been specially memorialized in this volume. But his own signature, "Ro. Trail," is before me, and that of his brother, "W. Trail."

1. Lieut.-Colonel James Trail (*born* 1600, *died* 1663); he settled at Tullochin, in the county of Down, Ireland.
2. Rev. Robert Trail, minister of Greyfriars, Edinburgh (*born* 1603, *died* 1676).

Lieut.-Colonel James Trail had a large family, but the male descent was continued by only one of them, viz., his eighth child, Hans, *born* 1658. Hans Trail was the father of James, who died in 1743. James was the father of Rev. Hamilton Trail (*born* 1720, *died* 1795), whose son, Rev. Archibald Trail (*born* 1755), was the last male descendant of Lieut.-Colonel James Trail of Tullochin, Ireland.

Descendants of Rev. Robert Trail, senior.

(1.) Rev. WILLIAM TRAIL (*born* 1640, *died* 1714). He was M.A. of Edinburgh in 1658, and was prepared for entering the ministry in 1661, but was obstructed by the introduction of Episcopacy into Scotland. He was licensed by a *Classis* of Presbyterian ministers in London in 1671, and in 1673 he went to Ireland, and was ordained as Presbyterian minister of Lifford. Being molested by the Irish Government, he removed to America in 1684, and ministered to a congregation in Maryland. Returning to Scotland in 1690, he became minister of Borthwick. He had three sons, namely :—

(2.) Rev. ROBERT TRAIL, minister of the Scots Church, London—*born* 1642, *died* 1716, unmarried.

1. Rev. JAMES TRAIL, minister of Montrose (*born* 1681, *died* 1723).

2. Rev. WILLIAM TRAIL, minister of Benholm (*born* 1683, *died* 1743). He had two sons in the ministry of the Church of Scotland :—
Rev. WILLIAM TRAIL, minister, first, of Logic Pert; secondly, of St. Monance (*born* 1712, *died* 1756); and
Rev. ROBERT TRAIL, D.D., who became Professor of Divinity in Glasgow University in 1761 (Moderator of General Assembly 1762), having been previously minister,
1st, of Kettins;
2dly, of Banff
(*born* 1720, *died* 1775).

3. Rev. ROBERT TRAIL, minister of Panbride (*born* 1687, *died* 1762). He had two clerical sons :—
Right Rev. JAMES TRAIL, Bishop of Down and Connor (*born* 1725, *died* 1783); and
Rev. ROBERT TRAIL, minister, 1st, of Rescobie; 2dly, of Panbride (*born* 1749, *died* 1798). The latter of these had two sons in the ministry of the Episcopal Church of Ireland, and other two sons in the ministry of the Church of Scotland, viz. :
(1) Rev. ROBERT TRAIL, Rector of Ballintoy (*born* 1754);
(2) Rev. ANTHONY TRAIL,

Descendants of Rev. Robert Trail, senior—continued.

The former of these (minister of St. Monance, Scotland) had a son in the Episcopal Church of Ireland, Rev. WILLIAM TRAIL, Rector of Lisburn, and Chancellor of the diocese of Connor (*born* 1746, *died* 1831).

The third son of the minister of St. Monance was JAMES TRAIL, Esq., M.P. in 1802 for Orford in Suffolk, Under-Secretary of State for Ireland in 1806, who died at his post in Dublin 18th August 1808.

Chancellor of Connor (*born* 1755);
(3) Rev. JAMES TRAIL, minister of St Cyrus (*born* 1757, *died* 1816);
(4) Rev. DAVID TRAIL, D.D., minister of Panbride (*born* 1765, *died* 1850).

Of whom the *second* (Anthony) was represented by his son, Rev. ROBERT TRAIL, D.D., Rector of Schull, county of Cork (*born* 1793, *died* 1847), known as the best translator of Josephus;

and the *fourth* (David) was the father of Rev. ROBERT TRAIL, LL.D., senior minister of the Free Church of Scotland at Boyndie, near Banff, now resident in London.

REV. ANTHONY TUCKNEY, D.D.

ANTHONY, son of Rev. Mr Tuckney, minister of Kirton in Lincolnshire, was born in September 1599. He was educated at Cambridge, and became Fellow of Emmanuel College. Boston, in the vicinity of which his native place was situated, became the scene of his pastoral labours, and he was much beloved as its vicar. In 1643 he removed to London, where he ministered to the church in Michael-Quern, in Cheapside. In 1645 he became Master of his College in Cambridge, and took up his residence there on his election to the vice-chancellorship of the University.

His grand occupation in London was attendance upon the Westminster Assembly. He was one of the most influential members, especially in the preparation of the Catechisms. To him we owe the beautiful exposition of the "Uses of the Law" in the Larger Catechism. [This Catechism, to the extent of 600 copies, was ordered by the House of Commons to be printed, 25th Oct. 1647.]

In 1653 Dr Tuckney became Master of St John's College, and, in 1655, Regius Professor of Divinity at Cambridge. At the Restoration, the king's letter, dated Whitehall, June 1, 1661, superseded him in both his offices, and granted him £100 per annum out of the Rectory of Somersham, which was attached to the professorship. He died in London in February 1670.

His residence in Cambridge had been signalized by a correspondence with his former pupil, Dr Benjamin Whichcote, concerning the use of reason in religion and the reconciliation of sinners to God. Four letters were written on each side, during the months of September and October 1651. It would have been well if Whichcote had met Tuckney's animadversions on his rationalism by cutting down his reply to the dimensions of a single sentence of his own in his first letter (omitting the "if"), "If I have done prejudice to saving grace, by idolizing natural ingenuity, the Lord reprove itt in me, and discover to me this sin by any hand whatsoever." Dr Tuckney, in his second letter, has one sentence which will convince every lover of the Gospel that in this encounter he was both a faithful reprover and a triumphant combatant : "Truly, sir, to say that either salvation or reconciliation *nascitur e nobis* [has its origin from ourselves] is, in my poor judgment, a very dangerous expression—(sure I am) a stranger to *Scripture-manner* of speaking, which, as *all* should much heed, so I expect that *you* will especially, who, before, in contradistinction of the fallible expressions and forms of words of man's making, judged (and that truly) Scripture expressions to be aptest to convey all saving truths to our understandings."

Dr Tuckney was one of the many living examples of the sympathy of evangelical ministers with learning. It is of him that the anecdote is told, that when the Master of St John's College was urged to favour the godly in the distribution of his academic patronage, his answer was : "I shall always have great regard for the godly, but I will choose none but scholars ; they may deceive me in their godliness, but they cannot in their scholarship." Of his "Forty Sermons" [printed in 1676] twelve are on counting all things loss for Christ (Philipp. iii. 5-8). While extolling the knowledge of Christ above all else, he says (*page* 7):— " Other knowledge and learning indeed there is, which in these schools of the prophets hath long flourished, and *long and long yet may and* (God grant) *more than ever*, which we hope Authority will yet countenance and advance, that our wars may not end in barbarism and our sun be turned into darkness whilst our moon is into blood—notwithstanding the mad rage of divers brutish men that decry learning because themselves have none, like the ape in the fable, &c." His great direction is (*page* 33). " We must take heed that we do not overdo in our studies that are lawful—not that I would have you to study *them* less, but *Christ* more."

" Teach that you may learn, but study that you may do both. For—however now-a-days every fool will be babbling—unstudied men are but poor learners and worse teachers."

"Seek if you would find, and study Christ if you would know Him. View Him as you use to do him whom you would know, and as the stung man did the brazen serpent."

(See Minutes of the Westminster Assembly, printed from transcripts of the originals, and edited by W. F. Mitchell, D.D., and John Struthers, LL.D. Edinburgh, W. Blackwood & Sons).

DEAN TURNER.[1]

WILLIAM TURNER was a native of Morpeth, in Northumberland. Of his career in the University of Cambridge we know that he was a companion of Nicholas Ridley, also a Northumbrian, afterwards the noble bishop and martyr, in Pembroke College. (Ridley entered the University in 1518, and his first public step in the direction of Protestantism was his signing the decree against the Pope's supremacy in 1534). William Turner studied medicine regularly, but left Cambridge without a degree. The date of his birth was probably 1500, in the days of Henry VII. When he was a young man he was converted to the gospel, or "to the opinions of Luther" (as would then be said). The first ascertained date in his career is 1538, when he translated a tract by Urban Regius, entitled, "A Comparison between the Old Learning and the New." Whether he received priest's orders from the Romish Church is doubtful. But upon his conversion to the gospel of the grace of God, he went (says Anthony à Wood) "through many parts of the nation and preached the word of God, not only in towns and villages, but also in cities." When thus employed he visited Oxford, and finding several Northumbrians there, he took up his residence in that University, cultivating books and literary society. Here, or somewhere else in England, his gospel-preaching was requited with imprisonment; "he was kept in durance for a considerable time," and then was banished. He went to Italy, and at Ferrara he was made a Doctor of Physic. During his whole life he served his generation both as a physician and as a clergyman, as a teacher, practitioner, and author.

Dr Turner visited Basle and Cologne, and probably Heidelberg also, as we conjecture from his translation of the Heidelberg Catechism. His son Peter (*born* 1542, *died* 1614) was Doctor of Physic of Heidelberg, "afterwards incorporated at Cambridge, where he had his first education," and also at Oxford. Peter married Pascha, sister of Dr Henry Parry, Bishop of Worcester, known in connection with the Heidelberg Catechism. But this is a digression.

[1] See Wood's "Athenæ," and the Parker Society's Index-Volume.

The year 1543 is the date of the publication of Dr William Turner's celebrated book, printed at Basle, "The huntyng and fyndyng out of the Romish Fox, whiche more than seven yeares hath been hyd among the Byshoppes of England after that the Kyngis Hyghnes had commanded hym to be dryven out of hys Realme." It has been said that Dr Turner had not sufficient confidence in "the King's Highness" to return to England during his reign; but there is a second book by him, entitled, "The Rescuynge of the Romish Fox—otherwise called The Examination of the Hunter—devysed by Steven Gardiner"—with the colophon, "imprynted at Winchester 1545."

The reign of Edward VI. was from 28th January 1547 to 6th July 1553. Dr Turner was now incorporated in Oxford as Doctor of Physic; he also became Physician to Edward, Duke of Somerset. As a clergyman he was made a Prebendary of York (stall of Botevant), Canon of Windsor, and Dean of Wells. His pen was busy both in medicine and in theology. He published in London "A New Dialogue, wherein is contained the examination of the Mass and of that kind of priesthood which is ordained to say Mass and to offer up for remission of sins the body and blood of Christ again." One of the speakers in the Dialogue he named MISTRESS MISSA—a name long remembered. He lectured at Thistleworth against Pelagianism. One of the auditory having attempted a reply, Dean Turner printed "A Preservative or Triacle against the poyson of Pelagius lately renewed and stirred up again by the furious sect of the Anabaptists." This publication is memorable on account of the Dedication to Bishop Latimer, whom the author had known in Cambridge. There he had listened to that Reformer's sermons, which were instrumental in delivering numbers in the University from "wyl-workes, as pylgrimage and settyng up of candels," and in bringing them "unto the workes that God commaunded expressedly in His holy Scripture and to the reading and study of God's worde, al dreames and unprofitable gloses of men set a syde and utterly despised." The Dean published the "Triacle" at London in 1551. In the same year he brought out "A New Herbal wherin are conteyned the names of Herbes in Greke, Latin, English, Duch, Frenche, and in the Potecaries and Herbaries Latin, with the properties degrees and naturall places of the same, gathered and made by Wylliam Turner Physscion unto The Duke of Somersettes Grace. Imprinted at London by Steven Mierdman Anno Domini 1551. Cum privilegio ad impremendum solum. And they are to be sold in Paules Churchyarde."

Dean Turner was an exile in Germany in the reign of Mary. He brought his combined medical and theological learning into play in a book which he produced on the Continent from an unknown printing office, though, according to the title-page, it was printed at "Rome in 1555" by Marcus Antonius Constantius, otherwise called "Thraso miles gloriosus." Strype (in his "Life of Cranmer," p. 357) thus described the book:—"A New Book of Spiritual Physick for divers diseases of the Nobility and Gentlemen of England. Dedicated to divers of the Nobility. It consisted of three parts. In the first he shewed who were noble and gentlemen, and how many works and properties belong unto such and wherein their office chiefly standeth. In the second part he shewed great diseases were in the nobility and gentry which letted them from doing their office. In the third part he specified what the diseases were, as namely, the whole palsy, the dropsy, the Romish pox and the leprosy—shewing afterwards the remedy against these diseases. For, being a very facetious man, he delivered his reproofs and counsels under witty and pleasant discourse."

The death of the Romish queen (17th November 1558) brought back the Protestant exiles. In 1559 Dr Turner was re-installed as Dean of Wells on the recommendation of the Archbishop of Canterbury (Parker). Although as a preacher and a physician he was well known in London, Wells could not reproach him as non-resident. He was evidently a general favourite because of his varied learning and humour, and his conscientious and courageous fidelity in his sacred office without respect of persons. As an ardent Protestant, he disapproved of the use of the old priestly vestments, by which some of the clergy hoped to entice an ignorant populace into bodily attendance on Protestant worship. His plan was to remove the poor people's ignorance, and to comfort their hearts and minds by pure Gospel teaching. Opposition to the vestments (strange to say) made an honest Englishman liable to persecution. Dean Turner braved that danger; but he underwent no prosecution, such was the general respect and popularity that had been earned by him.

In 1564 (March 23) the Bishop of Bath and Wells wrote to Mr Secretary Cecil : " I am much encumbered with master Dr Turner, Dean of Welles, for his undiscrete behaviour in the pulpitt, where he medleth with all matters, and unsemelic speaketh of all estates, more than is standing with discretion." Cecil took no practical notice of this, nor of a more serious complaint from Archbishop Parker, dated 30th April 1565 : " I was informed yesterday that Turner of Wells hath enjoined a common adulterer to do his open penance in a square priest's cap. If it be true, this is a strange toying with the prince's pleasure and injunctions. You of the council know what ye have to do." The Dean, in a Latin letter to Henry Bullinger, thus characterized the "old clothes" prosecutions :—" Our principal ministers and others, for the sake of an ass's appearance,[1] have thrown into prison many learned and godly pastors, stripped of all their dignities, and have exposed the flock of Christ unarmed to wolves, Papists, Lutherans, Sadducees, and Herodians." He also gave advice to Bullinger, who, as a foreigner, had written in a temporizing vein :—" You should candidly and openly and fearlessly bear witness in some published tracts, whether you are of opinion that

[1] [*Ob asini prospectum*—to carry out their determination that an officiating clergyman shall look like an ass]

princes or ecclesiastical prelates—whom you call *principal ministers*—have authority, without offence to Christian liberty and manifest injury to the Church, to obtrude upon the pastors of churches against their will, under pain of deprivation and imprisonment, certain prescribed vestments and corresponding ceremonies, whether borrowed from the heathen or transferred from the Levitical law, or invented and approved by the Pope, and destined, and employed, for the furtherance of idolatry." To this letter was added the signature, "William Turner, a physician delighting in the study of sacred literature." The ruling powers escaped from branding him as an ecclesiastical delinquent by regarding him as a beloved physician.

His publications as an author during this reign, of which I am informed, are connected with the medical faculty. He may be regarded as a father among English botanists. He published "The Seconde Parte of Uulliam Turners Herball wherin are conteyned the names of herbes in Greke, Latin, Duche, Frenche, and in the Apothecaries Latin and somtyme in Italiane, wyth the vertues of the same herbes, wyth diversse confutationes of no small errours that men of no small learning have committed in the intreatinge of herbes of late yeares. Hereunto is ioyned also a booke of the bath of Baeth in Englande and of the vertues of the same with diversse other bathes most holsum and effectuall both in Almany and Englande, set furth by William Turner Doctor of Physik. Imprinted at Collen by Arnold Birckman In the yeare of our Lorde MDLXII." He also wrote "Notes on Wines used in England," 1568.

Dean Turner died 7th July 1568, and on the 9th he was buried in the chancel of the Church of St Olave, Hart Street, London. According to Strype there was a monument to him in Crutched-Friars Church. His translation of the Heidelberg Catechism was printed in 1572. Although Mr Thelwall mentions a translation printed in 1570,[1] I reckon Dean Turner's as the first, because he left it in manuscript in 1568. A. Wood catalogues it briefly as *The Palsgrave's Catechism*; but the title is :—

"THE CATHECHISME
or manner to teach Children
and others the Christian faith :
used in all the laudes and dominions that are under the mighty Prince Frederike, the Palsgrave of the Rhene, Elector of the Empyre, &c.

"Translated out of Latin into Englysh by William Turner, Doctor of Phisicke; easely to be understanded and read as well of the people of the North cuntry as others.

"Imprinted at London by Richarde Iohnes, dwelling in the upper end of Fleet lane. 1572."

[1] "John Harrison the elder, a printer and stationer in London, in 1570, printed 'Frederic Count Palatine his Catechisme, translated out of Latin and Dutch.'"—*Thelwall*, p. 15.

"Quest. 1. Which is the anely comforte both in lyfe and in death? Ans. That both concernyng my soule and my body whether I live or I dye, I am not mine owne, but belong only unto my most faithfull Lord and Saver Jesus Christ, who with His precious blud moste fully makyng amendes for all my sinnes, hath delyvered me from the power of the Devyll, and keepeth mee so that without the wyll of my heavenly father ther cannot so much as an heire fall from my head. Yea, and further that all things must serve for my salvation, wherefor he hath made mee sure of everlasting lyfe by His holy Spirite and maketh mee prompt and redy from henceforth to lyve according to His wyll."

The tract finishes off thus :—

"Finis.

"Imprinted at London in y⁰ upper end of Fleet lane by Richard Jones, and ar to be sold at his shop joynyng to the Southwest Dore of St Paules Church."

The prejudices in favour of Popery, lingering among "the people of the north country [Northumberland] and others," might yield to a Doctor of Physic, when they would hold out against a Dean; so that he did not put his ecclesiastical office much forward; neither did his brother ecclesiastics, when they alluded to him (for a reason which I have already indicated). Bishop Parkhurst wrote to his Zurich correspondents, "Dr William Turner, a good physician and an excellent man, died at London. Lever preached at his funeral." [This was Rev. Thomas Lever, M.A., formerly Master of St John's College, Cambridge.]

ZACHARIAS URSINUS.

ZACHARY BEER was born at Breslau, 18th July 1534. He studied at Wittemberg under Melancthon from 1550 to 1557. The rough and raging quadruped, whom the English call "bear," has a German name of exactly the same sound, though spelt "Bär." Our student's surname having also the same pronunciation, he as a learned man was called *Ursinus*. He accompanied Melancthon to the religious conference at Worms, and in his visit to Heidelberg in 1557. Ursinus then went on a literary tour on his own account. He visited France and Switzerland, making the personal acquaintance of Bullinger and Peter Martyr at Zurich, and of Calvin and Beza at Geneva. Calvin presented him with his works "with best wishes." On his return to Wittemberg in 1558 he received a call to the rectorship of the great school at Breslau, called Elizabeth College. The death of Melancthon seems to have been the birth of so-called *Lutheran* zeal. The consequence was that Ursinus was dismissed from his office, and in October 1560 went to Zurich, intending to settle in that University town.

But in September 1561, on the invitation of Frederick III., he settled at Heidelberg as Professor of Theology. The Heidelberg Catechism is known as the Catechism of Ursinus, probably because he was a greater theologian than his colleague Olevianus. But though they finally welded their workmanship together harmoniously and successfully, both Olevianus and Ursinus diligently laboured apart, and several drafts in German and two in Latin[1] were executed. The judgment of Olevianus was well adapted for the work of revisal. On the death of Frederick III. in 1576, the Lutheran Elector Ludwig (Louis VI.) deposed and banished six hundred reformed ministers and teachers; of these Ursinus was one, and he did not live to be restored to Heidelberg. He found a refuge at Neustadt an der Hardt in John Casimir's territory, and there he founded a theological seminary, labouring from May 1578 till 6th March 1583, when he died.

His *Sum of the Christian Religion*, in the form of Lectures on his own Heidelberg Catechism, seems not to have been written out and prepared for the press by himself, but to have been compiled from Notes. We miss in the printed discourses the joyous spirit of the first question and answer, which were not a digest of his opinions only, but were the utterances of his heart. He used to say, "I would not take a thousand worlds for the blessed assurance of being owned by Jesus Christ." His works were collected by his only son and published in 3 vols. folio. The English deputies to the great Synod of Dort, said of the Heidelberg Catechism, that "neither the English nor the French church have a catechism so suitable and excellent. Those who compiled the Heidelberg Catechism were remarkably endowed and assisted by the Spirit of God therein. In several of their works they had excelled other theologians, but in the composition of this Catechism they have outdone themselves."

PASTOR JOHANNES VAN DER KEMP.

Mr Thelwall, in his edition of the Heidelberg Catechism, gives interesting details regarding the work of catechizing as carried on in Holland by pastors, catechists, and *Ziekentroosters* (comforters of the sick). He also commends Pastor Van Der Kemp's Exposition—a closely printed quarto volume of nearly one thousand pages, published in 1717, and frequently reprinted (18th edition, 1773). The Pastor died in 1718. As to the first question he added to the commentary an exhortation to self-examination, for the solemn consideration of the

[1] The Latin version, which was printed by the Elector's order, and is the version which has always been reprinted, was not one of those drafts, but was translated from the authorized Catechism by Joshua Lagus and Lambert Ludolph Pithopœus.

scholar who has declared, as learnt by rote, what is "MY only consolation in life and in death"—lest (says Mr Thelwall) "the learner should be beguiled into taking for granted, that he can adopt and apply to himself such language, as lightly and easily as he might learn and repeat a catechism of mere historical or scientific facts."

REV. JAMES WARDLAW.

MR WARDLAW was born in the parish of Saline in 1673. His father removed to the neighbouring parish of Carnock where his estate was, and he is known as Henry Wardlaw, Esq., of West Luscar. James was brought up in Episcopacy, which he renounced at an early age; he studied philosophy and divinity at St Andrews along with a brother who died young. While a divinity student he was ordained as an elder by the Rev. James Hog of Carnock, and was transferred to the Kirk-Session of Dunfermline in 1715, he having become in 1709 a preacher at the same time and place as his future colleague, Mr Ralph Erskine. He was ordained as minister of Cruden, in Aberdeenshire, in 1717, but finding that his parishioners were Episcopal in their leanings, he gladly accepted the offer of the second charge of Dunfermline in 1718. He succeeded to his father's estate, and was thus an heritor of the parish of Carnock, and quite in accord with his colleague and with Mr Hog as to "The Marrow" controversy, and as to the election of ministers by congregations. His life was simply that of an exemplary pastor and gospel preacher, and his name would not have descended to posterity had he not been one of "the twelve" who signed the famous Representation. With his brilliant colleague he lived and acted most harmoniously, and did not refuse the Associate Presbytery the shelter of his hospitable roof. It is not at all to his discredit that, according to the custom of the times, he declared from the pulpit, in his own vindication and as his opinion, that secession was not the true way to cure the corruptions of the Church; while it is much to his credit that, loyally ignoring the deposition of Mr Erskine as being an unconstitutional and malignant act, he continued to recognize him as his colleague. Nevertheless, it is a fact that Mr Wardlaw's plan was tried, without any success, in the year 1744 by Rev. John Willison of Dundee (*born* 1680, *died* 1750), in "A Fair and Impartial Testimony, containing Humble Pleadings with our Mother Church to exert herself to stop defection and promote reformation."

Mr Wardlaw died on 7th May 1742. He was the maternal grandfather of Dr Samuel Charteris, minister of Wilton.

REV. CHARLES WATSON, D.D.

CHARLES WATSON, a native of Edinburgh, was a pupil of the High School of that city, and a graduate of its University. He was licensed by the Metropolitan Presbytery in 1817, and was ordained by the Presbytery of Kirkcaldy as assistant and successor to the minister of Burntisland, 30th June 1820. He entered upon the full charge of that church and parish in 1822, but after a few years he had to withdraw from much public duty, owing to feebleness of voice and weakness of sight. In 1827 the Rev. John Aikman Wallace was ordained his assistant and successor, and he, on being translated to Hawick, was in 1834 succeeded by Rev. David Couper. In 1833 Mr Watson received the degree of D.D. from Marischal College, Aberdeen. In 1837 he resigned his charge, and resided in Edinburgh till his death on 11th August 1866. In 1843 Dr Watson became an Emeritus minister of the Free Church of Scotland. In my First Book I have devoted a chapter to his "Hints on Christian Experience" (1st edition, 1825; 2nd edition, 1833). He also published "Three Addresses on subjects connected with the Lord's Supper," 1827; "Preparation for Death," 1828; "Prayers for the use of families," 1831 (several times reprinted); "Prayers for young persons," 1831. The diction of his Family Prayers is beautiful.

REV. THOMAS WATSON.

THOMAS WATSON is quite equal to the greatest Nonconformist divines, his books being eminently useful and attractive, written in a sententious style, pithy and sensible, sparkling and musical. But having been a Cambridge man, of Emmanuel College, and having never been connected with the sister University, he has not been memorialized by the industrious Oxford antiquary. His pastoral charge in the Church of England was St Stephen's, Walbrook, in the city of London. From this he was ejected by the Black Bartholomew Act on 24th August 1662. He continued to labour in London for many years; "but (says Calamy) his strength wearing away, he retired into Essex, and there died suddenly in his closet at prayer." His laborious professional life did not afford materials for a biography; he escaped not only notice, but ill-will, as he was respected by all parties. (One of his admirers is spoken of by Dr Calamy as Bishop Richardson, probably the Venerable John Richardson, Archdeacon of Derry, who became Bishop of Ardagh, in Ireland, in 1663.)

Several quotations from Watson appear in the second part of my First Book. They are all from his "Body of Divinity," which consists of Discourses on the Westminster Shorter Catechism. He also published an "Exposition of the Beatitudes in our Lord's Sermon on the Mount," which is a small volume, and a gem. His views as to the beginning of consolation in a believer's heart are not very decided, having sometimes more of the spirit of a Saviour's welcome, at other times more that reminds us of a sentinel's warning off. There is in the Discourses on the Lord's Prayer, in his "Body of Divinity," a long and fine passage on the comforts of a pardoned soul, of which I shall quote the heads :—

"1. God looks upon a pardoned soul as if he had never sinned. Where sin is remitted, it is as if it had not been committed (Jer. l. 20).

"2. God, having pardoned sin, will pass an act of oblivion. When our sins are laid upon the head of Christ, our scape-goat, they are carried into a land of forgetfulness.

"3. The pardoned soul is for ever secured against the wrath of God. From the avenging wrath of God every pardoned soul is freed ; though he may taste of the bitter cup of affliction, yet he shall never drink of the sea of God's wrath. Being justified by His blood, we shall be saved from wrath through Him (Rom. v. 9). Christ's blood quencheth the flames of hell.

"4. Sin being pardoned, conscience hath no more authority to accuse. If the creditor discharge the debtor, what hath the serjeant to do to arrest him?

"5. Nothing that befalls a pardoned soul shall hurt him. The best things hurt the wicked, but the worst things which befall a pardoned soul shall do him no hurt—the sting, the poison, the curse is gone.

"6 To a pardoned soul everything hath a commission to do him good.

"7. A pardoned soul is not only exempted from wrath, but invested with dignity. A pardoned soul is made a favourite of heaven. Whom God pardons, He crowns. Whom God absolves, He marries Himself to (Jer iii. 12, 14).

"8. Sin being pardoned, we may come with holy boldness to God in prayer.

"9. Forgiveness of sin makes our services acceptable. God takes all we do in good part.

"10. Forgiveness of sin is the sauce which sweetens all the comforts of this life. Pardon of sin gives a sanctified title and a delicious taste to every comfort. As Naaman said to Gehazi, Take two talents (2 Kings v. 23), so God saith to the pardoned soul, Take two talents—take the venison and take a blessing with it—take the oil in the cruse, and take My love with it ; *take two talents.*

"11. If sin be forgiven, God will never upbraid us with our former sins. Mary Magdalen (a pardoned penitent),—after Christ arose, He appeared first to her (Mark xvi. 9) ; so far was Christ from upbraiding her, that He brings her the first news of His resurrection.

"12. Sin being pardoned is a pillar of support in the loss of dear friends.

God hath taken away thy child—thy husband—but withal He hath taken away thy sins. He hath given thee more than He hath taken away.

"13. Where God pardons sin, He bestows righteousness. With remission of sin goes imputation of righteousness. I will greatly rejoice in the Lord, He hath covered me with the robe of righteousness (Isa. lxi. 10). If a Christian can take any comfort in his inherent righteousness, which is so stained and mixed with sin, O then what comfort may he take in Christ's righteousness, which is a better righteousness than that of Adam! Adam's righteousness was mutable, but suppose it had been unchangeable, yet it was the righteousness of a man; but that righteousness which is imputed is the righteousness of Him who is God (2 Cor. v. 21).

"14. The pardoned soul needs not fear death. He may look on death with joy who looks on forgiveness with faith. Death will do a pardoned sinner the greatest good turn, therefore it is made a part of the inventory (1 Cor. iii. 22), *Death is yours.*"

REV. JOHN WILLIAMSON.

THE Rev. David Williamson, the ejected minister of the West Church (*alias* St Cuthbert's), Edinburgh, a godly covenanter, had a son, John, born in 1679. In the absence of particulars regarding John Williamson's studies, we may say that his call to the Christian ministry was suggested by some things which he himself suggested to a younger minister in an ordination sermon :—" A providential call to the study of theology either by a continued course of education or some singular providence determining that way—the Lord's blessing and countenancing these studies, so that an observable progress is made therein—a humble inclination and desire (if the Lord should think fit) to serve Him in the Gospel of His Son—a fervent love to souls and tender compassion for poor sinners, and an earnest desire of their salvation—a sweet concurrence and gracious assistance of the Spirit of God in and with meditation and prayer about this design—a shining on the soul with the light of His countenance, even under the exercise of the resolution to follow this work, and a powerful influence of grace drawing forth the soul to a humble dedication thereunto—fervent supplication for the Divine presence and blessing, and a firm dependence on Him for all necessary furniture and assistance—a being hedged in (as it were) by Providence from all other kinds of generation work—a patient waiting for the external call without any disorderly methods to obtain it—a humble submission to the trial [examinations] of Christ's ministers—and a fixed purpose (through grace) of diligence, faithfulness, and constant recourse to the Chief Shepherd upon all occasions, through the whole course of that work."[1]

On 14th January 1702 he was unanimously called by the congregation of Inveresk and Musselburgh, and was ordained as their minister by the Presbytery of Dalkeith on April 30th. During his whole life he was a faithful and popular minister. He came into public notice as one of the twelve representers against the Act condemning "The Marrow of Modern Divinity." In 1718, observing the outcry against the reprint of the First or Doctrinal Part of that book, he reprinted the Second or Practical Part, with a Preface and Appendix. He did not give his name to that publication, and "The Parents' Catechism" by him was also anonymous. He did not assist in drawing up the celebrated *Representation*. In May 1721 Boston says: "Mr John Williamson of Inveresk made his first appearance amongst us at signing the last draft, but was very useful after, being a man of a clear head, a ready wit, and very forward." The epithet "forward" is intended to be complimentary, and to denote alacrity, public spirit, and presence of mind. He took a creditable part before the General Assembly of 1721.

In Boston's account of this affair he perplexes modern readers by calling the Court *The Commission*. And therefore I must state that the Commission of the General Assembly has no power except in items of business committed to it by the previous Assembly; it has regular quarterly meetings. The General Assembly sits under the eye of a nobleman sent by the Sovereign, and called the Royal Commissioner, who remains during the time supposed to be necessary for an average programme of business. This programme is sketched at first, but may be added to. The Commissioner takes his departure at the usual time; but if the programme has not been exhausted, the General Assembly continues to sit, under the technical name of "the Commission," but only to finish the business already placed in the programme. In 1721 the Marrow-men's Representation was in the programme of Wednesday's business; but the Royal Commissioner had left Edinburgh on account of indisposition. The General Assembly was thus *dissolved*, or rather *resolved*, into a Commission; but it was in reality the General Assembly and open to the public—the only effect upon the *Marrow* affair was that sympathising members, who might have added their signatures to the Representation at any time during *the Assembly's* sittings, could not sign in *the Commission*, to which the Representation *of twelve ministers* had been referred. Having made this explanation, I still call the Court by the name of the General Assembly, for the sake of distinctness.

On Thursday, eleven ministers appeared at the bar of the Assembly. Their Representation was read. Mr Boston and Mr Hog were heard in elucidation of it. The Moderator then permitted thirteen speeches on the other side to be delivered, Mr Hog being put down when he rose to reply to one or other of

[1] "Gospel Method of Conquering Sinners," page 266.

them. This was for the benefit of the audience. The Moderator then called on Mr Boston to reply, and he made a short speech ; but a member of Assembly made a counter-speech. The parties at the bar were about to be removed, when Mr Williamson said : "Moderator, we have heard a multitude of speeches against us—such a multitude, indeed, that it is not possible to remember them, so as to answer them offhand. But if allowed time for recollection, we will answer them afterwards." The Assembly appointed a committee (a sub-committee of the Commission).

On Friday the Assembly met, and had the representers before them again. A member proposed that the case should go on with closed doors, and said that this was the wish of the representers. Mr Wilson of Maxton strongly asserted that he and his brethren wished the Court to be open. The audience therefore remained, and were greatly impressed in favour of the representers. Mr Williamson triumphantly refuted a speech by Mr Allan Logan of Culross ; and, on Principal Hadow's rising to the rescue, he was, in turn, refuted by Mr Boston. The consequence was, that although many appointments were made, no more discussions took place ; but the representers were summoned to the August Commission. In August they were merely informed that the Committee had prepared an overture for the Assembly of May 1722. Next, the November Commission concocted twelve queries for the twelve brethren (nicknamed *apostles*), and they were allowed till March to answer them. The March Commission received the answers. The Act of 21st May 1722 rebuked and admonished the representers. Mr Kid handed in their written protest, "but the Assembly would not read it, and quickly closed the sederunt."

When the Synod of Merse and Teviotdale were carrying on proceedings against Mr Wilson of Maxton for his sermon, "The Trust," Mr Williamson, along with the Erskines, went to Kelso and sat beside him.

Mr Williamson was industrious as an author. In 1721 he published with his name a volume of 500 pages, entitled "The Gospel Method of conquering sinners unto Christ, opened and applied in several sermons preached before the Sacrament of the Lord's Supper, upon Luke xiv. 23, compared with 2 Cor. x. 4, 5." This book was dedicated "Unto the Right Honourable the Society in Scotland for propagating Christian Knowledge."[1] In 1722 he published anonymously a pamphlet of 148 pages, "The Scope and Substance of the Marrow of Modern Divinity, wherein several passages, excepted against therein, are explained and vindicated. Being an Introductory Essay to a more particular confutation of Principal Hadow's pretended *Detection* of the *Antinomianism* of the *Marrow*." In 1726 he produced a volume of 200 pages, "Gospel Truth

---

[1] "In several places where their schools are erected, matters are on such a footing that the Popish priests have entirely lost their credit. Barbarity and the Irish language are almost entirely rooted out ; and the children have made considerable progress in the knowledge of Christianity." Page viii.

and Holiness, considered in their nature and necessity, and in their harmony and influence, in several Sermons before and after the Lord's Supper" (his texts being Ps. xliii. 3, 4, and John xvii. 19) ; and in 1727, another volume of 140 pages, entitled, " Gospel Preaching and Gospel Conversation, considered in several Sermons " (the texts were Mark xvi. 15, and Phil. i. 27). To the last volume was appended a Sermon by Rev. Charles Mastertoun, M.A., of Ireland, on John viii. 32.

His other pieces, which I have not seen, may be named for biography's sake. " Reasons why several ministers did not read the Act of Parliament relating to the murderers of Captain Porteous," 1737. " Seasonable Testimony," 1738, from which *Brown's Gospel Truth* quotes this lamentation, " Speaking of *Christ*—being in HIM—drawing strength from union or communion with Him—dependance on His righteousness, and such like, are obsolete, antiquated notions among many of our young divines." His last publication was entitled, " Plain dealing for the conviction of the Seceding Brethren," 1739. He disapproved of secession, though he loved the Seceders. He did not live to protest against the outrageous step of deposing them, for he died on 2nd February 1740, aged sixty.

Mr Williamson's sermons are not attractive to readers. Hearers, anxious for Gospel teaching, would listen to such sermons with thankfulness. Mrs Balderston, the sister of the Erskines, repeatedly praises him in her Diary. At one time she heard him preach at Edinburgh from the text (Sol. Song i. 5), " I am black but comely," and she notes, "It was a very great sermon, which I felt." At his sacramental services so many strangers from a distance attended that they could not be accommodated with lodgings, and their singing of psalms resounded among the woods in the night-watches. Patient readers of his three volumes of sermons would be rewarded by finding choice sentences. Thus, as to Christian simplicity, he says : " *Simplicity* imports a readiness to believe in Christ, and to comply with duty—a being void of wiles and cunning to contrive evil. The upright man is harmless, and *an even, downright man*."--III. 116.

" The Apostle earnestly presseth the necessary branches of holiness from the consolations that are in Christ (Phil. ii.). And how great these are, who can conceive ? who can express ? Must it not be owned that He, who is expressly called *The Consolation of Israel*, hath an inexhaustible store of consolations in Him ?"—III. 98.

REV. GABRIEL WILSON, M.A.

GABRIEL WILSON, born about 1679, held a bursary from the Presbytery of Edinburgh, took the degree of M.A. at the University 28th June 1697, and was licensed by the Presbytery of Kirkcudbright in 1705. As a preacher he was associated with veteran Presbyterians, being, first, the assistant at Jedburgh of Mr Gabriel Semple (formerly the covenanting minister of Kirkpatrick-Durham in Dumfriesshire), and next, assistant of Mr Robert Edgar, minister of Maxton, in the Presbytery of Selkirk. He was ordained as Mr Edgar's colleague 23rd February 1709, and came into the full charge in December 1713. In 1721 he comes into notice as one of the twelve representers against the Act of the General Assembly of 1720, which condemned the *Marrow*. He also printed in 1721 "A Letter to a Gentleman at Edinburgh concerning the proceedings of the Assembly, 1720, with reference unto doctrines chiefly." In March 1722 he gave the finishing touches to the answer of the twelve brethren to twelve questions addressed to them by the General Assembly's Commission. Mr Boston described those answers as "begun by Mr Ebenezer Erskine, but much extended and perfected by my friend Mr Wilson, where his vast compass of reading, with his great collection of books, were of singular use and successfully employed." Boston throughout his diary characterizes Mr Wilson as "a plain preacher, but deep in his thoughts," and among all the brethren "the most clear and distinct as to the nature of faith; zealous and faithful to a pitch, with much of the spirit of the old Presbyterians." On 7th October 1721, as retiring Moderator of the Synod of Merse and Teviotdale, he opened the Synod with a sermon on 1 Tim. vi. 20. Mr Kid [*see* KID] took the responsibility of printing it in 1723, when it had been referred to the General Assembly's scrutiny, entitling it in accordance with its text "The Trust." His opponents wished to detect Antinomianism in it—so that it was under discussion before four meetings of Synod and as many committees, before two Commissions (November 1722 and March 1723), and before the General Assembly, May 1723. In the supreme court Boston informs us that "Mr Wilson came off honourably, not one error being fixed on his sermon, notwithstanding all the clamour that had been made against it. For his peculiar zeal and faithfulness his brethren had shot at him particularly, but his bow abode in strength. And the truth is, he was never, till that his trial, known to them; but it set him in a clear light, and exceedingly raised his reputation."

Mr Wilson did not join the Associate Presbytery, but he protested against the Act which led to its formation in 1733, viz., the suspension of four ministers by the November Commission of the General Assembly. The Act went further than suspension, because it "loosed them from their pastoral charges and declared them no ministers of the Church of Scotland." But in effect it was suspension only, for nothing more was carried out for six years and a half. During that interval of time the whole church virtually adopted the course described in Mr Wilson's protest, and he adhered to it for life. This was the protest:—

"EDINBURGH, *November* 16, 1733.—I, Mr Gabriel Wilson, minister at

Maxton, do hereby, in mine own name, and in name of all those that shall adhere to me, protest against this sentence of the Commission in the case of the four brethren—and that it may be lawful for me to complain of the said sentence, and of the several Acts of Assembly that have occasioned the same, to any subsequent Assembly of the Church of Scotland—as also, that it may be lawful for me in a becoming manner, on all proper occasions, to bear testimony against the same, with all other defections and severities of this Church in her sentences—and, finally, that I may in the meantime, as in Providence I shall find opportunity, hold ministerial communion with my said dear brethren, as if no such sentence had been passed against them. Upon all which I take instruments in the clerk's hands. GABRIEL WILSON."

"The above Protest is adhered to by us,
RALPH ERSKINE, Minister at Dunfermline.
THOMAS MAIR, Minister at Orwell.
JOHN M'CLAREN, Minister in Edinburgh.
JOHN CURRIE, Minister at Kinglassie.
JAMES WARDLAW, Minister at Dunfermline.
THOMAS NAIRN, Minister at Abbotshall."

The severities of the Church Courts and the dark prospects as to religion led Mr Wilson to found a communion in Maxton on the principles of the Congregationalists. To this church he preached on Sabbath evenings, and to it alone he administered the Lord's Supper. Mr Davidson, of Galashiels, joined him [see DAVIDSON]. The Church Courts did not suspend him or even censure him. The only symptom of displeasure appeared in 1742 at Cambuslang, where, from among the thirty thousand visitors, every minister was called forward to preach to the people or to address communicants, *Mr Wilson alone excepted.* He died 11th February 1750. His son, Andrew Wilson, M.D., physician in London, attended his surviving friend, Mr Davidson, on his deathbed six years later.

The noble sermon, "The Trust," was printed from Mr Wilson's notes, which were handed in to the Synod's Committee, although he had not had time to preach so much. The elaborate divisions and subdivisions are almost a discourse by themselves. His *Doctrine* or thesis was, "Our Lord Jesus Christ is very earnest and importunate with every one of His ministers, that they would faithfully keep the trust He has committed to them. 'Tis His commission—'tis His command—'tis His request to every one of them, that they may do so. *O Timothy, keep that which is committed to thy trust* (1 Tim. vi. 20)."—Page 20.

THE THEOLOGY OF CONSOLATION.

I. As to this Trust, with the Committing of it—

1. (1.) 'Tis a steward's trust.—(2.) 'Tis an ambassador's trust. (3.) 'Tis a workman—a labourer's trust. (4.) 'Tis a watchman's trust. (5.) 'Tis a shepherd's trust. (6.) 'Tis a soldier's— a warrior's trust.

2. (1.) The mystery of the doctrine of Christ. (2.) The institutions of Christ. (3.) His holy commandments—1. To bind the holy commands on people in their due order; 2. To hedge people in both from licentiousness and from legalism; 3. To bind on Christ's yoke with His own cords—Gospel motives and arguments.

3. How and by whom is this trust committed?—(1.) By our Lord Jesus Christ and by the Holy Ghost. (2.) Ministerially and instrumentally by them who ordain. (3.) In and by the Holy Scriptures, as the charter of the office and the record and register of the commission and instructions. (4.) From preceding generations of believers, faithful ministers, and martyrs.

4. The qualities of the trust.—(1.) 'Tis a divine and heavenly trust. (2.) 'Tis a goodly, great, and precious trust. (3.) 'Tis an honourable trust. (4.) 'Tis a weighty and difficult trust. (5.) 'Tis a sealed trust.

5. Why is such a trust put into hands weak and unskilful?—(1.) In condescension and compassion to sinners. (2.) That the excellency of the power may be of God. (3.) Our Lord will have reprisals made on Satan and his kingdom by means even of the very people whom he had subdued, ruined, and destroyed. (4.) For the security, encouragement, and confidence of sinners. (5.) For the trial of people's faith, love, and obedience.

II. As to the Keeping of the Trust.

Part 1.—*The Theory.*

1. *In different actings.*—(1.) Give all diligence to be apprized and possessed of it. (2.) As stewards, diligently and wisely dispense it. (3.) Let them in their own persons be delivered into the very mould and likeness of that trust. (4.) Maintain and defend it. (5.) Suffering for the adhering to, and maintaining it. (6.) Commit it, for its safe transmission to posterity, unto faithful men.

2. *With reference to the subject or the receptacles where it must be kept.*—(1.) They must keep it in their heads; (2.) in their hearts; (3.) in their lips; (4.) in the whole of their conversation; (5.) in the world; (6.) in the Holy Scripture, and other approved standards of doctrine.

3. *With reference to its contraries.*—Keep it, in opposition (1.) to losing or letting it slip; (2.) to the fraudulence, deceit, and subtilty of men; (3.) to main force, violence, and robbery; (4.) to a voluntary surrender or sale of it; (5.) to contemptuous rejection and throwing of it away.

Part 2.—*The Manner of Keeping.*

(1.) With care and diligence; (2.) punctually, critically, and with the utmost exactness; (3.) with wisdom and prudence; (4.) without partiality or respect of persons; (5.) with a single eye; (6.) with zeal and resolution; (7.) stedfastly; (8.) believingly and dependently.

[There are also some more heads as to the earnestness and importunity of Christ in committing this trust to His servant's keeping.]

While the above summary gives some idea of the excellence of the sermon, it also suggests that there might be much in it to give offence to worldly churchmen. Take one paragraph as an example. Referring to our Lord's address to the Scribes and Pharisees (Matt. xxiii. 13), the preacher said: "If one does not preach Christ and life and salvation in Him to the worst of sinners—though he should otherwise (which no doubt a man may do) preach sound doctrine all his days—he *takes away* the key of knowledge, and *shuts* the kingdom of heaven against sinners, in the sense of our Lord's words. Yea, not only may a man preach sound doctrine without preaching the Gospel, but he may preach many things well about Christ, yet never *preach Christ* in the sense of the New Testament. Whosoever then would keep the *Trust* must mind to set open, and keep open, the door of the kingdom of heaven to the worst of sinners. Upon some, indeed, he must shut the door to *Church Privileges*, but upon none may he shut the door to *Christ and free grace*. No! But, in a diligent and faithful dispensation of the word and sacraments, is he plentifully to deal forth and scatter abroad the doctrine of Christ—His Person and Offices—His free grace—and of His exuberant, overflowing, overflowing fulness to all, to be received, believed, and applied every one to himself in particular."—pp. 88, 89.

NOTE.

If Mr Gabriel Wilson's library had been kept together, we might have perhaps known more about the various editions of the *Marrow*. In his printed anonymous letter, dated April 1721, he says: "How came your Committee to call upon the Assembly to condemn books, till at least they themselves knew something more about them? To say nothing of some former editions of the *Marrow*, that were entirely free of the alleged offensive passages for which they condemned it, the ninth edition, printed at London, 1690, has the passage anent faith, and that anent the law as the covenant of works, with many other seeming asperities (even more than the committee thought fit to single out), all smoothed according to the style of the Westminster Confession. . . . I could, I think, be bold to chide with Mr James Hog on the single particular, that he did not choose the last edition of the *Marrow*, against which they could not have found these shows of occasion they have taken hold of in the edition recommended by him. Yet I must own there seemed to be something in the reply one made me when talking to this purpose. 'Why,' said he, 'perhaps Mr Hog has not known there was any later edition of the book than that which fell into his hands. . . . We know not what Providence has to bring out of these proceedings for the behoof of Gospel truth. For as it befel our Lord Himself, so when Gospel truth is undervalued, dropped, and trodden down, many are at length left to bury it, that it may rise more glorious.' . . . Tell Mr Hog I sympathize with him under his reproach and contempt. He needs not, I hope, be put in mind, there is a resurrection of names, and of books too, as well as of persons."

REV. THOMAS WILSON.

DILIGENT readers of the Bible were wont to consult *Wilson's Christian Dictionary*. It is not generally known that the author was one of the very old worthies of the Church of England. Thomas Wilson, when a young man, was befriended by Dr Henry Robinson, Provost of Queen's College, Oxford, who "cherished" him in his college, and sent him to Canterbury in 1584 or 1585 to become one of the Six Preachers in the Cathedral. He was chaplain to "Lord Wotton, Baron of Marleigh," Lord-Lieutenant of Kent. When Mr Wilson was accused of nonconformity, Lord Wotton induced Archbishop Abbot to take no notice of the charge. It was probably in 1615 that Mr Wilson became minister of St George's, Canterbury. He was eminent as a preacher, a pastor, and an author during a ministry of thirty-six years. He died in January 1621, leaving the reputation "that not one of a thousand could be found like this worthy servant of Christ." He was a champion on the side of the free Gospel, and against semi-Romish superstitions. His funeral sermon was preached by Mr Swift.

His celebrated dictionary was his first publication. The Dedication to Lord Wotton was dated December 1611. There was also another epistle to his first patron, the Bishop of Carlisle (Dr Henry Robinson); to his old friend the Bishop of Worcester (Dr Henry Parry); and to his colleague, Dr Neville, Dean of Christchurch, Canterbury. As the second edition was more worthy of the author, I copy its title-page :—

DICTIONARY OF WRITERS.

"A CHRISTIAN DICTIONARY
Opening the signification of the chiefe words dispersed generally throughout Holy Scriptures of the Old and New Testament, tending to increase Christian knowledge.

Whereunto is annexed a Particular Dictionary { For the Revelation of S. John. For the Canticles or Song of Salomon. For the Epistle to the Hebrewes.

The second edition,
Augmented by addition of divers thousands of words, phrases and significations, and by explication of Leviticall rites. Also, of most difficult and ambiguous speeches, with farre more profitable Annotations than before.
By Thomas Wilson, Minister of the Word at S. Georges in Canterbury.

Every word of God is pure. Prov. xxx. 5.
Ye erre because ye know not the Scripture. Mat. xxii. 19.
Words are notes and markes of things. Aristotle.

Galen. lib. 1 de Method. cap. 5. *Whosoever is ignorant of words shal never judge well of things.*

¶ *Ubi plura aut diversa ejusdem vocis significata offeruntur, prima sunt propria et genuina, cætera metaphorica.* Mercerus in Pagn.
Distinctio vocis ambiguæ, primùm sit in omni rerum consideratione.
Keckerman System. Log.
London,
Printed by William Jaggard, dwelling in Barbican. 1616."

The title-page explains the object. Ministers and Christians are apt to string sermonic sentences together, without weighing the exact signification of the words which they are using. He also gave explanatory rhymes. For instance—

"As stars from heaven much light afford,
So do the words we find in Word;
But stars shine not, till they appear,
Nor words do teach, till sense we hear."

A friend who signed himself "*R. Rauen,*" contributed additional explanations of the object—

"Our English tongue from many tongues a snatch and smack hath taken,
As English men from foreign men their coats and suits have shapen;
Some words from French and some from Greek, more from the Latins flow,
Some new, some old—some dark, some plain—some hard, and strange to know.

Some to some place do give great light—some darken much the text—
Some, general in the first place—some, special in the next—
Some, properly found in this clause, improperly in that;
What some words sound thou know'st right well; some sound thou know'st not what."

I can give only one specimen of the Dictionary :—

"[CONSOLATION or COMFORT]. That inward spiritual refreshing and strengthening of the heart by the consideration and feeling of God's merciful promises in Christ. Ps. cxix. 50, Thy promises have comforted me in my trouble. 2 Cor. i. 4, God comforteth us in all our troubles; ver. 5, Our consolation aboundeth through Christ. Rom. i. 11, 12, Where consolation and strengthening are put the one for the other. The Holy Ghost, being the worker of comfort, is therefore called *the* Comforter, by an excellency. The promises of the Word are the grounds of comfort; our believing hearts are the seats of comfort; Godly ministers and the faithful are the helpers of our comfort. John xvi. 7, I will send the Comforter. 1 Thess. iv. 18, Comfort yourselves one another with these words. 2 Cor. vii. 7."[1]

Mr Wilson's other works were—"A Commentary on Romans," 1614 [2nd edit. 1627; another edit. 1658]; "Christ's Farewell to Jerusalem," 1614; "Theological Rules," 1615; "Holy Riddles," 1615; "A Dialogue about Justification;" "A Receipt against Heresie." The following is the title-page of his "Commentary":—

"A Commentarie upon the most Divine Epistle of S. Paul to the Romanes. Containing for matter the degeneration of our nature by Adams Fall, and the restauration thereof by the Grace of Christ. Together with the perfection of Faith and the imbecillity of Workes in the cause of Justification of elect sinners before God.

{ For forme and maner of handling, it hath } { The Coherence and Method, The Summe and Scope, The Interpretations and Doctrines, The Reasons and Uses, of most texts. }

All which are set downe very familiarly and compendiously in forme of a Dialogue betweene Timotheus and Silas.

By Thomas Wilson, one of the six Preachers in the Cathedrall Church of Canterbury.

¶ Our beloved Brother Paul, according to the wisedome given him of God,

---

[1] Wilson's "Christian Dictionary" was enlarged into a folio volume after the author's death. The first editor was Mr John Bagwell, who published the fifth edition in 1647, describing the work as "Begun by that famous and worthy man of God, Mr Thomas Wilson." The Rev. Andrew Symson (as he signs his name, though his title-page has it Simson) next took it up, and I have read descriptions of the sixth edition, dated 1655, attributed to him, and of the seventh edition, 1661. I have before me the eighth edition, 1678, with a preface by Symson, dated 25th March 1665, and an Epistle to the Reader, by Rev. Edmund Calamy.

hath written unto you, which the unlearned and unstable pervert to their owne destruction. 2 Pet. iii. 15.

¶ What Epistle of Paul is not more sweete than Honie?—AUGUST.

¶ The sublimity of Paul's minde went beyond the Heavens.—CHRYSOST.

¶ This Epistle is a Catechisme for Christians, and a perfect body of Apostolicall Doctrine.—PARÆUS.

London : Printed by W. Jaggard, dwelling in Barbican. 1614."

The idea and execution of his "Christian Dictionary" had shown that Thomas Wilson valued both the truth itself and accuracy in preaching it. A specimen of his "Commentary on the Romans" has been given in Book I., Part 2nd, Chapter 3. I conclude here with some of his comments on chap. xii. 1 : *I beseech you, therefore, brethren, by the mercies of God, &c.*

"The mercies of God, even His spiritual mercies, are in our text called *mercies* in the plural number, because they are many—to wit, election of grace, calling to Christ, justification by faith, sanctification by the Spirit. By all these mercies (which are every one of them more worth than a thousand worlds) he beseecheth them to obey God by the mortification of their lusts.

"The meditation of God's mercies in Christ are a most effectual motion and sharp spur to a godly life. As if a mother should beseech her child to do something by the womb that bare him, the paps which suckt him, the knees which dandled him, and all her entire compassions towards him. How flinty should his heart be not to yield to her ! So we should show ourselves more than stony-hearted if we yield not to God when He, that might condemn, doth *beseech*, even by those tender mercies whereby He begat us, pardoned us, called us, renewed us, and saved us."

* * * * * * * *

" Tim. *What is the lesson we are to take from hence ?*

Silas. That Christians are to be moved unto duty towards God and man after the doctrine of His grace and love towards them be manifested. For as the eye guides the body, so doctrine governs duty. And what a foundation is unto a house, that the doctrine of grace is unto a holy life—even the groundwork, root, and spring of all good works.

Tim. *What use of this instruction ?*

Silas. It confutes them which hold the doctrine of grace to be an enemy to a good life, and to open a window or gap unto liberty in sinne, from which it recalleth rather. Also it serves to reprove them that teach duties without doctrine, or do not lead their lives answerable to the doctrine of grace which they do know and profess."

REV. WILLIAM WILSON, M.A.[1]

In the covenanting times in Scotland Mr Gilbert Wilson, a small proprietor, was deprived of his estate in the parish of East Kilbride. He had to fly from his house. For a whole winter he lived on Mearns moor, "unsheltered and alone," provisions being secretly brought to him by a female servant. Thereafter he retired to Holland. He returned home at the Revolution, and lived in Glasgow in expectation of receiving compensation for the loss of his land. At this time he married Isabella Ramsay, niece of the widow of the martyred James Guthrie, and daughter of the Laird of Shielhill in Forfarshire, a bigoted Jacobite, who had long ago disowned and disinherited her on account of her religious principles. Their son was born in Glasgow on 19th November 1690, and was named after King William III. (Mr Gilbert Wilson was made Comptroller of Customs at Greenock).

William Wilson became M.A. of the University of Glasgow, and was licensed by the Presbytery of Dunfermline 23rd Sept. 1713. The Town Council of Perth in 1715 resolved that a third minister was required by the increasing population. The West Kirk, a wing which had fallen into disuse and disrepair, was therefore fitted up beneath the spacious roofs of St John's cathedral. It was opened in 1716. A call was given to Mr Wilson on the 21st August, and he was ordained on 1st November 1716.

There is one entry in his Diary concerning "The Marrow of Modern Divinity":—"6th March 1721. I went to Edinburgh to meet with some ministers who were to consider about some grievances—particularly the affair of the last Assembly concerning 'The Marrow.' We met and discoursed and prayed together. Our meetings continued for several days. We had much sweet satisfaction in so meeting, and in our praying and conversing together. At length it was agreed that a representation to the Assembly should be drawn up and signed, *complaining of their condemnation of several precious doctrines* contained in the book entitled 'The Marrow of Modern Divinity.'"

Mr Wilson did not take any further charge of this business; but it is believed that it was at his suggestion that a similar conference took place at Perth in 1731 and 1732. The following is from his Diary:—"November and December 1731. About this time a few ministers met together to consider what might be proper for them to do in the present juncture. Those who first met were Mr Gillespie, Strathmiglo; Mr Laing, Newburgh; Mr Lauchlan M'Intosh, Errol; Mr Fisher, Kinclaven; Mr Moncrieff, Abernethy. I was with them at all their meetings. After prayer and conference, we agreed to a repre-

[1] See "Memoirs of Rev. Wm. Wilson," by Rev. Andrew Ferrier, 1830; and "Life and Times of Rev. Wm. Wilson," by Rev. Dr. Eadie, 1849.

sentation and petition to the next General Assembly, relating to the grievances the church is at present under. We thought that if the Assembly should not regard it, it would be at least a standing testimony to future generations against the present courses that have such a visible tendency to ruin the Church of Scotland. A draft of a representation was prepared, and it was agreed to write to some ministers to meet with us at Perth on the 21st day of February 1732, and that copies of the representation should be sent them, that they might give their judgment upon it at meeting, and might be ready to sign it."

"February 1732. About eighteen ministers having met together from several places, the representation was read over and amended; and a fair copy being written, it was signed by us all who were present, and afterwards it was signed by several other ministers, together with a commission to some of our number to present it to the ensuing General Assembly."

It was signed by forty-two ministers and three elders (the latter were Alex. Swinton of Strathore, Tho. Trotter, and William Walker). The following were the ministers:—

Marrow-men.— Rev. Ebenezer Erskine, Ralph Erskine, John Bonar, Gabriel Wilson, Henry Davidson, and James Wardlaw, along with whom may be mentioned their friend, Rev. Alexander Hamilton.

Ministers who afterwards seceded.—Rev. William Wilson; James Fisher; Alexander Moncrieff, laird of Culfargie, minister of Abernethy in Perthshire (born 1695, died 1761); Thomas Mair, minister of Orwell (born 1700, died 1768); James Thomson, minister of Burntisland (died 1766); Thomas Nairne, minister of Abbotshall (died 1764).

Ministers who died before the deposition of the seceders.—Rev. James Goodsir, minister of Monikie (born 1679, died 1733); Robert Gray, minister of Brechin (died 1738); William Henderson, minister of Dalgety (born 1690, died 1737); John Johnston, minister of the second charge of Brechin from 1710 to 3rd November 1732; John M'Claren, minister of the Tolbooth Church, Edinburgh (born 1667, died 1734), author of a valuable book exposing Professor Simson's errors; George Mair, minister of New Deer from 1722 to 1736; Charles Moore, native of Armagh, minister from 1715 to 1736, first of Culross, second of West Church, Stirling, voted against the Anti-Marrow Act of 1722, father of John Moore, M.D., and grandfather of General Sir John Moore, K.C.B.; James Noble, minister of Eckford (born 1656, died 1739); Thomas Thomson, minister of Auchtermuchty (born 1666, died 1st January 1733).

Other Ministers.—Rev. George Gillespie, minister of Strathmiglo (born 1674, died 1755); was a member of the General Assembly of 1740, and dissented from the deposition of the seceders.

Rev. Robert Coventrie, minister of Kilspindie from 1727 to 1761; John Cranstoun, minister of Ancrum (born 1664, died 1748, father of the Church of

Scotland); John Currie, minister of Kinglassie (born 1679, died 1765); John
Drummond, minister of Crieff (born 1676, died 1754); Andrew Eliot, minister of
Auchtertool (born 1674, died 1745); James Farquhar, minister of Nigg, Aberdeenshire (born 1665, died 1756); John Forbes, laird of Pitnacadel, minister of
Deer (born 1687, died 1769); George Freer, laird of Eassindie, minister of
Lethendy from 1698 to 1750; John Gib, minister of Cleish (born 1667, died
1741); John Gow, minister of Cargill (born 1680, died 1742); William Haly,
minister of Muthill (born 1677, died 1754); Walter Hart, minister of Bonkle
from 1706 to 1761; James Innes, minister of Merton from 1718 to 1767;
James Ker, minister of Dun from 1701 to 1752; Robert Laing, minister of
Newburgh (died 1749); Lauchlan M'Intosh, laird of Dalmunzie and Dalreoch,
minister of Errol (born 1690, died 1744), moderator of the General Assembly
of 1736; George Meik, minister of Redgorton (born 1678, died 1756); John
Row, minister of Navar and Lethnot (born 1676, died 1745), signed the Rev.
John Willison's "Fair and Impartial Testimony" in 1744; David Stevenson,
minister of Glendevon (born 1689, died 1751). Here ends a brief account of
the ministers who signed the Representation to the General Assembly of the
Church of Scotland in 1732. The Assembly refused even to receive it.

When the Town Council of Perth founded the Third Charge, they took the
stipend out of the rent of some hospital lands. This was unknown to Mr Wilson, but as soon as he heard of it he refused to receive the money. The consequence was, that the Town Council surrendered the rents to the hospital, by a
decision of the Court of Session, affirmed by the House of Lords. But the judge
in the Scotch court being struck with the disinterestedness of Mr Wilson in
being the first objector, suggested a scheme of assessment which was adopted.
However, on a vacancy occurring in the Second Charge, the Town Council "presented Mr William Wilson to the second minister's stipend" (Minute dated 22nd
October 1733). On the 6th December of that year he joined the Associate
Presbytery; but it was not till the first Sabbath after the General Assembly of
1740 that, on the ground that he had been deposed from the ministry, he was
banished from the pulpit of the West Church. He had begun to preach in the
open air within the Glovers' Yard (by permission of that corporation) in the year
1737; he was permitted "to preach the Gosspell there when it is not his turne
to preach in the church." To that yard he retired, as his only place of worship,
in May 1740, until a church was built for him. He continued, in the service
of the people, to be practically "the third minister." A new minister had been
appointed to "the second charge" in 1737; but after Mr Wilson's final separation the Town Council of Perth declared that there was no need of a third
minister; and accordingly the Court of Session decided that there was no
vacancy with which the Presbytery could concern itself, "the third minister
being now suppressed."

Mr Wilson's exclusion from the Church of Scotland's pulpit, to which he publicly demanded admission, occasioned some official heat and some popular murmurs. An old woman was in his domestic service, the very girl who had conveyed food to his father on the Mearns Moor. Mr Wilson, when leaving his house on that eventful Sabbath forenoon, was thus accosted by her:—"Tak tent, Mr William, tak tent what ye're doing; for I fear, if things gang on this way, I'll get ye're meat to carry to the muir, as I did ye're guid father's before ye."

The varied labours of this admirable minister were too much for his bodily strength. His Presbytery having received about seventy applications "for supply of sermon" during the years 1737-8, resolved to form a Divinity Class, and he was elected Professor; and it was necessary, according to academic usage, that he should lecture in Latin. He had also to labour as an author. Preaching in the open air told severely on his health. He died on the 14th November 1741,[1] in his fifty-first year.

Tradition has called Mr Wilson "the Tongue of the Associate Presbytery;" and some have interpreted this as a testimony to the superiority of his pulpit eloquence, even to that of the Erskines. But his sermons permit no such claim. He was *the Tongue*, as the author of the standard book on the principles, of his Presbytery. The book was published in 1739, and a continuation in 1741, and is entitled "A Defence of the Reformation Principles of the Church of Scotland." It contains the following paragraph:—"If the acts and deeds of the several assemblies, 1720 and 1722, with respect to some propositions contained in the book called 'The Marrow of Modern Divinity,' as also with respect to the representation of twelve ministers, are duly and seriously considered, it may be found that a deep wound has been given by the present Judicatories to the Reformation Testimony—as it has been stated against the Church of Rome—for the doctrine of justification and eternal salvation, by the free grace of God, through the imputed righteousness of our Lord Jesus" (page 461). Brown of Haddington said that Mr Wilson preached "that marrow of the Gospel, MY GOD."

The following is a list of Mr Wilson's printed sermons:—

1. The watchman's duty and desire, or the prayer of faithful ministers for the Lord's beauty on His church, and success in their work. On Ps. xc. 17. A Sermon at the opening of the Synod of Perth and Stirling, 1727.

2. The Father's promise to the Son, a clear bow in the darkest cloud; or, the spiritual seed of Christ preserved in all ages. Several Sermons on Ps. lxxxix. 29, preached at Perth in the years 1729 and 1730.

3. Steadfastness in the faith recommended. A Sermon on 1 Cor. xvi. 13, preached at Perth, 22nd July 1733.

---

[1] EXTRACT from the manuscript Family Register of Rev. James Fisher: "Our two children, Margaret and James, were born in Perth, Saturday, Oct. 31, at three in the morning. They were baptized next day, being Sabbath, November 1, by Mr William Wilson, minister at Perth, which was the last piece of public ministerial work performed by that eminent servant of Jesus Christ. He died Nov. 14, 1741."

4. The blessedness lost in the first Adam, to be found in Christ the second Adam. The substance of some Sermons on Ps. lxxii. 17.

5. The Church's extremity, Christ's opportunity. On Micah iv. 10, And thou shalt go even to Babylon, there thou shalt be delivered. Preached at Abernethy sacrament, 17th July 1738.

6. The Lamb's retinue attending Him whithersoever He goeth. The substance of two Sermons on Rev. xiv. 4, preached at Orwell, 6th August 1738.

7. The day of a sinner's believing in Christ—a most remarkable day. A Sermon on Song iii. 11, preached in the New Church of Perth, Sept. 20, 1741, "Edinburgh, printed for and sold by David Duncan, at his House in the Grass-Market, opposite to the Corn-Market, second Door up the Timber-ravel'd Fore-Stair.   MDCCXLII."

Dr Eadie gives the following specimen of Mr Wilson's Gospel preaching. It is from a sermon preached in the open air on a communion Monday:—"There are a vast number gathered together here, and (I am afraid) a great many strangers to Christ, the worthy Lamb. O Sirs, ye come to sacraments, ye come to a communion table, ye come to sermons, but ye never come to Christ, the Lamb of God. O Sirs, we tell you, the Lamb this day invites you to come to Him—to come and follow Him. This day you are called and invited in the word of the Gospel, *Whosoever will, let him come and take the water of life freely* (Rev. xxii. 17). What shall I say?—Does the Lamb invite you, and will you not come? O will you not come, upon His invitation and call? What should hinder your compliance with the Lamb's call? What though you have been bearing arms against Him all your days to this very moment? yet I say unto you there is room in the Lamb for you, room in the grace of the Lamb for you, room in the heart of the Lamb for you, and you are by the Lamb invited this day to come in. Are you a poor graceless sinner? Why, then, I tell you, there is room in His grace for you, there are inexhaustible treasures of grace in Him, and these inexhaustible treasures of grace are just for them that have rebelled and carried arms against the Lamb. O that ye knew and would be persuaded that the Lamb hath received gifts for men for such as did rebel, that the Lord God might dwell among them! (Ps. lxviii. 18)."

In his last sermon he expatiated on (1) *Wisdom*, (2) *Righteousness*, (3) *Sanctification*, and (4) *Redemption*, thus:—

"(1.) Are you fools—ignorant fools—besotted with stupidity? Christ is ready—wisdom is ready for you—God hath made Him wisdom. There is light in Him—the light of knowledge is in Him; He is the light of the world, and He is just that light given for light and sight to the blinded Gentiles. O Sirs, come and behold Him.

"(2.) Are you guilty? Righteousness is ready for you—Christ is made of God unto us righteousness. He hath brought in an everlasting righteousness, and this—being imputed unto you put on your score, and reckoned on your account—will lay a foundation of an indefeasible title unto eternal life and happiness. Is Christ made of God unto us righteousness? then, to be sure, there is a sufficient righteousness in Him for you that are guilty, for you that are hell-deserving.

"(3). Are you destitute of the image of God?—are you unholy and polluted?—are you carried down the stream by the power and prevalency of sin?—are you led captive by your lusts? O, sanctification is ready for you. Christ is made sanctification. O sirs, come and behold Him.

"(4.) Are you in bonds and fetters? And indeed many of you are in bonds, the bonds of unbelief, the bonds and fetters of spiritual death and carnality. *Christ is made of God unto us redemption*—redemption from every spiritual evil and plague we are under. And, indeed, what are you by nature?—a mass of sin and guilt. If you have seen yourselves, you have been ready to say, I have a heart as black as hell. But, let your hearts be never so black, there is relief in the Lord Jesus Christ for you."

REV. JOHN WITHERSPOON, D.D., LL.D.

THE father of this great and good man was Rev. James Witherspoon, M.A., who was minister of Yester, in the Presbytery of Haddington, from 1719 to 1759, and one of his Majesty's chaplains for Scotland, who married, 21st October 1720, Anne, daughter of Rev. David Walker, minister of Temple. John Witherspoon was born in the manse of Yester 5th February 1722, and his school education was obtained in the grammar-school of Haddington. He was M.A. of the University of Edinburgh, and was licensed as a preacher 6th September 1743. He was ordained as minister of Beith, in Ayrshire, on 11th April 1745. In the course of this year the Rebellion broke out, and during 1745-6 he was a volunteer officer and a prisoner in the hands of the rebels, but he escaped from the Castle of Doune, and was received with enthusiasm on his return to Beith manse. His ardent patriotism was a part of his zealous piety.

In the year 1753 his zeal kindled into holy concern and indignation at the conduct of the leaders of the Church in prosecuting and deposing faithful ministers. He wrote and printed his famous satire, "Ecclesiastical Characteristics," as his contribution to the exposure and discomfiture of worldly churchmen. This publication, which was his first, was anonymous. He gave his name to his next piece, which was "An Essay on the connection between the Doctrine of Justification by the Imputed Righteousness of Christ, and Holiness of Life, with some reflections upon the reception which that doctrine hath generally met with in the world," Glasgow, 1756. He addressed it to the Rev. James Hervey, M.A., Rector of Weston-Favell, to whom he said, "You, Sir, are one of those happy few who have been willing to consecrate the finest natural talents to the service of Christ in the Gospel, and are not ashamed of His cross. You have been able to procure attention upon some subjects from many who would hardly have given it to any other writer. This hath made me observe with particular attention the effect of your last performance, 'Theron and Aspasio,' the character given to it, and the objections raised against it. And I have always found that the most specious and plausible objection, and that most frequently made against the doctrine of justification by imputed righteousness, has been in this case (as, indeed, usually before), that it loosens the obligations to practice. This is what I have particularly applied myself to refute in the following essay. And I have addressed it to you as a testimony of my esteem of your excellent and useful writings, as a public declaration of my espousing the same sentiments as to the terms of our acceptance with God. It was also no small inducement to it that thereby it might appear to all that no external distinctions or smaller differences ought to be any hindrance to a cordial esteem and affection among the sincere servants of our common Master."

In 1756 he received a presentation to the Laigh Church of Paisley, with the unanimous concurrence of the congregation. But the Presbytery of Paisley, taking into consideration a report that he was the author of a book [The Ecclesiastical Characteristics] which "is of a very bad tendency to the interests of religion, and injurious to the characters of many ministers of this Church," refused to take steps for enabling the congregation to sign a call, and appointed a committee of inquiry. This resolution was disorderly. The conduct of Mr Witherspoon was under the superintendence of the Presbytery of Irvine. If that Presbytery had considered the book a censurable one, it was their duty, in the first place, to demonstrate its errors and crimes ; and, in the second place, to discover the anonymous author—the former being the question of *relevancy*, and the latter being the personal accusation and proof. The action of the Presbytery of Paisley brought up all parties as appellants to the Provincial Synod. This gave Mr Witherspoon the opportunity of showing the irrelevancy by reviewing and vindicating the book without entering upon the question of its authorship. In the course of his speech he mentioned that the Bishop of London [Sherlock] and the celebrated Warburton had pronounced the book to be a good one, which might be read with profit by the English clergy. (To these testimonials he afterwards added that of the Bishop of Bristol.)

It appears from the records of the Synod of Glasgow and Ayr that there was a long debate at its meeting in October 1756. The appeal was by the Magistrates and Town Council of Paisley. And other appellants were present, representing the Kirk-Session, the Trades, and other seat-holders, and the Rev. James Baine, minister of the High Church, Paisley ("the Swan of the West"),

Mr John Dalrymple, advocate, appeared for the appellants. Mr Witherspoon's speech must have been made by him as a member of Synod during the "long reasoning" which followed the pleadings. The Synod appointed a small committee to converse with the parties, in the hope of bringing about an amicable accommodation. The committee returned with the draft of a motion in which all the parties had acquiesced, and this became the Synod's decision: "The Synod, without limiting the Presbytery's power of inquiring into the *fama clamosa* relating to the 'Ecclesiastical Characteristics,' and without approving or disapproving of the Presbytery's sentence, appoint the Presbytery of Paisley to proceed to the moderation of a call to Mr Witherspoon with all convenient speed according to the rules of the Church."

The call was transacted on 9th December, and on 16th June 1757 Mr Witherspoon became minister of Paisley. In 1763 he published "A Serious Apology for the 'Ecclesiastical Characteristics,'" dedicated to "The nobility and gentry of Scotland, particularly such of them as are elders of the Church and frequently members of the General Assembly." The pamphlet concludes thus:—
"We plead the cause that shall at last prevail. Religion shall rise from its ruins ; and its oppressed state at present should not only excite us to pray, but encourage us to hope, for its speedy revival."

For this result, as the leader of the Evangelical party in the General Assembly, Dr Witherspoon (D.D. of St Andrews in 1764) prayerfully laboured. But the new world summoned him to inaugurate a new era of learning and religion there. In the eighteenth century a minister, removing to America, was regarded as a Foreign Missionary. Zeal and a sense of duty conveyed Dr Witherspoon away from Scotland. He arrived in America in August 1768, and entered upon his work as President of Princeton College, New Jersey. The American Revolution called forth his talents as a statesman ; he was a member of the Congress of the United States from 1776 to 1783. His College was dispersed by the first outbreaks of war, but soon revived. He did not relax his attentions to the College and its pulpit, even when, in 1792, he lost his sight. With abiding mental powers, his body gradually decayed, and he died 15th November 1794, aged seventy-two. For the sake of students in the young Republic, President Witherspoon's writings were all printed ; they fill nine duodecimo volumes.

WITSIUS.

HERMAN WITT was a native of Enckhuysen in Holland (*born* 1636, *died* 1708). His great theological works are in Latin, and thus his surname was translated into Witsius. *Witt* is the same word as our *White*, and, according to the fashion of old and contemporary scholars, he might have handed down his name as Candidus. This he was content to remember as a hint to himself to be candid, and on his seal there was engraved the adverb, CANDIDE; on one occasion he pleasantly addressed Le Clerc, assuring him that he was writing with his accustomed *candour* (quo soleo candore). Witsius was a pastor from 1657 to 1675; he was Professor of Theology from 1675 to 1707, at Franeker, Utrecht, and Leyden successively. The event in his life most important to the British churches was his visit to England in 1687 as chaplain to Dykveldt, the Dutch envoy, when he made the acquaintance of the leading English divines.

This led to the appeal made to him by London ministers some years afterwards, to arbitrate on the differences of doctrine, which I have already described in my chapter on Crisp's "Christ Alone Exalted," and in my abstract of Robert Trail's celebrated "Letter from London." The result was the publication, in 1696, of the book known as *Witsius's Irenicum*, which was received with gratitude and admiration by readers acquainted with Latin. It was not till the year 1807 that an English translation was published, the work of the late Rev. Thomas Bell of Glasgow, a minister of the Relief Synod—(an ecclesiastical body founded by the Rev. Messrs Gillespie of Carnock, and Thomas Boston, junior, of Ettrick, Oxnam, and Jedburgh). The title of the English work, which is a literal translation of the original, is "Conciliatory or Irenical Animadversions (Animadversiones Irenicæ) on the controversies agitated in Britain under the unhappy names of Antinomians and Neonomians."

That Dr Crisp's soundness in the faith should have been so largely vindicated by the erudite and candid Witsius, is all the more gratifying, because, the great preacher of Christ having been for more than half a century in his grave, the vindication had to be carefully obtained from his posthumous volumes alone. On the other hand, the so-called Neonomians escaped censure only through explanations regarding their private evangelical creed, specially furnished to the arbiter—explanations as to which it may be said of the Neonomian party as a whole, that these were not samples of their regular pulpit ministrations. It would have been better to bring glad tidings to sinners, and to bind up the broken-hearted, Sabbath after Sabbath, than to please Witsius with one or two plausible missives.

As to honest difficulties regarding the hope of eternal life, it would be well to remember a sentence by Witsius :—

"We must accurately distinguish between a right to life and the possession of life. *The right to life* must so be assigned to the obedience of Christ, that all the value of our holiness may be entirely excluded. But certainly our works, or rather those which the Spirit of Christ worketh in us and by us, contribute something to *the possession of life.*"—Chap. xvi., § 2; [that is, *heaven must begin upon earth*].

The following is the Dutch arbiter's concluding charge, which, on the whole, is excellent, though the Apostle Paul would have disobeyed one of its counsels at least :—

"Leaving the dangerous precipices of opinion, let us walk upon the easy, plain, and safe way of Scripture, the simplicity of which is vastly preferable to all the sublimity of high-swollen science. Let us not be afraid to say what Scripture says, as if any of its seemingly rugged sayings could be polished by our more convenient phrases. Let us not by rigid, stubborn, and hyperbolical phrases, unsanctioned by the wonted words of the Holy Spirit, sharpen any moderate language which we encounter in the Scriptures. Let us give none occasion to the adversary to speak reproachfully. If we find that some rather incautious expressions have dropped from us, let us candidly and generously cancel, correct, or retract them; and as to expressions that have unwittingly fallen from others, if it appear that they were not from an evil design, let us rather assist them with a favourable interpretation than torture them with a literal reproduction. Let us so assert the free grace of God, that no pretext be given to the licentiousness of the flesh. Let us so extol free justification, that nothing be derogated from sanctification. Let us so inculcate the one righteousness of Christ,—the only righteousness that can stand accepted at the divine tribunal,—that neither the utility nor the reward be denied which Scripture assigns to our piety. In fine, let us so preach the saving grace of the Gospel, that the most holy law may still have its place and its use.

"If on both sides we sincerely do these things, it will follow, through the goodness of God, that instead of the quibbles of obscure controversy, the clear day will begin to shine, and the day-star arise in our hearts. Instead of the briars and brambles of thorny disputation, righteousness and peace will spring out of the earth. Banishing the contentions of unhappy differences, we shall all, as with one voice, celebrate the glorious grace of God in Christ, and shall, with united strength, eagerly adorn the chaste bride, the Lamb's wife, with the golden chain of Christian virtues. With which benefit, through the unsearchable riches of His free grace, may we be graciously honoured by the blessed God, the only potentate, the King of kings and Lord of lords, who only hath immortality, dwelling in light inaccessible, whom no man hath seen or can see, to whom be honour and power everlasting. Amen.

"So I wrote and warmly urged at Utrecht on the 8th of the Kalends of March 1696, and again at Leyden 1699."

PASTOR ALBERT WOLTERS.

ALBRECHT WOLTERS, pastor of Bonn, the picturesque university seat on the Rhine, deserves our gratitude for having given to the world a reprint of *the first edition* of the Heidelberg Catechism, accompanied with a useful history of the text, and with other biographical and illustrative matter. The size of the original catechism has been preserved, and a woodcut facsimile of the title-page is prefixed. The catechism itself is reproduced page by page, and line by line, in as exact facsimile as modern types will admit of. The words of the title-page are, " Catechismus oder Christlicher Underricht wie der in Kirchen und Schulen der Churfürstlichen Pfalz getrieben wirdt. Gedruckt in der Churfürstlichen Stad Heydelberg, durch Johannem Mayer, 1563." The Scripture references on the margins of the catechism give book and chapter, but not verse.

In 1562, when the catechism was still in manuscript, and immediately after its approbation and sanction by the Heidelberg Synod of December, a Lutheran dissentient wrote an attack upon it. In 1867 this Lutheran manuscript, which had just been discovered, was printed by Pastor Wolters. The unique copy of the catechism was reprinted by him in 1864. Its existence had been known, and it had been traced in its migrations through several libraries before the tercentenary of the Heidelberg Catechism in 1863. But it had not been available for publication in the tercentenary volume. Pastor Wolters was, soon after the year 1864, translated to Halle.

ADDITIONAL MEMOIRS.

MELCHIOR ADAM, PH.M.

OF Melchior Adam, to whom all lovers of biography and history owe so much, no regular biography has appeared. Romanists have not requited the impartiality which he meted out to them. Professor Peter Lorimer, of London, has done him justice in an article in the "Imperial Cyclopedia of Biography," which I here abridge.

Melchior Adam was a native of Grothau, in Silesia, born in the last quarter of the sixteenth century. He was educated, at the expense of a nobleman, at the Protestant gymnasium of Brieg, where he attended for eight years. As a member of the Evangelical Reformed Church, he went to the University of Heidelberg, and studied theology there from 1598 to 1601. He was prize poet, and took the degree of Master of Philosophy. He officiated as co-rector of the Gymnasium of Heidelberg from 1606 to 1613, when he succeeded to the rectorship of the gymnasium and to a chair in the University. It is said that latterly he was parish pastor of Heppenheim. His life was shortened by natural delicacy and by excessive study. He died in 1622.

Melchior Adam's great work was his "Lives of German Philosophers, Lawyers, Physicians, and Theologians," written in Latin. His zeal in collecting materials was such that he possessed upwards of sixty large volumes of funeral sermons, eloges, programmes, &c., in manuscript and in print. All his theologians (including twenty foreigners) were Protestants, but he showed no sectarian partiality, and did full justice to his Lutheran heroes. And in the other three series of lives he was equally fair to Roman Catholic literati. He omitted no names except from a want of materials; even *his* powers as a collector being not unlimited.

REV. JAMES ANDERSON.

THE Rev. James Anderson was born at Kirriemuir, in Forfarshire, in 1807, and was educated at Marischal College, Aberdeen, and at the Theological Hall of the

Original Secession Synod in Edinburgh, presided over by Professor Paxton. He was for some years a minister of his Synod in his native town, but owing to an affection of the chest, he resigned his charge. He settled in Edinburgh, and devoted himself to biographical literature. He first appeared as an author with distinguished literary partners, viz. Dr M'Crie, Hugh Miller, Dr Fleming, and Professor J. H. Balfour. Their joint work, the preface to which was dated *December* 1847, was entitled, "The Bass Rock," and Mr Anderson's share consisted of lives of "The Martyrs of the Bass." In 1850 he brought out his most celebrated book, "The Ladies of the Covenant," containing memoirs of female worthies of Scotland. In 1852, in consequence of an ecclesiastical union, Mr Anderson became an Emeritus minister of the Free Church of Scotland. His other works were, "The Ladies of the Reformation," *two series* (1854, &c.), and "Memorable Women in Puritan Times," two volumes, (1862). He died on 15th September 1875.

REV. JOHN ANDERSON.

THE father of this scholarly and beloved man was Andrew Anderson, a Renfrewshire miner. John, the second son in the miner's family, born in 1804, was educated for the ministry in the parish school of Eastwood, the University of Glasgow, and the Divinity Hall at Perth, presided over by Dr William Taylor. He became the first Presbyterian minister in the rising village of Helensburgh (now, partly owing to his popularity, a town) in 1827. The ecclesiastical body to which he belonged was a good old dissenting one, denominated the Associate Burgher Synod, which, under the leadership of the Rev. Dr Michael Willis, was incorporated in the Church of Scotland in 1839. Believing that Ebenezer and Ralph Erskine would have regarded the General Assemblies of that time as "free, faithful, and reforming," Mr Anderson heartily agreed to become a minister of the Established Church. When the law-courts by decisive blows disabled the succeeding General Assemblies of the Establishment, Mr Anderson became a minister of the Free Church of Scotland as organised in 1843. He died at Helensburgh on 10th January 1867 in his sixty-third year.

The name of "Anderson of Helensburgh" had become celebrated in authorship. John Anderson had a vein of poetry which gracefully pervades his prose writings. In 1839 he produced a tale of the Covenanting times, entitled, "Patrick Wellwood"; in 1841, a book for the young, "Precept and Example"; in 1843, "The Footsteps of the Flock" (two editions); in 1845, "Lays and Laments for Israel" (original and selected), with introductory essay; in 1846, "Luther's Spiritual Songs" (translated); in 1848, "Chronicles of the Kirk"; in 1850, "Pencillings in Palestine"; superseded in 1852 by "Wanderings in the Land of Israel"; and in 1855, by "Bible Light from Bible Lands." His travels in the East resulted in the publication of a larger work of permanent value, entitled, "The Life of Christ from the Cradle to the Cross," the preface of which was dated December 1869.

Mr Spurgeon, in his London Tabernacle, took the first opportunity of paying a tribute to Mr Anderson's memory. He said : "During nearly all the term of my ministry in London I have had the privilege of knowing a dear friend in Christ Jesus, to whom my heart has been greatly knit—one of the noblest and happiest of the sons of men. Yet it was not bodily vigour which made him so uniformly joyous; for, as long as I have known him, he has been of very weakly constitution, so that, as often as the wintry months came on, he had to wend his way to Egypt, Madeira, or South America, there to pass through the winter in banishment, and return to his ministry as soon as the season allowed. A loving heart and a large mind were blended in him ; he was always making friends, and (I should say) never lost one. He was deeply interested in the work here, and was much at home in the midst of this great assembly ; for our songs and praises, which he compared to the noise of many waters, were sweet to his ear. Now it pleased the Lord but a day or two ago that he should fall asleep. He thought that perhaps he could labour through this winter, and his soul was warmed with holy zeal to stay with his people if he could, and preach the gospel which he loved so well. That zeal has cost his life. He wrote me one or two sweet letters on his dying bed ; and when at last he closed his eyes, he uttered for his last testimony words so like my own John Anderson, that I am sure nobody could have invented them. His last words were, *All right !* Yes—that is how a Christian man can live, and how he can die. 'It is all right (saith he), it is well with me. It is right here ; I have done my work and God accepts it. It is right up there ; Christ has finished His work on my account.' . . . All right is it now, and all right it shall be, *with us also,* if we are depending upon the finished work of the Well-Beloved."

NOTE.

Mr John Oatt, of Glasgow, whose memoir I have abridged, does not mention "Hymns from the Land of Luther," *first series,* which I have hitherto regarded as a series of translations by Rev. John Anderson, of Helensburgh ; the second, third, and fourth series being by anonymous poetical partners. As the complete collection is before me, I cannot resist quoting a stanza from *page* 172 :—

> Hallelujah ! I believe !
> Now no longer on my soul
> All the debt of sin is lying;
> One great Friend has paid the whole.
> Ice-bound fields of legal labour
> I have left with all their toil,
> While the fruits of love are growing
> From a new and genial soil.

Rev. JAMES BANNATINE.

"AN Essay on Gospel and Legal Preaching" was the title of a crafty pamphlet fired off at the Marrow-men, in the same spirit as Erasmus challenged Luther, by publishing a treatise on the Freedom of the Will. The author with some eloquence and fervour discoursed on Gospel and Law, with affected impartiality, but with a vein of most unfair insinuation against Mr Hog of Carnock and his friends. The aim of his pamphlet was to disparage Gospel preachers, and to throw a shield round those who neglected to preach the Gospel, by almost disowning that there is such a thing as legalism. The pamphlet was anonymous, and Mr Brown of Whitburn, and others, though professing to know, do not say, who the author was. I have found a list of pamphlets in the handwriting of that period with this item: "An Essay upon Gospel and Legal Preaching, by Mr Ballantine, minister att Edr., anno 1723." That the author was a minister, popularly known as "Mr Ballantine," appears from Riccaltoun's reply. Among the Errata is the following in capital letters, "page 101. For Balentinus read Valentinus." On turning to the page, I find this sentence, "Tertullian tells us that Balentinus, the author of the sect of the Valentinians, was so swelled with the conceit of his merit that it made him think of being made a bishop. I do not think our Essayer is so very aspiring, &c." The *erratum* seems to have been a jocular device to let the anonymous champion see that he was found out. The tone and style are internal evidence in the same direction, as will afterwards appear. [*See* RICCALTOUN.]

His name was James Bannatine. He first appears as tutor in the family of a Scotch Judge, Lord Arniston. While thus employed, he was licensed as a preacher by the Presbytery of Dalkeith, 26th October 1703, being then in his 30th year. On 5th March 1707, he received a call to the Church of Whittingham, in the Presbytery of Dunbar, and was ordained 19th June. On 30th June 1714, he was translated to the senior Colleagueship of Trinity College Church, Edinburgh. Although not advanced to a Bishop's see or to a Professor's chair, he was rewarded for appreciated services, by elevation to the Moderatorship of the General Assembly in 1739, being preferred to two other candidates, Rev. John Willison of Dundee, and Rev. James Naismyth of Dalmeny. I have not seen his pamphlet published in 1737,—" Mistakes about religion amongst the causes of our defection from the Spirit of the Gospel." It is said to be written in a faultless style; and probably it contained insinuations against the seceding brethren. I conjecture this from the tone of his closing address as Moderator—the insinuations in which address came with a bad grace from the majority of unevangelical ministers whose mouth-piece he was. Alluding to the seceders, he said, "When we behold others insisting so much on their *Act and Testimony*, let us insist upon the testimony of Jesus Christ, the glorious Gospel of God our Saviour."

In 1745 he and Mr Maxwell [see MAXWELL] were candidates for the Moderatorship, but Principal Wishart was elected. In 1748 Mr Bannatine's daughter, Catherine, "a woman of great good sense and spirit," was married to the famed Hugh Blair, D.D., described as "her cousin." Mackenzie, in his "Life of Home," speaks of an Edinburgh clergyman of the name of "Ballantine" as one of the moderate party, and an associate of Home, Alexander Carlyle, Robertson, &c. If Mr Bannatine be meant, he must have been admitted into such society as an admired veteran of the party. He died on 10th April 1756, in his 82nd year. He left two sons—Rev. Hugh Bannatine, minister of Dirleton; and Rev. George Bannatine, minister of the West Church, Glasgow (afterwards St George's), who both died in 1769, and were eulogised by Alexander Carlyle.

NOTE.

Dr Scott attributes the *Essay on Gospel and Legal Preaching* to Bannatine's colleague, George Logan. But this is a mistake, arising from mixing up colleagues. Bannatine came to Edinburgh in 1714; Logan not till 1732. The "Essay" was written by a "minister of good abilities, with common consent of the leading clergy," [says Brown, pp. 24]; it was, in all probability, concocted in Edinburgh, in 1722-23. The style was flowing and sometimes eloquent—quite different from the style of George Logan, the lumbering antagonist of Thomas Ruddiman.

REV. JOHN BROWN [OF WHITBURN].[1]

THE Rev. John Brown of Haddington had two sons in the Christian ministry, John and Ebenezer. John, the eldest, was born in Haddington, 24th July 1754. He was educated in the University of Edinburgh, and in the Divinity Hall of the Associate Synod, and was licensed by the Associate Presbytery of Edinburgh, 21st May 1776. He was ordained as its minister at Whitburn, in Linlithgowshire, on 22nd May 1777, and continued there until his death on 10th February 1832. He was the father of John Brown, D.D., of Edinburgh, whose association with

[1] See the Memoir of Rev. J. Brown, by Rev. David Smith of Biggar, prefixed to "Letters on Sanctification."

him in the preparation of " Letters on Sanctification," has already been described (see HERVEY.)

To Brown of Whitburn I am specially indebted for his doctrinal and biographical compilation on *The Marrow*, which is entitled, " Gospel Truth accurately stated and illustrated," 1st edition, 1817 ; 2nd edition, 1831. This is quoted with implicit reliance by Dr Hew Scott, in his " Fasti Ecclesiæ Scoticanæ." Mr Brown's letter to his son in 1806, on his ordination over the Associate Church at Biggar, contains the principles of his own ministry,—" Be deeply concerned about your own soul. This will fill you with concern for others. Read the Word of God much, and be frequent in secret prayer. Be more [*more than you now are?*] acquainted with evangelical and practical divinity, such as Ebenezer Erskine's, Dr Owen's, Trail's, &c. You cannot preach long without laying in from these stores. Also, consult and be acquainted with your grandfather's works. Besides what you have, or can get from some of your people, I shall send you divinity books. Dress as neatly as you please in sermons, but let the matter be always solid and savoury. Be kind and affable to all. Be diligent among the young."

This faithful father and pastor was exemplary, not only in congregational work, but also in deeds and undertakings, animated by a world-wide spiritual philanthropy, the principles and theories of which were explained in a manual, entitled, " Means of doing Good: proposed and exemplified, in several Letters to a friend, by John Brown, Minister of the Gospel, Whitburn," Edinburgh, 1820.

He may be said to have died in harness ; " he had been confined to bed only ten days, and spent only three silent Sabbaths," when, on the 10th February 1832, he breathed his last. As to the solemn experience of dying, his principle had been expressed by Robert Trail (in the sermons on the Throne of Grace), in these beautiful words :—" To shut the eyes and give the hand to Christ—and to quiet the mind by trusting our Guide in this last step—is a mighty blessing."

The following is the beginning of Letter VI. of his " Letters on Sanctification," which was written by the author alone :—" My dear friend, I earnestly wish you to rejoice in holiness as a great and unspeakable privilege. This is the Scriptural view of it; and, under this conviction, I cordially agree with a judicious and evangelical divine (William Arnot of Kennoway) in the following sentiments :—' When the exercise of grace in the believer, and good works performed by him, are confined to the list of his duties and virtues—and not considered in the first place as his gracious privileges, and beginnings of eternal life within him—things obtain not their proper place in the system of grace. Grace and good works in the believer are no less than the Holy Spirit working in him both to will and do God's good pleasure. Therefore the exercise of grace and good works in the believer, instead of entitling him to eternal rewards, are a part of the eternal crown and reward, put in his possession while yet in the body.'

"At the same time we are not to forget that holiness is a duty, and this always supposes a law—the law of God. In the law there is both direction and obligation.

"There is a direction, and so it is called a light and a lamp. In this view God deals with us as reasonable creatures.

"It also has in it an obligation, as an exhibition of the Divine authority. A regard to this constitutes duty—a disregard to it, sin. Let us always remember that the law shews us our duty and binds us to it."

The opening of the First Letter is an example of Mr Brown's writing as embellished in Herveian style by his son:—"It is with real satisfaction, my dear Theron, that I sit down to pursue, by epistolary communication, those subjects which have formed the principal theme of so many delightful, and, I trust, not altogether useless, conversations. From the library window I perceive those fields over which we saw the sower scattering the precious seed, covered with rich verdure, and giving the promise of an abundant harvest. May I not indulge the hope that the still more precious seed of the word, sown in your heart by the great Husbandman through my humble endeavours, is already springing up in holiness and consolation, and will one day ripen into perfection of purity and felicity? The subject before me is peculiarly engaging, nor is it wonderful that I am partial to it. It is the foundation of all my present comfort, and all my hopes for eternity; and earnestly desiring, as I do, the happiness of my friend, I know no better method of promoting it than by endeavouring to build him up, ON THE MOST HOLY FAITH."

PROFESSOR WILLIAM DUNLOP.

Mr Brown ("Gospel Truth," p. 23) informs us that "Professor Dunlop published *Strictures on the Marrow Doctrine*, in his account of the Rev. W. Guthrie of Fenwick, and in his Preface to his Collection of Confessions of Faith." But this lamented young Professor does not appear to have taken any part in ecclesiastical proceedings against Mr Hog, &c. He died 29th October 1720, aged twenty-eight. William Dunlop was the son of a great covenanter, Principal Dunlop, and was born in Glasgow in 1692. He was licensed as a preacher in 1714, and in 1716 he became Professor of Church History in Edinburgh University, having been presented to the chair by the king, on the recommendation of Principal Wishart. His Sermons, in two volumes, are much prized. Here is an extract:—

"The principal act of faith is a relying on the Redeemer alone for salvation —the resting and trusting in Him for eternal life. Such expressions, however vilified and ridiculed by some who would impose upon the world a new scheme of divinity, and turn Christianity into refined heathenism or a bare morality, are the dialect of the Scriptures."—Vol. ii, p. 239.

The following is an interesting family group:—

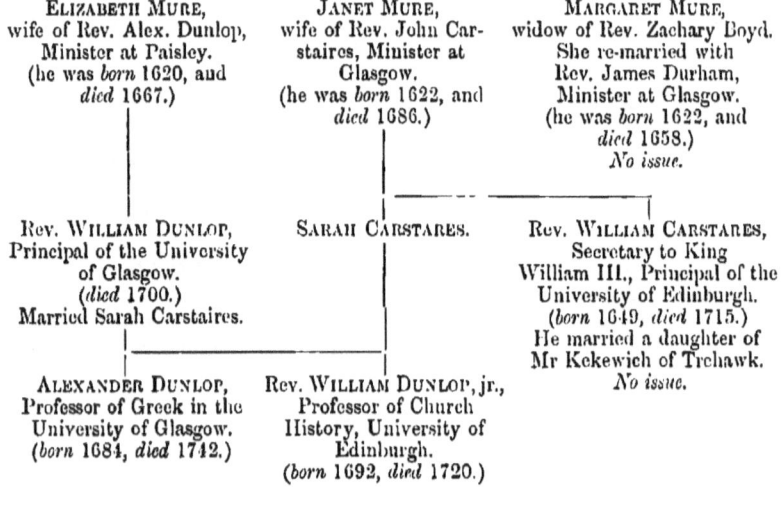

THREE SISTERS of WILLIAM MURE of Glanderson.

ELIZABETH MURE,
wife of Rev. Alex. Dunlop,
Minister at Paisley.
(he was born 1620, and
died 1667.)

JANET MURE,
wife of Rev. John Carstaires, Minister at
Glasgow.
(he was born 1622, and
died 1686.)

MARGARET MURE,
widow of Rev. Zachary Boyd.
She re-married with
Rev. James Durham,
Minister at Glasgow.
(he was born 1622, and
died 1658.)
No issue.

Rev. WILLIAM DUNLOP,
Principal of the University
of Glasgow.
(*died* 1700.)
Married Sarah Carstaires.

SARAH CARSTAIRES.

Rev. WILLIAM CARSTARES,
Secretary to King
William III., Principal of the
University of Edinburgh.
(*born* 1649, *died* 1715.)
He married a daughter of
Mr Kekewich of Trehawk.
No issue.

ALEXANDER DUNLOP,
Professor of Greek in the
University of Glasgow.
(*born* 1684, *died* 1742.)

Rev. WILLIAM DUNLOP, jr.,
Professor of Church
History, University of
Edinburgh.
(*born* 1692, *died* 1720.)

PRINCIPAL HADOW.

JAMES HADOW was a native of Douglas, in Lanarkshire. He is first met with as minister of Cupar, second charge, where he was settled in 1692 in succession to the episcopal "curate" of the past persecuting era. He was promoted to the first charge on 30th October 1694, but left Cupar for the chair of divinity in St Mary's College in St Andrews, on 5th April 1699. In the minutes of the college he is called Principal Hadow for the first time in the year 1708. The office of Principal of St Mary's College is a piece of Crown patronage. He was also Rector of the College from 1725 to 1737. The *Scots Magazine* gives the date of his death 4th May 1747.

He was generally respected, and was an excellent professor of Systematic Theology; but he seems to have failed to apprehend the scriptural method of preaching the gospel to the poor and to sinners. It is strange that men of the world are content to dream that Trail and Boston and the Marrow-men were rigid Calvinists, and were censured as such. The fact is they were Calvinists like Calvin; but they did not admit that a sinner must become a theologian before he can be a believer in Jesus. Principal Hadow, unlike Calvin, was the type of what is called an ultra-Calvinist, who seems to hold that an enquirer must have an intelligent acquaintance with the literature of the doctrine of Particular Redemption, before he can lay hold of the hope set before us and possess this anchor of the soul. Though the great champion of theological strictness, he was content to carry out his views by means of the votes of non-theological and anti-theological members of Church courts. His ministerial and professional life having been always within the bounds of the Synod of Fife, that Synod was specially severe on Marrow-men. Principal Hadow published a sermon preached before the Synod at St Andrews on 7th April 1719, entitled, "The Record of God and Duty of Faith therein required;" dedicated "To the Right Reverend the Moderator, and the Reverend and Worthy the Ministers and Elders of the Synod of Fife." Having a variegated but compact majority on his side, he relied more upon the dignity and power of the church, and the necessity of uniformity and subordination, than upon scriptural proofs. His sermon is a creditable performance, which is more than can be said of his other work, "A Detection of the Antinomianism of the Marrow of Modern Divinity." Riccaltoun, who styled the author of the alleged "Detection" a *politick disputant*, severely condemned its personalities. Any reader of Hadow's works may easily see that it is to him, rather than to the Marrow-men, that imputations of rigidity and uncharitableness apply. Yet both his pieces are valuable as having called out valuable statements of gospel grace and truth in reply to them; while they themselves, if read in the light of the comments of the other side, may be profitably consulted as containing able representations of some precious truths as to which both sides were at one.

REV. HUGH MAXWELL, M.A.

Mr Maxwell was the author of a volume, the appendix to which contains an unfavourable review of "The Marrow of Modern Divinity," and also of the

Catechism by Mr Hamilton of Airth. As the anti-Marrow men relied more upon votes than arguments, it is interesting to chronicle a book on their side. Whether the author claimed relationship to the family of Maxwell of Pollock, I know not, but his volume is dedicated thus:—" To the Honourable Sir John Maxwel of Pollock, one of the Right Honourable the Lords of Council and Session, a sincere lover of the orthodox faith which is after godliness, a true son of the Church of Scotland, and her stedfast friend in all times and of the Protestant succession by law established, a candid judge of learning, and a worthy pattern of holiness and virtue. In testimony of the greatest esteem, this Sermon with the Appendix and the Remarks upon the Marrow of Modern Divinity, published at the desire of several ministers, is humbly dedicated. And with earnest prayer for the increase of all grace and happiness unto his person and honourable family, and in particular for his continuance in health, for the lasting advantage of Church and State, is offered by his Lordship's most obedient and much obliged servant, HUGH MAXWEL." The title-page, which is without his name, runs as follows :—" The Beauty and Purity of the Gospel Church, held forth in a Sermon on Psalm xciii. 5 before the Synod of Angus and Mearns at Brechin, April 19, 1720, somewhat enlarged since, with an Appendix, and with some remarks and reflections upon the doctrines contained in the *Marrow of Modern Divinity*. Edinburgh, printed for the Author, Anno Dom. MDCCXXI." Sermon, 147 pp.; Appendix, 91 pp.; Remarks, 48 pp.

Hugh Maxwell was M.A. of the University of St Andrews, 2d March 1702, and licensed in the same year as a preacher (July 1) by the united Presbytery of Dundee, Meigle, and Forfar. He was minister of Tealing from 1703 to 1717, minister of Forfar from 1717 to 1744, and minister of Strathmartin from 1744 till his death 30th January 1751, aged about sixty-nine. His daughter was married to Rev. William Moncrief, minister of Kinnell, Forfarshire, and was the mother of the Rev. David Moncrief, M.A., minister of Redgorton, Perthshire, from 1763 to 1811.

REV. NATHANIEL MORREN, M.A.

To this accomplished author I feel indebted for his two volumes of " Annals of the General Assembly of the Church of Scotland," with appendixes of biographical sketches, illustrative documents, and notes ; the period is from 1739 to 1766. In 1835 he published vol. i. of " Biblical Theology," which, it is to be regretted, was not continued ; he proceeded no further than " The Rule of faith." He was a good linguist, and translated Rosenmuller's " Biblical Geography." Nathaniel Morren, who claimed good Huguenot descent, was born in Aberdeen 3rd

Feb. 1798, and became M.A. of Marischal College in 1814. He was one of the ministers of Greenock from 1823 to 1843, and died as minister of the first charge of Brechin, 28th March 1847.

REV. HEW SCOTT, D.D.

THE great obligations under which I lie to the magnificent volumes of Scottish Church Annals, entitled *Fasti Ecclesiæ Scoticanæ*, are acknowledged by this brief memoir of the learned and patriotic author. Hew Scott was a native of Haddington, born about 1798. He studied at the Universities of Edinburgh and Aberdeen, and was licensed as a preacher by the Presbytery of Haddington in 1820. He was ordained in 1829 for a foreign charge, but did not enter upon the active duties of the ministerial office until 12th June 1839, when he was inducted to the charge of Anstruther Wester. His talent for research led to his receiving the status of a fellow of the Scottish Antiquarian Society. And in 1867 he received the degree of D.D. from the University of St Andrew's, where he was known as an influential parish minister, and as having made a successful start in the publication of his *Fasti*. The plan of his great work was to arrange, under Synods and Presbyteries and Parishes, all the ministers of the Church of Scotland since the Reformation, giving all ascertainable dates in their respective careers, and every available biographical incident, accompanied with occasional quotation of panegyrics earned by them. His leisure time for nearly fifty years was devoted to this serviceable compilation, not only from printed books, but specially from manuscript records of Presbyteries, Synods, and General Assemblies, and from testamentary and other registers throughout Scotland. This elaborate information is carried on to June 1839. His own memoir, therefore, is not included; but himself, and ministers settled after his own induction, are recorded in lists of names, with dates of inductions. The volumes appeared in the following order:—

Vol. I., part 1. Synod of Lothian and Tweeddale, . . .		1866
,, part 2. Synods of Merse and Teviotdale, Dumfries, and Galloway, ...		1867
Vol. II., part 1. Synod of Glasgow and Ayr, , . .		1868
,, part 2. Synods of Fife, and Perth and Stirling, .		1869
Vol. III., part 1. Synods of Argyll, Glenelg, Moray, Ross, Sutherland and Caithness, Orkney and Zetland,		1870
,, part 2. Synods of Aberdeen, and Angus and Mearns, .		1871

All the parts were published by Mr W. Paterson, 67 Princes Street, Edinburgh.

Dr Scott has done hearty justice to the Marrow-Men. For instance, he says as to Hog of Carnock : "To a vigorous judgment and solid learning, joined to singular piety and tenderness, was added a degree of fortitude, which qualified him, in no common degree, for the maintenance of his opinions. His stand in defence of the doctrines in the Marrow of Modern Divinity was both ingenuous and manly, though keenly opposed by the ecclesiastical politicians of the day;" and as to Ebenezer Erskine, he was "distinguished for straightforward good sense, incorruptible integrity, and dauntless intrepidity."

The date of Dr Scott's death was 12th July 1872. His funeral sermon was preached by Rev. John Millar, his old friend and neighbour, minister of Largoward.

THE END.

INDEX.

I.—TEXTS OF SCRIPTURE.

GENESIS.			I. KINGS.		xxxiii. 22	130	cvi. 5	192
iii. 15	85,	PAGE 237	xix. 11, 12	PAGE 128	xxxiv. 14	159	cviii. 7	163
iv. 16		151			xxxv. 12	179	cx. 3	57, 73
v. 9		224	II. KINGS.		27	156	cxvi. 1	18
22, 24		162	v. 23	371	xl. 2	160	12, 13	222
xxxii. 28		166	vi. 15	201	8	73	16	78
					xli. 1	292	cxviii. 22	251
EXODUS.			II. CHRONICLES.		4	292	cxix. 32	136
xiv. 15		339	xiv. 11	180	11	164	49, 50	223
xv. 6		114			xlii. 2	301	50	145, 382
xvii. 11, 12		165	JOB.		xliii. 3, 4	375	50, 76	223
xx. 1, 2		76	i. 5	179	5	84	165	143, 149
			vi. 10	223	xlvi. 1, 2	302	166	85
LEVITICUS.			xiv. 4	114	l. 15	296	cxxii. 6	156
xvi. 21, 22	108, 371		xv. 11	224	li. 5	114	cxxv. 1	160
			xvi. 2	201	12	15	cxxx. 3, 4	7
NUMBERS.			7	223	lv. 6	161	4	78, 322, 358
xxi. 8, 9		363	xvii. 8, 9	188	lx. 6	163	cxxxviii. 3	18
xxiii. 21		107	xix. 25	331	lxviii. 13	303	8	144
			xxii. 21, 22	6	18	388		
DEUTERONOMY.			xxiii. 10	296	lxxii. 17	388	PROVERBS.	
iv. 1		157	xxxiii. 23, 24	147	lxxiii. 17	180	iv. 18	188
xix. 6-10		335	xxxvi. 8, 9, 10	291	lxxvii. 10	84	ix. 5	114
xxix. 29	21, 66		xlii. 6	302	lxxix. 8	9	xiii. 20	144
xxxii. 6		79			lxxxi. 13-16	73	xv. 8	249
xxxiii. 25	18, 280		PSALMS.		lxxxii. 6	173	xvi. 32	169
			iv. 6	204	lxxxviii. 7	223	xx. 9	114
JUDGES.			ix. 18	215	lxxxix. 29	388	xxiii. 3	262
ix. 9, 13		185	xv. 1-5	152	30-31	108, 296	xxiv. 16	160
xiii. 19		262	xvii. 15	170, 223	xc. 17	388	xxviii. 9	249
23		161	xix. 11	164	xcii. 12-14	184	xxx. 5	381
			xxiv. 7	262	xciv. 13	201		
I. SAMUEL.			xxv. 11	14	ciii. 3, 4	54, 343	SONG OF SOLOMON.	
vii. 12		145	xxvi. 3	85	cv. 15	173	i. 5	375
xiv. 29		48	xxxii. 1, 2	14	cvi. 3	158	ii. 14	161, 303

408 INDEX.

	PAGE		PAGE		PAGE		PAGE
iii. 11	387	xxxi. 33	73	v. 48	333	xvii. 4, 5	179
v. 10	255	xxxii. 27	275	vi. 12	176	10	222
viii. 6	181	l. 20	48, 371	28	113	xviii. 13	248
				vii. 18	148	xix. 6, 8	39
ISAIAH.		**LAMENTATIONS.**		21	158	10	114
i. 18	114, 265, 303	iii. 23	182	viii. 26	319	42	265
iii. 10	397			ix. 13	114	xxi. 28	190
vi. 5	302	**EZEKIEL.**		29	83, 130	xxii. 28-30	223
viii. 13	104	xxxv. 1	265	xi. 28	227, 265	xxiii. 28	300
ix. 6	182	xxxvi. 25	114	28, 29	4	42	97
xxvi. 3	130	26	275	28-30	276	xxiv. 47	95
xxvii. 4	108	26, 27	167	xiii. 12	188	**JOHN.**	
xxviii. 15-17	263			xiv. 31	138		
xxxviii. 19	214	**DANIEL.**		xviii. 8, 9	85	i. 12	44, 264, 352
xl. 31	188	xii. 3	223	11	114	iii. 15	20
xlii. 6	47			xix. 16	71	16	20, 28, 66, 102, 112
xliii. 5	25	**HOSEA.**		xx. 8	159	17	6
24, 25	263	ii. 14	263	15	296	36	264
25	55	19, 20, 23	281	xxii. 19	381	v. 24	12
xlv. 9, 10	296	23	137	37-40	32	25	47
22	20, 264	iii. 5	77, 358	xxiii. 13	379	35	213
17, 22, 24	114	vi. 6	155	27, 28	265	vi. 24	12
xlviii. 17	114	xi. 4	118	xxv. 35, 36	149	28, 29	7, 95, 340
l. 10	18, 138, 139	xiii. 9	114			29	228, 243
li. 1-5	20	xiv. 2	11, 166	**MARK.**		32	251
liii. 6	42, 49	3	154	iv. 26	67	35	44
6-8	28	4	114	26-28	292	37	20, 44, 113, 252
liv. 17	108	5-8	184	28	188	44, 45, 63	20
lv. 1	113, 265			ix. 24	84, 138	47	349
1-3, 7	114	**MICAH.**		xi. 24	83	69	8
6, 7	98	iv. 10		25	178	vii. 37	112, 116
7	220			xvi. 9	371	viii. 32	375
lvii. 17, 18	263	**ZEPHANIAH.**		14	352	46	8
19	154	iii. 16-18	156	15	66, 375	56	238
lix. 1, 2	13			**LUKE.**		ix. 31	151
lxi. 10	372	**HAGGAI.**		i. 38	201	38	9
lxiii. 11, 12	145	ii. 7	190	74, 75	77	x. 10	187
lxiv. 4, 5	222	**ZECHARIAH.**		77-79	5	28	161
lxvi. 10, 11	156	xiii. 1	114	ii. 10	47	xiii. 34	172, 243
JEREMIAH.		xiv. 7	255	25	224, 375	34, 35	17
				iv. 24	11	xiv. 3	191
iii. 12, 14	371	**MALACHI.**		vi. 32-34	250	6	42, 46, 52
10	137	iii. 3	56	45	244	13, 14	151
xiii. 23	114			vii. 47	78	15	73, 77
xvii. 9	114	**MATTHEW.**		viii. 47	177	21	138, 158
xviii. 1, 2, 3	296	i. 21	13	xi. 4	177	21, 23	143
xxiii. 6	51	iii. 7	119	27	158	23	104
29	183	v. 4	3	xii. 15	342	26	130, 224
xxxi. 1, 2	296	16	54, 143	xiv. 23	373	xv. 2	187
20	265	46, 47	250	xv. 20	265		

INDEX.

	PAGE		PAGE		PAGE		PAGE
xv. 5	114	iii. 25	9, 118	viii. 16, 17	136	xvi. 13	166, 388
5, 6	143	27	107	18	296		
8	73	28	290	28 55, 212, 296		**II. CORINTHIANS.**	
14	73, 170	28, 31	50	30	39, 148	i. 3	201
16	97	31	105	33, 34	135	4, 5	382
xvi. 7	382	iv. 1, 2	237	34	182	5	223
8, 9	7	5	43, 48, 96,	37	166, 299	12	143
14	130		113	ix. 15	46	20	201
23, 24	151	11	181	20, 21	296	22	145
31	8	16	231, 239	33	20	24	119
33	80	17	83	x. 3	236	iii. 5	14
xvii. 6	65	20	320	4	76, 330	18	141, 303
9	20	20, 21	8	6-8	215	iv. 17, 18	296
17	144	22-25	230	11	20	v. 5	137, 145
19	375	25	182	14	290	14	39
xix. 35	8	v. 1	39	14, 15	350	14, 19, 20	20
xx. 31	120	1, 2	135	17	229	17	242
		1-5	15, 25	xi. 26, 27	114	20	243
ACTS.		1-5, 11	152	xii. 1 42, 279, 284,		21	50, 235, 298,
i. 21-23	293	3, 4, 5	136		312, 383		349, 372
ii. 37	264	4, 5	138	10	172	vi. 16	284
39	11	6	60	11, 12	16	vii. 1	187
43	228	9	371	xiii. 1	325	4	156
iii. 26	114	10	182	8, 9, 10	171	6	224
iv. 12	72, 264	12	204	xiv. 17	128, 156	6, 7	224
v. 17-41	338	19	231	xv. 4	39	7	382
ix. 20	119	20	96			viii. 1	175
22	188	20, 21	105	**I. CORINTHIANS.**		12	161, 219
31	142	21	222	i. 27-31	81	x. 4, 5	374
x. 34, 35	11	vi. 1	59	30	39, 66, 89,	15	189
43	349	1, 2	96		264, 388	xii. 9	129, 165
xi. 13, 14	11	2-11	219	ii. 1, 2	137	xiii. 5	141, 213
xiii. 38, 39	120	14	106, 167,	2	60, 120, 185	5, 6	68
39	264		218, 244	4, 5	138	8	292
xiv. 1	228	vii. 4	330	12	138		
xv. 9 144, 216, 220		6	105	15, 16	116	**GALATIANS.**	
11	12, 137	7	204	iii. 22	372	i. 4	26
xvi. 31 20, 66, 205		15	161	vi. 9, 10	36	6	292
xvii. 2, 3	120	16-20	156	17	332	7, 8	337
xviii. 27	119	18	13	19, 20	77	ii. 5	278
xx. 23	234	21	223	20	85, 284	20	62, 66, 142,
xxiv. 15	9	24, 25	276	vii. 14	11		309, 338
16	142	viii. 1	160	viii. 3	171	21	65
xxvii. 25	8	1, 5, 9, 14	152	xi. 31	146	iii. 1	306
		1, 34	10	xii. 3	14, 185	2	139, 290
ROMANS.		3	205	xiii. 1	174	10	34, 157
i. 11, 12	382	7, 8, 2	114	13	170, 238	13	72, 182
24	67	14	149	xiv. 22	350	14	171
ii. 13	158	15	333	xv. 3, 4	6	29	144
iii. 20	92	16 137, 111, 158		10	223	iv. 28	144

v. 6	151	**I. THESSALONIANS.**		iii. 5	244	ii. 21	169
22	171		PAGE	8	70, 73	24	145
22, 23	46	i. 4, 5	145	18	54, 144	iii. 2, 9, 10	169
vi. 2	296	5	84, 137			iv. 7	244
10	174	10	119	**HEBREWS.**		v. 13	296
		iii. 13	144	i. 1	249		
		iv. 1	188	3	60, 117	**I. PETER.**	
EPHESIANS.		13	143	iii. 6	4, 10	i. 5	59
i. 6, 7	11	14	382	14	4	6, 7, 8	296
13	146	16	192	iv. 3	4	8	145
14	145	v. 8	244	16	150	13	20
17-23	120	9	343	v. 19	153	16	143
ii. 1	47	23	249	vi. 2	20	ii. 17	174
1-3, 10	114	**II. THESSALONIANS.**		6, 10, 11	223	19	143
3	108	i. 3	189	10	178	iii. 16	144
10	59	ii. 13	144	11	244	v. 10	200
iv. 11, 15	187	16	8	11, 12	15		
15	184	16, 17	19	18	8, 119, 231,	**II. PETER.**	
30	137	17	85		321, 342	i. 3	86
v. 1	158			19	9	4	144, 173
1, 2	170	**I. TIMOTHY.**		vii. 25	182	6, 7	152
6	205	i. 4	231	27	182	7	174
30	235	8	70	viii. 1	117	9	13
vi. 18	165	13	352	10	52, 281	10	148, 157
		15	94, 114, 182,	ix. 14	105	10, 11	16
PHILIPPIANS.			333	x. 19-22	7	iii. 4	190
i. 6	14, 145	16	116	22	20, 137	13	190, 191
11	148	iii. 16	184, 205	25	180	16	228
20, 21	214	vi. 12	163	31	150	17, 18	184
27	375	20	376	xi. 1	25, 237	18	186, 217
ii. 1	5, 375			27	238		
1, 2	200	**II. TIMOTHY.**		xii. 6	55, 330	**I. JOHN.**	
12, 13	86	i. 2	8	7	223	i. 3, 4	119
24	145	7	166	11	296	7	51
iii. 3, 4	146	9	12	14	143	ii. 1	50, 234
5-8	362	12	280, 343	24	51	1, 2	42
13	187	ii. 19	171	28, 29	358	7, 8	172
iv. 4	136	iii. 5	68	xiii. 1	172	12	16
		iv. 8	190, 193	5	215	14	165
				15, 16	154	14, 15	166
COLOSSIANS.		**TITUS.**				17	164
i. 10	189	i. 2	9	**JAMES.**		27	41
13	77, 145	15	114	i. 6	151	iii. 3	9
16, 19, 27-29	122	ii. 10	143	6, 7	137	9	59
27	145	11, 12	42, 57	17	14	14	17, 147
ii. 2	20	11-14	90	25	164	15	104
6, 7	119	14	39, 59, 143,	26	169	18, 19	16
19	184		153	ii. 8	171	18-21	18, 118
iii. 1, 2	39, 192	iii. 3	177	18	143	19	141, 148
13	178	3 7	114	20	148	22, 23	18

INDEX.   411

iii. 23	7, 20, 95, 120	v. 10	340	REVELATION.	xiv. 4		388
24	152	10, 11	137		13		164
iv. 7	171	13	139	i. 6	41, 352	xvii. 14	164
13	152	13-15	18	7	180	xxi. 7	163
14, 16	137	14, 15	343	8	54	xxii. 1	192
17	150			ii. 4	77	17-20	47, 112,
18	104	JUDE.		19	188		114, 388
19	171, 341			iii. 19	55	20	180, 190
21	17, 73	3	165	iv. 9	276		
v. 1	301	12, 13	59	v. 6	300		
4, 5	166	20	401	xii. 11	167		

II.—WRITERS MEMORIALISED.

Adams, T., 157, 163, 187, 191, 197, 199
Alting, H., 39, 148, 197, 201, 311
Ames, W., 170, 198, 203
Bastingius, 74, 197, 206, 210
Bates, W., 78, 122, 197, 206, 322
Bathgate, J., 198, 207, 251, 294
Bonar, J., 198, 208, 385
Boston, T., 39, 64, 65, 69, 77, 97, 99, 101, 109, 133, 177, 180, 183, 198, 210, 217, 229, 241, 282, 283, 301, 304, 373
Bridge, W., 176, 178, 179, 188, 198, 216
Brisbane, J., 149, 198, 217, 282, 288
Brown, J. (Haddington), 3, 89, 113, 183, 198, 221, 289, 387, 399
Brown, J. (Whitburn), 99, 198, 252, 284, 375, 399
Calvin, 37, 71, 198, 224, 252, 264, 278, 318, 367, 403
Cole, T., 198, 226
Colquhoun, J., 133, 142, 156, 181, 184, 190, 198, 209, 229

Coward, W., 114, 198, 231
Crisp, T., 42, 69, 91, 93, 115, 197, 233, 343, 392
Cross, W., 198, 237
Cudworth, W., 20, 85, 198, 240
Davidson, H., 198, 211, 241, 377, 385
De Witte, P., 38, 197, 243
Dwight, T., 198, 248
Erskine, E., 99, 101, 109, 143, 198, 207, 225, 250, 261, 262, 275, 282, 319, 376, 385, 405
Erskine, R., 100, 143, 144, 198, 218, 220, 221, 262, 282, 369, 377, 385
Felltham, O., 197, 255
Fisher, E., 61, 70, 73, 97, 197, 211, 259
Fisher, J., 143, 144, 198, 221, 253, 384, 385, 387
Flavel, J., 77, 92, 156, 182, 197, 264
Frederick III., Elector Palatine, 31, 197, 266
Fuller, A., 140, 172, 192, 198, 271, 273
Gill, J., 17, 42, 80, 98, 149, 153, 154, 164, 171, 172,

180, 193, 197, 234, 272, 283, 344
Gillet, J. F. A., 197, 276
Goodwin, T., 185, 198, 277
Goodwin, T., jun., 197, 278
Guyse, J., 115, 124, 198, 279
Hamilton, A., 198, 218, 280, 385, 404
Hamilton, W., 198, 261, 282, 288
Hervey, J., 85, 109, 198, 240, 283, 389, 401
Hog, J., 97, 99, 198, 208, 251, 285, 314, 332, 369, 373, 380, 405
Hooker, R., 198, 297
Hubbard, J., 115, 198, 298
Hunter, W., 198, 301
Kid, J., 198, 304, 374, 376
Leydekker, M., 197, 285, 305
Luther, 25, 65, 69, 97, 100, 197, 252, 260, 276, 278, 306, 348
Manton, T., 145, 149, 169, 198, 207, 310
Maresius, 197, 204, 311
Marshall, W., 81, 93, 198, 278, 283, 284, 294, 312

Mylius C., 176, 197, 315
Nevin, J. W., 197, 316
Olevianus, 31, 197, 266, 317, 354
Owen, J., 93, 123, 198, 238, 278, 318, 336
Pareus, D., 148, 197, 210, 269, 324, 383
Parry, H., 197, 325, 363, 380
Reynolds, E., 198, 319, 328
Riccaltoun, R., 198, 220, 259, 275, 309, 314, 334, 398
Ridgley, T., 76, 145, 168, 178, 183, 197, 234, 305, 341
Roëll, H., 197, 344
Romaine, W., 168, 169, 198, 283, 345
Sandys, E., 26, 197, 297, 347
Simpson, S., 198, 349
Strackius, T., 197, 353
Trail, R., sen., 198, 354, 360
Trail, R., jun., 93, 100, 198, 226, 319, 344, 356, 400
Tuckney, A., 174, 198, 361
Turner, W., 38, 197, 363
Ursinus, 31, 74, 148, 197, 266, 326, 354, 367
Van der Kemp, 197, 368
Wardlaw, J., 198, 251, 253, 254, 369, 377, 385
Watson, C., 127, 198, 370
Watson, T., 144, 145, 165, 179, 189, 198, 370
Williamson, J., 100, 198, 372
Wilson, G., 101, 198, 211, 241, 304, 374, 375, 385
Wilson, T., 153, 198, 225, 380
Wilson, W., 198, 253, 384, 385
Witherspoon, J., 79, 125, 197, 322, 389
Witsius, H., 42, 197, 274, 283, 391
Wolters, 31, 197, 394

III.—WRITERS QUOTED.

Anderson, James, 198, 234, 395
Anderson, John, 29, 198, 307, 396
Augustin, 158, 316, 383
Bonar, Arch., 209
Caryl, J., 61, 260
Chrysostom, 298, 383
Clark, Sam., 121
Cowper, W., 125
Currie, J., 125, 377, 386
D'Aubigné, J. H. M., 224, 306
Dunlop, W., 198, 401
Gibson, Edmund, 123
Goulburn, E. M., 126
Henry, Matthew, 121
Jennings, J., 12, 116
Justin Martyr, 298
Mather, Increase, 123, 264
Mohn, Wilibert, 38
Moncreiff, Sir H. W., 21
Rainy, Robert, 318
Schaff, P., 40, 197, 316
Scott, Hew, 198, 217, 242, 295, 304, 405
Sibbes, R., 260, 277
Spurgeon, C. H., 235, 397
Stevenson, J., 20
Strype, J., 364
Thelwall, J., 31, 327, 366, 368
Walker, James, 62
Watts, Isaac, 115
Wood, Anthony a, 61, 233, 259, 320, 327, 363
Wood, James, 115

IV.—SURNAMES, &c., FOR STUDENTS OR GENEALOGISTS.

Abercorn, Earl of, 232
Adam, Melchior, 198, 306, 395
Alting, J., 203, 311
Ames, W., jun., 203
Anderson, A., 290
Anglesea, Earl of, 239
Angus, J., 199
Annan, 356
Ap Harry, 326
Areskine (see *Erskine*).
Aristotle, 64, 381
Arminius, J., 225
Arniston, Lord, 398
Arnot, W., 400
Athol, Marquis of, 357
Badger, 200
Bagwell, J., 382
Baine, J., 390
Balderston, 263, 275
Balfour, J. H., 396
Balgay, N., 297
Bannatine, J., 198, 337, 398
Barnes, 326
Baxter, R., 207
Bayle, 263, 311
Beard, T., 270, 307

INDEX. 413

Bell, B., 282
Bell, T., 392
Bellamy, J., 83, 109
Bellarmine, 203, 325
Beza, 264, 318, 319, 367
Birch, 312
Birckman, 366
Blackhall, J., 242, 301
Blackwood, 363
Blair, H., 399
Blanchard, 310
Bland, 347
Bliss, P., 257
Bloome, 200
Bogue and Bennett, 235, 279
Bohemus, M., 246
Bolingbroke, Viscount, 283
Bonar, 209
Boston, M., 213
Boston, T., jun., 213, 392
Bouillon, Duc de, 311
Bourignon, A., 290
Bradshaw, W., 204
Bradwardine, 278
Bragge, 279
Brantius, 353
Brown, 223
Brown, Eb., 222, 263, 399
Brown, J., D.D., 223, 261, 399
Brown, J., M.D., 223
Brown, R., 211, 294
Brown, W., 292
Bruce, A., 289
Bruce, J., 342
Buchan, 263
Buchanan, T., 253
Bullinger, H., 365, 367
Burroughs, J., 260
Cadogan, W. B., 345
Calamy, E., 318, 382
Callander, 347
Campbell, G., 210
Campbell, Sir H., 290
Campbell, J., 338
Candlish, R. S., 19
Carlyle, A., 209, 399
Carmichael, Lord, 287
Carstaires, 402
Cato, 256
Chalmers, J., 290

Chalmers, T., 21
Chambers, R., 254
Chandler, S., 115, 279
Charteris, S., 369
Chauncy, T., 341
Chester, J. L., 236
Cicero, 169, 178
Clarke, Matthew, 232
Clarkson, D., 207, 320
Clemens, Alexandr., 165
Coccejus, 197, 305
Cole, P., 351
Conder, J., 280
Coppenstein, J. A., 353
Couper, D., 370
Coventrie, R., 386
Coward, 232
Cranstoun, J., 386
Crisp, Sir N., 233
Crocius, L., 364
Crosse, R., 327
Crum, 263
Culverwell, 360
Cumming, James, 257
Currier, 209
Dalrymple, J., 390
Dandrige, B., 342
Darling, 213
Deans, A., 334
De Coetlogon, 345
Desmarets, 310
D'Espagne, 290
Dick, J., 110
Dicky, N., 292
Doddridge, P., 232, 342
Dolins, Lady M., 342
D'Outrein, 197
Drummond, J., 212, 386
Drummond, Lt.-Gen., 239
Du Moulin, 324
Duncan, David, 388
Dunlop, 402
Dysert, J., 210
Eadie, J., 384
Eames, J., 341
Edgar, R., 376
Edwards, John, 91
Edwards, Jonath., 248
Electors-Palatine, 266, 271
Eliot, A., 386
Elizabeth, Q., 286

Elliot, Sir G., 342
Ellys, Sir R., 342
Elzevir, 38
Emett, 320
Erastus, 318
Erskine, H., 209, 251, 253, 263
Erskine, J., 312
Erskine, J., D.D., 253
Essenius, 210
Ewan, 209
Ewing, 263
Farquhar, J., 386
Feltham, 258
Ferrier, A., 384
Fishar, 261
Fisher, 263
Fleming, J., 396
Forbes, D., 342
Forbes, J., 386
Fowler, C., 236
Fox, G. T., 345, 347
Fraser, D., 250, 253
Frederick V., 200
Freer, G., 386
Galen, 381
Gaunt, Elizabeth, 237
Gib, A., 289
Gib, J., 386
Gillespie, G., 384, 385
Gillespie, P., 280
Gillespie, T., 392
Glas, J., 242
Goold, W. H., 319
Goode, W., 345
Goodsir, J., 385
Gouge, T., 341
Govett, 347
Gow, J., 396
Gray, 263
Gray, A., 357
Gray, R., 385
Gregory, Nyssen, 161
Guilnomma, 197
Guthrie, J., 280, 356, 384
Haag, E. and E., 206, 311
Hadow, J., 198, 251, 280, 294, 335, 374, 402
Halcro, 251, 263
Hall, J., 255
Haly, W., 386

Halyburton, T., 287, 291
Hamilton, Duchess of, 287
Hamilton, J., D.D., 345
Hamilton, J., M.D., 282
Hamilton, R., 282
Harding, J., 328
Harper, J., 250
Harrison, 366
Hart, W., 386
Haweis, T., 345
Haworth, 279
Hay, J., 282
Henderson, W., 385
Heppe, H., 269
Herzog, J. J., 305
Heshusius, 266
Hill, R., 274
Hill, T., 274
Hog, T., 286
Homer, 178
Hooker, T., 260
Hoornbeck, 245
Horsley, S., 282
Hulsius, 197
Hunter, D., 289
Huntingdon, Countess of, 222, 240
Hurrion, J., 342
Hyde, 263
Ignatius, 173
Innes, J., 386
Jackson, 258
Jacomb, 122, 207
Jaggard, 381
Jamieson, J., 289
Jansen, C., 305
Jenks, B., 283
Jerome, 159
Jewel, J., 297, 326
John Casimir, 269
Johnes, 366
Johnston, J., 385
Jones, T., 274
Josephus, 361
Junius, F., 350
Keckerman, 381
Kekewich, 402
Kempis, T. a, 90
Ker, J., 386
Killigrew, H., 268
Klebitz, 266

Kyngston, 200
Lagus, 354, 368
Laidlie, 317
Laing, R., 384, 386
Lampe, 197
Latimer, H., 364
Laud, W., 216, 328
Leechman, W., 125
L'Enfant, J., 197
Lever, T., 367
Lieber, T., 318
Lindsay, Lord, 359
Lindsay, H., 342
Lob, S., 278
Logan, A., 374
Logan, G., 399
Lookup, J., 208
Lorimer, P., 395
Lorimer, W., 278
Lovelace, W., 326
Luther, Paul, 306
Lye, T., 216
M'Claren, J., 377, 385
M'Crie, Tho., 38, 396
M'Euen, J., 293
M'Intosh, L., 384, 386
Macky, J., 293
Maclae, 263
Mainwaring, 320
Mair, G., 385
Mair, T., 253, 375, 385
Maitland, 291
Mar, Earl of, 250
Marckins, 235, 345
Marshall, J., 312
Martin, J., 292
Martyr, Peter, 175, 367
Mason, 222
Massie, R., 306, 307
Mastertoun, C., 375
Mawbey, Sir J., 274
Maxwell, H., 198, 399, 403
Maxwell, Sir J., 404
Mayer, 394
Meik, G., 386
Melancthon, 30, 266, 367
Menius, J., 306
Mercerus, 381
Mierdman, 364
Millar, J., 405
Miller, H., 396

Minto, Lord, 211
Mitchell, W. F., 363
Moncrief, D., 404
Moncrief, W., 404
Moncrieff, A., 221, 253, 384, 385
Moncur, 291
Moore, C., 385
Moore, Sir J., 385
Morren, N., 198, 404
Mossman, J., 293
Motley, J. L., 225
Mount, C., 268
Murray, M., 295
Myrton, 359
Nairne, T., 253, 377, 385
Naismyth, J., 398
Negus, 273, 274
Neve, T., 274
Neville, 380
Nichol, 200, 277
Nisbet, 310
Noble, J., 385
Nye, P., 350
Oatt, J., 397
Ogle, 357
Otto, Henry, 266
Owen, David, 325
Palmer and Calamy, 227
Parker, M., 348, 365
Paterson, T., 357
Paterson, W., 405
Patterson, J. B., 224
Paxton, G., 396
Pembroke, Earl of, 326, 327
Pickering, 257
Pithopæus, 354, 368
Porteous, 375
Preston, J., 260
Prittie, S., 260
Pythagoras, 64
Ramsay, 384
Raven, R., 381
Ravensteyn, 316
Regius, Urban, 363
Reid, 213, 290
Reuter, 197
Richardson, J., 370
Ridley, N., 363
Rippon, J., 273
Robinson, H., 380

INDEX

Rogers, J., 320
Rohan, Duc de, 355
Rolfe, J., 307, 308
Ross, Mrs, 295
Row, J., 386
Ruddiman, T., 399
Rutherford, S., 356
Ryssenius, 210
Sales, Francis de, 90
Schilling, C., 324
Scotstarvet, 356
Scott, 211, 324
Scott, J., 357
Scougal, H., 90
Seckendorf, 235, 306
Semple, G., 376
Sherlock, 390
Sherman, J., 199
Shiell, Mrs, 214, 295
Simeon, C., 222
Simonides, 256
Simson, J., 212, 292, 385
Skepp, J., 273
Slade, J., 342
Smith, Jean, 209
Smith, Samuel, 270
Socrates, 218
Somerset, Duke of, 364
Somervel, W., 338
Spalatin, G., 306
S. P. C. K., 229, 374
Spinniker, 312
Spurgeon, C. H., 273

Stähelin, 197
Stevenson, D., 386
Stewart, Sir J., 287, 357
Stoughton, John, 232
Stowell, W. H., 199
Strathmore, Earl of, 342
Strong, G1, 260
Struthers, J., 363
Sutherland, Earl of, 264
Swift, 380
Swinton, 385
Sylburgius, F., 38
Sympson, A., 382
Taylor, W., 396
Tegg, 216
Tertullian, 159
Thomond, Earl of, 257
Thomson, Sir J., 239
Thomson, Rev. J., 253, 285
Thomson, James, 338
Thomson, T., 385
Tingey, T., 342
Tomlyns, S., 313
Toplady, A. M., 273, 274
Trail, 342, 359
Trotter, 209, 385
Turpie, 251
Tweeddale, Marquis of, 253
Twisse, W., 236
Van Alpen, 197
Vandergucht, 342
Van der Honert, 345
Vauquet, 310

Voun, H., 274
Wackernagel, 306
Walker, D., 389
Walker, W., 385
Wallace, J. A., 370
Wallis, J., 259
Warburton, 390
Ward, Constancy, 237
Warden, J., 289
Wardlaw, R., 263
Warner, 59
Watson, 218, 290
Webster, J., 212, 291, 292
Wesley, J., 240, 283
West, 226
Whatley, 75
Whichcote, B., 362
Whitby, D., 273
Whitefield, G., 283
Wightman, R., 214, 295
Wilkinson, H., 216
Wilkinson, R., 355
William of Orange, 311, 384
Williams, D., 91
Willichius, 353
Willis, M., 396
Willison, J., 369, 386, 398
Wills, T., 345
Wilson, Walter, 232, 237
Wollebius, 21
Wotton, Lord, 380
Wren, M., 216
Zwinglius, 308

ERRATA.

Page 221.
For "William Moncrieff" read "Alexander Moncrieff."

Pages 214, 295.
Mr Robert Wightman, of Edinburgh, was Treasurer of the city.

Page 361.
Rev. R. Trail, of Boyndie, LL.D., was born in 1805, and died in London in 1880.

INDEX

Rogers, J., 320
Rohan, Duc de, 355
Rolfe, J., 307, 308
Ross, Mrs, 295
Row, J., 386
Ruddiman, T., 399
Rutherford, S., 356
Ryssenius, 210
Sales, Francis de, 90
Schilling, C., 324
Scotstarvet, 356
Scott, 241, 324
Scott, J., 357
Scougal, H., 90
Seckendorf, 235, 306
Semple, G., 376
Sherlock, 390
Sherman, J., 199
Shiell, Mrs, 214, 295
Simeon, C., 222
Simonides, 256
Simson, J., 212, 292, 385
Skepp, J., 273
Slade, J., 342
Smith, Jean, 209
Smith, Samuel, 270
Socrates, 218
Somerset, Duke of, 364
Somervel, W., 338
Spalatin, G., 306
S. P. C. K., 229, 374
Spinniker, 312
Spurgeon, C. H., 273

Stähelin, 197
Stevenson, D., 386
Stewart, Sir J., 287, 357
Stoughton, John, 232
Stowell, W. H., 199
Strathmore, Earl of, 342
Strong, G1, 260
Struthers, J., 363
Sutherland, Earl of, 264
Swift, 380
Swinton, 385
Sylburgius, F., 38
Sympson, A., 382
Taylor, W., 396
Tegg, 216
Tertullian, 159
Thomond, Earl of, 257
Thomson, Sir J., 239
Thomson, Rev. J., 253, 285
Thomson, James, 338
Thomson, T., 385
Tingey, T., 342
Tomlyns, S., 313
Toplady, A. M., 273, 274
Trail, 342, 359
Trotter, 209, 385
Turpie, 251
Tweeddale, Marquis of, 253
Twisse, W., 236
Van Alpen, 197
Vandergucht, 342
Van der Honert, 345
Vauquet, 310

Venn, H., 274
Wackernagel, 306
Walker, D., 389
Walker, W., 385
Wallace, J. A., 370
Wallis, J., 259
Warburton, 390
Ward, Constancy, 237
Warden, J., 289
Wardlaw, R., 263
Warner, 59
Watson, 218, 290
Webster, J., 212, 291, 292
Wesley, J., 240, 283
West, 226
Whatley, 75
Whichcote, B., 362
Whitby, D., 273
Whitefield, G., 283
Wightman, R., 214, 295
Wilkinson, H., 216
Wilkinson, R., 355
William of Orange, 311, 381
Williams, D., 91
Willichius, 353
Willis, M., 396
Willison, J., 369, 386, 398
Wills, T., 345
Wilson, Walter, 232, 237
Wollebius, 21
Wotton, Lord, 380
Wren, M., 216
Zwinglius, 308

ERRATA.

Page 221.
For "William Moncrieff" read "Alexander Moncrieff."

Pages 214, 295.
Mr Robert Wightman, of Edinburgh, was Treasurer of the city.

Page 361.
Rev. R. Trail, of Panmure, LL.D., was born in 1805, and died in London in 1880.

TURNBULL AND SPEARS, PRINTERS, EDINBURGH.

www.ingramcontent.com/pod-product-compliance
Lightning Source LLC
Chambersburg PA
CBHW030549300426
44111CB00009B/919